Fragmented Urban Images

Für Janet + Boone
— ein kleines Dankeschön
für ein wunderbares
Jahr in Chapel Hill!

Neue Studien zur Anglistik und Amerikanistik
Herausgegeben von Willi Erzgräber und Paul Goetsch

Band 52

PETER LANG
Frankfurt am Main · Bern · New York · Paris

GERD HURM

Fragmented Urban Images

The American City in Modern Fiction
from Stephen Crane to Thomas Pynchon

PETER LANG
Frankfurt am Main · Bern · New York · Paris

CIP-Titelaufnahme der Deutschen Bibliothek

Hurm, Gerd:

Fragmented urban images : the American city in modern fiction from Stephen Crane to Thomas Pynchon / Gerd Hurm. – Frankfurt am Main ; Bern ; New York ; Paris : Lang, 1991
    (Neue Studien zur Anglistik und Amerikanistik ; Bd. 52)
    Zugl.: Freiburg (Breisgau), Univ., Diss., 1989
    ISBN 3-631-43226-7

NE: GT

Diese Arbeit wurde mit einem Druckkostenzuschuß
der Wissenschaftlichen Gesellschaft Freiburg
im Breisgau unterstützt.

D 25
ISSN 0170-8848
ISBN 3-631-43226-7

© Verlag Peter Lang GmbH, Frankfurt am Main 1991
All rights reserved.

All parts of this publication are protected by copyright. Any
utilisation outside the strict limits of the copyright law, without
the permission of the publisher, is forbidden and liable to
prosecution. This applies in particular to reproductions,
translations, microfilming, and storage and processing in
electronic retrieval systems.

Printed in Germany 1 2 3 4 5 6 7

Meinen Eltern,
Petra und Lukas

Contents

Preface

1	Introduction: The Modernist Search for Meaning in the Fragmented City	1
2	The Modern American City	18
3	A Sociology of Fragmented Experience	45
4	Attitudes toward the American City	73
5	Literary Criticism	86
6	Urban Fiction and Urban Theory: A Synthesis	105
7	Stephen Crane. Maggie: A Girl of the Streets	110
8	Theodore Dreiser. Sister Carrie	133
9	Upton Sinclair. The Jungle	166
10	F. Scott Fitzgerald. The Great Gatsby	192
11	John Dos Passos. Manhattan Transfer	213
12	Richard Wright. Native Son	245
13	Hubert Selby. Last Exit to Brooklyn	273
14	Thomas Pynchon. The Crying of Lot 49	300
15	Conclusion	326
	Bibliography	337
	Index	358

> The cause of America
> is in a great measure
> the cause of all mankind.
>
> Thomas Paine

Preface

Appearances can be deceiving. Yet when we watch the sun rise or set, we tend to be aware that the sun does not actually set or rise. Similar deceptions hold true for cities. In popular thought, literature, and science, however, cityscapes, looming large through their material presence, have long been linked to effects and features which were not of their making. Cities were blamed or praised for what society as a whole had generated. Only in the last two decades, a new urban theory has begun to challenge such traditional assumptions. One of the reasons for persisting misjudgments is that the rise of the metropolis coincided with the rise of positivism. This type of scientific inquiry, which looked for the cause of things primarily in things themselves, tended to confirm the seeming self-evidence of surface observations. As science, it often gave credit to rather than questioned distorted views about the capacity of cities which thus have lingered in minds in the twentieth century. But city crime and city glamour, urban wealth and urban misery cannot be attributed to inherent qualities of cities. Rather, they are expressions of more encompassing structures, of the entire cultural, political, and economic relations of society. The examined novels, providing detailed accounts of modern urban experience, have indeed set the city mostly within such a general framework.

One of the chief aims of the present study is to disclose in which ways certain distortions and biased perceptions of American urban experience have evolved as well as to show to what great degree city images are influenced by social interests and preconceived cultural notions. In contrast to generalizing concepts which posit the existence of a generic urban mind, urban personality, or urban culture, this study emphasizes the fragmentation and diversity of the ways in which the modern city may be experienced depending on the class, gender, and ethnicity of the urbanite.

Understanding social processes around us more fully, for example through the analysis of interested projections of fictional cityscapes, on a globe that has become virtually urbanized, may hopefully help change the direction of a world which has become alarmingly more violent, self-destructive, and endangered. In my opinion, the ways in which we live, work, consume, and enjoy ourselves today in the urban environments of the industrial nations have to change if we are to secure our children, future generations, and economically less powerful regions at least the chance to live lives in dignity, peace, and happiness. In this sense, the cause of urbanized America also is, in Thomas Paine's words, "the cause of all mankind."[1]

I would like to generally thank the many people who allowed me to see, understand, and cherish American culture and, especially, the culture of its cities. What began more than eleven years ago as a romance has, somewhat cooled off, been turned into an intellectual venture since. As criticism may also be a form of love and appreciation, I hope the following pages with their sometimes harsh comments on tendencies in American culture may be understood as a token of such feelings.

Beyond the expression of general gratitude and the acknowledgment of the great indebtedness to preceding scholarship in urban studies and literature, I would like to extend thanks specifically to those people who have helped this study to be completed. My thanks go most of all to my teacher Paul Goetsch, who supervised the thesis at the University of Freiburg. I am profoundly indebted to him for his generous help, advice, and encouragement. He alone knows the many weaknesses and mistakes which have been omitted due to his astute criticism. I have learned a lot from him in the past years. Cordial thanks extend to Townsend Ludington who was my tutor during the academic year 1984/85 at the University of North Carolina at Chapel Hill. He has had a strong influence on the study in its early stages and has helped me to focus it with his knowledge and advice. My thanks also go to Eric Mottram who in 1983 read a seminal essay on *Manhattan Transfer* at King's College, London, and whose initial encouragement to continue remained very important to me. Finally, I would like to thank Leo Marx and Heinz Ickstadt who at different stages read and discussed parts of my work and who shared their knowledge on the subject with me.

I am very grateful to friends who were involved both personally and intellectually in the story of this book. Steve Alford and Suzanne Ferriss have not only shared their friendship and generosity with me, but also their wide reading and knowledge of modern literature. Their comments and suggestions have been very helpful to me. To my friend Shamoon Zamir I am grateful for discussing central ideas of the study with me. Bob Shannon and Lisa Goldberg, whom I met in the final stages of this project, have my thanks for adding clarity to my writing. Wherever this has not been achieved, it is my fault. Finally, thanks go to my friends and colleagues at the English department of the University of Freiburg, to Susanne Bach, Wolfgang Hochbruck, Mabel Lesch, Beatrix Reichel, Elmar Schenkel, and Martina Wächter who were perceptive critics in discussions as well as patient listeners. I also have to thank them for proofreading the manuscript.

I am grateful for the institutional help which I received in preparing and writing this study. I am generally indebted to those who established the social grant system (BAföG) and in particular for the grant which allowed me to study a year at King's College, London in 1982/83. I am also grateful for the scholarship and research support provided by the German Academic Exchange Service (DAAD) and by the John-F.-Kennedy-Institute in Berlin (West). I would also like to thank the staffs of the libraries of the University of Freiburg, of the John-F.-Kennedy-Institute, of the Massachusetts Institute of Technology, of Hunter College, of Columbia and Harvard University. Special thanks go to Ilse Repplinger at the John-F.-Kennedy-Institute and to Frauke Vrba in the English Department of the University of Freiburg.

Finally, thanks go to individuals who were influential in more than one way for this study. I owe a great deal to Jürgen Bunzel who made me speak English and roused my interest in different cultures. I also owe a great deal to my friend Andreas Götze with whom I first explored the United States--an experience which led me to study its language, literature, and culture. My greatest debt is to my friend, lover, and now wife Petra for the invaluable assistance and encouragement during the past years. She has had a profound influence on this study.

[1]Thomas Paine, *Common Sense*, 1776, ed. with an introduction by Isaac Kramnick, Harmondsworth, 1976, p. 63.

1

Introduction:
The Modernist Search for Meaning in the Fragmented City

The city has become the dominant environment in Western civilization in the twentieth century.[1] The giant cities of the United States were at the forefront of modern capitalist urbanization: their vastness, dissociation, and segregation, their concentration, heterogeneity, and sprawl, their downtowns, slums, and suburbs, their skyscrapers, tenements, and Levittown houses have suggested a path for others in what has by now become a worldwide transformation. Hence images and myths of modern American cities have attained universal significance.[2] Fiction about New York, Chicago, or Los Angeles, the poetic transfiguration of Manhattan's skyline or the naturalist record of conditions in Chicago's stockyards point beyond the singularity of a national culture: their analysis pertains to Western civilization as a whole.[3]

The novel, the literary genre which has focused from the beginnings of modernity on both the relation and the conflict between individual and environment, has become a major forum for the investigation into the tensions produced in modern cities.[4] An "ex-

---

[1] In this study, 'city' and 'urban' are used as interchangeable terms for the diverse forms of large settlements, the city, metropolis, and megalopolis. As it is argued that the terms 'urban' or 'city' do not possess a generic status, a more detailed typology of settlement forms is not necessary. For a further delimitation of the concepts, see chapters 2 and 3.

[2] Raymond Williams, *The Country and the City*, London, 1973, p. 351.

[3] Upton Sinclair's image of the modern American city in *The Jungle*, for instance, had an impact on artists and intellectuals like George Bernard Shaw, Charlie Chaplin, Bertolt Brecht, and Herbert Marcuse and influenced their reactions to urban issues. Leon Harris, *Upton Sinclair: American Rebel*, New York, 1975, pp. 4, 83ff. Dieter Herms, *Upton Sinclair, ein amerikanischer Radikaler. Eine Einführung in Leben und Werk*, Frankfurt, 1978, p. 42.

[4] No affinity, however, is posited between the modern city and a specific literary genre as in Volker Klotz' study which relates the form of the city to the form of the novel (Volker Klotz, *Die erzählte Stadt: eine Herausforderung des Romans von Lesage bis Döblin*, München, 1969). Other genres and media have captured the changes in the modern city in ways no less congenial. Indeed, Irving Howe holds that T. S. Eliot's poem *The Waste Land* has generated its most powerful image. Irving Howe, "The City in Literature," *The Critical Point*, New York, 1973, p. 53.

pression of transcendental homelessness,"[5] the novel as a genre has implied a search for meaning in man-created environments. In the twentieth century, the fragmentation in giant cities has precluded valid generalizations or metaphysical speculation in the modernist search and has radically annulled aspirations toward the anachronistic totality constitutive of the epic.[6] The world which the modern city novel transforms is partial, incomplete, dissociated, and contrary.[7]

Segregation in the metropolis and dissociation in fiction are intricately related as they are both setting and forum in the writers' modernist search for meaning. But even though this relationship has become a commonplace in literary criticism, the specific connections and interrelations between novel and city have not yet been analyzed extensively.[8] A causal relationship cannot be posited. It is only on the surface that metropolitan and modernist dissociation seem to determine each other as the violent disruptions and upheavals in Western industrial cities happened to coincide with the emergence of the arbitrary signifiers of modern fiction.[9] However, in what follows it will be argued that both city and novel are dialectically linked to more comprehensive transformations in modern capitalist societies.

This study will examine the specific ways in which modern novel and modern city, fictional perception and urban theory have interacted in the United States. It analyzes eight novels which have concentrated on modern urban experience: *Maggie: A Girl of the Streets* by Stephen Crane, *Sister Carrie* by Theodore Dreiser, *The Jungle* by Upton Sinclair, *The Great Gatsby* by F. Scott Fitzgerald, *Manhattan Transfer* by John Dos Passos,

---

[5] Georg Lukács, *Theory of the Novel*, trans. Anna Bostock, Cambridge, Mass., 1971, p. 41.

[6] For an extended critique of Marxist concepts of totality in the twentieth century, see Martin Jay, *Marxism and Totality*, Oxford, 1984.

[7] For Burton Pike, the city in modern literature "became fragmented and transparent rather than tangible and coherent, a place consisting of bits, pieces, and shifting moods; it came to stand under the sign of discontinuity and dissociation rather than community." Burton Pike, *The Image of the City in Modern Literature*, Princeton, 1981, p. 72.

[8] There are many valuable contributions in articles and monographs to various aspects of American urban literature (as will be discussed in chapter 5), but a historical overview of developments in the city and the novel has not been attempted. Blanche Gelfant's comprehensive account of early modern city novels from 1954 is dated. Blanche Housman Gelfant, *The American City Novel*, Norman, Oklahoma, 1954.

[9] Analyzing this process for Western civilization in general, Raymond Williams has suggested in his essay "The Metropolis and the Emergence of Modernism," a connection through the breakdown of social, cultural, linguistic, and aesthetic conventions. For him, modernism was a socially grounded reaction to the disruptions in exploding urban centers. The arbitrariness of tradition became material as the links of convention were violently dissolved by industrial capitalism. Raymond Williams, "The Metropolis and the Emergence of Modernism," *Unreal City: Urban Experience in Modern European Literature and Art*, eds. Edward Timms and David Kelley, Manchester, 1985, pp. 21f. See also Malcolm Bradbury, "The Cities of Modernism," *Modernism, 1890-1930*, eds. Malcolm Bradbury and James Mc Farlane, Harmondsworth, 1976, 96-104.

Native Son by Richard Wright, *Last Exit to Brooklyn* by Hubert Selby, and *The Crying of Lot 49* by Thomas Pynchon. The selection includes some of the most influential novels in the canon of urban literature and urban studies. In this sense, the choice is taken to be representative.[10] The novels also provide a historical cross-section as they record and project the changes in the modern American city from the 1890s to the 1960s.

For an analysis of their interrelation, both the novel and the city require proper investigative categories and tools. Imaginative texts can neither be reduced to function as mere social or historical documents nor be limited to the realm of purely literary and aesthetic categories. On the other hand, the modern city cannot be treated as a given *a priori* to the investigation.[11] It is contended, indeed, that a fruitful insight into modern urban experience can be won precisely at the intersection of these two cultural phenomena, that is, at the point where the city and the novel, the social and aesthetic, the material and imaginative, the concrete and abstract converge and shape one another.

Defining the modern city, the setting, subject, and impulse for the writers' search, is the foremost task for this investigation. City and urban are, as all theorists in the field agree, particularly complicated and elusive terms.[12] The modern city not only implicates, in Robert E. Park's famous words, the crucial dissolution into "a mosaic of little worlds

---

[10] The choice of novels reflects the study's intention to reexamine the dominant view of American urban fiction and to analyze the reciprocal relation between urban fiction and urban theory in establishing the myth of the uniform, autonomous, and generic city. This necessarily has led to the exclusion of less influential, though no less important, ethnic or female accounts. Since, due to their momentous impact, the study had to include Theodore Dreiser's and John Dos Passos' widely interpreted city novels, further upper- and middle-class accounts of the central city were excluded. This does not imply that the urban fiction by William Dean Howells, Edith Wharton, Willa Cather, Thomas Wolfe, Saul Bellow, or Donald Barthelme could be qualified as less creative or important as fiction. Similarly, female accounts were not included, although Anzia Yezierska in *Bread Givers* writes about the immigrant Lower East Side of Stephen Crane, or Willa Cather in *The Song of the Lark* treats the urban artist theme of Theodore Dreiser. Again, the choice reflects the impact that these male novels had in discussions in urban studies. Analyzing novels of an established canon does not imply its uncritical acceptance, but simply acknowledges that their city images were influential in the development of the dominant perception of American cities. Canons can be challenged both by extending them as well as by critically reassessing them. A study of the distinct female experience, for instance, as actually lived and as formulated in female city fiction has yet to be written. For a first assessment, see Catherine R. Stimpson, Elsa Dixler, Martha J. Nelson, and Kathryn B. Yatrakis, eds., *Women and the City*, Chicago, 1980. Susan Merrill Squier, ed., *Women Writers and the City: Essays in Feminist Literary Criticism*, Knoxville, 1984.

[11] Manuel Castells, *The Urban Question*, trans. Alan Sheridan, London, 1977, pp. 83ff.

[12] Raymond E. Pahl, *Whose City?* London, 1970, p. 209. David Harvey, *Social Justice and the City*, London, 1973, p. 22. Philip Abrams, "Towns and Economic Growth: Some Theories and Problems," *Towns in Societies*, eds. Philip Abrams and E. Wrigley, Cambridge, 1978, pp. 9-33. R. J. Holton, *Cities, Capitalism, and Civilization*, London, 1986, pp. 1-18.

4 Fragmented Urban Images

which touch but do not interpenetrate,"[13] but also means a multiplicity of divergent perspectives and a profusion of judgments about conflicting and mutually exclusive urban modes of existence.[14] Grounded in different class practices and social relations, the segregated city implies very different things to different groups; varying forms of spatial organization, socially produced and constituted, generate distinct class perspectives. The single common denominator among this variety of experiences and images is their partiality and fragmentation.[15]

A generic core of the modern city cannot be defined from this multiplicity of divergent and contradictory mental maps. Urban areas contain a wide spectrum of social behavior and cultural ties.[16] In the twentieth century, *urban* may denote vastness, density, heterogeneity, alienation, artificiality, impersonality, and impenetrability; it may suggest narrowness, enclosure, sameness, deprivation, and constriction; but it may also mean homogeneity, cohesion, community, and embeddedness, or signify tolerance, openness, anarchism, and freedom. Whatever the particular perspective, the definition remains partial. All attempts in urban theory have failed to produce a universally valid concept or a satisfactory ontological definition of the city through either physical categories or psychological archetypes.[17] *Urban* does not have any value in an epistemological sense and derives its meaning solely from specific economic, historical, social, and cultural conditions.[18]

This state of theory contrasts starkly with the host of fixed images which pretend to capture the American city in its totality. In popular, literary, and even scientific usage, *urban* has been used as a relatively stable concept: it often simply meant downtown as

---

[13] Robert E. Park, "The City: Suggestions for the Investigation of the Human Behavior in the City Environment," *The American Journal of Sociology*, 20 (1915), p. 608.

[14] Kevin Lynch stressed the subjective cognition of cityscapes in his pathbreaking study, *The Image of the City*, and introduced mental maps as a new field of investigation to urban studies. Kevin Lynch, *The Image of the City*, Cambridge, Mass., 1960. See also, Sam Bass Warner, "The Management of Multiple Urban Images," *The Pursuit of Urban History*, eds. Derek Fraser and Anthony Sutcliffe, London, 1983, 383-94. Mark Gottdiener, "Culture, Ideology, and the Sign of the City," *The City and the Sign*, ed. Mark Gottdiener, New York, 1986, 202-18.

[15] Castells, pp. 75-85; A. L. Strauss, *Images of the American City*, New York, 1961, p. 303. Warner, p. 384.

[16] Michael Peter Smith, *The City and Social Theory*, New York, 1979, p. 175.

[17] R. J. Holton summarizes: "The failure to produce a generic definition of the city is not so much the result of some inexplicable logical error in urbanist discourse, as the outcome of an increasing awareness of heterogeneity in what are conventionally regarded as 'urban' forms." Holton, p. 26.

[18] Holton concludes: "The generic notion of city survives uneasily . . . as an ungrounded conceptual residue in contemporary discussion of urbanism and urbanization. Its resilience is in fact remarkable in view of the powerful logical and empirical objections that have been made to ideas of some universal quality that cities possess across time and space." Holton, p. 27.

perceived from a male middle-class perspective.[19] Generally speaking, the city was materially enticing, but at the same time it was a moral and social cauldron. This particular image was raised to the status of a general symbol since it reflected the privileged view of an influential group. Certainly, the predominance of such imagery is linked to the paradigmatic quality of downtown conditions in the early phase of the modern city and also to the centrality, density, and mixture of the core city, yet the claim that this part of the city characterizes the whole is untenable and expresses an ideological purpose. Generically vast, overwhelming, anonymous, and chaotic, such imagery removes the American metropolis from meaningful involvement and demands adjustment to the 'moloch,' whatever the specific form or cost of accommodation. Seen from this angle, the political interest in perpetuating such an image becomes apparent.

In contrast to such a view of urban totality, the present study argues that none of the various segments, neither the experience in the central city, in the ghetto, nor in suburbia may conclusively represent *the* modern American city. Pervasive contradictions constitute the modern capitalist metropolis. What the city is and what it means is the object of a continuing debate. Images of the city which seemingly proclaim quintessential insights and objective truths can only be partisan and inevitably reflect specific social interests. Thus contemporary I-love-New-York promotions attempt in their commercial smoothness to gloss over the conflicts which caused the urban crisis in the sixties and seventies.[20] Concomitantly, other facets of the metropolis, the cruel inhumanity and desperate bleakness of life in crime-ridden ghettos, are accepted as generic urban deficiencies. The neoconservative visions of an urban jungle suggest the benign neglect of such areas by official politics.[21]

It will therefore be more interesting to analyze why certain types of images have prevailed and why particular attitudes have persisted. In general, the loss of universally binding beliefs and norms and the weakening of ties to socially produced space in the modern city have led to the predominance of, and bifurcation into, physical-empirical and psychological-archetypal concepts. The physical-empirical definition, the most important trend, is best represented by the Chicago School of sociology which defined urbanism using the physical factors of size, density, and heterogeneity. The city as a psy-

---

[19]For a discussion of the limitation of this urban image see, Herbert J. Gans, "Urbanism and Suburbanism as Ways of Life: A Re-evaluation of Definitions," *Human Behavior and Social Processes,* ed. Arnold Rose, Boston, 1962, 625-48, repr. *American Urban History,* ed. Alexander B. Callow, Jr., New York, 1969, 504-519.

[20]For a general discussion of this tendency, see Harald Jähner, "Tour in die Moderne: Die Rolle der Kultur für städtische Imagewerbung und Städtetourismus," *Die Unwirklichkeit der Städte. Großstadtdarstellungen zwischen Moderne und Postmoderne,* ed. Klaus R. Scherpe, Hamburg, 1988, 225-242.

[21]For such a position see Edward C. Banfield, *The Unheavenly City,* Boston, 1970.

6 Fragmented Urban Images

chological-mythical category has found its most complex expression in Lewis Mumford's writings, especially in his great opus *The City in History*, and, in fictional form, in James Joyce's *Ulysses*, in which the urban community is defined through archetypal constellations of the modern nuclear family.[22] Both concepts, the physical-empirical and the psychological-archetypal, are similarly flawed since they play down the social constitution and political implementation of images by suggesting a disinterested assessment through either positivist objectivity or psychological universality.

Ahistorical images such as Babylon, hell, moloch, or jungle have indeed been very influential in the United States. Such images have persisted, beyond their controlled proliferation in the mass media, for they convey the impression of stability, coherence, and universality in the midst of contradiction and fragmentation. But whether based on an objective-rational or a subjective-psychological concept, any image of the modern American city has also been profoundly affected by the tendency toward individuality, naturalness, and totality in bourgeois ideology.[23] As Henri Lefebvre has indicated, the city is produced twice, once in its class-based spatial transformation and once in its mental representation.[24] Interest and image are dialectically related: regardless of one's perspective, partiality, fragmentation, and totality are strongly interconnected. Class[25] and urban ideology[26] are linked since social experience suggests the particular

---

[22] Louis Wirth, "Urbanism as a Way of Life," *The American Journal of Sociology*, 44 (1938), 1-24, repr. Louis Wirth, *On Cities and Social Life*, ed. Albert J. Reiss, Chicago, 1964, pp. 60-83. Lewis Mumford, *The City in History: Its Origins, its Transformation and its Prospects*, 1961, Harmondsworth, 1966. James Joyce, *Ulysses*, 1922, New York, 1934.

[23] Ideology and class are among the most contested terms in materialist theory. The ongoing discussion with its broad differences cannot even be sketched here. Both concepts as used in this study are described below. For a further discussion of urban ideology see Raymond Williams' study *The Country and the City*. See also, Roland Barthes, *Mythologies*, trans. Annette Lavers, London, 1972, pp. 109-59. Neil Smith, *Uneven Development*, New York, 1984, pp. 1-31.

[24] Mario Rui Martins, "The Theory of Social Space in the Work of Henri Lefebvre," *Urban Political Economy and Social Theory*, eds. Ray Forrest, J. Henderson, and Peter Williams, Aldershot, 1982, 160-85.

[25] Class is used in this study in a broadly Marxist sense and signifies a group's relation to the means of production. This contrasts with a Weberian definition which sees class primarily in relation to property and which further splits the concept into class, power, and status. Yet the traditionally monolithic definition of class in Marxism, in which the instrumental action became the single motor of history, has been challenged and refuted, above all by Jürgen Habermas (Jürgen Habermas, *Knowledge and Human Interests*, trans. Jeremy J. Shapiro, Boston, 1971). The present study conceives of members of a class as actively participating in defining themselves as a class and not as mere determined functions of a transcendental process as in structuralist readings of Marx in the 1960s and 1970s. Ira Katznelson has recently summarized the developments in materialist theory to distinguish different levels of class without cutting the close connection to the means of production. Class is a junction term which allows "to specify more precisely the points of connection *between* the structure of class relations at the macroeconomic level; the lived experience of class in the workplace and in the residence community; groups of people disposed to act in class ways; and class-based collective action" (Ira Katznelson, "Working-Class Formation: Constructing Cases and Comparisons,"

focus and selection in the city image and since ideology provides the objectified shape and organic roundedness. Only in the last two decades has urban theory recognized and examined this partial and class-based cognition of the city.

Such findings in urban studies affect the approach toward modern city novels. If the modern city lacks a definition *sui generis*, an ontological genre of urban fiction cannot be fruitfully defined. Indeed, city novels vary immensely in content and form. Suburban decadence and black belt cohesion, reportorial realism and esoteric avantgardism exist side by side. A direct correspondence between subject and genre does not exist. Without a uniform experience in and without a transhistorical definition of the city, there can be no prototypical or archetypal *urban* perception, state of mind, or culture. Each experience will have to produce its own poetic transformation.

Moreover, it is questionable whether there are any novels dealing with purely *urban* concerns. By their very constitution, fictional city images exceed their topographical and social boundaries. In his pathbreaking analysis of English literature in *The Country and the City*, Raymond Williams has shown that projections of the classical, medieval, or modern industrial city have embodied meaning and incorporated historical conflicts beyond the spatial and ecological confines of their setting. Images of the city give figurative presence to wider issues and ideas about society. According to Leo Marx, in "imaginative literature, indeed, the concept of the 'city' must be understood as in large

---

Working-Class Formation: Nineteenth-Century Patterns in Western Europe and the United States, eds. Ira Katznelson and Aristide Zolberg, Princeton, 1986, p. 21). In this study, class implies historical constriction and political choice, contingent determination and human agency.

[26]In materialist theory, ideology has received two chief definitions. For one, Georg Lukács saw ideology as the second nature of an alienated and reified consciousness. Emancipatory action and demystification could dismantle its seemingly natural objectifications and indicate authentic relations. In contrast to this traditional conception, Louis Althusser, extending Jacques Lacan's structural reading of psychoanalysis, defined ideology as the unavoidable expression of all social practice and as the natural projection of an imaginary unity. Man as an "ideological animal" cannot escape from ideology, only the theoretical practitioner may achieve the scientific knowledge of totality (Jay, pp. 385-422). With Jürgen Habermas, who extended the traditional Lukácsian formula, the present study argues that ideology may be demystified. To the extent that the projected harmony is connected to class-based social practice, the criticism of ideology is a necessary step to achieve the economic, social, and cultural liberation. The study follows Jürgen Habermas' radical reassessment of cognition in *Knowledge and Human Interests*. Still, as will be proposed later, Pierre Macherey's literary model, based on Althusser's concept, may be fused with Habermas' definition as both theories view totality as "a decentered whole in in which no one level [is] the basic determinant of the others" (Jay, p. 486). The crucial difference, Martin Jay points out, is that Habermas "persisted in conceiving of one of the levels, that of social integration, in intersubjective terms, rather than reducing all of them to structural 'practices' without any subjective determination." Ibid., p. 486. See also Myra Jehlen, "Introduction: Beyond Transcendence," *Ideology and Classic American Literature*, ed. Sacvan Bercovitch and Myra Jehlen, Cambridge, 1986, 1-18.

measure an abstract receptacle for displaced feelings about other things."[27] The tensions and contradictions generated by American capitalism and the complexities of modern life are embodied in cityscapes, but the issues cannot always be specified or grasped as particularly *urban*. Topography mostly functions as metonymy.[28] Any restriction to purely *urban* concerns would narrow the scope of such fiction. Besides, if one searches for *urban* flaws, one may only detect *urban* flaws. This study instead conceives of city novels as novels which treat general social and cultural issues with a specifically urban focus.

As Raymond Williams has indicated, *urban* approaches run the danger of turning the city into the scapegoat for general deficiencies in society. Neglecting the crucial question of whose fragment was projected, writers and critics have often defined the city in generic contrast to the country. Thus they have turned conflicts in modern cities into environmental issues: they have associated country and city with an ontological opposition between innocence and corruption, nature and civilization, repression and freedom, and backwardness and progress.[29] Such ideologies of space further cemented the division of cities and villages whose visual and material presence already deceptively suggested an environmental division.[30] Ideologies of space were formulated both on the political left and right: Karl Marx claimed that he wished to save urban workers from "the idiocy of rural life," whereas T. S. Eliot or Oswald Spengler identified the modern necropolis as being the end of civilization.[31] A proper assessment of social and economic inequality, however, will overcome a simplistic physical division and indicate the variety

---

[27]Williams, *The Country and the City*, p. 350; Leo Marx, "The Puzzle of Anti-Urbanism in Classic American Literature," *Literature and the Urban Experience*, eds. Michael C. Jaye and Ann Chalmers Watts, New Brunswick, N.J., 1981, p. 64.

[28]The figurative conception of topography has been argued in several studies: David R. Weimer, *The City as Metaphor*, New York, 1966, p. 6. Alan Trachtenberg, "The American Scene: Versions of the City," *Massachusetts Review*, 8 (1967), p. 284. Leo Marx, "Pastoral Ideals and City Troubles," *Journal of General Education*, 20 (1969), p. 270. Burton Pike, *The Image of the City in Modern Literature*, Princeton, 1981, pp. 10f.

[29]Williams, pp. 9, 347-68. James L. Machor writes: "There is no denying that a belief in the superiority of either rural or urban environments has been central to America, for beneath their divergence these two ideological strains share a common assumption in forming much of our history: the conviction that city and country embody diametrically opposed values." James L. Machor, *Pastoral Cities: Urban Ideals and the Symbolic Landscape of America*, Madison, 1987, p. 5.

[30]Abrams, p. 9. The dichotomies formed around the American city, although they have persisted nominally, differed significantly in their specific content. The city was not only contrasted to the country, but in different functions it was seen deficient in comparison with nature, wilderness, arcadia, the farm, the West, or the suburban home. Blaine Brownell, "The Agrarian and Urban Ideals: Environmental Images in Modern America," *Journal of Popular Culture*, 5 (1971), 576-87.

[31]Karl Marx, *The Communist Manifesto*, *The Marx-Engels Reader*, ed. Robert C. Tucker, New York, 1978, p. 476. T. S. Eliot, *The Waste Land*, London, 1922. Oswald Spengler, *The Decline of the West*, trans. C. F. Atkinson, New York, 1928.

Introduction 9

in both country and city. After all, inequality, exploitation, and alienation cannot be causally connected to geographical or narrowly environmental categories.

Two interrelated strands thus fundamentally characterize the fragmentation of the modern American city. Split into socially contradictory fragments, the American city, as a mosaic aggregate, constitutes only a fragment in the totality of all settlement space. American class society provides the appropriate frame for a full examination of this double fragmentation both *in* the city and *of* the city. Urban and literary theory converge in this assumption. Literary criticism has indicated the figurative use of topography, while urban theory has succinctly characterized the city as "a projection of society on space."[32] The city, indeed, is a "terrific lens" to put society in focus.[33] The present study, therefore, examines the forces which led to booming urbanization on the national scale to understand the framework for processes in individual cities. In addition, it tries to show how experience in the American city has become fragmented and how images reflect particular class perspectives.[34]

Finally, the examination of fictional city images requires one more specific qualification. Owing to the sheer variety of urban perspectives, any city portrayal will undergo an inevitable reduction beyond its class-based fragmentation and ideological bias.[35] Geographical and political, sociological and economic, architectural and literary images of the city have been shown to differ extensively.[36] But if images are colored by thematic perspectives, this channeling will become significant to city novels. Thus, fictional city images are crucially shaped by the particular issues chosen for treatment.[37] The thematic perspective for the fictional city is constituted by the novel as a whole.[38] The frame of reference is the comprehensive range of incidents and motifs which the novels assemble: authors mold their cities and shape the setting, characters, and atmosphere according to their particular focus and fictional theme. The image of John Dos Passos' cubist metropolis as simultaneous chronicle in *Manhattan Transfer* differs substantially

---

[32]Castells, p. 115.

[33]Bruce M. Stave, "A Conversation with Sam Bass Warner, Jr.: Ten Years Later," *Journal of Urban History*, 11 (1984), p. 90. Also, see Asa Briggs, "The Environment of the City," *Encounter*, 59 (1982), p. 26.

[34]Peter Orleans, "Differential Cognition of Urban Residents: Effects of Social Scale on Mapping," *Image and Environment*, eds. Roger M. Downs and David Stea, Chicago, 1973, 115-30.

[35]Many reductions, however, are not related to the subject *per se*, but pay tribute to the fact that each academic discipline has fractured and compartmentalized the city for its purposes.

[36]Lloyd Rodwin and Robert Hollister, eds. *Cities of the Mind*, New York, 1984, p. 6.

[37]Williams, p. 349; Marx, "The Puzzle of Anti-Urbanism in Classic American Literature," p. 74; Rodwin and Hollister, p. 6; Pike, p. 10.

[38]David R. Weimer, *The City as Metaphor*, p. 3. Pike, p. 12.

from F. Scott Fitzgerald's image of the American dream as a Long Island romance in *The Great Gatsby*. Urban *experience*, fictional *theme*, and city *image* are intricately related.[39] Modifying David R. Weimer's hyperbolical assertion that "there are as many cities as there are imaginations,"[40] one could say that each city image is as creatively unique as it also is typical for its class perspective.

The experiences and images projected for the American city in the twentieth century, for the Lower East Side, Great Neck, or Brooklyn, are diverse and contradictory; the selection of city novels in this study testifies to these differences and extremes in the American metropolis. Some accounts are based on autobiographical experiences, others present a congenial perspective of author and group. Each novel evidences a unique relation to the people, to the quarters portrayed. Stephen Crane roamed the Bowery as a journalist and used accounts by Jacob A. Riis to compose *Maggie: A Girl of the Streets*. Theodore Dreiser intimately knew the glamorous and ghastly sides of the industrial city as he had submitted both Chicago and New York to journalistic scrutiny. Under an assumed identity as a stockyard worker, Upton Sinclair collected information in the meat factories for *The Jungle* and spent time among immigrants in Chicago. John Dos Passos lived in Brooklyn and Greenwich Village while he was composing *Manhattan Transfer*. F. Scott Fitzgerald, as a celebrated young writer, had access to the New York upper class in Great Neck and incorporated his insights into *The Great Gatsby*. Richard Wright, in his autobiographical *Black Boy* and *American Hunger*, described how he moved to Chicago and what his experience was like in the black ghetto. Hubert Selby grew up in Brooklyn and, for a while, lived the life of his characters himself. Finally, the Californian outcasts in Thomas Pynchon's *The Crying of Lot 49* relate to the Watts rebels of his *New York Times*' essay from 1966.[41]

The fictional city of each novel presents its unique search for meaning as it examines the deformations under which people failed or succeeded in the segregated American city, or how they generally coped with the dehumanizing conditions in twentieth-century Western civilization, or how they suffered under the capitalist exploitation

---

[39] Eberhard Kreutzer, *New York in der zeitgenössischen amerikanischen Erzählliteratur*, Heidelberg, 1985, p. 98; Trachtenberg, p. 284. For a detailed definition of the terms *experience*, *theme*, and *image* see chapter 6.

[40] Weimer, p. 6.

[41] James B. Colvert, *Stephen Crane*, New York, 1984. W. A. Swanberg, *Dreiser*, New York, 1965. Leon Harris, *Upton Sinclair. An American Rebel*, New York, 1975. Townsend Ludington, *John Dos Passos. A Twentieth Century Odyssey*, New York, 1980. Andrew Turnbull, *Scott Fitzgerald*, New York, 1962. Michel Fabre, *The Unfinished Quest of Richard Wright*, trans. Isabel Barzun, New York, 1973. John O'Brien, "Interview with Hubert Selby, Jr.," *The Review of Contemporary Fiction*. 1 (1981), 315-35. David Seed, *The Fictional Labyrinths of Thomas Pynchon*, London, 1988.

Introduction 11

in the stockyards in the early modern city or from the atmosphere of desperation and brutality in Brooklyn housing projects in the 1950s. In these modern quests for meaning, the questions and answers have differed widely. The artistic solutions cannot be reduced to a single, uniform category--not to modernism, urbanism, or materialism. Written with the post-structuralist challenge to totality in mind,[42] this study of American city novels does not assume an apodictic certainty about correct readings or provide presumptuous glimpses of incontestable urban truths. Nevertheless, the study sees philosophical-scientific models as important attempts to approximate a socially valid, if historically changing, frame of totality. It rejects the reverse holism of post-structuralist concepts with their claims to universal fragmentation.[43] In this sense the following investigation is part of the project of modernity which, as Jürgen Habermas has remarked, is uncompleted as yet.[44]

In evaluating actions, in examining proposed options for emancipatory change, or in recognizing the peculiar forms of resistance in the novels, this study cannot but apply a set of values. Believing in human agency within given material and historical constraints, it bases its judgments on the materialist and Western humanist tradition. It underwrites what Herbert Marcuse has called the *a priori* of critical theory in *One-Dimensional Man*, namely the simple but important conviction that "human life is worth living or rather can be and ought to be made worth living."[45] The values which direct the following assessments of the novels spring from this belief. The analysis tries to reconstruct the possibilities which historically existed in order to accomplish this goal and evaluates them, from a contemporary perspective, as paths. In contrast to orthodox materialist approaches, the realm of culture is conceived as being relatively autonomous. The study follows Jürgen Habermas who has argued that "*liberation from hunger and misery* does not necessarily converge with *liberation from servitude and degradation*, for there is no automatic developmental relation between labor and interaction."[46] Hence,

---

[42]See Michel Foucault, *The Archaeology of Knowledge*, trans. A. M. Sheridan Smith, New York, 1972. Michel Foucault, *The Order of Things: An Archaeology of the Human Sciences*, trans. Alan Sheridan, New York, 1973. Jacques Derrida, *Writing and Difference*, trans. Alan Bass, Chicago, 1978.

[43]For a discussion of the arguable claim to the universality of fragmentation in post-structuralism, see Jay, pp. 462-537. Terry Eagleton, *Literary Theory*, Oxford, 1983, pp. 127-50.

[44]Jürgen Habermas, "Die Moderne: ein unvollendetes Projekt," *Kleine politische Schriften, I-IV*, Frankfurt, 1981, 444-64.

[45]Herbert Marcuse, *One-Dimensional Man*, Boston, 1964, p. x.

[46]Jürgen Habermas, *Theory and Practice*, trans. John Viertel, London, 1974, p. 169. Even though this study will use insights from traditional Marxist theory, it nevertheless rejects the base-superstructure model as a frame for its investigation. Jürgen Habermas has pointed out in *Knowledge and Human Interests* that the

12 Fragmented Urban Images

the investigation focuses on the specific relationship between image and condition, between fictional projection and actual perception of city life.[47] It wishes to uncover the source and impact of urban images, to lay bare the interest behind ideological restrictions in *urban* concepts, to discover viable forms of experience and emancipatory practice in the American city. Thus it hopes to continue the modernist search of the novels through a scientific-philosophical inquiry.

Within given material and historical constraints, men and women have actively shaped cities. As they continue to found and rebuild them, as they interpret and evaluate them, they can redefine and change them. Such traces of human agency too are present in the novels even though there is a tendency in modern fiction to project the metropolis as a 'superhuman' environment and as a seemingly uncontrollable force. Literature which remains quasi-autonomous in its playful, indirect, and aesthetic relation to reality and which may not provide direct political or social solutions, nevertheless may correct distorted assessments about human experience in the city. Even though literature cannot change urban conditions, as action takes place beyond texts, it can shape perceptions and influence decisions. Indeed, many American writers and intellectuals were said to be hostile toward their cities because their outspoken opposition to degradation and exploitation in general was misinterpreted as antiurbanism.[48]

As the modern city changes with differing perspectives, the analysis of fictional urban experience cannot confine itself to an assessment of the aesthetic coherence, complexity, or ambiguity in portraying urban life. Rather, it presupposes a precise conception of the urban problems that are projected, a knowledge of what specific historical conditions meant. As no single, self-contained discipline may fully elucidate the city, the present study fuses the compartmentalized strands of urban studies to achieve a better understanding of the topic.[49] Its materialist approach to American society and cities does not claim to have access to superior and apodictical insights, yet it professes to offer the most advanced and comprehensive framework for this type of investigation. As

---

model blurs rather than illuminates the distinct modes of power relations in the "instrumental" and "communicative" field. Habermas, *Knowledge and Human Interests*, p. 59.

[47]This connection has been stressed by Michael C. Jaye and Ann Chalmers Watts, eds., *Literature and the Urban Experience*, New Brunswick, N.J., 1981, p. ix; David M. Fine, *The City, the Immigrant, and American Fiction, 1880-1920*, Metuchen, N.J., 1977, p. ix.

[48]See Lucia and Morton White, *The Intellectual versus the City*, pp. 1-15, 209-39. Claude S. Fischer, *The Urban Experience*, New York, 1976, pp. 15-25. Their thesis has been refuted by Leo Marx, Alan Trachtenberg, Michael Cowan, and Gregory L. Crider. Michael Cowan, *City of the West: Emerson, America, and Urban Metaphor*, New Haven and London, 1976. Gregory L. Crider, "William Dean Howells and the Antiurban Tradition: A Reconsideration," *American Studies*, 19 (1978), 55-64. For a detailed discussion, see chapter 5.

[49]Briggs, p. 26.

any interpretation may only perceive what its urban concept allows to visualize and recognize, fiction is approached with a critically reflected concept of what is urban.

City fiction, however, cannot be exhausted by assessing class perspectives or urban ideologies. As important as it is to specify the ideological perspective, it is important to move beyond claims to documentary mimesis. The analysis of the ideological bias in the depiction of life in American cities is thus only a first step. The second one is the interpretation of the aesthetic transformation of reality. Both, the ideological perspective and aesthetic transformation, are dialectically related. This is true for modern and postmodern novels alike. As dissociated and decentered as the aesthetic fragment may be, it springs from a particular perspective on the city.[50]

The modern novel in its search for meaning is understood as an attempt to create artistic stability and as a frame for orientation in fragmented social worlds. The aesthetic totality which is developed is necessarily partial. Pierre Macherey has explored in *A Theory of Literary Production* the specific ways in which fiction uses, changes, and transcends social ideologies.[51] For Macherey, literature refutes ideology by dissolving its feigned coherence. It exposes ideology by redoubling it in the form and content of the text. Absences, contradictions, and incongruities in a text thus become eloquent and dismantle the false closure and roundedness of ideology. The fragments are recaptured from a feigned aesthetic totality. Beyond Macherey, this study argues that creative novels can generate innovative modes of city perception.

Thus far the historical dimension of the city has been neglected in concentrating on the social constitution of images. Yet ideologies relate to both class and history. Urban imagery as historical imagery reveals the partial needs expressed in class perspectives at different stages. It also indicates how ideological images aim at rendering the temporary in cities as transhistorical. In order to perpetuate the *status quo*, ideology defines the present as transcendental. Especially psychological, archetypal, or metaphysical explanations level the crucial historical variations which exist among the seemingly per-

---

[50]Thus Donald Barthelme's preoccupation with nature and civilization in his short fiction *City Life* can be linked to traditional middle-class and suburban perspectives which are concerned with similar issues and which employ this metaphoric dichotomy (Donald Barthelme, *City Life*, New York, 1970). Italo Calvino's *Invisible Cities*, in their numerical arrangement according to Edwin Hubble's theory of the universe, may be linked to the author's concept of an ahistorical universality of cities and his interpretation of historical Venice (Italo Calvino, *Invisible Cities*, trans. William Weaver, New York, 1972). See Laura Marello, "Form and Formula in Calvino's *Invisible Cities*," *The Review of Contemporary Fiction*, 6 (1986), 95-100.

[51]Pierre Macherey, *A Theory of Literary Production*, trans. Geoffrey Wall, London, 1978. See especially his essays "Lenin, Critic of Tolstoy," pp. 105-35, and "Literary Analysis: The Tomb of Structures," pp. 136-155. For a more detailed explanation of his theory, see chapter 6.

sistent images of the city.[52] Traditional urban and literary theories show similar deficits here. Often, the historical forms of urbanism have been reduced to timeless qualities in images of Babylon or New Jerusalem, of hell or jungle. Similarly, the specific reactions to disruptions in early modernist accounts of the city have been elevated to aesthetic universals as montage, fragmentation, or dissociation.

Frequently in discussions of urban imagery, crucial historical and political distinctions are intentionally levelled: a novel is interpreted as displaying a generic ambivalence toward city life, as depicting a timeless urban impersonality, or eternal urban chaos.[53] Yet the notion of urban chaos, for example, implies contradictory views when spelled out: chaos may mean disorder and instability; but it may also just stand for the opposite, that is the incapacity to perceive a distinctive order; moreover, chaos can be a willed attempt at subverting an imposed order.[54] Urban chaos, then, is too general a concept to be useful: the evaluation of chaos differs according to the distinct needs for order. In Stephen Crane's *Maggie: A Girl of the Streets* and Hubert Selby's *Last Exit to Brooklyn*, the differing definitions of chaos are related to the momentous changes over three quarters of a century. To speak of urban chaos in general then is only possible when attributing to cities a supposedly ontological quality of chaos. But this is the very strategy of *urban* ideology.[55]

The tendency to ahistorical city definitions has been especially strong in connection with *New World* cities. The vast expanse of nature in the West and American myths about the untouched, primal state of frontier territory have been important. This ahistorical attitude combined with the fact that the modern American city was continually rebuilt and changed due to capitalist expansion and that a possible sedimentation of historical forms was erased by the pace of these changes.[56] Hence time categories are frequently used to capture a supposed essence of the American city. According to Claude

---

[52]Barthes, pp. 144f; Williams, pp. 347ff.

[53]Urban is used in this general way in the studies by Blanche Gelfant, Volker Klotz, Monroe K. Spears, Gerhard Hoffmann, Diana Festa-McCormick, and Burton Pike, to name some of the most important. Monroe K. Spears, *Dionysus and the City: Modernism in Twentieth-Century Poetry*, New York, 1970. Gerhard Hoffmann, *Raum, Situation, erzählte Wirklichkeit*, Stuttgart, 1978. Diana Festa-McCormick, *The City as Catalyst: A Study in Ten Novels*, Rutherford, 1979.

[54]Heinz Ickstadt, "Black vs. White City: Kultur und ihre soziale Funktion im Chicago der Progressive Period," *Amerikastudien*, 29 (1984), pp. 199f., 207. William F. Whyte, *Street Corner Society*, Chicago, 1955.

[55]Castells, pp. 75-85. Philip Abrams notes that the city is an "*explanandum*, not an *explanans*." Abrams, p. 30.

[56]Sam Bass Warner, Jr., *The Urban Wilderness: A History of the American City*, New York, 1972, p. 3.

Lévi-Strauss, American cities are particularly prone to obliterate their past because they "are new cities, whose newness is their whole being and their justification."[57]

All in all, the analysis of class perspectives must be accompanied by an examination of the historicity of views. Both the prevailing attitudes toward the city and the state of urban conditions at the time of composition must be analyzed; the vague concept of a *modern* city must be specified for each period. There are visual images of the American city which clearly mark the historical differences: the teeming pedestrian and streetcar center at the turn of the century, the skyscraper-topped downtowns of the 1920s, or the sprawling metropolis of the 1970s. Less visibly, the social and cultural conditions in American cities have altered just as drastically from the widespread visions of progress and success as embodied in the urban version of the American dream early in the century, to the isolation and frenzied desperation in consumption and violence in the crime-ridden metropolis of the 1970s and 1980s.

In the distinct transformations of urban experience, urban aesthetics also reflect historical changes.[58] Raymond Williams has called attention to the fatal academic habit of treating modernism and the metropolis as unchanging universals.[59] Often, critics seem to assume that the city is montage and montage is the city: reciprocally, two historical modes testify to their classical, universal form. Yet the notion of a modernity which is supposed to be stable, conclusive, and static is a contradiction in terms. As the conditions for modernism change continually, the classical forms need not be the only valid answer to capitalist contradictions in cities. Indeed, literary responses have evolved and changed. Walt Whitman's inchoate embracing of early modern New York in the nineteenth century anticipated and triggered various modern reactions. Its rounded totality has, however, become unacceptable for his followers, for John Dos Passos, whose Manhattan has become a web of contingent and autonomous structures, or for Allen Ginsberg whose Fifties' metropolis has become so fragmented as to be "too vast to know, too myriad windowed to govern."[60]

In sum, the complex processes which have produced the unique form of the American city in this century can only be comprehended adequately if the insights of several disciplines are fused. The specific achievement in the fictional transformation of the city can only be grasped if the text is placed into its cultural and historical context: this un-

---

[57]Claude Lévi-Strauss, *Tristes Tropiques*, New York, 1961, p. 100.

[58]Kreutzer, p. 121.

[59]Williams, "The Metropolis and the Emergence of Modernism," p. 14.

[60]Allen Ginsberg, "Waking in New York," *Planet News: 1961-1967*, San Francisco, 1968, p. 72. See also Kreutzer, pp. 278ff.

derstanding of the fragmented fictional city, however, must be preceded by insights into the basis of the fragmented American metropolis itself. Neither can urban idiosyncrasies be separated from the economic and political developments in U.S. society at large, nor can they be reduced to a deterministic reflection of its processes. To establish the relationship between the economic, political, and cultural basis and its spatial manifestations may be difficult, but must be attempted.

In the past, the interpretations of the modernist search in American city novels were often biased and in fatal circularity simply mirrored the dominant perspective. Including material from urban studies is a step towards breaking the vicious circle and revealing difference in the American city where there was difference: the modernist mosaic of refracted and contrary pieces is obviously related to profound transformations which have generated both the fragmented metropolis and the modern novel.

The structure of the study follows from the preliminaries elaborated above. First, the economic origins and the historical evolution of the segregated American city will be sketched as these processes crucially prefigured its modern shape. In the next step, the novels will then be interpreted within this context. The study provides information about the relation between city and society for each phase because a great deal of information on the specific historical conditions has simply been obliterated by the incredible pace of change in the twentieth century. For example, it may be necessary to point out that, unlike today, in the New York of Stephen Crane's *Maggie: A Girl of the Streets* streetcars indicated status and middle-class users, and thus may function both as symbols of modernity and of class in the novel. However, only some of the material will acquire such direct relevance for the analysis. On the whole, the sketch of historical changes in the American city will illumine the tendencies and issues surfacing in the novels.

Chapter 2 will begin with a basic outline of the development of American cities and explain the specific economic, political, and geographical processes which led to their present shape, size, and hierarchy. It will discuss the wider social and cultural processes which have shaped the urban experience of American city dwellers. The synopsis of urban development is geared towards the issues most relevant for the interpretation of the novels used in the study. Moving from American urbanization in general to specific processes within each city, chapter 3 will deal in detail with the diverse modes of life within the fragmented metropolis. It thus intends to establish the historical background of the specific urban experiences of the fictional characters. After an examination of the traditional explanations of urbanism as a way of life, alternate concepts from urban studies will be introduced which are thought more appropriate to grasp the evident multiplicity in urban areas. Insights from urban case studies, research in cognitive mapping and urban semiotics will be presented in this section.

In chapter 4 the popular and intellectual attitudes toward the American city will be sketched. Important as sources of urban images, such attitudes influence the meaning and hence the reception of novels. Against the background of economic and sociological developments, image and condition can be related in greater detail. This chapter will be followed by a discussion of the various city concepts which have been applied in literary criticism to interpret modern urban novels. Finally, the approach of the present study will be fully elaborated.

In the main part of this study, each novel will be interpreted in detail. The concluding chapter will relate the results of the individual readings to developments in U.S. society and modern fiction, sketching the general tendencies in the modernist search for meaning in American city novels.

The first perspective on the American city, however, is a European perspective. The "Citty upon the Hill" precedes the modern metropolis by three centuries: a brief look at the initial image reveals a crucial link.

2

The Modern American City

1. The Boston Paradigm

Aboard the *Arabella* in 1630, John Winthrop, the spiritual and political leader of a fleet of English emigrants, envisioned a Christian brotherhood of farmers and artisans living in a "Citty upon the Hill."[1] Boston would be founded to become a "New Jerusalem": guided by godly love and piety, a united and stable community was to evolve. However, when John Winthrop died in 1649 less than two decades later, the urban utopia had evaporated, the Christian ideals had been readjusted.[2] Materialism and individualism prevailed, trade flourished: the "City upon the Hill" fully embodied the interests of Boston's merchants; New Jerusalem was redefined to mean commercial success. As a citizen remarked, it "hath pleased God to dispose that o[u]r Towne chiefly consists of Trade."[3] In what became a paradigmatic struggle between idealist aspirations and material power, between communal responsibility and unrestrained individualism, this conflict was decided by the power of mercantile considerations in colonial society.[4] In this way, Boston was established as the leading New World town.[5] A sketch of its development may demonstrate the paradigmatic and distinctively American features of this process.

---

[1] Darrett B. Rutman, *Winthrop's Boston: Portrait of A Puritan Town, 1630-1649*, Chapel Hill, 1965, p. 4.

[2] As Darrett B. Rutman shows, the dissolution and secularization of the Christian community was already discernable after just a few years. Rutman, p. 164.

[3] Rutman, pp. 200f.

[4] Darrett B. Rutman stresses the exemplary mode underlying this change: "Individualism and materialism, a Franklinesque morality, a clear distinction between the sacral and secular affairs of men, the associational nature of society--none of these qualities found in Boston as the second decade gave way to the third were Winthropian; none had had a place in that paen delivered aboard the *Arabella* in the grand moment of beginning. Then Winthrop had spoken of society being united in deed and purpose; of men singly and collectively devoted to God; of a subordination of self in the interest of the community for the greater glory of the deity. . . . In Winthrop's Boston the ideal of the medieval community was transformed into the reality of modern society." Ibid., pp. 278f. See also, Howard P. Chudacoff, *The Evolution of American Urban Society*, Englewood Cliffs, N.J., 1981, pp. 2f.

[5] Sam Bass Warner, *The Urban Wilderness: A History of the American City*, New York, 1972, p. 10.

In *Winthrop's Boston: Portrait of A Puritan Town, 1630-1649*, Darret B. Rutman shows that members of the European mercantile elite reestablished themselves in New England and dominated politics in Boston from the beginning. In the crucial question of land distribution it was decreed that acreage could be allotted according to the individual's ability to improve the land. As settlers with large funds and servant laborers could claim much more acres than the common citizen, Boston as a town was soon divided into gentry and generality: by 1649, in a town of three thousand, some 30 families had received almost one half of all the land granted.[6] A severe economic crisis ensued after almost a decade of feverish expansion when the supplies of an argricultural surplus production surmounted the demands of newcomers. Now Winthrop's vision of community, his "Modell of Christian Charity," was further demolished: Boston's elite fully focused on the prosperous future that lay in overseas trade. Boston became a port town of merchants, tradesmen, and seamen--and not of farmers and artisans as had been envisaged in the paen of the founders.[7]

Beyond the unique history of Boston's rise to preeminence in the colony, this pattern of growth forecasts a paradigmatic mode of interaction among capital, state, and culture which would direct the distinctive evolution of towns and cities in North America.[8] The nascent town discloses the interplay of forces more immediately. In economic terms, surplus production fully established mercantile capitalism in New England; politically, though feudal dependencies were loosened in the colony, the settlers favored privilege and hierarchy over communal solidarity; culturally, Christian tenets were interpreted in favor of individualism against the Winthropian ideal, the "Modell of Christian Charity."[9]

If this triad of economics, politics, and culture is intricately interrelated, economic interests have turned out to be the most decisive in the urbanization process and the subsequent imbalance among towns, cities, and regions. In Boston colonial mercantilism came to rule unchallenged as the economy faltered, when supply exceeded demand, when prices for goods plummeted, and profits stagnated.[10] Whatever the religious tenets

---

[6]Rutman provides drastic examples of unequal land distribution: a working family of nine was assigned 36 acres of land, while the son of a gentry family alone was assigned 200 acres. Rutman, pp. 76, 82, 87.

[7]Rutman, pp. 187, 278.

[8]In *The Urban Wilderness*, Sam Bass Warner stresses the enormous influence of decisions by the early settlers. Warner, pp. 3-19.

[9]Warner, p. 16. The "ten," a select committee established in 1636, consisted solely of men who represented the interest of the economic and religious elite. Rutman, p. 81.

[10]Rutman, pp. 185ff.

or communitarian ideals at this point, material considerations ranked foremost with Boston's elite. This clearly is an American paradigm. Admittedly, the general path of the colonial order was decided in England and settlers imported remnants of European thought and a feudal mercantilism;[11] yet the peculiar features in Boston's evolution, its early withdrawal from communal positions--other townships for example preserved them much longer[12]--renders this development paradigmatic, a precursor of that of other prospering towns.[13]

In the following, the specific mode will be described in which economic, political, and cultural factors were interrelated in the United States, how they influenced the location and size of cities and how their interplay shaped the internal structure of the modern segregated city.[14] To discern a decisive influence in the colonial-mercantile phase of American history in which neither towns nor cities existed that were anywhere near the size and heterogeneity of contemporary agglomerations, punctuates that urbanization, even though manifested in towns, cities, and metropolises, is generated by forces which produce the spatial organization of society as a whole.[15] Space is inert until economic and social forces transform it. If capitalism hence achieves great importance in this study, the American city cannot be reduced to a simple reflection of its processes: each culture develops its unique urban form.[16] In this sense, Boston too foreshadowed the distinctively American pattern of city growth.

---

[11]Charles N. Glaab and A. Theodore Brown, *A History of Urban America*, New York, 1967, p. 3.

[12]Warner, p. 10.

[13]Charles N. Glaab and A. Theodore Brown similarly stress that "All of the colonial cities and towns were planned communities in origin; the idea that their growth might be shaped by individuals' interest in real estate speculation was to emerge only slowly." Glaab and Brown, p. 7.

[14]In its summary of recent scholarship the study draws heavily on: Howard P. Chudacoff, *The Evolution of American Urban Society*, Englewood Cliffs, N.J., 1981. Sam Bass Warner, *The Urban Wilderness: A History of the American City*, New York, 1972. Charles N. Glaab and A. Theodore Brown, *A History of Urban America*, New York, 1967. R. J. Johnston, *The American Urban System. A Geographical Perspective*, New York, 1982. Blair Badcock, *Unfairly Structured Cities*, Oxford, 1984. Mark Gottdiener, *The Production of Urban Space*, Austin, Texas, 1985.

[15]Howard P. Chudacoff similarly proposes a comprehensive approach to urbanization. He points out that the "creation and growth of cities were important, but it must be remembered that urbanization is an economic and social process that occurs in a society as a whole, not just in its cities." Chudacoff, p. 34.

[16]Badcock, p. 168. Elisabeth Lichtenberger, *Stadtgeographie*, vol. 1, Wien, 1985, p. 19.

2. The Growth of American Cities

With Boston leading the way, mercantile capitalism soon completely dominated the New World. As yet, colonial interests in the mother country directed social and political life. It is not surprising to note that due to the focus in activity effected by trade, the major colonial settlements spread along the eastern seaboard. Coastwise trade and connections to England predominated the economic performance of the towns.[17] A loose string of port cities evolved along the Atlantic fringe in the seventeenth and eighteenth centuries, with Boston, Newport, New York, Philadelphia, and Charleston as leading settlements. Their size resulted from high economic growth rates. In 1690, Boston led the colonial towns with seven thousand inhabitants, while Philadelphia and New York counted approximately four thousand each.[18]

Eastern port towns profited from the transatlantic mercantilism in two ways: on the one hand, arriving ships brought goods and new settlers who bought supplies in the port of entry; on the other side, ports became centers for the shipment of agricultural goods from the inland. Each port town functioned as a gateway to its hinterland which produced raw materials or harvested the crops for mercantile transactions. An expanding economy pushed towns, farms, and settlers further west opening possibilities to found additional inland towns. It was not primarily Turner's independent frontiersmen but a network of mercantile towns pushed further and further westward taking possession of the land from the natives.[19] Port merchants had most to gain from the colonial economy and they and their towns prospered as they used their initial advantage to predominate inland settlements and thus profited in two directions: both by sea and by land.[20]

---

[17] Even though trade must be thought of in distinct dimensions from today's figures--in the second decade some twenty to twenty-five ships reached Boston harbor annually--this enterprise was sufficient to turn Boston into the center of the Massachusetts settlements. By the middle of the century it already counted one-fifth of the total population of Massachusetts. Rutman, p. 191.

[18] Chudacoff, p. 4. Boston turned its regional hegemony and maritime supremacy into a dominant position in the New World: its vessels carried most of the trade, its shipbuilding industry flourished. Carl Bridenbaugh, *Cities in the Wilderness: Urban Life in America, 1625-1742*, New York, 1938, p. 330.

[19] The basic tenets of Frederick Jackson Turner's influential 'frontier theory' from 1893 were challenged and corrected in Richard C. Wade's *The Urban Frontier, 1790-1830*. Turner saw the frontier as the place where the self-reliant American democrat was formed. Wade showed that an urban frontier colonized the West: "The towns were the spearheads of the American frontier. Planted as forts or trailing posts far in advance of the line of settlement, they held the West for the approaching population." Richard C. Wade, *The Urban Frontier, 1790-1830*, Cambridge, Mass., 1959, p. 1. See also J. W. Reps, *The Making of Urban America: A History of City Planning in the United States*, Princeton, N.J., 1965.

[20] Carl Bridenbaugh, *Cities in Revolt: Urban Life in America, 1742-1776*, New York, 1955, p. 70.

22 Fragmented Urban Images

Competition for market shares was high among the rising number of port merchants on the Atlantic fringe. By the third quarter of the eighteenth century New York had superseded Boston in size.[21] Its merchants and financiers had won the struggle for trade and profits against their rivals from Massachusetts.[22] Boston now began experiencing the drawbacks of commercial stagnation due to uneven development--characteristic of an economic system based in inequality.[23] The growing inequities and contradictions among port towns, conflicts stemming from the very structure of colonial mercantilism, became a decisive element in the 'urban' revolution, in the secession from the British Empire.[24]

Linkages between towns were further extended under mercantile capitalism as the colonies achieved national sovereignty in the late eighteenth century. Since profits could be augmented by enlarging old or adding new markets, merchants were very interested in cheap and reliable transportation links.[25] Thus the first railroads garnered nearby trade to East Coast towns. The canals and railroads financed by merchants and speculators rearranged the surface of the country and accelerated the pace of urbanization in heretofore unseen dimensions. Hundreds of towns and cities boomed along these lines of transportation as nodes in the national economy.[26] The location pattern of

---

[21] While Boston was still the largest town a century after its foundation in 1742 with 16,382 inhabitants, Philadelphia and New York had considerably gained in size and importance. By 1775, New York counted 25,000 inhabitants, Philadelphia as second biggest had 24,000, while Boston had stagnated at 16,000 inhabitants. Chudacoff, pp. 5ff.

[22] There were both political and economic reasons for this rise of New York to preeminence. For one, as Carl Bridenbaugh explains, New York became the center of British military operations in the French and Indian War and profited highly from this decision (Bridenbaugh, *Cities in the Wilderness*, p. 392). Second, until about 1730, New York merchants relied heavily on Boston vessels but then freed themselves from this New England domination (Bridenbaugh, *Cities in Revolt*, p. 45). Finally, New York merchants utilized a major natural asset to keep and extend their leading role: the canal built in the Hudson-Mohawk gap in New York's hinterland allowed easy access to the expanding inland market. Johnston, p. 65.

[23] Neil Smith, *Uneven Development*, Oxford, 1984, p. xi. Since 1735 Boston's commercial activities had stagnated and its growth had stopped. Thus, its merchants and leading citizens were hyperactive in the battle against tributes and taxes levied by the mother country: not surprisingly, Boston was the site of the Tea Party protest. As the English closed off Boston port in turn, the town's leaders saw the certain ruin of their commerce and turned protest into rebellion--a rebellion which eventually culminated in the War for Independence. This chain of events again testifies to the importance of national developments for the conditions in cities. A hundred years later, a similar process of economic decline led Charleston to play a crucial part in the outbreak of the Civil War. Chudacoff, pp. 65f.

[24] Chudacoff, p. 25; Glaab and Brown, pp. 2, 15.

[25] Blair Badcock points out the interest of British manufacturers in the nineteenth century to develop the infrastructure in the former colony. Badcock, p. 91.

[26] The first half of the nineteenth century saw two spurts of canal construction: the first from 1815 to 1834, and a second from 1836 to 1854 (Warner, p. 68). The most successful venture, the 363 miles of the Erie Canal were completed in 1825 and infused the capacities of the thriving Western cities of Buffalo, Chicago,

the railroad indicates to what considerable degree the implementation of a new technology depended on existing surplus capital. From 2,800 miles of track in 1840, to 30,600 in 1860, the railroad network exploded to 210,000 miles by 1904.[27] An expression of financial power, the size and density of linkages was highest in the East.

Directed by the investments of East Coast merchants, unprecedented growth could take place in the American urban system in the nineteenth century. The network itself and its parts expanded. There were five towns with a population over ten thousand in 1790, 37 towns could be counted in 1840, and 168 in 1870. Within the same time the absolute number of people living in towns and cities mushroomed from some two hundred thousand to over six million. The cities of the nation became increasingly integrated. As yet, the urbanization was directed by a predominantly mercantile economy: new towns originated primarily on the basis of commercial activities and good transportation connections.[28]

This pattern of investment changed in the antebellum years: rather than earning money through buying, delivering, and selling goods, more and more entrepreneurs began profiting directly by investing in workers producing goods in factories.[29] Before the Civil War few companies' work force exceeded three hundred laborers, but with the shift to industrial production, factories with several thousand became common.[30] Technological innovations, the *sine qua non* of industrial progress, were thus implemented most profitably. This change in the mode of production, the shift from independent producers to proletarian wage-earners, with its basic tendencies of accumulation and specialization profoundly affected the further evolution of cities. The industrial phase of capitalism generated the basic structures of the U.S. urban system as it exists to date. This transi-

---

Cleveland, and Detroit into New York merchants' network (Russell B. Nye and J. E. Morpurgo, *The Growth of the U.S.A.*, 2 vols., Harmondsworth, 1970, p. 358). By mid-century, this water transportation was challenged by the new communication technology of the railroads. The railroads fully transformed semirural towns into cities (Chudacoff, p. 95). Owing to these new linkages New Orleans would lose virtually all of its Upper Mississippi trade to East Coast merchants (David C. Perry and Alfred J. Watkins, "Contemporary dimensions of Uneven Development in the U.S.A.," *City, Class, and Capital*, eds. Michael Harloe and Elizabeth Lebas, London, 1981, p. 122).

[27] Douglas F. Dowd, *The Twisted Dream: Capitalist Development in the United States since 1776*, Cambridge, Mass., 1977, p. 63. This meant that the U.S. at this point possessed more mileage than all of Europe together. The use of the railroad climaxed in 1916: 254,000 miles stretched all over the United States, transporting 77% of the freight tonnage and 98% of all passengers. Warner, pp. 89ff.

[28] United States Department of Commerce, *Historical Statistics of the United States--Colonial Times to 1957*, 2 vols., Washington, D.C., 1951, p. 14; Chudacoff, p. 37.

[29] Ira Katznelson, *City Trenches: Urban Politics and the Patterning of Class in the United States*, New York, 1981, pp. 48f.

[30] Blake McKelvey, *The Urbanization of America, 1860-1915*, New York, 1963, p. 130.

tion did not occur abruptly; both economic modes existed side by side for some time. By the last third of the nineteenth century, however, industrial production was dominant and specialization took place on a large scale.[31]

Industrialization was based mainly on the investments of merchants and financiers, that is by capital they had accumulated by exploiting an agricultural economy. The hierarchy of cities reflected this persistence: those cities grew strongest where industrial production was preceded by commercial activities. Thus, eight of the nine cities which exceeded a population of 100,000 by 1860 were port cities.[32] In general, urban growth followed two dominant patterns in the late nineteenth century. First, it occurred in the old mercantile centers; port cities and major inland gateways experienced the most rapid increase.[33] Second, specialized industrial cities developed and boomed in the vicinity of mineral deposits.[34]

If predominantly economic interests have been emphasized so far, this is not to deny the influence of political will or cultural convictions in the process of urbanization. At this point in American history, however, the urban growth is dictated almost exclusively by economic forces. Current ideologies precluded any intervention. Thus Jacksonian politics opposed the interference with the market forces which were thought basic to personal freedom. Yet laissez-faire capitalism, following its inherent logic, increased concentration, accelerated minority ownership and thereby destroyed the very independent producer it was meant to protect.[35] Despite this development, economic freedom and social equality remained associated with laissez-faire politics in popular belief--a helpful bourgeois myth perpetuated long after its basis had vanished.[36]

---

[31] Katznelson, pp. 46-52; Badcock, p. 89.

[32] Chudacoff, p. 97. Brooklyn, the ninth city, had grown within the vicinity of a major port. McKelvey, p. 4.

[33] New York ranked first with 813,600 inhabitants in 1860, Philadelphia was second with 565,500, while Chicago still ranked ninth with little over one hundred thousand citizens. In 1910, New York as the leading metropolis had 4,766,900, Chicago as second biggest had mushroomed to 2,185,300 and Philadelphia ranked third with 1,549,000 inhabitants. Chicago had become the major center of the manufacturing belt as the hub of the world's most extensive railroad system. Chudacoff, pp. 63, 102.

[34] Those cities thrived which functioned as entrepots or where raw materials would be processed: Buffalo, Cleveland, Detroit, or Pittsburgh belonged to this new category of the industrial city. Warner, pp. 86-92.

[35] Warner, pp. 78f.

[36] Even in the West, where conditions seemed closer to popular notions of individual freedom this claim does not withstand careful examination: land distribution and commodity prices were regulated by speculators and merchants long before the individual settler could compete for his individual share. Warner, p. 19; Michael Spindler, *American Literature and Social Change*, Bloomington, 1983, p. 21.

Thus, national urban developments were shaped by the destructive potential, the irresponsible boom and bust of industrial capitalism.[37] Toward the close of the nineteenth century, large corporations, trusts, and monopolies increasingly shaped the path of the American economy. The twelve corporations estimated at $10 million or more in 1896 mushroomed within seven years to fifty valued at over $50 million in 1903.[38] The production of industrial goods in large factories further concentrated the labor force in cities. Monopoly and metropolis coincide at this stage: the concentration of capital translates into the geographical concentration of labor. Directed by the same economic mechanisms, industrial and urban development almost become identical: by the turn of the century nine tenths of all industrial output was being produced in cities. In the financial field, a parallel concentration had accompanied this development. The extreme dominance of New York as major metropolis was also reflected by its supremacy in the banking hierarchy.[39]

As a result of these economic and political conditions, urban centers underwent uncontrolled expansion into giant metropolises in the late nineteenth and early twentieth century. With the shifts in economic production, millions of natives and immigrants felt the material need to move to cities. Workers, aggressively recruited in Europe,[40] contributed strongly to U.S. urbanization: altogether 35 million immigrants entered the United States between 1850 and 1930, providing American industry with almost unlimited cheap labor.[41] The urban population multiplied nine times, from 6.2 million in 1860 to 54.4 million in 1920--a period in which the total population of the United States tripled. The total number of urban places mushroomed in the same time from 392 to 2,722. In 1840, only New York had more than 250,000 inhabitants and just two cities had passed the 100,000 mark. By 1910, however, there were 31 places with a population over 100,000, 16 cities had more than 250,000, and three metropolises even contained over a

---

[37]If the state intervened to protect economic freedom its decisions were often determined by the interests of the ruling class: thus the Sherman Anti-Trust Act in 1890 was not used against concentration trends in ownership but against unions and workers' organizations. Samuel Eliot Morison, Henry Steele Commager, and William E. Leuchtenberg, *A Concise History of the American Republic*, New York, 1983, p. 380.

[38]McKelvey, p. 42.

[39]Ibid., pp. 45, 48, 57; Badcock, p. 89.

[40]Fine, *The City, the Immigrant, and American Fiction*, p. 145. Sidney L. Harring, *Policing A Class Society: The Experience of American Cities, 1865-1915*, New Brunswick, N.J., 1985, p. 10.

[41]*Historical Statistics*, p. 8. For a discussion of their social background see John Bodnar, "The European Origins of American Immigrants," *Essays from the Lowell Conference on Industrial History 1982 & 1983*, ed. Robert Weible, North Andover, Mass., 1984, 259-275.

26 Fragmented Urban Images

million inhabitants.[42] What these figures suggest but hardly capture are the immense changes in the ways of life of both native and immigrant Americans under the unrestrained dictate of a 'free' market.

Concentration and specialization were the two basic trends urbanization followed under industrial capitalism. Those cities which had an initial advantage in capital or resources prospered most. Established imbalances and hierarchies were thus cumulatively reinforced.[43] Port cities and inland gateways basically kept the leading positions they had gained during the mercantile period; only a few centers in the vicinity of industrial resources were added. The physiognomy of the present urban system in the United States was formed then: the concentration on the East Coast, in the manufacturing belt of the heartland, and in the regional centers of the South and the West.

This expansion of the national system of cities had occurred unimpeded and almost unaccompanied by political or cultural adjustments. Cities boomed, driven by a compound of forces beyond the grip of single municipal governments. Although developments in cities, such as the growing dissatisfaction in slums, were perceived as a threat to stability, reforms on the federal, state, and local level remained inadequate.[44] Progressivism in the beginning of the century was a first nationwide attempt to ameliorate the situation, but the corrections were often fatally tied to nineteenth-century principles: paradoxically business initiative and interest, which was responsible for the dilemma in the first place, were proposed as remedies.[45] Only in the 1920s, when for the first time more Americans lived in the city than in the countryside, conditions in the exploding metropolises received more and more attention. With the debacle of laissez-faire capitalism at the close of the third decade, symbolized by the collapse of Wall Street, the first federal program set up exclusively for urban areas gave expression to the new coalition of urban liberals and progressive scientists and the subsequent collective spirit of the New Deal. As late as 1937, the first study on federal urban policy was conducted.[46] Still, as Howard Chudacoff has argued, federal programs for urban areas only

---

[42]*Historical Statistics*, p. 14.

[43]Gottdiener, p. 46. As major cities expanded, they diversified their economy. Besides incorporating new manufacturing industries they also kept and increased their commercial and financial hegemony. Cities which ranked low in the urban hierarchy lost their initial diversity and became monoindustrial parts in the national network, the mixed use of the mercantile era gave way to specialization. Warner, pp. 72, 87.

[44]Roy Lubove, *The Progressives and the Slums. Tenement House Reform in New York City, 1890-1919*, Greenwood, 1962, p. 6.

[45]Michael B. Katz, *In the Shadow of the Poorhouse: A Social History of Welfare in America*, New York, 1986.

[46]The United States Conference of Mayors, constituted in 1933, was the first organization to bring urban concerns before the administration and Congress. Chudacoff, p. 237.

accentuated existing trends on the private market and were never conceived of as catering to the good of all groups. Besides, following the progressive tradition, housing and environmental solutions were preferred to social ones; freeways were constructed, slums cleared, loans for housing were provided: the economic plight and social inequality remained untouched. In general, those who profited most from federal subsidies were the white middle-class clientele of politicians.[47]

If federal politics generally had a stronger impact on the development of cities by mid-century, it was nevertheless the U.S. economy which dictated urban rhythms as industrial capitalism moved into its multinational phase. In the second quarter of the century, the American economy underwent further quantitative and qualitative changes in which three related if seemingly contradictory trends of concentration, centralization, and decentralization could be noticed.[48] Above all, the occupational pattern changed. Whereas industrialization had been characterized by a domination of non-agricultural over agricultural employment, a dividing line which was crossed in the 1880s, in the twentieth century white collar occupations rose steadily among manual workers and by the 1950s service sector employment dominated.[49] This boom of the tertiary sector resulted from the rising concentration of corporate power. As companies expanded and coerced mergers to augment their share of the market, their bureaucracies directing and coordinating the activities of the various departments had to enlarge.[50] Also, Federal Government increasingly took over regulatory functions, which substantially augmented its number of civil servants.[51]

The minority control over large sections of the market increased. In the early nineteenth century 80 percent of the working population still consisted of independent producers. This figure fell to 41 percent in 1870, and eventually dropped as low as 18 percent in 1940. Also, by 1933 some six hundred corporations owned more than half of

---

[47]Chudacoff, pp. 284-94.

[48]Castells, pp. 383-92.

[49]Michael P. Conzen, "The American Urban System in the Nineteenth Century," *Geography and the Urban Environment*, 4 (1981), p. 320; Charles H. Hession and Hyman Sardy, *Assent to Affluence. A History of American Economic Development*, Boston, 1969, p. 831.

[50]Between 1919 and 1930 altogether eight thousand businesses disappeared. The two hundred largest non-financial companies already owned one third of all corporate assets in 1909, but twenty years later this share had mounted to almost fifty percent. Dowd, p. 71; Spindler, p. 103.

[51]From virtually no money in 1920, federal expenditures for urban programs rose to hundreds of millions in the 1960s. See Mark I. Gelfand, *A Nation of Cities: the Federal Government and Urban America, 1933-1965*, New York, 1975. The financial crises of the 1970s had their basis in the resulting conflict: while profits remained private and corporate, the rising costs to buffer conflicts became the responsibility of the general taxpayer and the state. Castells, p. 415.

all corporate wealth, while the rest was distributed among 388,000 companies.[52] Concentration at this stage induced centralization: corporation headquarters were located in the major metropolitan centers, with New York at the top of the hierarchy.[53] In banking, the leading metropolis kept its hegemony which it had established early in the century.[54]

This process of economic concentration directly affected the shape of the national system of cities. In the second quarter of the twentieth century, U.S. society moved from an urban to a metropolitan stage in which large cities were further accentuated: from eight and a half million inhabitants in 1920, to eleven and a half in 1940, the population in New York's metropolitan area rose to over nineteen million in 1970.[55] However, urbanization now also incorporated smaller places and formerly untouched areas as the implementation of new communication and transportation technology facilitated existing decentralizing tendencies. Power was exerted from sprawling metropolitan areas: the fifty largest companies, all situated in the fifty-five metropolitan areas with a population over 500,000 inhabitants, controlled over ninety percent of the employees in the manufacturing, retailing, utilities, transportation, banking, life insurance, and financial sectors of the U.S. economy.[56] The majority of people consequently had to work and live in metropolitan areas; 51,4% of the population were urban in 1920, 56,5% in 1940, and 73,5% in 1970.[57] Within an interrelated and hierarchically organized structure, metropolitan areas developed into multicentered corridors, into huge agglomerations: "megalopolis" was the final consequence.[58] As Lewis Mumford noted, "The electric grid,

---

[52] T. B. Bottomore, *Classes in Modern Society*, London, 1965, p. 42 (cited in Spindler, p. 25); Morison, p. 584.

[53] In 1960, one third of the largest five hundred manufacturing companies had their management in Manhattan. Another index to the degree of centralized power is the number of jobs directed from metropolitan centers: again, 8.5 million employees were controlled from New York headquarters in 1970--more than four times as much as from the two next largest centers, Detroit and Chicago. Johnston, pp. 70, 133.

[54] In 1910, New York handled $100 billion of business, while Chicago and Boston only handled $12 respectively $8 billion. Johnston, p. 70.

[55] Kenneth T. Jackson, "The Capital of Capitalism: The New York Metropolitan Region, 1890-1940," *Metropolis 1890-1940*, ed. Anthony Sutcliffe, London, 1984, p. 320. Chicago, as second largest metropolis, similarly increased from 3,376,400 in 1920, to 4,569,600 in 1940, and eventually to 6,981,300 in 1970. Irving Cutler, *Chicago: Metropolis of the Mid-Continent*, Chicago, 1973, p. 179.

[56] Johnston, p. 135.

[57] On the regional level concentration was even higher. Robert Estall, *A Modern Geography of the United States*, Harmondsworth, 1976, p. 51.

[58] Jean Gottmann first described this phenomenon in the "Boswash" megalopolis in 1960: six hundred miles of continuous urban settlement extend from Boston to Washington, D.C. Jean Gottmann, *Megalopolis: The Urbanized Northeastern Seaboard of the United States*, Cambridge, Mass., 1961.

not the Stone Age container, provides the new image of the invisible city and the many processes it serves and furthers."[59]

The emerging pattern of urbanization was closely tied to general tendencies in U.S. postindustrial society. Produced for mass consumption, private cars and prefabricated housing units changed cities into multicentered, low-density areas.[60] Economic pressure and lobbying made the private car the single most important means of transportation in the American city. Automobile corporations even acquired streetcar and railway companies to dismantle their networks of mass transportation. Above all, Federal Government provided huge subsidies to automobile companies in form of highway construction programs.[61] Suburbanization, begun in the nineteenth century alongside streetcar lines, now flourished fully: a million single-family houses were built in 1950 alone in the vicinity of agglomerations. By 1970, 76 million Americans lived in suburbs.[62] Particularly in those regions which experienced their major growth after 1930, metropolitan settlement sprawled under the dictate of individualized consumption. Los Angeles, for instance, had to yield two thirds of its space to private traffic.[63] In general, real estate speculators, developers, and car manufacturers profited most, while public transportation became less and less efficient with low residential densities. In turn, additional highway programs increased the debts of metropolitan municipalities.

The nation's altered role in world politics profoundly influenced these urbanization patterns in the second half of the twentieth century. The rise to economic power, followed by the rise to military and political power after World War I and World War II, were highly influential for U.S. urban developments.[64] Its novel role as a super power found expression in the federal budget: the slice assigned to the military and industrial sector rose rapidly. Through major expenditures in these fields, the U.S. government could influence and direct regional urban development. Money which flowed into the research of military and aeronautic projects chiefly helped industrial corporations in the

---

[59]Mumford, p. 645.

[60]Ibid., p. 386. In 1908, 63,500 cars were sold in the United States. This figure jumped to 1,525,600 in 1916 and to a first relative high in 1929 with 4,445,200 car sales. In 1965 alone, 9,306,000 new automobiles were sold. Lance E. Davis, Richard A. Easterlin, and William N. Parker, *American Economic Growth. An Economist's History of the United States*, New York, 1972, p. 259.

[61]Castells, p. 387.

[62]Chudacoff, pp. 209ff., 264f.

[63]Morison, p. 706.

[64]The share of U.S. manufactured goods in world export was about four percent in the 1890s. It rose to thirteen percent in the second decade of the present century and by the fifties the United States' share exceeded 25 percent. Davis, p. 576.

West and the South.[65] As a consequence, these areas showed incredible urban growth rates. By 1970, California had surpassed New York in population and had become the largest state in the union; nine out of ten Californians lived in metropolitan areas. Moreover, subsidized research generated spin-off innovations. Growth industries which were initially linked to developments in the military-industrial complex such as new electronic and communication technologies boomed in these regions and, as they had the initial advantage in know-how, shifted economic power to these areas. California thus became the most urbanized state.[66] Sam Bass Warner names the forces behind these developments: "Since World War II the magnitude of the corporate and federal effort has in large measure determined the national location of jobs."[67]

Corporate concentration on the national and international level and high federal spending shaped developments in U.S. urbanization in the second half of the twentieth century: the high degree of control is expressed in research expenditures, which are indispensable for innovations and new ventures. Some six hundred firms control ninety-five percent of industrial research; Federal Government funds half of the total research in the United States. The control, previously concentrated in metropolitan centers, now has been decentralized with the aid of modern communication systems. The dependence of major metropolises on non-local decisions has reached incredible dimensions: forty percent of San Francisco's jobs, a major regional center, are controlled from New York City--which itself has also over half a million jobs controlled elsewhere.[68]

The national and international dimension of American urbanization is bluntly evident on this economic and geographical level: metropolitan growth, the form and location of cities, was directed by U.S. capitalism. This was the energy which fuelled developments in single cities, in adjacent towns and villages. And yet, in American culture and politics, the old polarity between country folks and city dwellers, between seemingly

---

[65]Raymond Mohl, "The Transformation of Urban America Since the Second World War," *Amerikastudien*, 33 (1988), pp. 64f.

[66]Another result of this spending pattern was the increase of urbanization in the Southwest and the Old South in recent years. Cities in the Northeast declined or stagnated in the seventies and eighties, while the major centers of the South had incredibly high growth rates. Urban space and labor were cheaper there. Corporations could bypass the industrial legacies of the North: they could evade unionization and progressive workers' legislation, evade the costs for renewing the outdated and deficient infrastructure, evade the critical potential which accumulated and exploded in the urban crisis of the Sixties. Some factions in northern metropolitan centers, however, in the financial and quarternary sector, profited from Southern developments: if the New York area as a whole stagnated, the construction craze in the business and finance district of Manhattan in the eighties testified to undiminished corporate profits. See David C. Perry and Alfred J. Watkins, *The Rise of Sunbelt Cities*, Beverly Hills, 1977; Mohl, pp. 53-71; Johnston, p. 149.

[67]Warner, p. 148.

[68]Johnston, pp. 137, 147f.

autonomous rival cities, each with identification formulae for its citizenry, dominated the discussion and blurred the conflict underlying the inequality among settlements. In the first half of the century legislation remained in the hands of rural politicians who were biased against federal programs to leaven the problems in cities: the ideology of division, the spatial antagonism between country and city seemed to provide an adequate answer to the problems. Only in 1960, the U.S. Supreme Court mandated a political reapportionment long overdue; yet by the time it redistributed power, it only helped the white middle class and its suburbs which had already benefitted most from previous housing and development programs.[69]

Uneven development, the hallmark of capitalism, appears on all levels: if cities themselves form a hierarchy and appear unequal in power and influence, if country and city seem to have conflicting interests, their differences become secondary when looking at the social division within each of the settlements. The black working-class child in Chicago's South Side and the poor hill-billy kid from the Appalachians have more in common than their geographical and cultural animadversion suggests.

The process which led to segregation in modern American cities, regardless of their rank in the national hierarchy, will be examined in the next section. For some, at the lower rungs of the economic ladder, there even was a reverse relation to metropolitan importance: manufacturing wages in New York City were lower than those in Birmingham, Alabama.[70] The distribution of wealth and power expressly follows class and not urban lines.

3. The Segregated City

The unequal distribution of resources which caused regional imbalances and produced a hierarchy among American cities reappears on a lower scale in the fragmented structure of the modern American city. Yet although the segregated metropolis results from the inequalities inherent in a capitalist economy, its specific fragmentation, as Sam Bass Warner has pointed out, was strongly shaped by fundamental decisions of the early settlers.[71] Two major legacies of the seventeenth and eighteenth centuries were influential in creating the peculiar mosaic of the U.S. city: property law and the gridiron

---

[69]Chudacoff, pp. 39, 291.

[70]Warner, p. 120.

[71]Ibid., pp. 3-19.

layout. Both contributed to the idiosyncratic physiognomy which developed in the American metropolis under industrial capitalism.

Individual ownership of land was conceived as a superior civil liberty from the very beginning. The Puritan land tenure which evolved as a response to oppression and restriction by feudal landlords promised to hold a fair solution to the allocation of resources.[72] Even though the shortcomings of this system were clearly palpable by the eighteenth century, the American Constitution codified the practice, for politics in this field was dominated then by the interests of traders, financiers, and speculators. The conflict between private and public control of urban space only became a central issue in the late nineteenth century; by then a legal moat surrounded the private exploitation of land fending off public interference and democratic control.[73]

The force behind the seemingly free development in cities became visualized through the gridiron pattern, the dominant American layout. The grid not only helped speculators to maximize their profits; its controlled geometry and its unrelenting efficiency expressed the very spirit underlying capitalist land use.[74] If property law prevented democratic control of communal interests, the layout facilitated the subordination of public concern to private speculation. The belief in the superiority of private over public ownership of land accompanied historical changes in American cities without appropriate adjustments. But the lack of adequate democratic measures against capitalist control of urban space was only conceived problematic as cities exploded to segregated metropolises in the last third of the nineteenth century.

Until then, the 'walking city' was characterized by its compactness, its high density, its mixing of different land uses. Sam Bass Warner asserts that if the mixture of social classes and ethnic groups is regarded as the criterion for urbanity, the zenith of the American city is to be dated around the mid-nineteenth century.[75] Interesting to note, it thus coincides with the city which Walt Whitman celebrates in his New York poems. However, the urbanity of this period is not to be confounded with urban equality.

---

[72]The restraining influence of close-knit communities in early townships and the seemingly illimitable availability of land (ancient land-use rights of Native Americans were simply disregarded) rendered private ownership attractive to all white settlers. Warner, pp. 8ff.

[73]Chudacoff, p. 34; Warner, p. 26.

[74]Chudacoff, p. 49. It was applied in Charleston in 1672, in Philadelphia in 1682, and was firmly engrained as the American pattern with the Land Ordinance in 1785. The block layout in Manhattan was implemented in 1811 under the pressure of speculators and land developers. Harold Carter, *The Study of Urban Geography*, 1972, London, 1981, p. 57; McKelvey, *The Urbanization of America*, p. 10.

[75]Warner, p. 84.

Blacks, Indians, and women were excluded from the political and social life of society.[76] Besides, De Tocqueville's egalitarianism too has been dismantled as myth: urban communities were already highly stratified in the eighteenth century and contained the seeds for the gigantic disruptions to follow.[77] Services in the city were distributed along class lines, sanitation existed solely for those who could afford it. Under closer inspection, the seeming hodgepodge reveals the virtually unrestrained rule of economic forces, with Boston having paved the way.[78]

The deficits of the land-use practices were aggravated by the immense growth of cities in the late mercantile and early industrial phase. In 1700, the largest town had 6,700 inhabitants, one hundred years later New York had just passed the 60,000 mark, but by the beginning of the twentieth century the leading metropolis had mushroomed to 3,437,200.[79] In the early modern city, the inequality and social stratification of capitalist industrialism was reproduced in segregated land-use patterns and separate social neighborhoods. The inherent tendency in capitalist production to concentrate and specialize also ruled the use of urban space. As Ira Katznelson stresses, the American exceptionalism was closely tied to the particular division between work and home which was established then for the male faction of society.[80]

In the modern city segregation meant that the male workplace and the residence of the families became divided, that the land-use demands for industry and housing were separated. Economic interests ruled these processes without constraint:

> The Jacksonian entrepreneurial ethos and land use control by the community were mutually exclusive. Jacksonian liberalism precluded any planned and orderly development of the human and material resources of the urban community.[81]

---

[76] For an account of the female city in this period see Barbara J. Berg, *The Remembered Gate: Origins of American Feminism, The Woman and the City, 1800-1860*, New York, 1978.

[77] In Boston, for instance, five percent owned 44 percent of all taxable property in 1771, and by 1833, four percent of Bostonians even possessed 59 percent. Chudacoff, p. 51.

[78] Warner, p. 204; Chudacoff, p. 43; Katznelson, p. 49.

[79] Bridenbaugh, *Cities in the Wilderness*, p. 143; Ira Rosenwaike, *Population History of New York City*, Syracuse, 1972, p. 63.

[80] Katznelson, pp. 19f.

[81] Roy Lubove, *The Progressives and the Slums. Tenement House Reform in New York City, 1890-1919*, Greenwood, 1962, p. 3.

34 Fragmented Urban Images

The city builder controlled urban land, the successful townsman was involved in speculation. Real estate speculators invested both in land and housing developments.[82] With innovations in short-range transportation implemented by financiers in the second half of the nineteenth century, speculators could offer residences in green environs to their upper-class clientele, residences which were closely linked to the commercial center. Northeastern cities which were endowed with the required capital dispersed first: omnibuses, commuter railroads, and eventually streetcars spread in the growth areas and became the vehicles of a mobile upper and middle class.[83] Speculative construction ventures were closely linked to this development in inner-city transport. Developers bought tracts of land along streetcar lines and built suburban houses for affluent customers. Social distance was thus enhanced by spatial segregation in the early modern city: downtown was the place where for the time being the mixture was retained.[84] Those who could afford it fled the discomfort and noise of the urban core and were provided with spacious housing on the fringes of the booming cities. The ideal of true womanhood and domesticity among the upper and middle class assisted this move:

> If the city was place of filth, disease, and disorder, the Victorian home was to be a model of impeccable cleanliness and order, where each item had its place. If physical health was vital to moral health, then the true woman practiced preventive medicine by providing a good diet, thoroughly washing everything in sight, and keeping the house free from dust. In this manner, cooking and housekeeping were transformed, in theory, from drudgery into a domestic science.[85]

Speculative construction of inner-city tenements was not as lucrative as suburban ventures. Therefore, dwellers in the center constantly suffered from overcrowding and from housing shortages--which, on the other hand, kept rents high.[86] As a result, slums expanded rapidly. The filtering process in which the housing vacated by the rich was to trickle down to poorer residents produced insufficient and inferior housing.[87] Besides, if petty speculators decided to have tenements built, this meant that lots had to be used most intensively, regardless of the detrimental effect on the health of prospective

---

[82]McKelvey, *The Urbanization of America*, p. 12. Speculators controlled the land in the central business district and on the urban periphery making immense profits with the rise in real estate values. Chudacoff, pp. 85, 203.

[83]Glaab and Brown, p. 155; Chudacoff, pp. 81f.

[84]Katznelson, p. 38.

[85]Marlene Stein Wortman, "Domesticizing the Nineteenth-Century American City," *Prospects*, 3 (1977), p. 536.

[86]Castells, p. 390.

[87]Warner, p. 269.

tenants. This speculative system, which lacked any control by housing or health regulations, introduced the overcrowding, the bad sanitation, the diseases, and the dilapidated structures which have since typified inner-city areas. Those buildings which needed improvement most remained unrepaired because the landlords were unwilling or unable to procure money for proper maintenance. With the population pressure created by American industrial capitalism, by the aggressive recruitment of European immigrants and the indigenous migration from rural areas, the majority of the people in cities dwelled in inhuman conditions. By the 1890s seven out of ten New Yorkers lived in tenements.[88]

Mounting violence in cities testified to the tensions produced by laissez-faire capitalism: crime and riots increased in frequency and severity by the middle of the nineteenth century, especially in times of economic crisis.[89] Crime, riots, and the fear of epidemics in densely populated areas horrified upper- and middle-class citizens.[90] Yet, the measures taken in response attacked the symptoms, but did hardly anything to remove or alleviate the causes. One answer, a salaried, professional police force was introduced to the leading cities in the 1840s and 1850s. Though the police force multiplied in the 1860s more quickly than the urban population, crime figures and rioting rose just as rapidly.[91] New York alone saw eight major riots between 1834 and 1871, protests climaxing in 1863 with two thousand people killed during the draft riots.[92]

Such upheavals and the news of an imminent cholera epidemic in 1865 produced a novel response to the problems by New York municipal leaders. In 1867, with the enactment of the Tenement House Law, a first, inefficient step was taken toward a municipal regulation of construction business. Also, middle-class philanthropists gradually began to notice the discrepancy between the claims of the Constitution and the harsh realities of growing American cities. Private charity organizations were founded, and

---

[88]Lubove, pp. 9, 43. Robert G. Barrows has pointed out that the extent of New York tenement crowding was unique among cities in the United States. Still, in each city the majority lived in indecent dwellings. Robert G. Barrows, "Beyond the Tenement: Patterns of American Urban Housing, 1870-1930," *Journal of Urban History*, 9 (1983), 395-420.

[89]McKelvey, p. 93.

[90]Lubove, p. 6. It is telling to see that the elite only reacted to the riots, but not to the problems and needs of these people. The official language has remained revelatory to date: slums are seen as disease, as blight, as menace to existing conditions. Warner, p. 24.

[91]Chudacoff, p. 43; McKelvey, p. 93. Contrary to what upper- and middle-class critics claimed, the police controlled the urban labor force efficiently by the end of the nineteenth century. Harring, p. 150.

[92]Warner, p. 79.

churches eventually discovered the social gospel.[93] But help still was closely linked to laissez-faire principles.[94] The same processes which had brought about the inhuman conditions for working-class families, had made the rich lose touch with the plight of the lower classes. An autonomous working-class culture evolved in cities by the middle of the nineteenth century.[95] Tenement districts increasingly became foreign territory for wealthy members of society; the term "slumming" came to mean a fashionable pursuit for the affluent, a visit to slum areas for enjoyment or charitable purposes.[96] In reform programs, upper- and middle-class blindness of slum reality took on grotesque forms at times: destitute women were taught how to serve tea from silver trays.[97] All in all, the division in the early modern city extended well beyond income and residence.

Toward the close of the nineteenth century, the insight into the necessity for urban reforms increased. Approaches differed considerably: some wide-eyed settlement workers wanted to help the needy and organize them politically; other middle-class factions saw in reforms nothing but the means for enhanced social control; patriotic groups, finally, saw their national ideals threatened by the mass of alien intruders and recognized in reforms a tool to further the Americanization of the immigrant.[98] The business elite also saw the necessity to respond to inefficiency in urban management. It was not only that their values seemed questioned by conditions in cities,[99] but also powerful competitors, the political machines, had emerged in municipal affairs in the second half of the nineteenth century.

After the old Protestant elite had withdrawn from municipal affairs earlier in the century, party machines had filled the political vacuum of Jacksonian cities. Based on lo-

---

[93] Ibid., p. 219; Chudacoff, p. 179.

[94] Michael B. Katz points out that there was a concerted drive to make relief solely private: "Alarmed by the disorder of American cities in the last third of the nineteenth century, frightened by the spectre of a militant, organized, and undeferential working class, the charity organizers responded as harshly as employers and governments confronted with similar problems. The task charity organizers set themselves was to teach the poor that they had no rights. Afraid that relief was turning into a right, the new reformers put all their energy into transforming it back into charity." Michael B. Katz, *In the Shadow of the Poorhouse: A Social History of Welfare in America*, New York, 1986, p. 58.

[95] Katznelson, pp. 58f.

[96] Warner, "The Management of Multiple Urban Images," pp. 387f.

[97] Chudacoff, p. 185.

[98] Ibid., pp. 174f.; Glaab and Brown, p. 259; Blake McKelvey, p. 174. Richard Hofstadter, *The Age of Reform*, New York, 1955, p. 180f.

[99] Martin Shefter, "Images of the City in Political Science: Communities, Administrative Entities, Competitive Markets, and Seats of Chaos," *Cities of the Mind*, eds. Lloyd Rodwin and Robert M. Hollister, New York, 1984, p. 81.

cal organizations at the beginning, they had developed centralized structures in and around City Hall.[100] They had recognized the importance of urban politics: votes in a democracy meant power. Through political influence, they could acquire the means for pragmatic help among immigrants, for the distribution of jobs, services, and bribes among their clientele--and also for personal enrichment. Of course, their extralegal activities and amoral code of conduct aroused middle-class opposition, but it was the increasing control over municipal affairs of the political machines, the resulting patronage and corruption, and their cooperation with big business which increased cries for reforms.[101]

Machine politicians helped millions of immigrants in an unbureaucratic manner: their organizations assisted the newcomers in adjusting to strange surroundings by providing vital community services. Many leaders were sons of immigrants, and thus intimately knew of the problems in the city and how to find a job or cheap housing.[102] Political power in City Councils was used to secure the economic funds for the party machine: bribes and grafts were accepted means, franchises and charters were profitably sold to the business world. By 1880, all major cities had seen machine rule. Clearly, without the help of the machine the urban poor would have been in a worse predicament. The close relation between machines and police departments at times even ensured protection against middle-class prudery or harassment. Nevertheless, the strength of the political organization, its pragmatism and community orientation, also was its flaw: it deflected and appeased political struggle for more profound changes.[103] Above all, the most damaging development at this stage was the division into politics at work and politics of community among the emerging working-class. Workers were politically united as labor but virtually mute in the community. Ira Katznelson writes:

> What is distinctive about the American experience is that the linguistic, cultural, and institutional meaning given to the differentiation of work and community, a characteristic of all industrialist capitalist societies, has taken a sharply divided form, and that it has done so for a very long time.[104]

Thus, the growing urban working class found itself controlled by both economic and political structures which precluded their self-determination and freedom. Their

---

[100]Katznelson, pp. 56ff, 67; Chudacoff, p. 142.

[101]Ibid., p. 141. See also Lincoln Steffens' articles on municipal corruption: Lincoln Steffens, *The Shame of the Cities*, 1904, New York, 1957.

[102]Hofstadter, p. 177; Chudacoff, pp. 143ff.

[103]Ibid., pp. 146f., 159, 163.

[104]Katznelson, p. 19.

working schedule was decided by entrepreneurs, housing conditions were regulated by speculators, and their political power was buffered by party machines. On the other side, the middle class was frightened and horrified by the conditions in industrial cities, neglecting its share in producing the very environment. As Richard Sennett explains, the gigantic upheavals produced by industrial capitalism left many middle-class families insecure and frustrated; the aggression which resulted from this conflict was directed against the forces of chaos and subversion: mob rule was projected and feared, a better policing of immigrants was demanded.[105]

This continued hegemony of a relatively small but powerful group over the majority of urban society cannot be adequately understood and explained unless American peculiarities and their reflection in dominant ideologies are taken into consideration. The orthodox explanation for the acquiescent working class in the United States, the belief that "American socialism had been shipwrecked on shoals of apple-pie and roast beef,"[106] cannot be upheld in the face of recent wage comparisons.[107] Rather, the unique division into local party organizations and business unions split and integrated the powerful male electorate. Rivalries among ethnic groups were used by ward politicians and thwarted mutual action.[108] Besides, strong individualist myths and the nineteenth-century belief in progress obstructed political solidarity. For Sam Bass Warner, the special irony in the widespread 'privatism' of the New World is an "almost universal faith in private property as the anchor of personal freedom" and the "recurrent recognition of private property's social, economic, and political tyrannies."[109] The burgeoning proletarian movements were also invalidated as the hope to participate in the American dream made many move from city to city to better their lot. Consequently, the turnover in the

---

[105] Richard Sennett, *Families Against the City: Middle Class Homes of Industrial Chicago, 1872-1890*, New York, 1974. See also Pike, *The Image of the City in Modern Literature*, pp. 110f.

[106] Werner Sombart cited in Peter R. Shergold, *Working-Class Life: The American Standard in Comparative Perspective, 1899-1919*, Pittsburgh, 1982, p. 224.

[107] American workers were not generally more affluent than their European counterparts, rather the differences in wages within the labor force were stronger. Peter Shergold concludes: "The profound socioeconomic divisions stunted the growth of any mass movement based upon the concept of a united working class. It is the comparative inequality of wage rewards in the United States, an income gulf widened by ethnic heterogeneity and racial prejudice, that must provide the socioeconomic context within which to analyze the American labor movement. American workers found it profoundly difficult to perceive their very different lifestyles as the product of a common exploitation. It was not a high average standard of living that dictated how they behaved." Shergold, p. 229.

[108] Marc Fried, Ellen Fitzgerald, Peggy Gleicher, Chester Hartman, et al., *The World of the Urban Working Class*, Cambridge, Mass., 1973, p. 256.

[109] Warner, p. 15.

neighborhoods was high and the ties among the working class were weakened.[110] Finally, populism and religious fundamentalism deflected criticism to the innate and timeless evils of cities.[111] Such myths and ideologies, spread through the commerical mass media, aided the upper and middle class to advance their views.

The business elite supported and spread cultural ideals which allowed them to forge control. It thus promoted boosterist competition and civic pride to gloss over the fundamental material inequality within each city. As Heinz Ickstadt shows, the City Beautiful movement which originated with the Columbian Exposition in Chicago in 1893 proposed architectural and political solutions in which the mob was rigorously submitted to upper-class leadership.[112] Though genteel reformers may have believed in their calling, they were certainly not blind to their own interests:

> All thinking people agree we must humanize these communities of mixed people; we must raise the standard of living among them, and they must become more rational in their thinking and acting, to make them good and safe citizens. If we can do this we will make our cities more desirable for the home-seeker, and a safe place for business enterprise and development.[113]

With the proliferation of high-rise architecture, skyscraper and skyline competition was promoted among American cities so that patriotic citizens would identify with their city and their local elite.[114] Such ancillary ideological influences were accompanied by repressive measures and overt campaigns for social control. Unionization was impeded under the Sherman Anti-Trust Act, the police forced workers to comply to middle-class views of order and propriety, public opinion was molded through the commercial press which agitated against the unruly mob of foreigners, and protestant missions imposed their values on the lower classes.[115]

---

[110] See David Ward, *Cities and Immigrants: A Geography of Change in Nineteenth-Century America*, New York, 1971.

[111] Josiah Strong, for instance, held that the "first city was built by the first murderer, and crime and vice and wretchedness have festered in it ever since." Josiah Strong, *The Twentieth Century City*, New York, 1898, p. 181.

[112] Heinz Ickstadt, "Öffentliche Fiktion und bürgerliches Leben--der amerikanische Roman der Jahrhundertwende als kommunikatives System" *Amerikastudien--Theorie, Geschichte, interpretatorische Praxis*, eds. Martin Christadler und Günter Lenz, Stuttgart, 1977, p. 224.

[113] Cited in Ickstadt, "Black vs. White City: Kultur und ihre soziale Funktion im Chicago der Progressive Period," p. 204.

[114] Warner, p. 393.

[115] Chudacoff, p. 146. In Chicago alone, more than a million laborers were arrested for violation of public order in bars between 1890 and 1915. Harring, p. 159.

40 Fragmented Urban Images

By the beginning of the twentieth century, the fight against the urban dilemma, the reform of deficient municipal governments, was seen as a foremost challenge for American society. James A. Bryce had asserted in 1888 that there "is no denying that the government of cities is the one conspicuous failure of the United States."[116] Early reform movements now saw their cause resumed by 'muckraking' journalists and progressive politics. In the early twentieth century, the coalition of social groups which constituted urban progressivism tried to correct the crying injustice in urban areas and municipal government which they perceived foremost in corruption, child labor, and slum housing.[117] However, by the time when urban liberals, the new urban coalition of reformers and of an immigrant-stock working class, were to hold political power in the 1930s, the problems had mushroomed beyond the control of individual municipal councils as urban issues had acquired a pronounced national dimension. Vital decisions had long before passed into the hands of trusts and corporations which operated on a national and international level. The regulation of corporations by municipal governments was invalidated as the leading companies by mid-century had themselves reached the size of major nineteenth-century cities. In addition, groups opposing government intervention had gained in numbers within cities as the nation prospered.[118] While the dominance in the world market enabled more Americans to rise to the middle class, the peculiar effect of metropolitan growth in which the service sector increases disproportionately with the size of a metropolis, led to the development of a numerous petty-bourgeois clientele beside the traditional faction of working-class households.[119] In addition, the administration of cities had become a mosaic of segregated areas with conflicting interests and fragmented governmental structures.[120]

As the 1920s brought an incredible increase in private automobiles, the new mobility of the middle class allowed many to move to the suburbs. The suburbs which had begun to attract the wealthy in the second half of the nineteenth century now were open to millions of Americans. Individualized consumption and the new transportation pattern produced the typical low-density sprawl outside the metropolitan cores. By 1950, a

---

[116] Cited in McKelvey, *The Urbanization of America*, p. 97.

[117] Chudacoff, pp. 190-196; Katz, p. 113.

[118] Warner, pp. 125f., 132f.

[119] In 1955, the United States counted six percent of the world population but produced fifty percent of all goods. Morison, p. 703; Warner, p. 133.

[120] Gottdiener, pp. 61f. By 1970, Chicago alone embraced 1,172 administrative units of which 1,100 could levy taxes. Estall, p. 418.

ring of white middle-class citizens surrounded the central district which contained the least mobile and underprivileged. Howard Chudacoff stresses the ethnic dimension:

> Since World War II the division between cities and suburbs has assumed a racial dimension--whites on the outside, blacks on the inside. Between 1950 and 1966, 70 percent of the increase in the nation's white population occurred in the suburbs, while 86 percent of the increase in the black population took place in central cities.[121]

With manufacturing and retailing relocating on the urban fringe, jobs for the deprived became even scarcer in the center and the inner cities were drained of tax revenues. Although some white ethnic neighborhoods were well-maintained owing to higher portions of homeowners, inner-city decay generally advanced: social inequality was enhanced by unequal access to metropolitan facilities.[122] The filtering process did not procure sufficient housing units, public housing projects were negligible,[123] and overcrowding led to the quick wear of tenements.[124] The tenements and rowhouses built around the turn of the century formed the environment of the central districts by the 1970s; much of this housing, however, did not fulfill standards of 1900.[125] Housing shortages and subsequent overcrowding were further aggravated in post-war decades as highway construction picked inner-city areas with the cheapest land and the least juridical resistance.[126] In the seventies, the large-scale abandonment of housing units in the inner city blatantly visualized the deficits of urban policies.[127] Still, the central business districts retained the symbols of success and wealth, displayed the American dream in teasing, glittering towers right before the eyes of those who had failed or were to fail in the system.[128]

Suburbs continued to grow and multiply as white collar occupations continued to profit most from the shifts in corporate capitalism. By 1970, more people lived in suburbia than in central districts. The suburban middle class, which had managed to receive

---

[121] Chudacoff, p. 276.

[122] Castells, pp. 388ff.

[123] Less than two percent of Americans dwelled in public housing projects in 1970. Warner, p. 241.

[124] At the density at which blacks had to live in Harlem in 1960, the entire population of the United States could have been housed within the five New York boroughs. Estall, p. 411.

[125] Warner, p. 51.

[126] Urban renewal projects commonly meant a net loss of cheap housing. Chudacoff, p. 288.

[127] Castells, p. 408. For 1973 alone, the official figures have one hundred thousand units abandoned in New York City.

[128] It is important to stress the difference in the inner city between the wealth in the CBD and the decay of residential areas at large. Castells, p. 389.

42 Fragmented Urban Images

the greatest share of federal loans, denied their responsibility in municipal matters and refused to assist the underprivileged who were left helpless in the impoverished core.[129] Suburbia secured that their communities became unincorporated and thus would not have to contribute with their taxes to metropolitan expenditures. The poor thus paid for the commuters' highways to the suburbs--for the very roads which further decimated cheap housing.[130] Also, the poor in inner cities paid more for the maintenance of parks, art galleries, and museums than those from the periphery who primarily used these facilities.[131]

Federal urban policy under the influence of a rural majority had long been biased against aid for the central cities. When electoral reapportionment was finally achieved in the sixties, white suburbs and rural interests formed a new alliance which opposed innercity needs.[132] The alarming rise in crime, the race riots in the 1960s, the fiscal crises in the 1970s, but also the spread of a new collectivity in tenant and grass roots movements resulted from these disparities. Those living in the center, especially in the black ghetto, saw themselves trapped. Blacks suffered most: the socioeconomic disadvantage has always been exacerbated by prejudice and racial oppression.[133] Actively recruited by Northern companies in times of labor shortage during the two World Wars, they were the first to lose their jobs with the return of veterans.[134] Through rent restrictions they were crammed in highly segregated ghettos.[135] Only with the Civil Rights Movement in

---

[129] Chudacoff, pp. 243, 264; Warner, p. 230.

[130] Johnston, p. 238.

[131] Ann R. Markusen, "Class and Urban Social Expenditure: A Marxist Theory of Metropolitan Government," *Marxism and the Metropolis*, eds. William Tabb and Larry Sawers, New York, 1984, p. 93. Suburban dwellers and real estate agents were interested in keeping undesirable population groups out, as any intrusion of blacks or other lower-class groups would have lowered real estate values. Hence, they used zoning laws and minimum lot sizes to stabilize their privileges (Warner, p. 33). For general trends in the eighties see Andreas Falke, "Die amerikanischen Städte zwischen Niedergang und Revitalisierung: Stadtentwicklung, Politik und soziale Probleme in den 80er Jahren," *Amerikastudien*, 33 (1988), 21-51.

[132] McKelvey, *The Emergence of Metropolitan America*, pp. 140f; Chudacoff, p. 291.

[133] Castells, pp. 405f.

[134] A vicious circle has left them virtually no solution for their dilemma in cities: either blacks remained powerless among a white majority which had not altered its attitude toward the rights of disadvantaged groups, or if they attempted to assume power in inner cities through politics or nonincorporation, it meant that the flight of industry and capital would bring certain ruin to the communities (Castells, p. 417ff). Black percentage in cities rose from 23 percent in 1900, to 73 percent in 1960. In 1970, only five percent of blacks lived in suburbia (Chudacoff, p. 273). This trend has not been reverted in the 1980s. John R. Logan and Mark Schneider, "Racial Segregation and Racial Change in American Suburbs, 1970-1980," *American Journal of Sociology*, 89 (1984), 874-88.

[135] Warner, p. 172. See also Arnold Hirsch, *Making the Second Ghetto: Race and Housing in Chicago, 1940-1960*, Cambridge, 1983.

the fifties and sixties and the riots in Harlem and Watts did the suppression of blacks receive national attention--though hardly much changed after the protests. In 1972, Blacks constituted eleven percent of the American population but had one third of the poor among them.[136]

Inequality, the basis of capitalist economy, was thus reproduced in a uniquely American way within the urban environment. It was a society stratified by class segregated in socially homogeneous areas.[137] The discrepancy between rich and poor persisted despite the rise in national wealth: in 1929, the upper fifth received 54 percent of the total income, the lower fifth four percent. In 1965, this relation had not altered for those at the bottom: now the upper twenty percent owned 43 percent and the lower fifth five percent.[138] Because of this perversion of the ideals of American democracy, urban neighborhoods became more and more divergent and unequal. Besides, the political fragmentation in U.S. cities cemented existing disparities. Schools, which offer the major opportunity for social and occupational advancement, fix the *status quo* as the quality of teaching is directly dependent on the wealth of the neighborhood: bussing alone could not undo the imbalance.[139] Local autonomy and zoning tend to perpetuate the socioeconomic segregation of neighborhoods.[140] Private interest has managed to shift the scope of urban planning to zoning legislation, which, although inappropriate, remains the sole device in municipal politics to achieve at least some democratic control over urban resources.[141]

The fatal preference of viewing the possession of land as a superior civil liberty and not as a social resource runs as basic weakness through all stages of the segregated American city. Americans gave the right answers to this conflict in urban planning, Philip S. Broughton ironically remarked, but they had asked the wrong questions.[142] The basic cause lies beyond the spatial division: the socioeconomic division of American ci-

---

[136]Robert A. Wilson and David A. Schulz, *Urban Sociology*, Englewood Cliffs, N.J., 1978, p. 80.

[137]Badcock, p. 189.

[138]Cited in Fried, p. 246.

[139]Castells, pp. 385, 391.

[140]If attempts were made to solve the problems in cities, politics meddled with symptoms, as in the unsuccessful bussing policy in the seventies (Castells, p. 413). Also, such positive developments as inner-city gentrification by a new urban middle class only transferred slum conditions to other areas. Chudacoff, p. 299.

[141]Chudacoff, p. 260; Warner, p. 36.

[142]Philip S. Broughton, "Foreword," *The Progressives and the Slums. Tenement House Reform in New York City, 1890-1919*, Roy Lubove, Greenwood, 1962, p. xii.

ties into multiple, socially divergent areas mirrors to a great degree the fundamental fact of capitalist inequality.

Each of the novels discussed in this study contains specific tensions and portrays distinctive fractions of the modern American city. To know about the issues that loomed large for each period--the importance of municipal reform, machine politics, or the role of environmentalism--helps to recognize what the writers stress, what they leave out, and how they evaluate developments. As the urban environment changes constantly, the awareness of the historical and social differences achieves paramount importance. The disruptions in the American city in the twentieth century cannot be reduced to a stable core: the fictional responses have differed as American social conditions have changed.

3

A Sociology of Fragmented Experience

1. Urbanism as a Way of Life

The development of segregated American cities exhibits a complex interplay of economic, political, and cultural factors. They have determined the shape and use of urban space in the United States. In contrast to traditional geographical and historical explanations, the explosion of towns to giant cities with millions of inhabitants cannot be simply explained by referring to an indigenous urban force. In a related pattern, urbanist theory in sociology argues that urbanization led to a specifically *urban* way of life. Thus an assessment of the diversity of urban modes of life must begin with a discussion of the classical concepts formulated early in the twentieth century.[1]

The conditions which evolved in the segregated American cities of the late nineteenth century demanded new, progressive explanations. What developed as a slow, but in the end pervasive process, with shifts occurring in the mercantile and industrial environment, culminated in the early modern city. Characteristic were its large numbers and huge expanses, its heterogeneity and anonymity, its strangeness and impenetrability. Conditions appeared to have undergone a qualitative shift away from previous cultural modes. New types of behavior developed. The social and mental constitution of modern metropolitans seemed altered.

Urban sociology emerged as an academic and political response to the changed situation. It attempted to describe, classify, and examine the changes in the contemporary environment.[2] John Berger calls attention to the wider epistemological framework for this investigation and the particular attitude evidenced in its research:

---

[1] In its analysis of urban sociology, the following discussion draws heavily on: Herbert J. Gans, "Urbanism and Suburbanism As Ways of Life: A Re-evaluation of Definitions," *American Urban History*, ed. Alexander B. Callow, New York, 1969, 504-518. Manuel Castells, *The Urban Question*, trans. Alan Sheridan, London, 1977. Michael Peter Smith, *The City and Social Theory*, New York, 1979. Peter Saunders, *Social Theory and the Urban Question*, London, 1981. R. J. Holton, *Cities, Capitalism, and Civilization*, London, 1986.

[2] From the beginning, the research of the Chicago School of sociology was closely related to reform and practical concerns. Elisabeth Pfeil, *Großstadtforschung*, Hannover, 1969, p. 100. Glaab and Brown, p. 249.

> Positivism and the camera and sociology grew up together. What sustained them all as practices was the belief that observable quantifiable facts, recorded by scientists and experts, would one day offer man such a total knowledge about nature and society that he would be able to order them.[3]

Classical urban sociology assumed that the conditions to be experienced by future generations were already to be seen in the modern city. Urbanism as a way of life would soon dominate the world.[4] The hectic and anonymous throngs in downtown areas with their depersonalized, alienated, and anomic city dwellers epitomized the shift in the quality of social life.[5] Urbanism in its highest form was to be found in the city center. The larger the metropolis the more apparent these idiosyncracies would become. With the United States leading the way, urbanism took grip of the Western world.

Two concepts excelled among the many attempts to explain these urban phenomena. Georg Simmel's essay "The Metropolis and Mental Life" was published in 1903 and responded to conditions in Berlin, the booming capital of Germany. Louis Wirth's article "Urbanism as a Way of Life" appeared in the *American Journal of Sociology* in 1938 and summarized sociological observations made in Chicago, the industrial giant of the Mid-west.[6] While Simmel's essay was the first attempt to probe the new field in depth, Louis Wirth's theory climaxed the efforts to define urban characteristics in traditional sociology. Their essays became the two most often cited models to delimit a distinctive urban mode of life.[7]

The two concepts are closely connected. Georg Simmel profoundly influenced American urban sociology through his writings which were published in the *American Journal of Sociology* and, personally, through Robert E. Park, who received his "only formal instruction in sociology" from Simmel in Berlin in 1899.[8] Park, one of the major figures of the evolving Chicago School, soon established human ecology as the dominant

---

[3] John Berger and Jean Mohr, *Another Way of Telling*, New York, 1982, p. 99.

[4] Smith, *The City and Social Theory*, p. 35.

[5] Gans, "Urbanism and Suburbanism As Ways of Life: A Re-evaluation of Definitions," p. 505.

[6] Georg Simmel, "The Metropolis and Mental Life" *The Sociology of Georg Simmel*, trans., and ed. Kurt H. Wolff, repr. *Cities and Society*, eds. Paul K. Hatt and Albert J. Reiss, 1951, New York, 1963, pp. 635-46. Louis Wirth, "Urbanism as a Way of Life," *The American Journal of Sociology*," 44 (1938), 1-24, repr. Louis Wirth, *On Cities and Social Life*, ed. Albert J. Reiss, Chicago, 1964, pp. 60-83.

[7] Peter Saunders called the essay by Louis Wirth the most famous sociological article ever published. Saunders, p. 92.

[8] David Frisby, *Georg Simmel*, Chichester, 1984, p. 148. Martin Bulmer, *The Chicago School of Sociology*, Chicago, 1984, p. 38.

mode of explanation in urban sociology.[9] Louis Wirth, trained in Chicago, developed his concept of urbanism by ingeniously fusing Simmel's sociopsychological analysis with Park's human ecology.

The strong interrelation among the major theoreticians of urbanism is striking: conceivably, their concepts had to resemble one another. The similarity is significant since these theories were frequently employed as the sociological frameworks of literary interpretations of modern city fiction.[10] Georg Simmel had a profound influence on the assessment of the modern metropolis. Walter Benjamin, for example, applied Simmelian insights in his analysis of Charles Baudelaire's flaneur.[11] It will thus be illuminating to examine how these theories define *urban* and how they evaluate urban modes of life, especially what they consider typically urban behavior.

In "The Metropolis and Mental Life," Georg Simmel, the "quintessential individualist,"[12] chiefly concerns himself with the ways in which the individual reacts to the altered conditions in the modern metropolis.[13] The urbanite faces both positive and negative possibilities in the new environment. On the one hand, the metropolis offers the chance of accomplishing a higher degree of individual freedom and uniqueness than ever achieved before in the course of human history. On the other hand, urban dwellers are immersed in impersonality. According to Simmel, this leads to "the atrophy of individual culture through the hypertrophy of objective culture."[14] Owing to the size and high degree of differentiation, the individual is confronted with more superficial contacts, faster rhythms, rapidly changing images, and sharper discontinuities in the metropolis. For Simmel, the "psychological basis of the metropolitan type of individuality consists in the intensification of nervous stimulation which results from the swift and

---

[9]It has prevailed as the mainstream method in textbooks to date. Mark Gottdiener, *The Social Production of Urban Space*, Austin, Texas, 1985, p. 5.

[10]Among the many studies which have used this framework are: Blanche Housman Gelfant, *The American City Novel*, Norman, Oklahoma, 1954. John Henry Raleigh, "The Novel and the City: England and America in the Nineteenth Century," *Victorian Studies*, 11 (1968), 291-328. Volker Klotz, *Die erzählte Stadt: eine Herausforderung des Romans von Lesage bis Döblin*, München, 1969. Robert H. Walker, "The Poet and the Rise of the City," *American Urban History*, ed. Alexander Callow, New York, 1969, 363-73. Gerhard Hoffmann, *Raum, Situation, erzählte Wirklichkeit*, Stuttgart, 1978. Hana Wirth-Nesher, "The modern Jewish Novel and the City: Franz Kafka, Henry Roth, and Amos Oz," *Modern Fiction Studies*, 25 (1978), 91-101.

[11]Frisby, p. 147.

[12]Smith, p. 116.

[13]The first sentence in "The Metropolis and Mental Life" establishes his focus: "The deepest problems of modern life derive from the claim of the individual to preserve the autonomy and individuality of his existence in the face of overwhelming social forces, of historical heritage, of external culture, and the technique of life." Simmel, p. 635.

[14]Ibid., p. 645.

uninterrupted change of inner and outer stimuli."[15] Metropolitan dwellers adjust to this psychological overstimulation. They develop the intellectual capacity at the expense of emotion and cultivate a blasé attitude which protects their personal space in a veil of reserve and indifference.

For Simmel, metropolitan life differs from small cohesive communities in exactly these psychological effects. Such conditions also set off the modern metropolis from other historical forms of the city as the Greek polis or the medieval town, and distinguish it from the contemporary small town; the prejudice and pettiness in small settlements hinder the development of a truly individual personality. The path of modern society, in Simmel's eyes, was toward the development of the unrestrained individual.[16]

Simmel's essay describes the metropolis as an autonomous agent which creates its own conditions. The effect exerted by the city extends beyond its physical boundaries and influences the urban hinterland. Contrary to this assessment, the essay also attributes metropolitan characteristics to the advanced money economy in modern societies. In this context, the city functions solely as the "seat," "locale," and "arena" for the economy.[17] Both the blasé attitude of metropolitan individuals and the preponderance of intellectual capacities are causally linked in such passages to the money economy which indiscriminately levels distinctions and furthers a calculative, rational spirit.[18] Simmel does not resolve this crucial ambiguity. For him, the metropolis is both the product of the money economy and the autonomous producer of its own conditions.[19]

It is important to stress the status Simmel assigns to size. In opposition to the assessments of the modern city by Karl Marx, Max Weber, or Emile Durkheim, Georg Simmel reestablishes the metropolis as agent and generic environment. Marx and Weber drew clear distinctions between the feudal city which they saw as an active participant in overcoming feudalism, and the industrial metropolis which they believed had lost

---

[15]Ibid., p. 635.

[16]Ibid., pp. 640f.

[17]Ibid., pp. 636, 642.

[18]Simmel had a profound influence on Marxist thinkers, especially on Georg Lukács and his concept of reification. Frisby, pp. 107, 145f.

[19]Peter Saunders has referred to this as the "Simmelian dualism." On one side, Simmelian theory describes the modern capitalist city which is wholly dependent on external forces, but at the same time, it also attributes causal power to the metropolis because of its large numbers. In Simmel's work, the two dimensions are "inextricably confused." Saunders, p. 92. See also Lothar Müller, "Die Großstadt als Ort der Moderne: Über Georg Simmel," *Die Unwirklichkeit der Städte*, ed. Klaus R. Scherpe, 14-36.

this autonomy and was ruled by economic and political forces beyond its grip.[20] For Simmel, however, the size of settlements became a factor in itself.

"The Metropolis and Mental Life" contained a split assessment on the status of the urban. Simmel's student, Robert E. Park, and the school of human ecology, however, did not hesitate to regard the urban environment as a determinant of social life. They proposed the most systematic conceptualization of the urban in this century.[21] Their laboratory was one of the booming centers of American industry, the Chicago of the twenties and thirties. There, ecologists examined how human beings adapted to 'natural' surroundings created through biotic processes which operate "in the human as well as in the plant and animal communities."[22] Within such *natural areas*, homogeneous groups congregated to form the famous "mosaic of little worlds."[23] For Park, the city essentially reproduced and reflected human nature:

> It is the structure of the city which impresses us by its visible vastness and complexity, but this structure has its basis, nevertheless, in human nature of which it is an expression.[24]

Posited as a natural process, the conditions in the modern city were turned into essentials of an inevitable development. Western cities were seen as part of a teleological evolution in which urban modes of life replaced outdated rural ones. Groups naturally adjusted to the forms which developed under such unassailable laws. This ecological explanation of social processes, refined and partly altered over the years, imprinted its seal on American urban sociology for decades, and fully established the urban as an independent determinant in urban studies.[25]

---

[20]Peter Saunders summarizes: "What appears as the most striking (and, given the divergences in their methods, astonishing) feature of any comparative reading of the works of Marx, Weber, and Durkheim in relation to the urban question is thus their unanimity in their approach to the city, for all three see the medieval city as historically significant while addressing the modern city simply as the most visible expression of developments in the society as a whole." Ibid., p. 47.

[21]Ibid., p. 48.

[22]Robert E. Park, "Human Ecology," *The American Journal of Sociology*, 32 (1936), p. 8.

[23]Robert E. Park, "The City: Suggestions for the Investigation of the Human Behavior in the City Environment," *The American Journal of Sociology*, 20 (1915), p. 608. As society expanded, ecologists argued, new forms of living developed which were directed by the processes of competition and selection. This biotic evolution was accompanied and finally overcome by cultural systems based on consensus and cooperation. Society advanced from lower to sublimated stages, from simple to complex forms, from homogeneous folk ways to heterogeneous urban life, from community to society. The focus of human ecology was to describe the biotic aspect of this evolution. Park, "Human Ecology," pp. 1-15.

[24]Park, "The City: Suggestions for the Investigation," p. 578.

[25]First solely criticized for internal contradictions in its theories, the very basis of the ecological system has been refuted since. Its critics argued that historical conditions in the modern American city were transformed into transhistorical generalities and man-made processes were naturalized in comparisons to plant

50 Fragmented Urban Images

In the late thirties, Louis Wirth combined two strands, Simmel's sociopsychological approach and the environmental determinism of human ecology, in his famous theory of the modern city, "Urbanism as a Way of Life." Here, the city received its classic urbanist definition as a "relatively large, dense, and permanent settlement of socially heterogeneous individuals."[26] The triad of size, density, and heterogeneity rule the urban experience and produce the features of urbanism. The size of the population, Wirth argued, leads to differentiation and segregation, to anonymity and superficiality; density reinforces the differentiation and specialization and causes friction and irritation; heterogeneity, finally, leads to increased mobility and subcultural conflicts, to eccentricity and depersonalization, and also to the fragmentation of the city into a mosaic of social worlds. For Wirth, disorganization and alienation are characteristic of the urban way of life.

Like the ecologists, Wirth adhered to an evolutionary model in which ruralism and urbanism were defined in ideal types and placed at the opposite ends of a scale.[27] He anticipated the progressive unfolding of reason and science in history.[28] As human culture developed from rural-folk to urban-industrial types, it would proceed from the dominance of primary bonds to secondary bonds and community would evolve into society. In agreement with Simmel, Wirth also assumed that the forms of urbanism were not confined to the physical boundaries of the city but extended beyond. For Wirth, "the ongoing changes in urbanism will for good or ill transform not only the city but the world."[29]

The tenets of traditional urban theory have been challenged on several grounds. Above all, there is a fundamental contradiction in its environmentalism. If urban qualities are to appear independent of setting, then the factors of size, density, and hetero-

---

communities. Like animals, human beings were seen competing, invading, succeeding, and dominating in space. The underlying teleology rendered the evolutionary process highly evaluative, the view of social forms as natural ones led to conservative system maintenance rather than scientific enquiry. Saunders, pp. 48-67.

[26] Wirth, p. 66.

[27] Saunders, pp. 98ff.

[28] Smith, p. 35. The concept of cultural evolution found its most explicit formulation in Robert Redfield's folk theory. As Anthony Leeds points out, in Redfield's theory 'rural' is fatally associated with untouched tribal conditions (Anthony Leeds, "Cities and Countryside in Anthropology," *Cities of the Mind: Images and Themes of the City in the Social Sciences*, eds. Lloyd Rodwin and Robert M. Hollister, New York, 1984, 291-312). Philip Abrams concludes: "Few if any now defend the most ambitious and thorough-going version of the effort to constitute the town as a social object--Robert Redfield's notion of the folk-urban continuum." Abrams, p. 15f.

[29] Wirth, pp. 63, 83.

geneity cannot be valid categories in the first place.[30] Conversely, if such forms of behavior appear outside the determining ecological locale, then the theory rather applies to the whole of society and cannot be attributed to a single settlement type.[31] As has been frequently pointed out, the theories set forth by Wirth, Park, and Simmel confused the relationship of tendencies in capitalist mass society with urbanism.[32]

In addition, the accuracy of descriptions in Wirth's model was seriously challenged.[33] Herbert J. Gans early contended that the conclusions Wirth derived from his study of the inner city could not be generalized to the entire urban area.[34] Raymond E. Pahl later indicated that an overwhelming body of evidence had been gathered which suggested that inner areas differed considerably from what Wirth had described.[35] Moreover, the concept of stimulus overload, crucial to Simmel's and Wirth's model, has been criticized and revised.[36] Urban environments are primarily overstimulating for the newcomer and the outsider but not necessarily for inner-city residents. In addition, the capacity for stimulation crucially varies with a person's activities and purposes in the city. As the stimuli can be both stressful or beneficial, the onesided evaluation of the effect of changing sights and fast pace is misleading.[37] In the seventies, Manuel Castells and the new urban theory launched the most comprehensive critique of traditional con-

---

[30] Peter Saunders argues that Wirth failed to prove that size, density, and heterogeneity are the key determinants for the behavior and attitudes that his theory claimed to expound. Saunders, p. 102.

[31] Saunders, pp. 91f. Related to this, Wirthian theory also is inconsistent in assuming the simultaneity of rural and urban forms of life in the modern city. If size, density, and heterogeneity act as ecological determinants, ruralism cannot persist in this advanced settlement type, or, on the other side, if Wirth postulates an evolutionary process from a rural to an urban type, the cultural development cannot be captured with size, density, and heterogeneity as causal factors.

[32] Castells, p. 83. Ray Francis, "Symbols, Images, and Social Organization in Urban Sociology," *Urban Social Research: Problems and Prospects*, eds. Valdo Pons and Ray Francis, London, 1983, p. 119. Curiously enough, Wirth himself warned in his essay not to confound urbanism with industrialism and capitalism. Wirth, p. 66.

[33] Wirth himself had warned not to use his theory uncritically; he conceived of it as a hypothesis which had yet to be verified by further research. Wirth, p. 83.

[34] Gans, p. 505.

[35] Raymond E. Pahl, "The rural-urban continuum," *Readings in Urban Sociology*, ed. Raymond E. Pahl, London, 1968, p. 267.

[36] This too applies to stimulus overload concepts which, like Stanley Milgram's model, were derived from a fusion of Simmel's and Wirth's theory (Stanley Milgram, "The Experience of Living in Cities," *Science*, 167 (1970), 1461-68). For a critique of the concepts, see Daniel M. Geller, "Responses to Urban Stimuli: A Balanced Approach," *Journal of Social Issues*, 36 (1980), pp. 86-97. See also Eike Gebhardt, "Die Stadt als moralische Anstalt: Zum Mythos der kranken Stadt," *Die Unwirklichkeit der Städte*, ed. Klaus R. Scherpe, 279-303.

[37] Geller, p. 97.

cepts of the city indicating how Wirth's model of cultural progress was profoundly based upon ideological assumptions.[38] Castells' *The Urban Question* particularly challenged Wirth's use of physical factors to explain historical and social processes.[39]

The sum of criticism Wirthian theory received (including the features derived from the work of Simmel and Park) has affected the foundations of classical urban sociology. All in all, urban theory has failed to isolate generic environmental features which might be convincingly applied to all social experiences in the city.[40] The urban environment by itself has not produced a uniform mode of living. The majority of recent studies suggest that there are diverse and multiple modes of living in cities which are related to the entire economic, political, and cultural practices of society. *Urban* acquires a more precise, if socially and historically limited meaning, as Raymond E. Pahl points out:

> If, then, 'urban' has no final ontological status this does not, of course, mean that *at a given period of time under given conditions of political economy*, the term cannot be used with very clear and potent meaning.[41]

In this sense, the models by Simmel, Park, and Wirth can be taken as theories describing, rather than explaining, general social tendencies in industrial capitalism during the early decades of the present century when capitalist production and urbanization grew parallel to one another. However, when regarded as a specific description of social behavior, urbanism only applies to a restricted number of social groups in the city. The distinction is important. Either the urban as defined by traditional theory represents a historical phase in which the modern city and capitalist economy almost become identical in locale and cause; or, when it is used as a description of urban behavior, it must be limited to specific groups in the inner city.

The strong connotations the urban-rural dichotomy has accumulated in Western culture acquired a supposedly objective status through Chicago sociology.[42] Wirth's

---

[38] On the various meanings of ideology in urban theory, see Saunders, pp. 149f.

[39] Castells, p. 83. Peter Saunders similarly concludes: "What is basically at fault with the theories of Simmel, Wirth, Redfield and other similar writers is not that they chose to focus their attention on, say, the question of how size affects the pattern of social relationships, but that they failed to recognize the very limited scope of such an approach and in consequence attempted to explain a wide range of culturally variable phenomena though an illegitimate physical reduction." Saunders, pp. 107f.

[40] Holton, p. 26.

[41] Raymond E. Pahl, "Concepts in Context: Pursuing the Urban in 'Urban Sociology'," *The Pursuit of Urban History*, eds. Derek Fraser and Anthony Sutcliffe, London, 1983, p. 382.

[42] Sidney H. Aronson, "The City: Illusion, Nostalgia, and Reality," *Readings in Introductory Sociology*, eds. Dennis H. Wrong and Harry L. Gracey, New York, 1972, p. 293.

theory is anchored in such evaluative categories.[43] In his model, cohesive folk behavior is idealized, but, at the same time, described as anachronistic and irrecoverable in the evolutionary process.[44] Urbanism as an inevitable development, on the other hand, is attributed the traditional flaws of Sodom and Gomorrha. Thus, the city is a destroyer, a "consumer of man," it reduces natural fertility and is held responsible for other conventional deficits:

> Personal disorganization, mental breakdown, suicide, delinquency, crime, corruption, and disorder might be expected under these circumstances to be more prevalent in the urban than in the rural community.[45]

Yet crime, for instance, cannot simply be linked to the size or density of cities. Contrary to popular belief, there is no clear correlation between crime rate and city size, even though cities as focal points of social tension are frequently the site of violence and crime.[46]

The similarities in the theories forwarded by Simmel, Park, and Wirth are due to the researchers' personal contacts and intellectual interactions. More important, their concepts reveal the influence of social Darwinist thought. They clearly evidence the impact of Herbert Spencer's teleological evolutionism, an ameliorated version of the ideology of natural selection:[47]

> The Lamarckian character of the struggle for survival in Spencer is fundamental. The reason why welfare-statism is counter to the principles of evolution is not that the weakest must be made to go to the wall in order for improvement of the race to occur by natural selection, but that welfare measures will prevent people adapting themselves through their own efforts.[48]

---

[43] Saunders, p. 102. Although his argument does not show an extreme bias--he indicates the positive features of an urban way of life as well as the negative aspects of ruralism--his community ideal which is epitomized by close, cohesive, and primary bonds and which is identified as a rural-folk mode of life evokes a pattern which Raymond Williams has dismantled as a typical form of environmental nostalgia. The stick of the past is used to beat the degraded present. Williams, p. 21.

[44] Smith, p. 35.

[45] Wirth, p. 82.

[46] Herbert Jacob, *Crime and Justice in Urban America*, Englewood Cliffs, N.J., 1980, pp. 14-28. Herbert Jacob concludes: "When we compare smaller central metropolitan areas with larger ones, we find that the largest cities are not the most dangerous." Jacob, p. 20.

[47] For assessments of Herbert Spencer's theory see Richard Hofstadter, *Social Darwinism in American Thought*, 1944, Boston, 1955, pp. 31-50. T. J. Jackson Lears, *No Place of Grace: Antimodernism and the Transformation of American Culture, 1880-1920*, New York, 1981, p. 20ff.

[48] J. D. Y. Peel, *Herbert Spencer: The Evolution of a Sociologist*, London, 1971, p. 148. Peel explains the Lamarckian version of adaptation as follows: "Animals confront challenging circumstances and must adjust to them if they can, the successful passing on their organic achievements to their descendants" (Peel, p. 147). For the parallels and differences in the theories of Darwin and Spencer see Peel, pp. 131-65.

54 Fragmented Urban Images

Charles Darwin and Herbert Spencer were important catalysts in the development of Georg Simmel's sociology and the Spencerian theory of evolution, differentiation, and heterogeneity became the cornerstone of human ecology.[49] This philosophical background explains the teleology in the evolutionary process of the Chicago School which postulated the progression from rural to urban and from lower to sublimated forms of cultural life.

The crucial point is not that values influenced the scientific model, but rather, that the chief ideology of liberal capitalism reappeared in the guise of disinterested objectivity testifying to the naturalness of urban development in the United States. Exactly those urban idiosyncrasies as had been caused by entrepreneurs, speculators, and corporations were now being sanctioned in a philosophical model which rationalized capitalist ruthlessness as inevitable and beneficial.[50] While conceding that human culture restrained natural competition, Robert E. Park for instance wrote in 1936:

> Human ecology, in so far as it is concerned with a social order that is based on competition rather than consensus, is identical, in principle at least, with plant and animal ecology.... The ties that unite its individual units are those of a free and natural economy, based on a natural division of labor. Such a society is territorially organized and the ties which hold it together are physical and vital rather than customary and moral.[51]

In the sixties and seventies, the skewed basis of many of the findings in traditional sociology was criticized and dismantled by liberal, Weberian, and Marxist studies.[52] Despite considerable differences in the philosophical background of criticism, all assessments agree that traditional theory muddled the relationship between cause and effect. The modern city should be viewed as a product of society; it did not autonomously generate new and distinct modes of life. If the role to be attributed to space in the new urban theory is not clarified, certainly space cannot be treated as an independent entity and a purely physical category. It must be held to be socially constructed.[53]

---

[49]Frisby, pp. 71f.; Gottdiener, p. 26.

[50]Gans, p. 514; Spindler, pp. 28ff.

[51]Park, "Human Ecology," p. 14f.

[52]For a summary of recent developments see Sharon Zukin, "A Decade of the New Urban Sociology," *Theory and Society*, 9 (1980), 575-601. Charles Jaret, "Recent Neo-Marxist Urban Analysis," *Annual Review of Sociology*, 9 (1983), 499-524.

[53]While most sociologists agree that classical urban theory confused the relationship between cause and effect, a wide and contradictory variety of alternative models have been proposed to advance the state of theory. The status to be assigned to space and, in particular to the urban, is much under discussion. Leading the way, Herbert J. Gans, Raymond Pahl, Henri Lefebvre, Manuel Castells, and David Harvey introduced innovative ideas to urban theory. Structural Marxism became a dominant explanation in urban theory in the seventies. By now, its models have been questioned and superseded (Peter Newman, "Urban Political Eco-

American urban sociology was long complacent about the chief contradictions in ecological theory. An urban factor was incorporated into the underlying anthropological model: ecological context and behavior were related through philosophical tenets which assumed but did not question or verify their very connection.[54] In some instances, empirical research simply chose the ecological context so that the size and shape of the community would fit its proposed hypothesis.[55] In other cases it uncritically applied data which appeared to verify the hypotheses. Robert E. L. Faris' and H. Warren Dunham's study of insanity, for example, claimed that the degree of mental health could be related to size, density, and heterogeneity. Insanity would be highest in the central parts of the city and decline toward its fringe.[56] The figures even bore out their thesis. Yet, as Manuel Castells has indicated, the study is flawed in its selection of empirical material for it solely employed statistics from public hospitals. This created a bias toward poor patients from the central city who had to rely on public health services. Affluent suburbanites who received treatment in private clinics did not appear in the statistics employed by the urbanists.[57] The myth of the sickening city predominated over the careful analysis of empirical evidence.

The definition of an ideal type of the urban was questionable. In addition to this, the effects empirically described as urban in Simmelian and Wirthian theory only applied to a few groups of urbanites. The superficial acquaintance with one's neighbors, the multiple but shallow contacts in the city, the fast rhythm dictated by Franklinesque clocks--these urban characteristics in the Wirthian model strongly resembled the experiences of a few inner-city residents, of transients in the middle class, and of the socially isolated in slums, as Herbert J. Gans has pointed out.[58] It did not capture the urban modes of life of large groups of urbanites in traditional quarters, in ethnic districts, in working-class areas, in black ghettos, and in slums, all those whose urban way of life

---

nomy and Planning Theory," *Urban Political Economy and Social Theory*, eds. Ray Forrest, J. Henderson, and Peter Williams, Aldershot, 1982, 186-202). For the present study of urban fiction, the complex branchings and specifics of the ongoing discussion are only marginally significant. They are relevant in so far as the importance of spatial identity is conceived as a real need of humans and cannot be simply refuted as ideological. The specific form of the need, however, is not simply given with space itself but is created by its use and thus reflects social and historical conditions.

[54]Castells, p. 78.

[55]Paul K. Hatt, "The Concept of Natural Area," *American Sociological Review*, 11 (1946), 423-427. Hatt shows that evidence for the existence of homogeneous, natural areas in human ecology could be produced simply by altering the size of the sample.

[56]Robert E. L. Faris and H. Warren Dunham, *Mental Disorders in Urban Areas*, Chicago, 1939.

[57]Castells, p. 105.

[58]Gans, pp. 505ff.

was rather characterized in differing degrees by embeddedness, group cohesion, and informal networks but also by enclosure, narrowness, economic deprivation, and violence.[59]

Furthermore, it is important to an understanding of early modern city novels (which often portray the experience of migrants from rural backgrounds) to keep in mind that the image of a hectic, disorganized, and anonymous social life represents the typical perspective of a newcomer, traveler, or transient urbanite. Michael Smith locates major contradictions in Wirthian theory in the context of such misinterpretations by an outsider:

> Curiously, Wirth never makes clear why it is reasonable to expect that urban residents will be exposed to abrupt juxtapositions of divergent personalities, areas, and ways of life if they spend most of their time living in relatively homogeneous social worlds. Nor does he attempt to reconcile the contradiction between his picture of the urban dweller as a normless social isolate with his picture of social life as consisting of a mosaic of cohesive 'social worlds.' . . . Only an outside social analyst or perhaps an automobile passenger 'passing through' the city can be expected to be overstimulated by abrupt transitions among specialized urban zones.[60]

Although such a contradictory assessment is characteristic of the outside social analyst, it also resembles the view of a slumming flaneur or a detached reporter, unacquainted with the urban milieu and its distinct social organization.[61]

William F. Whyte, for instance, argued in respect to the inner city that "behavior that seemed to the outside middle-class world disordered and unregulated conformed to definite standards within the community."[62] In an explanatory essay on his slum study *Street Corner Society*, Whyte reports a paradigmatic incident and how appearances may be deceiving for the detached observer. Whyte, a participant observer in Cornerville, was searching for a local resident of whom nobody would even admit to knowing.[63] Later he found out that it was the fear of the unknown outsider, and hence a potential welfare agent, which made the people pretend not to know their area and neighbors. They simply wanted to protect their friend from enquiries. An interviewer, Whyte concludes, might deduce a high degree of anonymity from their answers as they ap-

---

[59]Wirth himself had analyzed such attitudes in his study *The Ghetto*. He writes that "two groups can occupy a given area without losing their separate identity because each side is permitted to live its own inner life and each somehow fears or idealizes the other." Louis Wirth, *The Ghetto*, Chicago, 1928, p. 283.

[60]Smith, p. 17f.

[61]William F. Whyte, *Street Corner Society: The Social Structure of an Italian Slum*, 1943, Chicago, 1955.

[62]William F. Whyte, "On Street Corner Society," *Urban Sociology*, eds. Ernest W. Burgess and Donald J. Bogue, Chicago, 1964, p. 157.

[63]Whyte, pp. 156-68.

A Sociology of Fragmented Experience 57

peared not to know their immediate neighbors. As Whyte shows, this would be a fatal misinterpretation of their urban experience and an assessment diametrically opposed to the evident cohesion in this quarter. Often, studies of working-class and lower-class areas have revealed the values of middle-class academics rather than anything else.[64]

For assessments of the early modern metropolis it is interesting to note that Georg Simmel, Jacob A. Riis, Stephen Crane, Theodore Dreiser, Robert E. Park, or John Dos Passos, to mention the most prominent in this study, encountered city life primarily as detached observers and newspaper reporters. Park's doctrines that "detachment is the secret of the academic attitude,"[65] and that the sociologist as a scientific "reporter" was an observer and not a participant, could only prove fatal to investigations into the different social worlds in early modern cities.[66] In his theory, Georg Simmel who was characterized as a disengaged "wanderer"[67] in the city, also generalized impressions of transience and anonymity as standard metropolitan features: "We frequently do not even know by sight those who have been our neighbors for years."[68] As David Frisby explains, the distance in such views is clearly social:

> Indifference and a blasé attitude can be readily incorporated into a wider aestheticization of reality that seeks to emphasize the distance between the individual and the world. . . . Reserve and indifference as defence mechanisms in the metropolis are most likely to be used by those social strata who, from a relatively secure social position, can afford to adopt this response.[69]

All in all, the effects listed in traditional theory as genuinely urban qualities are incomplete, incoherent, and reveal a selective social perspective. Traditional theory perceives the chaos in the center from a distance and fuses it with traditional Babylonian flaws. To put it poignantly, it objectifies an outside view from upper- and middle-class suburbs whose residents now find conditions in the central cities disturbing and disorderly. Traditional urban sociology which had set out to explain the city in objective

---

[64] Whyte remarked in *Street Corner Society* that, "The middle-class person looks upon the slum district as a formidable mass of confusion, a social chaos. The insider finds in Cornerville a highly organized and integrated social system." Whyte, *Street Corner Society*, p.xviii. See also Gerald D. Suttles, *The Social Order of the Slum*, Chicago, 1968, pp. 3-12.

[65] Robert E. Park cited in Stow Persons, *Ethnic Studies at Chicago, 1905-1945*, Urbana, Ill., 1987, p. 28.

[66] Persons, p. 30; Bulmer, pp. 90f.

[67] Frisby, pp. 16, 21f.

[68] Simmel, p. 640.

[69] David Frisby, *Fragments of Modernity: Theories of Modernity in the Work of Simmel, Kracauer, and Benjamin*, Cambridge, 1985, pp. 82f.

and universal terms, could only produce a selective and partial image. Herbert J. Gans summarizes the central failure of its theory:

> If ways of life do not coincide with settlement types, and if these ways are functions of class and life-cycle stage rather than of the ecological attributes of the settlement, a sociological definition of the city cannot be formulated.[70]

From this state of theory in classical urban studies, important conclusions can be drawn for the interpretation of city novels. Of a major consequence, a generalized concept of *the* modern city cannot serve as a valid measure for the relation between form and content in modernist urban fiction since the city lacks autonomous, generic features. Furthermore, interpretations which employed the theories of Georg Simmel, Robert E. Park, or Louis Wirth as extraliterary models necessarily tend to overemphasize the inherent, environmental features of the modern city and, in the peculiar ecological perspective, tend to reify antiurban sentiments as seemingly disinterested assessments, while in actuality they give scientific credence to prejudices and middle-class myths about urban life.

Such qualms about an urbanist influence in previous interpretations of modern fiction are well justified. The circularity in traditional urban theory, literary criticism, and urban studies is remarkable. For example, invoking Chicago theory in order to testify to the accuracy and authenticity of Dreiser's fiction clearly is tautological.[71] Since Spencerian and Darwinian models informed both Park's, Wirth's, and Dreiser's city, the one view can hardly be more objective than the other.[72] Moreover, when Robert E. Park projected the agenda for urban sociology he noted that "we are mainly indebted to writers of fiction for our more intimate knowledge of urban life."[73] A practical outcome of this insight, Dreiser's city novels, among others, were used in Chicago classes to teach sociology.[74] Such direct interaction between urban sociology and literature continued.

---

[70]Gans, p. 515.

[71]See Gelfant, pp. 51, 62ff.

[72]Park and Dreiser developed a similar detached stance toward the city which they both acquired as urban journalists. Park wrote about his first essay which became the research agenda for uban sociology: "In the article I wrote about the city (1915) I leaned rather heavily on the information I had acquired as a reporter regarding the city." Park cited in Bulmer, p. 91.

[73]Robert E. Park, "The City: Suggestions for the Investigation of the Human Behavior in the City Environment," repr., and rev. *The City*, eds. Robert E. Park, Ernest W. Burgess and Roderick McKenzie, Chicago, 1925, p. 3. Heinz Ickstadt has pointed to the similarity in Park's and Dreiser's language with which they described the city. Heinz Ickstadt, "New York und der Stadtroman der Amerikanischen Moderne," *Medium Metropole: Berlin, Paris, New York*, eds. Friedrich Knilli und Michael Nerlich. Heidelberg, 1986, p. 119.

[74]Bulmer, p. 91.

Writers of the next generation, James T. Farrell and Richard Wright received instruction in Chicago before they wrote their city novels.[75]

Urban fiction, traditional sociology, and literary criticism were often fused uncritically to testify to the accuracy of what plainly was an urbanist, middle-class myth.[76] Without exaggerating the influence or positing a causal nexus, it is important to recollect that the effects of this interrelation did not remain purely academic as Herbert Gans indicates:

> The planner can recommmend changes in the spatial and physical arrangements of the city. ... He has been attracted to ecological explanations because these relate behavior to phenomena which he can affect. For example, most planners tend to agree with Wirth's formulations, because they stress number and density, over which the planner has some control. If the undesirable social conditions of the city could be traced to these two factors, the planner could propose large-scale clearance projects which would reduce the size of the urban population, and lower residential densities. Experience with public housing projects has, however, made it apparent that low densities, new buildings, or modern site plans do not eliminate anti-social or self-destructive behavior.[77]

The failure to develop a grand urban theory to link physical environment and social behavior, however, cannot justify a complete dismissal of sociological studies as extraliterary models for the novels. Rather, commonsense opinions and intuitive approaches to urban modes of life in fiction have been responsible for a long tradition of misrepresenting the many shades of experience in the American city. Traditional theory in many respects only reified conventional middle-class notions about the city.[78] Challenging this uniform urbanist view, varied and multiple urban cultures have been examined in recent sociology. Several case studies concentrate on the tension and interaction between the dominant culture and smaller social networks in the city by describing the conflict in the proximity of discordant cultures.

Sociological case studies can indeed provide helpful extraliterary models. They assist in perceiving the difference of urban groups beyond the expected or prejudiced image which has persisted owing to the very segregation and fragmentation in cities.[79]

---

[75] Bulmer, p. 96. Constance Webb, *Richard Wright: A Biography*, New York, 1968, p. 102.

[76] Both Theodore Dreiser and James T. Farrell received special and detailed treatment as generic urban novels in Blanche Gelfant's study which was based on Wirthian theory (Gelfant, pp. 11f). James T. Carey tentatively noted: "Literary and sociological circles were linked by similarities in conceptual orientation, similar world view, and personal associations." James T. Carey, *Sociology and Public Affairs: The Chicago School*, Beverly Hills, 1975, p. 183.

[77] Gans, p. 514.

[78] Castells, p. 85.

[79] As Heinz Ickstadt has generally cautioned, the assessment of subcultural views by an outsider cannot be taken as authentic since the recorded views of the observer may not assume to represent the group's own

Ira Katznelson has remarked that "ordinarily, the cultural patterns of most working and poor people are hidden from view."[80] The use of models from urban studies attempts to uncover the crucial distinctions among seemingly similar views of the city, acknowledging that order, chaos, or anonymity may mean very different things to different groups. It may help to recognize the achievement of urban fiction which treated such conflicts.

Three strands in recent urban research seem especially relevant to the interpretation of modern American city fiction: sociological case studies, studies in cognitive mapping, and studies in urban semiotics. Sociological case studies of particular groups may provide a more accurate conception of alternate urban experiences. Cognitive mapping, which analyzes subjective conceptions of the city, directly relates to the modes of perception in fiction. Urban semiotics, finally, examines the meaning of the urban environment and analyzes how verbal, visual, and mental images of the city are formed.

2. Urban Case Studies

Of the various areas in the American city, suburbs have received the most attention. Life on the urban fringe differs visibly from the bustle and pace in inner districts. The interest in suburban ways of life boomed especially with the mass migration to the fringe in the second half of the present century. It is necessary, however, to distinguish between two chief types of studies. A first group of case studies, among them Bennett Berger's *Working-Class Suburb* and Herbert J. Gans' *Levittowners*, examine specific types of suburbs and discuss the life-style of the social groups in them.[81] A second, vast group of literature generalizes conditions in suburbia and frequently contrasts the new type of living with modes in the central city. Similar to the emergence of concepts which defined urbanism as a way of life early in the century, such generalizations about suburbia responded to visible changes in U.S. society around mid-century, a tendency in the middle

---

view. If such misgivings are not to be pushed aside, a critical approximation is considered a valid attempt and an improvement over previous neglect and misrepresentation. Heinz Ickstadt, "Black vs. White City: Kultur und ihre soziale Funktion im Chicago der Progressive Period," *Amerikastudien*, 29 (1984), p. 200.

[80]Katznelson, p. 1.

[81]Bennett Berger. *Working-Class Suburb: A Study of Auto Workers in Suburbia*, 1960, Berkeley, Cal., 1968. Herbert J. Gans, *The Levittowners: Ways of Life and Politics in a New York Suburban Community*, New York, 1967.

class ironically described by Lewis Mumford as "a collective attempt to lead a private life."[82]

The studies which tried to define suburban qualities *sui generis* resumed the environmentalist tradition. U.S. society which had proceeded from a rural to an urban mode of life, now progressed toward a suburban one.[83] A new ecological way of life was hypothesized in which the male suburbanite was typified as socially mobile and transient, other-directed and conformist, family- and consumer-oriented.[84] Suburbia received the cultural attributes which had become common in middle-class America by mid-century. Bennett Berger summarizes the shortcomings of suburbanist theory:

> The studies that have given rise to the myth of suburbia have been studies of *middle-class suburbs*, that is, suburbs of very large cities populated primarily by people in the occupational groups often thought of as making up the 'new middle class'--the engineers, teachers, and organization men mentioned earlier. If the phrase 'middle-class suburb' strikes the eye as redundant, it is testimony to the efficacy of the myth, for as I have suggested, there is certainly no reason to believe that residence in a new tract suburb in and of itself immediately (or even within a few years) generates a uniquely new middle-class style of life.[85]

The tenets of suburbanism were refuted by case studies which indicated that class, profession, and life-cycle were more important than physical environment for the formation of a new way of life.[86] What had been described as a homogeneous culture turned out to differ considerably, depending on the occupational or social group which resided in the suburb. The multitude of subcategories within the suburban typology overtly disclosed the misconception underlying environmentalism. If upper-class, middle-class, and working-class suburbs had to be differentiated as producing different ways of life, the suburb *qua* suburb evidently did not exert a decisive influence. An ecological category suburban came to be regarded as meaningless.[87]

---

[82] Lewis Mumford, *The Culture of Cities*, London, 1940, p. 125.

[83] Sylvia F. Fava, "Suburbanism as a Way of Life," *American Sociological Review*, 21 (1956), 34-38.

[84] Berger, pp. 3ff.

[85] Berger, pp. 11f.

[86] Berger, p. xxi; Gans, pp. 509ff.

[87] Several case studies showed that features isolated as suburban were inaccurate and incomplete. Herbert J. Gans showed in *The Levittowners* that lower-class suburbanites had much closer bonds than commonly assumed. P. O. Muller distinguished among four suburban types with distinctive modes of social ties and different degrees of cohesion: upper income suburbs, middle-class family suburbs, suburban cosmopolitan centers, and working-class suburbs (P. O. Muller, *The Outer City*, Washington, D.C., 1976). While upper-class and middle-class suburbanites meet through voluntary associations and rely less on local neighboring, working-class communities develop a strong local cohesion based in a 'person-oriented' life-style. Paul Knox, *Urban Social Geography: An Introduction*, London, 1982, pp. 46f.

62 Fragmented Urban Images

The research which Bennett Berger conducted among auto workers in Detroit most clearly dismantled the environmentalism of a uniform suburban culture. He showed that the working-class culture was little affected by the move to the new environment and that distinctive patterns of working-class interaction remained intact.[88] For Berger, a major deficit of previous studies was that the suburb posed a false harmony:

> The myth of suburbs is the latest attempt to render America in this homogeneous manner, to see in the highly visible and proliferating suburban developments a new melting pot which would receive the diverse elements of a new generation from a society fragmented by class, region, religion, and ethnicity, and from them create the American style of life.[89]

Only the interplay between social class and spatial form generates the specific culture of an area. Suburbanization seemed to produce a distinct way of life as the suburban withdrawal coincided with the changing experience of a social class.

A second, major group of sociological case studies has a long tradition and reaches back to nineteenth-century reform literature: writings on ethnic districts, on working-class quarters, and on lower-class ghettos. Jacob A. Riis' famous journalistic account of New York's tenement population in *How the Other Half Lives* was among the first of these enquiries. They were resumed by human ecologists who conducted studies in the city's "little worlds" in the twenties.[90] This second strand of research in the Chicago School was closely linked to the influence of Durkheim's theory and Park's journalistic penchant for the urban mosaic.[91] Among the first studies which examined Chicago's *natural areas* were Harvey W. Zorbaugh's *The Gold Coast and the Slum* which analyzed life-styles in the near North Side, and Louis Wirth's *The Ghetto*, which examined a Jewish community in Chicago.[92]

Early ecological studies were often flawed, however, since they subsumed the cohesive types of urban neighborhoods under outdated rural or folk modes of life. Such a classification is questionable in two respects. For one, it imposes an unjustifiable evaluation on the modes of life in the inner city, and second, it describes the reality of urban villagers inaccurately. In other words, the social behavior examined is devalued as a residual, dissolving form of life and it is compared to an idealized but irrecoverable type of

---

[88] Berger, pp. 91ff.

[89] Berger, p. xviii. For a similar criticism, see also Chudacoff, p. 271.

[90] Jacob A. Riis, *How the Other Half Lives*, 1957, New York, 1890.

[91] Saunders. p. 44; Strauss, *Images of the American City*, p. 53.

[92] Harvey W. Zorbaugh, *The Gold Coast and the Slum: A Sociological Study of Chicago's Near North Side*, Chicago, 1929. Such studies often showed that primary bonds and traditional community dissolve under the impact of urbanism.

A Sociology of Fragmented Experience 63

community.[93] In contrast to rural forms of life, however, urban neighborhoods in American cities are characterized by vast cultural differences within a few blocks: little Italy is adjacent to Chinatown, an Irish colony occupies the next block over from Jewish immigrants. Charlotte Mayerson has beautifully recorded in *Two Blocks Apart: Juan Gonzales and Peter Quinn* how greatly different New York neighborhoods may be for two seventeen-year-old boys, the one from a poor Puerto Rican, the other from an Irish middle-class family.[94] Cohesive urban communities are influenced by the proximity of other cultures, by the potentially threatening, unfamiliar surrounding beyond the neighborhood, and by a substantial rate of turnover due to economic transience. They are affected by the disruptive influence of dominant cultural values which are infused into these seemingly self-contained urban worlds through work, school, and mass culture.[95]

Notwithstanding the problematic question of evaluation in early ecological assessments, each case study reveals the necessity to distinguish among the forms of social organization in the fragmented city. Each type of neighborhood has responded to specific needs and interests of its inhabitants within the boundaries set by U.S. society at large.[96] The cohesion in ethnic quarters, in working-class districts, or in lower-class slums can be seen as an attempt to cope with situations of deprivation, discrimination, and suppression.[97] Although solidarity often was a conscious response to inequalities, the formation of such communities is not a completely voluntary choice, but also a reaction to material and cultural pressures. The fragility or solidity of neighborhoods depends highly on external forces and whether the quarter may organize economic resources or political power.[98] Even though mechanisms to cope with deprivation are somewhat similar, the various groups in the working class have developed distinctive subcultures. For the range of urban experience projected in the novels it is useful to distinguish between working-class, lower-class, and black ghetto studies.

---

[93]Smith, p. 35; Castells, pp. 388f; Robert Allen Slayton, *Back of the Yards: the Making of a local Democracy*, Chicago, 1986, pp. 4-10.

[94]Charlotte Leon Mayerson, ed., *Two Blocks Apart: Juan Gonzales and Peter Quinn*, New York, 1965.

[95]Gans, p. 507. To describe such groups as rural is imprecise as their communities differ in the length of existence, as the inhabitants of a quarter may have a wide variety of regional and cultural backgrounds compared to tendentially immobile villagers, and as the variety of professions and skills differ considerably from the range of occupation in an agrarian community.

[96]Robert A. Wilson and David A. Schulz, *Urban Sociology*, Englewood Cliffs, N. J., p. 164.

[97]Marc Fried, Ellen Fitzgerald, Peggy Gleicher, Chester Hartman, et al., *The World of the Urban Working Class*, Cambridge, Mass., 1973, pp. 224-58.

[98]Ida Susser, *Norman Street: Poverty and Politics in an Urban Neighborhood*, New York, 1982, pp. 3-17.

64 Fragmented Urban Images

The persistence of close-knit working-class areas in the American city most clearly gainsays the influence of a dissociating urbanist agent. Even though fragile, class solidarity has persisted within the city.[99] As the research group around Marc Fried has shown, a lower working-class community in Boston possessed a strong sense of group identity, a quarter in which close kinship bonds and ties to local friends played an important role in social life. Fried and his group found friendliness, warmth, embeddedness, loyalty, trust, and community involvement--all attributes usually deplored as lacking in urban areas. Moreover, they demonstrated that physical factors lacked the decisive impact that the ideology of ecological studies attributed to them: often associated with high density figures, bad housing conditions were only of marginal importance for deviant behavior in the area.[100] Only when coupled with poverty and unemployment, may delapidated housing produce negative effects.[101] All in all, West Enders developed strong emotional ties to what a middle-class observer might describe as slum:

> But for many people, local commitments and satisfactions provide recompense for inadequacies of housing and life situations. More than that, many working-class people become so deeply involved with their residential communities that we can only describe it as a sense of territorial identity. The price of such investment is frequently a narrow conception of the world and restricted boundaries which people feel free to carry out their daily lives. . . . The image of home, of a feeling of kinship among unrelated individuals, and a sense of belonging and proprietary rights establish the quality of working-class conceptions of neighborhood.[102]

To stress community, as Fried does, is not to romanticize a certain life-style. Cohesion is also a response to the accompanying deficits, an alternative option compared to the non-local organizations of an individualistic middle class. The pressure on the lower working class is indeed strong. Their local bonds must be seen in conjunction with their feeling of

---

[99] Among the many sociological studies in this field Herbert J. Gans study of a working-class neighborhood in Boston's West End *The Urban Villagers*, Marc Fried's *The World of the Urban Working Class*, and Ida Susser's *Norman Street* stand out. Herbert J. Gans, *The Urban Villagers: Group and Class in the Life of Italian-Americans*, New York, 1962.

[100] Fried, pp. 202, 226, 232.

[101] Whyte, p. 160.

[102] Fried, p. 226. Such attitudes cannot simply be generalized. Some studies correctly deny the existence of true communities within American neighborhoods, seeing affirmative and nostalgic community studies often as part of an ideological exercise (Charles Bowden and Lew Kreinberg, *Street Signs Chicago: Neighborhood and other Illusions of Big-City Life*, Chicago, 1981). Paul Knox similarly notes: "The mutuality of the urban village is underlain by stresses and tensions which follow from social intimacy and economic insecurity, and several studies of working-class neighborhoods have described as much conflict and disorder as cohesion and community." Knox, p. 45.

worthlessness, insecurity, derogation, and powerlessness within the dominant culture of American society.[103]

If deprivation exceeds limits of strain, communal solidarity may dissolve and working-class areas deteriorate to ghettos.[104] Although social networks in slum areas are less stable since they suffer severely from economic disadvantage (and thus may approach the way of life which Louis Wirth generalized for the city),[105] there are nevertheless many indications of extensive informal ties in such areas.[106] William Whyte was the first to point out in *Street Corner Society* in 1943 that the dominant view of slums as disorganized mostly reflected the perspective of the middle-class analyst.[107] Cornerville has its own hierarchical form of social organization and life conforms to the proper norms of the area. Whyte writes:

> The man who looks at slum districts through the glasses of middle-class morality is not, in fact, studying the slum district at all but only noting how it differs from a middle-class community. He seeks to discover what Cornerville is not. My study was undertaken to discover what it was.[108]

But ways of life ruled by subcultural norms and the values of middle-class America often are mutually exclusive. Hence, either the disadvantaged continue to suffer from their limited opportunities within the stratified U.S. society and attempt to compensate for deficiencies in restrictive group coherence, or the rise of a single member of the group (as only individual improvement is possible) can be achieved only by breaking local loyalties.[109] Community life among lower-class urbanites then cannot be idealized; it is continually threatened by economic crises and political decision beyond their control, disruptions which often pose a direct threat to their form of life. The fragility, insecurity, and tension, the delinquency and violence are part of the threat. If such lower-

---

[103] Fried, p. 225.

[104] Fried, p. 229. The deviant modes of life associated with the urban lower class--divorce, child neglect, occupational instability, and delinquency--are found no less among groups of higher status, only that the latter tend to have the resources to alleviate or conceal these 'moral' deficits. Fried, p. 153.

[105] Elliot Liebow writes: "Living on the edge of both economic and psychological subsistence, the street-corner man is obliged ot spend all his resources on maintaining himself from moment to moment." Elliot Liebow, *Tally's Corner*, Boston, 1967, p. 65.

[106] Gans, p. 508. William Whyte argues in his article "On Street Corner Society" that even in highly unstable rooming-house districts informal networks would develop. In Cornerville, the social isolate was the exception not the rule. Whyte, pp. 157f.

[107] Whyte, "On Street Corner Society," p. 157.

[108] Whyte, p. 158.

[109] Smith, *The City and Social Theory*, p. 182.

class communities react with cohesion and create their own conflicting forms of organization, this frequently is the only viable option for survival.[110]

Finally, many case studies have investigated conditions in black ghettos.[111] While racial discrimination has added a peculiarly bitter note to black suppression, the great majority suffered from economic and social disadvantages similar to the two preceding groups. Whereas most ethnic groups which came to American cities dispersed and were incorporated into the American class system, racial and social discrimination prevented any alleviation of black suppression: the black ghetto stands for their separateness. Urban black communities developed in a pattern different from those of the other disadvantaged. Blacks were exploited at the workplace and, in addition, segregated into ghettos with the help of zoning laws and rent restrictions. Viewed from the inside, however, the ghetto community also came to represent positive values: the solidarity among blacks gave security against the repression in a surrounding circle of white culture.[112] In contrast to the white working class, which was divided in its political allegiance between neighborhood and workplace, between ethnic and religious ties, black communities would mobilize in the 1960s in the fight against the ruling majority.[113]

In sum, the evidence of case studies indicates how greatly urban experience may differ. Urban ways of life may range from cohesion to isolation, from embeddedness to insecurity, from closeness to anonymity, and from policed safety to uncontrollable violence. The American city did not produce a single mode of life: in its fragmented space, class attitudes were enhanced or mollified; it expressed and concentrated tendencies of U.S. society at large. If authentic urban novels mostly did not portray communal life in the city affectionately, it is because novelists took issue with those forces which threatened and destroyed humane modes of existence in the city.

---

[110]Susser, p. 14. What appears as subversive and beyond the norms of the dominant culture often represents a willed and organized counterculture opposing dominant norms. Opposition among immigrant workers to native, protestant temperance movements which threatened the freedom to consume alcohol and to hold assemblies in pubs also defended a distinctive working-class culture. Ickstadt, "Black vs. White City--Kultur und ihre soziale Funktion im Chicago der Progressive Period," pp. 199-214.

[111]See, for instance, St. Clair Drake and Horace C. Cayton, *Black Metropolis: A Study of Negro Life in a Northern City*, 1945, New York, 1970. Allan H. Spear, *The Making of a Negro Ghetto, 1890-1920*, Chicago, 1967. David Ley, *The Black Inner City as Frontier Outpost*, Washington, D.C., 1974.

[112]Toni Morrison, "City Limits, Village Values: Concepts of the Neighborhood in Black Fiction," *Literature and the Urban Experience*, eds. Michael C. Jaye and Anne Chalmers Watts, New Brunswick, N.J., 1981, pp. 37f. In 1978, 38 percent of the black population selected the large city as their first residential choice, whereas only 13 percent of Americans preferred the metropolis. *A Survey of Citizens Views and Concerns About Urban Life*, Louis Harris and Associates, Inc., final report, conducted for the Department of Housing and Urban Development, study H-2835, 1978, p. 17.

[113]Katznelson, pp. 115ff.

3. Cognitive Maps

Different groups possess different images of the American city as their experiences vary within the city. The mental representations of such partially perceived cities are examined in cognitive mapping studies. Any view of the city is fragmented since it is grounded in a particular class practice. As David Ley explains, all "roles imply a bias in knowledge of the city, the objective map is an abstraction that does not correspond with any personal or group mental map."[114] Mental map research thus can be made useful for an analysis of urban fiction. The frequency and the extent of movements, the width of the characters' radius and the predominant perspective in the fictional city may indicate the specific urban life-style and the peculiar fragmentation of the city image. As Manuel Castells has remarked, "Every image is linked to a social practice."[115]

Kevin Lynch conducted the pathbreaking study in this field, *The Image of the City*, in 1960. Lynch was interested in the design, the legibility and imageability of cities, that is how people perceived their city and the ways they mentally organized the stimuli for orientation.[116] Lynch chose to focus on the physical structure of images rather than on their social meaning.[117] In the seventies, Peter Orleans paradigmatically examined the socioeconomic dimension and ideological bias of urban perception in a study of Los Angeles images.[118] Orleans' analysis departed from previous investigations by linking social status to the range of knowledge and variety of experience in the city. He explicitly warned against the fallacy of a physical determinism: "It is all too easy to reify the concrete manifestation of the city, to assume that its symbolic representation is equivalent for all its residents. This is especially dangerous if the perceptions of middle-class analysts are taken as representative of the population at large."[119] Though not all of his conclusions can be generalized, Orleans' study of composite class maps of Los Angeles is

---

[114] David Ley, *A Social Geography of the City*, New York, 1983, p. 107.

[115] Castells, p. 217.

[116] From this initial impulse, the research in environmental cognition has taken several paths in which such different topics as the design of cities, the development of urban cognition in children, or the maps from neighborhoods to complete cities and global regions have been examined. Gary T. Moore, "Knowing about Environmental Knowing: The Current State of Theory and Research on Environmental Cognition," *Remaking the City: Social Science Perspectives on Urban Design*, eds. John S. Pipkin, Mark La Gory, and Judith R. Blau, Albany, N.Y., 1983, pp. 21-49.

[117] Kevin Lynch, *The Image of the City*, Cambridge, Mass., 1960, pp. 6-10.

[118] Peter Orleans, "Differential Cognition of Urban Residents: Effects of Social Scale on Mapping," *Image and Environment*, eds. R. M. Downs and D. Stea, Chicago, 1973, 115-30.

[119] Orleans, p. 129.

suggestive.[120] Class and the extent of the maps can be linked: the higher the status of the group, the more they possess an extensive map of the city.[121] Thus upper-class residents had an expansive knowledge and a virtual overview of Los Angeles owing to their economic means and wide range of contacts, whereas the Los Angeles for a lower-class, Spanish speaking community from Boyle Heights extended but a few blocks. On the other hand, as extensive as the composite maps of white upper-class and middle-class urbanites were, they tended to suppress black areas within Los Angeles.[122]

Mental maps from other American cities support such a social interpretation. Stanley Milgram's analysis of New York images by middle-class professionals also shows that areas of other classes are excluded.[123] Similarly, maps reflect the unequal economic power and role of gender. Men tend to have larger maps than women because of their wider radius of activity.[124] Mapping is primarily a social process: blanks can be eloquent, the gaps in perception indicate class perspectives and reveal biases.[125] The fear of crime, so prominent in the mind of contemporary Americans, is only part of the answer to the segregated maps.

Findings in cognitive mapping verify and refine well-known statements about the discrepant perception and knowledge of cities. In the very beginning of segregated industrial cities, Friedrich Engels noted the selective perception in mid-century Manchester: "Owing to the curious lay-out of the town it is quite possible for someone to live for years in Manchester and to travel daily to and from his work without ever seeing a working-class quarter or coming into contact with an artisan. He who visits Manchester

---

[120] Peter Orleans himself pointed to some uncertainties in his study. Thus, he had misgivings about the small sample of analyzed persons and the adequacy of some of the methods used (Orleans. p. 128). For a survey and a critical discussion of research, see Gary T. Moore, "Knowing about Environmental Knowing: The Current State of Theory and Research on Environmental Cognition," *Remaking the City: Social Science Perspectives on Urban Design*, eds. John S. Pipkin, Mark La Gory, and Judith R. Blau, Albany, N.Y., 1983, pp. 21-49. Miriam J. Boyle and M. E. Robinson, "Cognitive Mapping and Understanding," *Geography and Urban Environment*, eds. R. J. Johnston and D. T. Herbert. London, 1979, 59-82. Thomas F. Saarinen, David Seamon, and James L. Sell, eds., *Environmental Perception and Behavior: An Inventory and Prospect*, Chicago, 1984.

[121] The difference reflects their social experience in the city. Research has shown that the extent or exactness of mental maps cannot be correlated to the intelligence or the verbal reasonong skills of the respondent. Moore, "Knowing about Environmental Knowing," p. 33.

[122] Orleans, pp. 121ff.

[123] For an interview and a summary of Milgram's study see Susanna Duncan, "Mental Maps of New York," *New York*, (Dec. 19, 1977), p. 54. See also Stanley Milgram et al., "A Psychological Map of New York City," *American Scientist*, 60 (1972), 194-200.

[124] Ley, p. 109.

[125] Stanley Milgram explains: "There is a city culture that is transmitted from one generation to the next focusing on or highlighting certain parts of the city, while actually suppressing a knowledge of other parts. In this sense, the mental maps are social facts, not just individual facts." Milgram quoted in Duncan, p. 54.

simply on business or for pleasure need never see the slums."[126] At the turn of the century, Jacob A. Riis similarly reported the restricted New York image of immigrant pupils from the Lower East Side: the great majority had never seen Central Park or even Brooklyn Bridge, the outstanding monument of modern technology in America then, which was only a few blocks away from their homes.[127] The findings in social mapping studies underline what Henry Roth's *Call it Sleep* had projected forcefully in 1934: the early modern city for non-English speaking immigrants was extremely narrow.[128] The rapid change of impressions, the psychic overstimulation, or the ignorance of neighbors and one's close environs did not apply to their constricted modern city.

For the present study it will be illuminating to analyze the range and frequency of movements and to examine the gaps in the perception of the fictional city. The incomplete and distorted image of the metropolis will provide clues. The novel excludes certain areas not because characters do not see the entirety of their city but rather that they cannot see its entirety. Since space and class often coincide, such gaps may be particularly illuminating to connect ideological perceptions of the American city to narrative strategies in urban fiction.

4. Urban semiotics

Urban semiotics conceives of the city as an agglomeration of signs which can be read and interpreted.[129] As Mark Gottdiener points out, the codes of the city are deciphered along ideological lines. For Gottdiener, urban semiotics concentrates on the articulation of ideology with settlement space and it is interested in how mental, visual, or verbal images are used, directed, and changed by ideology.[130] It assumes that the city cannot be limited to a single image, but offers conflicting views. Semiotic analysis, in this

---

[126]Friedrich Engels, *The Conditions of the Working Class in England*, trans., and eds. W. O. Henderson and W. H. Chaboner, Stanford, 1958, p. 54.

[127]Riis, p. 180. Robert E. Park and Louis Wirth too have pointed out that social groups were ignorant of any other but their own area in the city. Similarly, Anselm Strauss indicated in *Images of the American City* that groups are only cognizant of a small area. Strauss concludes: "The various kinds of urban perspectives held by the residents of a city are constructed from spatial representations resulting from membership in particular social worlds." Strauss, *Images of the American City*, p. 67.

[128]Henry Roth, *Call it Sleep*, New York, 1934.

[129]For the various approaches which exist within urban semiotics, see Mark Gottdiener and Alexandros Ph. Lagopoulos, eds., *The City and the Sign: An Introduction to Urban Semiotics*, New York, 1986.

[130]Mark Gottdiener, "Urban Semiotics," *Remaking the City: Social Science Perspectives on Urban Design*, eds. John S. Pipkin, Mark La Gory, and Judith R. Blau, Albany, N.Y., 1983, p. 101.

sense, is a necessary extension to cognitive mapping which often failed to incorporate meaning into its analysis.[131] For an interpretation of the meaning of buildings, of streets, or of urban form, it can be telling to depict the interest behind the perception, to indicate who particularly promoted which view. Such distinctions are necessary in the segregated city since it contains a multitude of codes. Sam Bass Warner concludes:

> Therefore, it seems obvious to me, in approaching the subject of urban imagery, to insist that as historians we collect and deal with multiple urban images, and that we do not retreat to constructs of a predominant perception of something called a city and something which is not a city.[132]

Two types of studies can be distinguished which are useful in the present context. The first group contains analyses which examine how perception can be influenced and how ideological meaning can be attributed to specific forms of urban space or architecture.[133] Thus, the social significance of urban layout has been treated by Lewis Mumford and his readings of the grid pattern in *The City in History*.[134] Urban design, too, may express the ideology of dominant groups: Heinz Ickstadt has shown the interest of the elite behind the neoclassicist plan and architecture of the Chicago World Fair in 1893.[135] Finally, as Gerhard Fehl explains, private parcel parks, the lobbies and atria of skyscrapers in downtowns of the 1980s are designed to function as illusionary places of a new consumer harmony in the central city which, protected by deterrent architectural design and private police, exclude adjacent lower-class urbanites from these places of consumer and employee tranquility.[136]

---

[131] Castells, p. 216. For a self-critique see Kevin Lynch, "Reconsidering *The Image of the City*," *Cities of the Mind: Images and Themes of the City in the Social Sciences*, eds. Lloyd Rodwin and Robert M. Hollister, New York, 1984, 151-162.

[132] Warner, "The Management of Multiple Images," p. 384.

[133] Again, Friedrich Engels provided a lead: "It is therefore possible for anyone who knows Manchester to judge the social character of any district merely by observing the appearance of the buildings fronting the road through which he is passing." Engels, p. 56. See also Paul D. Cherulnik and Scott K. Wilderman, "Symbols of Status in Urban Neighborhoods: Contemporary Perception of Nineteenth-Century Boston," *Environment and Behavior*, 18 (1986), 604-22.

[134] Mumford for instance connected the geometrical pattern of the grid to the rise of a monetary, efficient economic order in Miles. Lewis Mumford, *The City in History: Its Origins, its Transformation and its Prospects*, Harmondsworth, 1966, p. 223ff, 346f.

[135] Burnham's layout and buildings in the White City were an expression of a hierarchical order in which the leading representatives exactly claimed to know what was best for the disorderly masses. Heinz Ickstadt, "Black vs. White City--Kultur und ihre soziale Funktion im Chicago der Progressive Period," p. 204.

[136] This analysis is indebted to a lecture by Gerhard Fehl, University of Aachen, given at a weekend seminar "Politics and Architecture in the United States," at the Elisabeth-Selbert-Kolleg, Saarbrücken, April 24-26, 1987.

A Sociology of Fragmented Experience 71

A second group of studies focuses on the origin, development, and continuity of certain images and perspectives that have accompanied the modern American city. Thus Sam Bass Warner relates the changing meaning of the term 'slum' to the interest of the political groups fighting over the causes of poverty and degeneracy. All in all, the concept had ambiguous effects. In denying a distinction between deserving and undeserving poor, 'slum' was egalitarian and democratic. At the same time, the term also obscured the cause of the problem. Warner summarizes:

> The political success of the symbol slum and its accompanying visual images thus derived part of its power from their environmental quality. The success also derives from its mystifying, or obscuring function in the overall contemporary ideological structure of secular, democratic, liberal capitalism. Neither in old-fashioned Christian terms, nor in the new manner of capitalistic economics, did the symbol slum suggest any cause for the new environment. Slums were just there, facts of life, found objects. The symbol concentrated attention on the attributes of the new found place as if it were like any other fact of science, something which was always there, but which we have recently discovered, like cholera germs. By not suggesting any cause--by refusing the old explanation that evil people made evil places--the symbol neatly assumed a special role in contemporary ideological structure.[137]

Another group of semiotic studies devoted itself to the ideological transformation which occurred with the rise of the skyscraper. In "Image and Ideology: New York in the Photographer's Eye," Alan Trachtenberg examines the attempt to soften the disruptive appearance of skyscrapers at the turn of the century.[138] Trachtenberg analyzes an essay by the popular journalist Alfred Corbin from 1903 in which Corbin gave exemplary readings of New York photographs by Alfred Stieglitz. The skyscraper and the skyline, Corbin suggests to his readers, can be appreciated by the flaneur from the distance, and the dematerialized buildings may become a source of aesthetic pleasure. Corbin thus imposes a longed-for order on the threatening urban chaos (for which the skyscraper was a central symbol then) and introduces a mode of perception which soon came to prevail.[139]

---

[137]Warner, p. 389. Also see William R. Taylor, "Psyching Out the City," *Uprooted Americans*, eds. Richard L. Bushman et al., Boston, 1979, 247-86. Hans Bergmann, "Panoramas of New York, 1845-1860," *Prospects*, 10 (1985), 119-37.

[138]Alan Trachtenberg, "Image and Ideology: New York in the Photographer's Eye," *Journal of Urban History*, 10 (1984), 453-64.

[139]Trachtenberg, pp. 462f. Not all groups in the upper and middle class then shared the enthusiasm for the modern aesthetic. Lucia and Morton White remark that, "Henry James spoke most profoundly for those who saw the city as a scene of chaos as it presented itself to 'the painter's eye.' It lacked order, structure, history, and dignity in 1907. . . ." White, p. 237. See also Merrill Schleier, *The Skyscraper in American Art, 1890-1931*, Ann Arbor, Mich., 1986.

72 Fragmented Urban Images

Sam Bass Warner extends this argument to a discussion of the ideology of the skyline. He shows that the proliferation of skyline photography assisted in mollifying the debate over skyscrapers of monopoly capitalism. High-rise architecture, which at first was experienced as disruptive and threatening, was soon promoted by the elite in smooth silhouettes, and could thus become part of popular urban perception.

> The skyline photographers by their special point of view, by stepping away, and by turning skyscrapers into abstract compositions, solved this political and economic conflict between the democratic and capitalistic elements of contemporary ideology. In their hands the skyscrapers are not corporate towers at all, they are art objects, and a landscape, and as such they moved the skyscraper's image from a position of conflict in the ideology to the older tradition of civic pride. So transformed, the corporate tower became a universal American symbol for a city, something every city wanted as part of its image, like a fancy railroad station or a jazzy airport.[140]

In sum, this survey of fragmented experience indicated that the variety of urban modes of life are substantially defined by different social contexts, to a great degree they are a function of class, gender, and cultural values. There is no single urban behavior as such. Urbanist ideology, however, functions to provide completeness and coherence where there is fragmentation and inconsistency; notions of an urban ontology have prevailed because they most perfectly fitted the dominant white middle-class perception of the American city.

---

[140]Warner, "The Management of Multiple Images," p. 393.

4
Attitudes toward the American City

1. Divided Images

Despite the evident fragmentation of experience, American culture has produced a stable set of city images. Such images and metaphors express attitudes toward the city and provide a framework for orientation in the complex urban world. Anselm Strauss explains:

> Characterization of the city, and of the life lived in it, is indispensable for organizing the inevitably ambiguous mass of impressions and experiences to which every inhabitant is exposed, and which he must collate and assess, not only for peace of mind but to carry on daily affairs. When the city has been symbolized in some way, personal action in the urban milieu becomes organized and relatively routinized. To be comfortable in the city--in the widest sense of these words--requires the formulation of one's relations with it, however unsystematically and crudely.[1]

Aside from their psychological significance, the symbols are related to class perspectives as well and thus incorporate an ideological assessment of conditions in the city. The preceding chapters on urban form and urban experience have produced an important backdrop for this investigation of images: a homogeneous and unified American city did not exist. Since even the first "Citty upon the Hill" was divided into gentry and generality, a unanimous attitude toward images of New Jerusalem or Babylon is highly improbable. Nevertheless, the examination of dominant attitudes and images--chiefly developed by upper- and middle-class thinkers, professionals, writers, and journalists--is important as they generally affected urban perceptions and behavior. The following survey sketches the context in which the modern imagery evolved. It includes a wide variety of images, consisting of religious emblems, archetypal symbols, popular icons, and sociological metaphors, as these constitute the overall frame for the specific images in the city novels.

---

[1] Strauss, *Images of the American City*, p. 17.

74 Fragmented Urban Images

American culture has developed a relatively stable set of city images, many of which reach back to the beginnings of Western civilization.[2] Some ideas originate with nascent Judaeism and Christianity, others develop in classical antiquity. Once created, the images are handed down as denominated myths, emptied of the original conflict and significance.[3] Western tradition has developed polar terms and worked with the opposition of city and country, civilization and nature:

> On the country has gathered the idea of a natural way of life: of peace, innocence, and simple virtue. On the city has gathered the idea of an achieved centre: of learning, communication, light. Powerful hostile associations have also developed: on the city as a place of noise, worldliness and ambition; on the country as a place of backwardness, ignorance, limitation.[4]

As the discussion of evaluative categories in American urban sociology has shown, scientific models were affected by such traditional and stereotyped attitudes toward the city. Moreover, the associations developed in American urban sociology indicate the multinational validity of images within Western culture. Although the Chicago School emphasized an indigenous bias, reflecting the singular conditions in the United States with its vast expanse of land in the West, it perpetuated, as well, a tradition of European, and especially of German thought in which the industrial city was seen as deficient.[5]

Within this Western tradition, Americans presumably have developed a particularly strong hostility toward their cities. This view was vigorously proposed by Lucia and Morton White in *The Intellectual versus the City: From Thomas Jefferson to Frank Lloyd Wright* and buttressed by other studies which also claimed to have detected an antiurban leaning in the United States.[6] Yet the existence of such a unison animadversion has been seriously questioned. There is sufficient evidence to argue for a diametrical, prourban tendency in American culture.[7] Several studies of American

---

[2] Glaab and Brown, *A History of Urban America*, p. 53.

[3] Barthes, *Mythologies*, pp. 144f; Williams, p. 29.

[4] Williams, *The Country and the City*, p. 9.

[5] Sidney H. Aronson, "The City: Illusion, Nostalgia, and Reality," *Readings in Introductory Sociology*, eds. Dennis H. Wrong and Harry L. Gracey, New York, 1972, p. 293; Wilson, *Urban Sociology*, p. 7; Smith, *Uneven Development*, pp. 1-31.

[6] Claude S. Fischer, *The Urban Experience*, New York, 1978, pp. 15-20. Diana Festa-McCormick, *The City as Catalyst: a Study in Ten Novels*, Rutherford, 1979, p. 14. Robert H. Walker, "The Poet and the Rise of the City," *American Urban History*, ed. Alexander Callow, 1969, 363-73.

[7] James L. Machor sees "urban pastoralism" as a "significant component of American values." James L. Machor, *Pastoral Cities: Urban Ideals and the Symbolic Landscape of America*, Madison, 1987, p. xiv.

urban thought detected a fair amount of city celebrations.[8] Charles N. Glaab for example notes: "If one were to judge only by quantity taking into account newspapers, gazetteers, local history, promotional tracts and the like--then writing in praise of the American city would outweigh writing that condemned it."[9] While not denying the existence of antiurban sentiments, Andrew Lees too argues for a positive view among American intellectuals, writers, and journalists:

> Their writings call into serious question the familiar view that American intellectual energies were directed overwhelmingly during these years against the course of urban development. At a minimum, it is quite clear that Americans were just as favorably disposed towards their cities as Europeans were towards theirs, and a good case can be made that the balance of opinion was made more favorable in the United States.[10]

One need not choose sides, however. Many studies indicate that both positive and negative attitudes have existed side by side in a complex and ambivalent relation.[11]

Yet, a more serious challenge, the assumptions underlying the division itself, must be questioned. The verbal umbrella of pro- or antiurbanism blurs rather than explains the attitudes toward the city. Certainly, some fundamentalist groups in American society were directly opposed to the city and its influence. Likewise, for farmers at the turn of the century, facing drought, debt, and inflation, the spatial division represented the economic suppression exerted from the centers of industrial capitalism.[12] More often, however, the label itself is incorrect and the antiurbanist position is but a misconception because larger issues are at stake. A closer look indeed reveals that considerable disagreement exists within similar positions and that arguments supposedly from the same corner contradict one another.[13]

---

[8] Adrienne Siegel, "When Cities were Fun: The Image of the American City in Popular Books, 1840-1870," *Journal of Popular Culture*, 9 (1975), 573-82. Anselm Strauss, "Urban Perspectives: New York City," *The American City*, New York, 1968, pp. 4-18.

[9] Charles N. Glaab, "The Historian and the American Urban Tradition," *Wisconsin Magazine of History*, 57 (1963), p. 18.

[10] Andrew Lees, *Cities Perceived: Urban Society in European and American Thought, 1820-1940*, London, 1985, p. 103.

[11] Glaab and Brown, p. 53. Blaine A. Brownell, "The Agrarian and Urban Ideals: Environmental Images in Modern America," *Journal of Popular Culture*, 5 (1971), 576-87. Janis P. Stout, *Sodoms in Eden: The City in American Fiction before 1860*, Westport, Conn., 1976. Christine Bolt, "The American City: Nightmare, Dream, or Irreducible Paradox?" *The American City: Literary and Cultural Perspectives*, ed. Graham Clarke, New York, 1988, 13-35. Daniel Aaron, "The Unholy City: A Sketch," *American Letters and Historical Consciousness*, eds. J. Gerald Kennedy and Daniel Mark Fogel, Baton Rouge, 1987, 177-190.

[12] Castells, p. 85; Walker, p. 364.

[13] Glaab and Brown, p. 54.

If Walt Whitman who praised Manahatta and its masses, and Ralph Waldo Emerson who projected an "organic city" could be said to respond favorably to the city as city, they, at the same time, fought the tendency toward the dehumanizing materialism which another group of prourbanists, the local patriots and boosters, strongly promoted.[14] Similarly, antiurbanism is said to mourn the loss of nature and wilderness in big cities as in the writings of Henry David Thoreau,[15] whereas for the cosmopolitan Henry James, the turn of the century American city is still too rough and not civilized enough.[16] Such puzzling contradictions result from a warped perspective. More often than not, the city is not attacked as city, but rather the setting metonymically represents broader issues about class, culture, and civilization. This is particularly true for imaginative literature. Some writers may have opposed urban life itself, but mostly, Leo Marx points out, the use of topography in literature was metaphoric.[17] If, however, fictional texts are taken as reportorial accounts of the city and if images are excised from their context, interpretations may in a fatal way define a bias against the city which did not exist in the first place.

Critics have called attention to such misinterpretations in Lucia and Morton White's influential study of American urban thought, *The Intellectual versus the City*. Several interpretations have since been conducted which on the whole refute the vast majority of their claims. Their judgments about attitudes in the writings of Emerson, Thoreau, Hawthorne, Howells, and Henry James were corrected.[18] Nonetheless, in a parallel process, the Whites' findings have been quoted extensively in literary and sociological studies to evidence a strong hostility toward cities among American

---

[14]Michael Cowan, *City of the West: Emerson, America, and Urban Metaphor*, New Haven, 1976. Brownell, p. 585.

[15]As Thoreau attacked both the country and the city, the options of the division cannot hold the solution to his criticism. Stout, p. 18.

[16]The Whites notice the two divergent strands of antiurbanism but resolve the contradiction by attributing the positions to different historical stages in which first, the city posssessed too little, and later, too much civilization (White, pp. 228f). The divergent views, however, also appear at the same time: the period of Henry James saw a major effort at reintroducing nature into the city. See Peter J. Schmitt, *Back to Nature: The Arcadian Myth in Urban America*, New York, 1969.

[17]Marx, p. 75. See also, Alan Trachtenberg, "The American Scene: Versions of the City," *Massachusetts Review*, 8 (1967), p. 284. Weimer, p. 4.

[18]Their findings were refuted in studies by Leo Marx, Alan Trachtenberg, Michael Cowan, and Gregory L. Crider. Michael Cowan, *City of the West: Emerson, America, and Urban Metaphor*, New Haven and London, 1976. Gregory L. Crider, "William Dean Howells and the Antiurban Tradition: A Reconsideration," *American Studies*, 19 (1978), 55-64.

intellectuals and writers.[19] In a vicious circle of compartmentalized knowledge in urban studies, the reliance on one or two sources may have reified a cultural legacy that did not actually exist in this extreme form as the academic record now suggests.[20] This is not to argue that antiurbanism did not exist in the United States, but that the dual tradition has been distorted and that intellectuals and writers became scapegoats for general deficiencies.[21] The Whites' contention about the antiurban tradition in the United States thus deserves another look.

The Whites' initial goal in the study is above criticism. They argue that the American city should not be blamed for social problems in general; antiurban attitudes, bathed in the romantic vocabulary of the natural and organic, only prevent the rational treatment of the city's troubles.[22] To replace the victim, however, to assign antiurbanism simply to intellectuals, is a questionable strategy in solving the dilemma.[23] The Whites denigrate much of what the intellectuals said as being "the product of doctrinaire ideology, of blindness, and prejudice."[24] While it is not denied that such thinkers as Emerson, Thoreau, or Mumford opposed materialist ways of life as epitomized in cities, they cannot be simply reduced to intellectuals who are hostile to the American city. Moreover, some of the study's assessments are shaky. The Whites use suggestive phrasing to support their argument. In a single reference to Stephen Crane and Upton Sinclair they write that, "Stephen Crane did not mean to praise the city in *Maggie* when

---

[19]Their results are used, among others, in the studies by Burton Pike, Adrienne Siegel, Elisabeth Pfeil, Malcolm Bradbury, Blaine Brownell, David Hummon, Lutz Holzner, Sidney H. Bremer, and John J. McDermott. Malcolm Bradbury, "The Cities of Modernism," *Revue des Languages Vivantes*, 40 (1974), 442-448. John J. McDermott, "Nature, Nostalgia, and the City: An American Dilemma," *Soundings*, 55 (1972), 1-20. Lutz Holzner, "Stadtland USA - Zur Auflösung und Neuordnung der US-amerikanischen Stadt," *Geographische Zeitschrift*, 73 (1985), 191-205. David M. Hummon, "Urban Views: Popular Perspectives on City Life," *Urban Life*, 15 (1986), 3-36.

[20]Spout, p. 7.

[21]Without challenging the assumptions of the pro- and antiurban division, the dichotomy often is replaced by another set of opposites. Anselm Strauss sees writers as prourban, but intellectuals and sociologists as antiurban (Strauss, "Urban Perspectives: New York City," *The American City*, pp. 4-18); Adrienne Siegel divides into prourban writers of popular fiction and the antiurbanism of alienated intellectuals (Siegel, p. 574); Sidney H. Bremer, finally, stresses the distinction between positive female and negative male accounts of the city. Sidney H. Bremer, "Lost Continuities: Alternative Urban Visions in Chicago Novels, 1890-1915," *Soundings*, 64 (1981), 29-51.

[22]White, p. 200.

[23]The Whites conclude: "The fact that our most distinguished intellectuals have been on the whole sharply critical of urban life helps explain America's lethargy in confronting the massive problems of the contemporary city in a rational way. It is not the only element in the explanation, but the fact that so many of our intellectuals have been so antipathetic toward urban life has had a profound, even though not numerically measurable effect on popular consciousness." White, p. 200.

[24]White, p. 4.

he likened it to a jungle, nor did Upton Sinclair."[25] This statement says little about Crane's or Sinclair's actual attitude toward the city; it does, however, evoke the impression that they opposed it. Similarly, in treating Lewis Mumford's ideas on the city, the Whites, critical of his utopian model and his "blurry blueprints," show their bias claiming that he is the most thorough and unrelenting antiurbanist in the romantic vein and that he batters the city page after page in his writings.[26] The Whites' foremost fault, however, is to approach literature with inappropriate methods. They disregard fictional autonomy, excise opinions from the context, and often take passages as simple reflections, as accounts with seemingly reportorial accuracy.[27]

The Intellectual versus the City is not the only study which has misread attitudes in American city literature and which claims a powerful legacy of antiurbanism. Claude S. Fischer's sociological study, *The Urban Eperience*, similarly claimed to have detected a bias against the city among writers. His argument, however, rather indicates the strong fragmentation in urban studies. Fischer's study, written against the determinism of the Chicago School of sociology and its inherent bias against the city, argues that traditional urban theory does not present an isolated case but that American writers and intellectuals have also strongly opposed the city.[28] He then, paradoxically, backs his argument with literary interpretations conducted exactly within the urbanist framework of the Chicago School. Both Blanche Gelfant and Robert Walker, the two critics whose findings he cites, link their evaluation of urban literature to Louis Wirth's theory. A consequence of their sociological models, both may unwittingly read antiurbanism into the texts--the hostility against the city *qua* city need not be actually present, it is inherent in the focus of the interpretation.[29]

---

[25]White, p. 228.

[26]White, p. 236. For a different assessment of Mumford's attitude see Elisabeth Pfeil, *Großstadtforschung*, Hannover, 1972, p. 110; Lees, p. 293.

[27]Marx, pp. 74f. Alan Trachtenberg similarly concludes: "But when we look in detail at the Whites' evidence we find that their method raises more problems than it solves. Their approach is to search through the written works of their authors to find articulations of attitude and opinion. What matters for their thesis is the opinion itself, not its context, not its place within a total work." Trachtenberg, p. 283.

[28]Fischer, pp. 15-25.

[29]Walker, p. 372. Fischer's conclusion contains exactly such a simplification: "Depending on which horn of the dilemma they have grasped, philosophers and poets have become either pro-urbanists or (as is usually the case) anti-urbanists" (Fischer, p. 18). In fatal circularity he reifies the skewed perspective of his analysis into an objective tradition: "By and large, Western culture--particularly American culture--has made its assessments *against* the city. Accurate or not, that is the intellectual heritage bequeathed to us all." Fischer, p. 20.

The "alienated intellectual elite"[30] then, is no more prourban or antiurban than any other group, even though they admittedly tend to be more critical of society in general. But if intellectuals, writers, and journalists cannot be said to have been antiurban and if prourban attitudes were as widespread in American culture, the thesis of a general American antiurbanism has to be revised. It is more accurate to say that American society has developed diverging strands of urban thought.[31] What Americans inherited was not so much an unequivocal tradition of hostility toward the city as ready images and environmental ideologies which hid deeper inequalities and buffered social insecurity in times of disruption. The important question is how images were applied and who specifically used them. In fact, the notion of a national antiurbanism itself is a tendentially useful argument against federal or state assistance to cities and a handy excuse for the nonexistence of such urban programs.

2. Urban Thought in American History

Images of cities in Western civilization reach back to the dawn of the Judaeo-Christian tradition. Positive and negative ideals, the City of God and the City of Man, New Jerusalem and Babylon have existed side by side. Even then, the antiurban sentiments in respect to Sodom and Gomorrha and the crushing punishment for these flourishing, sinful cities were expressions of an actual animadversion of nomadic people on the desert fringe.[32] According to Jacques Ellul, 'city' in ancient Hebrew was related to the words for enemy and terror.[33] Handed down through the generations, emptied of the initial conflicts, Jewish and Christian images became potent myths. Medieval literature devised powerful and lasting images: hell, for example, was depicted as an overcrowded city.[34] Still, each religious image also had its ideological function: Augustine's "City of God" which saw the city as a haven and refuge, was turned into a political instrument in medieval towns to legitimize ecclesiastical jurisdictions against feudal claims.[35]

---

[30]Siegel, p. 574.

[31]Marx, p. 78.

[32]Janis P. Stout, *Sodoms in Eden: The City in American Fiction before 1860*, Westport, Conn., 1976, pp. 7f. Carter, *The Study of Urban Geography*, p. 252.

[33]Jacques Ellul cited in Pike, p. 5.

[34]Jay Martin, *Harvests of Change: American Literature, 1865-1914*, Englewood Cliffs, N.J., 1967, p. 4.

[35]Holton, p. 6.

Puritans imported the divided stream of Christian imagery to the New World. Boston's very secular failure-in-success as "Citty upon the Hill" could thus be qualified as New Jerusalem overcome by Babylon. As city and countryside became more and more divided in economic interest in their distinct roles in the nation, polar images multiplied. The use of city images then began to follow a recurring pattern. Social and economic progress was favorably associated with the city. Its positive image was nurtured by the aspiration for wealth and success.[36] On the other side, as life in the booming industrial cities was experienced more and more as oppressive and destructive and when expectations for material gains failed or material security seemed endangered, moral attacks were directed against the urban moloch.[37] The metaphysical imagery is indeed a helpful tool: by stressing the eternal evil of the city, it diverts the criticism from secular flaws and political deficits.

Janis P. Stout has analyzed this very division of argument in city novels before 1860. During this period, cities generally appear as insecure ground morally but offer material advantages.[38] Other studies have discovered similar patterns throughout the nineteenth century.[39] As Blaine Brownell points out, the success story genre has been highly favorable to the city; Adrienne Siegel too finds praise in popular city novels for the charms of urban life, for its wealth and cultural attractions.[40] On the other hand, the evil character of New York had achieved the dimension of a national myth by mid-century.[41] At the close of the nineteenth century, city guidebooks formalize moral attitudes toward the city providing advice on how to pass unscathed through Sodom.[42] To put it poignantly: success is secular in the city, failure is attributed to its eternal perfidy.[43]

Similar responses can be discerned with the sharp deterioration of conditions in the industrial city. 1893 is a significant date for the early modern American city. It marks

---

[36] Brownell, "The Agrarian and Urban Ideals: Environmental Images in Modern America," p. 581. The opposition between country and city appears by mid-eighteenth century. Bridenbaugh, *Cities in Revolt*, p. 5.

[37] Stout, pp. 7f.

[38] Ibid., pp. 21f.

[39] Aaron, pp. 177-88.

[40] Brownell, p. 579; Siegel, pp. 573-82.

[41] Eugene Arden, "The Evil City in American Fiction," *New York History*, 35 (1954), p. 259.

[42] Laura Hapke, "Down There on a Visit: Late Nineteenth-Century Guidebooks on the City," *Journal of Popular Culture*, 20 (1986), 41-56.

[43] Laura Hapke writes: "To the nineteenth-century popular imagination, the city was as much a symbol of moral evil as economic good." Hapke, p. 41.

Attitudes toward the American City 81

both the year that the glamorous city at Chicago's World Fair attracted 27 million people and one of the most severe depressions which left approximately a quarter of the urban work force unemployed.[44] In 1893, too, the City Beautiful Movement emerged and Frederick Jackson Turner proposed his frontier theory at the Fair.[45] Both responses, incidentally at the same moment, are telling reactions to the threat of the capitalist boom and bust in the modern city. They decline to solve the deficiencies of the contemporary city with modern political programs.[46] The erection of civic buildings strove for the aesthetic and moral rejuvenation by imposing neoclassical architecture and order, while the frontier myth defined the wilderness as a moral setting where male American democrats had been formed--now that the frontier was closed.[47] Both strongly invoke the past and anachronistic ideals, the civic order of the slaveholder polis and the natural virtue in the wilderness; both see ethical values primarily in the past and are unwilling to address urban problems except in these moral and aesthetic terms. At a time when millions of urbanites were unemployed and starving, they avoid facing the contradictions of the industrial city and instead propose powerful mythical images.

As social distress worsened in the early modern city, the virulent opposition to degradation was indeed channeled and diverted in a variety of moral and antimodern attitudes. Protestant groups condemned Babylon,[48] the elite proposed outdated hierarchical models,[49] while others turned to nature in seek of virtue to quench feelings of guilt over their materialism by idealizing America's rural culture.[50] Personal experience underlined this moral polarity of space, its simplistic division into the healthy country and the corrupt city. A constant feature in biographies at the height of industrial uprootedness and migration, countryside and childhood become inevitably associated

---

[44] Glaab and Brown, p. 260; Michael B. Katz records that the best modern estimates assume a national unemployment rate of 17 to 19 percent. In New York, thirty-five percent of the labor force were out of jobs. Michael B. Katz, *In the Shadow of the Poorhouse: A Social History of Welfare in America*, New York, 1986, pp. 147f.

[45] See Alan Trachtenberg, *The Incorporation of America: Culture and Society in the Gilded Age*, New York, 1982, pp. 11-37.

[46] Chudacoff writes that in the City Beautiful movement "problems of slums and social inequalities were seldom addressed." Chudacoff, p. 189.

[47] Daniel Aaron writes: "Perhaps the note of pessimism in his [Turner's] famous announcement of the closing of the frontier derives in part from his memories of immigrants penned up in cities and doomed to remain alien and un-American because denied the cleansing frontier experience." Aaron, p. 186.

[48] Josiah Strong, *The Twentieth Century City*, New York, 1898.

[49] Ickstadt, "Black vs. White City," p. 204.

[50] For the strong tendency to criticize the city with reference to the land, nature, and wilderness, see the accounts by Lucia and Morton White, pp. 231-39; Peter J. Schmitt, pp. xvff; McDermott, pp. 1-20.

with care, shelter, and humanism, whereas the modern city is the place of uncertainty, inhuman toil, and disillusionment for most of the rural newcomers. This was extremely important to the impact these images had and explains their acceptance beyond the partisan promotion in mass culture. The moral division of city and country was experienced as emotionally genuine.[51]

It is important to indicate the different quality of prourban and antiurban images in order to perceive their usefulness in upper- and middle-class ideology. As mass culture spread both derogatory and laudatory images of the American city, the urban lure became identified with a belief in material wealth and social well-being, with progress, future, and modern insecurity.[52] The solution for its deficits were directed toward the past, tradition, and nostalgia, suggesting a social harmony and safety which seemed irrecoverably lost.[53] Images which stress the generic opacity of the urban moloch deny collective forms of opposition and strongly suggest adjusting to the urban wilderness or, if possible, fleeing its destruction.

The American upper and middle class developed a peculiar mode of dealing with the disruptions in the modern city and of overcoming the division between moral rejection and material profit. Moving to the fringe of the industrial city, rural modes of life became incorporated into a sophisticated urban life-style. The out-of-doors was made fashionable and Boy Scouts organizations were founded.[54] The discovery of nature happened within a conservative frame of mind as rural virtues were conceived to be politically useful.[55] Endangered nature is defined as transhistorical and preserved in wilderness parks, it is adored and esteemed in its wildness, its sublime grandeur, and its overwhelming force. By the time the industrial ruling class has bought physical labor and may do without, Roland Barthes explains in his *Mythologies*, it attempts to retain the

---

[51] Georg Simmel, Robert E. Park, and Louis Wirth grew up in villages. Wilson, p. 7; Lees, p. 299.

[52] Utopian novels mostly projected positive images of the city. Brownell, p. 579.

[53] Blaine A. Brownell provides a psychological interpretation in his essay "The Agrarian and Urban Ideals: Environmental Images in Modern America." For Brownell, images reflect environmental preferences and provide as emotional stability during times of change and insecurity. He concludes: "In the final analysis, each individual maintained an image of his environment that reflected his own peculiar background and personality, an environmental image that was, in many ways, a mirror of his needs, fears, and aspirations." Brownell, p. 584.

[54] James Machor points toward a larger pattern in the imagery of white middle-class America: "Viewing pastoralism as inadequate in itself, the urban-pastoral vision conceives of an alternate 'middle realm' in which the city blends harmoniously with the countryside or contains within its own boundaries urbanity, complexity, and sophistication combined with the physical or social attributes of simple rusticity." Machor, p. 14. See also Schmitt, p. 177-89; Smith, pp. 9ff.

[55] George Mowry, *The Urban Nation, 1920-1960*, New York, 1960, p. 2.

value and virtue of labor at least in metaphors and sights; to these ends, wilderness becomes a suitable object.[56] Criticism of the unnatural and debased city follows the familiar pattern. Value lies in the past, virtue resides in the untouched realm of nature or in the crabgrass frontier of suburbs. In contrast, morals are lacking in the corrupted and artificial environment of the modern city. Neil Smith has described this ideology of space: once nature is exploited, pervaded, and subdued, the dominant class romanticizes the object of its conquest.[57] It is no coincidence that nature is often linked to femininity in this context. Barbara Berg explains the broader connection between patriarchy, domesticity, and the city:

> By transforming their conceptions of an agricultural paradise into a set of prevailing images and perceptions of womanhood, Americans could preserve the qualities they valued most, while enjoying the advantages and opportunites of a new era.
> The woman, quietly tucked away at home, creating a haven of peace and order, provided a salubrious contrast to the shrill urban milieu. As the repository of all virtue and morality, woman became the substitute for a bountiful nature who nourished and nurtured, purified and sustained. Blissfully noncompetitive, she remained unsullied by a corrupt world. She emulated the serene garden, free from rampant vying for money, power, and position so characteristic of industrial cities.[58]

The division of urban images thus incorporates a major contradiction in American society, a conflict which is an important source for ambivalent feelings toward the city to date. Most people have to work in the American city but positive value is only offered in images that evoke conditions which lie buried in the past or outside the modern environment. The myth of traditional community thus has loomed large in the American mind and has served as an ideological alternative to degenerate modern ways of life and proverbial urban alienation.[59]

Mainstream culture proposed a new compromise for the conflict as suburbia expanded rapidly in the twentieth century. Suburbs were stylized as the perfect embodiments of the American dream. Such images of a suburban Arcadia did not emerge at random, nor were they proliferated voluntarily. Mary Corbin Sies concludes for the early phase of suburban myth-making:

> In architectural journals, mass circulation magazines, home economics courses, and department stores, both the suburban ideal and the P-MS (the professional-managerial

---

[56] Barthes, p. 74. Manuel Castells, *City, Class, and Power*, London, 1978, p. 153.

[57] Smith, pp. 13f.

[58] Berg, p. 264.

[59] Charles Bowden and Lew Kreinberg, *Street Signs Chicago: Neighborhood and Other Illusions of Big-City Life*, Chicago, 1981; Katznelson, p. 26.

stratum) life-style that it embodied were aggressively advertised as the goal towards which all American families should strive.[60]

In the suburban ideal, the city fringe perfectly united the moral profit of the country and the economic advantages of the city. Upper- and middle-class Americans could possess both, material gains and frontier virtue. Suburbia continued the middle-class tradition of urban pastoralism which James Machor analyzed:

> By conceiving of cities that unite the best of urban activities with pastoral values, it [urban pastoralism] addresses the desire for a way of life in which the personal conflict between self-fulfillment and group identification and the cultural tension between change and continued stability are reconciled.[61]

A 1972 Gallup poll, which has often been cited as evidence for the persistence of antiurbanism, discloses the very pattern of contradiction. According to the survey only 13 percent preferred to live in the city, whereas 31 percent chose the suburb, 32 percent the small town, and 23 percent the farm.[62] Important to note, the poll was conducted when American urbanization had reached its phase of megalopolitan sprawl and when for the first time more people lived in suburbs than in inner cities. If only 13 percent wanted to live in the city, those selecting the surburb, the small town, and the farm as preferable settings did not need to be cut off from the positive materialism of urban culture since they had them within reach by means of modern communications. In fact, many people which preferred a rural or small town setting wanted to remain within 30 miles of a large city.[63] What this antiurbanism opposes (without spelling it out), are conditions in the inner city--its poverty, filth, decay, and crime--the very disruptions of social and cultural life which the upper and middle class helped produce. The 1969 report of the National Commission on Urban Problems unmistakenly indicates them as the groups most responsible for the dilemma in inner cities:

---

[60]Mary Corbin Sies, "The City Transformed: Nature, Technology, and The Suburban Ideal, 1877-1917," *Journal of Urban History*, 14 (1987), pp. 105f.

[61]Machor p. 18.

[62]Fischer, p. 21; Kreutzer, p. 11.

[63]Hummon, p. 33. The Harris' survey of attitudes toward the American city from 1978 backs this conclusion: 60 percent of Americans saw the best employment opportunities in large cities, while 82 percent also considered it the worst place for the family. The study concludes: "Many suburbanites and those in town and rural areas remain tied economically, socially and culturally to the city in varying degrees. Central cities are far from irrelevant to the lives of many in the suburbs and outlying areas, even if many do not find large cities desirable as residential areas." *A Survey of Citizens Views and Concerns About Urban Life*, Louis Harris and Associates, Inc., final report, conducted for the Department of Housing and Urban Development, study H-2835, 1978, pp. 5, 7.

The people in the slums are the symptoms of the urban problems, not the cause. They are virtually imprisoned in slums by the white suburban noose around the inner city, a noose that says 'Negroes and poor people not wanted.' It says this in a variety of ways, including discriminatory subdivision regulations, discriminatory fiscal and planning practices. In simple terms, what many of these practices add up to is a refusal of many localities to accept their share of housing for poor people. But the problem is more than that.[64]

The remarks point at the chief contradiction of present day antiurbanism among the American upper and middle class: the negative image of the city is a moral rejection of the very deprivation from which the upper and middle class have profited. Evidently, it is easier to condemn selected features of society and modernity rather than face the question of which processes have shaped past and present, downtown and suburbia, as well as city and countryside.

Urban fiction, however, has generally set the city in more encompassing metaphorical contexts and has not been content with mere praise of or opposition to the city. If the city was criticized, it was because the city was the prominent spatial manifestation of the contradictions of industrial capitalism. Space is part of the identity: one cannot help but also criticize the immediate, graspable forms of suppression.

In sum, the history of attitudes toward the American city does not yield a homogeneous and unequivocal tradition, rather diverse groups used images for their own purposes.[65] It may be shown that authentic modern fiction did not fall into the trap of a prourban and antiurban discussion but rather laid bare the complexities of urban experience. To do justice to city writers, it is necessary to provide an adequate framework so that the intricate and often contradictory assessments of the fragmented city may be discerned. A perspective which posits antiurbanism can only discern antiurbanism--the question already provides the answer.[66]

---

[64]National Commission on Urban Problems, *Building the American City*, House Document No.19-34, 91st Congress, 1st Session, Washington, D.C., 1969, p. 1.

[65]Marx, p. 78. David Hummon concludes: "Urban experience plays a complex, socially mediated role in the maintenance of diverse urban perspectives." Hummon, p. 32.

[66]Cowan, p. 4.

5
Literary Criticism

1. Urban concepts in criticism

Considering the multitude of perspectives on the city, the variety of approaches to American city fiction need not be surprising. The critical analysis of American city novels spans from George A. Dunlap's published dissertation *The City in the American Novel 1789-1900* in 1934 to Eberhard Kreutzer's interpretation of New York fiction in 1985.[1] It ranges from Yi-Fu Tuan who analyzes fictional texts primarily for behaviorist and geographical purposes,[2] to David Weimer's aesthetic approach in which the city is present only in singular metaphors of American writers.[3] There are studies which offer insights from novels into urban planning[4] and others which are guides to the city's writers and literary settings.[5] In the wake of the urban crisis in the sixties and the growth of

---

[1] George A. Dunlap, *The City in the American Novel 1789-1900: A Study of American Novels Portraying Contemporary Conditions in New York, Philadelphia, and Boston*, 1934, New York, 1965.

[2] Yi-Fu Tuan, "Literature, Experience, and Environmental Knowing," *Environmental Knowing*, eds. Gary T. Moore and Reginald G. Golledge, Stroudsburg, Penn., 1976, 260-72. There are several studies in which city novels predominantly serve as evidence for non-literary questions. Thus W. J. Lloyd's article "Landscape Imagery in the Urban Novel: A Source of Geographic Evidence" reflects on how to use urban novels for geographic research (W. J. Lloyd, "Landscape Imagery in the Urban Novel: A Source of Geographic Evidence," *Environmental Knowing*, eds. Gary T. Moore and Reginald G. Golledge, Stroudsburg, Penn., 1976, 279-285). David L. Rankin's dissertation "Urban and Rural Syntax: An Analysis based on American Fiction from 1920-62" examines random excisions from fictional texts from a linguistic standpoint and searches for differences between urban and rural sentence structure. David L. Rankin, "Urban and Rural Syntax: An Analysis based on American Fiction from 1920-62," diss. Renselaer Polytechnic Institute, 1973.

[3] Weimer, *The City as Metaphor*, pp. 1-13.

[4] Michael Cowan, "Walkers in the Street: American Writers and the Modern City," *Prospects*, 6 (1981), 281-311.

[5] Susan Edminston and Linda Cirino have compiled such a guide to New York's writers and intellectuals, to their neighborhoods, streets, apartments, and bars. Susan Edminston and Linda Cirino, *Literary New York: A History and a Guide*, Boston, 1976. See also Rufus R. Wilson and Otilie Wilson, *New York in Literature*, New York, 1947.

urban studies, complete issues of periodicals have been dedicated to the subject, anthologies, essay collections, and conference lectures have been published.[6]

The various literary approaches to urban fiction have recently been summarized in detail by Eberhard Kreutzer.[7] In order not to repeat his findings, the following synopsis rather concentrates on the urban concepts which have been applied in literary criticism. Such an analysis is important as the city concept directs the assessment of the fictional city. In particular, the model used in Blanche Gelfant's *The American City Novel* in 1954, the first comprehensive account in the field and the most influential study as yet, deserves careful attention. Gelfant's study has been cited most often in geographical and sociological studies to evidence literary judgments on the American city and has become a model for many studies which followed.[8]

Blanche Gelfant analyzes how novelists reacted to the dissociation of the individual in modern civilization and, in particular, how city writers transfigured the social fragmentation experienced in twentieth-century American metropolises. Gelfant not only uses Wirthian theory as a background study, but conducts her investigation within an ecological framework.[9] Hence, she may contend that the metropolitan environment produces a typical way of life and that the city determines modern behavior in a way similar to the frontier previously. After establishing the modern city as agent and force, she defines the urban novel as a twentieth-century literary genre. The "active participation of the city in shaping character and plot"[10] distinguishes the modern genre from local color fiction in which the city only functions as scenery. Gelfant distinguishes three types of city novels: the 'portrait' type, which reveals the city through a single character

---

[6]*Modern Fiction Studies*, "The Modern Novel and the City," 24 (1978). *Zeitschrift für Linguistik und Literatur*, "Stadt und Literatur," ed. Wolfgang Haubrichs, 12 (1982). David R. Weimer, ed., *City and Country in America*, Meredith, N.Y., 1962. Alan Trachtenberg, ed., *The City. American Experience*, New York, 1971. H. Pickering, ed., *The City in American Literature*, New York, 1977. Michael C. Jaye and Ann Chalmers Watts, eds., *Literature and the Urban Experience*, New Brunswick, N.J., 1981. Berndt Ostendorf ed., *Amerikanische Ghettoliteratur: zur Literatur ethnischer, marginaler und unterdrückter Gruppen in Amerika*, Darmstadt, 1983. David M. Fine, ed., *Los Angeles in Fiction: A Collection of Original Essays*, Albuquerque, 1984. Susan Merrill Squier, ed., *Women Writers and the City: Essays in Feminist Literary Criticism*, Knoxville, 1984. Edward Timms and David Kelley, eds., *Unreal City: Urban Experience in Modern European Literature and Art*, Manchester, 1985. *AvantGarde*, "Metropolis," 1 (1988). Graham Clarke, ed. *The American City: Literary and Cultural Perspectives*, New York, 1988. Klaus R. Scherpe, ed., *Die Unwirklichkeit der Städte. Großstadtdarstellungen zwischen Moderne und Postmoderne*, Hamburg, 1988.

[7]Kreutzer, *New York in der zeitgenössischen amerikanischen Erzählliteratur*, pp. 15-22.

[8]Pike, *The Image of the City in Modern Literature*, p. 10. Kreutzer, p. 17. Gelfant's results are used in the studies by Claude Fischer and Andrew Lees.

[9]Gelfant, *The American City Novel*, pp. 28ff.

[10]Ibid., p. 5.

(Theodore Dreiser's *Sister Carrie*), the 'synoptic' type in which the city is the protagonist (John Dos Passos' *Manhattan Transfer*), and the 'ecological' type, in which the neighborhood manners of a specific area in the city receive prime attention (James T. Farrell's *Studs Lonigan*).[11]

As Kreutzer has already pointed out, Gelfant's typology is not fully convincing: *Studs Lonigan* is as much the portrait of a single character as of an urban collective.[12] Moreover, seen in the light of the new urban theory, only an 'ecological' type may be said to exist. Any novel, however wide its range, may only present a partial segment of urban society.[13] Even the synoptic image of the metropolis in *Manhattan Transfer* is ruled by a particular class perspective. Gelfant's division into a 'synoptic' and an 'ecological' type however suggests that one fragmented perspective is more urban and objective than the other. Moreover, Gelfant's city concept restricts the variety of experiences that she defines as urban. This bias can be noticed in the reasons she gives for the inclusion or exclusion of novels in her study. Conceiving of the city novel as an "organic whole," she rejects Stephen Crane's *Maggie: A Girls of the Streets* as too "fragmentary."[14] Obviously, the clash of two distinct urban cultures, the differences between Bowery and Uptown in the novel, contradict her uniformism. She too excludes Upton Sinclair's *The Jungle* because the novel uses the city within a broader context. Such a concept contradicts her urban ontology.[15] Finally, she cannot categorize F. Scott Fitzgerald's *The Great Gatsby* as urban, since its well-ordered upper-class setting does not produce the anonymity, isolation, and dissociation which by definition are to be expected in the heterogeneous American city. Her approach is most convincing for *Sister Carrie* and *Manhattan Transfer* where the modern city metonymically represents general tendencies in Ameri-

---

[11] Ibid., pp. 11ff.

[12] Kreutzer, p. 16. Kreutzer points out that if Gelfant's criteria for the urban genre are strictly applied, only *Manhattan Transfer* could be categorized as city novel.

[13] The ecological type is problematic for Gelfant since the neighborhood as determining setting does not produce primarily the anonymous, hectic, and alienating ways of life that she has isolated as urban. She thus redefines this type as a study of manners (Gelfant, pp. 12f). As the stagnation in Farrell's South Side contradicts the gaudy materialism of her city, she has to attribute the bleak mood to a distinct phase in the history of Chicago and to the supposedly distinct experience of children (ibid., pp. 185ff). However, Chicago boomed no less in the teens and twenties of Farrell's novels than in Dreiser's Chicago at the turn of the century. Similarly, both Crane and Dreiser describe New York at the same time: the difference in atmosphere clearly is social and not historical.

[14] Ibid., pp. 6, 63.

[15] For Gelfant, *The Jungle* is disqualified as a 'problem novel.' In contrast, *Sister Carrie* is "concerned with a total way of life." Her argument reveals the class restriction in her model: since the totality of working-class experience in the city contradicts the Chicago School features, it simply does not present a total *urban* way of life. Gelfant, pp. 7f.

can society at a point when urbanization, industrialization, and capitalism become almost indistinguishable as forces. The achievement of Gelfant's monograph thus lies in its detailed examination of literary techniques of expressing the dissociation of the modern subject, but not in its restrictive definition of an urban genre.[16]

The approaches toward American urban fiction can broadly be divided into three groups. There are studies which concentrate on psychological-archetypal, aesthetic-thematic, and sociological-historical aspects of American city novels.[17]

2. The Psychological Approach

This group of studies observes city fiction through a psychological lens and applies a variety of archetypal, mythical, or symbolic patterns to the novels. The interpretations examine the specific psychological reactions of the characters to the environment or analyze the significance of urban symbols. Such investigations into the stock of urban imagery may be relevant to discover conflicts or deficiencies which repeatedly appear in large settlements. They may also be helpful in discerning the received vocabulary on which descriptions of modern city life are based.

As Raymond Williams has explained, a powerful link between urban conditions and archetypal myths has developed in modernity. Myth and revolution, in their variable forms, have dominated the responses to altered conditions in the fragmented metropolis. Myth, as collective unconscious, creates a new community among the dissociated urban monads in and through intense subjectivity. The fragmented daily experiences in the modern environment are stabilized in the link to universal constants and metaphysical patterns.[18] On the other hand, psychological approaches tend to confine the city to a few generalized features and thus reduce the wide and contradictory variety in the modern city. As Williams has pointed out, however, "in the nineteenth and twentieth centuries it often matters more what else is being said than what is being said, in conventional ways, about the city."[19]

---

[16]Kreutzer, p. 16.

[17]This grouping is not intended as a typology, almost any study could be cross-classified. Felice Witzum Dickstein proposes a similar division. Felice Witzum Dickstein, "The Role of the City in the Works of Theodore Dreiser, Thomas Wolfe, James T. Farrell, and Saul Bellow," diss. The City University of New York, 1973, p. 2.

[18]Williams, pp. 294ff.

[19]Ibid., p. 349.

Burton Pike's *The Image of the City in Modern Literature* is the most extensive and elaborate monograph in this field. The study examines Western urban literature from the eighteenth to the twentieth century. For Pike, who draws on theories by Sigmund Freud and Lewis Mumford, city imagery has a dual character. On the one hand, there are transhistorical patterns in the attitudes toward the city. They express our "culture's restless dream about its inner conflicts."[20] On the other hand, the surface features of city representations change with history. An ordered and static city in the early nineteenth century thus is replaced by a city in flux. This individualized city then dissolves further into the fragmentary modern mosaic. These variations, however, are secondary to Pike: "At a deeper level . . . the widely varying historical cities of Western culture are the same city, a powerful archetype-emblem representing deep-rooted social and psychological constants."[21]

Since Pike's archetypal image implies a city which is a compact, circumscribed entity, he has difficulties assessing the changes in the post-industrial city. Rather than criticizing those forces which have produced isolation and fragmentation in sprawling cities, he attacks the dispersal itself. On the one hand, he blames sociology and geography for blurring the archetypal city core:

> Sociologists generally prefer to talk about 'megalopolis,' 'conurbation,' or 'commutershed,' rather than city. Obliterating the shape of the city by extending it to include a diffuse amount of territory beyond it is a way of defining the contemporary situation of the city by its shapelessness. But these terms might represent more a projection of cultural attitudes than a neutral description of realities. This preference for abolishing the shape of the city seems to imply a de-mythification of the city of monuments which has for so long expressed positive as well as negative attitudes towards culture. . . .[22]

On the other hand, the sprawl itself is criticized for the deficiencies in postindustrial environments:

> The dispersed city has signally failed to give rise to meaningful monuments or a meaningful culture. Central city cores, even chaotic ones, remain the magnets for those things which give meaning to civilization.[23]

---

[20]Pike, *The Image of the City in Modern Literature*, p. 8.

[21]Ibid., p. 17. Pike concedes that the fundamental assumption of archetypal criticism has yet to be proven. The question of "how attitudes are transmitted on the level of cognition remains a problem. Some authorities reject the idea of continuity in the archetype of the city." Ibid., p. 6.

[22]Ibid., p. 130.

[23]Ibid., p. 133.

Such an assessment may be challenged, however, for even the Hellenistic "polis" was dispersed in a sense and included the rural environs in its image. Town and hinterland were seen as a unity in Greek and Roman concepts of the city.[24] Pike's supposedly transhistorical concept of cities as "things apart"[25] is a modern view. It is related to traditional urban theory and its attempt at turning the city into an autonomous object for scrutiny.

Interpretations by Joyce Carol Oates and Leslie Fiedler similarly display some of the drawbacks of an archetypal approach. For Oates, the archetypes of the City of God and the City of Man have been fused in the modern city. Because of the diminished importance of "communal religion" in modernity, the secular city is read as utopian.[26] The inevitable disappointment about the heavenly city then is expressed in infernal images. For this reason, a hellish city prevails in modern American city fiction. Oates' claim, however, is too broad and undifferentiated.[27] As she reduces the diverse criticism to a necessary disappointment over secular shortcomings, she turns all efforts at improvement into inevitable failures. Moreover, Oates' scattered remarks about what city life means, reveal a familiar view of the American city. It receives the attributes of the Chicago School: her city is amoral, anonymous, suprahuman, and materialistic.[28] In places, the archetype evokes a middle-class city of choice and pushes the distinct conditions of ghetto or working-class environments to the margin.[29]

Leslie Fiedler too examines the continuity in images.[30] Dante's image of the city as hell survives in modern culture because the archetypal division between city and nature lives on. Rich and poor alike feel the alienation from the natural world in cities.

---

[24] Holton, p. 3.

[25] Pike, p. 3.

[26] Oates analyzes fiction by Stephen Crane, Theodore Dreiser, Upton Sinclair, Anzia Yezierska, Saul Bellow, and Donald Barthelme. Joyce Carol Oates, "Imaginary Cities: America," *Literature and the Urban Experience*, eds. Michael C. Jaye and Ann Chalmers Watts, p. 11.

[27] Upton Sinclair's hellish city, for instance, does not condemn the city as such. Rather, Chicago is the place of proletarian hopes. Oates, p. 13.

[28] Ibid., pp. 18, 30. She holds that Augie learns "the lesson of the city: to plot, to calculate, to negotiate, to press forward, never allow himself to be manipulated, never to allow others to define his limits." Ibid., p. 20.

[29] Oates writes: "Bellow's unique synthesis of the humanistic and the tragic, his apparently effortless synthesis of the 'classic' and the defiantly modern, greatly outdistances the time- and place-locked 'naturalism' of James T. Farrell. Like his creator, Augie refuses to be 'determined' beforehand. He defines himself. . . ." Ibid., p. 21.

[30] Leslie Fiedler, "Mythicizing the City," *Literature and the Urban Experience*, eds. Michael C. Jaye and Ann Chalmers Watts, 113-21.

Hence the image of an urban hell has dominated in literature and has been invoked both by leftists and rightists. But the cityscapes in Dante, T. S. Eliot, Stephen Crane, or Richard Wright are not specified by Fiedler, the very different contexts of the infernal imagery remain untouched. In his interpretation, Fiedler is content with broad generalizations, such as Spengler's dictum that the city contradicts and denies all nature. Hell stands for an eternal resentment of the city because of our "instinctive, impulsive undermind yearns" for nature.[31]

Such an archetypal approach is of limited use because the mere replacement of an ahistoric city concept with timeless images of Hell, Babylon, or New Jerusalem does not advance the understanding of the diverse and historically unique conditions in the modern city. Moreover, in Monroe K. Spears' *Dionysus and the City*, a class-directed version of the contemporary city appears in the guise of a timeless archetype. For Spears, modernity begins as Dionysus enters the City.[32] This archetype of the City is defined as an autonomous environment which is "both cause and symptom."[33] The economic or historical constitution of the city is not discussed. Spears' brief catalogue of characteristics discloses the bias of the city concept:

> The city is both massive fact and universally recognizable symbol of modernity, and it both constitutes and symbolizes the modern predicament: the mass man, anonymous and rootless, cut off from his past and from the nexus of human relations in which he formerly existed, anxious and insecure, enslaved by the mass media but left by the disappearance of God with a dreadful freedom of spiritual choice, is the typical citizen of Megapolis, where he enjoys lethal and paralyzing traffic, physical decay and political corruption, racial and economic tension, crime, rioting, and police brutality.[34]

This obviously is a most contemporary archetype which has received characteristics of urbanist ideology.

The psychological approach includes studies in which city and archetype merge completely. In Alan Rose's "Sin and the City: The Uses of Disorder in the Urban Novel," an amoral city exclusively functions as the locale for the "fruitful Fall," for initiation into adulthood.[35] For Rose, the city as representation of crime, degradation, and amorality

---

[31] Fiedler, p. 118.

[32] Monroe K. Spears, *Dionysus and the City: Modernism in Twentieth-Century Poetry*, New York, 1970, p. 68f.

[33] Spears, p. 71.

[34] Ibid., p. 74.

[35] Alan H. Rose, "Sin and the City: The Uses of Disorder in the Urban Novel," *Centennial Review*, 16 (1972), 203-20.

no longer fulfills its traditional function to initiate men into maturity but only offers frustration and barrenness in modern times.[36]

A mythical approach to American city fiction need not be confined to such openly ideological uses of the city. There are studies of archetypal imagery which inquire into historical and social differences. Heinz Ickstadt examines how the metaphors of New Jerusalem and Babylon have altered their function in modern literature. He shows that in each novel city imagery is linked to larger criticism of society and that each myth is redefined through the actual conflicts present in the fictional city.[37] The utopian city which Hart Crane would still like to project in *The Bridge* is on the wane in the twentieth century; with the protagonists of *Sister Carrie, Manhattan Transfer,* or *The Great Gatsby,* who are all immersed in struggles within the city, utopian belief is present only as reminiscence in negative imagery.[38]

Ihab Hassan offers a reading of the internal city in "Cities of Mind, Urban Words: The Dematerialization of Metropolis in Contemporary American Fiction." He sees the city as an "inscape of mind."[39] For Hassan, the central urban archetype is the complicity of language, knowledge, and artifact. Its early manifestation is Babel with its tower and polyglottism. While Hassan also notices a recurrent conflict between the city and nature, this opposition for him does not lead to Spenglerian gloom or cyclical views of necropolis. The city traditionally has been many fictions, both good and evil. Its contemporary shapelessness may lead to a broader scope in which urban forms will be treated in an analysis which encompasses civilization as a whole.[40]

In *The Art of the City: Views and Versions of New York*, Peter Conrad provides interpretations of the aesthetic transformation of New York in literature, painting, and photography.[41] For Conrad, any city is founded by an epic hero--through him, human life is reprieved from its brevity. Yet the myth which records the heroism also presents a delusion. Man fatally considers himself and his cities as central on earth.[42] Since Conrad

---

[36] Rose, p. 204.

[37] Heinz Ickstadt, "Gesichter Babylons: Zum Bild der Großstadt im modernen amerikanischen Roman," *Jahrbuch für Amerikastudien*, 16 (1971), 60-76.

[38] Ickstadt, p. 76.

[39] Ihab Hassan, "Cities of Mind, Urban Words: The Dematerialization of Metropolis in Contemporary American Fiction," *Literature and the Urban Experience*, eds. Michael C. Jaye and Ann Ch. Watts, p. 94.

[40] Hassan's thesis that the fictional city becomes dematerialized cannot be generalized. He restricts his analysis chiefly to postmodernist writings by Burroughs, Barthelme, and Pynchon in which text and subject are dissolved. Hassan, p. 108.

[41] Peter Conrad, *The Art of the City: Views and Versions of New York*, New York, 1984.

[42] Conrad, pp. 3f.

selects Walt Whitman and his unconventional treatment of New York as the *genius loci* of his book, a differentiated, if idealistic and male, portrayal of the artistic transformation of New York results. While the city, as 'a crime against nature,' often infringes upon Conrad's judgments, the division into nature and civilization does not seriously impair his interpretation. Nature and culture are essentially linked in Whitman's universe.

3. The Aesthetic Approach

Among the approaches which primarily deal with the literary transformation of the modern American city, several studies follow Blanche Gelfant's pattern. Hana Wirth-Nesher applies Louis Wirth's model in "The modern Jewish Novel and the City: Franz Kafka, Henry Roth, and Amoz Oz," and tries to show how social and spatial urbanism translates into the aesthetics of the novels.[43] Analogous to Gelfant's synoptic type, Diana Festa-McCormick's *The City as Catalyst* intends to examine "the city as protagonist in fiction, projecting visions and molding individuals." Except for defining the city as a "force in man's universe," she does not explicate the basis for this assumption and defines the city rather vaguely as "dynamic energy incessantly in motion" and "immutable in its way while constantly renewing itself."[44] Festa-McCormick does not elaborate what the city is and why it can be protagonist in a novel.[45]

Gerhard Hoffmann's *Raum, Situation, erzählte Wirklichkeit*, draws on Blanche Gelfant's classification and uses Louis Wirth's theory in its section on the modern city.[46] Hoffmann's aim at producing a general typology of the literary transfigurations of space may explain why he predominantly focuses on the city as a spatial rather than as a social phenomenon.[47] His neglect of the social aspect is a major drawback. Hoffmann posits the Wirthian city as ontological model and equates it in its status with nature. Size, density, and heterogeneity function as explanatory categories in his analysis. For example, he claims that the heterogeneity of the metropolis generates the problems of class

---

[43] Hana Wirth-Nesher, "The modern Jewish Novel and the City: Franz Kafka, Henry Roth, and Amos Oz," *Modern Fiction Studies*, 25 (1978), 91-101.

[44] Diana Festa-McCormick, *The City as Catalyst: a Study in Ten Novels*, Rutherford, 1979, p. 15.

[45] Interpreting *Manhattan Transfer* she relies on a vaguely biotic concept: "The bloodline or nerve centers of a metropolis are totally polymorphous, interdependent entities held together by that nebulous thread called atmosphere." Ibid., p. 144.

[46] Gerhard Hoffmann, *Raum, Situation, erzählte Wirklichkeit: Poetologische und historische Studien zum englischen und amerikanischen Roman*, Stuttgart, 1978.

[47] Kreutzer, p. 20.

formation and causes the conflict between rich and poor, between employee and employer.[48] His analysis of the symbolization of urban space, though, is not seriously impaired by this restrictive model (beyond the confusion in the relationship between cause and effect) because he choses novels which possess an affinity to Wirth's particular concept. And yet, in his interpretation any image of the American city can only refer to itself as autonomous essence and cause. Thus the diverse metaphoric uses of space and topography tend to be marginalized.

Heinrich and Renate Plett's examination of expressionistic New York plays in the Twenties shows that the analysis of urban space need not necessarily lead to an ecological reduction.[49] Here, the diverse images of New York are fruitfully combined with an analysis of specific conditions in the Machine Age. An interesting turn in perspective, Michael Cowan analyzes fiction in "Walkers in the Street: American Writers and the Modern City," to offer insights for more humane city planning. He examines the implications of authorial viewpoints and the uses of the motif of walking in city fiction. He distinguishes three perspectives on the city: the vista from above, which frequently implies contemplation, judgment, or domination; the view from below, which often suggests subversion; finally, the active glimpses from the maze on the street level. For Cowan, walking, that is participating in street life, constitutes the creative choice; the novelists' observations should be considered when designing urban space to emphasize the pedestrian, humane scale in the city.[50] Studies by Graham Clarke, Blanche Gelfant and Richard Hanley also examine the implications of perspective and standpoint. Clarke sees a dual tendency in images of New York. The followers of Whitman emphasize the upward perspective and the view of the skyline, while the followers of Melville stress the downward perspective and the experience of the street.[51] Gelfant sees the view from below in the subterranean city as a correlative to pastoral retreat in previous fiction.[52]

---

[48]Hoffmann, pp. 389f.

[49]Heinrich F. und Renate Plett, "New York. Variationen über das Thema Metropolis im amerikanischen Drama der zwanziger Jahre," *Zeitschrift für Literaturwissenschaft und Linguistik*, 12 (1982), 103-33.

[50]Cowan, "Walkers in the Street: American Writers and the Modern City," pp. 281f.

[51]Graham Clarke, "A 'Sublime and Atrocious' Spectacle: New York and the Iconography of Manhattan Island," *The American City*, pp. 38f.

[52]Blanche Gelfant, "Residence Underground: Recent Fictions of the Subterranean City," *Sewanee Review*, 83 (1975), p. 437.

For Hanley, the movement between city, country, and suburb is the most important American pattern, rather than an adherence to one setting.[53]

Several studies followed Gelfant's examination of literary technique in *The American City Novel*. Rudolf Haas closely examined exemplary passages from modern city novels in "Großstadtmotive im Spiegel moderner amerikanischer Prosa."[54] Renate Schmidt-von Bardeleben compared the different techniques employed by Theodore Dreiser and John Dos Passos in *Das Bild New Yorks im Erzählwerk von Dreiser und Dos Passos*.[55] While her analysis of novelistic tools is convincing, the examination is too uncritically based upon the assumption that the city in the novel directly relates to the real city and thus its topography tends to be analyzed regardless of its function within the metaphoric design of the novel.[56]

Felice Witzum Dickstein also examines the aesthetic and thematic use of the city in twentieth-century fiction.[57] Further predominantly thematic analyses of urban fiction can be found in George A. Dunlap's *The City in the American Novel 1789-1900*, Robert E. Fleming's "The Chicago Naturalistic Novel, 1930-1966,"[58] Joan Zlotnick's *Portrait of an American City: the Novelists' New York*,[59] and Carl S. Smith's *Chicago and the Literary Imagination*.[60] These studies include documentary information about the social and economic development of each city, yet mostly confine themselves to a descriptive paraphrase rather than a critical analysis of the contents of the fiction. A recent collection of essays similarly examines aesthetic and thematic aspects in the literary treatment of individual cities.[61] In his dissertation "Lure of the City: Urban Landscape and Metaphor in

---

[53]Richard Eugene Hanley, "Place to Place: A Study of the Movement Between the City and Country in Selected Twentieth-Century American Fiction," diss. State University of New York at Binghampton, 1981, p. 247.

[54]Rudolf Haas, "Großstadtmotive im Spiegel moderner amerikanischer Prosa," *Die neueren Sprachen*, 6 (1957), 497-510.

[55]Renate Schmidt-von Bardeleben, *Das Bild New Yorks im Erzählwerk von Dreiser und Dos Passos*, München, 1967.

[56]Thus Schmidt-von Bardeleben focuses only on Dreiser's portrayal of New York even though New York and Chicago only receive full significance within their duality in *Sister Carrie*.

[57]Felice Witzum Dickstein, "The Role of the City in the Works of Theodore Dreiser, Thomas Wolfe, James T. Farrell, and Saul Bellow," diss. The City University of New York, 1973.

[58]Robert E. Fleming, "The Chicago Naturalistic Novel, 1930-1966," Diss. University of Illinois, 1967.

[59]Joan Zlotnick, *Portrait of an American City: the Novelists' New York*, Port Washington, N.Y., 1982.

[60]Carl S. Smith, *Chicago and the Literary Imagination, 1880-1920*, London, 1984.

[61]Graham Clarke's collection includes among others: Henry Claridge, "Chicago: 'The Classical Center of American Materialism,'" 86-104; Graham Clarke, "'The Great Wrong Place': Los Angeles as Urban Milieu,"

American Literature, 1870-1920," Lester Roy Zipris illumines the changes in city novels which occurred at the turn of the century when writers developed outmoded fictional forms to include the new contents of city life.[62]

David R. Weimer first emphasized the symbolic transformation of the city in *The City as Metaphor* and thus opened a new dimension to the interpretation of fictional cities. Even in the works of a documentary writer as Theodore Dreiser, the city, Weimer writes, is "abundantly wrought, fashioned, made over."[63] Stressing that fictional cities require metaphoric categories most, Weimer corrects previous approaches in which fiction is reduced to a literal reflection of reality. His refusal to analyze urban conditions and his decision to concentrate solely on the diversity of the imaginative cities moves the pendulum to the other extreme, however.[64] Weimer's conclusion restricts the image of the American city to singular meanings or vague metaphors. For him, the modern city is a miracle and fantasy, order and fate.[65]

Weimer's metaphoric approach was resumed and further refined by Alan Trachtenberg and Leo Marx who both stressed the necessity of analyzing both the autonomus constitution of the image in urban fiction and the social or historical conditions which informed it.[66] Leo Marx showed in his readings of urban fiction by Nathaniel Hawthorne and F. Scott Fitzgerald that the "topography here--place in a literal sense--is a vitally important but nonetheless secondary subject, or vehicle, of the great central figurative conception whose primary subject, or tenor, is the search for inner freedom and fulfillment."[67] For Marx, the alleged antiurbanism in nineteenth-century city novels is more a misconception than an actual bias against the American city.[68]

The most sophisticated examination of narrative technique has recently been conducted in Eberhard Kreutzer's *New York in der zeitgenössischen amerikanischen Er-*

124-45; Arnold Goldman, "Life and Death in New Orleans," 146-78; Julian G. Hurstfield, "The Truths of Washington, D.C.," 105-23; A. Robert Lee, "Harlem on my Mind: Fictions of a Black Metropolis," 62-85.

[62]Lester Roy Zipris, "Lure of the City: Urban Landscape and Metaphor in American Literature, 1870-1920," diss. State University of New York, 1981.

[63]Weimer, *The City as Metaphor*, p. 6.

[64]Declining to define what city precisely means for him, Weimer proposes rather commonplace views and prejudices about urban life where he has to refer to the actual city. Thus, the metropolis contains "anonymous cubicles" and there are "city-bred logistical difficulties of moving. . . ." Weimer, p. 68.

[65]Ibid., p. 13.

[66]Alan Trachtenberg, "The American Scene: Versions of the City," *Massachusetts Review*, 8 (1967), 281-95. Marx, "The Puzzle of Anti-Urbanism in Classic American Literature," pp. 63-80.

[67]Marx, p. 74.

[68]Ibid., p. 79; see also Pike, p. 12.

zähliteratur. Incorporating the latest insights in urban studies, the chief interest of Kreutzer's interpretation of post-war New York fiction lies on the narrative strategies employed to convey urban experience.[69] His socio-psychological approach examines the perception of fictional characters. The selective use of city perspectives and of socio-topography receive foremost attention. Including information about the social and historical background, the study leads to many illuminating insights into the relation between city conception and narrative technique. Kreutzer's reading of *Last Exit to Brooklyn*, for instance, shows how Hubert Selby's naturalism attempts to project the desperation and the atmosphere of brutality among juvenile drop-outs in Brooklyn in motif repetition and circular form.[70] While the study fully succeeds in analyzing literary techniques, it remains too descriptive at times.[71]

Several studies discuss the relation between city and fictional form. Diane Wolfe Levy and Barabara Lee Hussey examine the connection between the city and its fictional dematerialization.[72] Walter Göbel analyzes the link between the naturalist novel and Chicago.[73] Using an ecological concept of city growth, Göbel tentatively argues that changes in the novel correspond to developments in the city. Yet his claim is too broad and deterministic.[74] Thus his contention that the focus of fiction narrows as the city grows is inaccurate.[75]

The most encompassing claim was made by Volker Klotz who posited in his monograph *Die erzählte Stadt: eine Herausforderung des Romans von Lesage bis Döblin* an affinity between the city and the form of the novel. The result of the examination, however, is disappointing.[76] Klotz fails to give convincing arguments for his parallelism. Above all, the study is flawed by the vagueness of its city definition. The author freely

---

[69] Kreutzer, p. 23.

[70] Ibid., pp. 231-244.

[71] Kreutzer's summary of urban research does not include studies from the new urban theory which link the production of space to economic or political interest and which indicate the connection between urban image and social practice. Ibid., pp. 10-15.

[72] Diane Wolfe Levy, "City Signs: Towards a definition of Urban literature," *Modern Fiction Studies*, 24 (1978), 65-74. Barbara Lee Hussey, "The Disappearance of the City in the Modern Novel: From Spatiality to Textuality," diss. Purdue University. 1980.

[73] Walter Göbel, "Schreckbild Stadt: Chicago im naturalistischen Roman," *Zeitschrift für Literaturwissenschaft und Linguistik*, 12 (1982), 88-102.

[74] Göbel, p. 95.

[75] Ibid., p. 94. His hypothesis that the city in the naturalist novel represents circumstance while the city in poetry and painting stands for hope is not convincing. For different reasons, Chicago signifies hope both for Theodore Dreiser and Upton Sinclair.

[76] See also Isernhagen, *Ästhetische Innovation und Kulturkritik*, pp. 140-4.

concedes that he is not interested in sociological or geographical aspects of his subject.[77] To suit his thesis, he defines the city as an autonomous system. Yet Klotz's claim that the city, like the novel, contains many subordinate elements which aggregate to a unique whole is too vague. Such an organization also holds true of society or of civilization in general. Nonetheless, the approach is important. Philip Fisher correctly stresses in "City Matters: City Minds," the necessity to examine closely the correspondences between urban experience and fictional form: mere thematic-descriptive interpretations cannot grasp the complex interrelation.[78]

Several studies examine the relation between metropolis and modernism. For Hartwig Isernhagen, city fiction incorporates the modernist tendencies of disorientation and reorientation.[79] According to Malcolm Bradbury, "the cultural chaos bred by the populous, evergrowing city, a contingent and polyglot Tower of Babel, is enacted in similar chaos, contingency, and plurality in the texts of modern writing."[80] Clearly, the metropolis was the locale where modernism originated and where cultural life was influenced most profoundly by avantgarde practices.[81] On the other hand, it would be misleading to suggest a direct, deterministic link between the metropolis and modernism.

In "New York und der Stadtroman der Amerikanischen Moderne," Heinz Ickstadt links the representation of the modern city and its modernist dynamism to a diminuition of its content, its meaning.[82] As his examination of novels from Howells to Fitzgerald suggests, the concept of the city is gradually emptied, whereas the complexity of form increases. Ickstadt's thesis that formal elements become dominant is corroborated by Raymond Williams' generalizations about the interrelation between early urban experience and modernist techniques in "The Metropolis and the Emergence of Modernism."[83] Williams writes that the widespread move to segregated cities at the turn of the

---

[77]Klotz, p. 9. When he elaborates his ideas about the city, he presents a concept which is based on a dated geographic and ecological determinism. Klotz, p. 436.

[78]Philip Fisher, "City Matters: City Minds," *The Worlds of Victorian Fiction*, ed. Jerome H. Buckley, Cambridge, Mass., 1975, p. 373.

[79]Hartwig Isernhagen, "Die Bewußtseinskrise der Moderne und die Erfahrung der Stadt als Labyrinth," *Die Stadt in der Literatur*, eds. Cord Meckseper and Elisabeth Schraut, Göttingen, 1983, 81-104.

[80]Bradbury, "The Cities of Modernism," pp. 98f.

[81]Eric Homberger, "Chicago and New York: Two Versions of American Modernism," *Modernism, 1890-1930*, eds. Malcolm Bradbury and James Mc Farlane. Harmondsworth, 1976, 151-161.

[82]Heinz Ickstadt, "New York und der Stadtroman der Amerikanischen Moderne," *Medium Metropole: Berlin, Paris, New York*, eds. Friedrich Knilli und Michael Nerlich, Heidelberg, 1986, 111-24.

[83]Williams, "The Metropolis and the Emergence of Modernism," 13-24.

century was disruptive for both social groups and individuals in Western cultures.[84] The veil of naturalness was removed from social and cultural conventions, artists and intellectuals became alert to the arbitrariness of signs and systems and felt insecure about the function and significance of art in modern society. Artists in this situation relied on their techniques, on the media of expression. The play with conventions and the disruptive or assertive use of generic material created a new sense of community among the avantgarde. A genuine response initially, modernism soon became a convention itself.[85]

Similarly, Klaus R. Scherpe argues that modernist authors, though overcoming the traditional, moralistic symbolizations of the city, still mystify metropolitan complexity in their concentration on a purely aesthetic free play of signifiers.[86] Irving Howe generally reflects on the influence which the modernist stance has exerted on the perception of cities.[87] For Howe too, the genuine doubts of modernists have deteriorated to stale clichés. He concludes:

> We are the children, or step-children, of modernism. We learned our *abc*'s lisping "alienation, bourgeoisie, catastrophe." As against those who brushed aside the 20th century, we were right in believing our age to be especially terrible, especially cursed, on the rim of apocalypse. But today loyalty to the tradition of modernism may require a rejection of its academic and market-place heirs, and far more important, a questioning of its premises and values.[88]

4. The Sociological Approach

While there are several sociological interpretations, only a few historically comprehensive studies exist in this field. If one disregards Gelfant's pathbreaking but dated study from 1954, a detailed sociological analysis of twentieth-century American city fiction has yet to be written.[89] Often, when sociological or historical concepts are applied,

---

[84]See also Bradbury, pp. 100ff.

[85]Williams, p. 14.

[86]Kaus R. Scherpe, "Nonstop nach Nowhere City? Wandlungen der Symbolisierung, Wahrnehmung und Semiotik der Stadt in der Literatur der Moderne," *Die Unwirklichkeit der Städte*, p. 130.

[87]Irving Howe, "The City in Literature," *The Critical Point*, New York, 1973, 39-58.

[88]Howe, p. 54.

[89]Kreutzer, p. 22.

the subject of investigation has been limited to a specific city or period as in the interpretations by Kreutzer, Smith, or Fine.[90]

A collection of essays edited by Susan Merrill Squier provides the first detailed assessment of the distinct female experience in cities and of views of the city by women writers.[91] Sidney H. Bremer gives an account of the literary and cultural activities of women in Chicago at the turn of the century.[92] Christine W. Sizemore applies Kevin Lynch's categories to Doris Lessing's *The Four-Gated City*.[93] In an overview of twentieth-century American fiction, Blanche Gelfant examines the city's "hungry heroines," that is women who oppose the passivity and domestic orientation expected of them. Several novels indicate that the modern metropolis provides women with the opportunity to escape the narrow environs of the home and the family. "All the confusions of urban life usually considered devastating,"[94] Gelfant notes, imply freedom for these urban heroines. Mostly, it is a thirst for experience, knowledge, and art that these heroines try to quench in the city. The pattern, as Blanche Gelfant admits, is often associated with middle-class women.[95] Thus it is no surprise that her favorite heroines, Carrie Meeber in *Sister Carrie* and Oedipa Maas in *Crying of Lot 49* live and move in middle-class cities.

The activity noted by Blanche Gelfant stands in contrast to the gender dichotomy that Sidney Bremer developed for the city in her essay "Lost Continuities: Alternative Urban Visions in Chicago Novels, 1890-1915." Bremer holds that the artifical city of alienated, isolated, and independent individuals was a masculine view of the city, whereas women stressed the family and communal concerns:

> In response to the same forces ... Chicago's "scribbling women" dramatized the possibilities of opening up communalism to embrace diverse perspectives. Instead of regretting the loss of local autonomy, they affirmed interdependence as an essential fact of urban life--

---

[90]David M. Fine, ed., *Los Angeles in Fiction: A Collection of Original Essays,* Albuquerque, 1984.

[91]Susan Merrill Squier, ed., *Women Writers and the City: Essays in Feminist Literary Criticism*, Knoxville, 1984.

[92]Sidney H. Bremer, "Willa Cather's Lost Sisters," *Women Writers and the City: Essays in Feminist Literary Criticism*, ed., Susan Merrill Squier, Knoxville, 1984, 210-29.

[93]Christine W. Sizemore, "Reading the City as palimpsest: The Experiential Perception of the City in Doris Lessing's *The Four-Gated City*," *Women Writers and the City: Essays in Feminist Literary Criticism*, ed. Susan Merrill Squier, Knoxville, 1984, 176-190.

[94]Gelfant, p. 267.

[95]Blanche Gelfant, "The City's 'Hungry' Woman as Heroine," *Women Writers and the City: Essays in Feminist Literary Criticism*, ed. Susan Merrill Squier, Knoxville, 1984, p. 271.

linking past and present, country and city, family and family. Not static homogeneity within limits, but interactive, expansive familiarity was their preferred basis for community.[96]

While it cannot be denied that the experience of women in the city has differed crucially from that of men and that their perspective has been marginalized and neglected, Bremer's claim to divide into a masculine urbanist and a feminine communal view of the city is too rigid. Moreover, class issues pervasively shape the gender question in cities.[97] As Barbara Berg has pointed out, even in the suffrage movement in the beginning of the century class considerations came to dominate over gender divisions.[98]

Several studies focus on the specific experience and perception of the American city by minorities and ethnic groups.[99] In *The City, the Immigrant, and American Fiction, 1880-1920*, David M. Fine shows the groping for new ways of seeing among urban immigrants and illustrates how immigrant fiction responded to both the times and literary conventions.[100] Impeded by literary formulae in slum fiction and in the romantic tenement tale, it took some time for immigrant fiction not to repeat inauthentic stereotypes but to project genuine views. According to Fine, novels by Abraham Cahan, Stephen Crane, or Upton Sinclair provide such immigrants' views from below.[101] In "City Limits, Village Values: Concepts of the Neighborhood in Black Fiction," Toni Morrison asserts the distinct perception by black writers. Because they have been collectively excluded from the decisions which shaped the modern American city, black city novelists do not resent the curtailing of the mandates of individualism as the majority of

---

[96]Sidney H. Bremer, "Lost Continuities: Alternative Urban Visions in Chicago Novels, 1890-1915," *Soundings*, 64 (1981), p. 48.

[97]Sidney Bremer's argument that Chicago novels by men tend to idealize nature, while women use "seasonal extremes in weather" to epitomize the city's oppressive weight (Bremer, p. 37), is questioned by the class pattern in Upton Sinclair's *The Jungle*. Sinclair indicates how much stockyard families suffered from seasonal changes. Upton Sinclair, *The Jungle*, 1906, New York, 1960, p. 104. See also chapter 9.

[98]Barbara Berg concludes: "In their fight for the vote, women both ignored and compromised the principles of feminism. The complexities of American society at the turn of the century induced the suffragists to change the basis of their demand for the franchise. They had originally argued that it was the natural right of every *woman*, as well as every man, to participate in the legal system that govern them. Now, however, the suffragists moderated their platform as massive immigration once again transformed the texture of life in the United States. Seeking wide support among other middle-class Americans, the campaigners urged that women be given the vote to balance the impact of the foreign born. Thus the suffrage rationale of the early twentieth century used the persuasion that native-born women outnumbered foreign-born men and women combined." Berg, p. 269.

[99]Berndt Ostendorf ed., *Amerikanische Ghettoliteratur: zur Literatur ethnischer, marginaler und unterdrückter Gruppen in Amerika*, Darmstadt, 1983.

[100]David M. Fine, *The City, the Immigrant, and American Fiction, 1880-1920*, Metuchen, N.J., 1977.

[101]Fine, p. ix.

white city writers, but instead stress the values of the black city within the city.[102] The ghetto accumulates positive associations as it provides neighborly ties and assistance against the suppression in the surrounding white society. If the urban environment is described in a negative manner, this often means that a black ancestor is missing in Northern cities.[103]

Amy Beth Kaplan's reading of city novels in her dissertation "Realism Against Itself: The Urban Fiction of Twain, Howells, Dreiser, and Dos Passos" is similar to the present study in focus and interest.[104] Kaplan sets images of cities in the wider context of social and historical changes and sees cityscapes as metonymic representations of larger processes.[105] The novels actively shape rather than passively reflect the historical tendencies in cities. Conflicts and contradictions appear in the incongruities in the style and form of the novels. In contrast to the present approach, Kaplan discusses the city images primarily in their metonymic function.

The present study was influenced most profoundly in method and aim by Raymond Williams' interpretations in *The Country and the City*. Williams examines the partisan treatment of city and country in English literature and traces the roots of views to literary images in Western antiquity. He stresses the historical changes in the recurrent use of Golden Age yearnings or the stereotyped evil city. For him, it is important to analyze both the change and the evident persistence in images:

> Clearly the contrast of country and city is one of the major forms in which we become conscious of a central part of our experience and of the crises of our society. But when this is so, the temptation is to reduce the historical variety of forms of interpretation to what are loosely called symbols or archetypes: to abstract even these most evidently social forms and to give them a primarily psychological or metaphysical status. This reduction often happens when we find certain major forms and images and ideas persisting through periods of great change. Yet if we can see that the persistence depends on the forms and images being changed, though often subtly, internally and at times unconsciously, we can see also that the persistence indicates some permanent or effectively permanent need, to which the changing interpretations speak. I believe that there is indeed such a need, and that it is created by the processes of a particular history. But if we do not see these processes, or see them only incidentally, we fall back on modes of thought which seem able to create the permanence without the history.[106]

---

[102]Toni Morrison, "City Limits, Village Values: Concepts of the Neighborhood in Black Fiction," *Literature and the Urban Experience*, eds. Michael C. Jaye and Ann Chalmers Watts, 35-43.

[103]Morrison, p. 39.

[104]Amy Beth Kaplan, "Realism Against Itself: The Urban Fiction of Twain, Howells, Dreiser, and Dos Passos," diss. Johns Hopkins University, 1982.

[105]Kaplan, p. xiii.

[106]Williams, p. 347.

104 Fragmented Urban Images

Williams' main goal is to overcome the polarity of the destructive city and a pastoral countryside. The opposition of city and country is only part of the story and has long distracted attention from more profound divisions and inequalities. If in comparison to *The Country and the City*, the present approach is rather limited in historical scope, its concept of the city image as a subjective, class-based fragment permits a more detailed reading of individual urban novels.

6
Urban Fiction and Urban Theory: A Synthesis

Modern fiction not only is congenially related to the fragmentary metropolis but both are conceived as products of a deeper transformation. The city participates in a wider system: urban studies investigates the relation between American society and the conditions in its cities and mediates between a fragmented knowledge of the city and its basis in social practice. Similarly, the fictional city image is part of a more comprehensive design, as the metonymic use of topography is linked to the partial reflection of the city and prominent issues in the novel. This analogy between the actual and fictional city is striking. It ought to be made fruitful: the compartmentalized knowledge in urban studies must be fused and linked to the critical analysis of the literary city image.

And yet, the connection between the fictional city and the real city cannot simply be solved by positing a homology, as Lucien Goldmann's *Towards a Sociology of the Novel* has generally proposed for value in capitalism and in fiction.[1] There is no one-to-one reproduction of reality in literature. The relation has been subject to many suggestive solutions in materialist criticism: from Bertolt Brecht's apercu that art reflects reality but with special mirrors to Herbert Marcuse's contention that the progressive character of art is contained in its aesthetic form.[2] Such theories, however, still start with an essential coherence in a work of art, and in their concepts of aesthetic reflection, they cling to a model of totality which has been since challenged.[3]

Post-structuralist theory has stressed the essential inconsistency and incoherence of texts and concepts--a contradictory fragmentation which, as argued in the beginning, has been particularly prominent in modern urban fiction.[4] In contrast to deconstruction

---

[1] Lucien Goldmann, *Towards a Sociology of the Novel*, trans. Alan Sheridan, London, 1975.

[2] Bertolt Brecht, *Kleines Organon für das Theater*, Frankfurt, 1961, p. 42. Herbert Marcuse, *The Aesthetic Dimension: Toward a Critique of Marxist Aesthetics*, Boston, 1978.

[3] Jay, *Marxism and Totality*, pp. 510-537.

[4] Jacques Derrida, *Writing and Difference*, trans. Alan Bass, Chicago, 1978. William Sharpe and Leonard Wallock write that Derrida's "missing center" has already influenced urban theory itself. They explain: "Like

theory, this study does not see fragmentation as inevitable. Ideas conceived by Pierre Macherey achieve importance for the present study because his *A Theory of Literary Production* applies deconstructionist techniques within a materialist frame.[5] His basis in Althusser's structuralist reading of Marx, however, is replaced in this study with the reconstruction of critical holism by Jürgen Habermas. This seemingly ecclectic fusion is possible as both theories view totality as a decentered whole with no single level functioning as a basic determinant of all others. The important difference, as Martin Jay has remarked, is that Habermas "persisted in conceiving of one of the levels, that of social integration, in intersubjective terms, rather than reducing all of them to structural 'practices' without any subjective determination."[6]

For Pierre Macherey, any literary text is based on ideology. Authors do not invent a particular ideology but they use ideologies which have already been formed in society. In the specific case of American urban fiction, the city novelist incorporates the traces of an interested perspective in transforming current experiences and views of the American city. But since the novel is written within a particular ideological concept, the text transforms the very ideology through the material coherence which the form generates for the artistic whole. For Pierre Macherey, the specific character of fiction is to reveal, in its texture, the omissions and contradictions which necessarily appear if the false totality of ideology is projected as coherent.[7]

Literature creates tensions through its special quality: by "redoubling" ideology in content and form, the displacement produces revealing conflicts and incongruities in the feigned coherence of the text. The absences expose the meaning of the artifact as they disclose the partial and incomplete reproduction of reality. Macherey denies the existence of an essential structure or a hidden meaning which might articulate an artistic truth above contradictory social practice.[8] Critics have to learn how to read the omis-

---

language, the city is a system of signification dependent on certain fixed relations and shared values for its comprehensibility or 'interpretation.' But if traditional functions of the city as social, political, and economic center are extended to other parts of a more homogeneously urbanized environment, then the effect will resemble the loss of semiotic apprehensibility that Derrida describes." William Sharpe and Leonard Wallock, "From 'Great Town' to 'Nonplace Urban Realm': Reading the Modern City," *Visions of the Modern City: Essays in History, Art, and Literature*, eds. William Sharpe and Leonard Wallock, 1984, Baltimore, 1987, p. 23.

[5]See especially his chapters "Lenin, Critic of Tolstoy," and "Literary Analysis: The Tomb of Structures," Macherey, *A Theory of Literary Production*, pp. 105-156. See also Frederic Jameson, *The Political Unconscious*, London, 1981, pp. 56ff.

[6]Jay, p. 486.

[7]Macherey, pp. 115, 131ff, 154ff.

[8]Ibid., pp. 154f.

sions and contradictions which literature produces.[9] Conceivably, his claim to discern gaps and to reveal contradictions, necessitates a knowledge of what the underlying totality might be.

For Macherey, such a totality is still given in the process of history as revealed through a stucturalist reading of Marx. However, the various concepts of totalization proposed by Marxist theory in the twentieth century, and especially Louis Althusser's concept of transcendental structures, have been seriously challenged.[10] This study too assumes that any model may only approximate an intersubjective truth. A materialist analysis cannot claim to be infallible. And yet, Jürgen Habermas' theory, in which he has integrated psychoanalysis, linguistics, and systems theory to further the materialist understanding of culture, points toward a new mode of overcoming fragmentation. In agreement with his argument developed in *Knowledge and Human Interests*, this study replaces the obsolete model of a dialectical relationship between base and superstructure in the critical analysis of quasi-autonomous cultural processes.[11] The dialectic of labor and the dialectic of symbolically mediated interaction must be analyzed separately before they can be linked. In this study of urban culture, urban case studies, cognitive mapping, and urban semiotics are employed to examine the forces which have influenced experience in the modern American city.

Fiction does not in any simplistic way 'reflect' reality. Hence, an unmediated expression of what the fictional city may signify cannot exist. The image of the city in fiction must be interpreted using the tools of literary theory. On the other hand, the relative autonomy of literature does not obliterate the basis of recorded experience in real life. In this study, any transformation of urban reality is viewed as a partial and interested process. The fictional city is constituted on different levels. These combine to create the meaning of the city image. In this study they are distinguished as urban *experience*, urban *theme*, and urban *image*. These levels are only separated for analytical purposes but they appear in interrelated form in the novels.

Urban *experience* denotes the various modes of life in the city which the novels present. It stands for the recognizable social practices which come to constitute the urban milieu in the fictional world and which may be analyzed using the insights provided through urban case studies, cognitive maps, and urban semiotics. Conceivably, urban experience is projected in both form and content, plot and motif; the generic arrangement

---

[9] Ibid., p. 133.

[10] Jay, p. 537.

[11] Jürgen Habermas, *Knowledge and Human Interests*, trans. Jeremy J. Shapiro, Boston, 1971, pp. 36-59. See Martin Jay's discussion of the development of Habermas' theory. Jay, pp. 483-509.

of the narrative can be as telling as the incidents themselves. Therefore the literary mode and its aesthetic techniques are carefully examined for they shape the fictional city.

Urban theme represents the specific perspective from which the novel perceives urban experience. Theme refers to the particular focusing exerted on the selection of urban incidents through the wider issues of the novel. In its broadest sense, urban theme can signify the metaphoric frame of the urban experience in the novel, the perspective on the social topography, so to speak. Theme and experience are intricately interrelated; social relations may rule particular perspectives on the city.

Urban image, finally, acquires its full meaning in the unique fusion of these two levels in each novel. As Wolfgang Clemen noted in regard to Shakespeare's imagery, "an isolated image, an image viewed outside of its context is only half the image."[12] The image of the city exists within the interrelated levels of aesthetic creation; it is the fusion of generic form, narrative strategy, and the urban experience, it is the resulting gaps and contradictions of an interested perspective. In a sense, it is the aggregate evocation of the city as fiction. Any image of the city cannot but reflect the specific cultural practices and tensions which are infused in the novel as fragmented perspective. Each of the levels and the levels among themselves may reveal tensions and contradictions.

If this framework of *experience*, *theme*, and *image* aspires to coherence and completeness as any systematic model, clearly, with regard to the diversity of the novels, the presence of these strands will differ considerably in each case. Based in typicality, each novel uniquely creates its city image. The cities of Theodore Dreiser and John Dos Passos, for example, employ documentary details much stronger in their portrayal of urban experience than the selective expressionism in Stephen Crane's episodic model. Similarly, the figurative tendency of the romance genre in F. Scott Fitzgerald's *The Great Gatsby* and the formal experiments of Hubert Selby's naturalism in *Last Exit to Brooklyn* will necessarily have different effects on the aesthetic transformation of the city.

Finally, each author differs in the emphasis he attributes to the city within the fictional structure as a whole. Thus the city in *Sister Carrie* becomes the embodiment of disruptive change and is virtually omnipresent; in Thomas Pynchon's *The Crying of Lot 49* it is but a significant part of the post-industrial grid and has lost its dominant role. The city in the novel often exists within a wider human landscape; it may be marginal or central to the novel. To qualify for selection in this type of study, a novel has to use the topography as urban focus to cultural and social concerns. To deal exclusively with novels in

---

[12]Wolfgang Clemen, *The Development of Shakespeare's Imagery*, London, 1951, p. 3.

which the city predominates form and content would *a priori* restrict the enquiry to a specific view of the modern city.

It takes a perspective beyond the city to recognize its characteristics. F. Scott Fitzgerald illustrates such a viewpoint in *My Lost City*:

> From the ruins, lonely and inexplicable as the sphinx, rose the Empire State Building and, just as it had been a tradition of mine to climb to the Plaza Roof to take leave of the beautiful city, extending as far as eyes could reach, so now I went to the roof of the last and most magnificent of towers. Then I understood--everthing was explained: I had discovered the crowning error of the city, its Pandora's box. Full of vaunting pride the New Yorker had climbed here and seen with dismay what he had never suspected, that the city was not the endless succession of canyons that he had supposed but that it had limits--from the tallest structure he saw for the first time that it faded out into the country on all sides, into an expanse of green and blue that alone was limitless. And with the awful realization that New York was a city after all and not a universe, the whole shining edifice that he had reared in his imagination came crashing to the ground.[13]

---

[13]F. Scott Fitzgerald, "My Lost City," *The Crack-Up*, ed. Edmund Wilson, New York, 1945, p. 32.

7

Stephen Crane
Maggie: A Girl of the Streets

1. Dual New York: Bowery and Uptown

The subtitle in the 1893 edition of *Maggie: A Girl of the Streets* announces the novel as *A Story of New York*.[1] In fact, Stephen Crane tells the story of two New Yorks. The segregation of the early modern city is central to the novel. The world in *Maggie* is divided into Bowery and Uptown, into the working-class New York of the Lower East Side and the upper- and middle-class New York of northern Manhattan. The modern city has disintegrated into mutually exclusive fragments. The focus in *Maggie* is on the Lower East Side which provides the chief setting and the main characters. While the presentation of Bowery experience clearly dominates, Uptown culture is represented by its values, its luring riches, and in occasional encounters with working-class people.

Maggie depicts the New York of the 1890s in which the two-part division loomed large in the mind of its citizens. By the time that Stephen Crane takes issue with the segregated city, its division has already become a "conventional trope."[2] Crane's novel resumes and transcends paths previously explored by didactic tracts, reform literature, and popular Tenement Tales.[3] *Maggie* distinguishes itself from these predecessors in the

---

[1] Rejected by New York publishers, Stephen Crane had his manuscript privately printed and published it under the pseudonym of Johnston Smith. In 1896, Appleton released a cleansed and slightly revised edition. For a long time, this 1896 version was the only available edition and directed the reception of *Maggie: A Girl of the Streets*. Since the textual revisions however are minor, Crane's original version from 1893 may be used here. All subsequent quotations are taken from Thomas A. Gullason's edition. References to *Maggie* will be incorporated in the text abbreviated to MGS. Stephen Crane, *Maggie: A Girl of the Streets*, 1893, ed. Thomas A. Gullason, New York, 1979.

[2] Alan Trachtenberg, "Experiments in Another Country: Stephen Crane's *City Sketches*," *Southern Review*, 10 (1974), p. 268.

[3] For a discussion of the novel's sources, see Marcus Cunliffe, "Stephen Crane and the American Background of *Maggie*," *American Quarterly*, 7 (1955), 31-44. Thomas A. Gullason, "The Sources of Stephen Crane's *Maggie*," *Philological Quarterly*, 37 (1959), 497-502. David M. Fine, "Abraham Cahan, Stephen Crane, and the Romantic Tenement Tale of the Nineties," *American Studies*, 14 (1973), 95-107.

mode in which it incorporates urban experience in the Bowery. Crane approaches what he calls New York's "dual existence"[4] with a dual perspective: he renders his impression of the Bowery, but he also renders the view from within.[5] This inclusion of the perspective from below is a major accomplishment of *Maggie*. Yet this doubling of viewpoint also is disruptive. The recorded Bowery experiences blend uneasily with Crane's superimposed interpretation.

Duality thus dominates this slum novel. It appears in various modes in *Maggie*, for example as a separation and juxtaposition in place, in perspective, in culture, and in world view. Duality is evident in the division in diction and in composition. It is mirrored in Crane's double mode as a social critic and as a moral ironist. The novel presents a complex response to the segregated New York of the 1890s. The separation is not drawn in a picturesque manner. It is characterized by the crushing momentum generated in the clash of two unequal urban cultures. The incongruous juxtaposition of the two cities produces the "double mood"[6] of the novel and assists in generating its vitality and formal complexity. Yet it also underlies the stylistic and generic dissonances in *Maggie*.

2. The Lower East Side in the 1890s

The 1890s saw New York develop from a trade and manufacturing city to become the commercial and financial center of the nation. Unaffected by this general shift, light manufacturing industries continued to flourish in New York. With an immense capacity for cheap labor, New York boomed. Its harbor, which had helped trade and the city's elite to prosper, served as a major port of entry for millions of immigrants. In the 1890s, Greater New York added more than a hundred thousand citizens to its population annually.[7]

---

[4]Crane uses the term in regard to Sixth Avenue. Stephen Crane, *The New York City Sketches of Stephen Crane*, ed. Robert W. Stallmann and E. R. Hagemann, New York, 1966, p. 117.

[5]Aida Farrag Graff has stressed Crane's conception of a dual setting. Graff distinguishes between the tenement and the city and relates these places to metonymic and metaphoric modes of representation. Aida Farrag Graff, "Metaphor and Metonymy: The Two Worlds of Crane's *Maggie*," *English Studies in Canada*, 8 (1982), p. 426.

[6]Robert Wooster Stallmann, "Crane's *Maggie*: A Reassessment," *Modern Fiction Studies*, 5 (1959), p. 252.

[7]Half of the nation's trade passed through New York's harbor. David C. Hammack, *Power and Society: Greater New York at the Turn of the Century*, New York, 1982, p. 38; Rosenwaike, *Population History of New York City*, p. 63.

Prerequisites for a sharp contrast were thus given. Riches accumulated faster and were more ostentatious in the financial metropolis than anywhere else. One third of the nation's millionaires were estimated to live there in 1892.[8] Conspicuous display and Fifth Avenue became synonymous. On the other side, the immigrant labor force was exploited in small, unregulated firms, accepting demeaning conditions with one eye fixed on the American dream. Visions of progress, nourished by boosterist propaganda and advertising, helped to ignore inhuman working and housing conditions and made people adjust to what they thought were temporary hardships. By the 1890s, New York society was fully segregated. The rich moved north in the city, whereas a teeming Southern Manhattan contained a mosaic of ethnic and working-class quarters.

Most working-class people were crammed into narrow multistory buildings. The tenements housed well over a million people, that is seven out of ten New Yorkers lived in them.[9] Aware of the imbalance, the reformer Jacob A. Riis himself called attention to the euphemism in the title of his popular study of poverty *How the Other Half Lives*. This was true, Riis declared, in the 1870s.[10] Many of the immigrant boarders and families were concentrated in Lower East Side tenements.[11] Lots, originally plotted for one family, now housed eight. Lower New York had the world's highest density rates which even exceeded figures in congested Bombay.[12]

The Bowery, a mile long street cutting through tenement areas in the Lower East Side came to signify the immigrant and working-class city. The signs of poverty showed themselves most conspicuously in that vicinity. As wages were low, the majority of families lacked the means for a dignified existence.[13] Here, children faced filth, hunger, and disease. Moreover, since child labor was not illegal, it was common for working-

---

[8]Hammack, p. 46.

[9]Roy Lubove, *The Progressives and the Slums: Tenement House Reform in New York City, 1890-1919*, Greenwood, 1962, p. 43. Although the standard of multistory buildings differed, the conditions in the Lower East Side were worst. Chudacoff, p. 117.

[10]Jacob A. Riis, *How the Other Half Lives*, New York, 1890, repr. 1957, p. 2. Even in the 1860s, as Roy Lubove indicates, almost two thirds of the New York populace lived in tenements. Lubove, p. 18.

[11]In the worst crammed district, the Tenth Ward, people lived as densely as 986 persons per acre in 1894. Lubove, p. 94.

[12]A competition for model tenements was one of the answers to the housing problems. But the Housing Committee had to declare that the design of model tenements did not satisfy the "requirements of physical and moral health." Still, the dumbbell model was awarded the prize. It met the second requirement: it guaranteed maximum profitability for investors. Thus dumbbells came to dominate tenement construction in the last quarter of the nineteenth century. Its largest rooms measured ten by eleven feet. Lubove, pp. 28f, 94.

[13]Chudacoff, p. 125. Riis reports that in the worst tenements in the Bowery rents were up to one third more expensive than those in Uptown. Riis, p. 8.

class children to help in sweatshops (an investigator even discovered three- and four-year-olds assisting cigar making).[14] In the tenements, women and children, otherwise romanticized in society, had to toil in the lowest paid jobs. Indeed, conditions in textile manufacturing, the major occupation for female workers in New York, were notorious since the work in sweatshops was not regulated by labor legislation. A congressional committee investigating practices in the textile industry in 1893 declared that "the clothing worn by the majority of our people is made under conditions not merely revolting to humanity and decency, but such as to endanger the health of the wearer."[15] In general, long working hours, the absence of safety regulations and of workers' compensation in case of accident meant that work was physically devastating. An early death at the age of thirty to thirty-five for working-class people was not uncommon.[16]

The increasing discrepancy between rich and poor as well as the conflict between modern metropolitan needs and the outdated municipal administration characterized New York. Brooklyn Bridge, the most celebrated symbol of technology, and the overcrowded tenements stood side by side. Modern commodities, teasingly present in the vicinity of working-class quarters, simply could not be afforded. The ride on a streetcar, for instance, was largely restricted to middle-class employees. The geographer John P. Radford asserts: "The relationship between fares and wages made streetcars essentially a white-collar mode of transportation until late in the nineteenth century."[17] The frequent references to streetcars in *Maggie* thus acquire significance beyond their function as motifs of modernity. They also imply upper- and middle-class privilege. They represent an unattainable New York.

In the 1890s, cheap amusement facilities continued to multiply in the Lower East Side. The Bowery was part of an extensive red light district. Here, slumming was fashionable. Riis computed forty saloons for each church on Manhattan's southern tip.[18] Saloons and clubs became important places where the working class could organize their own culture and oppose subordination to middle-class norms. Yet working conditions, poverty, and saloons combined unprofitably for the working class in the last analysis:

---

[14]Chudacoff, pp. 123f.

[15]Cited in Lubove, pp. 97f.

[16]Chudacoff, p. 125.

[17]John P. Radford, "The Social Geography of the Nineteenth Century U.S. City," *Geography and the Urban Environment*, 4 (1984), p. 282. Distinctions among cities are important, however. A different policy in Chicago made streetcars available a lot earlier to workers. Here, their need to take the cars made expensive yet affordable fares very profitable. Harring, p. 10.

[18]Riis, p. 158.

amusement and alcohol not only compensated for a pursuit of happiness in self-determination, but profits also flowed outside to Uptown places. New York theaters, so prominent in *Maggie*, were controlled by a few strong businessmen by the 1890s. They dictated the contents of performances.[19] Thus the Lower East Side was exploited at work, at home, and in amusement halls. The working class was flooded with middle-class aspirations which could not be fulfilled under these conditions: "She [Maggie] wondered if the culture and refinement she had seen imitated, perhaps grotesquely, by the heroine on the stage, could be acquired by a girl who lived in a tenement house and worked in a shirt factory" (MGS, p. 28).

Roused by the split in the modern city and by the threat of impoverished slum dwellers, reform groups took an interest in conditions in working-class areas. In the 1890s, the journalist Jacob A. Riis became the foremost spokesman for those who crusaded in favor of an improvement in the moral and physical surrounding of the poor. Environmentalism was seen to provide valid and palatable answers.[20] The refom groups argued that not even the willing and resolute dweller could succeed under such bleak conditions. Moral and hygenic education, but also general improvements in the tenement ecology seemed necessary. Reform movements, however, did not ponder on contradictions in their paternalistic concepts. Upper- and middle-class privileges were not touched by their propositions. Most reformers agreed that the provision of housing was to be conceived as a business and not as a right.[21] Capitalist real estate which had produced the inhuman environment in the first place, was now to solve the housing crisis.

Tenement construction thus remained in the hand of speculators. Housing conditions hardly improved. Only the most scandalous extremes reached the public who were greatly outraged when the Legislative Tenement House Commission finally revealed in 1894 that some of the worst slum pockets were enriching the accounts of America's wealthiest church. Tenements belonging to the Trinity Church, the largest single owner of tenement property in New York, had a death rate which was one third higher than that of the rest in the city. Crane's criticism of religious hypocrisy must certainly also be seen in this context.[22]

---

[19] Jack Poggi, *Theater in America: The Impact of Economic Forces, 1870-1967*, Ithaca, N.Y., 1968, p. 11.

[20] Glaab and Brown, pp. 237f.

[21] Lubove, pp. 82, 104.

[22] Lubove, pp. 114f. When Stephen Crane revised *Maggie* for the 1896 edition, the only substantial extension occurs where Bowery churches and mission practices are criticized. Crane added, "He [Jimmy] clad his soul in armour by means of happening hilariously in at a mission church where a man composed his sermons of

3. Bowery Experience

Stephen Crane responds to New York's division with a dual perspective. He records views from inside the Bowery and projects his own impressions of its people, "as they seem to me."[23] The viewpoints are intertwined: the one perspective means documenting and selecting, the other evaluating and arranging. To have treated *Maggie* as an objectively recorded novel, as in earlier naturalist assessments, was misleading.[24] Although Crane stresses the forces of environment, he does not render reality as an arbitary naturalist slice. At close sight the episodic novel reveals Crane's extensive composition and indicates, as Joseph X. Brennan has noted, "a degree of subtlety and calculated artistry . . . that existing critical estimates have generally overlooked."[25] *Maggie* is not an artless sociological record of slum reality and cannot be explained solely as exhibiting naturalist techniques. The novel questions Stephen Crane's own assertion to provide but "a slice out of life"[26] to his readers.

In *Maggie*, Crane overcame the picturesque perspective so prominent in the tenement portrayal of his days.[27] Trained as a journalist, Crane roamed the Lower East Side for material and informed himself in tenement literature about conditions.[28] A truthful documentation could be achieved, Crane argued, if the personal impressions were recorded honestly.[29] In his 1894 New York sketch "An Experiment in Misery," he explicates his procedure in fictional terms. The experiment of "the younger man" is to assume the position of a Bowery tramp in order to "discover his point of view or

---

"you's." *Once a philosopher asked this man why he did not say 'we' instead of 'you.' The man replied 'What?'"* (MGS, p. 13; Crane's additions are in italics).

[23] Stephen Crane, *Stephen Crane: Letters*, ed. Robert W. Stallmann and Lilian Gielkes, New York, 1960, p. 133.

[24] Frequently, when treated as a naturalistic novel, the passages which do not fit the paradigm are said to be failures of technique or method. Arno Karlen, "The Craft of Stephen Crane," *The Georgia Review*, 28 (1974), 473-77.

[25] Joseph X. Brennan, "Ironic and Symbolic Structure in Crane's *Maggie*," *Nineteenth Century Fiction*, 16 (1962), p. 303.

[26] Crane, *Letters*, p. 158.

[27] Trachtenberg, p. 273.

[28] Crane composed *Maggie* in several stages. As in *The Red Badge of Courage*, he drew a great deal of information from literature on the topic. Particularly Jacob A. Riis' *How the Other Half Lives* contains many incidents which recur in fictional form in *Maggie*. Crane also attended Riis' lectures in Ashbury Park. See Gullason, "The Sources of Stephen Crane's *Maggie*," pp. 497-502; Colvert, p. 40.

[29] Crane, *Letters*, p. 109.

something near it."[30] What originates in an atmosphere of Bohemian playfulness in the story, results in a profound questioning of a world view:[31]

> The people of the street hurrying hither and thither made a blend of black figures, changing, yet frieze like. They walked in their good clothes as upon important missions, giving no gaze to the two wanderers seated upon the benches. They expressed to the young man his infinite distance from all that he valued. Social position, comfort, the pleasures of living, were unconquerable kingdoms. He felt a sudden awe....
> "Well," said the friend, "did you discover his point of view?"
> "I don't know that I did," replied the young man; "but at any rate I think mine own has undergone a considerable alteration."[32]

In the New York sketches, which Crane considered as some of his best work,[33] the writer, as Alan Trachtenberg has noted, "transmutes social fact into felt experience."[34] *Maggie* is the first of these Bowery experiments. The novel compactly elucidates the effects of segregation in New York. In contrast to the sketches, *Maggie* is characterized by its duality in which the characters' viewpoints and the dominant perspective of the author are juxtaposed.

The characters' urban perception and experience are constricted in *Maggie*. The Bowery figures are defined by their slum environment. Stephen Crane emphasized his intention to show the force of circumstance in the famous inscription to the 1893 edition:

> It is inevitable that you will be greatly shocked by this book but continue please with all possible courage to the end. For it tries to show that environment is a tremendous thing in the world and frequently shapes lives regardless. If one proves that theory one makes room in Heaven for all sorts of souls (notably an occasional street girl) who are not confidently expected to be there by many excellent people.[35]

Crane translates his belief that "environment is a tremendous thing" into a fictional strategy. The characters' position in the social hierarchy conditions their perception,

---

[30] Crane, *Sketches*, p. 34.

[31] As Alan R. Slotkin has indicated, the transformation is also mirrored in the changing diction of the experimenter. The young man gradually accepts and takes over the dialect of his companion. Alan R. Slotkin, "Dialect Manipulation in 'An Experiment in Misery'," *American Literary Realism*, 14 (1981), 273-76.

[32] Crane, *Sketches*, pp. 42f.

[33] Crane, *Letters*, p. 135.

[34] Trachtenberg, p. 280. Trachtenberg analyzes in which ways newspaper strategies reacted to the impenetrability of the modern metropolis. The big city daily claimed to dispel the mystification of the city as news, yet, at the same time, abetted it as sensationalism (Ibid., p. 269). Crane experiments within this framework. He employs the journalistic device of disengagement to delete social identity and to overcome the very distance that had been put up for middle-class self-protection. He tricks the reader into the new perspective: "In each case the narrative point of view projects the youth's consciousness; he is made into a register of the world-as-it-is-felt of the particular setting." Ibid., p. 280.

[35] Crane, *Letters*, p. 14.

which in turn, influences their behavior. Their vision affects their urban experience: in Crane's fiction, generally, as Milne Holton has pointed out, the event of seeing represents the achievement of understanding.[36]

In his Bowery novel, Crane presents the urban experience of Maggie, Pete, and Jimmy. The episodes trace their fictional lives from childhood.[37] Readers are to see how their New York experience differs from that in Uptown and how their young lives are shaped "regardless."

The opening passage of *Maggie* situates Jimmy Johnson in a context that will remain characteristic for him throughout the novel. He is in the tenement district and he is fighting. Rum Alley defines his urban experience and educates him:

> The inexperienced fibres of the boy's eyes were hardened at an early age. He became a young man of leather. He lived some red years without labouring. During that time his sneer became chronic. He studied human nature in the gutter, and found it no worse than he thought he had reason to believe it. He never conceived a respect for the world, because he had begun with no idols that it had smashed. (MGS, p. 13)

The Bowery law that physical force rules is involuntarily engrained in the child.[38] Jimmy's path is predetermined. He becomes one of the notorious street-corner boys on the Bowery and soon has a "fair record" as a juvenile delinquent.[39]

Even though Jimmy broadens his urban experience as a truck-driver in the lower parts of Manhattan, he remains bound to his Bowery attitudes. He rejects Uptown culture and fights middle-class New York represented in the novel by "well-dressed men" (MGS, p. 14), by chrysanthemums in button-holes, and by mission sermons. "Fine raiment" (MGS, p. 14) is weakness and aggravated idiocy is connected with people on streetcar platforms. Jimmy only respects force. He yields to a fire engine as it threatens to annihilate him (MGS, p. 16). Steeped in biting irony, Crane depicts him as cruel, selfish, and irresponsible, consciously exploiting the contrast to the noble characters of popular tenement fiction.

Pete, in contradistinction, is to tenement people a "man of the world" (MGS, p. 17). He is introduced as a Bowery tough who knows places beyond the Lower East

---

[36] Milne Holton, "The Sparrow's Fall and the Sparrow's Eye: Crane's Maggie," *Studia Neophilologica*, 41 (1969), p. 118. A slightly revised version of the article is reprinted as a chapter in Milne Holton, *Cylinder of Vision: The Fiction and Journalistic Writing of Stephen Crane*, Baton Rouge, 1972.

[37] Mary Johnson also is an important figure. But she *is* a Bowery figure, whereas the others are shown in which way they *become* typical Bowery people.

[38] The Bowery language testifies to this attitude; Jimmy's father typically answers his fighting with a physical threat: "It's like I can never beat any sense into yer damned wooden head" (MGS, p. 7).

[39] Juvenile street-gangs, as Jacob A. Riis reports, spread all over lower Manhattan. Riis, p. 165.

Side. He takes Jimmy to a boxing-match in Williamsburgh and impresses Maggie with his tales of an unknown city. To show off, Pete relates himself to Uptown, a strange territory in which he even may boast of a victory:[40]

> "I met a chump deh odder day way up in deh city, "he said. 'I was goin' teh see a frien' of mine. When I was a-crossin' deh street deh chump runned plump inteh me, an' den he turns aroun' an' says, 'Yer insolen' ruffin', he says, like dat. . . . He says I was a contempt'ble scoun'el, er some'ting like dat, an' he says I was doom' teh everlastin' pe'dition an' all like dat. 'Gee,' I says, 'gee! Deh hell I am,' I says. 'Deh hell I am,' like dat. An' den I slugged 'im. See?" (MGS, pp. 19f)[41]

Eventually, Pete is overcome too by women he has exploited.[42] Despite his frequent trips outside the Bowery, Uptown remains barred to him. To emphasize the cultural gap, Crane has Pete literally "discover" (MGS, p. 26) the Museum of Arts. It is Pete's and Maggie's exploration of the elite's cultural center which forcibly indicates the incompatibility of the two cities. Middle-class treasures are ludicrous to Bowery people. They are "outa sight" (MGS, p. 26) as Maggie notices:

> "What deh hell," he demanded once. "Look at these little jugs! Hundred jugs in a row! Ten rows in a case an' 'bout a t'ousand cases! What deh blazes use is dem?" (MGS, p. 27)

Pete and Jimmy's city, the New York of the male Bowery, is small, yet, it expands much further than Maggie's. Both men ruthlessly exploit this advantage over women. Jimmy's machoism in the novel parallels Pete's behavior toward Maggie. In the beginning, when Maggie's knows only the environs of her block, she may only watch Jimmy and Pete leave from her window. Later, when taken to theaters and museums, Maggie is attracted by this world. Her dreams and her illusions of escape, infused and shaped by middle-class melodrama, make her succumb to Uptown attractions. As a Bowery woman, she is victimized both by her male surrounding and the false promises of middle-class culture.

Until she meets Pete, Maggie's life is ruled by the Rum Alley tenement and by the alienating work at the sweatshop. Even though she seems naive, she contrasts with the innocent tenement girl of popular fiction: she curses, she treats her brother rudely, and she steals flowers (MGS, p. 12). Pete introduces her to an unknown New York: with

---

[40]Pete works in a saloon which, for all its fake respectability, visibly contrasts with tenement filth and disorder: "The elementary senses of it all seemed to be opulence and geometrical accuracy" (MGS, p. 34).

[41]In Crane's sketches, Bowery characters always win their fights. In his sketch "An Ominous Baby," Tommy on excursion in "a strange country," defeats his middle-class opponent when they quarrel over a toy. Crane, *Sketches*, pp. 59-62.

[42]Pete's degradation is prefigured in the declining quality of halls which he visits. As Aida Farrag Graff has pointed out, the arrangement of halls testifies to Crane's conscious use of places. Graff, p. 430.

him she is always out, leaving, or returning. He takes her to Bowery beer halls, to theaters, parks, and museums. Once her experience widens, her social contacts diminish. Eventually, she is rejected in both cities.[43] Hers is the pattern of lower-class success in which the individual rise means the exclusion from the neighborhood group.

Crane draws a gloomy yet authentic picture of the New York as it existed for many people in the Lower East Side. In contrast to the riches and opportunities of upper- and middle-class New York, the Bowery is an "enclosed world."[44] Its modern city consists of crowded lanes, filthy tenements, and dingy rooms. "Gruesome" (MGS, p. 6) doors and dark stairways dominate. The penitentiary on Blackwell Island, not Brooklyn Bridge is their perspective in the novel. Crane does not willfully exclude imposing mansions, spectacular high-rise architecture, or cosmopolitan achievements. He does not show them since they are "outa sight" (MGS, p. 26) for Bowery people. In *How the Other Half Lives*, Jacob A. Riis reported an actual survey of Bowery experience in which children of a downtown school were asked about supposedly popular landmarks of Manhattan:

> Out of forty-eight boys twenty had never seen the Brooklyn Bridge that was scarcely five minutes' walk away, three only had been in Central Park, fifteen had known the joy of a ride in a horse-car.[45]

The Bowery experience of poverty, limitation, and violence and the affluence and amusement of Uptown New York are juxtaposed in *Maggie*. Upper- and middle-class culture influences the Lower East Side:

> In the finale she fell into some of those grotesque attitudes which were at the time popular among the dancers in the theatres up-town, giving to the Bowery public the phantasies of the aristocratic theatre-going public at reduced rates. (MGS, p. 23)

Uptown intrudes into the Bowery in a variety of forms. It is associated with neighborhood missions and religious hypocrisy. Crane shows the discrepancy between middle-class ideals and behavior in their encounters with working-class people. Even the clergy sidestep charity when accosted in the novel (MGS, p. 51). Uptown does not know Bowery conditions. It does not see its needs:

---

[43] The desperation in her question "But where kin I go?" (MGS, p. 50) refers to more than a room to stay. In her last appearance, reduced to a prosperous member of the "crimson league," she futilely tries to solicit men and to establish contact.

[44] Donald Pizer, "Stephen Crane's *Maggie* and American Naturalism," *Criticism*, 7 (1965), p. 191.

[45] Riis, p. 180.

> He [Jimmy] clad his soul in armour by means of happening hilariously in at a mission church where a man composed his sermons of "you's." While they got warm at the stove, he told his hearers just where he calculated they stood with the Lord. Many of the sinners were impatient over the pictured depths of their degradation. They were waiting for soup-tickets. (MGS, p. 13)

Including the Bowery point of view is a major achievement in *Maggie*. Stephen Crane's widened scope of analysis distinguishes the novel from other accounts in the 1890s. He objects to the individualistic moralism in popular tenement fiction. He also does not limit the Bowery degeneration to environmentalist causes but extends it to a complex set of factors. The small, dirty, overcrowded, and violent metropolis of the working class is confronted with unreachable goals and false ideals.

On the whole, Crane's own image of the modern city organizes the novel. With his diction and his ironic comments, he distances himself from his characters. Despite recording views from below, he remains a slumming reporter in the Bowery. The arrangement of incidents, of motifs, and of images combine to evoke his view of the Bowery as conclusive. It is an enclosed chaos. Constant quarreling, fighting, and wrecking of apartments accumulate to a vision of violence and an all-pervasive chaos,[46] while circular motifs, animal imagery, and the limitations in the Bowery add up to indicate the inescapable closure of a cyclical process.[47] In places, Crane fuses these two motifs. Chaos and closure embody the Bowery--the very first paragraph initiates the reader into this world:[48] "A very little boy stood upon a *heap of gravel* for the honor of Rum Alley. He was *throwing stones* at *howling* urchins from Devil's Row who were *circling madly about the heap* and *pelting* at him" (MGS, p. 3; my italics) Clearly, the concept of an amoral struggle in the Bowery is closely associated with the "survival of the fittest" of Social Darwinism. It sustains one of the growing city myths then: the urban jungle.

---

[46] Crane explicitly refers to fights as chaotic: "He began to kick into the chaotic mass on the ground" (MGS, p. 6).

[47] Aida Farrag Graff has called attention to this connection between closure and circular motifs. Graff, pp. 423f.

[48] Bettina L. Knapp, *Stephen Crane*, New York, 1987, p. 43.

4. Bowery Chaos

Crane's image of a chaotic city has dominated interpretations of *Maggie* as urban fiction.[49] His view of the modern city is related to larger issues. Critics have interpreted the novel in two chief ways. Either, the all-pervasive violence, the disorder of the environment were seen as basic to a naturalist meaning of the novel;[50] or, Crane's implication of relationships and causes and his stress on ethical responsibility were emphasized.[51]

It would be misleading to see Stephen Crane as a spokesperson for the working class in the Bowery. His openness and empathy are important facets, yet there are other, conflicting sides. True, there is the "young radical"[52] who according to William Dean Howells spoke wisely and kindly about the Bowery poor and whose dominant impulse,

---

[49] Blanche Gelfant excluded the novel from her book. Conceding that Crane had raised the slums to an aesthetic level never reached before, yet she dismisses it as fragmentary lacking the scope of a city novel (Gelfant, p. 63). David R. Weimer interprets *Maggie* as a "landscape of hysteria." Weimer sees the emotional disorder of the city reflected by the impression of disorder in the novel. For him Crane's city is an extension of the psyche (David R. Weimer, *The City as Metaphor*, New York, 1966, pp. 52-64). Thomas A. Gullason marginalizes the factualism and naturalism in Crane's Bowery to read it as a modernist account: "In *Maggie*, Crane purposely avoids much that a "good" naturalist would never avoid. There is really nothing about hunger and poverty; nothing about crime . . . nothing about the cramped, unsanitary and unsafe tenement quarters. . . . " Thomas A. Gullason, "The Prophetic City in Stephen Crane's 1893 *Maggie*," *Modern Fiction Studies*, 24 (1978), pp. 130f.

[50] Several articles attempted to define the ideology of *Maggie*. Max Westbrook argued that Crane linked determinism with individual responsibility. "The ethical action expected of individual characters changes according to individual circumstances" (Max Westbrook, "Stephen Crane's Social Ethic," *American Quarterly*, 14 (1962), p. 591). In contrast, David Fitelson claimed that Crane adhered to popular Darwinism: the city is in an amoral environment and only survival decides between right and wrong (David Fitelson, "Stephen Crane's *Maggie* and Darwinism," *American Quarterly*, 16 (1964), 182-94). Donald Pizer emphasized the impact of moral forces: "Crane's desire, however, was to stress that the vicious deterministic force in the slums was its morality, not its poor housing or inadequate diet, and it is this emphasis which controls his characterization" (Pizer, p. 172). Charles Child Walcutt, finally, saw the interdependence between conditions and ethics in *Maggie*. Walcutt's interpretation regards chaos as a key to the novel as it represents "a moral madhouse" (Charles Child Walcutt, *American Literary Naturalism*, Minneapolis, 1956, p. 69). Interpreting *Maggie* as a primarily naturalistic novel, he must strain literary terminology to call it "entirely consistent and coherent." *Maggie* both stands for "pure naturalism" and "frantic impressionism" (ibid., pp. 66, 72). For Walcutt, Crane's unscientific distortions become exact naturalism.

[51] For James B. Colvert, the double viewpoint is the chief structure in Crane's oeuvre. Colvert interprets the tension between the standpoints in its function to reveal "false pride, vanity, and blinding delusion." (James B. Colvert, "Structure and Theme in Stephen Crane's Fiction," *Modern Fiction Studies*, 5 (1959), p. 200). Maggie is "the victim not so much of the blind impersonal force of her environment as of the inadequate morality of the unreal world view rooted in perverse pride and vanity" (Ibid., p. 203). For Milne Holton, perception is central to Crane's work. *Maggie* deals with an "incapacity of vision" in the Bowery--Crane's irony springs from the disparity between two ways of seeing, between author and characters. Holton, "The Sparrow's Fall and the Sparrow's Eye," p. 120.

[52] Crane, *Letters*, p. 32.

Frank W. Noxon asserted, was a desire to serve the helpless.[53] But Crane also displays aristocratic arrogance, he indulges himself in clever aestheticism, and, while writing about Bowery plight, he chiefly dreams of fame in the literary world of Uptown.[54] Introducing a distinctly modern viewpoint, he treats his low-life characters condescendingly. Crane's ambivalence toward working-class culture pervades the novel on all levels.[55]

Crane's investigations into the Bowery are characterized by a contradictory attitude. His New York sketch "An Experiment in Luxury" provides a good example. Crane dismantles church propaganda about the suffering rich as a helpful lie, but then concludes that nobody could be held responsible for this ideology.[56] *Maggie* and the New York stories are characterized by this inconsistency. In the last analysis, they deny the results of their investigation. Examining social defects, Crane strangely claims that social speculation is not possible.[57] Not surprisingly, Crane varies a great deal in comments on his Bowery writings. According to the 1893 inscription to *Maggie*, he wanted to demonstrate that environment shapes lives regardless. Three years later, in a letter to Catherine Harris, he individualizes and moralizes, displaying the very middle-class attitude he had shown incongruent with Bowery reality in his novel:

> A person who thinks himself superior to the rest of us because he has no job and no pride and no clean clothes is as badly conceited as Lilian Russell. In a story of mine called "The Experiment in Misery" I tried to make plain that the root of Bowery life is a sort of cowardice. Perhaps I mean a lack of ambition or to willingly be knocked flat and accept the licking.[58]

---

[53] Ibid., pp. 306, 335.

[54] Ibid., pp. 31, 115; Colvert, p. 47.

[55] Stanley Wertheim has described the writer as revealed in his letters as "simultaneously egocentric and generous, conscientious and irresponsible, rebellious and overly concerned about his reputation." Stanley Wertheim, "Stephen Crane," *Hawthorne, Melville, Stephen Crane*, ed. Theodore L. Gross and Stanley Wertheim, New York, 1971, p. 217.

[56] Crane, "An Experiment in Luxury," *Sketches*, p. 44.

[57] Crane, "The Men in the Storm," *Sketches*, p. 92. Malcolm Bradbury links Crane's fictional method to general problems of artists in the 1890s and to the ways in which writers attempted to recover their lost function. When the literary imagination sensed the weakness in its visions of society, writings became explicitly more sociological. Though *Maggie* is such "a species of accurate observation," another strand in the novel also suggests "a profound romantic dissatisfaction with the world as it is given" (Malcolm Bradbury, "Sociology and Literary Studies. II. Romance and Reality in *Maggie*," *Journal of American Studies*, 3 (1969), pp. 118f). This opposition produces a strong ironical impulse, which in Bradbury's eyes almost turns *Maggie* into a failure. Yet it also poses a solution to the problem of objectivity. Crane does not respond to the changed conditions with more accurate reportage but with impressionism. Increased irony and ambiguity combine to create in *Maggie* a piece of early modernist writing. For Bradbury, Crane's solution is "a kind of negative vision, perplexed between realism and impressionism." Ibid., p. 121.

[58] Crane, *Letters*, p. 133.

The image of the early modern city which Crane projected in *Maggie* reflects these tensions. He indicates causal relations, yet simultaneously provides complex and contradictory explanations for these dependencies.

Crane's intention of showing environment as a relentless force did not imply a didactic mode for him. Explicit commentaries are absent in *Maggie*. For Crane, art precluded preaching: "if there is any moral or lesson in it [the literary work], I do not try to point it out, I let the reader find it for himself."[59] Thus, he developed techniques of indirect commentary, some of which Joseph X. Brennan described and analyzed in his study of irony in *Maggie*: parallelism, contrast, reversal, and ironic repetition.[60] With these methods Crane may unobtrusively indicate relations and dependencies in his novel. These parallels and contrasts are constituted within the novel, in which Maggie's unsuccessful rise is an anti-model to the success of stage heroines in the melodramas she visits, and outside the novel, where they refer to current patterns in popular Bowery fiction. Thus the irony poured on some characters, their incredible vileness and irresponsibility can be linked to Crane's opposition to the image of the poor in Romantic Tenement Tales.[61]

Stephen Crane does not merely show the inevitable destruction of hopes in a working-class slum but also investigates the origin of forces responsible for this. Therefore, Crane opens the novel with a new, unspoiled generation and indicates the context of failure. In a letter to Catherine Harris, he explained that children could be saved if the environment were changed.[62] Crane employs a double strategy in his novel. He shows the inevitable cycles in the Bowery and the impossibility of dignified life in such conditions--Tommy dies very young, Jimmy is directly compared with his father, and Maggie, in her final appearance, is associated with her mother 'Mary'--but Crane also hints at responsible agents for their defeat.

The novel's duality illustrates a major reason for their failure: Uptown and Bowery are thoroughly segregated. Bowery people cannot cope with outside influences adequately since their environment restricts in its poverty, filth, crowdedness, and

---

[59] Ibid., pp. 158f.

[60] Brennan, pp. 303-15.

[61] Several articles have illumined the literary context of *Maggie* connecting it to slum novels of the time. They indicate Crane's conscious reception and critical use of popular models. Eric Solomon, *Stephen Crane: From Parody to Realism*, Cambridge, 1966. Fine, "Abraham Cahan, Stephen Crane, and the Romantic Tenement Tale of the Nineties," 95-107.

[62] Crane, *Letters*, p. 133; Fine, p. 100.

violence. Life in the Bowery is cheap. Crane records death in laconic sentences: "The babe, Tommy, died" (MGS, p. 13).[63]

Maggie Johnson's cycle is central to the novel. Despite his ironic detachment, Crane directs sympathy toward her character. Her belief in values set her apart both from an amoral Bowery and a false Uptown.[64] Maggie is the only person in the family who cares for others: even after her brother has struck her, she offers her help. Her defeat is the most complete and the most complex. She rises to wealth from the "broken furniture, grimy walls, and general disorder and dirt of her home" (MGS, p. 18). But when she has succeeded materially, as her "handsome" (MGS, p. 52) clothes indicate, she commits suicide.

Crane depicts Maggie as naive but not as innocent. She fights, she curses, and she steals flowers for Tommy's coffin. She is pragmatic about her Bowery surroundings: it is "composed of hardship and insults" (MGS, p. 20). Her ignorance of affluent New York disposes her to romance. She does not dream in a vacuum: her phantasies become directed by Uptown values. When she first takes notice of Pete, she associates him vaguely with chivalry, with strange countries. Her dreams are bluntly romantic, if biblical, but not yet shaped by the contact with the upper- and middle-class New York:

> Maggie perceived that there was the beau ideal of a man. Her dim thoughts were often searching for far away lands where, as God says, the little hills sing together in the morning. Under the trees of her dream-gardens there had always walked a lover. (MGS, p. 19)

As her experience broadens, the contents of her dreams change. Now they are overtly directed toward Uptown attractions. "She began to note, with more interest, the well-dressed women she met on the avenues. She envied elegance and soft palms" (MGS, p. 25). Her work threatens her youth and with it the only advantage she possesses. The shirt factory now becomes destructive and begins "to appear to her mind as a dreary place of endless grinding" (MGS, p. 20).

Crane juxtaposes the small world of the Bowery with its inhuman working and housing conditions to the attractions of the glamorous New York:

> Her cheeks were blushing with excitement and her eyes were glistening. She drew deep breaths of pleasure. No thoughts of the atmosphere of the collar and cuff factory came to her.

---

[63]"His father died and his mother's years were divided up into periods of thirty days" (MGS, p. 14).

[64]Malcolm Bradbury argues that she becomes something of a middle-class heroine transcending both cultures by her "higher-than-Darwinian motives and desires." Bradbury, p. 120.

When the orchestra crashed finally, they jostled their way to the sidewalk with the crowd. Pete took Maggie's arm and pushed a way for her, offering to fight with a man or two. (MGS, p. 24)

Amusement is associated with Uptown. The Bowery receives its theater phantasies from upper- and middle-class New York. The ambience of Maggie's final appearance recalls the underlying connection:

> Two or three theatres emptied a crowd upon the storm-swept pavements... Men stepped forth to hail cabs or cars, raising the fingers in varied forms of polite request or imperative demand. An endless procession wended toward the elevated stations. An atmosphere of pleasure and prosperity seemed to hang over the throng, born, perhaps, of good clothes and of having just emerged from a place of forgetfulness. (MGS, p. 51)

Crane alters the patterns of the 'fallen-woman' tale significantly.[65] Maggie's decision to abandon the Bowery is not rendered as being immoral or irresponsible.[66] Yet the escape from poverty is denounced by the morals of the very society which had nourished and shaped Maggie's aspirations. Mary Johnson condemns her daughter using the rhetoric of their church missions.[67] The scene in which Maggie is rejected in the tenements connotes the very Uptown institutions which had fostered her idea to leave the Bowery--the entertainment halls, the theaters, and the Museum: "Children ventured into the room and ogled her, as if they formed the front row at a theatre.... Maggie's mother paced to and fro, addressing the doorful of eyes, expounding like a glib showman at a museum" (MGS, p. 48).

Defying the formulae of popular tenement fiction, Crane excludes the moral struggle and psychological distress of the sentimental heroine.[68] The moralizing of the Tenement Tales only reappears as parody, in the hypocritical damnation which Maggie receives from the residents of her tenement. Crane rather concentrates on the impact of wealth and amusement in Maggie's new environment. Street walking appears as the only option for a woman once she has been excluded from her community. The individual

---

[65] Fine p. 101; Bradbury, p. 119.

[66] Maggie Johnson continues to care for her family. Crane even has her symbolically change the tenement environment. She decides to leave when her attempt to embellish the room has failed and when the furniture is wrecked once again. Although Uptown lures have captured her mind--the individual rise of the poor heroine is offered as a model in the plays attended by her--she cannot imagine daily life outside her former surrounding. Crane points toward her lack of knowledge: "She imagined a future, rose-tinted, because of its distance from all that she previously had experienced" (MGS, p. 39).

[67] Knapp, p. 58.

[68] Fine, p. 101.

126 Fragmented Urban Images

rise which was proposed in the plays brings isolation and exclusion: "The shutters of the tall buildings were closed like grim lips" (MGS, p. 53).

Chapter 17, in which Maggie Johnson commits suicide, compresses the themes of separation, dislocation, and isolation.[69] Movement characterizes the episode: it is the only instance in which a Bowery figure is actually seen to cover the gap between glittering avenues and dark tenements. The scene ends with death. Crane translates the impossibility of Maggie's rise in spatial terms. Although she hurries forward "as if intent upon reaching a distant home" (MGS, p. 52) her walk only makes her see, in the end, how "the lights of the avenues glittered as if from an impossible distance" (MGS, p. 53). The walk stresses her dislocation from the Bowery but also links Maggie to her former life.[70] Her final movement reverses her ascent: Maggie proceeds from wealthy to impoverished clients. The contrast between darkness and light, between blackness and glitter recalls the division of Bowery and Uptown visually. Moreover, Uptown merriment intrudes into the dreary atmosphere as sounds from an unreachable distance. As Rudolf Haas has indicated, Crane underlines its lure with a onomatopoeic effect: "Street car bells jingled with a sound of merriment."[71] Uptown sounds thus drown out Maggie's silence--the last word in the chapter. The final paragraphs elaborate on the segregation of social classes as the context of her failure:

> She went into the darkness of the final block. The shutters of the tall building were closed like grim lips. The structures seemed to have eyes that looked over her, beyond her, at other things. Afar off the lights of the avenues glittered as if from an impossible distance. Street car bells jingled with a sound of merriment.
> When almost to the river the girl saw a great figure. On going forward she perceived it to be a huge fat man in torn and greasy garments. His grey hair straggled down over his forehead. His small, bleared eyes, sparkling from amidst great rolls of red fat, swept eagerly over the girl's upturned face. He laughed, his brown, disordered teeth gleaming under a grey, grizzled moustache from which beerdrops dripped. His whole body gently quivered and shook like that of a dead jelly fish. Chuckling and leering, he followed the girl of the crimson legions.
> At their feet the river appeared a deathly black hue. Some hidden factory sent up a yellow glare, that lit for a moment the waters lapping oilily against timbers. The varied sounds of life, made joyous by distance and seeming unapproachableness, came faintly and died away to a silence. (MGS, p. 53)

---

[69] So far, most interpretations have read the chapter as a symbolic telescoping of time (Brennan, p. 309). The spatial organization also holds important clues. Graff, p. 433.

[70] The river of the opening chapter reappears and Maggie Johnson again encounters the clergyman she accosted earlier. Finally, the man with "disordered teeth" (MGS, p. 53) and beerdrops in his moustache is strongly reminiscent of the Rum Alley environment.

[71] Haas, p. 501.

Congruent with the author's credo that preaching is fatal to art, the novel denies the reader an explicit explanation for Maggie's death.[72] Moreover, the suggestion of relationships which the interpretation has indicated thus far is questioned in the novel. Crane seems unwilling to probe deeper into Bowery conditions. *Maggie* nurtures the impression that the Bowery indeed is an impenetrable chaos: physically, socially, and morally.

Crane prided himself that his account of Bowery reality was regarded as sincere.[73] Critics accepted his city image of closure and especially of chaos as authentic projections of New York.[74] Incongruent exaggerations were attributed to his shock intention, or if interpreted as pre-expressionistic, the grotesque and unreal side of his modern city were stressed.[75] Some interpretations, however, called attention to his extreme emphasis on disorder in the tenements. Thus the constant wrecking of furniture in the Johnson household found opposition.[76] This willed bias toward chaos contrasts with Crane's claim to have rendered Bowery experiences sincerely.[77] This is not to argue that the Bowery could not be seen as violent and disorganized. Crane chose the extreme case of the Johnson family--three of five family members die early and the rest turn alcoholic and criminal--to evoke the extreme conditions in this part of New York.[78] In places, however, chaos stands in contrast with the experience of the enclosed world which Crane recorded. The Johnson apartment is demolished more than six times in the novel and the monotonous line of familiar backyards is described as "darkening chaos"

---

[72] Bergon, pp. 74f.

[73] Crane, *Letters*, p. 109.

[74] Frank Bergon claimed that "Crane was to present for the first time this lower class of society from a seriously rendered, insider's point of view." Frank Bergon, *Stephen Crane's Artistry*, New York, 1975, p. 75.

[75] Larzer Ziff has interpreted these exaggerations as Crane's "outstripping the event." It is not slum reality that the novel renders but the author's extreme vision; it is devoid of factual reference and intends to shock. Larzer Ziff, *The American 1890s: Life and Times of a Lost Generation*, New York, 1966, p. 185; Gullason, p. 131; Weimer, p. 57.

[76] Ziff, p. 191; Walcutt, p. 69.

[77] Crane saw a personal responsibility for the honesty of one's vision: "I go ahead, for I understand that a man is born into the world with his own pair of eyes, and he is not at all responsible for his vision--he is merely responsible for his quality of personal honesty. To keep close to this personal honesty is my supreme ambition. There is a sublime egotism in talking of honesty. I, however, do not say that I am honest. I merely say that I am as nearly honest as a weak mental machinery will allow." Crane, *Letters*, pp. 109f.

[78] Hamlin Garland was the first to draw attention to Crane's particular focus. In the next tenement, Garland argued, hard working people tried to endure the strain. Hamlin Garland, "An Ambitious French Novel and a Modest American Story," *Arena*, 8 (1893), xi-xii, repr. *Maggie: A Girl of the Streets*, 1893, ed. Thomas A. Gullason, New York, 1979, pp. 144f.

(MGS, p. 8). This sheds a different light on Crane's claim to honesty. In such instances, Crane does not record but he intentionally evokes chaos.

These distortions which overemphasize disorder in the Bowery link Crane's novel to the typical slum image of an outsider. As William Whyte has shown, chaos is in the mind of the middle-class observer rather than in the structure of the slum society. Whyte has argued that "the middle-class person looks upon the slum district as a formidable mass of confusion, a social chaos. The insider finds in Cornerville a highly organized and integrated social system."[79] Clearly, Crane as detached observer superimposes his impressions on a strange and obscure part of the city.

Crane's concept of the chaotic city becomes the overall stance. In his famous tenement description, he carefully selects and arranges the odors, noises, and movements in order to convey an impression of disorder and impenetrability:

> Eventually they entered into *a dark region* where, from a careening building, a dozen gruesome doorways gave up *a load of babies* to the street and the gutter. A wind of early autumn *raised yellow dust* from cobbles and *swirled* it against an hundred windows. Long streamers of garment *fluttered* from fire-escapes. In all handy places there were *buckets, brooms, rags and bottles*. In the streets infants played or *fought* with other infants or *sat stupidly in the way of vehicles*. Formidable women, with *uncombed* hair and *disordered* dress, gossiped while leaning on railings, or *screamed in frantic quarrels*. Withered persons, in curious postures of submission to something, sat *smoking pipes* in *obscure corners*. A *thousand odors* of cooking food came forth to the street. The building *quivered and creaked* from the weight of humanity stamping about in its bowels. (MGS, p. 6; my italics)

The scene is consciously composed in its chaotic appearance: this is not an insider's view, of Jimmy and his father returning home to their familiar tenement block.[80] It is the view of a stranger giving his impression of a confusing street in the Lower East Side.[81] The tenement community whose closeness is shown in the damnation and hypocritical mourning of Maggie is excluded. Neighbors here function as an anonymous crowd. "Ol' Johnson" does not recognize anyone among these strangers who appear as an opaque conglomerate.[82] It is, as Kenneth Lynn has noted, the Bowery image of an "outsider looking in."[83]

---

[79] Whyte, *Street Corner Society*, p. xviii.

[80] For Milne Holton, the passage renders the perspective of the frightened Jimmy returning home. Holton, p. 119.

[81] Crane's view of the Bowery as chaotic is mostly considered accurate. Only recently, Andrew Lees has remarked that the famous tenement passage secured Crane's reputation as a "penetrating observer." Lees, *Cities Perceived: Urban Society in European and American Thought*, pp. 129f.

[82] The anonymity is improbable as the Johnsons live in the same tenement for years.

[83] Kenneth S. Lynn, "Introduction," *Sister Carrie*, New York, 1957, v-xvi, repr. *Sister Carrie*, ed. Donald Pizer, New York, 1970, p. 510.

A further conclusion can be drawn from the tenement scenery. Crane links chaos to masses. He interprets Bowery tenements as disorderly and impenetrable, whereas in Maggie's individual case he still implies causes and dependencies. Investigating the relationship between the tenement world and the glamorous city, Crane suggests causal connections. He distinguishes, however, between the knowable individual and the anonymous mass. Crane shies away from crowds. He analyzes limited, personal ethics, but not extended social structures. Interestingly, *Maggie* omits any traces of the most obvious order in the Bowery. By excluding the pervasive influence of the political machines, Crane consciously neglects a major factor in the cohesion in working-class tenements.

This too is a response to the booming New York in the 1890s: the modern city is depicted as impenetrable and incomprehensible.[84] With his fragmentary glimpses from the Bowery, he pays tribute to new conditions, but his analytic focus on a sympathetic heroine nonetheless indicates his adherence to older fictional models. In a logical step, his later work provocatively excludes the social and political context. Crane presents ahistorical and existential situations: four men in a boat battling against a wild sea.[85] *Maggie*'s power derives from its inclusion of American society in the 1890s.

Crane interprets Bowery reality in terms of chaos and closure. His documentation of social opportunity and of urban experience indicate the restrictions in the working-class environment. This closure then is linked with chaos, his perception of the Bowery. From the beginning, when the fighting boys are surrounded by a "bobbing circle" (MGS, p. 5), Crane fuses images of circles and disorder. Social Darwinist ideas form the framework for this connection and in true naturalistic manner, he sees social conflict in biological terms. He anthropomorphizes buildings. They have "bowels" (MGS, p. 6), "eyes" (MGS, p. 51), and "lips" (MGS, p. 53).[86] He also compares characters in the Bowery jungle to animals. Maggie is a "pursued tigress" (MGS, p. 9), Pete a "panther" (MGS, p. 36). Crane reduces the historical conflict to an ontological condition and denounces his own insights: man-made cycles become unchangeable, natural ones. If closure restricts, chaos excludes further scrutiny of conditions. This tension lies at the core of *Maggie* and forms the source for its power and its weakness.

The chaos image leads in two directions. One path has just been described. Chaos stands for the inscrutable force of Social Darwinism and the struggle for survival in

---

[84]Trachtenberg, pp. 266f.

[85]Klaus Poenicke, *Der amerikanische Naturalismus*, Darmstadt, 1982, pp. 58f.

[86]In his sketch "A Mournful Old Building," he turns the struggle between old and new buildings into a generational conflict. Crane, *Sketches*, pp. 16f.

cities. But chaos also allows Crane to stress subjectivity and irony.[87] If theories are fallible and deep insights into urban society impossible, then honesty to subjective impressions poses an alternative. Moreover, the irony which springs from the juxtaposition of disparate perceptions may question, subvert, and distance subjective views. It may objectify subjectivity to a certain degree.

The double perspective profoundly shapes *Maggie*. Both versions of urban reality appear side by side in the novel. Order and disorder, closure and chaos are oppositions and complementations in Crane's view. The form of *Maggie* expresses this duality: one strand indicates relationships, while the other denies them. Order and disorder hold a precarious balance. On the one side, there is the structured *Maggie* with its perfect determinist plot,[88] with the circular closure of its motifs and of the sequence of events; there is the subtle yet extensive network of cross-references, of reversals and parallels in *Maggie*. On the other side, there are the loosely related episodes, the disruptive clash of diction, the disconnected sentences with their tendency to ellipsis,[89] the frequent abrupt images, and the recurrent motifs of wreckage and chaos.

The dual mode allows Crane to merge his interpretation of the modern city with the New York seen from a Bowery standpoint. Honesty in perception and the exchange of viewpoints produce vital tension. However, such a fusion of disparate standpoints also results in incongruities. Crane's ambivalence toward the slum world creates the contradictory strands in the text. It produces the stylistic breaks in the hard juxtaposition of Bowery sociolect and pretentious images.

The doubling into a New York perceived from both a middle-class and a working-class standpoint also offers two diverging options to read the text. If the chaos image has prevailed in interpretations of Crane's cityscape, this reflects an actual bias toward disorder and the novel's attempt to project the distinct quality of segregation and impenetrability. But as important, it reflects predominant urbanist concepts and the middle-class experience by most critics. Established notions of what to expect in the modern city prevented a proper perception of the enclosed New York and its particular constraints. For Thomas Gullason, Crane projects a "City of Unreality."[90]

---

[87]Malcolm Bradbury has noted that Crane's subjectivism does not lead "simply to a more accurate reportage, but to impressionism." Bradbury, p. 121.

[88]Walcutt, p. 67.

[89]Frank Bergon analyzed Crane's fragmented style. It is characterized by "shorthand prose, suggestibility, shifts in perspective, slowness, and ellipses between and within sentences." Bergon, p. 26.

[90]Gullason, "The Prophetic City in Stephen Crane's 1893 *Maggie*," p. 131.

The chaos image, which suggests that city life is fragmented and which questions concepts of order and truth, also relates to Crane's detached mode of writing. Inflated diction and artificial similes are his stylistic means to achieve distance from Bowery plight and disorder. Juxtaposed upon lower-class sociolect, this generates the irony which serves Crane's need for detachment and self-defense.[91] His sarcasm removes him from the Bowery and the violent chaos of the masses. It is the major weakness of the novel.[92] Dealing with Bowery conditions in a progressively modern way, Crane at the same time treats the immigrant and working-class world in a condescending manner.

In fact, Dietmar Haack pointed to the journalist movement of the "clever school" as a source for Crane's inflated diction.[93] Crane had been part of this writing school, before he published his novel. In a letter to Lily Brandon Munroe in 1892, he explains that "there must be something more in life than to sit and cudgel one's brains for clever and witty expedients."[94] *Maggie*, however, still contains 'clever' residues in some of its facetious comparisons. The cub writer draws attention to himself and his skill rather than to the situation described:[95] "The little boy ran to the halls, shrieking like a monk in an earthquake" (MGS, p. 9). In other passages, awkward phrasing clearly relates to disengagement as emotional self-defense. Describing a cruel fight between mother and son, Crane cannot but compare them ludicrously to struggling gladiators and then turn the episode into parody: "'Whoop!' said the Rum Alley tenement house" (MGS, pp. 29f).

In sum, the dual code signifies a divided city. The clash of incongruent registers and of distinct generic styles need not be attributed to artistic incapacity or immaturity. The duality reproduces the contradiction in Crane's attempt to fuse disparate perspectives. The incongruity of vision becomes an incongruity of style. On the whole, the novel profits from the duality in viewpoint. The essential openness of Crane's double vision enables him to present a previously unacknowledged image of New York. It allows him to transcend the current modes of genteel realism and narrow environmentalism in dealing with the early segregated metropolis. The offending immorality of

---

[91] Trachtenberg has called *Maggie* parodic. Trachtenberg, p. 274.

[92] Frank Bergon and Malcolm Bradbury among others, have called attention to this inconsistency. Bergon, p. 76; Bradbury, p. 120.

[93] Dietmar Haack, "Stephen Crane und die 'kühne Metapher'," *Jahrbuch für Amerikastudien*, 14 (1969), 116-23.

[94] Crane, *Letters*, p. 31.

[95] Walcutt, p. 71. Crane's romantic expectations of success and fame in connection with the publication of the novel under a pseudonym have been pointed out (Colvert, p. 47). Crane hired people to sit on streetcars, ostentatiously reading his slum novel. To no avail though--he only sold a handful of copies. Crane, *Letters*, p. 336.

132 Fragmented Urban Images

the novel stems from the double viewpoint: it consciously deletes the didactic stance of Tenement Tales.

The presentation of two distinct urban cultures and Crane's superimposition of a unifying image resulted in rifts and incongruities. This discontinuity and openness was long overlooked by literary criticism.[96] A source of complexity, organicist and holistic patterns could not be applied satisfactorily to *Maggie*. The frequent shifts in assignment to critical paradigms, to naturalism, impressionism, expressionism, and modernism, underline its intricacy.[97]

As an urban novel, *Maggie* is important as its disconnected images overcome the hierarchical totality of the nineteenth-century city novel. Its disjointed, episodic structure prefigures the montage form of John Dos Passos' *Manhattan Transfer*.[98] In addition, Crane no longer concentrates on the opposition between country and city but projects the grave fissure within the American city. *Maggie* is the first exploration into the segregated American metropolis. It is an acknowledged precursor to Richard Wright's and Hubert Selby's explorations into inner-city slums. The disruptions in upper- and middle-class New York, however, an experience which Crane only presented indirectly, were projected more completely by Theodore Dreiser and John Dos Passos. Hence *Sister Carrie* and *Manhattan Transfer* became the representative New York novels in the twentieth century, and not Stephen Crane's fiction about the tenement majority.

---

[96] Poenicke, pp. 55ff.

[97] Interpretations of *Maggie* document the various paradigms of literary criticism and its changes in focus. In the beginning, naturalist readings and biographical approaches dominated. Later Crane's impressionism, his focus on perception, his irony, and his anticipation of expressionism and modernism followed. See Poenicke, pp. 46-75.

[98] Dietmar Haack, "Formen der Darstellung bei Stephen Crane," diss., Berlin, 1968, p. 96.

8

Theodore Dreiser
Sister Carrie

1. A World of Change

Change in its various shades of evolution, progress, mobility, transience, and displacement is the ruling theme of *Sister Carrie*.[1] In the 1890s, more than in any other period, disruptive change became an all-pervasive experience. In *Sister Carrie*, it appears in several forms: in geographic terms as Carrie's exemplary migration from country to city, as the dislocation from Chicago to New York, and as the instability in urban residences; in economic terms as the aggressive transition from a production-oriented industrialism to the commodity-filled environments of corporate capitalism; in ideological terms as the partial replacement of the Protestant ethic by Social Darwinism and Herbert Spencer's benevolent evolution; in social terms as the transition from the inner-directed to the outer-directed personality, as the fragmented identities of different roles and names, as the transience in careers, and as the emergence of the new woman; and finally, in terms of plot, it appears as the dynamism in the contrapuntal movement with Carrie's ascent and Hurstwood's descent, as Carrie's education from light acting to serious literature, as the ceaseless motion in the novel's sequences, incidents, and motifs, and as the nautical city imagery of the ocean, the sea, and the tide. Change is omnipresent.[2]

---

[1] The importance of the theme is documented by the many studies which directly focused on it. See Kenneth S. Lynn, "Introduction," *Sister Carrie*, New York, 1957, v-xvi, repr. *Sister Carrie*, ed. Donald Pizer, New York, 1970, 509-18. Jay Martin, "The Visible and Invisible Cities," *Harvests of Change: American Literature, 1865-1914*, Englewood Cliffs, N. J., 1967, pp. 256-59. Robert James Butler, "Movement in Dreiser's *Sister Carrie*," *Dreiser Newsletter*, 11 (1980), 1-12. Philip Fisher, *Hard Facts: Setting and Form in the American Novel*, New York, 1985. Heinz Ickstadt, "New York und der Stadtroman der Amerikanischen Moderne," *Medium Metropole: Berlin, Paris, New York*, eds., Friedrich Knilli und Michael Nerlich, Heidelberg, 1986, 111-24.

[2] Charles C. Walcutt enhances the "principle of change" to underlie all forms of life in Dreiser. Walcutt, *American Literary Naturalism*, p. 191.

In *Sister Carrie*, the continually changing city figuratively represents modern American society. For Dreiser, the metropolis embodies natural progress. *Sister Carrie* projects a new social and economic totality in which the anachronistic polarity of country and city is obliterated. The novel subsumes all tendencies to the ceaseless motion and overwhelming dynamism in the modern metropolis. In this sense, *Sister Carrie* has justly been called the "generic novel" of modern American city fiction.[3]

The novel's totality, however, in which society and city are interchangeable, is construed. The community-oriented groups in the ethnic and working-class quarters as well as the tightly separated upper-class areas are blind spots in the naturalist picture as they contradict ceaseless change. The city image is indicative of the mental maps of middle-class transients at the turn of the century.[4] Their particular segment of the city pretends to comprehensiveness and universality in the novel, while it clearly shows only a class experience. While the city is restricted to the urban experience of the middle-class, Dreiser diagnoses a deep rift within this group in its attitude toward the modern city. Contrary modes of adjustment to a disruptive economy pervade *Sister Carrie*.

The vast upheavals of the 1890s not only affect the presentation of urban experience in *Sister Carrie* but are crucially linked to the form and function of the novel.[5] Dreiser controverts traditional patterns of nineteenth-century city novels and especially assails their outdated strategies for success.[6] In addition to projecting a distinct transition from country to city for his protagonist, the novelist incorporates in the story the paradigmatic change of an artist figure. For Dreiser, the quality of disruptions necessitates a distinctly new response. Arguing for changed ethics of perception, he writes in 1903:

> The sum and substance of literary as well as social morality may be expressed in three words--tell the truth. It matters not how the tongues of the critics may wag, or the voices of a partially developed and highly conventionalized society may complain, the business of the author . . . is to say what he knows to be true, and, having said as much, to abide the result with patience.
> Truth is what is; and the seeing of what is, the realization of truth. To express what we see honestly and without subterfuge: this is morality as well as art.[7]

---

[3] Gelfant, p. 64.

[4] Fisher, p. 17.

[5] For an extended study of the specific response of naturalism to the social disruptions of the time, see June Howard, *Form and History in American Naturalism*, Chapel Hill, 1985.

[6] Kathy N. and Arnold E. Davidson, "Carrie's Sisters: The Popular Prototypes for Dreiser's Heroine," *Modem Fiction Studies*, 23 (1977), p. 407.

[7] The essay "True Art Speaks Plainly" was one of the few articles Dreiser published after the failure of *Sister Carrie*. Theodore Dreiser, "True Art Speaks Plainly," *Booklover's Magazine*, February 1903, p. 129.

Dreiser intends to portray the city honestly from an aesthetic and scientific vantage point. However, his decision to concentrate merely on the "surface scene"[8] as a disengaged observer is a withdrawal from evaluation. Also, the bias of perspective and arrangement are blurred by the claim of providing a disinterested picture of conditions. Dreiser, like many writers who faced the instability of reference and communication in the disrupted social relations of the early modern city, came to base his judgment on values of the literary community.[9] Among the avantgarde, aesthetic bonds and ideals partly replaced social ones.

The partiality of the city portrait is disclosed by the ideals of honesty and totality in Dreiser's naturalistic model.[10] The urban experience, truthfully recorded, jars with the condescending tone of scientific omniscience and ideals in Dreiser's philosophical passages. The diverse, even diametrical, readings of *Sister Carrie* document this rift. Critics have claimed Dreiser both to condemn the evil materialism of cities and to revel in their material pleasures.[11] Pointing beyond the author's intention and his well noted ambivalence toward the American metropolis, on its fringes the novel displays a truly radical city image.[12]

---

[8] Theodore Dreiser, *Dawn*, New York, 1931, p. 129.

[9] The New York City that Theodore Dreiser worked and communicated with was precisely such a city of artist-minded people. F. O. Matthiesen, *Theodore Dreiser*, New York, 1951, p. 43; Martin, p. 254.

[10] Such friction becomes especially discernible in *Sister Carrie* as most of the events are based on autobiographical experiences in which the immersion in social relations prevented clinic detachment. For a full analysis of the biographical parallels see, Donald Pizer, *The Novels of Theodore Dreiser: A Critical Study*, Minneapolis, 1976.

[11] The rejection of the city was argued by Blanche Gelfant and Lucia and Morton White. The Whites, for instance, claimed that Dreiser "made anti-urban use of . . . materialism" (White, p. 135). David Weimer, Philip Fisher, Walter Benn Michaels, and Heinz Ickstadt have stressed the affirmative stance of the novel.

[12] Since this study focuses on the reception of the novel and its influence on the perception of the American city, the 1900 edition of *Sister Carrie* will be used despite the fact that it was bowdlerized and cut. For relevant deleted passages, the extended 1981 Pennsylvania edition will be consulted (Theodore Dreiser, *Sister Carrie*, The Pennsylvania Edition, Historical Editors, John C. Berkey and Alice M. Winters; Textual Editor, James L. West III; General Editor, Neda M. Westlake, Philadelphia, 1981). All subsequent quotations are taken from Donald Pizer's edition (Theodore Dreiser, *Sister Carrie*, ed. Donald Pizer, New York, 1970); references to *Sister Carrie* will be incorporated in the text abbreviated to SC.

136 Fragmented Urban Images

2. White City and Black City

In the period in which *Sister Carrie* portrays the journey from country to city, Chicago and New York added another million of migrants to its booming populace.[13] Because of the momentous transformations which occurred with the restructuring of industrial capitalism, American cities in the 1890s faced unseen upheavals. Migration by the millions loosened and severed economic, social, and cultural ties. Finding employment predominantly in industrial factories and in related services for the increasing number of urban households, most people had to make their living in continually threatened neighborhoods. Especially in the last decade of the nineteenth century, the feeling of insecurity was pervasive.

Capitalist agglomeration which directed the economic boom and bust underwent a phase of substantial reorganization in the 1890s. Capital concentration advanced. On the national scale, this focusing of power made New York the banking and service center of the United States.[14] In addition, the economic concentration also meant that American trusts and corporations had to find further outlets for their supplies as focused manufacturing saturated markets more rapidly. The shift to the mass production of private commodities was one solution. In its wake, the prominence of industrial production was replaced in the following years with policies to trigger private consumption.

In the concomitant social restructuring, white-collar and managerial employment grew in American cities in the 1890s and with it spread the attitude of specialized and noncommitted professionals. As the agents and overwhelmed participants in the process of change, middle- and upper-class groups also faced problems of adjustment. Uncertain about developments in the future, these groups in the bourgeoisie were split as to the specific path that the American city should take. They were tacitly unified, however, in assuming that the goal of progress continued to be their undemocratic share of wealth, profit, and power.[15] The professionalization and beautification of cities, two of their

---

[13]Greater New York exploded from 1,772,962 inhabitants in 1880, to 2,321,644 in 1890, and to 3,437,202 at the turn of the century (These figures include Brooklyn which was only incorporated officially in 1898; Rosenwaike, p. 63). Chicago expanded similarly: from 503,185 inhabitants in 1880, to 1,099,850 in 1890, to 1,698,575 in 1900. Cutler, p. 179.

[14]Hammack, *Power and Society: Greater New York at the Turn of the Century*, pp. 50f.

[15]Jackson T. Lears and Richard Sennett have analyzed the insecurity of the upper and middle class toward the close of the century. Most solutions aimed at overcoming problems attempted to contain the disorder without touching the root cause. Richard Sennett, *Families Against the City: Middle Class Homes of Industrial Chicago, 1872-1890*, New York, 1974; Jackson T. Lears, *No Place of Grace: Antimodernism and the Transformation of American Culture, 1880-1920*, New York, 1981.

ideologies which responded to the urban threat, appear in fictional form in *Sister Carrie*. Their influence is clearly exhibited in Dreiser's treatment of Chicago and New York.

Demands for urban efficiency and professionalism became widespread toward the end of the nineteenth century. The Progressive movement which then emerged, promoted entrepreneurial management, statistical assessments, and social engineering as solutions to regain better control of the overwhelming process of urbanization. The Pittsburgh Survey of 1907 and the foundation of the Chicago School of sociology are the best known results of the Progressive ideology and its scientific attitude toward the problems of the early modern city.[16] Howard Chudacoff writes:

> Most urban progressives believed that trained professionals could best define the public interest and execute proper policies in that interest through specialized, independent agencies. This faith in scientific management blinded reformers to the contradictions between disinterested (nonpolitical and uncorruptible) social engineering and democratic self-determinism. Thus they could advocate more trust in the people and more popular involvement on the one hand while they worked for centralized power and impersonal bureaucratic administration on the other. Moreover, they confused the independence of experts and bureaucrats with neutrality, when in fact bureaucracies became as self-serving as the machines that the reformers wished to replace.[17]

Significantly, Bob Ames, the figure who educates Carrie to a refined attitude toward the modern city in *Sister Carrie*, is a scientist.

Another group in the upper and middle class, however, turned away from analyzing the urban dilemma and instead celebrated achievements of traditional elites and high culture. For them, the "White City" of Chicago's World Fair in 1893 became a national model. Neglecting everyday problems and menaces benignly, the way to unify the city was to instill admiration for commercial and civic architecture and to induce urbanites to identify with the local elite through elevating scenery. Thus, $46 million was spent for the temporary attraction of the White City.[18] Alan Trachtenberg explains the broader implications:

> White City implied not only a new form of urban experience but a new way of experiencing the urban world: spectacle. Visitors to the fair found themselves as *spectators*, witnesses to an unanswerable performance which they had no hand in producing or maintaining.[19]

---

[16]Glaab and Brown, pp. 237-47.

[17]Chudacoff, pp. 192f.

[18]Ewen, p. 199.

[19]Trachtenberg, *The Incorporation of America*, p. 231.

Daniel Burnham, the leading Chicago architect and one of the organizers of the Columbian Exposition, would consequently demand in 1897 that "the time has come for Chicago to make herself attractive."[20]

Trained as a journalist, Theodore Dreiser was immersed in both ideologies. On the one hand, he practiced professional detachment to urban affairs, on the other, he promoted aesthetic contemplation of industrial cityscapes in essays on art. In fact, the majority of magazine articles written before his first novel were dominated by topics concerning the arts or the city.[21] Not unexpectedly then, a congenial affinity can be detected between Dreiser's fictional strategy and the new progressive approach; Dreiser clearly possesses traits of the superreporter which his journalist colleague, Robert E. Park, soon demanded of the urban sociologist.[22] Dreiser's penchant for a recorded totality led him to incorporate a variety of materials. In his narrative, he records starvation, superfluity, and the strike of streetcar workers with the same scientific detachment as he includes a phone-booth as the latest technological achievement (SC, p. 194).

Practicing disengagement toward his subject, Dreiser too incorporates the incertitudes which induced such a distancing. In an attempt to control his experience in his fiction, he carefully mapped the fictional chronology in *Sister Carrie* so that Hurstwood's failure in the novel would parallel his own defeat searching for work in New York. Dreiser had come to know what it meant when suddenly 800,000 people became unemployed, when approximately 35 percent of the workforce in New York were without jobs in the severe depression of the mid-nineties.[23] Trying to compensate for his social impotence in the pose of a professional onlooker, recorded plight and insecurity continually disrupt his disengaged approach to the material. An omniscient Dreiser vicariously rebukes his pupil, Carrie Meeber, for her "uncritical upwelling of grief for the weak and the helpless" (SC, p. 107). In such passages, the disengagement is overtly revealed as insecurity translated into distance.

In his essays on art, Dreiser similarly advised detachment by aestheticizing urban experiences. He too had indulged himself in the artifice of the Columbian Exposition

---

[20]Burnham quoted in Bowden and Kreinberg, *Street Signs Chicago: Neighborhood and Other Illusions of Big-City Life*, p. 147.

[21]Joseph J. Kwiat, "The Education of Theodore Dreiser in the World of the City: 'Exercises' for the Early Novels," *Americana-Austriaca*, 5 (1980), p. 99.

[22]Bulmer, *The Chicago School of Sociology*, pp. 90f.

[23]Katz, *In the Shadow of the Poorhouse: A Social History of Welfare in America*, p. 147; McKelvey, *Urbanization of America*, p. 148.

and had praised the upper-class mirage of an ecclectically neo-classicist cityscape as a "realized dream of beauty" and as a "splendid picture of the world's hope for itself."[24]

The splendor and enjoyment embodied in the White City were a consequent development at a time when industrial cities were changing to function as playgrounds for consumers. Stuart Ewen writes that, "display ... was magnified and utopianized in the shadowless dazzle of the White Cities."[25] In downtown streets, the middle-class urbanite now is encouraged to desire goods in shopping-windows and burgeoning department stores infuse desire by employing the openness of cityscapes as a technique of display.[26] Concomitantly, one is advised to cherish the threat and insecurity of industrial cities in aestheticized panoramas as flaneur. Detachment and immersion become the two interrelated sides of consumerist behavior.

With the Chicago Exposition in 1893, civic beautification and aesthetic appreciation became fully established as responses to the dangerous city.[27] The White City had a lasting national impact through the subsequent City Beautiful Movement. Its impact, however, then was mainly limited to upper- and middle-class citizens who formed the majority of the visitors to the White City.[28] An estimated 5 to 10 percent of American society, mostly from the upper level, had been subjected to its "scenic architecture."[29] After all, the disengaged flaneur was a person of means and not yet the mass consumer of the post-industrial age.

The Ferris Wheel with its trivialization and domestication of technology and the illuminated scenery of the White City became the great magnets of the Fair.[30] Using lighting for the first time, the cluster of buildings consumed three times as much electric-

---

[24]Theodore Dreiser, *A History of Myself*, New York, 1922, p. 248. Also, see Guy Alan Szuberla, "Dreiser at the World's Fair: The City Without Limits," *Modern Fiction Studies*, 23 (1977), 369-79.

[25]Stuart Ewen, *Channels of Desire: Mass Images and the Shaping of American Consciousness*, New York, 1982, p. 200.

[26]Fisher, p. 137.

[27]The elitist and antimodernist impulse underlying the White City failed. Its neoclassical architecture was a last attempt to regress to older forms of hierarchical stability in which, however, the modern professional would also find his place now. Exceeding its original intention, the spectacle of the Fair generated a new mode which viewed the industrial cityscape as an illusion, attraction, and amusement. Ickstadt, "Black vs. White City," p. 204; Trachtenberg, *The Incorporation of America*, pp. 208-234.

[28]Reid Badger writes that most immigrants, migrants, blacks, and large portions of the working class were economically barred from seeing the Exposition. For people in Chicago, the high admission fee was restrictive. R. Reid Badger, *The Great American Fair: The World's Columbian Exposition and American Culture*, Chicago, 1979, p. 109.

[29]Montgomery Schuyler quoted in Badger, pp. 109, 127.

[30]Badger, p. 108.

ity as all of industrial Chicago to promote its image of progress.[31] This mirage was well received in the upper and middle class as the florid city seemed to obliterate the actual problems of industrial capitalism in beauty. A consequent development, urban solutions which were created in the spirit of the Exposition, as Burnham's 1909 plan for downtown Chicago, marginalized the needs of people and neighborhoods in their grandiose schemes.[32]

At the turn of the century, however, not all factions in the upper and middle class favored urbanized solutions. Many, especially in the old elite, withdrew to the privacy of the home, upholding tradition in the image of the bourgeois family against urban insecurity.[33] In American fiction, William Dean Howells became the critical chronicler of this attitude toward the modern city.[34] Not surprisingly, Howells is said to have told Dreiser that he did not like *Sister Carrie*.[35] The ideal of domesticity which praised traditional values and which kept women in their accustomed place in the home produced a distinct response to the city. Although such middle-class urbanites also sought the benefits of the expanding economy, they were unwilling to adjust their social patterns to the changed environment. For many families, as Richard Sennett has indicated, the resulting situation was utterly frustrating. The impulse to succeed in the urban world was defeated by the anxiety generated in the withdrawal to privacy. Influential as a group, the feeling of impotence was released as aggression toward those symptoms of disruption which now were seen at its roots: the immigrant, the mob, the Haymarket anarchists, or the chaotic and evil city.[36] A paradigmatic process, anti-urbanist sentiment in the middle class did not simply spring from false consciousness; it was deeply rooted in social practice.

---

[31] At a time when the elite demanded proper municipal management, this city was designed so inefficiently that it could not be kept in use. After it had served some homeless as shelter in the winter, it was destroyed by incendiaries during a labor dispute in 1895. Badger, p. 130.

[32] Ickstadt, p. 205; Wortman, pp. 563f. Howard Chudacoff concludes: "The City Beautiful usually spawned projects to make commercial districts more attractive--and more profitable--for business and government personnel who lived on the urban fringe. The problems of slums and social inequality were seldom addressed." Chudacoff, p. 189.

[33] Wortman, "Domesticizing the Nineteenth-Century American City," p. 535.

[34] Walter Benn Michaels, "*Sister Carrie*'s Popular Economy," *Critical Inquiry*, 7 (1980), p. 389. Ickstadt, "New York und der Stadtroman der Amerikanischen Moderne," pp. 113ff.

[35] Quoted in R. Lingemann, *Theodore Dreiser: At the Gates of the City, 1871-1907*, New York, 1986, p. 330.

[36] Richard Sennett, "Middle-Class Families and Urban Violence: The Experience of a Chicago Community in the Nineteenth Century," *Nineteenth-Century Cities: Essays in the New Urban History*, ed. Stephan Thernstrom and Richard Sennett, New Haven, 1969, pp. 412-18.

These backward looking groups in the upper and middle class had their compromise already under construction then. Emerging suburbs were promoted as perfect physical surroundings for domesticity.[37] Rich suburbanites thought they could do without the aesthetic or scientific detachment from the turmoil of downtown and simply purchased themselves the geographic and political distance in unincorporated places on the urban fringe. Many, as Daniel Burnham, took the best of both sides. Indulging himself in grand urban visions, he fled to the suburban fringe because he could no longer bear "to have my children run in the streets of Chicago."[38] For those who had to stay and use Chicago's streets, Burnham's plan of 1909 did not improve the situation.

Sister Carrie fictionally reproduces this fissure in the upper and middle class. Withdrawal from or involvement in urban affairs was a prominent issue. The novel's power and its initial rejection by middle-class readers stem from its antimoralist, antidomestic, and antigenteel position. Only participation in urban change counts for Dreiser. To live in the city is to be in tune with a natural process. Carrie, the new independent woman, is educated to become the urbanite of the future.[39]

3. Middle-Class Transience

Despite its claims to represent the city as a whole, *Sister Carrie* only depicts the segment of the middle class. Interpretations which saw Dreiser present a generic modern city usually took two related standpoints.[40] They played down or ignored the fact that other modes of living existed in the metropolis and elevated the middle-class segment to embody an inherently metropolitan life-style.[41] Dreiser himself neglects the community-oriented experiences of immigrant and working-class families for their modes of living contradicted his individualistic model of change. Increasing the isolation and independence of his characters, Dreiser has Carrie Meeber and George Hurstwood move from a relatively familiar Chicago to a New York in which they do not have any

---

[37] G. Wright, *Building the Dream: A Social History of Housing in America*, New York, 1981, pp. 107-13.

[38] Burnham quoted in Bowden and Kreinberg, p. 136.

[39] Ickstadt, "New York und der Stadtroman der Amerikanischen Moderne," pp. 119f; Fisher, pp. 129ff.

[40] For Blanche Gelfant, Dreiser creates "urban types" (Gelfant, p. 92); for Jay Martin, he projects the new "urban mind" (Martin, p. 255); for Walter Göbel, he shows the paradigmatic urban isolate (Göbel, p. 95); and, finally, for Philip Fisher, he imagines the urban consumer (Fisher, pp. 131f).

[41] Few called attention to the restriction in Dreiser's selection of figures who capture only a small if powerful segment of the urban populace in the 1890s. See Warner, p. 110; Rolf Högel, "Chicago, 1880-1900: Seine Darstellung in Theodore Dreisers Roman *Sister Carrie*," *Der Fremdsprachliche Unterricht*, 15 (1981), p. 24.

social or cultural bonds. Dreiser's city image primarily encompasses mental maps of transients and of middle-class urbanites which, however, range from the lower middle-class thrift of the Hansons to the upper middle class of the Hurstwoods.[42]

Only recently having risen to prominence, Dreiser concentrates on the effects of social transience in the city. In Carrie Meeber's rise and George Hurstwood's fall, the novel incorporates a wide variety of urban experiences and makes its description seem comprehensive. Moreover, Dreiser's images of sea, ocean, and tide suggest the universality of his partial city segment. The events in the novel, however, modify Dreiser's explanation of the city as "magnet" (SC, p. 1) and lone cause of conditions. While anomie, alienation, anonymity, or the breakdown of familial bonds dominate the novel--features which Chicago sociologists identified as generically urban--*Sister Carrie* attributes most of these effects to social transience. Yet transience, as Herbert J. Gans asserted in his refutation of Chicago theory, is found in all types of settlement, rural and urban.

Social transcience explains most behavior. Carrie Meeber and George Hurstwood frequently move in New York and become isolated not because of urbanism or the huge size of the Hudson metropolis, but because of the socioeconomic segregation in the industrial city which generally had established itself by the 1890s.[43] Money dictates the affordable place in the grid.[44] Anonymity is also important, but it clearly is delimited in the metropolis. Hurstwood may propose to keep Carrie hidden as a mistress in Chicago (SC, p. 110), but the lack of anonymity among managers later leads to his economic failure in New York: "He did know some hotel owners in several cities, including New York, but they knew of his dealings with Fitzgerald and Moy. He could not apply to them" (SC, p. 251). Total professional anonymity does not exist, not even in an "ocean like New York" (SC, p. 214). The control over good managerial positions make his former customers unreachable for Hurstwood and eventually lead to his decline.[45]

---

[42] The Hansons, of course, are nominally working class in the novel. Their function in *Sister Carrie*, however, defines them more precisely. They are the noble poor of the working-girl novel tailored on bourgeois values (Davidson, p. 400). Their urban experience does not represent that of a working-class family.

[43] Warner, p. 108. For Dreiser, the change of residence need not imply a characteristic of a metropolis. Because of their poverty, the Dreiser family had to move frequently in their small town. Robert H. Elias, *Theodore Dreiser: Apostle of Nature*, 1948, New York, 1970, p. 7.

[44] Carrie Meeber is perfectly conscious of her shabby address as Mrs. Wheeler (SC, p. 262). The figures of the New York grid indicate status and social radius (Schmidt- von Bardeleben, p. 28).

[45] Similarly, Carrie's initial rejection in the theater world hints at the power of the syndicate.

In *Sister Carrie*, urban isolation and economic control are juxtaposed. Yet Dreiser does not critically investigate the economic and political relations which inform his modern city: its conditions are the product of a natural evolution. He primarily concentrates on the urban scenery and intends to provide a comprehensive record of its surface materials. Reassessing his espousal of Spencerian doctrines in *Sister Carrie*, the novelist later claimed to have been politically naive: "I saw only the surface scene, and other than artistically my mind was a blank. I had no gift for organic sociology. Trade and all that related to it was interesting as a strange, at times even lovely, spectacle, but as a problem or compulsion . . . I was not able to register it."[46] Contrary to this statement, the novel's philosophical passages evidence that Spencer's theory of progress directed Dreiser's social commentaries in 1900.[47]

The novel opposes two mutually exclusive middle-class life-styles in the city. In the course of her urban education, Carrie is made to experience both of them. Contrast being one of the pervasive principles in *Sister Carrie*,[48] Theodore Dreiser conceives of the Hansons as an anti-model to Carrie's rise. They are used to illustrate the incompatibility of traditional middle-class behavior with the changed conditions in the modern city. The Hansons cling to the old Protestant work ethic and traditional morals. Yet the ideal of domesticity, as Dreiser indicates, has degenerated into a dull imprisonment in their apartment. Marriage thus cannot hold the solution for Carrie; instead, it too is a devastating "round of toil" (SC, p. 10). At the Hansons, the work ethic has permeated every aspect of family life and has reified the bond to relatives. Carrie is used to finance a house in the suburbs, but is sent away when she needs assistance: "Unless Carrie submitted to a solemn round of industry and saw the need of hard work without longing for play, how was her coming to the city profit them?" (SC, p. 24). The saving spirit from Horatio Alger tales has deteriorated to thrifty lifelessness, Sven Hanson is as "silent as a deserted chamber" (SC, p. 38). Dreiser presents Hanson's way of life as incompatible with evolutionary necessity. In a most devastating judgment, inverting Thomas Jefferson's assessment which declared the city as cancer on the body politic, Dreiser now sees diligence, perseverance, and morality as disease in the natural urban environment: in American consumerist society, Sven Hanson's "I'm after bread" reveals his "contagion of thought" (SC, p. 39). The home cannot function as rescuing port

---

[46]Dreiser, *Dawn*, p. 327.

[47]Christopher G. Katope, "*Sister Carrie* and Spencer's *First Principles*," *American Literature*, 41 (1969), pp. 64-75.

[48]Gelfant, p. 52.

in this "ocean." The deadly silence in the apartment evidences its inferiority to the sounds of the lively city streets:

> To Carrie, the sound of the little bells upon the horse-cars, as they tinkled in and out of hearing, was as pleasing as it was novel. She gazed into the lighted street when Minnie brought her into the front room, and wondered at the sounds, the movement, the murmur of the vast city which stretched for miles and miles in every direction. (SC, p. 9)

> When Hanson came home at seven o'clock, he was inclined to be a little crusty--his usual demeanor before supper. This never showed so much in anything he said as in a certain solemnity of countenance and the silent manner in which he slopped about. He had a pair of yellow carpet slippers which he enjoyed wearing, and these he would immediately substitute for his solid pair of shoes.... He would then get his evening paper and read in silence.
> For a young man, this was rather a morbid turn of character and so affected Carrie. Indeed, it affected the entire atmosphere of the flat, as such things are inclined to do, and gave to his wife's mind its subdued and tactful turn, anxious to avoid taciturn replies. (SC, p. 22f)

Dreiser exaggerates the drabness of this life-style in order to discredit the underlying ideology. Only a lethargic and doomed Hurstwood finally comes close to Sven Hanson's inertia who "sat every evening in his front room and read his paper" (SC, p. 9). In its last analysis, the novel implicates the utter failure of this mode of life. The final sequence of *Sister Carrie* reassembles all figures who introduced Carrie Meeber to the city, in order to provide the backdrop for her success and development. The domestic Hansons, however, the nominal working-class family of sentimental conception, do not reappear.[49]

Carrie moves beyond the Hansons and resumes her urban education in different middle-class circles. Dreiser has her recognize early in the novel that effort and reward no longer correlate in American society. Injustice and chance rule. Conventional morality which relies on the traditional work ethic seems out of place as the days in the factory and at the Hansons have taught her. Dreiser's protagonist also cannot push back the evolutionary wheel and return to the past, to Columbia City.[50] Participation in, and not withdrawal from, Chicago will mean success. Nevertheless, firm ethics which might point the way through this immoral and unstable world, Dreiser philosophizes, are yet in the making (SC, pp. 68f). Old morals, he knows for certain, are incompatible, however. Carrie Meeber thus does not achieve material security by selling her body at the workplace and by resisting worldly temptation, but by yielding herself to private male consumption for financial comfort and an even greater freedom than she could achieve

---

[49]Davidson, p. 400.

[50]Weimer, p. 76.

as a working girl. Not yet fully adjusted, the omniscient narrator explains, Carrie's conventional conscience rebels at the decision:

> Her conscience, however, was not a Drouet, interested to praise. There she heard a different voice, with which she argued, pleaded, excused. It was no just and sapient counselor, in its last analysis. It was only an average little conscience, a thing which represented the world, her past environment, habit, convention, in a confused way. With it, the voice of the people was truly the voice of God. (SC, p. 70)

Yet, the impressionable heroine soon overcomes her misgivings and adjusts to the prevalent manners of bourgeois society. The Hansons' absence in the end, thus, is significant in another sense: Carrie as Drouet's "sister" (SC, p. 54) succeeds, while her married working-class sister, toiling for a place in the suburbs, disappears.

Movement correlates to success in this novel of change.[51] Initially barred from rides in streetcars as a worker, Carrie's advancement is depicted by her mobility. Train and coach rides become symbols of wealth in the novel. Carrie elopes to middle-class security in a vehicle with Drouet: "Got here safe, did you? Well, we'll take a car" (SC, p. 60) and later, during a coach ride, she is won by George Hurstwood. But mobility is qualified in its function. One is to use vehicles, not service them: Hurstwood finally fails as a scab in the streetcar workers' strike.[52] Similarly, Carrie Meeber learns that shoes and clothes are to be desired and worn, not produced in factories.

Carrie Meeber's city is permeated with material aspirations. In his heroine, Dreiser projects the model consumer of the twentieth century.[53] John Berger has described the process which generally defines Carrie's change: "The interminable present of meaningless working hours is 'balanced' by a dreamt future in which imaginary activity replaces the passivity of the moment. In his or her daydreams the passive worker becomes the active consumer. The working self envies the consuming self."[54] Thus, without fear of losing orientation among the "wall-lined mysteries" (SC, p. 13) of Chicago's streets, the rural newcomer drifts to the center of commodities on her second day. In contradistinction to actual working-class arrivals in the city, as for instance in Upton Sinclair's *The Jungle*, it seems as if Carrie Meeber had already internalized the map of middle-class shoppers and their 'palaces of consumption' in

---

[51]Fisher, p. 155.

[52]Fay M. Blake writes that "the strike has marked the end of Hurstwood's existence as a strong and decent human being." Fay M. Blake, *The Strike in the American Novel*, Metuchen, N. J., 1972, p. 84.

[53]Amy Beth Kaplan, "Realism Against Itself: The Urban Fiction of Twain, Howells, Dreiser, and Dos Passos," diss., Johns Hopkins University, 1982, p. 177.

[54]John Berger, *Ways of Seeing*, Harmondsworth, 1972, p. 149.

downtown Chicago.⁵⁵ Although she is as yet the poor, rural applicant, the frustration which accompanies her search for a job is overcome in the attraction to goods in department stores and the pleasure in looking at imposing buildings:

> Carrie passed along the busy aisles, much affected by the remarkable displays of trinkets, dress goods, stationery, and jewelry. Each separate counter was a show place of dazzling interest and attraction. . . . The dainty slippers and stockings, the delicately frilled skirts and petticoats, the laces, ribbons, hair-combs, purses, all touched her with individual desire, and she felt keenly the fact that not any of these things were in the range of her purchase. . . . She realized in a dim way how much the city held--wealth, fashion, ease--every adornment for women, and she longed for dress and beauty with a whole heart. (SC, p. 17)

For Carrie Meeber, as for her tutors Charles Drouet and George Hurstwood, the city represents consumption and amusement. Freedom and happiness are redefined as leisure and entertainment: Hurstwood is the manager of one of the best restaurants in Chicago, and Carrie later succeeds in the theaters of New York. Not accidentally, Dreiser introduces Chicago through the eyes of a distanced, "casual wanderer" (SC, p. 12).⁵⁶ His city is the environment of a strolling consumer in which seeing and being seen is all that counts. In the introductory chapters of the novel, the verb 'to see' rules the text. Carrie first is to see and visit Lincoln Park, the latest achievement of urban landscaping in Chicago.⁵⁷ As Richard Poirier has noted, "the floods of language by which he [Dreiser] embraces things outside himself are a verbal equivalent to the visual obsessions of his characters."⁵⁸

The fact that Dreiser's city image is limited to a middle-class segment can be best seen in the ways that he uses street-life in the novel. Marked in its opposition to the imprisonment at the Hansons, where Carrie should not even stand in the street door and watch the neighborhood ballet (SC, p. 42), avenues in Chicago and New York function as arenas for indulging gazes and conspicuous representations. One is to take a bath in urban throngs. Even the window's functions change.⁵⁹ Display ranks foremost:

> The large plate of window glass, now so common, was then rapidly coming into use, and gave to the ground floor offices a distinguished and prosperous look. The casual wanderer could see as he passed a polished array of office fixtures, much frosted glass, clerks hard at

---

⁵⁵Ewen, *Channels of Desire*, p. 155.

⁵⁶Urban sociology and aesthetic cityscape are linked in *Sister Carrie* through their common foundation in Herbert Spencer's theories and in the detachment of professionals. Similar to Dreiser's distance as "wanderer," Robert E. Park claimed that "detachment is the secret of the academic attitude." Robert E. Park cited in Persons, p. 28.

⁵⁷The beautification of cities by building parks was the precursor of City Beautiful trends. Machor, p. 204.

⁵⁸Richard Poirier, *A World Elsewhere: The Place of Style in American Literature*, New York, 1966, p. 237.

⁵⁹Fisher, p. 156. On the function of windows for the detached spectator, see Howard, pp. 116f.

work, and genteel business men in 'nobby' suits and clean linen lounging about or sitting in groups. (SC, p. 12)

The use of streets in *Sister Carrie* particularly well reflects Dreiser's perspective bias in the 1890s. The vital street life of ethnic and working-class neighborhoods which was the dominant social and political space in their distinct urban culture, is completely absent in Dreiser's city. The teeming virility of Stephen Crane's Bowery seems continents away. In *Sister Carrie*, community space is obliterated and redefined as commodity space.[60]

> Carrie stepped along easily enough after they got out of the car at Thirty-fourth Street, but soon fixed her eyes upon the lovely company which swarmed by and with them as they proceeded . . . Jewelers' windows gleamed along the path with remarkable frequency. Florist shops, furriers, haberdashers, confectioners--all followed in rapid succession. The street was full of coaches. Pompous doormen in immense coats, shiny brass belts and buttons, waited in front of expensive salesrooms. Coachmen in tan boots, white tights, and blue jackets waited obsequiously for the mistresses of carriages who were shopping inside. The whole street bore the flavor of riches and show, and Carrie felt that she was not of it. She could not, for the life of her, assume the attitude and smartness of Mrs. Vance, who, in her beauty, was all assurance. She could only imagine that it must be evident to many that she was the less handsomely dressed of the two. It cut her to the quick, and she resolved that she would not come here again until she looked better. At the same time she longed to feel the delight of parading here as an equal. Ah, then she would be happy! (SC, p. 227)

4. Real Immersion

Through its heroine, *Sister Carrie* expresses approval of the latest changes in society. In tune with the ideology of progress, the novel advises participation. Dreiser's celebration of Chicago's advantages in chapter two could well have been written by its Bureau of Commerce (SC, pp. 11f). It is a well-meaning affirmation of the comfort gained through technological developments. Dreiser welcomes material progress. Although he simultaneously criticizes superciliousness, lavish materialism at least allows comfort and distance. Inner change may follow outer progress.[61] But there is no justification to continue the anachronism of restraint--Hansons' deadly thrift, for instance--in a world in which effort and reward, morality and success are not

---

[60] Fisher, pp. 133f.

[61] Dean McWilliams, "The Profound Superficiality of Dreiser's 'Sister Carrie'," *The DLSU Graduate Journal*, 13 (1988), p. 49.

interconnected and in which chance directs Carrie's rise and leads to Hurstwood's defeat.[62] The inappropriate formulae presented in earlier fiction had to be corrected.[63]

Dreiser's suspension of middle-class morality is a radical response. Having himself experienced the poverty of his protagonist, Dreiser knew that the satisfaction in food, clothes, and housing was not reprehensible. The poor needed and deserved material security. This distinguishes the transient Dreiser from other upper- or middle-class critics. Thorstein Veblen had only recently condemned leisure and materialism and had demanded restraint from conspicuous consumption in his *Theory of the Leisure Class* in 1899.[64] Dreiser shows that restraint takes a full belly. Material comfort is held in high esteem. In a melange of satisfaction, pride, and envy, Dreiser thus celebrates the culture of American hotels:

> Once seated, there began that exhibition of showy, wasteful, and unwholesome gastronomy as practiced by wealthy Americans, which is the wonder and astonishment of true culture and dignity the world over. The large bill of fare held an array of dishes sufficient to feed an army, sidelined with prices which made reasonable expenditure a ridiculous impossibility.... On the walls were designs in color, square spots of robin's egg-blue, set in ornate frames of gilt, whose corners were elaborate moldings of fruit and flowers, with fat cupids hovering in angelic comfort. On the ceilings were colored traceries with more gilt, leading to a center where spread a cluster of lights--incandescent globes mingled with glittering prisms and stucco tendrils of gilt. The floor was of a reddish hue, waxed and polished, and in every direction were mirrors--tall, brilliant, bevel-edged mirrors--reflecting and re-reflecting forms, faces, and candelabra a score and a hundred times. (SC, p. 234f)

Unwilling to look deeper into the connection between dominant ethics and modes of production, Dreiser adheres to promises in Spencer's evolutionary optimism which claims eventually to provide material satisfaction for all.[65] Dreiser's decision not to examine beyond the surface is the reason for the striking opportunism which influences the narrative on several levels. One should not forget that the author himself risked his financial basis for artistic distance when he entered the literary market as a novice and that he had to vie for a middle-class audience for his product.[66]

---

[62]Julian Markels, "Dreiser and the Plotting of Inarticulate Experience," *Massachusetts Review*, 2 (1961), pp. 431-448.

[63]Davidson, p. 395.

[64]Michaels, p. 389.

[65]Katope, pp. 64-75.

[66]Elias, pp. 110ff. Dreiser's social position was unstable and money troubles actually interrupted the composition of *Sister Carrie*. Pizer, p. 43.

The disclosure of hypocritical morality constitutes the critical thrust of the novel.[67] Contemporary fiction still adhered to truths which were no longer valid. In *Newspaper Days*, Dreiser explains:

> I set to examining the current magazines and the fiction and articles to be found therein: *Century, Scribner's, Harper's*. I was never more confounded than by the discrepancy existing between my own observation and those displayed here, the beauty and peace and charm to be found in everything, the almost complete absence of any reference to the coarse and the vulgar and the cruel and the terrible. How did it happen that these remarkable persons--geniuses of course, one and all--saw life in this happy roseate way? Was it so, and was I all wrong? Love was almost invariably rewarded in these tales. Almost invariably one's dreams came true, in the magazines. . . . But as I viewed the strenuous world about me, all that I read seemed not to have so very much to do with it.[68]

Dreiser is intentionally iconoclastic and consciously dismantles the moralist and antiurbanist stance in such tales. Using a reversal pattern he had developed in editorials for *Ev'ry Month*, Dreiser first proposes sentimental clichés and then has events disprove their validity.[69] Thus he ironically projects the expected path to be taken by Carrie Meeber at the beginning of the novel: "When a girl leaves home at eighteen, she does one of two things. Either she falls into saving hands and becomes better, or she rapidly assumes the cosmopolitan standard of virtue and becomes worse. Of an intermediate balance under the circumstances, there is no possibility" (SC, p. 1). Carrie, however, in Dreiser's naturalist novel, comes to the city, falls, and succeeds. Dreiser even has her find a balanced "middle state" (SC, p. 51) as a mistress. Drouet, similarly, is not the mean seducer of conventional urban fiction, but to Carrie, "and indeed to all the world, he was a nice, good-hearted man. There was nothing evil in the fellow" (SC, p. 48). Generally, as Cathy and Arnold Davidson have pointed out, the novel "controverts almost all of the basic messages preached in the popular fiction of the time."[70] Dreiser repudiates the patterns of the working girl novels which middle-class professionals offered to a willing audience and disproves the sentimental ideology with its triad of restraint, suffering, and eventual success.[71]

---

[67]Matthiesen, p. 61.

[68]Theodore Dreiser, *A Book About Myself*, New York, 1922, pp. 490f.

[69]Donald Pizer points out that Dreiser frequently employed a straw man technique in his "Reflections" as "The Prophet" in *Ev'ry Month*. Pizer, p. 86.

[70]Davidson, p. 407.

[71]Lydia Schurman Godfrey, "Theodore Dreiser and the Dime Novel World; Or, the Missing Chapter in Dreiser's Life," diss., University of Maryland, 1984, p. xx.

150 Fragmented Urban Images

This reversal strategy profoundly influences the language of the novel as Dreiser consciously employed the difference in sentimental and realistic registers.[72] Often, what seems like a stylistic incoherence is not a failure of the raw and untutored autodidact, but the willed juxtaposition of distinct modes of expression as fictional method.[73] Fitting other strategies of premeditated craftsmanship which criticism has revealed,[74] a clash of stylistic codes is partly intended.[75] Attracting readers with the facade of sentimental fiction, Dreiser dismantles its anachronistic paradigms with his documentary realism.[76]

Dreiser thus attacks the moral opposition to urban ways of life in these tales. His novel reverses the common nineteenth-century pattern of attraction to the city and eventual retreat to the countryside.[77] But against the grain, Carrie stays and succeeds in a city with "cunning wiles" (SC, p. 1). The countryside and her family do not exist as valid options to return to. Her heart revolts at the thought to go back to the "dull world" of her village (SC, p. 52).[78] Despite sentimental clichés about the hypnotic influence of the "magnet" city, there is no moral opposition to its pleasures or a longing for the superior qualities of rural communities. Life in Chicago simply is better, it is "livelier, sprightlier" (SC, p. 21).

Such views differ considerably from those of the Chicago sociologists whose theories have often been applied to Dreiser.[79] Such readings impose a nonexistent

---

[72]Sandy Petrey, "The Language of Realism, the Language of False Consciousness," *Novel: A Forum on Fiction*, 10 (1977), p. 109.

[73]Donald Pizer, for instance, argued that Dreiser "unconsciously falls into the language of the sentimental novelists." Pizer, p. 37; Matthiesen, pp. 59f; Weimer, p. 68.

[74]Ellen Moers, "The Finesse of Dreiser," *American Scholar*, 33 (1963), 109-114; Pizer, p. 41.

[75]The differing accounts of the novel's composition may provide a further clue to the question of Dreiser's conscious craftsmanship. As in his account of the novel's suppression, Dreiser contradicts himself. Promoting chiefly a romantic version of composition which stressed his intuitive beginning, he indicated in other places that he never started a novel unless he had mapped it out. "I cannot imagine myself," he recalls, "ever sitting down and figuring out a plot without its characters, their emotions, environment, and the ensuing scenes being quite clearly in my mind" (Dreiser quoted in Pizer, p. 43). There is evidence that he had fully outlined a novel prior to *Sister Carrie* (Godfrey, p. 89). All this may indicate (further evidence seems unlikely as all diaries and records of the 1890s are destroyed or lost) that Dreiser, who seemed interested in perpetuating the myth of spontaneous composition, may have consciously mapped *Sister Carrie* as an anti-romance. See Davidson, pp. 395-407.

[76]Petrey, p. 113.

[77]Dickstein, p. 29.

[78]Davidson, pp. 397ff. Only in times of stress in the early stages, nostalgia for life in the countryside is evoked (SC, p. 31).

[79]The twenty or thirty years which passed between the writing of *Sister Carrie* and the formulation of Robert E. Park's or Louis Wirth's theory become very important in the assessment of the modern American city. In the 1890s, Dreiser could believe more readily in an urban path of progress as envisioned by Herbert

antiurbanism on *Sister Carrie*. They take the sentimental rebuffs of the city at face value and link urban experience in the novel to the rural bias of the Chicago School.[80] Quotations from Dreiser which are used to back such moralist readings are taken from statements in the 1920s. In them, Dreiser looks at the city in retrospect, just at a time when he began reintroducing moral judgment into his fiction and opposed the "untrammeled individualism" that he promoted in his early oeuvre.[81] The essays written in the 1890s do not contain moral objections to city life as yet. But accounts of *Sister Carrie* as antiurbanist fiction became so widespread that by the 1970s a sociological textbook would cite the novel as an outstanding example of antiurbanism in American literature.[82] Urbanist ideology had closed another circle.[83]

More recent interpretations have corrected this bias. Philip Fisher has argued that, "far from being in any simple way estranged in the city, man is for the first time surrounded by himself. In every direction is a mirror, every sound is an account of his affairs."[84] Dreiser sees mankind and its cities obeying the laws of a natural evolution.[85] Being one with society and nature, however, implies a consumer city and not the withdrawal to outdated forms of security within the metropolis. *Sister Carrie* paradigmatically projects this urban shift from production to the ambiance of desire. Carrie does not revolt at work but she is upset by the poor clothes she has to wear on the streets (SC, p. 31). Drouet persuades Carrie to become his mistress as he introduces her to the lively Chicago of strolling consumers: "Drouet selected a table close by the window, where the busy rout of the street could be seen. He loved the changing panorama of the street--to see and be seen as he dined" (SC, p. 44). The city is a spectacle, it is most itself as sight for the distanced and yet continually desiring

---

Spencer. This ideology, however, lost its credibility with the rise of corporate capitalism (Spindler, p. 30). When the Chicago School applied Spencer for their purposes in the twenties, the positive ideal of rural communities was infused into the system of thought.

[80]Blanche Gelfant in her important analysis, for instance, argued that "his literary picture of the city is best illuminated not by reference to aesthetic theories but by an analysis of the impact of urbanism upon his mind and feeling." Gelfant, pp. 62f.

[81]Elias, pp. 257f.

[82]Wilson, p. 145.

[83]Lucia and Morton White had claimed that Dreiser, even though ambivalent, hated the city and that he could be the "most anti-urban of American novelists." White, pp. 125, 138.

[84]Fisher, p. 132.

[85]Dreiser writes in 1896: "From that law [of segregation] there is no escape and both men and planets obey it. It makes towns, cities, nations and worlds, and does nothing perhaps, except show what mites we are in the stream of nature." Theodore Dreiser, "The City," *Theodore Dreiser: A Selection of Uncollected Prose*, ed. Donald Pizer, Detroit, 1977, pp. 95f.

consumer. Dreiser as narrator sets the pattern in the way he introduces Chicago. Before readers are to follow Carrie in her search for employment, Dreiser wants his audience to "look at the sphere in which her future was to lie" (SC, p. 11). Carrie's future then is identified with the promising sights of a "casual wanderer" (SC, p. 12). Similarly, Dreiser's protagonist first enters the city in the early evening when the panorama is particularly attractive, when, according to Dreiser, even working people perceive the city as a consumer spectacle:[86]

> They were nearing Chicago. Signs were everywhere numerous. Trains flashed by them. Across wide stretches of flat, open prairie they could see lines of telegraph poles stalking across the fields toward the great city. . . . To the child, the genius with imagination, or the wholly untraveled, the approach to a great city for the first time is wonderful thing. Particularly if it be evening--that mystic period between the glare and gloom of the world when life is changing from one sphere or condition to another. Ah, the promise of the night. . . . Says the soul of the toiler to itself, "I shall soon be free. I shall be in the ways and the hosts of the merry. The streets, the lamps, the lighted chambers set for dining, are for me. The theater, the halls, the parties, the ways of rest and the paths of song--these are mine in the night. (SC, pp. 6f)

The city often is such a panorama viewed by a distanced spectator.[87] Even poverty can be contained as a visual experience; cheap clothes and raggedness seem the worst injustice when Carrie observes workers from her window:

> She was constantly pained by the sight of the white-faced, ragged men who slopped desperately by her in a sort of wretched mental stupor. The poorly clad girls who went blowing by her window evenings, hurrying home from some of the shops on the West Side, she pitied from the depths of her heart. (SC, p. 107)

In this way, material insecurity is overcome by imagining poverty as distanced event. On a more abstract level, Hurstwood's plot of decline continually recalls the actual vagaries in the 1890s and allows Dreiser to control his fear of defeat in aesthetic-philosophic detachment. The strict parallelism to Carrie's rise indicates the underlying impulse toward stability and detachment in a world of incertitude.

Society's tendency to define progress in terms of consumption is also reflected in the plot, the pattern of determined action which in naturalism defines protagonists. Here too, the novel projects the transition from the inner-directed self to the outer-directed facade. Hurstwood who has risen "by perseverance and industry" (SC, p. 33) complies to the old pattern. He fails to adjust to the new situation into which he has fallen

---

[86]Kenneth Lynn writes that "much of *Sister Carrie* takes place at night, when the city is most artificial and most fascinating." Lynn, p. 514.

[87]Kwiat, p. 108.

accidentally but irreversibly by the clicking of a safe.[88] As Kurt Müller has shown, the portrait of Hurstwood incorporates features of David Riesman's inner-directed type.[89] This lends Hurstwood traces of a moral dignity that critics valued and which led them to elevate his fall to quasi-tragic dimensions.[90] But his death not only seems caused by the personal, biological decay, as Dreiser's naturalist explanation seems to imply, but also his personality clearly is out of tune with the urban evolution (SC, pp. 239f).

On the other hand, Carrie Meeber's ascent symbolizes the victory of the outer-directed personality. Carrie adjusts to new situations without endangering the coherence of her self. In the nineteenth-century realist novel, character was still defined by inner autonomy, but Dreiser now identifies it with "desire, an involvement with the world so central to one's sense of self that the distinction between what one is and what one wants tends to disappear."[91] Carrie's mind is obsessed with commodities and material power. Relations to the world around her are reified. Dreiser masterfully records the facade of desire.[92] Her first seduction, for instance, poignantly defines the quality of yearning among the new middle-class:

> "I wish I could get something to do," she said.
> "You'll get that all right," said Drouet. "What's the use worrying right now? Get yourself fixed up. See the city. I won't hurt you."
> "I know you won't," she remarked, half truthfully.
> "Got on the new shoes, haven't you? Stick 'em out. George, they look fine. Put on your jacket."
> Carrie obeyed. (SC, p. 58)

Show your shoes and see the city. What the sentimental cliché mystifies as the hypnotic influence of the city, or of a Drouet, who at times represents it,[93] here is rendered in its graspable, material form. The fragmented personality of the consumer perfectly adjusts to changing situations: role-playing dominates and actually becomes

---

[88] Matthiesen, pp. 74ff.

[89] Kurt Müller, "Identität und Rolle in Theodore Dreisers *Sister Carrie*. Teil 1: Rollenverhalten, Identität und soziale Struktur," *Literaturwissenschaftliches Jahrbuch*, 21 (1980), pp. 272-77.

[90] Donald Pizer, for instance, writes that "because we ourselves are also creatures of place--that is, we are middle-class--we can sense the tragic import for our lives in the fall of a Hurstwood." Pizer quoted in Howard, p. 105. See also Kurt Müller, "Identität und Rolle in Theodore Dreisers *Sister Carrie*. Teil 2: Überanpassung und Anomie," *Literaturwissenschaftliches Jahrbuch*, 22 (1981), p. 209.

[91] Michaels, p. 381.

[92] McWilliams, pp. 48f.

[93] Drouet and Chicago receive the same attributes by Dreiser: both are said to have wiles and exert a magnetic attraction, but the action dismantles such sentimental clichés (SC, pp. 2f., 48ff).

personality.[94] Indeed, Dreiser's characters change names as frequently as locations. Ironically consequent, the city becomes the most real for Carrie behind a theater stage where role-playing and detachment may be practised: "Here was no illusion. Here was an open door to see all of that" (SC, p. 129). Here, role rehearsal in play and life may coincide.[95]

The change in *Sister Carrie* from an inner- to an outer-directed personality need not be taken as a tight pattern. Still, the transition captures the general direction of society. Carrie Meeber succeeds, George Hurstwood commits suicide, and the Hansons disappear even earlier. Change rules the novel. As Philip Fisher points out, "the wealth of motion in the novel insists that the society itself is, by means of its new streetcars, railway systems, steamships, carriages, and endless places to walk, most itself when in motion."[96] This truly captures the message of events as translated into plot. Dreiser's city is the future as continuing evolution.

On a deeper level, however, this pattern in which change represents continual progress is contested. Its contradiction touches on the origin of incongruities in *Sister Carrie*. The final movements in the novel hint at a hidden incompatibility with the world depicted and provide a clue to Dreiser's difficulties in concluding the novel.[97] The initial impetus to transcend the rural past, to break the link to America's Columbia City, an evolutionary thrust which is kept alive in the novel through images of movement and mobility, comes to a halt at the end. The plot and its distinct endings can be seen in two ways.[98] First, in the original ending, the plot stops with Hurstwood's death and thus indicates the extinction of the inner-directed type and with it the impossibility of Carrie becoming a self-controlled observer of urban change. Second, in the Doubleday, Page version,[99] the plot ends in circular motion with Carrie ceaselessly rocking in her chair thus expressing the futile hope of continued progress which, however, had nurtured the very plot in its vision of eventual benevolence. Dreiser's novel on motion and change ends in lethal stasis or in semi-circular paralysis.

---

[94]See Rachel Bowlby, *Just Looking: Consumer Culture in Dreiser, Gissing and Zola*, New York, 1985, pp. 52-65.

[95]Müller, pp. 253-58.

[96]Fisher, p. 155.

[97]Elias, p. 108.

[98]For a detailed discussion of the various versions of the ending, see Berkey et al., "Historical Commentary," pp. 501-541.

[99]The moralistic overtones in the final paragraph resulted from corrections by Dreiser's wife, Sara Dreiser. Berkey et al., "Historical Commentary," pp. 514-19.

Carrie's dual function in the novel provides the key to these contradictions. She not only succeeds as a naive and sentimental consumer in the city projecting a future life-style, but Dreiser at the same time intends to educate her in the pattern of the *bildungsroman* to become a serious actress and reader of realist novels.[100] Throughout *Sister Carrie*, Dreiser indicated in condescending omniscience that as much as he understands the power of materialism, he also advises against it. Charles Drouet, the Hurstwoods, the Vances are as much chided for their shallowness as Carrie whose sentimentality in the early sections was increased by Dreiser in textual revisions to punctuate her development.[101] The pale engineer Bob Ames, who often is claimed to be Dreiser's mouthpiece, educates Carrie eventually.[102] But the lessons Ames teaches, are invalidated by the recorded events. The ideological transformation from materialist to aesthetic sensibility, to the sublimated satisfaction that lies in observation alone, usually tends to omit the steps that lead to this position of privilege.[103] By recording Carrie's ascent, however, *Sister Carrie* exactly lays bare the social costs of achieving such detachment. An important foil, Hurstwood's decline in the second half continually recalls the insurmountable barriers erected for some to remain human in dignity and distance.

Having reached the final stage of Ames' education, her supposedly true artistic vein awakening with the reading of Balzac's *Père Goriot*, it is significantly from a hotel room that Carrie Meeber ponders on general poverty, but at the same time remains blind to her specific responsibility toward George Hurstwood. At the time that she has become receptive for grand realist ideas and humanist pity, the novel presents scenes in which her ex-husband is barred from accosting her and in which a person, like Hurstwood previously, is seen falling in the street outside. While it is questionable whether the effect was consciously intended, the incident nevertheless fits the novelistic pattern of dismantling sentimental or idealist clichés.

Such a discrepancy between deeds and words is used extensively throughout *Sister Carrie*. Carrie's conventional complaint that the metropolis is a "cold place socially" (SC, p. 324) in which only money counts, is preceded by her final note to Hurstwood which shows Carrie, herself, acting irresponsibly: "I wouldn't mind helping you, if I could, but I can't support us both, and pay the rent. I need what little I make to pay for my clothes"

---

[100] Howard, p. 108; Fisher, p. 170.

[101] Pizer, p. 39.

[102] Ellen Moers, *Two Dreisers*, New York, 1969, p. 109.

[103] The autobiographical parallels of this education have been well researched. Philip L. Gerber, *Theodore Dreiser*, New Haven, Conn., 1964, pp. 51-70.

(SC, p. 320). Similarly, the lack of warm family life is sentimentally deplored, but the recorded behavior discounts even the possibility of its existence (SC, p. 63). In compact form, Carrie's final residence in the rent-free hotel embodies smooth relations in a consumer society in which all commodities are provided for those economically able to participate, but where the underlying working relations are hidden from view. Similarly, for the flaneur, buildings do not indicate the sweat of production but may shine in attractive facades. Carrie Meeber's education to this privileged perspective of the indulging and yet distanced observer, materialized in her position at the hotel window, is contradicted by Dreiser's portrayal of a society which produces unrestrained desire and whose economic elite no longer is interested in consumer restraint.[104]

Dreiser himself had only recently obtained a financially secure position--he was included in the 1899 *Who's Who* for his journalistic work--which allowed him to write the novel.[105] In his magazine days he had interviewed celebrities and opportunistically trumpeted American success stories which featured the very belief in perseverance, diligence, and reward which he now denigrated in Hanson's and Hurstwood's stories. In his novel, however, his artistic integrity discredits any attempt at superficially whitewashing Carrie's path.[106] Morals are now subsumed in the honesty of perception. Criticism has shown that recorded urban experience in *Sister Carrie* disproves any attempt at restraint.[107] As Walter Benn Michaels concludes, "the power of Sister Carrie, then, arguably the greatest American realist novel, derives not from its scathing 'picture' of capitalist 'conditions' but from its unabashed and extraordinarily literal acceptance of the economy that produced those conditions."[108]

Since the ideal of restraint is merely superimposed on a society which forcibly disproved the possibility of ascetic behavior, protagonists of such ideals must remain vague. The flaws in characterization in *Sister Carrie*, as frequently criticized in formalist and biographical approaches, are better understood as the result of an incompatible strategy that the text unintentionally but uncompromisingly discloses.[109] The failure of

---

[104]Michaels, p. 386.

[105]W. A. Swanberg, *Dreiser*, New York, 1965, p. 97.

[106]See Theodore Dreiser, "Life Stories of Successful Men--No. 10," *Selected Magazine Articles of Theodore Dreiser. Life and Art in the American 1890s*, vol. 1, ed. Yoshinobu Hakutani, London, 1985, pp. 120-39.

[107]Fred G. See, "The Text as Mirror: *Sister Carrie* and the Lost Language of the Heart," *Criticism*, 20 (1978), 144-66.

[108]Michaels, p. 377.

[109]Gelfant argues that Dreiser "does not explore the inner feelings that give these people the capacity to appreciate and express aesthetic values. His own ineptness at handling language, revealed in the flatness and banality of his style, contributes partly to the failure in characterization" (Gelfant, p. 92). She too notes that

Dreiser's idealism to produce credible protagonists in Bob Ames and Carrie Meeber need not be solely blamed on Dreiser's artistic incapacity, little formal education, or verbosity. Carrie's whole experience contradicts her turn to become a serious actress. Dreiser's aesthetic project which intended to distill ideals from a society without ideals, which sought a moral stance in a world which he depicted as blatantly immoral, was doomed to fail. Instead, Dreiser authentically records the intermittent and now forgotten steps which mystify aesthetic distance as yearning for timeless beauty.[110] It is the very same contradiction which informs the image of the modern city that criticism has tended to generalize as Dreiser's ambivalence. The novel provides real answers. If Dreiser later recalls an urban romanticism, "the city of which I sing was not of land or sea or any time or place. Look for it in vain! I can scarcely find it in my soul now,"[111] the disappearance relates to the incompatible imposition of the White City spectacle to bleak streets. Its solution was a mirage from the beginning.

5. The Awkward City

One of the most autobiographical writers of the twentieth century, Dreiser was fully immersed in the events that he transformed into fiction.[112] Brought up in poverty, in a family which broke apart under the pressures of small town conventionalism and the demands of a modern society, the young boy became further alienated when he moved to the unfamiliar world of Chicago.[113] His menial jobs and later the experience as a journalist led him to seek detachment from cruel and inhuman conditions.[114] In Herbert Spencer's theory he found an ideology that facilitated both rebellion and adjustment to mainstream society. Spencer's philosophy justified optimism for the wealthy or the professionally distanced, but it also explained and ascertained the pessimism he had

---

"in exploring the soul-hunger for an undefined spiritual quality, he is usually vague and ineffectual" (ibid., p. 72). See also Matthiesen, p. 73; Pizer, pp. 68f; Müller, p. 230.

[110]Dreiser himself upheld this ideal. He would later write that "Carrie is an illustration of the by what devious ways one who feels, rather than reasons, may be lead in the pursuit of beauty." Dreiser quoted in Pizer, p. 47.

[111]Dreiser, *Dawn*, p. 163.

[112]For an extended reading of Dreiser's involvement and its implication for his novel, see the interpretation by Amy Beth Kaplan. Kaplan argues that "the force of Dreiser's realism lies not in his objective empirical account of social conditions, but in a full immersion in those social processes that the text reproduces." Kaplan, p. 197.

[113]Swanberg, pp. 27ff.

[114]Elias, p. 110.

gained as an unsuccessful, isolated worker immersed in the struggle. Even though Dreiser tacitly accepted the suspension of democratic values in this modified form of Social Darwinism, in contrast to other upper- and middle-class followers of Spencer, he radicalized the moral implications of the theory in *Sister Carrie*.[115]

The opportunism of the ideology appears in authorial passages where Dreiser justifies distance with philosophical-professional authority. 'Middle' is a key term for Dreiser and significantly connotes the suspension of extremes in a middle-class position. Material equilibrium is the precondition for restraint:

> There is nothing in this world more delightful than that middle state in which we mentally balance at times, possessed of the means, lured by desire, and yet deterred by conscience or want of decision. When Carrie began wandering around the store amid the fine displays she was in this mood. (SC, p. 51)

Even though he sides with the bourgeoisie in his desire for material security, he reproaches them for not transcending their anachronistic moralism which does not fit demands in the "middle stage" (SC, p. 54) of evolution. As a consequence, the author does not criticize Carrie for achieving a "middle state" (SC, p. 51) by yielding herself to Drouet. If this condition of society is natural, Dreiser concludes, its moralism is out of place: "For all the liberal analysis of Spencer and our modern naturalistic philosophers, we have but an infantile perception of morals" (SC, p. 68).

But Dreiser also knew that such a "middle state" was hard to achieve. A critical novel endangered his material security. Robert Elias points out that "therefore, whether he could remain detached depended upon his success in getting the book published, or at least in being persuaded that his efforts would be rewarded."[116] The mental breakdown which followed the novel's initial rejection indicates the lability of the position from which Dreiser had portrayed the modern city. Composing *Sister Carrie*, he had tried to rely on a different ethical basis from which he could judge society for he rejected its bourgeois morals and claimed that new social ethics were only evolving. Such a stability he found in the artistic circles in the metropolis. Aesthetic integrity replaced social ethics and allowed him to treat poverty and success side by side.

Much more than the professionalism as a journalist which only resulted in disappointment and frustration for Dreiser, his aesthetic practice seemed to secure order and detachment for him. His articles and short stories from this period indicate the

---

[115] Generally, Spencer's philosophy then helped to appease an insecure upper and middle class by arguing that if society was cruel and immoral at present, a benevolent evolution would help those in tune with it. Lears, pp. 20ff.

[116] Elias, p. 110.

struggle for a morally sound standpoint toward the treated material.[117] In "Nigger Jeff," written in 1899, he projects the development of a journalist, the uninvolved observer of a lynching, who is to become an artist. Dreiser's aesthetic stance surfaces in the attitude of the novice:

> Davies swelled with feeling. The night the tragedy, he saw it all. But also with the cruel instinct of the budding artist that he already was, he was beginning to meditate on the character of the story it would make--the color, the pathos....
> "I'll get it all in!" he exclaimed feelingly, if triumphantly at last. "I'll get it all in!"[118]

Where newspaper editors had kept Dreiser from writing what he had seen, the ideals of artistic honesty and positivist comprehensiveness now made Dreiser venture to "get it all in." But the withdrawal to an artistic integrity delegated solely to novelistic practices leaves its marks on *Sister Carrie*.

Among the evolving literary responses to modernity, the detachment in scientific naturalism congenially fit the attitudes of the journalist Dreiser. In New York, his connection to painters further shaped the mode of his novelistic explorations. Dreiser knew that his friends and acquaintances, painters like Everett Shinn, William Louis Sonntag, John Sloan, or the photographer Alfred Stieglitz were attempting to redefine the visual artist's function within the new industrial landscape.[119] In the 1890s, they transformed the threatening environment into panoramas of the city's festive moods. They also treated its buildings impressionistically as an integral part of a natural scenery. "Skyscraper"-lined streets then became "canyons."[120] In its detachment from social problems, such aestheticism prepared the ideology with which the upper and middle class would take visual possession of the modern city in the next two decades.[121] Alan Trachtenberg has shown that their magazines collaterally promoted aesthetic sensibility as an attitude to overcome the threatening chaos in the city. Thus Alfred Corbin wrote in *Scribner's*: "What our cities most need to render them beautiful is an artist who will body forth to our duller eyes the beauties already there."[122] The city needs flaneurs and its crudities and problems will vanish. Dreiser's image of the city is deeply influenced by such positions as he aestheticizes perception and withdraws to professional-scientific

---

[117]Swanberg, pp. 87f; Howard, p. 111.

[118]Theodore Dreiser, "Nigger Jeff," *Free and Other Stories*, New York, 1918, p. 111.

[119]Dreiser had written about Stieglitz in 1899. Moers, pp. 12f, 32-42.

[120]Merrill Schleier, *The Skyscraper in American Art, 1890-1931*, Ann Arbor, Mich., 1986, p. 36. Wanda Corn, "The New New York," *Art in America*, 11 (1973), p. 60.

[121]Taylor, "Psyching out the City," p. 284.

[122]Corbin quoted in Trachtenberg, p. 460.

heights.[123] He elaborates on such ideas in "The Beauty of Life," one of the essays later included in the collection aptly titled *The Color of a Great City*, in which the urban environment is reduced to mere scenery:

> For one not so mentally equipped a world of imagery is closed, with all that that implies: poetry, art, literature . . . To be dull to the finer beauties of line and curve that are forever beating upon the heart and mind--in earth, in air, in water, in sky or space--how deadly! The dark places of the world are full of that. Its slums and depths reek with the misery that knows no response to the physical beauty of nature, the wonder of its forms. To perceive these, to see the physical face of life as beautiful, to respond in feeling to the magnificent panoramas from which the eye cannot escape, is to be at once strong and wise mentally and physically, to have in the very blood and brain the beauty, glory and power of all that ever was or will be here on this earth.[124]

Read against the events of the novel and the insight that detachment takes a full belly, the omissions in the essay become eloquent. Here, only the aesthetic transformation of poverty yields the necessary detachment for Dreiser. In *Sister Carrie*, he also promotes an exchange between art and economics. The honesty in perception he called for in "True Art Speaks Plainly" correlates to the honest usage of money he demands in one of the philosophical passages in *Sister Carrie* (SC, p. 48). But since a moral economy does not exist in American society, honesty is restricted to the artistic subject. Dreiser writes: "The realm of all reality is the realm of the author's pen, and a true picture of life, honestly and reverentially set down, is both *moral* and *artistic* whether it offends the conventions or not."[125] The closeness to what Lucien Goldmann has called the homology of value in his study *Towards a Sociology of the Novel* is striking.[126] Value in *Sister Carrie* can only be defined as aesthetic practice and resides beyond the urban world depicted.

This aesthetic focus in Dreiser's city image further explains why economic and historical criticism of urban conditions are marginalized in *Sister Carrie*. Explaining a natural process, Dreiser defines Spencer's theories revealingly as "beautiful laws."[127] The inevitable and cruel path of society could best be mastered in aesthetic distance. Wealth and poverty become mentionable as the janus-faced sides of the same natural process. In his early essay "The City," Dreiser bluntly proposed such an aesthetic strategy: "There are shades of suffering innumerable as the countless tints of a roseate sky; grades of

---

[123]Kwiat, pp. 91-109; Fisher, p. 129.

[124]Theodore Dreiser, "The Beauty of Life," *The Color of a Great City*, New York, 1923, p. 170.

[125]Dreiser, "True Art Speaks Plainly," p. 129 (my italics).

[126]Lucien Goldmann, *Towards a Sociology of the Novel*, London, 1975.

[127]Elias, p. 90.

poverty as various as the hues of a changeful sea."[128] While the recorded action in *Sister Carrie* challenges any pure aestheticism, the strike of streetcar workers may yet create urban atmosphere and the breadline of the Bowery poor may be conceived of as urban scenery.[129] Without commentary, the poverty of the homeless is set against the city's "lightsome atmosphere" (SC, p. 343):

> At that hour, when Broadway is wont to assume its most interesting aspect, a peculiar individual invariably took his stand at the corner of Twenty-sixth Street and Broadway--a spot which is also intersected by Fifth Avenue. This was the hour when the theaters were just beginning to receive their patrons. Fire signs announcing the night's amusements blazed on every hand. Cabs and carriages, their lamps gleaming like yellow eyes, pattered by. . . . Across the way the great hotels showed a hundred gleaming windows, their cafés and billiard-rooms filled with a comfortable, well-dressed, and pleasure-loving throng. All about was the night, pulsating with the thoughts of pleasure and exhilaration--the curious enthusiasm of a great city bent upon finding joy in a thousand different ways. (SC, p. 342)

Juxtaposing the spectacle of a booming cityscape upon descriptions of misery, filth, or sexual desire, however, was a progressive step in a time when picturesque and genteel accounts deleted all reference to the brutal sides of everyday life in the working city. As F. O. Matthiesen has pointed out, sex and poverty were virtually nonexistent in popular fiction then.[130] Dreiser's positivist program to "get it all in," allows him to dismantle the falsified picture of conditions. However, since his portrait is restricted to mere aesthetic integrity, his superimposed idealization of art and beauty can easily be integrated into an idealist reversal of the novel's events. Accordingly, Dreiser's celebration of the immoral world of corporate capitalism and his mystified concept of beauty were reinterpreted as a humanist opposition to degrading and unjust *urban* ways of life. Dreiser's later explanation of aestheticism as the timeless "beauty of instability" was accepted as an Emersonian and idealist response.[131] Yet the naturalist record in *Sister Carrie* exactly dismantles the outdated myth of beauty as truth.

While Dreiser avoids to probe more deeply into the politics of a disengaged, 'objective' perception, the artistic ideal allows him to incorporate two distinct strands into the text, an affirmative and a critical one. The privilege of position is justified as a

---

[128]Dreiser, "The City," p. 99.

[129]This aesthetic detachment which is inchoately present in Dreiser's panoramas has been perpetuated as an upper- and middle-class attitude toward cityscapes. Jane Jacobs' critical and influential account in *The Death and Life of Great American Cities* in 1961, for instance, adopts a similar perspective and perceives the promise of lively neighborhoods in its "sidewalk ballet." Jane Jacobs, *The Death and Life of Great American Cities*, New York, 1961, p. 50. See also Jähner, pp. 233f.

[130]Matthiesen, pp. 79f.

[131]Dreiser, "The Beauty of Life," p. 168; Walcutt, pp. 180f.

superior, that is scientific perception: objectivity silences objection. Dreiser's attitude toward his former, ignorant self that he envisions in his female protagonist is full of condescending vocabulary. Throughout the beginning, Carrie Meeber is but a sentimental "little knight" (SC, p. 2), a "little soldier of fortune" (SC, p. 45) in a "little world" (SC, p. 39). The arrogance in authorial aloofness obviously is meant to hide insecurity. Professionalism which then emerged as a new mode of masculine dominance is employed to educate a female marionette.[132] Still, Dreiser may be called a "fellow traveller" in the female struggle against patriarchy through the freedom of choice and action he attributes to his protagonist.[133] Many upper- and middle-class women disliked Dreiser's antisentimental city for these reasons: for them domestic competence and security seemed the proper basis for emancipation.[134]

Most important, the honesty in perception allowed Dreiser to include a wide variety of urban facets and to record the unsmoothened surface of insecurity at the turn of the century.[135] Dreiser transcends nineteenth-century determinism in his novels by depicting the world in terms of chance and rule.[136] Carrie Meeber, George Hurstwood, or later Clyde Griffiths in *An American Tragedy* are never fully determined by circumstance but are also not free to choose. Dreiser may thus build a balanced novel with controlled architecture out of a world ruled by insecurity and chance. Probability and not certainty counts--his description in *Sister Carrie* points beyond determinism. Dreiser's artistic honesty allows his partial view to become authentic.

The text as a whole, however, reproduces the incongruities underlying Dreiser's ideology of the detached observer who cannot interfere with the course of natural developments. *Sister Carrie* is notorious for a stylistic awkwardness in which disparate codes mingle in the novel: bad writing, it can be shown, is related to an uneasiness in detachment rather than to artistic incapacity *per se*.[137] Stylistic incongruities appear on all levels of the novel. Sentences, sequences, and chapters mix incompatible styles and

---

[132] Howard, pp. 142-182.

[133] Susan Wolstenholme, "Brother Theodore, Hell on Women," *American Novelists Revisited: Essays in Feminist Criticism*, ed. Fritz Fleischmann, Boston, 1982, 243-64.

[134] Harper rejected Dreiser's manuscript arguing that female readers would not like the novel. Berkey et al., "Historical Commentary," pp. 519f; Wortman, pp. 531-72.

[135] Ford Maddox Ford regarded this as Dreiser's main achievement: ". . . it is because he renders for us this world of fantastic incertitude that Dreiser's work is of such importance." Ford Maddox Ford quoted in Gelfant, p. 58.

[136] Müller, p. 282.

[137] See also Petrey, p. 113.

genres. Thus the denigration of Hanson's work ethic, praised by Dreiser in magazine tales on success, recurs in the stylistic break between two sentences.

> "I'm after bread," was all he said as he passed.
> The contagion of thought here demonstrated itself. (SC, p. 39)

Recording surfaces is Dreiser's forte. The first sentence aptly translates monotony into the sentence rhythm and thus indicates the deficiency of a lifeless Hanson. Switching to omniscience, however, his voice falters and becomes vague and construed. The reason is obvious: the novelist Dreiser who opposed a belief in rewarded effort in Hanson's case hoped that his own literary efforts would be acknowledged. In another example, Dreiser distances his projection of the failed self in a gesture of rational control: Hurstwood is awkwardly belittled to "a fine example of great mental perturbation" (SC, p. 174).

The strike episode is similarly disrupted for Dreiser has to justify his disengagement and noninvolvement with scientific-political insights. The comic portrayal of policemen who have the evolutionary duty to punish workers but not the sympathy of the onlooker, creates tension within a predominantly documentary mode:

> Infuriated by this, the latter plunged left and right, laying about madly with his club. He was ably assisted by his brother of the blue, who poured ponderous oaths upon the troubled waters. No severe damage was done, owing to the agility of the strikers in keeping out of reach. They stood about the sidewalk now and jeered. (SC, p. 308f)

Distance here reappears as a jump to a different genre. The comic battles in Henry Fielding, one of Dreiser's favorite novelists, appropriately come to mind. They awkwardly clash with the documentary style in the rest of the chapter. The narrator tries to justify his distance as he alone knows the "true social significance" (SC, p. 300) of the event, but only with the description of the workers' victory in the final sentence, does he regain the stability of his naturalist diction.[138]

In general, the resulting awkwardness has dissatisfied both admirers and detractors of Dreiser. To understand the reason for the incongruities, the "aesthetic ideology"[139] of naturalism must be reintroduced to the novel and its portrait of a middle-class city in the 1890s. *Sister Carrie* appears complicated and muddled as Dreiser uses the sentimental code both to intentionally mark the rejection of an outdated middle-class moralism and when he idealizes his aesthetic stance. But beauty in Dreiser's consumer

---

[138] Naturalism's basic contradiction was, June Howard writes, that the reform impulse evident in the recording of social inequality and poverty is simultaneously questioned by its distancing of poverty. The artistic treatment means human assistance but at the same moment it denies involvement in social matters because of the claim to professional autonomy. Howard, pp. 142-82.

[139] Howard, p. 147.

city has either been reified or emptied. Thus, Bob Ames, his mouthpiece, who as an outsider remains ignorant of conditions in the city, or Carrie Meeber, who is noticeably more vague as the New York actress than as the lively consumer in the Chicago section, could only be flat as idealistic, inner-directed characters. All Dreiser could record, was a society in which desire undermines restraint and moderation as possibility. To be in tune with the developments Dreiser described, meant that paradigms from realist fiction had become invalid.

Immersed as Dreiser was in the vast upheavals of the 1890s, the promise of evolution fused with Bohemian aloofness seemed a walkable path to capture the new quality of the city. The transient wanted to incorporate acceptance and protest: Dreiser dreamt of success and felt that disadvantage was not an outcome of natural conditions. When the novel failed on the market and Dreiser's material safety was endangered, the dream of a pure artistic standpoint evaporated.[140]

Readings which took the superimposed ideals at face value, often inverted Dreiser's apt characterization of reified consumers to imply artistic failure, and thus failed to see the radical, contrary elements in *Sister Carrie*.[141] Such interpretations often quoted the later Dreiser to prove that he had rejected materialism already in his first novel. A vague concept of beauty, broadened to fit definitions in the various phases in Dreiser's oeuvre, pretended coherence where world view and fictional strategies had changed substantially.[142] Only later, for instance in *An American Tragedy*, did Dreiser adjust his fictional focus and examine the relation between morals and material conditions. This is not the case in *Sister Carrie*. Readings could not be convincing which saw Dreiser as a humanist novelist, regardless whether the interpretations were based on a formalist, idealist, or Marxist model.[143] Dreiser's blatant opportunism and immersion in the world of commodities in his early work does not match notions of the humanitarian critic or ascetic idealist.[144] In *Sister Carrie*, consuming defines being, while traditional morals are irrelevant.

In 1900, the novel posed a challenge in a time of momentous changes. The late reception among middle-class readers indicates the effrontery of Dreiser's radical view.

---

[140] Similar to the rocking motions of his protagonist, Dreiser, during his psychic breakdown, walked in circles. Robert Forrey, "Theodore Dreiser: Oedipus Revividus," *Modern Fiction Studies*, 23 (1977), p. 349.

[141] Gelfant, pp. 72, 92.

[142] The ideal could contain the aestheticism, nihilism, social engagement, and idealism of his various phases. See Walcutt, pp. 180-193.

[143] Poenicke, p. 115.

[144] Michaels, p. 377.

His libertarian critique was bowdlerized and attempts were made to restrict its effect.[145] Today, the critical aspects of the urban hedonism postulated by Dreiser has been blunted by the emergence of corporate-directed desire.[146] It is thus important to see the two contradictory sides in Dreiser's image of the early modern city. The inclusion of poverty and plight in contemporary fiction was a radical attempt to elevate the forms of perception to modern conditions. On the other hand, his purely aesthetic commitment was opportunistic and created incongruities. Its stance was soon affirmatively used by the corporate mass media which promoted an urban aestheticism to cover conflicts with glamorous facades. *Sister Carrie* dismantles smooth surfaces and records the pervasive insecurity of the 1890s. Then as today, the text contains a critical message in its gaps and ruptures. *Sister Carrie* records the labor neglected in views which treat the city solely as an aesthetic spectacle and amusing playground for consumers.

---

[145] Matthiesen, pp. 61ff; Berkey and Winters, "Historical Commentary," pp. 501-41.

[146] See Stuart Ewen, *Captains of Consciousness: Advertising and the Social Roots of Consumer Culture*, New York, 1976.

9

Upton Sinclair
The Jungle

1. Revolution and the City

With unequalled intensity, Upton Sinclair's "story of Chicago" projects the early modern city as it existed for American working-class families.[1] The industrial factory, represented by the stockyard meat-packing companies, is the center of the novel and of working-class life. *The Jungle* shows the modern industrial world without embellishment: a degrading and alienating mode of production dominates people both on the assembly line and at home. Whether American, Irish, German, Bohemian, Polish, Slovak, or Lithuanian, whether black or white, these working-class families toil day for day but receive too little money to live a humane existence. Outside the factory, no respite or homey refuge exists for them. Chicago, which claimed to be an "urbs in horto,"[2] a city in a garden, offers for its working people only the foul water of "Bubbly Creek," the contaminated soil of former dumping grounds, and the unsanitary conditions of shack housings. Industrial capitalism ruthlessly devastates the environment, animals, and human beings. In contradistinction to its technological progress, it has lowered modern culture to a state where beasts prey on beasts in an economic wilderness.

---

[1] Upton Sinclair subtitled the novel as "A Story of Chicago" in its first serial appearance in the Socialist newspaper *Appeal to Reason* (Upton Sinclair, *The Jungle, Appeal to Reason*, (February 11, 1905), p. 1). Here, the Doubleday, Page book edition of 1906 will be used which directed the reception of the novel (Upton Sinclair, *The Jungle*, 1906, New York, 1960. References to *The Jungle* will be abbreviated to TJ and incorporated into the text). In 1988, Gene DeGruson edited a new, compiled version of the longer serial novel as it was originally published in the *Appeal to Reason* and the *One Hoss Philosophy*. The version in the *Appeal to Reason* ended with the book chapter 28. The final chapters only appeared in the *One Hoss Philosophy* and were strongly cut and revised for the Doubleday, Page edition. For a discussion of the textual history see Michael Brewster Folsom, "Upton Sinclair's Escape from *The Jungle*: The Narrative Strategy and Suppressed Conclusion of America's First Proletarian Novel," *Prospects*, 4 (1979), 237-66. Gene DeGruson, "Introduction," Upton Sinclair, *The Jungle*, ed. Gene DeGruson, Memphis, Tenn., 1988, xiii-xxxi.

[2] Glaab and Brown, p. 262.

The hope for a revolution pervasively shapes the city image in *The Jungle*. Here, the metropolis and the modern idea of revolution are interrelated. For Sinclair, Socialism with its intention of bringing about individual freedom through collective self-determination, becomes the *sine qua non* for a dignified urban existence. This hope for change is transformed into the literary strategy of the novel. Although in a somewhat crude manner, *The Jungle* suggests a politicizing of form which Walter Benjamin later demanded of modern art in general.[3] This inference to Benjamin need not be surprising as Sinclair's novel impressed Bertolt Brecht and influenced his political theater.[4] But while Sinclair links the literary strategy to political concerns, it is still a long way away from the formal experiments of Brecht's epic drama. On the contrary, the "proletarian"[5] novel unthinkingly perpetuates literary clichés and various chauvinistic expressions hoping to reach a wide readership. Sinclair reproduces popular forms in his conviction that "great art has always been popular art, and great artists have swayed the people."[6]

Sinclair primarily expands the subject matter and function of the modern novel. Formal innovations seem secondary since for him art and literature are determined by the material base of society. Around the time that *The Jungle* was composed, Sinclair argued in the essay "Our Bourgeois Literature--The Reason and the Remedy":

> The point is that we have now a system of society which makes wage-slaves of the vast mass of humanity, and shuts them out forever from all hope of sharing in civilization, progress, and light; and the failure of all our efforts at reform, of all our dreams of joy and beauty, is simply the justice of Nature, the vengeance of this downtrodden class. . . . There can be among us neither political virtue, nor social refinement, nor true religion, nor vital art, so long as men, women, and little children are chained up to toil for us in mines and sweatshops, are penned in filthy slums, and fed upon offal, and doomed to rot and perish in soul-sickening misery and horror.[7]

As a result of such a determinism, *The Jungle* moves from urban fiction to political agitation and climaxes with the hopeful slogan of the 1904 election, when Socialists succeeded in the stockyards: "CHICAGO WILL BE OURS!" (TJ, p. 341). In a genuine response, which soon became a stale pattern in proletarian fiction,[8] the transformation

---

[3] Walter Benjamin, *Das Kunstwerk im Zeitalter seiner technischen Reproduzierbarkeit*, 1936, Frankfurt, 1963, p. 44.

[4] Leon Harris, *Upton Sinclair: Amercian Rebel*, New York, 1975, p. 84. Dieter Herms, *Upton Sinclair, ein amerikanischer Radikaler. Eine Einführung in Leben und Werk*, Frankfurt, 1978, p. 42.

[5] Upton Sinclair, "What Life Means to Me," *Cosmopolitan*, 41 (1906), p. 594.

[6] Upton Sinclair, *Mammonart*, Pasadena, Cal., 1925, p. 9.

[7] Upton Sinclair, "Our Bourgeois Literature--The Reason and the Remedy," *Collier's*, 34 (October 8, 1904), pp. 24f.

[8] Fine, *The City, The Immigrant, and American Fiction*, p. 75.

of the Lithuanian peasant to the American comrade Jurgis Rudkus was meant to lead to further conversions in the urban working class and to strengthen the Socialist movement.

Though the aesthetic concept may have been appropriate to rouse indignation among readers, the literary strategy generates a blatant incongruity in the description of the working class in *The Jungle*. As the revolutionary plot unfolds, the novel marginalizes the ethnicity which was passionately celebrated in the opening *veselija*.[9] For Upton Sinclair, immigrant culture seemed outmoded. Omitting ethnic bonds and partisanship, his conversion plot posits an assimilated worker who cuts his ties to Lithuanian culture and overcomes the racial dissent of the stockyard mosaic. In maturing politically, Jurgis Rudkus degenerates to the pale pupil of Socialist lectures, while the underlying conflict between emancipation and paternalism leads to a modification of the revolutionary momentum. Sinclair, who directs his immigrants in omniscient propriety from the beginning, has forgotten their capacity for rebellion by the time he reaches the last chapters. The modern city novel, which was to revolutionize Chicago, closes with a genteel, preaching voice.

2. The Stockyard Paradigm

The continuing power of *The Jungle* results from its paradigmatic analysis of industrial working-class experience.[10] The object which Sinclair chose for his scrutiny of the contradictions and disruption in monopoly capitalism was indeed exemplary. After consolidating a number of small firms in 1865, Chicago's Union Stock Yards had expanded under railroad leadership to become one of the largest U.S. corporations by the turn of the century. An ingeniously efficient division of labor which broke slaughtering into small steps left workers only with unskilled, monotonous, and alienating tasks.[11] Because of this lowering of skills, workers could be replaced at any time and became an exchangeable part of the industrial machine. In this way, the stockyards advanced to become the largest employer in Chicago, the "total urban-industrial landscape."[12]

---

[9] Heinz Ickstadt, "Exploring the Abyss: Die Entdeckung des sozialen Untergrunds in der amerikanischen Fiktion des späten neunzehnten Jahrhunderts," *Amerikanische Ghettoliteratur: Zur Literatur ethnischer, marginaler und unterdrückter Gruppen in Amerika*, ed. Berndt Ostendorf, Darmstadt, 1983, pp. 48f.

[10] Robert Allen Slayton, *Back of the Yards: the Making of a Local Democracy*, Chicago, 1986, pp. 12f.

[11] Barrett, p. xv.

[12] Warner, p. 104; Cutler, p. 76.

The Jungle presents the major forces which then fuelled American urbanization and which within a single generation turned Chicago from a manufacturing city into a major industrial metropolis. Capitalist production led to the concentration of economic power. From 1897 to 1905, 318 corporations swallowed over 5300 industrial firms in the United States. Parallel to this development, Chicago's Beef Trust manufactured $256 million worth of products by the turn of the century, that is more than the next six meat-packing centers combined.[13] Over three million cattle and six million hogs passed through the pens of the Chicago stockyards by 1910.[14] As Chicago's largest industrial complex with almost 30,000 employees, the stockyards affected the lives of several hundred thousand people. At the turn of the century, the Pullman settlement and the Back of the Yards neighborhood evidenced the altered quality of working-class dependence. The gigantic industrial plants moved to outlying zones of the city and with them went families, boarders, and workers who had little choice but to adapt to whatever labor conditions demanded. Such huge agglomerations around factories can well be called cities in themselves (TJ, p. 203).

The packers dominated the working-class city for they controlled its employment and wages. In 1900, Charles C. Bushnell reported that the average male worker was severely underpaid receiving between 9 and 27 cents per hour. Annual incomes were even lower because employees could be laid off whenever packers wanted; on the average, unskilled workers lost about two months work per year.[15] Official figures indicate that in 1914 stockyard jobs still only paid 35 to 49 percent of the amount that the Department of Labor considered to be the minimum for existence and beneath which a family could not go without the "danger of physical and moral deterioration."[16] Women, who made up more than one tenth of the stockyard work force, were paid even less. In addition to low pay, lay-offs, and slack time, working conditions were so dangerous that disease and injury abounded. At Armour, one of the major companies, half of the employees were injured or ill at work within one year. Yet illnesses due to accidents were rarely compensated.[17]

Exploitation continued beyond the factories and was evident in the degenerating working-class quarters of Back of the Yards. Here, Bubbly Creek, a branch of the South

---

[13] Dowd, *The Twisted Dream*, pp. 70ff; Slayton, p. 11.
[14] Mayer, p. 213.
[15] Slayton, pp. 10, 89.
[16] Ibid., p. 90.
[17] Ibid., pp. 82, 91.

River, was so contaminated that it caught fire several times.[18] Rancid stench and industrial pollution seeped into every crack and fissure. Such unsanitary conditions in conjunction with malnourishment made working-class people five to ten times more prone to illnesses such as bronchitis or diphteria than Chicago's upper- and middle-class residents. One out of three children died before the age of two--seven times more than in Chicago's affluent areas.[19]

The strains of keeping a job to ensure the minimum of livelihood were immense. Two-thirds of the workforce in the stockyards consisted of unskilled laborers earning only minimal wages. Since jobs were steadily reduced in requirements, most of the unskilled workers could be easily replaced. Demands for improved labor conditions could always be answered with the threat of hiring new immigrants or black workers from the South who were willing to start work for the same or even less. Chicago companies aggressively advertised in European countries and arriving immigrants were pitted against those who had accumulated profits and machines through their work. By 1900, three out of four Chicagoans were immigrants.

Working-class sections like Back of the Yards thus consisted of a mosaic of segregated ethnic groups. While employers promoted dissent among these diverse groups to divide the work force,[20] within the neighborhoods tight ethnic cohesion and solidarity aided accommodation to the otherwise unbearable conditions. Saloons, clubs, and churches created social networks and pragmatically assisted their members. Moreover, such ethnic and class institutions helped to retain a collective identity. As members, immigrants opposed attempts at Americanization and domination by middle-class standards of behavior and propriety.[21]

Saloons, alcohol, and drinking became vicarious issues for general conflicts of class and nationality. Workers who identified with neighborhood saloons, defended them as cultural and political institutions, whereas anti-saloon forces in the middle and upper class saw them as centers of vice, crime, and political opposition. Yet the division was not as simple as the traditional dichotomy of upper- and middle-class prohibitionists and working-class sympathizers might suggest. True, many saloon-keepers helped their

---

[18] James R. Barrett, "Introduction and Notes," *The Jungle*, ed. James R. Barrett, Urbana, Ill., 1988, p. 341. Sinclair also reports such fires in the novel (TJ, p. 97).

[19] Barrett, p. xvii. See also James R. Barrett, *Work and Community in the Jungle: Chicago's Packinghouse Workers, 1894-1922*, Urbana, Ill., 1987.

[20] Robert Slayton concludes: "Within the community, the packer's role was all-encompassing. . . . Packers also used the workplace to manipulate the social structure, fostering national and occupational segregation and blocking attempts at unity which might be turned against them." Slayton, p. 12.

[21] Ickstadt, "Black vs. White City," pp. 204, 212.

working-class customers by providing a place to organize politically. As Sidney Harring has shown, however, business and municipal interests also opposed restrictions on saloons. In the 1890s, liquor accounted for almost nine percent of all value manufactured and paid one tenth of Chicago's budget through high license fees. Besides, saloon-keepers were influential in machine politics and often protected through alliances with patrolling officers.[22] Thus, the anti-saloon faction in the upper and middle class could only impose restrictions on the unruly workers, the least powerful in the conflict. For disorderly conduct alone, over three hundred thousand workers were disciplined and detained by the Chicago police from 1901 to 1908.[23] This effective policing of the alien and supposedly criminal mob found support both among moral reformers and businessmen who for good reasons preferred a pacified work force. Above all, valuable jobs in the factory functioned as the best instance of control guaranteeing working-class submission. For workers and their families, days in jail could mean the collapse of the week-to-week security.[24]

The impact of *The Jungle* in 1906 can easily be explained: the novel presented a virtually unknown Chicago to the public. Previous accounts of the stockyards and of working-class life had ignored, suppressed, or stereotyped the conditions of immigrant families at work and at home. The saloon question dominated discussions. As political decisions loomed, The *Chicago Tribune*, one of the city's great dailies which was favorable to big business, ran front-page news about workers' violence, vice, and crime in saloons and argued for stricter control of these places.[25] When the *Tribune* took notice of *The Jungle*--after its managing editor had been involved in an unsuccessful attempt to denigrate Sinclair's findings--, the paper accused Upton Sinclair of making "fiction a cloak for calumny" and remained persistently negative about stockyards revelations.[26] Such unjustified imputations about the political "propagandist" have continued to cast doubt on the veracity of the record in *The Jungle*. Recent studies by

---

[22]Forty-two large breweries held three-quarters of all licenses for the eight thousand saloons in Chicago. Harring, *Policing A Class Society*, pp. 155ff, 165.

[23]Ibid., p. 172.

[24]Sidney Harring argues that working-class activities were well controlled: "An officer, then as today, dealt with situations almost entirely by personal discretion. Hence, the impact of the police on working-class communities and recreational activities was greater than the arrest data might suggest. The arrest power was a coercive weapon held in reserve." Harring, p. 199.

[25]Harring, p. 163.

[26]Harris, p. 81. Christine Scriabine, "Upton Sinclair and the Writing of *The Jungle*," *Chicago History*, 10 (1981), pp. 30, 33f.

172 Fragmented Urban Images

James R. Barrett and Robert Slayton have indicated, however, that Sinclair's facts were accurate.[27]

In 1906, the novel prevailed against the denunciatory campaigns of the Beef Trust.[28] Sinclair's story, which had already reached some 300,000 subscribers in the *Appeal to Reason*,[29] became one of the most influential and widely read novels in the twentieth century. Sinclair called attention to working-class plight and boosted support for a booming Socialist movement. The optimism in *The Jungle* about radical political changes, which may appear exaggerated to contemporary readers, was well justified then.[30] But the novel did not lead to the revolutionary changes for which it was agitating. Moreover, Sinclair had not intended its major political effect: Theodore Roosevelt passed a Pure Food and Meat Inspection Act in response to consumer protest.[31] Contrary to public outrage over spoiled food, the novelist argued that those who bought meat produced under such inhuman conditions deserved "all the poisoning" they received.[32]

For the immigrant families of the stockyards hardly anything changed. Many workers even resented Sinclair's meddling since one of the first measures compelled them to buy new outfits for work. A follow-up campaign in the stockyards in 1907 which intended to demonstrate that indeed little had been altered was successfully ignored. Two decades later, Sinclair concluded in *American Outpost*:

> I am supposed to have helped clean up the yards and improve the country's meat supply-- though this is mostly delusion. But nobody even pretends to believe that I improved the

---

[27]See Barrett, pp. xiii, xvii, xix; Slayton, p. 3-13. James R. Barrett concludes: "Amazing as they seem, then, Sinclair's descriptions of the physical conditions of daily life in the neighborhood are firmly grounded" (Barrett, p. xix). The denigration of the book continues to date. Quoting both Barrett and Slayton as evidence, Louise Carroll Wade has recently implied that the record indeed was inaccurate and that the reputation of the stockyard community "was stained by Upton Sinclair's unflattering portrait in *The Jungle* (1906)." Louise Carroll Wade, *Chicago's Pride: the Stockyards, Packingtown, and Environs in the Nineteenth Century*, Urbana, Ill., 1987, p. xi.

[28]In the beginning, the power of the Beef Trust was almost invincible. They nearly prevented the novel's publication through false accusations and testimonies. Scriabine, pp. 30ff. In 1914, the film version of *The Jungle* was banned in Chicago. Eric Homberger, *American Writers and Radical Politics, 1900-1939*, New York, 1987, p. 54.

[29]Folsom, "Upton Sinclair's Escape from *The Jungle*," p. 246.

[30]In their peak year in 1912, Socialists polled over a million votes and more than one thousand Socialists represented workers in city halls and parliaments. Barrett, p. 349.

[31]The meat-packing industry used the decision to its advantage and warned against the danger of the non-inspected meat of foreign competitors. In addition, Beef Trust practices soon rendered the new laws meaningless. Homberger, pp. 42f, 53f; Howard, p. 159.

[32]Sinclair, "What Life Means to Me," p. 592.

conditions of the stockyard workers. They have no unions to speak of, and their wages are, in relation to the cost of living, every bit as low as they were twenty-eight years ago.[33]

3. The Modern Working-Class City

The industrial factory dominates city life in *The Jungle*. The novel depicts the pervasive influence of capitalist production and the distinct experiences of the urban working-class. As it demonstrates, industrial capitalism affects working-class lives at work and at home; it infringes upon their freedom and pastime, limits their skills and traditions, and debases their housing and surrounding. Upper- and middle-class Chicago with its skyscrapers, theaters, and parks, the disruptions of social and residential transience which had dominated Theodore Dreiser's city image in *Sister Carrie*, only marginally affect the mental maps of working-class immigrants on the industrial fringe. The loop, which then represented the modern, progressive Chicago, stands in contrast to the life of working-class characters in *The Jungle*. This other Chicago is beyond their reach: "Four or five miles to the east of them lay the blue waters of Lake Michigan, but for all the good it did them it might have been as far away as the Pacific Ocean" (TJ, p. 105).

In keeping with the political strategy of the novel, the urban experience depicted, however, exceeds the limitations that might be expected from a naturalist portrait of Chicago's "slum districts" (TJ, p. 174). Sinclair uses an omniscient narrator to present a diversity of urban experience.[34] He empathetically records the restricted view of the Packingtown characters in the manner of a participant observer, but also extends the ethnic city beyond its constricted topography. The picaresque Chicago in the second part incorporates wider issues and dependencies which infringed upon local communities and which indirectly sustained the stockyards' exploitive system. With Jurgis Rudkus in the role of an urban tramp, readers learn more about "perfect spider-web[s] beneath the city" (TJ, p. 221). In addition, the omniscient narrator is used to demonstrate the wider ramifications of the economic and political determination of working-class neighborhoods.

A unification of urban experience in *The Jungle* is achieved through the working relations in the industrial factory. Capitalist exploitation drains the energy of all

---

[33] Upton Sinclair, *American Outpost: A Book of Reminiscences*, New York, 1932, pp. 175f.
[34] R. N. Mookerjee, *Art for Social Justice: The Major Novels of Upton Sinclair*, Metuchen, N.J., 1988, p. 52.

characters; it destroys family, friendship, and community and produces a floating proletariat of boarders, hobos, and tramps. Low wages, long working hours, physically devastating labor, illness, and injuries affect men, women, and children. The old and "worn-out parts of the great merciless packing machine" (TJ, p. 126) are replaced without resentment (TJ, p. 48); the young who cannot partake of the free education in municipal schools are subdued by Taylorist working routines. For little Stanislovas, who has to quit school to help the family survive, bleak monotony seems predetermined:

> Hour after hour, day after day, year after year, it was fated that he should stand upon a certain square foot of floor from seven in the morning until noon, and again from half-past twelve till half-past five, making never a motion and thinking never a thought, save for the setting of lard cans. (TJ, pp. 75f)

In analogy to the vast differences in the segregated city, contrast becomes the pervasive principle indicating the degradations of working-class life. The discrepancy between ideals and reality reveals flaws of American society. The early chapters of *The Jungle* forcefully indicate that traditional attitudes are incompatible with industrial conditions. Thus Jurgis Rudkus who is seen as a representative of the Protestant work ethic, merely repeats his phrase "I will work harder" (TJ, p. 22) as an answer to stockyard injustice, corruption, and exploitation. As the story demonstrates, however, toiling more is simply not enough in twentieth-century Chicago. The vagaries of capitalist production exceed and destroy the perseverance of even the fittest individual.

In addition, the novel indicates that saving, planning, and a general orientation toward future goals as the Protestant ethic would demand are incompatible with stockyard reality.[35] Slack time, seasonal work, lay-offs, unemployment, and uncompensated injuries render each day a day of material hardship and insecurity. Urban life is shaped by the unforseeable vagaries of such a present-oriented existence. All, except the very little and the very old, have to fight for survival with physically wasting and mentally stupefying work.

Sinclair confronts American ideals with actual conditions among working-class immigrants.[36] Jurgis Rudkus, whose pursuit of happiness stresses the happiness through work and who initially takes pride in being part of the great stockyards companies, comes to hate work, like all other employees (TJ, p. 46). His unwillingness to lose a day at work makes him lose months with an injured ankle and results in the near starvation of his family (TJ, pp. 120f). In contrast to conventional visions of happy childhood and

---

[35] Jon A. Yoder, *Upton Sinclair*, New York, 1975, p. 31.

[36] Jack London stressed this aspect in his 1906 preface to *The Jungle*. Jack London, "The Jungle," *Jack London, American Rebel*, ed. Philip S. Foner, New York, 1947, p. 519.

sheltered adolescence, Nikalojus and Vilimas, age ten and eleven, have to leave school and earn their living by selling newspapers (TJ, p. 123). In contradistinction to the upper- and middle-class ideals of true womanhood, female workers have to toil in the factory. Marriage becomes impossible under such conditions. Marija Berczynskas' plans to marry Tamoszius Kuszleika are thwarted by material needs; she has to contribute her savings for daily expenditures so that the family may overcome yet another financial crisis. Eventually, even though all of them work, the Lithuanian immigrants cannot afford a "Home, Sweet Home" (TJ, p. 49).

Sinclair compresses their experience to present the outcome of their American dream as a "nightmare" (TJ, p. 210). Virtually robbed of a promising material future, an aspiration which had dominated all nineteenth-century city novels, his working-class urbanites lose hope and with it the perseverance to sustain the daily struggle:

> They were beaten; they had lost the game, they were swept aside. It was not less tragic because it was so sordid, because that it had to do with wages and grocery billy and rents. They had dreamed about freedom; of a chance to look about them and learn something; to be decent and clean, to see their children grow up to be strong. And now it was all gone--it would never be! They had played the game and they had lost. Six years more of toil they had to face before they could expect the least respite, the cessation of the payments upon the house; and how cruelly certain it was that they could never stand six years of such a life they were living! (TJ, p. 138)

In *The Jungle*, capitalist exploitation extends beyond the factory to the private sphere of the working class and reveals the crucial interdependence of work and home. The shacks cannot serve as a refuge from the stockyards but are a part of the grotesque cityscape. The monotony of work is extended in the endless rows of dire shacks.

> Down every street they could see, it was the same--never a hill and never a hollow, but always the same endless vista of ugly and dirty little wooden buildings. Here and there would be a bridge crossing a filthy creek, with hard-baked mud shores and dingy sheds and docks and along it; here and there would be a railroad crossing, with a tangle of switches, and locomotives puffing, and rattling freight cars filing by; here and there would be a great factory, a dingy building with innumerable windows in it, and immense volumes of smoke pouring from the chimneys, darkening the air above and making flithy the earth beneath. But after each of these interruptions, the desolate procession would begin again--the procession of dreary little buildings. (TJ, p. 29)

Unable to choose housing freely within the city, working-class families are limited by their income and have to live in the polluted vicinity of the industrial factory. Soil, water, and air are contaminated and bear the marks of a ruthless, profit-oriented economy. The degenerate environment is the first impression received by the newcomers to the Middle West:

> A full hour before the party reached the city they had begun to note the perplexing changes in the atmosphere. It grew darker all the time, and upon the earth the grass seemed to grow less green. Every minute as the train sped on, the colors of things became dingier; the fields were grown parched and yellow, the landscape hideous and bare. And along with the thickening smoke they began to notice another circumstance, a strange, pungent odor. (TJ, p. 29)

In these dire surroundings, little Antanas has "all the diseases that babies" (TJ, p. 140) may be infected with and eventually drowns in a mudpool off the sidewalk (TJ, p. 209). Sinclair conceives of the Packingtown suburb as an anti-model to the "urbs in horto," to Chicago's official motto of civic affluence which promoted an urban pastoralism of upper- and middle-class boulevards, parks, and architecture.

However, as deteriorated as the surrounding may have become under stockyard and real-estate policies, these immigrants do not propagate a movement "back to nature," an ideology which then was widespread in upper-class suburbs. Sinclair's immigrants have only recently fled the oppression in the countryside. Moreover, they have never been sheltered enough from nature's hardships to romanticize it. Seasonal change implies plight for them:

> When the springtime came, they were delivered from the dreadful cold, and that was a great deal; but . . . warm weather brought trials of its own; each season had its trials, as they found. In the spring there were cold rains, that turned the streets into canals and bogs; the mud would be so deep that wagons would sink up to the hubs, so that half a dozen horses could not move them. Then, of course, it was impossible for anyone to get to work with dry feet, and this was bad for men that were poorly clad and shod, and still worse for women and children. Later came midsummer, with the stifling heat, when the dingy killing beds of Durham's became a very purgatory; one time, in a single day, three men fell dead from sunstroke. All day long the rivers of blood poured forth, until with the sun beating down, and the air motionless, the stench was enough to knock a man over; all the old smells of a generation would be drawn out by this heat--for there was never any washing of the walls and rafters and pillars, and they were caked with the filth of a lifetime. (TJ, p. 104)

Basically, Sinclair appreciates industrial work and does not propose a withdrawal to natural, rural forms of life to overcome inhuman modes of production and ownership.[37] Sinclair's overriding hope is a new social collectivity in the metropolis. Having built these cities, people can rebuild them. Not naturalist gloom and urban fatalism, but active opposition to man-made suppression and exploitation is the answer given in *The Jungle*.[38]

---

[37]Michael Brewster Folsom, "The Unredeemed Landscape: Industrial America in the Imagination of Whittier, Bellamy, and Sinclair," *Essays from the Lowell Conference on Industrial History 1982 & 1983*, ed. Robert Weible, North Andover, Mass., 1984, p. 73.

[38]Yoder, p. 32; Mookerjee, p. 42.

Sinclair's view of a hopeful urban future, however, denies the immigrants' roots in traditional culture. He marginalizes powerful bonds in the ethnic neighborhoods. Each group in the stockyards, as Robert Slayton has observed, maintained its ethnic culture and native folklore.[39] For Sinclair, such inadequate behavior belonged to the past and would inevitably be overcome in the new industrial society. He shows the positive sides of ethnic culture for a last time in the wedding celebration of *The Jungle* and expresses its anachronism through the a-chronological placement in the novel.[40]

The marginalization of the distinct forms of ethnic subculture and resistance in saloons, clubs, or neighborhood churches springs from a denigrating view of ethnic culture. Certainly Sinclair, who was intent to move his audience, vests Jurgis with an "innately American identity" to by-pass racial stereotypes and to present Socialism as something quintessentially American in its espousal of justice, equality, and freedom.[41] Clearly, for him, Socialists are not "enemies of American institutions" (TJ, p. 256). On the other hand, as Sinclair Americanizes and educates his foreign workers, he completely dominates them in his guidance toward superior bourgeois norms. Although Sinclair understands the plight of his working-class characters, he disapproves of their distinct modes for coping with capitalism.[42] Sinclair's genteel position directs his analysis: alcohol is devilish, the saloon a festering boil of vice, and sexuality reduces humans to wild beasts (TJ, p. 217).

Sinclair's modeling of workers according to his ideals is evident on several levels in the novel. Thus the bonds in the "myriad of villages" (TJ, p. 88) are narrowed to links of an isolated middle-class family. Ties beyond the home, so important in the resistance to packers in Back of the Yards, are virtually nonexistent in *The Jungle*. The many Lithuanian friends who peopled the *veselija* vanish. The Rudkus home might as well be built in a Lithuanian "wilderness" (TJ, p. 26) for as much as we hear from their neighbors. Sinclair's record of working-class life at times contradicts such omissions.[43] When Jurgis Rudkus tells Madame Haupt about the family's financial distress and why he cannot pay more to save his wife, the immigrant midwife poses the very question which cannot be answered by Sinclair's isolated Lithuanians: "Vere is your friends, dat ought to help you?" (TJ, p. 182).

---

[39] Slayton, p. 24.

[40] Ickstadt, "Exploring the Abyss," p. 48.

[41] Guy A. Szuberla, "Dom, Namai, Heim: Images of the New Immigrant's Home," *Prospects*, 10 (1985), p. 147. Yoder, pp. 47f.

[42] William A. Bloodworth, *Upton Sinclair*, Boston, 1977, pp. 60ff.

[43] Upton Sinclair, "Is '*The Jungle*' True?" *Independent*, 40 (1906), 1129-33.

4. Visions of a Collective Chicago

The idea of a Socialist revolution carries the hope for change in the capitalist "sore of a city" (TJ, p. 33). Not the withdrawal to suburbia, the countryside, or the West, but only self-determination through collective ownership is suggested as a solution for these urbanites. The title of the novel, often misread as a metaphor for a generically chaotic and barbaric city,[44] signifies the capitalist jungle which reduced human beings to helpless and hence wild animals.[45] When Sinclair discovered Socialism, he saw that he "was no longer obliged to think of civilization as a place where wild beasts fought and tore one another without purpose and without end."[46] Mutual political action will bring the fulfillment of hopes that the stockyards destroy for Jurgis Rudkus and Ona Lukoszaite step by step. From the beginning, their working-class city signifies the achievement of happiness through work:

> Jurgis and Ona were not thinking of the sunset, however--their backs were turned to it, and all their thoughts were of Packingtown, which they could see so plainly in the distance. The line of the buildings stood clear-cut and black against the sky; here and there out of the mass rose the great chimneys, with the river of smoke streaming away to the end of the world. It was a study in colors now, this smoke; in the sunset light it was black and brown and gray and purple. All the sordid suggestions of the place were gone--in the twilight it was vision of power. To the two who stood watching while the darkness swallowed it up, it seemed a dream of wonder, with its tale of human energy, of things being done, of employment for thousands upon thousands of men, of opportunity and freedom, of life and love and joy. When they came away, arm in arm, Jurgis was saying, "Tomorrow I shall go there and get a job!" (TJ, p. 34)

As in Theodore Dreiser's *Sister Carrie*, Chicago stands for the future. For Sinclair, however, Chicago signifies the collective future of liberated working people. Despite its present degeneration, the modern city functions as the symbol for culture, progress, and hope. The countryside as conventional antipode of progress is identified with an irrecoverable and dated stage of development.

In contrast to current patterns in popular city novels and to the suburban ideology of the upper and middle class, the countryside does not offer a viable solution to social and moral questions in *The Jungle*. The rural refuge solely represents a temporary and restrictively individualistic freedom for tramps, but does not hold a valid panacea for urban problems. Contrary to views in the upper and middle class, as for instance Henry Ford's, who claimed that the problems of cities would be solved by

---

[44] See Göbel, p. 96; Oates, p. 13.

[45] Ickstadt, p. 48.

[46] Sinclair, "What Life Means to Me," p. 592.

leaving them, Upton Sinclair asserts that the basic questions for laboring people are economic ones and that they have to be solved in the city and in the country.[47] Moreover, nature does not even offer a refuge for the individual: Jurgis returns to Chicago in winter as he does not see a chance of survival in the countryside (TJ, p. 219). While Sinclair sees a general necessity for healthier forms of life--a desire which would make Sinclair found the communitarian Helicon Hall in 1906[48]--the countryside stands in opposition to emancipation and enlightenment in *The Jungle*. As comrade Dr. Schliemann explains, the farmer is a "stunted, haggard, ignorant man" who scratches the soil with primitive tools and is "shut out from all knowledge and all hope, from all the benefits of science and invention" (TJ, p. 337).

Sinclair generally welcomes the city and the industrial factory. His next book would envisage the machine-based future of *The Industrial Republic*.[49] Despite his scathing attacks on exploitation, Sinclair approves of the latest accomplishments in industrial technology. Cattle butchering in the yards is praised as "applied mathematics" (TJ, p. 39). Jurgis Rudkus admires the speed and efficiency of machines as a "wonderful poem" (TJ, p. 41). In contrast to the nightmarish surface, Sinclair's account of the industrial city in 1905 is optimistic. He trusts human agency without qualification and is convinced of its eventual triumph. Sinclair ascertains in 1904 that a "mighty revolution . . . is gathering its forces, far down in the underworld of the poor."[50]

Fascinated and disgusted by what he had seen in the stockyards, Sinclair is most successful in translating working conditions into the prose of *The Jungle*. The alienating monotony and the inhuman pace are expressed in fragmented and mostly paratactical sentences and conveyed by use of parallelism, anaphora, alliteration, and assonance:

> One scraped the outside of a leg; another scraped the inside of the same leg. One with a swift stroke cut the throat; another with two swift strokes severed the head, which fell to the floor and vanished through a hole. Another made a slit down the body; a second opened the body wider; a third with a saw cut the breastbone; a fourth loosened the entrails; a fifth pulled them out--and they also slid through a hole in the floor. There were men to scrape each side and men to scrape the back; there were men to clean the carcass inside, to trim it and wash it. (TJ, p. 41)

The pace of the prose is determined by the number of different activities and the speed of the workers. Words are repeated and handed down the rhythmically structured

---

[47]Henry Ford, *Ford Ideals: Being a Selection from 'Mr. Ford's Page' in the Dearborn Independent*, Dearborn, Mich., 1922, p. 425.

[48]Harris, pp. 93ff.

[49]Folsom, p. 242. Upton Sinclair, *The Industrial Republic*, New York, 1907.

[50]Sinclair, "Our Bourgeois Literature," p. 24.

sentences as the pieces of meat in the assembly line. The consequent repetition of words--"each," "cuts," "swift," "floor," "work"--assists the impression of accelerated motion:

> They worked with furious intensity, literally upon the run. . . . It was all highly specialized labor, each man having his task to do; generally this would consist of only two or three specific cuts, and he would pass down the line of fifteen or twenty carcasses, making these cuts upon each: First there came the "butcher," to bleed them; this meant one swift stroke, so swift that you could not see it--only the flash of the knife; and before you could realize it, the man had darted on to the next line, and a stream of bright red was pouring out upon the floor. This floor was half an inch deep with blood, in spite of the best efforts of men who kept shoveling it through holes; it must have made the floor slippery, but no one could have guessed this by watching the men at work. (TJ, p. 43)

The innovative power lies in the approving and fresh mode in which the author presents industrial work. Sinclair follows Walt Whitman, whom he considered a Socialist forerunner in poetry,[51] in his focus on the ubiquitous, industrial, ugly, and unpoetical. A democratic inclusiveness in *The Jungle* assigns to previously unacknowledged labor the respect it deserves. The fascinating speed and efficiency of the industrial city are also expressed by the form of the narrative. While the summary narrative which Sinclair preferred in general cannot adequately convey the immediacy of scenic action, it congenially captures the pace of working-class life in the novel. Resuming the epic scope of Whitmanesque catalogues, *The Jungle* heaps industrial detail upon detail, motif upon motif, and event upon event.

The theme of revolution strongly shapes Sinclair's image of the city. The form of the novel incorporates the emancipatory momentum which is attributed to the city. Sinclair uses a dual strategy. He rouses indignation hoping to move readers politically and he also indicates the direction for change. In an explanation of his plans in the *Appeal to Reason* in 1905, Sinclair remarks:

> I have in *The Jungle* not merely to set forth a tragedy, but to drive home to the dullest reader the truth that this tragedy is, in its every detail, the inevitable and demonstrable consequence of an economic system: If that is to be done, the reader must first have the system in his mind; and concerning the system that prevails in Packingtown, the average American is as ignorant as an unborn babe.[52]

Both elements have been generally important for Sinclair's oeuvre as a whole. Noticing his powerful and often melodramatic grip on readers, Vladimir Ilyich Lenin called

---

[51]Ibid., p. 24.

[52]Upton Sinclair, "Comrades of the Appeal," *Appeal to Reason*, (March 10, 1905), p. 1.

Sinclair a "socialist of the emotions."[53] Indeed, Sinclair's nightmarish fiction wants to shake "the country out of its slumber."[54] The other facet characterizes the idealist and educator who became a persistent propagandist for emancipation and change. These two elements which on the whole complement one another are in opposition by the last chapters of the novel. By then, the genteel lecturer and Socialist educator predominates.

Sinclair explicated his poetics in essays written around the publication of *The Jungle* and later formulated his ideas generally in *Mammonart*. Sinclair's theory repeats basic convictions of materialist determinism. For him, literature primarily mirrors society. All art is social and hence ideological: "The artist is a social product, his psychology and that of his art works [are] determined by the economic forces prevailing in his time."[55] Art reflects the dominant ideology and like any other cultural product is used as a weapon in the class struggle. Art distinguishes itself from pure ideology through its playfulness: "If it [the propaganda] is to remain art, it must keep the play form."[56] At the turn of the century, when leisure, conspicuous consumption, and Bohemian hedonism characterized a decadent bourgeoisie to him, Sinclair posited other priorities: "I have become like a soldier upon a hard campaign--I am only thinking of the enemy."[57] Sinclair thus stresses *movere* and *prodesse* over *delectare*. He writes in 1906:

> The proletarian writer . . . does not find the life of his fellows an opportunity for feats of artistry; he finds it a nightmare inferno, a thing whose one conceivable excellence is that it drives men to rebellion and to mutual aid in escaping. The proletarian writer is a writer with a purpose: he thinks no more of "art for art's sake" than a man on a sinking ship thinks of painting a beautiful picture in the cabin; he thinks of getting ashore, and of getting his brothers and comrades ashore--and then there will be time enough for art.[58]

The artist is the "forerunner" of the revolution and lends his voice to the working people.[59] Following Marx who rejected a merely contemplative practice of philosophy, Sinclair refuses to be restricted to the literary realm. The important thing to do, as he expounded in *Mammonart*, is to change the world:

---

[53]Vladimir Ilyich Lenin, *On the United States of America*, Moscow, 1967, pp. 105f. Cited in Dieter Herms, *Upton Sinclair: Zwischen Pop, zweiter Kultur und herrschender Ideologie*, Berlin, 1986, p. 94.

[54]Sinclair, "What Life Means to Me," p. 593.

[55]Sinclair, *Mammonart*, p. 21.

[56]Ibid., p. 20.

[57]Sinclair, "What Life Means to Me," p. 594.

[58]Ibid., p. 594.

[59]Upton Sinclair, "The Muckrake Man," *Independent*, 65 (1908), p. 519.

That is the message of this book, the last word I have to say: that your creative gift shall not be content to make art works, but shall at the same time make a world; shall make new souls, moved by a new ideal of fellowship, a new impulse of love, and faith--and not merely hope, but determination.[60]

This intention shapes the form of *The Jungle*. The novel moves from the self-enclosed set-piece of the wedding to the actuality of a Chicago election and the vision of a Socialist victory. The last words of the novel point toward political involvement that lies beyond literature: "CHICAGO WILL BE OURS!"[61]

The political form of *The Jungle* not only marked, in Sinclair's words, "the beginning of proletarian literature in America"[62] but it also functioned as a catalyst for ideas in the literary theories of Bertolt Brecht and Walter Benjamin.[63] Sinclair's achievement was to readjust the conventional function of the didactic *movere*. He turns its individual-moralistic bias into a collective-political focus and replaces the purely psychological effect of catharsis with political reflection and social emancipation. Prefiguring Brecht's *Lehrtheater* plays, *The Jungle* exceeds mere artistic contemplation and involves readers in political decisions.

Sinclair appropriates traditional and popular forms for his political purposes. The stockyard sections in *The Jungle* are modeled after naturalist paradigms.[64] The modern city here is limited to the documentary slice of Packingtown. As Jurgis Rudkus becomes part of the floating proletariat, Sinclair applies picaresque strategies used by Daniel Defoe and Charles Dickens in the classical city novels of the eighteenth and nineteenth centuries. In spite of the use of such different narrative strategies, the novel retains a consistent atmosphere as the improbabilities of the picaresque plot resume the grotesque conditions in the stockyards. Extending the moral focus in the picaresque tales of his forerunners, Sinclair concentrates on economic, political, and moral forces and

---

[60] Sinclair, *Mammonart*, p. 386.

[61] The end in the Doubleday, Page edition of 1906 differs from the version in the *One Hoss Philosophy*. Sinclair changed his intentions several times. At one point, Sinclair even considered writing a sequel to *The Jungle* (Sinclair quoted in Folsom, p. 249). In the version of the *One Hoss Philosophy*, a final paragraph reports the imprisonment of Jurgis Rudkus--which retained the possibility of a sequel. For the book publication, he thoroughly revised the lengthy ending and deleted the final paragraph. In *American Outpost*, he later acknowledged his difficulties with the last chapters: "I did the best I could--and those critics who didn't like the ending ought to have seen it as it was in the manuscript! I ran wild at the end, trying to solve all the problems of America. . . ." (Sinclair, *American Outpost*, p. 161). For a detailed discussion of the textual history see Folsom, 237-63; DeGruson, pp. xiii-xxxi.

[62] Sinclair, "What Life Means to Me," p. 594.

[63] Herms, p. 42.

[64] Howard, p. 157. Sinclair knew the naturalist novels of Frank Norris and Jack London. Harris, pp. 60, 65.

defines characters primarily through their social roles. Sinclair explicitly rejects a psychological approach which he sees as the mark of "middle-class writers."[65] The concentration on the social facets of character has often been regarded as a major flaw of Sinclair's novel. Typical is William Bloodworth's assertion: "As a work of modern fiction measured against the aesthetic achievements of a Henry James or a William Faulkner or a James Joyce, *The Jungle* hardly merits any discussion at all. Psychological complexity is alien to Sinclair's characterization...."[66]

The Jungle certainly displays weaknesses. As much as the novel transforms traditional patterns to suit its modern subject matter, *The Jungle* reveals Sinclair's apprenticeship as hack novelist and genteel writer. His early literary practice was notorious: within little more than a year in 1898, a full-time student at Columbia then, the young Sinclair spurted out well over four thousand pages of popular fiction. Sinclair never lost the characteristics of fast literary production. In another sense, however, this involvement in pulp production also assisted the political project.[67] The familiarity with popular models helped Sinclair to know what the majority of readers expected and how he could keep them interested in proletarian concerns through stock plots, events, and motifs. As his predominant intention was to agitate for changes, he needed to reach as many readers as possible. Sinclair was fully aware of the resulting dilemma:

> First of all I was an artist, and I wished to write a piece of literature; but I wished also if possible to make a popular book, one that would be read by the people and would shake the country out of its slumber.[68]

Inevitably, the popular and tendentially conservative elements clash with his radical image of the modern city. The concentration on the individual hero of nineteenth-century fiction in a political novel that proposes collectivity, Sinclair's penchant for the spectacular and melodramatic, and his use of stale metaphors and idioms are a result of such incongruous juxtaposition. Also the genteel prejudices and clichés which the novel unthinkingly reproduces must be seen in this context. Despite its passionate commitment to the working class, *The Jungle* uses a number of typical stereotypes about the underprivileged.[69]

---

[65]Sinclair, "What Life Means to Me," p. 594.
[66]Bloodworth, p. 60.
[67]Harris, p. 34; Herms, pp. 93f.
[68]Sinclair, "What Life Means to Me," p. 593.
[69]Folsom, pp. 259f.

The blatant juxtaposition of the conventional and radical is profoundly linked to Sinclair's adherence to nineteenth-century determinism. He sees repression predominantly in materialist terms.[70] All changes in the superstructure of society, in culture and art, are exclusively connected to changes in the industrial base, to the synthesis which Jürgen Habermas has described as the dialectic of instrumental action. Not surprisingly, literary authenticity is linked to the empiricism of the natural sciences; the description is true and disinterested.[71] The novel is a "statistical compilation."[72]

This materialism of Sinclair's literary theory accounts for both the power and the weakness of *The Jungle*. If popular paradigms clash with the radical content of the novel, this seems to be a tribute the novelist has to pay to reach the mass public. After all, the innovation of the artistic form is secondary to economic changes. On the other side, the novel forcefully captures the atmosphere of exploitation, alienation, and reification in its description of industrial labor. Its clarity and vigor were new and challenged reified modes of expression and perception. Most fictional techniques in *The Jungle* were implemented to shock, destabilize, and move readers to political action. This generates the "cumulative power" which has reminded critics of the mood in novels by Fyodor Dostoyevsky or Emile Zola.[73] Indeed, an atmosphere of restlessness and torment hovers over the working-class city. One dismal occurrence chases the next. The nightmarish cityscape is reinforced with every episode and forces readers to respond to the inhuman conditions. *The Jungle* is not an unreflected muckraking document as many critics seem to think, rather its strategy assists the artistic intention of the novel.[74]

Sinclair indicates the direction for political change through comparison, reversal, and contrast. *The Jungle* opens with the yearnings and ideals conventionally connected to the American dream. The novel shows how, one by one, virtually all hopes end in disillusionment. Work, wages, and wedding differ substantially from what the hard-laboring Lithuanians expect. Similarly, the ideals connected with factory, home, religion,

---

[70]In 1904, he asserts that "The bourgeois civilization is, in one word, an organized system of repression." Sinclair, "Our Bourgeois Literature," p. 23.

[71]Sinclair writes, "I mean it to be true, not merely in substance, but in detail, and in the smallest detail. It is as true as it should be if it were not a work of fiction at all, but a study by a sociologist." Sinclair, "Is 'The Jungle' True?" p. 1129.

[72]Sinclair, "What Life Means to Me," p. 593.

[73]Robert E. Spiller, et. al., *Literary History of the United States*, 1946, New York, 1974, p. 997.

[74]William Bloodworth, for instance, writes that "with *The Jungle* literature is less a way of ordering and interpreting experience--less the imposition of a particular artistic vision--than a way of simply presenting life. . . ." Bloodworth, p. 61. See also Walter B. Rideout, *The Radical Novel in the United States, 1900-1954*, New York, 1956, p. 37.

school, and politics in democratic America have been corrupted. Degeneration prevails where the immigrants hoped for improvement. This reversal technique is pervasive. Ona and little Stanislovas should not work; they have no choice (TJ, pp. 74f). Ona should nurse her baby; she has to return to the factory (TJ, p. 110). The children should attend school; they cannot (TJ, p. 123). Ona should have medical care; she dies because they lack the money to provide it (TJ, p. 179f).

Jurgis' experiences outside Packingtown complete the dismal picture. American ideals repeatedly clash with reality under capitalism. The laissez-faire economy with its alleged freedom for labor is revealed as an oppressive regimen with lay-offs, bribes, and black lists (TJ, p. 194). The American party system is undermined by graft and illegal ballots (TJ, p. 249). Official stockyard tours and the inofficial perspective of the workers below are juxtaposed (TJ, pp. 38, 65f).[75] Whereas signs stress cleanliness in meat production, Jurgis reveals that workers did not even have toilets where they could wash their hands (TJ, p. 136).

The accretion of injustices prepares for the political conversion of Jurgis Rudkus. His rejuvenation through Socialism becomes the fictional climax. The moment Jurgis Rudkus turns revolutionary, many tensions which have accumulated in the novel dissolve and negative contrasts acquire their positive counterparts: Jurgis returns "home" at last (TJ, p. 318). The last section refurbishes the ideals of freedom, equality, and community which had disappeared after the *veselija*.[76]

Repetition reinforces the effect of Jurgis' conversion to Socialism. The end which follows the necessities of the political aesthetic is tightly structured. The novel presents three conversions; Jurgis attends three main lectures and conversations about the inevitability of Socialist changes; workers are asked three times to "Organize! Organize! Organize!" (TJ, p. 340); finally, the novel climaxes with the typographical crescendo of a triple, "Chicago will be ours! *Chicago will be ours!* CHICAGO WILL BE OURS! (TJ, p. 341). Since Sinclair wants to incite a "revolt against capitalism,"[77] the final chapters prepare this step beyond the purely literary world and increasingly include the actual slogans, pamphlets, and ballot results of the 1904 election when the Socialist Party polled almost thirty percent of the vote and a Socialist candidate was elected in the

---

[75]During the Columbian Exposition in Chicago over a million visitors took part in such promotional tours in the stockyards. Wade, p. xiv.

[76]Franz-Peter Spaunhorst, *Literarische Kulturkritik als Dekodierung von Macht und Werten am Beispiel ausgewählter Romane von Upton Sinclair, Frank Norris, John Dos Passos und Sinclair Lewis*, Frankfurt, 1986, p. 197.

[77]Sinclair, "The Muckrake Man," p. 519.

stockyards.[78] In the final phrase, fiction and reality converge in the hope: "CHICAGO WILL BE OURS!"

As several critics have pointed out, however, the Socialist ending considerably differs in style from the preceding chapters.[79] The power which gave momentum to the events in Packingtown and Chicago is absent. The novel instead closes with a tedious voice: educating, lecturing, and debating. Suddenly, not action and rebellion, but rather talk dominates. The last paragraphs which ought to make readers actively join the Socialists and increase the revolutionary momentum lack the power of the stockyard narrative. Paradoxically, it is Jurgis Rudkus who recalls Sinclair's intention just before he is submitted to further Socialist lectures: "The thing was not to talk but to do; the thing was to get hold of others and rouse them, to organize them and prepare them for the fight!" (TJ, p. 305).

5. The Paternalist Revolution

The Jungle presents Chicago as the modern capitalist environment, but also as the future city of the "revolutionary Socialist movement."[80] Sinclair's Socialist city consists of two contradictory facets. Political emancipation will turn the metropolis into a community of free citizens, but the path toward this transformed city is paternally prescribed. Intending to liberate the working class, Sinclair poses as an omniscient and "trusty leader in the most wonderful adventure that the world has ever seen."[81] He gives voice to the experience of his "ignorant" pupils.[82] Guiding them his way, however, he silences their specific cultural experiences and needs.

The structure of *The Jungle* is shaped by repetition, contrast, and reversal. The opening *veselija* and the closing discussions are opposite poles in the novel. The wedding is modeled as a naturalist set-piece and nearly functions as a disconnected episode within the structure of the novel; the final sections are linear elements in the political plot which receives its full significance only in real life. The contrast of the doomed festivity of immigrants and the revolutionary rigor of Socialists is paradoxically

---

[78]Barrett, p. 352.

[79]For a detailed discussion see Folsom, "Upton Sinclair's Escape," pp. 237-66; Bloodworth, p. 60; Harris, pp. 75ff; Fine, p. 85; Mookerjee, p. 57.

[80]Sinclair, "What Life Means to Me," p. 594.

[81]Ibid., p. 595.

[82]Ibid., p. 592.

connected to literary form. The celebration of the bourgeois version of the American dream forms the basis for the most jubilant scene in Sinclair's novel which Leon Harris called "the best he ever wrote."[83] On the other hand, the presentation of the Americanized Socialist Rudkus lacks the vitality of the rest of the novel.[84] By the end, ethnic culture and political ideals contradict one another: Sinclair, the Socialist lecturer, can only envision debating intellectuals but not active workers.

The major parallels and contrasts in *The Jungle* exist between the traditional wedding celebration of the first chapter and the political education in the rest of the novel. The opening *veselija* presents an outdated form of the American dream. The future is equated with progress achieved through honesty, diligence, and perseverance. The wedding cake is topped with the Eiffel tower, a symbol of industrial progress (TJ, p. 9).[85] But the ideals displayed during the *veselija* cannot withstand the destruction of communal culture through the stockyards. In the midst of capitalism, traditional solidarity becomes impossible. The family may expect no compensation for their *veselija* expenditures as was custom in Lithuania. Young Lithuanians, grown up in the stockyards, profit from the revels without contributing their share of expenses (TJ, pp. 17f). Also, the saloon-keeper takes advantage of their situation (TJ, p. 21). Nevertheless, Jurgis closes the ceremony with a belief in the power of the individual: "I will work harder" (TJ, p. 25). These words will ring in Jurgis' ears throughout the following plot of decline. Success in this world does not reward diligence, but is directed by power, corruption, or the mere luck of survival.

The *veselija* anticipates the political strategy as it prepares the conversion in the end. In the first chapter, Sinclair projects a fundamental change from Lithuanian values to American ideals. The Lithuanians who recall "best home traditions" in the beginning (TJ, p. 7), dream of returning to their Packingtown "home" by the end of the wedding (TJ, p. 25). Similarly, the celebration opens with a Lithuanian song but closes with an "American tune" (TJ, p. 24). Lithuanian peasants are transformed into American workers adhering to the Protestant work ethic.[86] The arrival at the wedding is bathed in ethnic folklore, the departure indicates a resolution of Horatio Alger figures.

The chapters which follow the wedding celebration indicate why the conversion to middle-class ideals was not sufficient to cope with the new type of industrial

---

[83]Harris, p. 71.

[84]Mookerjee, p. 56.

[85]Spaunhorst, p. 181.

[86]Bloodworth, p. 50; Ickstadt, p. 49.

exploitation and why other major changes are inevitable. Throughout the story, the events of the first chapter provide important contrasts. Tamoszius Kuszleika who created the liveliness and sensuality of the *veselija* with his violin lilts, is poisoned and loses his fingers at work (TJ, p. 287). Marija Berczynskas, who was the most vital figure in the wedding ceremony, is compared to the rejuvenated Jurgis in the end: capitalism has reduced Marija to a drugged and apathetic prostitute (TJ, p. 325). Traditional society clearly is doomed: whereas Jurgis' acceptance of Socialism is projected as a virtual rebirth, the wedding fails to give birth to a new society and instead results in the death of many of the participants (TJ, p. 304). This duality of beginning and conclusion, of past and future expresses the contrast between the political models. The *veselija* as the novel's prologue functions as the rounded epilogue to a doomed Lithuanian culture, whereas the succeeding episodes, as the novelistic epilogue, become the prologue for a future community in, and beyond, the novel.

Despite their differences, however, both versions of the American dream are fundamentally related in their attitudes toward the ethnic working-class culture. The final section, the most discussed break in the novel, is not a disparate appendage to the main body, but rather the logical conclusion of tendencies present throughout *The Jungle*. Sinclair dominates his Lithuanian figures from the beginning. But as the novel proceeds, his voice more and more silences also those traits which constituted the power in the communal celebration of the wedding. The active and passionate working-class figures of the *veselija*, an actual wedding ceremony in which Sinclair had the chance to participate in the stockyards,[87] eventually stand in stark contrast to Jurgis Rudkus, the Socialist pupil, who has to submit himself to talky Socialists in the end. The paternalism which occasionally surfaced at the beginning becomes the novel's general stance.

Throughout *The Jungle*, the omniscient narrator shows his distance to working-class characters. Although Sinclair attacks inhuman conditions and sees that filth was not a generic feature of working-class life, he argues that the underprivileged are "spreading a slow contagion that was infecting the whole of civilization."[88] Sinclair seems to hope for a purifying and ennobling effect of the revolution.[89] Moreover, from the beginning, Sinclair likens some Lithuanian figures to animals and indicates that as rural people they still belong to a low stage in evolution. The rural immigrants cannot identify the sickening stench of pork, beef, and fertilizer as "their taste in odors" is not developed

---

[87]Sinclair, "Is 'The Jungle' True?" p. 1132.

[88]Sinclair, "What Life Means to Me," p. 592.

[89]Ickstadt, pp. 48f.

(TJ, p. 29). In Sinclair's writings about stockyard people these prejudices return. The workers were uneducated and in need of his guidance:

> But these wretches were ignorant; they did not know what was the matter with them. They were also voiceless, and could not have told even had they known. . . . I, alone of all men who had education and a voice, had been down into the social pit, and had lived the life of the proletarian.[90]

The Americanization of Lithuanians in the opening chapter then is a logical first step in Sinclair's concept. Since the immigrants are devoid of an adequate culture, they first need to lose their Lithuanian remnants. The *veselija* produces Americanized Lithuanians who then will be educated to become Socialists by the end of the novel. Sinclair completely controls their education: the lengthy discussions express this all-pervasive guidance. In the greater context of 1905, this ideal of teaching also reflects Sinclair's practical involvement in Socialism. He believed in advancing revolutionary changes through education and founded the *Intercollegiate Socialist Society*.[91] The city of the future was to be realized through a worker's revolution and their concomitant education.[92]

Sinclair shapes working-class characters according to his idealistic and genteel image. By the end of the novel, his conception of education, propriety, and moralism prevail over the depiction of working-class needs. The accretion of horrors does not induce action, but reinforces his conviction in the priority of agitation and paternalism. Sinclair silences their specific working-class culture and thereby robs his working families of their vitality in the early chapters. The wordiness of the end is certainly not caused by a lack of inventiveness.[93] From his time as a dime-novelist, Sinclair knew a variety of stock endings and ploys from marriage to revolt that he need not have his tale end with uneventful talk. Rather, this end seems suggested by the contradictory logic of Sinclair's political education. His remarks about the troubles he had finishing *The Jungle* assist such a reading.[94]

---

[90] Sinclair, "What Life Means to Me," pp. 592f.

[91] Homberger, p. 50. Jack London became its first president. In the sixties, the renamed institute was involved in the foundation of the student organization SDS. Herms, *Upton Sinclair, ein amerikanischer Radikaler*, pp. 44f.

[92] Of course, the marginalization of ethnicity in the novel must also be seen as an attempt to by-pass the racial division among workers and avoid prejudice among readers. The literary strategy thus merges political analysis with wishful thinking.

[93] Harris, p. 75; Folsom, p. 249.

[94] Folsom, pp. 249ff.

As William J. Bloodworth and R. N. Mookerjee have pointed out, Sinclair's middle-class notions clash with his portrait of working-class reality. His characters reveal a "prim propriety," and their language indicates genteel immigrants.[95] While graphic descriptions of working-class degradation supersede the picturesque treatment of workers, the novel still perpetuates the idealistic image of the noble laborer:

> Always the critics say--without knowing anything about it--that I "idealize" these characters. I can only say, if there is any finer type in the world than the humble workingman who has adopted brotherhood as his religion, and sacrifices his time and money and often his job for his faith, I have not encountered it.[96]

Consequently, alcohol, amusement, and sexuality are denigrated or marginalized in *The Jungle*. Workers are distracted from their real tasks in saloons if they are not cheated there. Jurgis significantly loses his $100 bill in a saloon (TJ, p. 241), and the lowest point in his degradation is drinking in bars. As Dr. Schliemann expounds, drink is a vice (TJ, p. 332). Thus, Marija, the most vital character of the beginning, ends as a dope addict in a brothel (TJ, p. 325). Sexuality is either omitted in best genteel tradition, or it is said to release people's lowest instincts (TJ, p. 217). Working-class forms of recreation, amusement, and resistance are rejected. Sinclair's propriety is ridiculous in passages in which he spells out what he dislikes about working-class culture:

> These revolutionists were not angels; they were men, and men who had come up from the social pit, and with the mire of it smeared over them. Some of them drank, and some of them swore, and some of them ate pie with their knives.... (TJ, p. 318)

Radical in its analysis of capitalist exploitation and suppression, Sinclair's novel kept to a middle-class path of well-behaved Socialists.[97] Years later, F. Scott Fitzgerald poignantly criticized such paternalism and the disregard for cultural forms of the working class: "That's the trouble with you radicals, you know all about communism . . . the Five-Year Plan . . . and the coming revolution, but you don't know a thing about football."[98]

Sinclair's attitude generally reflects the contradictions of paternalist policies as evidenced in the various forms of municipal planning and social engineering in modern societies. Sinclair espouses the basic assumptions of professionalist reformers. In his strategy to free the working class, expert guidance dominates over the emancipation of

---

[95] Mookerjee, p. 56; Bloodworth, p. 60.

[96] Sinclair, *American Outpost*, p. 174.

[97] Yoder, p. 18; Folsom, p. 248. In the Lake Shore episode, Jurgis in his "wolf-hunger," eats with "two shovels, the fork in one hand and his knife in the other" (TJ, p. 239).

[98] Fitzgerald cited in Gervais, p. 82.

all participants in the process. The actual needs of those to be helped are disregarded. Change is teleological. Workers have to do all the cultural adjustment. At the end of the novel, the Socialist propagandist revealingly wants to "drill" the workers (TJ, p. 341). This blatant incongruity in Sinclair's ideology underlies his wordy finale: he assumes that he has to do all the teaching. But domination and paternalism--not education--are incompatible with emancipation and liberation. True enlightenment, as Jürgen Habermas has pointed out, only knows participants.[99]

Although Sinclair opposes working-class crudities, his novel argues for real changes and against the fake ethnicity which was promoted by big business, political machines, and the mass media.[100] Moreover, the actual situation of American workers and their organizations must be taken into consideration. The working-class people imprisoned for disorderly conduct by the thousands, the suppression of their political protest in the Ludlow massacre, or their treatment during the *red scare* evidence an effective silencing of opposition. This fact should be recalled when one criticizes Sinclair's genteel silencing of his characters and his propagandist stance.

The vigor of Sinclair's image of industrial Chicago, his relentless depiction of injustice and cruelty by far supersede the genteel weakness of the novel. To see why Sinclair's urbanites are pale and lifeless as they approach their liberation is to recall the cultural vitality that has been obliterated in a one-sided model of change. Sinclair's momentous bequeathment to modernity is the belief in human agency. Those who have built cities may again change them to serve the needs of all. While other writers withdrew from the modern metropolis or developed a new urban aesthetic, Sinclair based his urban portrait on the vision of a liberated society. Arguing for solidarity and involvement, one of the most conventional of twentieth-century city novelists reveals himself as one of the most radical and modern critics of the industrial city.

---

[99] Habermas, *Theory and Practice*, p. 40.

[100] For a critical account of Chicago neighborhoods, see Charles Bowden and Lew Kreinberg, *Street Signs Chicago: Neighborhood and Other Illusions of Big-City Life*, Chicago, 1981.

10
F. Scott Fitzgerald
The Great Gatsby

1. The View from Outside

In a traditional combination for urban novels, F. Scott Fitzgerald's *The Great Gatsby* associates materialism and success with the modern city.[1] Jay Gatsby's corrupted vision of the American dream organizes Fitzgerald's "picture of New York."[2] The modern metropolis is both setting and issue in his romance about wealth, glamour, corruption, despair, and death. But the novel cannot be limited in its meaning to urban issues.[3] Fitzgerald himself projects the figurative use of the urban environment in his romance. His final title indicates the broader, national focus: he wanted to call his work *Under the Red, White, and Blue*, but his telegram reached the publisher too late to alter the plates.[4] Within the novel, Fitzgerald's narrator indeed views city conflicts more generally as he extends them to the mythic dichotomy of East and West, and to the opposition between sophistication and simplicity, civilization and nature. Beyond its figurative conception, the specific New York image of *The Great Gatsby* had a substantial impact on perceptions of the American metropolis.

The urban segment that F. Scott Fitzgerald selects for his fictional transformation astutely captures the latest developments on the fringes of American cities. In the twen-

---

[1] F. Scott Fitzgerald, *The Great Gatsby*, 1925, Harmondsworth, 1966. References to *The Great Gatsby* will be abbreviated to GG and incorporated into the text. Matthew J. Bruccoli has edited the remaining fragments of the various stages of the composition in F. Scott Fitzgerald, *The Great Gatsby: A Facsimile of the Manuscript*, ed. Matthew J. Bruccoli, Washington, D.C., 1973. See also Matthew J. Bruccoli, *Apparatus for F. Scott Fitzgerald's The Great Gatsby*, Columbia, S.C., 1974.

[2] F. Scott Fitzgerald mentioned this phrase as descriptive subtitle but rejected it because of its assertive ring. F. Scott Fitzgerald, *The Letters of F. Scott Fitzgerald*, ed. Andrew Turnbull, New York, 1963, p. 179. The theme has been noted in criticism: Marius Bewley, "Scott Fitzgerald's Criticism of America," *The Sewanee Review*, 62 (1954), 223-46.

[3] See Marx, "The Puzzle of Anti-Urbanism in Classic American Literature," pp. 75-79.

[4] F. Scott Fitzgerald, *Correspondence of F. Scott Fitzgerald*, ed. Matthew J. Bruccoli and Margaret M. Duggan, New York, 1980, p. 153.

ties, when suburban populations exploded, Fitzgerald conveys the commuters' perspective from the periphery and with it a view that would dominate city images in the decades to come. Furthermore, Nick Carraway's upper-class perception is linked through his pastoral language to a discussion in the upper and middle class where the advantage of simple, healthy, and natural forms of life over the debasing ambiance of the artificial metropolis was proposed. For its wealthy inhabitants, the suburbs represented a new Arcadia. Frederic Jackson Turner had metaphorically reached the crabgrass frontier.[5]

The view from outside, filtered through an upper-class lens, guaranteed the popularity of the novel's skyline image. Carraway's famous description from the Queensboro Bridge further romanticized the Manhattan silhouette. In the 1970s, New York middle-class professionals significantly selected skyscrapers seen from Hudson bridges as the most poetic city image.[6] The view of a broker who held that "the city seen from the Queensboro Bridge" is the city "seen for the first time, in its first wild promise of all the mystery and the beauty in the world" (GG, pp. 74f), continues to shape romantic perceptions.

As much as F. Scott Fitzgerald identifies with the glamorous sides of the modern city, he counterbalances the affirmative stance with a critical foil in *The Great Gatsby* and diagnoses corruption behind the white facade.[7] Describing the upper-class experience of the nouveau riche, the leisure class, and the traditional elite, Fitzgerald does not identify uncritically with Nick Carraway's standpoint even though he employs him as an authentic story-teller. Fitzgerald's "honest book"[8] challenges the self-proclaimed "honesty" (GG, p. 66) of its upper-class mouthpiece. The text questions all upper-class interpretations of the modern American city in which the actual politics of exclusion are mirrored in blind spots of perception.

F. Scott Fitzgerald's crucial achievement in *The Great Gatsby* is an openness which he would later define as a capacity to combine "two opposed ideas" without breaking apart.[9] His novel transcends the views of Jay Gatsby and Nick Carraway and

---

[5]This formulation is indebted to the title of Kenneth T. Jackson's study of American suburbs. Kenneth T. Jackson, *Crabgrass Frontier: The Suburbanization of the United States,* New York, 1985.

[6]Susanna Duncan summarizes research that Stanley Milgram had conducted among New York professionals. Duncan, "Mental Maps of New York," p. 59.

[7]In "My Lost City," Fitzgerald would write in 1936: "For the moment I can only cry out that I have lost my splendid mirage. Come back, come back, O glittering and white!" Fitzgerald, *The Crack-Up,* p. 33.

[8]F. Scott Fitzgerald, "Introduction," *The Great Gatsby,* New York, 1934, p. x.

[9]Fitzgerald, *The Crack-Up,* p. 69.

undertakes a radical criticism of American materialism. Fitzgerald's "consciously artistic"[10] though restrictively aesthetic effort to capture the crisis of American society in the twenties incorporates contrariness. A masterpiece in its unity of style, the city's aesthetic surface, however, reveals cracks.

2. The Suburban Twenties

The Great Gatsby is famous for its economy of structure and detail.[11] Its selection of incidents and motifs has the "solidity of specification" that Henry James demanded of the modern novel.[12] The romance scathingly projects the "business of America"[13] in the twenties--its corrupt politics and democratized materialism, its bootleggers and gamblers, its craze for cars, sports, and parties.[14] The novel depicts unembellished the manifestations of the decade's prosperity, prohibition, and ethnic fundamentalism.

Inherently related to wealth and love as generic topics, F. Scott Fitzgerald's romance is also associated through its language with a discourse on nature which was widespread among the affluent on the urban fringes.[15] In the first two decades of the twentieth century, the suburbs of metropolitan areas were elevated to a morally superior "middle landscape"[16] which reunified the virtues of country and city, of nature and civilization for its residents. Nick Carraway's pastoral vocabulary evokes the spatial ideology with which upper- and middle-class residents justified their separation from the social and environmental plight in the center.

Beginning in the mid-nineteenth century, railroad suburbs had been built for the upper class on the periphery of American cities. This trend was accelerated toward the

---

[10] Fitzgerald, *Letters*, p. 163.

[11] Scott Donaldson summarizes critical opinion when writing that there is "nothing accidental or haphazard" in the novel. Scott Donaldson, "Introduction," *Critical Essays on The Great Gatsby*, Boston, 1984, p. 4.

[12] James E. Miller, "Fitzgerald's Gatsby: The World as Ash Heap," *Critical Essays on The Great Gatsby*, ed. Scott Donaldson, Boston, 1984, p. 250.

[13] Calvin Coolidge compressed the decade's purpose in his phrase that the "business of America is business." In most fields, the American economy reached record profit levels. Nye, pp. 653f.

[14] Among other contemporary cases, Fitzgerald used the files on the Fuller-McGee corruption case for his novel. Turnbull, p. 155.

[15] See Schmitt, *Back to Nature*, pp. 177-189. Schmitt writes: "The flight from the crowd took various directions--to city parks, suburbs, country places or to the wilderness." Ibid., p. 182.

[16] Mary Corbin Sies, "The City Transformed: Nature, Technology, and The Suburban Ideal, 1877-1917," *Journal of Urban History*, 14 (1987), p. 90.

turn of the century and, by the twenties, suburban populations outgrew those in central areas.[17] Fuelled by the concentration of labor in industrial capitalism, this migration considerably shaped the specific fragmentation of the American metropolis. A prime objective of this willed segregation was that the bourgeoisie wanted to escape the social costs of capitalist destruction in downtown areas. Affluent enough to implement new technologies, they fled the unemployment, poverty, filth, crime, and class antagonism in inner cities.[18]

Moreover, the social withdrawal was implemented to further class politics. The annexation of outlying areas by cities and the incorporation of separate communities as suburbs were related processes. In the early phase, annexation was perceived as a viable tool to change the electoral balance in central cities to favor the elite. The incorporation of Brooklyn's middle-class voters into a Greater New York in 1898 to defeat the immigrant politics of Tammany Hall was one of the last and most prominent of these unsuccessful maneuvers.[19] Toward the close of the century, the rich fringe replaced this fruitless strategy with its opposite: now metropolitan annexations were rejected by claiming a right to home rule. Domination was replaced by segregation.[20]

A new phase of corporate concentration and increased profits in the twenties fuelled the construction of suburbs and skyscrapers. While one percent of the elite already controlled 31% of the total personal wealth in 1919, a decade later it controlled 36%.[21] With more high-rise architecture under construction than ever before in the central business district, the towers of finance and commerce created a new focal point and expressed the domination of corporations visually. Outside the core, the families of corporate managers and white collar employees were generating a similarly momentous transformation. Annually, about 800,000 new houses were erected, most of them on the metropolitan fringes. Long Island's Nassau County tripled its population in the decade.

---

[17]Peter O. Muller, *Contemporary Suburban America*, Englewood Cliffs, N.J., 1981, p. 22.

[18]Patrick J. Ashton, "Urbanization and the Dynamics of Suburban Development under Capitalism," *Marxism and the Metropolis*, ed. William Tabb and Larry Sawers, New York, 1984, p. 59.

[19]Ann R. Markusen, "Class and Urban social Expenditure: A Marxist Theory of Metropolitan Government," *Marxism and the Metropolis*, ed. William Tabb and Larry Sawers, pp. 88f.

[20]Small communities were seen to be more manageable. The taxes to maintain and expand a booming metropolitan infrastructure could be left to those remaining inside who, however, were obviously least endowed to cope with them (Chudacoff, p. 91). In the center, the protection of private property, of business and office buildings, accounts for the largest budget share amounting to approximately one third of total municipal expenditure. Markusen, pp. 91ff.

[21]Richard Parker, *The Myth of the Middle Class*, New York, 1972, p. 93.

By 1925, New York had 129 incorporated suburbs. The elite suburbs had reached their peak.[22]

The Great Gatsby deals with these urban developments. Most importantly, by focusing on the view from the outside, F. Scott Fitzgerald gives literary shape to the suburban perspective which became so prominent in the following decades. The romance includes an important assessment of the Manhattan skyline which would soon appear as natural as the island on the Hudson itself.

Based on an ideology that reaches back to the late nineteenth century, the withdrawal to the fringe was mystified as a necessary movement closer to nature.[23] At the Columbian Exposition in 1893, Frederick Jackson Turner had defined the frontier as a congenial environment for American democracy and had thus projected a way of reintegrating the outmoded duality of self-reliant agrarianism and cancerous urbanism in the form of a suburban frontier within a booming urban America. Professionals in the upper and middle class were involved in creating a new ideal in which a healthy environment with sports, boy scouts, recreation, and nature conservation would invigorate members of the class.[24] Nature, which was otherwise ruthlessly subdued in profitable exploitation, was at once refined through suburban planning and romanticized as *sine qua non* of a modern life-style.[25] Domesticity mystified the part played by women in homes close to mother 'nature.' Consequently, as Nick Carraway pastoralizes Jay Gatsby's view, he does not pastoralize it innocently.[26] Romantic language as the image of the "fresh, green breast" (GG, p. 187), which Carraway uses for his particular version of the original American dream, also connotes this suburban ideology. Yet, Fitzgerald critically examines the upper-class topography. Turning images topsy-turvy, he sees leisure-class morbidity and degeneracy underlying the suburban refuge. Still, the pastoral vocabulary of the "story of the West" (GG, p. 183) affirmatively retains what William Smythe projected as Eden in 1922. In his *City Homes on Country Lanes* Smythe offered to suburbanites

---

[22]Chudacoff, p. 213; Schmitt, p. 182; Jackson, pp. 102, 176.

[23]In middle-class circles, the domestic ideology of the home accompanied this impulse toward a natural environment. Since *The Great Gatsby* predominantly deals with the corruption among the upper class, the issue of domesticity is marginal in the novel. See Wortmann, "Domesticating the Nineteenth-Century American City," pp. 531-72.

[24]Sies, pp. 83f; Schmitt, pp. 4f.

[25]Smith, *Uneven Development*, pp. 13f.

[26]Marx, p. 76.

"the cream of the country and the cream of the city, leaving the skim-milk for those who like that sort of thing."[27]

3. The Homogeneous Metropolis

The Great Gatsby projects typical mental maps of upper-class residents. Their fragment is characterized by its broad overview, its social homogeneity, but also by its large-scale omissions of the working metropolis.[28] Exclusiveness implies exclusion in their cognitive maps. Indeed, their metropolis seems a "world complete in itself" (GG, p. 111). Upper-class experience in the modern metropolis differs substantially from other groups. Blanche Gelfant excluded Fitzgerald's "novel of the modern city"[29] from her study because the urban experience which was portrayed in the romance could not be grasped within the categories of Chicago urbanism.

The modern city in *The Great Gatsby* is based on a closed community. Above all, it is socially homogeneous. It has the small scale of villages; Carraway calls its residents the "nobility of the countryside" (GG, p. 51). Seemingly contradicting claims of metropolitan anonymity, people here are individuals and are known by name. Nick Carraway's list of visitors, beyond its function to ridicule the leisure-class and nouveau-riche partygoers, testifies to the small radius of this world. The circle of metropolitan figures is limited to those who count: Tom Buchanan has bought his Georgian Colonial mansion from "Demaine, the oil man" (GG, p. 14). In contrast to this individualizing, Carraway's servant never advances beyond the generality of her national identity as a "Finn." Not heterogeneity, density, and vastness, but lawns, mansions, and golf courts define the metropolis in *The Great Gatsby*. Meetings take place at parties and invitations match--even in Nick's youth: "'Are you going to the Ordways'? the Herseys'? the Schultzes'?'" (GG, p. 182). But the "dignified homogeneity" (GG, p. 51) is degenerate. Sidney Bremer concludes: "The transitory gestures of entertaining and having a good time--consumers' proofs of leisure and wherewithall--have become more important than the human relations they falsely proclaim."[30]

---

[27] William Smythe, *City Homes on Country Lanes*, New York, 1922, p. 60; cited in Schmitt, p. xvii.

[28] Orleans, pp. 118ff; Warner, *The Urban Wilderness*, pp. 111f.

[29] Malcolm Bradbury, "Style of Life, Style of Art and the American Novelist in the Nineteen Twenties," *The American Novel and the 1920s*, eds. Malcolm Bradbury and David Palmer, London, 1971, p. 31.

[30] Sidney Bremer, "American Dreams and American Cities in Three Post-World War I Novels," *South Atlantic Quarterly*, 79 (1978), p. 280.

Despite this homogeneity, Fitzgerald indicates tensions among the privileged. With the twenties' boom, more and more people invaded the exclusive fringe areas. *The Great Gatsby* divides the upper class into the nouveau riche (Jay Gatsby and his guests), the leisure class (the Buchanans and their friends), and Nick Carraway as a member of the old elite.[31] These upper-class factions are characterized by their attempts at internal delimitation and a constant bickering for status. Tom Buchanan sees Gatsby as a bootlegger with a circus wagon (GG, p. 127). Nick Carraway snobbishly discloses the shallowness and ignorance of both the Buchanans and Gatsby. The selective catalogue of party-goers is an excellent piece of ironic name-giving and reflects the narrator's sense of decorum.[32] Carraway's self-proclaimed modesty and tolerance are revealed as a deep-seated arrogance toward those with a less privileged background than himself as a member of the elitist Yale Club (GG, p. 63). Thus, gainsaying his boasted "honesty," he comments on Gatsby's situating San Francisco in the Middle West with an ironic "I see" (GG, p. 71).

Upper-class corruption is symbolically revealed through its privileged paraphernalia and hobbies. Owing to the prominence of the "back to nature" ideology, sports, recreation, and nature trips were in vogue among the upper and middle class. Fitzgerald thus employs sports to characterize his figures.[33] Tom Buchanan, the racist and brainless brute, has a background in football (GG, p. 12), and Jordan Baker is known in golf circles.[34] Yet Tom and Jordan are especially characterized by their disregarding the elite ideals identified with sports. Acting less than gentlemanly, Tom Buchanan breaks Myrtle Wilson's nose with his uncontrolled physical power (GG, p. 43) and Jordan Baker has a record of dishonesty for cheating in tournaments (GG, p. 64). Even here, in the field of fair play, the upper class is incurably corrupt.

Cars and houses, too, express qualities of their owners in *The Great Gatsby*.[35] The tasteless materialism of the nouveau riche is embodied in Gatsby's luxurious vehicle:

---

[31] James Light has stressed that Fitzgerald sees his world in terms of social class. James F. Light, "Political Conscience in the Novels of F. Scott Fitzgerald," *Ball State University Forum*, 4 (1963), p. 18.

[32] Peter Lisca, "Nick Carraway and the Imagery of Disorder," *Twentieth Century Literature*, 13 (1967), p. 21.

[33] Christian Messenger, "Tom Buchanan and the Demise of the Ivy League Athletic Hero," *Journal of Popular Culture*, 8 (1974), 402-10.

[34] An upper-class sport per se, nine out of ten golf courts belonged to private clubs in the 20s. Jackson, p. 99.

[35] Similar to the function of automobiles, architecture is revealing as the studies by Curtis Dahl and Eugen Huonder have indicated. Curtis Dahl, "Fitzgerald's Use of American Architectural Styles in *The Great Gatsby*," *American Studies*, 25 (1984), 91-102. Eugen Huonder, *The Functional Significance of Setting in the Novels of Francis Scott Fitzgerald*, Bern, 1974.

> It was a rich cream colour, bright with nickel, swollen here and there in its monstrous length with triumphant hat-boxes and supper-boxes and tool-boxes, and terraced with a labyrinth of wind-shields that mirrored a dozen suns. Sitting behind many layers of glass in a sort of green conservatory, we started to town. (GG, p. 70)

Similarly, reckless driving characterizes the upper class. Jordan Baker's near accident with workmen, in which the car's fender "flicked the button on one man's coat" (GG, p. 65), signifies the general carelessness of the leisure class. The cars of the rich symbolize their degeneracy: Gatsby's "green conservatory" is likened to a hearse (GG, p. 75).[36] Significantly, Myrtle Wilson is killed by an upper-class car.[37]

Above all, the assessments of the nouveau riche and the leisure class reflect Carraway's position as a member of a superior tradition. However, his criticism is undermined as he lacks all the qualities that he demands of others in the upper class. Writing in retrospect, his judgment and his behavior do not indicate the modesty, restraint, or honesty that he sees as privileged qualities. Although he claims that honesty is a cardinal virtue, Carraway lies several times in his story. A debased upper class thus is chided by an unreliable critic.[38] Strangely enough, George Garrett has pointed out, none of the traditional elite appear in *The Great Gatsby*.[39] The novel presents Carraway's claims to having ideals, but it does not show any upper-class figure who lives accordingly. An empty reality questions the ideal.

4. A Contrary Vision

The Great Gatsby exceeds a solely 'urban' reading. Yet, its divisions into metropolis and suburb, into Eastern urbanity and Western simplicity are crucial. The way the novel analyzes the corrupted and commodified American dream helps to focus its city image.

---

[36] Fitzgerald omitted an actual comparison of Gatsby's car and a hearse in the revision of the manuscript. Joan S. Korenman, "A View From the (Queensboro) Bridge," *Fitzgerald/Hemingway Newsletter*, 7 (1975), p. 96.

[37] Fitzgerald indirectly pointed toward the accident's symbolism when he wrote to Perkins that he could not omit the scene in New York because he wanted the accident to happen on the way back. *Letters*, p. 172.

[38] Eble, p. 95. For a discussion of the narrator's reliability, see Scott Donaldson, "The Trouble with Nick," *Critical Essays on The Great Gatsby*, 131-139.

[39] George Garrett, "Fire and Freshness: A Matter of Style in *The Great Gatsby*," *New Essays on The Great Gatsby*, ed. Matthew J. Bruccoli, Cambridge, 1985, p. 107.

The topography of the novel has been discussed intensively by critics. Richard D. Lehan distinguished the various levels which give meaning to the modern city image in Fitzgerald's romance.[40] The West is linked to the past and the first settlers' romantic yearnings.[41] The romance's dichotomy between East and West which relates modernity and the past to degeneracy and innocence, and to civilization and nature, is connected to this mythic level. The geographic duality defines the relationship between the metropolitan center and its fringe and even is repeated in the duality of suburbs, in East and West Egg.[42] New York and the characters' urban experience only receives meaning from the interdependence of these levels.[43]

Nick Carraway, an unreliable narrator modeled after the manner of Joseph Conrad, selects events and interprets their figurative relevance. Carraway's assessment mirrors his upper-class values of order, restraint, and decorum.[44] He dominates events, rewrites and explains Gatsby's vision of the American dream for the reader.[45] The novel's incidents reveal him as egotistic, snobbish, and judgmental. Yet, in his limited trustworthiness, he is a perfect narrator for *The Great Gatsby*.[46] Fitzgerald's revision which changed the third-person omniscience to a first-person narrative, removes the aura of objectivity in favor of a subjective bias, inducing readers to question the proposed analysis.[47]

Carraway's view of the American dream and the modern city indeed is biased. In the end, the class origin of his judgment is disclosed when he offers the dichotomy between East and West as the final explanation. As Carraway conclusively projects the

---

[40] Richard D. Lehan, *F. Scott Fitzgerald and the Craft of Fiction*, Carbondale, 1966, p. 118.

[41] Suggesting a biographical source for this yearning, Lehan stresses Fitzgerald's obsession with lost youth. Lehan, p. 104.

[42] David F. Trask, "A Note on Fitzgerald's *The Great Gatsby*," *University Review*, 33 (1967), p. 199.

[43] Lehan, pp. 116ff. Eugen Huonder's reading of the modern city, for instance, disregards the figurative conception which limits the interpretation to a contradictory analysis of single passages. Huonder, pp. 55-76.

[44] James E. Miller, Jr., *F. Scott Fitzgerald: His Art and His Technique*, New York, 1964, pp. 106ff; Lisca, p. 21.

[45] Richard Godden, "*The Great Gatsby*: Glamor on the Turn," *Journal of American Studies*, 16 (1982), pp. 369f.

[46] Since Carraway seems to have been too obviously dishonest, Fitzgerald revised his early characterization so that he has a figure who may relate the story sufficiently reliable and remain authentic. Donaldson, pp. 134, 139. See also Susan Resneck Parr, "Individual Responsibility in *The Great Gatsby*," *Virginia Quarterly Review*, 57 (1981), pp. 677ff.

[47] In the earliest surviving draft, the story was told from an omniscient standpoint. Matthew J. Bruccoli, *Some Sort of Epic Grandeur*, London, 1981, p. 185. See also Miller, p. 106.

meaning of events, he excludes some of the story's major victims. The dead George and Myrtle Wilson do not count; they are carelessly forgotten.

> I see now that this has been a story of the West, after all--Tom and Gatsby, Daisy and Jordan and I, were all Westerners, and perhaps we possessed some deficiency in common which made us subtly unadaptable to Eastern life. (GG, p. 183)[48]

Those who suffered most and were erased by the "vast carelessness" (GG, p. 186) of the leisure class still do not contribute to the romance's meaning for Nick Carraway. Tom Buchanan's upper-class mistress and her mechanic-husband who kept their cars and their suburban artificiality running, vanish from view. This omission, however, is not a singular incident.[49] Carraway's romanticized skyline similarly deletes labor just as the ash-grey workers are blurred earlier in his view of the valley of ashes, the Flushing Meadow dumping ground (GG, p. 29). The dichotomy of East and West is a superimposed, ideological explanation--some of the incidents in the novel and Carraway's omissions provide a more profound reading.

Fitzgerald's achievement was to transcend upper-class ideology. Undisputedly, he strongly identified with Gatsby's attraction to wealth and shared Carraway's reminiscences of luxurious ease as the well-known story of the Jazz Age protagonist indicates.[50] Fitzgerald, who already in 1922 called himself a "Socialist in politics,"[51] predominantly focuses on the potency of the luring upper-class facade because it formed his sole authentic experience. Only later did he formulate as politics what his "artistic conscience"[52] transformed into a novelistic strategy in *The Great Gatsby*. Fitzgerald said he held "a double allegiance to the class that I am part of and the Great Change I believe in."[53] The story about the modern city as viewed from the suburbs may have erased the underlying effort and conflict, but these reappear in revelatory gaps in the romantic facade.

Fitzgerald thus may identify with Gatsby and Carraway and yet overcome their upper-class position. Fitzgerald did not "carelessly" exclude the perspective from the

---

[48] The passage does not appear in this place in the manuscript. The revision proves Fitzgerald's mastery in building toward the climax and challenging his own romanticism about the American dream with contrary ideas. *Facsimile*, p. 253.

[49] Fitting the increased subtlety that Fitzgerald accomplished through revision, he omitted Carraway's overt scorn for the lower class. In the opening chapter, the manuscript has the narrator once again express his "disgust" for that "necessary evil, the garbage man." *Facsimile*, p. 3.

[50] Fitzgerald saw himself as Jay Gatsby. *Correspondence*, p. 175.

[51] Scott Donaldson, "The Political Development of F. Scott Fitzgerald," *Prospects*, 6 (1981), p. 321.

[52] Fitzgerald, "Introduction," p. x.

[53] Fitzgerald, *Letters*, p. 423. Cited in Ronald J. Gervais, "The Socialist and the Silk Stockings: Fitzgerald's Double Allegiance," *Mosaic*, 15 (1982), p. 79.

Wilson garage. His aesthetic strategy of a contrary vision integrates the antithesis as an absence, or rather, by emphasizing its marginal role in the upper-class milieu. His aesthetics fused "two opposed ideas" as he would theorize in *The Crack-Up*. "One should," Fitzgerald wrote, "be able to see that things are hopeless and yet be determined to make them otherwise."[54] In *The Great Gatsby*, this hopelessness correlates to the absence of a group or figure who could embody hope. Nevertheless, fissures in the suburban facade undermine Carraway's romanticized and ahistorical explanation of Gatsby's behavior and extend the critique to a radical assessment of American conditions. Fitzgerald's power, Malcolm Cowley has generally noted, is his "maximum of critical detachment . . . combined with the maximum immersion in the drama."[55] This capacity engenders a progressive image of the modern city.

Nick Carraway arranges the surface of *The Great Gatsby* and interprets events according to his traditionalist values. With an almost aristocratic arrogance he rails at recent leisure-class degeneracy. His aloofness, however, also allows a tolerant stance toward the low materialism of a mid-West boy who has risen to success in the East. "I snobbishly repeat," he misinterprets his father's advice to reserve judgment, "a sense of the fundamental decencies is parcelled out unequally at birth" (GG, p. 7). Carraway explains Gatsby's behavior in the ahistorical opposition between idealism and materialism, between romanticism and realism. As much as he notices Gatsby's corruption, he nevertheless clings to a belief in his innocence. He is ambivalent in his criticism of contemporary American society and openly oscillates between admiration and condemnation toward his object of observation. Reflecting on the disappointment he experienced in New York, Carraway introduces his ambivalent evaluation in the opening section: "Only Gatsby," he writes, "the man who gives name to this book, was exempt from my reaction--Gatsby, who represented everything for which I have an unaffected scorn" (GG, p. 8). Again, the Wilsons are exempt--and forgotten. The conflict which underlies Carraway's ambivalence is deeper than the spatial ideology of East and West may explain.

Carraway's easy acceptance of Gatsby, his "complete renewals of faith" (GG, p. 135) in the romantic readiness of a corrupt businessman is also related to the function of the American dream for the upper class. Carraway must believe in the integrity of his romantic vision, as it testifies to his own integrity. If the dream ever only was a set of hollow and disregarded rules, as in the fly-leaf in Gatsby's book (GG, p. 180), and not a

---

[54] Fitzgerald, *The Crack-Up*, p. 69.

[55] M. Cowley, "Fitzgerald: The Double Man," *Saturday Review of Literature*, 24 (February 24, 1951), p. 43.

viable reality in American society, this flaw will also taint his own ancestry and privilege. Similarly, only if the dream is still valid and all Americans can be rich through honest effort, can the hegemony of wealth be justified. His faith, which is so easily restored by a gesture or a smile, also is a restored faith in his own upper-class tradition and the faked genealogy of the "Dukes of Buccleuch" (GG, p. 8).[56]

A consequence of this traditional viewpoint, his critique of American urban society is not economic, political, or social, but ahistorical. His criticism is presented in moral, mythic, and metaphysical terms. The qualities he admires lie in an irrecoverable past like the tradition that he is part of. This is most evident in his vision of modern American society. He defines its "middle landscape," in which both city and country take part, as a valley of ashes:

> About half-way between West Egg and New York the motor road hastily joins the railroad and runs beside it for a quarter of a mile, so as to shrink away from a certain desolate area of land. This is a valley of ashes--a fantastic farm where ashes grow like wheat into ridges and hills and grotesque gardens; where ashes take the form of houses and chimneys and rising smoke and, finally, with a transcendent effort, of ash-grey men, who move dimly and already crumbling through the powdery air. Occasionally a line of grey cars crawls along an invisible track, gives out a ghastly creak, and comes to rest and immediately the ash-grey men swarm up with leaden spades and stir up an impenetrable cloud, which screens their obscure operations from your sight. (GG, p. 29)[57]

Only the past, the golden age of the old elite, seems to offer values: the lost West reappears as an ashen "fantastic farm."[58] As critics have pointed out, the life-in-death imagery is based on T. S. Eliot's elitist critique in *The Waste Land* and is perhaps indebted to Oswald Spengler's fatalistic view of history.[59] Although only the personal world view of Nick Carraway is shaken, he diagnoses metaphysical decay and expresses it through apocalyptic imagery. In this fallen world, God is an advertisement and blind.[60] But the reassurance in ahistorical views, which state an inevitably corrupt and eternally degenerate world, allows the White Anglo-Saxon Protestant to function again "back home" (GG, p. 184). The idealized past as imagined in Gatsby's romantic hope should not be tainted. In the end, Carraway erases an obscene word to keep the steps of Gatsby's man-

---

[56]Godden, p. 345.

[57]Again, Fitzgerald's revisions of the manuscript stress the blurring of workers. He added their screened "obscure operations." *Facsimile*, p. 73.

[58]Trask, p. 199.

[59]See Miller, "Fitzgerald's Gatsby: The World as Ash Heap"; Letha Audhuy, "*The Waste Land*: Myth and Symbols in *The Great Gatsby*," *F. Scott Fitzgerald's The Great Gatsby*, ed. Harold Bloom, New York, 1986, 109-22; Bruccoli, *Epic Grandeur*, pp. 206f.

[60]The manuscript explicitly labels the dumping ground as the "back alleyway of Hell." *Facsimile*, p. 73.

sion white: he is continually rewriting and purging the real story of the American dream (GG, p. 187).

Fitzgerald's double vision and contrary identification explain Carraway's complex reactions toward Gatsby and the modern city. Carraway develops two distinct versions of New York: it is a pastoral metropolis and an unreal fallen city. The one envisions material success, whereas the other indicates the moral rejection of materialism. Beyond their ambivalence, his images are congenial because they both exclude actual working relations in the city. But the marginalized and omitted working class is nevertheless crucial for Fitzgerald's story. An "ashen" figure (GG, p. 168), linked to the "ash-grey" workingmen in the dumping ground, eventually erases Gatsby's dream. George Wilson, misled by a luxurious automobile, kills Jay Gatsby.

The images of the modern city are shaped by Carraway's biased perception and his general tendency to conceal and purge disagreeable facts.[61] The language emphasizes his suburban perspective on events.[62] His Manhattan skyline is an assertive view of America's corporations devoid of effort and conflict:

> Over the great bridge, with the sunlight through the girders making a constant flicker upon the moving cars, with the city rising up across the river in white heaps and sugar lumps all built with a wish out of non-olfactory money. The city seen from the Queensboro Bridge is always the city seen for the first time, in its first wild promise of all the mystery and the beauty in the world. (GG, p. 74f)

As a literary motif, the view resumes William Wordsworth's romantic image of London seen from Westminster Bridge in which Wordsworth praises the sleeping city as the apex of civilization.[63] Congenial in its omission of a working city, the broker's view from the suburbs stresses corporate power as promising height. Even though on the bridge above, the viewer seems lower than the looming "white heaps" of "rising" skyscrapers. This view of the city as cleansed facade has become so natural that its historical origin is almost forgotten.[64] Yet in the first decades of the twentieth century, corpo-

---

[61] Richard Lehan writes that *The Great Gatsby* is a novel about seeing and mis-seeing: "Nick, as narrator, continuously sees and often mis-sees what is going on." Lehan, p. 120.

[62] Peter Lisca writes that "both *what* Nick takes note of and the language in which he notes it become important factors." Lisca, p. 23.

[63] William Wordsworth, "Composed Upon Westminster Bridge, September 3, 1802," *William Wordsworth Poetical Works*, ed. Ernest De Selincourt, Oxford, 1936, p. 214. Wordsworth's image of the city is ambivalently related to the nineteenth-century ideology of civic pride. See also Hans Bergmann, "Panoramas of New York, 1845-1860," *Prospects*, 10 (1985), 119-37.

[64] Warner, "Multiple Urban Images," pp. 391ff. The impressionist painter Childe Hassam wrote in 1911: "It is ... towering against the sky and melting tenderly in the distance that the skyscrapers are truly beautiful." Childe Hassam cited in Schleier, p. 17.

rations had to overcome inner-city protest against their oppressive buildings. From the distance, however, Manhattan's skyline becomes an impressive and impenetrable facade, and with its aesthetic glamor leads to civic pride. This view from the outside, attractively appeasing as it lacks all traces of labor, struggle, and conflict, was successfully launched by the corporate-owned mass media. In 1977, Stanley Milgram's analysis of mental maps among New York middle-class professionals indicated that the view from the Queensboro and other Hudson bridges had been established as the most popular and poetic city image.[65]

At second look, however, Carraway's romantic view of Manhattan is tainted. It is framed by Babylonian motifs of corruption, degeneracy, and death. The "white card" which bribes the policeman in the preceding scene (GG, p.74) anticipates the false innocence of New York's "white" skyline. The hearse "heaped with blooms" repeats the "heaps" of concrete seen from the Queensboro Bridge. Carraway's romantic facade, finally, is juxtaposed upon a cellar meeting with New York's underworld. As in Charles Dickens' *Great Expectations*, the ideal is disclosed to be grounded on foul practices. An image of hell underlies the wish for non-olfactory money.

The generally favorable views of central New York presented in the novel are ambivalent after all. The center, even though "overripe," (GG, p. 131) is in tune with nature and not the suburb:

> We drove over to Fifth Avenue, warm and soft almost pastoral, on the summer Sunday afternoon. I wouldn't have been surprised to see a great flock of white sheep turn the corner. (GG, p. 34)[66]

Carraway's urban pastoralism has two functions. For one, it serves as an affirmative view to underwrite the continued possibility of wealth and success in the modern city. But second, it also assists Carraway, as a member of the traditional elite, in showing corruption among the suburban nouveau riche and leisure class. In contrast to their ideology of a suburban Arcadia, Carraway shows an unnatural life-style in the countryside. The sole natural habitat beyond the lawns is Gatsby's monstrous vehicle as a "green conservatory" (GG, p. 70). The suburban garden is mechanized and artificial; it receives food for its parties from a pastoral Manhattan.

> Every Friday five crates of oranges and lemons arrived from a fruiterer in New York--every Monday these same oranges and lemons left his back door in pyramid of pulpless halves. There was a machine in the kitchen which could extract the juice of two hundred oranges

---

[65]Duncan, p. 59.

[66]This view of a pastoral Manhattan again is framed by the affair of Tom Buchanan and Myrtle Wilson.

in half an hour if a little button was pressed two hundred times by a butler's thumb. (GG, p. 45)

Carraway similarly redefines the dichotomy between East and West to suit his own ends. The geographical location of the two suburbs--the idealistic Carraway and Gatsby live in West Egg, the materialistic Buchanans in East Egg--evokes the traditional connotation. Even though Carraway's West retains its association with simplicity and innocence, it receives a very specific interpretation. Thus, his West does not signify the wilderness which as "frontier brothel and saloon" was only an environment for the "pioneer debauchee" (GG, p. 107). He also opposes the agrarian West with "the bored, sprawling, swollen towns beyond the Ohio, with their interminable inquisition which spared only the children and the very old" (GG, p. 183).[67] The Eastern city is superior in its wild promises for the upper-class flaneur:

> I began to like New York, the racy adventurous feel of it at night, and the satisfaction that the constant flicker of men and women and machines give to the restless eye. I liked to walk up Fifth Avenue and pick out romantic women from the crowd and imagine that I was going to enter into their lives, and no one would ever know or disapprove. (GG, p. 63)

But the West also cannot be identified with a distinct type of city.[68] In Lincoln Steffens' muckraking essays *The Shame of the Cities* from 1904, Carraway's and Fitzgerald's St. Paul-Minneapolis had been criticized as having allowed a "corruption which for deliberateness, invention, and avarice has never been equaled."[69] Not natural, agrarian, or urban, the West in *The Great Gatsby* is a class image: it is the upper-class childhood of the narrator. His elitist Middle West is the "Carraway house in a city where dwellings are still called through decades by a family's name" (GG, p. 183). Correspondingly, his lost youth is associated with invitations to the Ordways, Schultzes, and Herseys. Such White Anglo-Saxon Protestant homes indeed become America:[70]

> We drew in deep breaths of it as we walked back from dinner through the cold vestibules, *unutterably aware of our identity with this country* for one strange hour, before we melted indistinguishably into it again. (GG, pp. 182f; my italics)

---

[67]Fitzgerald opposed the twenties' idealization of the farmer as vital and close to the soil because this myth was a "stubborn seeking for the static in a world that for almost a hundred years had simply not been static." Fitzgerald, *Letters*, pp. 186f.

[68]Lawrence Larsen has shown that the West did not produce any cities that were significantly different from their Eastern counterparts. Lawrence Larsen, *The Urban West at the End of the Frontier*, Lawrence, Kansas, 1978, pp. 120f.

[69]Lincoln Steffens, *The Shame of the Cities*, 1904, New York, 1957, pp. 46f.

[70]Peter Gregg Slater, "Ethnicity in *The Great Gatsby*," *Twentieth Century Literature*, 19 (1973), pp. 58f.

The West is an upper-class projection of its superior though past values and emotionally evokes an innocent childhood. In a more abstract sense, it also points back to America's national childhood of Thomas Jefferson's independent farmer whose democratic vision is now readjusted to images of a natural frontier in suburbia. But Carraway can only produce class-based nostalgia--in fact, his West is as empty as his upper-class ideals.

The Dutch sailors' vision of the continent as a "fresh, green breast" (GG, p. 187) extends image and figurative meaning into an even more distant past, to another moment irrecoverably gone. In Carraway's view, male Protestants expected nourishment from mother America in vain. Correspondingly, *The Great Gatsby* projects a generally negative view of mothers, women, and romantic love.[71] The white veil of romance is linked to the mysterious facades of the corrupt city.[72] For Carraway, all female figures in the novel are dishonest and hollow--they no longer provide nourishment. Jordan is "slender and small-breasted" (GG, p. 17), Myrtle Wilson, wife of a "worn-out" garage owner (GG, p. 143), significantly dies with "her left breast swinging loose like a flap" (GG, p. 145), and Gatsby who expected that through his romance "he could suck on the pap of life, gulp down the incomparable milk of wonder," is disappointed by Daisy, the terrible mother (GG, p. 122).[73] The dream of "little boy[s]" (GG, p. 94), a term that Carraway uses for a love-stricken Gatsby, is a male projection which attributes suburban disappointment and faults to an absent mother. This patriarchal interpretation of gender is part of Carraway's upper-class view of wealth and love and figuratively shapes his romanticized image of New York.

The vacuity of Carraway's explanatory categories amounts to a stringent pattern. The American dream, the modern city, upper-class ideals, and romantic love are empty vessels. An upper-class narrator romanticizes ideals with a nonexistent basis. The ro-

---

[71] Carraway's chauvinism, which expects honesty only from men but not from women, has been analyzed in Parr, pp. 662-80.

[72] Daisy and her voice "full of money" (GG, p. 126) is described in strikingly similar terms as the false promise of New York facades: "Gatsby was overwhelmingly aware of the youth and mystery that wealth imprisons and preserves, of the freshness of many clothes, and of Daisy, gleaming like silver, safe and proud above the hot struggles of the poor" (GG, pp. 155f). Also, the city and Daisy are recurrently characterized with the epithet "white."

[73] Fitzgerald's own life provides several parallels for the disappointment with romantic love. The biographical basis to his fiction has been examined extensively. See Turnbull, pp. 137-57.

mance questions the whole concept of idealism by revealing absences.[74] Not surprisingly, Carraway cannot spell out what he admires as Gatsby's romantic readiness:[75]

> Through all he said, even through his appalling sentimentality, I was reminded of something--an elusive rhythm, a fragment of lost words, that I had heard somewhere a long time ago. For a moment a phrase tried to take shape in my mouth and my lips parted like a dumb man's, as though there was more struggling upon them than a wisp of startled air. But they made no sound, and what I had almost remembered was uncommunicable forever. (GG, p. 118)

A gesture, a smile is all there is. Jay Gatsby is a glittering facade that hides reified and corrupt practices.[76] The honest efforts that the Protestant ethic demands are retained only in Gatsby's piece of paper from childhood, but his actions shown in the story are all tinged by corruption. All Carraway may do is aestheticize a vacuous ideology.[77] F. Scott Fitzgerald felt this lack of substance in Gatsby's dream as he wrote in a letter to Edmund Wilson:

> The worst fault in [the novel], I think is a BIG FAULT: I gave no account (*and had no feeling or knowledge of*) the emotional relations between Gatsby and Daisy from the time of their reunion to the catastrophe. However, the lack is so astutely concealed by . . . the blankets of excellent prose that no one has noticed it. (my italics)[78]

Unutterable ideas and ideals without a basis--the story which Carraway relates seems a strange Hegelian history of suburban masters without servants. Since Carraway excludes the productive force of history, his story must be stagnant and action, deeds, and viable practice can only be attributed to a past period; indeed, without a motor of history, all this upper-class figure may imagine for the future are "boats against the current, borne back ceaselessly into the past" (GG, p. 188).

Critics of the novel's city image have for a long time accepted the internal division between Jay Gatsby and Nick Carraway, or between East and West Egg as the single windows on the story. Some readers have interpreted the novel as an affirmation of superior Western values which draws on Thomas Jefferson or Frederick Jackson Tur-

---

[74] The color white, Milton Stern has argued, represents in *The Great Gatsby* the "corrupting nothingness of appearances." M. R. Stern, *The Golden Moment: The Novels of F. Scott Fitzgerald*, Urbana, Ill., 1970, p. 282.

[75] Significantly, the communicated apotheosis of the romance again is wordless and expressed with silent lips (GG, p. 156).

[76] Posnock, p. 202.

[77] Heinz Ickstadt points out the vacuum of ideology. Both the city as future and the West as past are emptied of meaning. Ickstadt, "Stadtroman der amerikanischen Moderne," p. 124.

[78] Fitzgerald, *Letters*, p. 341.

ner.[79] Other critics have explained Jay Gatsby as a mythic American figure.[80] Still others saw correctly that America as a whole, both East and West, is criticized.[81] In most abstract terms, the story of lost youth shows the inescapable fate of a romantic "eternal lateness."[82]

Though Nick Carraway's views bear some affinity to ideas of Fitzgerald, Carraway's explanations cannot be taken as the final meaning.[83] Carraway's judgments are set against contrary evidence in the novel. As Richard Godden has shown, Fitzgerald created a novel within the novel. He contrasts the smooth explanation of Gatsby's idealism with its reified vacuity.[84] Fitzgerald's great achievement was to conceive for *The Great Gatsby* an aesthetic strategy that would generate contradictory strands and still function as a unified narrative. "This book," Fitzgerald wrote, "will be a consciously artistic achievement and must depend on that as the first books did not."[85] But his superb architecture and compressed language incorporate the contrary. In *The Crack-Up*, Fitzgerald retrospectively defined such a strategy as the "test of a first-rate intelligence" in its "ability to hold two opposed ideas in the mind at the same time, and still retain the ability to function."[86] This "double vision" allows Fitzgerald to present the irresistible enticement of wealth and yet indicate its destructive potential.[87]

Politically, this strategy meant that he could hold a "double allegiance." All hope is embodied in a future change which as yet has not emerged. Thus, the exclusion of the Wilsons can become the absence which dismantles both an insufficient present and a

---

[79] Kenneth Eble sees the story as a near fictional counterpart to Turner's thesis. Kenneth Eble, *F. Scott Fitzgerald*, New York, 1963, pp. 96f. Eugen Huonder similarly claims that Nick rejects the "corrupt and materialistic civilization of the East for the rural civilization of the West." Huonder, p. 76. See also Arthur Mizener, *The Far Side of Paradise: A Biography of F. Scott Fitzgerald*, New York, 1950, pp. 175f.

[80] Hans Günter Schitter, *Die letzten Romane F. Scott Fitzgeralds: Untersuchung zur Spiegelung von zeitgeschichtlichem und mythischem Bewußtsein im literarischen Kunstwerk*, Bonn, 1968. Brian Way, *F. Scott Fitzgerald and the Art of Social Fiction*, London, 1980. Susan Resneck Parr, "The Idea of Order at West Egg," *New Essays on The Great Gatsby*, ed. Matthew J. Bruccoli, Cambridge, 1985, 59-78. See also Lehan, p. 117; Stern, p. 165.

[81] According to Marius Bewley, Fitzgerald's novel offers "some of the severest criticism of the American dream that our literature affords." Bewley, p. 223. See also Miller, p. 254.

[82] Robert Ornstein, "Scott Fitzgerald's Fable of East and West," *College English*, 18 (1956), p. 142.

[83] Fitzgerald complained about the lack of an American aristocracy and railed against its wasting class in his story "What Kind of Husbands Do 'Jimmies' Make?" Bruccoli, *Epic Grandeur*, p. 192.

[84] Godden, p. 371. Ross Posnock, "'A New World, Material Without Being Real': Fitzgerald's Critique of Capitalism in *The Great Gatsby*," *Critical Essays on The Great Gatsby*, ed. Scott Donaldson, 201-13.

[85] Fitzgerald, *Letters*, p. 163.

[86] Fitzgerald, *The Crack-Up*, p. 69.

[87] Lehan, p. 117; Posnock, p. 201.

glorified past and yet also contains glimmerings of hope for change.[88] In *The Great Gatsby*, however, such politics are present solely as artistic strategy. In a novel devoid of viable ideals, modern aesthetics cannot supplant social content. Fitzgerald may present the original liberating vision only as an incomprehensible "aesthetic contemplation" (GG, p. 182), define romantic readiness as an "uncommunicable" quality (GG, p. 118) and cover the commodified ideals of Gatsby in "blankets of excellent prose."[89]

In the single passage which envisions an unembellished reality--the narrator imagines Gatsby's emptiness after his dream had evaporated--the novel discloses a crucial instability of this world:

> A new world, material without being real, where poor ghosts, breathing dreams like air, drifted fortuitously about . . . like that ashen, fantastic figure gliding toward him through the amorphous trees. (GG, p. 168)

Not accidentally, the passage strongly recalls both Karl Marx's description of a corrupt bourgeoisie in whose economic practices "all that is solid melts into air" and Friedrich Nietzsche's verdict of the weightlessness of the same society.[90] The seeming incompatibility of political ancestors need not be surprising, as F. Scott Fitzgerald had already called himself in a puzzling remark in 1924 a "communist (with Nietzschean overtones)."[91] Recently, in *All That is Solid Melts Into Air*, Marshall Berman has pointed out a crucial link between these contrary philosophies of modernity.[92] Hollow aesthetics and upper-class ideals cannot cover the nihilist essence of this society.

Fitzgerald's achievement in *The Great Gatsby* is the metamorphosis of his contrary philosophy into a critical form. "Das Formschaffen," Georg Lukàcs has noted in his *Theory of the Novel*, "ist die tiefste Bestätigung des Daseins der Dissonanz, die zu denken ist."[93] Although Fitzgerald did not elaborate his vision of a great change or of a revolutionary hope beyond the uncommunicable content of aesthetic contemplation, he incorporates the antithesis to a debased reality in contrary aesthetics. The novelistic form is political. In *The Great Gatsby*, as Karl Marx would say, "everything is pregnant

---

[88] Richard Godden writes that Carraway sees Wilson as an "ashen, fantastic figure" (GG, p. 168) because "Nick refuses to conceive of Wilson's world and of the world of Gatsby's origins." Godden, p. 371.

[89] Godden, p. 355.

[90] Karl Marx, "The Communist Manifesto," *The Marx-Engels Reader*, ed. Robert C. Tucker, New York, 1978, p. 475. Marshall Berman, *All That is Solid Melts Into Air*, 1982, Harmondsworth, 1988, p. 100.

[91] Fitzgerald cited in Donaldson, "Political Development," p. 321.

[92] Berman, pp. 15-36, 85-129.

[93] Quoted from Georg Lukàcs, *Die Theorie des Romans*, Darmstadt, 1971, p. 62.

with its contrary."[94] The romance's form blends two contrary strategies. On the one hand, *The Great Gatsby* is tightly structured, coherent, and unified.[95] On the other hand, Fitzgerald produces gaps and contradictions.[96] The contrary is evident in its use of irony, paradoxes, oxymorons, contrasting scenes,[97] and "double consciousness."[98] Thus its meaning may remain open for a negated hope without breaking apart into contradictory facets. It allows a class reading against a surface grain in which Carraway's conclusions seemingly encompass all human history.

However, Fitzgerald's purely aesthetic strategy is apolitical in content and its glittering surface blankets such shortcomings perfectly. The novel's interpretations have mostly taken issue with this surface. Yet, to see only the romantic aestheticism is fatal for the overall thrust of the novel. The Wilsons must be reintroduced as agents and victims to get an undistorted perspective of F. Scott Fitzgerald's radical image of the modern metropolis. Fitzgerald himself was disappointed about the novel's reception and said that only Edmund Wilson and H. L. Mencken had seen what the novel intended.[99] Mencken's review significantly had stressed the interrelatedness of style and politics: "Fitzgerald, the stylist, arises to challenge Fitzgerald, the social historian, but I doubt that the latter ever quite succumbs to the former."[100]

The Great Gatsby critically examines developments in the metropolis of the twenties and indicates the missing gaps in visions about an Arcadian suburbia or in an aestheticized skyline. The upper-class romanticism which underlies these ideologies of space was willingly accepted and repeated by middle-class readers who aspired to similar perspectives on the American dream. Yet, both pastoral and unreal city images are intricately and crucially related in the novel. They cannot be separated from the absences in the romance. From the beginning, *The Great Gatsby* shows that images of a Babylonian degeneracy and of I-love-Manhattan-skylines are biased perspectives and misleading promises. Although F. Scott Fitzgerald was strongly attracted by these facades,

---

[94] Marx cited in Berman, pp. 35f. Ross Posnock has convincingly shown "how deeply Marx's critique is assimilated into the novel's imaginative life." Posnock, 201.

[95] Garrett, p. 114. Kenneth Eble has praised the novel's "tight inevitability of construction." Eble, p. 91.

[96] Keath Fraser writes: "What *The Great Gatsby* seems about in part, and where it derives its suggestiveness and energy, lies in what is not accounted for, what is undisclosed." Keath Fraser, "Another Reading of *The Great Gatsby*," *English Studies in Canada*, 5 (1979), 330-43.

[97] Lehan, p. 109; Parr, p. 60; Posnock, p. 204; Korenman, p. 95.

[98] Posnock, p. 201.

[99] Fitzgerald, *Letters*, p. 342.

[100] H. L. Mencken, "As H. L. Mencken Sees It," *Baltimore Evening Sun*, May 2, 1925, p. 9; repr. F. Scott Fitzgerald, *The Critical Reception*, ed. Jackson R. Bryer, New York, 1978, pp. 211-14.

212 Fragmented Urban Images

his novel nevertheless dismantles the romanticized edifices of modern architecture.[101] Some years later, Fitzgerald explicitly told his daughter what his novel as yet only captured as aesthetic form: "Most questions in life" he wrote to her in 1939, "have an economic basis (at least according to us Marxians)."[102] Looking for this missing basis in the fissures and holes of the glittering facade then is the most productive way to comprehend the radical and hopeful side of the city image in *The Great Gatsby*.

---

[101]Fitzgerald wrote to Ludlow Fowler in 1924: "Thats the whole burden of this novel--the loss of those illusions that give such color to the world so that you don't care whether things are true or false as long as they partake of the magical glory." Fitzgerald, *Correspondence*, p. 145.

[102]Donaldson, "Political Development," p. 348.

11

John Dos Passos
Manhattan Transfer

1. The Paramount Visual City

The striking visuality of *Manhattan Transfer* renders John Dos Passos' treatment of the city unique in modern fiction.[1] The novel is totally immersed in the American city of the 1920s. The focus on metropolitan processes and spatial structures outweighs all other fictional concerns. *Manhattan Transfer* is, as Blanche Gelfant has pointed out, a "text on the art of the city novel."[2] Intended by John Dos Passos as a documentary novel in the style of the "straight writer,"[3] *Manhattan Transfer* is an embodiment of the urban decade.[4] In 1920, the Bureau of Census announced that for the first time the majority of Americans lived in urban areas; the city's share amounted to 51.2 % of the total population in almost three thousand separate urban places. The statistical watershed indicated that an overwhelming portion of economic, social, and cultural power was now visibly wielded from metropolitan centers.

As a fictional "architect of history,"[5] Dos Passos reconstructs the development of New York from 1897 to 1924. From its start, the novel projects hopes for a new era: the first section is permeated with beginnings, arrivals, births, inaugurations, and awakenings. The Hudson metropolis is at the very center of things; the apex of progress, it provides the ambiance for utopian visions. Its rhythm, pace, noises, tunes, images, and col-

---

[1] John Dos Passos, *Manhattan Transfer*, Boston, 1925. References to *Manhattan Transfer* will be abbreviated to MT and incorporated into the text.

[2] Gelfant, p. 135.

[3] John Dos Passos, "Introduction," *Three Soldiers*, 1921, New York, 1932, p. viii.

[4] James B. Lane, "*Manhattan Transfer* as a Gateway to the 1920s," *Centennial Review*, 16 (1972), p. 293.

[5] Dos Passos, "Introduction," *Three Soldiers*, p. viii.

ors give the novel a distinctly modern atmosphere. Showing the mark of specification, Sinclair Lewis noted that the novel captured the very spirit of Manhattan.[6]

The omnipresence of the city, however, also is conceived of as a physical entrapment. Bathed in the cultural pessimism of the 1920s, Dos Passos' depiction of New York has affinities to the sterile and unreal cities of T. S. Eliot or Oswald Spengler.[7] Its inanimate environment is generally opposed to nature, and the novel significantly opens with references to rotten fruits and vegetables floating on the Hudson. While Walt Whitman had seen the American city generally in accordance with natural phenomena, and Theodore Dreiser had conceived of it as part of a natural evolution, for John Dos Passos the metropolis stands in contrast to nature. People are lost in such an arid environment: corruption, degeneration, decay, and death abound. A hostile critic likened *Manhattan Transfer* to an "explosion in a cesspool."[8] The environment seems to rule and subdue the characters.

This duality of the city image is basic to *Manhattan Transfer*: the novel is both naturalist and modernist, the city both determined and free. This ambiguity is linked to the central social and thematic concerns of the novel. Thus, despite the sweeping focus of Dos Passos' "rapportage"[9] whose inclusiveness of detail makes the novel seem a comprehensive mosaic, the events in the novel still are selected and arranged from a single perspective. As the title suggests, *Manhattan Transfer* emphasizes social and geographical mobility. The three central figures, Jimmy Herf, Ellen Thatcher, and George Baldwin are upper- and middle-class transients and this perspective shapes most facets in the novel. As in *The Great Gatsby*, the preoccupation with the opposition of nature and city testifies to a particular class view.

The impression of totality in *Manhattan Transfer*, facilitated through the selective overview of a middle-class mental map, derives predominantly from the concentration on the visual city. The novelist describes his intention with spatial analogies:

> I started a rapportage on New York . . . The narrative must stand up off the page. Fragmentation. Contrast. Montage. The result was *Manhattan Transfer*.[10]

The visual arts proved highly influential, for *Manhattan Transfer* presents a multifaceted cubist city. Naturalism records surface phenomena, while cubism unifies narratives and

---

[6] Sinclair Lewis, "Manhattan at Last!" *Saturday Review of Literature*, 2 (Dec. 5, 1925), p. 361.

[7] E. D. Lowry, "*Manhattan Transfer*: Dos Passos' Wasteland," *The University Review*, 30 (1963), 47-52.

[8] Elmer More, *The Demon of the Absolute*, Princeton, 1928, p. 63.

[9] Allen Belkind, ed., *Dos Passos, the Critics, and the Writer's Intention*, Carbondale, Ill., 1971, p. xx.

[10] John Dos Passos, "What makes a Novelist?" *National Review*, 20 (1968), p. 31.

relates perspectives.[11] The "democratized modernism" of *Manhattan Transfer* reflects the collectivist intention to make experience commonly available.[12]

Most important, the metropolis as a setting and catalyst to innovative trends is recaptured as a human artifact through cubism. Its reconstruction presupposes an aesthetic and political choice. The cubist conception of space has been, as John Berger has indicated, one of the most radical and advanced approaches toward physical reality.[13] Cubist autonomy, contingency, and openness expressed a utopian hope. Even Manhattan, the most opaque and insurmountable of urban molochs, may be subdued to human action. The novel itself incorporates such glimpses in which the liberating breakup of urban form is envisioned. Phil Sandbourne's belief in human activity corresponds to Dos Passos' hope in his modernist poetic in *Manhattan Transfer*:

> Do you remember years ago old man Specker used to talk about vitreous and superenameled tile? Well I've been workin on his formula out at Hollis.... Man it would revolutionize the whole industry. Combined with concrete it would enormously increase the flexibility of the materials at the architects' disposal. We could make tile any color, size or finish.... Imagine this city when all the buildins instead of bein dirty gray were ornamented with vivid colors. Imagine bands of scarlet round the entablatures of skyscrapers. Colored tile would revolutionize the whole life of the city.... Instead of falling back on the orders or on gothic or romanesque decorations we could evolve new designs, new colors, new forms. If there was a little color in the town all this hardshell inhibited life'd break down. (MT, p. 257)

The tension between a naturalist determinism and a cubist openness is emphasized by gaps in the novel's attempted totality. Arguing for the necessity of change, *Manhattan Transfer* omits any traces of a possible agent of change. Collective human action is marginalized in the collectivist novel. *Manhattan Transfer* is foremost a kaleidoscope of sights and a document to collectivity through language and shared viewpoints, but a political group or class which might create alternative forms of life is not depicted. Critics so far have generally described this inconsistency as a division between the modernist aesthete and the social critic in Dos Passos.[14] In contrast, this study argues that Dos Passos intricately relates politics and art in *Manhattan Transfer*. He replaces the dated objectivism of naturalism with an open cubist diagram and thus may present the city as both free and determinate, random and ordered.

---

[11] See Ben Stolzfus, "John Dos Passos and the French," *Comparative Literature*, 15 (1963), 146-63. George Knox, "Dos Passos and Painting," *Texas Studies in Literature and Language*, 6 (1964), 22-38. Michael Spindler, "John Dos Passos and the Visual Arts," *Journal of American Studies*, 15 (1981), 391-406.

[12] E. D. Lowry, "The Lively Art of *Manhattan Transfer*," *PMLA*, 84 (1969), p. 1638.

[13] John Berger, "The Moment of Cubism," *The Sense of Sight*, New York, 1985, 159-88.

[14] Malcolm Cowley, "The Poet and the World," *New Republic*, 70 (Apr. 27, 1932), 303-5; Gelfant, p. 141.

2. The Decade of the Skyscraper

Manhattan Transfer is replete with documentary details. Such a combination of fiction and history, Dos Passos argued, was essential to the modern novel.[15] The novel depicts Manhattan as "simultaneous chronicle"[16] and it analyzes the historical process which has engendered this state. The optimistic beginning, so permeated with hopes, promises, and visions that D. H. Lawrence would call it almost "too warm, too passionate,"[17] is succeeded by an overall atmosphere of disillusionment.

Dealing with the period from 1897 to 1924, *Manhattan Transfer* covers momentous upheavals in American society. In this era, the economy generally shifted from industrial production to mass consumption; also, in the 1920s corporate concentration again accelerated. These changes greatly affected urban life. In the first quarter of the century, urban America doubled in population from 30 to 61 million, and the figure of those urbanites who lived in cities with more than half a million inhabitants exploded from eight to eighteen million. New York underwent severe restructuring. From its position as the leading commerce and manufacturing city it developed into the chief place for banking and big business. By 1920, three out of four companies of the largest national corporations had their headquarters in Manhattan.[18] The oligarchy of big business was further cemented in the 1920s. From 1919 to 1930, eight thousand firms disappeared in mergers in the United States.[19] In cities this development became visually evident in the profusion of corporate and banking skyscrapers in the business districts: "The abstractions of high finance produced their exact material embodiment in these buildings."[20] Similar to the first wave of monopolism in the 1890s, when the first skyscrapers and the Sherman Anti-Trust Act had coincided, the vertical city of the 1920s again corresponded with corporate enlargement. The twenties became the decade of the skyscraper and the skyline.

---

[15] John Dos Passos, "Statement of Belief," *Bookman*, 68 (Sept. 24, 1928), p. 26.

[16] John Dos Passos, "Contemporary Chronicle," *The Carleton Miscellany*, 2 (1961), pp. 25-29; cited in Linda W. Wagner, *Dos Passos: Artist as American*, Austin, 1979, p. 49.

[17] D. H. Lawrence, rev. of *Manhattan Transfer*, *Calendar of Modern Letters*, 1927, 70-72, repr. *Dos Passos: The Critical Heritage*, ed. Barry Maine, London, 1988, p. 76.

[18] 167 of the 232 largest companies were located there. Nestor R. Rodriguez and Joe R. Feagin, "Urban Specialization in the World-System: An Investigation of Historical Cases," *Urban Affairs Quarterly*, 22 (1986), p. 205.

[19] Dowd, p. 71; Spindler, p. 103.

[20] Mumford, p. 609.

New York saw an immense boost in high-rise office architecture as a result of its leading role in national finance and commerce. The demand in office space for enlarging bureaucracies increased immensely. This spatial concentration raised land values in urban areas twentyfold from 1920 to 1926.[21] The dominant position of Manhattan was expressed by its excessive number of skyscrapers: it possessed five times as many tall buildings as Chicago, the city ranked next, which itself was an outstanding center in the industrial Midwest. The absolute increase in New York's verticality was astounding. In 1900, Manhattan mainly contained buildings from nine to sixteen stories and only a few over twenty, but by 1920 more than 400 skyscrapers over twenty stories rose above the rest. This construction boost accelerated in the 1920s. In 1925, 350 tall buildings were under way.[22] By the end of the decade, New York had half the nation's tall skyscrapers over 200 feet.[23] The race for verticality, prestige, and power among the giant corporations was run on Manhattan's skyline in the first decades of this century: first the Singer Building in 1908, then the Metropolitan Tower, the Woolworth, the Chrysler, and finally the Empire State Building set new records for height.[24] Yet Manhattan's skyline as an embodiment of technological progress and as a symbol of the incredible power of big business was not the sole visible change.

New York also exploded in expanse and size. From 1.4 million in 1890 the population increased to 6.9 million in 1930 within the city limits and from 2.5 million to 10.8 million in the metropolitan area. Despite a strong migration to white-collar suburbs, Manhattan reached its highest density ever. By 1920, approximately two million people were crammed on the Hudson island.[25] The majority of New Yorkers had to live in overcrowded tenements; around the turn of the century this group of residents amounted to more than two thirds of the total population, most of them immigrants. In the first decade, over half of New York's populace was foreign-born.[26] The business districts on the southern tip and in Midtown existed uneasily side by side with such working-class and lower middle-class areas. In fact, the first zoning laws of 1916 were

---

[21]Chudacoff, p. 203.

[22]Schleier, p. 69; Warner, p. 29.

[23]In 1929, a survey found that 188 of 377 U.S. buildings over 200 feet stood in New York. Kenneth T. Jackson, "The Capital of Capitalism: The New York Metropolitan Region, 1890-1940," *Metropolis 1890-1940*, ed. Anthony Sutcliffe, London, 1984, p. 350.

[24]George Lankevich and Howard B. Furer, *A Brief History of New York City*, New York, 1984, pp. 173, 206. Edward Robb Ellis, *The Epic of New York City*, Toronto, 1966, pp. 495f.

[25]Manhattan's population peaked in 1910 with 2.3 million residents and then steadily declined to 1.2 million in 1980. Jackson, pp. 320, 328.

[26]Ibid., p. 325; Lankevich, p. 175.

implemented to prevent lowly garment workers from disturbing affluent customers of fashionable shops on Fifth Avenue with their brown lunch bags.[27]

In the wake of immigration, however, New York possessed an incredibly varied and cosmopolitan mixture of ethnic cultures and languages.[28] "This is certainly the city," one character declares, "for everyone being from somewhere else" (MT, p. 64). German, Jewish, Italian, French, Senegalese, Russian, Irish, Slavic, Chinese, Sicilian, Polish, Swedish, Norwegian, Danish, Syrian and Greek Manhattanites people the pages of the novel. Dos Passos conveys an impression of the many languages spoken in this heterogeneous community by suggesting their foreign accents in a varied phonetic orthography.

One important factor contributing to the rapid development of New York was its harbor, the center of U.S. overseas trade. In 1920, forty percent of the exports and more than fifty percent of the imports of the nation's trade passed through its docks. It was thus equipped to receive the majority of European immigrants. Of 23 million new citizens from the Old World between 1880 and 1919, 17 million alone disembarked on Ellis Island. Also, during wartime, one and a half million soldiers departed for Europe from New York's harbor.[29]

New York was thus characterized by an exceptional geographical and social mobility. The restructuring of capitalism allowed large numbers of Manhattan office clerks to rise within the middle class. In 1900, white-collar occupations only accounted for half of those of manual workers, but by 1930, this group, together with people in the service sector, equalled the number of physical laborers.[30] The professions introduced in the first pages of the novel reflect this prevalence of service and white-collar jobs in New York: readers encounter a nurse, an accountant, a printer, an import business manager, a construction worker, and a broker. Related to this economic shift, approximately one and a half million middle-class residents moved from more central areas to outlying boroughs and the suburban fringe in the decades that *Manhattan Transfer* spans.[31] The ceaseless motion and endless traffic in the novel reflects this increased division between work and home, shopping and residence, living and entertainment for the middle class:

> Red light. Bell.
> A block deep for ranks of cars wait at the grade crossing, fenders in taillights, mudguards scraping mudguards, motors purring hot, exhausts reeking....

---

[27] Jackson, p. 338.

[28] George-Albert Astre, *Thèmes et structures dans l'oeuvre de John Dos Passos*, Paris, 1956, p. 199.

[29] Rodriguez, p. 205; Jackson, p. 323; Ellis, p. 500.

[30] Spindler, p. 103.

[31] Jackson, p. 329.

> Green light. Motors race, gears screech into first. The cars space out, flow in a long ribbon along the ghostly cement road, between blackwindowed blocks of concrete, between bright slabbed colors of signboards towards the glow over the city. . . . (MT, p. 217)

The sense of motion, fast pace, and noisy traffic created in the novel, also derive from Manhattan's role as national and metropolitan hub for the exchange, transfer, and transportation of goods and people. The harbor is important in the novel and the many glimpses of oceanfront, docks, and vessels document this as well as the multitude of ferries, tugboats, ships, and oceanliners that appear in the narrative. The readers ferry into the novel and in the end again out of it. Manhattan is an island or, as Dos Passos later puts it, "a continent in itself."[32] Mass transportation rules the inner city. 1.2 million subway rides were recorded daily by the middle of the second decade. The number of cars tripled in the twenties.[33]

The peculiar coincidence of corporate-controlled industrialism and urban concentration had its peak in the 1920s. Social and spatial transformation produced political conflicts and aggravated social crises. Capitalist expansion altered the social fabric according to its needs. Organized labor was defeated in its struggle against corporate power. An effective alternative to existing machine politics did not develop. Despite the hysteria unleashed in the *red scare*, radical and collective solutions were only of marginal impact; conformism, fraudulence, and corruption dominated federal and municipal politics. Not until 1937 did the urban electorate acquire the means of influencing metropolitan decisions, at least through tools of planning.[34]

Social frustration and aggression reappeared in the shrill tensions between old and new immigrants, between black and white Americans. Racism, organized crime, and religious fundamentalism thrived as symptoms of the crisis in the 1920s. A conservative majority tried to fight the loss of moral standards and inner restraint through the prohibition of alcohol in a society whose economy and culture was more and more based on the indulgence of consumers.

A democratized materialism which reached most people in the middle class came to function as a safety valve. Consumer capitalism suggested equality by the choice among its products, directing the desires, wishes, and dreams of its customers toward affirmative channels. In the first three decades, the money spent for advertisements rose thirteenfold. Expenditures for magazine ads alone tripled in the twenties. Mass publica-

---

[32] John Dos Passos, *The Best Times: An Informal Memoir*, New York, 1966, p. 132.

[33] Jackson, p. 334. By 1918 there were eight million cars registered in the United States and only a decade later the figures had more than tripled to 26 million. Chudacoff, p. 212; Morison, p. 566.

[34] Jackson, p. 339.

tions spread the latest fashion in haircut, dress, or dance. Organized leisure boomed. Attendance in sport stadiums, dance halls, vaudevilles, cinemas, and theatres exploded.[35] Commercial icons loomed large. These consumerist trends, at the time, were almost identical with metropolitan behavior since the electronic media, which soon would penetrate even the most remote corner in the country, had not yet been implemented. Against genteel America which rejected popular culture as low and vulgar, the modernist avantgarde discerned a liberating and disruptive potential in the messages and media of mass culture. They posed an alternative to the bourgeois values dismantled as hollow and false in World War I.

New York became the outstanding venue for the fruitful interlinkage of popular culture and modernist thought. John Dos Passos had been deeply impressed by the New York Armory Show, which in 1913 presented modern European art to Americans for the first time. Greenwich Village, where the novel was partly written, became a fertile ground for cultural experiments. *Manhattan Transfer* is at the apex of this symbiosis. It presents a cubist collage of metropolitan paraphernalia and ephemeral mass products.[36] The novel contains advertisements, commercial slogans, and signs which Dos Passos had collected over the years in the city, it reproduces newspaper headlines and stories, it includes lyrics of popular tunes and Tin Pan Alley songs, and it even incorporates a list of shipped goods (MT, p. 144) and excerpts from an encyclopedia (MT, p. 87).[37] The multifaceted picture presents a jarring cosmopolitan mixture.

3. Social and Geographical Transfer

The reputation of *Manhattan Transfer* for capturing the generic essence of the modern city must be reassessed. Admittedly, among the attempts to present the modern cityscape it is the most successful one. Manhattan *is* the protagonist.[38] Yet despite the broad focus of the "synoptic" novel, the facets portrayed are selective and one-sided. The experience projected in the novel does not represent an urban way of life in general, but

---

[35]Ewen, *Captains of Consciousness*, pp. 32, 62; Chudacoff, pp. 210ff.

[36]Knox, p. 263. John Dos Passos was not the first to associate New York with the montage of cubism. In 1912, the cubist writer Blaise Cendrars had composed his first poem *Pâques à New York* in Manhattan. Two years later, the painter Francis Picabia called New York the "cubist city." Monique Chefdor, *Blaise Cendrars*, Boston, 1980, p. 37; Taylor, p. 248.

[37]Townsend Ludington, *John Dos Passos. A Twentieth Century Odyssey*, New York, 1980, p. 229.

[38]Gelfant, p. 161; Eugen Arden, "*Manhattan Transfer*: An Experiment in Technique," *University of Kansas Review*, 22 (1955), p. 1953; Astre, p. 145; Hoffmann, p. 414.

only captures the behavior of social transients in the inner city.[39] The episodes primarily focus on characters from the lower to the upper middle class, interspersed with some isolated lower-class figures. Hence, the distinct urban experience of a large number of New Yorkers and their particular perception of the city are not contained in *Manhattan Transfer*.

As the title of the novel and many of its episodes, motifs, and images indicate, urban experience is linked to social transience.[40] Geographical mobility, in a sense, is only a variant of the social. Competition in capitalism, whose hierarchical stratification is basic to transience, produces a pervasive isolation and atomization. Success empties, failure crushes people.

The three main figures are characterized by social and professional mobility. Jimmy Herf departs from the city as an unemployed journalist; George Baldwin succeeds as a lawyer and then moves into politics; and Ellen Thatcher achieves fame as an actress on Broadway. Ellen Thatcher and George Baldwin push forward without scruples; Ellen, to get ahead, is said even "to marry a trolleycar" (MT, p. 156). Their eventual union is the consummation of identical interests and an apotheosis to the victory of a reified materialism. Other figures also experience the pervasive insecurity of transience. Joe Harland, once the "Wizard of Wall Street" (MT, p. 146), ends as a beggar. Stan Emery loses his grip on the world, a stability that Bud Korpenning never gains when he tries to find a new place for himself in the city, away from rural brutality. Competition, rather than cooperation, ruthlessness, rather than solidarity, conformism, rather than creativity, count in this society.

In urban criticism, this behavior was often linked to generic conditions in the modern city.[41] Since the segment chosen by Dos Passos for special treatment coincided with the sociological focus of the Chicago School and with middle-class notions of innately urban features, it was elevated to capture the essence, the depravity of modern metropolitan life. Nature, on the other hand, was seen as a possible alternative and yardstick of evaluation.[42] In fact, the surface description in *Manhattan Transfer* seems to validate that size, density, and heterogeneity determine the anonymity, atomization, and anomie in large cities. Close examination reveals, however, that while clearly using environmental imagery, Dos Passos' assessment of experience is closer to Herbert J.

---

[39] Incidentally, a study of the novel was titled *Manhattan Transients*. Sharon Fusselman Mizener, *Manhattan Transients*, Hicksville, N.Y., 1977.

[40] John H. Wrenn, *John Dos Passos*, New York, 1961, p. 122.

[41] Gelfant, pp. 161ff.

[42] Michael Clark, *Dos Passos's Early Fiction, 1912-1938*, Selingsgrove, 1987, p. 99.

Gans' critique of the Chicago School urbanism. In his essay "Urbanism and Suburbanism as Ways of Life," Gans has pointed out that Louis Wirth's analysis only, and not very accurately, applies to a limited group of urbanites in the central city; it is true for social isolates (Bud Korpenning, Joe Harland, or Dutch Robertson), for social transients (Ellen Thatcher, George Baldwin, and Congo Jake), and it is partially true for inner-city students, intellectuals, and artists who conceive of their stays as intermezzos on the road to more distant goals (Ruth Prynne, Cassandra Wilkins, and Jimmy Herf). "The social features of Wirth's concept of urbanism," Gans says in summary, "seem therefore to be a result of residential instability rather than number, size, and heterogeneity."[43] Such instability, however, especially in economically tightly segregated areas, is a function of income and class, but not of urban, suburban, or rural modes of living.

The urbanist argument has often been extended to the novel's aesthetics: the form of *Manhattan Transfer* is said to reflect the generic disorder of the modern city.[44] The various strands seemed isolated and unrelated while connections between the facets of the montage were neglected.[45] Such an interpretation is deceptively circular. The city was defined as generically atomized and chaotic and then the form expressed the novelistic transformation of sociological insight. But montage as aesthetic technique does not have a fixed, innate meaning. For example, through montage Sergej Eisenstein's films, often mentioned in connection with Dos Passos' novel, portrayed collective rebellion, cohesion, and solidarity.[46] Admittedly, Dos Passos' fiction deals with single individuals and presents disconnected narrative lines, but the thematic and formal arrangement suggests the will to order and an attempt at collectivity. According to E. D. Lowry, "artist and reader form a community and the reconstruction of the communal idea is one of Dos Passos' major aims in *Manhattan Transfer*."[47]

---

[43]Gans, pp. 507f.

[44]Lees, pp. 290f. Hartwig Isernhagen discusses in detail the interpretations of Blanche Gelfant, Festa McCormick, Volker Klotz and others and their failure to provide convincing urban readings. For Isernhagen, Dos Passos distinguishes himself from other modernists as he does not provide a consistent abstract order. Isernhagen sees him as a proto-existentialist writer in his aesthetic negativity (Hartwig Isernhagen, *Ästhetische Innovation und Kulturkritik: Das Frühwerk von John Dos Passos 1916-1938*, München, 1983, pp. 130-48.) Monika Schiller too sees *Manhattan Transfer* characterized by a profound negativity. Monika Schiller, *Geschichte als Erinnerung bei John Dos Passos*, Heidelberg, 1983, p. 165.

[45]Landsberg, p. 120.

[46]Lowry, "The Lively Art of *Manhattan Transfer*," p. 1633. It has been a commmonplace to link the novel's technique to the films of Sergej Eisenstein and to *Battleship Potemkin* in particular. The first film of the Russian director, however, was released in Europe in 1925 and *Battleship Potemkin* only in 1926 so that there could have been no direct influence. Montage was a widespread technique by then. Spindler, "John Dos Passos and the Visual Arts," pp. 402f.

[47]Lowry, p. 1634.

The limits of Dos Passos' portrayal of urban experience in New York are most apparent when those groups characterized by different life-styles and cultural habits are taken into consideration. *Manhattan Transfer* omits suburban areas and commuters and thus excludes the distinct forms of homogeneous upper-class living which F. Scott Fitzgerald's *The Great Gatsby* scathingly attacked in the same year. It omits the narrow and enclosed metropolis of lower-class neighborhoods as depicted in Stephen Crane's *Maggie: A Girl of the Streets* or the claustrophobia in lower middle-class quarters that James T. Farrell described in *Studs Lonigan*. Finally, it omits the huge group of ethnic working-class communities whose perceptions and attitudes were very different, whether Manhattan was seen from Harlem or from a Jewish neighborhood, as in Henry Roth's *Call It Sleep*. Such divergent modes of experience are marginalized, as they do not fit the predominant perspective in *Manhattan Transfer*. Their exclusion is a telling blindspot in the multifaceted totality. Significantly, working-class and lower-class quarters are almost invisible in this novel which otherwise celebrates the visual city. Often, these areas only intrude as stench into the middle-class panorama:

> He walked without hearing the yells of the children or the annihilating clatter of the L trains overhead or smelling the rancid sweet huddled smell of packed tenements. (MT, p. 10)
>
> He crossed Sixth Avenue and followed the street into the dingy West Side, where there was a smell of stables and the sidewalks were littered with scraps of garbage and crawling children. Imagine living down here among low Irish and foreigners, the scum of the universe. (MT, p. 51)
>
> Through the smell of the arbutus she caught for a second the unwashed smell of his body, the smell of immigrants, of Ellis Island, of crowded tenements. Under all the nickelplated, goldplated streets enameled with May, uneasily she could feel the huddling smell, spreading in dark slow crouching masses like corruption oozing from broken sewers, like a mob. (MT, p. 395)[48]

The novel captures a cross-section of New York society, of its locales, types, and professions, and assesses each of them from the perspective of individual mobility. Transience, both social and geographical, furthers atomization and isolation. Even where love, kindness, or solidarity appear in *Manhattan Transfer*, it appears as a sympathy for individual nonconformism or anarchism. Thus Congo Jake, the bootlegger, deserves more respect than all the characters of big business. "If I'd been God," Jimmy Herf tells him, "and had to decide who in this city should make a million dollars and who shouldn't

---

[48] Dos Passos does not altogether exclude views of tenements (MT, p. 10), but he never portrays them as a social community. In Ellen's view, he both records and criticizes the middle-class fear of dangerous aliens as an unruly and subversive mob. Her perceptions link her to the denunciations of Densch (MT, p. 288).

I swear you're the man I should have picked" (MT, p. 383). But sympathetic characters are also infected by the adverse conditions. Dutch Robertson, unemployed and hungry, at least resents his unjustified use of power:

> Dutch stuck out his jaw and talked tough. 'Give us a swig o milk will yez?' The milkman was a frail pinkfaced youngster. His blue eyes wilted. 'Sure go round behind the wagon, there's an open bottle under the seat. Dont let nobody see you drink it.' He drank it in deep gulps, sweet and soothing to his parched throat. Jez I didn't need to talk rough like that. He waited until the boy came back. 'Thankye buddy, that was mighty white.' (MT, p. 316)

Manhattan Transfer only deals with isolated individuals. In this "collectivist novel"[49] which demands the active participation of the reader, community is primarily an aesthetic idea and collectivity an intellectual concept.

Beyond the restricted social focus in the novel, the portrayal achieves its power through its unique fusion of transient experiences and the concern for the visual Manhattan. The city, viewed by dislocated, mobile citizens, corresponds closely to the perspective of newcomers, outsiders, strangers, or commuters to the city. Indeed, Dos Passos would later say of himself in *The Best Times*: "I delighted in exploring the creeks and channels and backwaters of the city . . . always as the visitor, the tourist on his way to the railroad station."[50] Approaching a city, its physicality dominates perception as it provides a first orientation. Such city sights abound in the novel: "As the boat drew near the buildings densened to a granite mountain split with knifecut canyons" (MT, p. 251). Similarly, readers and newcomers first must assemble the puzzling multitude of urban facets to a tendentially consistent whole, linking it to expectations or prior knowledge about the place.

But even here, a specific class view organizes Dos Passos' visual representation of New York. First, only the middle and upper class possess the map-like overview projected in *Manhattan Transfer*. A portrait of New York in 1925 centered in working-class tenements in the Lower East Side would no doubt be strikingly different. Second, the identification of Manhattan as the center of New York corresponds with the middle-class maps, as Stanley Milgram has indicated, and relates to the location of principal economic and cultural institutions for this class in Manhattan.[51] Its museums, avenues, parks, and high-rise architecture are delightful for the flaneur, traveler, and tourist: in

---

[49] Joseph Warren Beach, *American Fiction, 1920-40*, New York, 1941, p. 41.
[50] Dos Passos, *Best Times*, p. 149.
[51] Duncan, p. 56.

1925 this meant membership in the upper or middle class.[52] Little Jimmy Herf receives such a sightseeing tour of Manhattan's 'classical' spots:

> Look deary you're missing things . . . There's the Statue of Liberty. . . . And there's Governors Island the other side. There where the trees are . . . and see, that's Brooklyn Bridge. . . . That is a fine sight. And look at all the docks . . . that's the Battery . . . and the masts and the ships . . . there's the spire of Trinity Church and the Pulitzer building. (MT, p. 69)

But if the power of *Manhattan Transfer* stems from this particular perspective which both captures the view of outsiders *to* the city, of immigrants, visitors, and tourists and of outsiders *in* the city, of commuters, shoppers, and suburbanites, the city at the same time is reduced to a mere physical object or a distanced panorama: "Against a sootsmudged horizon tangled with barges, steamers, chimneys of powerplants, covered wharves, bridges, lower New York was a pink and white tapering pyramid cut slenderly out of cardboard" (MT, p. 276).

Dos Passos' city does not present the knowable community of a working-class or ethnic neighborhood with its saloons, clubs, neighbors, friends, or relatives which he otherwise appreciated.[53] Rather, Dos Passos seems visually obsessed with the city. Manhattan after all is, a figure asserts, "the greatest sight in the world" (MT, p. 276). Even in the most unlikely of situations he has his characters record glimpses of the physical city. Why should a waiter take notice of familiar and everyday scenery, if it were not for the author's desire to present more of New York's panorama?

> When the waiter leans over to take away the empty oystershells he can see through the window, beyond the greystone parapet, the tops of few buildings jutting like the trees at the edge of a cliff and the tinfoil reaches of the harbor littered with ships. (MT, p. 287)

Yet recording the visual Manhattan, Dos Passos does not restrict himself to the totalizing view of panoramas. His splitting the city into cubist facets allows change of focus and distance. Like a camera, he may move from a close-up view to more distant objects:

> Dusk gently smooths crispangled streets. Dark presses tight the steaming asphalt city, crushes the fretwork of windows and lettered signs and chimneys and watertanks and fireescapes and moldings and patterns and corrugations and eyes and hands and neckties into blue chunks, into black enormous blocks. (MT, p. 112)

---

[52] Stanley Milgram explains: "There is a city culture that is transmitted from one generation to the next focusing on or highlighting certain parts of the city, while actually suppressing a knowledge of other parts. In this sense, the mental maps are social facts, not just individual facts." Milgram quoted in Duncan, p. 54.

[53] Melvin Landsberg, *John Dos Passos' Path to U.S.A.*, Boulder, Col., 1972, p. 98.

The multiple perspectives of a cubist image allow the approximation of wholeness through variety. The fact that Manhattan represented a spearhead of modern Western culture added extra power to this attempted totality.

4. Politics and the Cubist City

The "pronounced visual quality" of *Manhattan Transfer* has been praised in criticism.[54] Thematic concerns conventionally associated with the city, the striving for success, the destruction of familial bonds, the corrupting effects of materialism, or the hectic pace of life, are present too in *Manhattan Transfer*,[55] but they are dominated by immersion in the visual city. Dos Passos' emphasis on the visual city springs from personal predilections and his conviction that modern life had produced an "eyeminded" culture. Dos Passos studied architecture and later, when he thought of a profession, he did not know whether he should turn writer or painter. In the 1920s, he exhibited paintings in New York galleries.[56] Thus, the visual modern city had to be Dos Passos's *sujet*. He later recalled, "New York was the first thing that struck me. It was marvelous. It was hideous. It had to be described."[57]

Dos Passos' interest in the visual is translated by a dual strategy in the novel. First, Manhattan is recorded in a naturalist documentation of its topography, layout, and architecture and through the cumulation of selected facets from its segregated social mosaic. Second, the visual city is dissected into segments which are then reassembled in a cubist montage. Critics have frequently underestimated the powerful attempts at order in the novel and have interpreted the separate fragments as an expression of the disorderly modern city.[58] Some studies have examined the coexistence of randomness and order. For example, Joseph Warren Beach introduced an important paradigm of interpretation by claiming that the novel's form represented the moral disorder of urban dissociation, but also pointed out that an extensive aesthetic design structured *Manhattan Transfer*. The novel, Beach asserts, has "the disposition to build up a composition out of

---

[54]Lowry, p. 1630.

[55]Becker, p. 46; Iain Colley, *Dos Passos and the Fiction of Despair*, Totawa, N.J., 1978, p. 60.

[56]John Dos Passos, "Grosz Comes to America," *Esquire*, 6 (1936), p. 131. Ludington, p. 223.

[57]Dos Passos, "What makes a Novelist?" p. 31.

[58]See Colley, p. 60; Wrenn, pp. 129f.

elements which, however unrelated they may at first appear, are found to have their cunningly related correspondences and to result in the end in a significant pattern."[59]

The naturalist treatment of space in *Manhattan Transfer* has been analyzed in detail.[60] The environmental determinism has often been seen as the major drawback of the novel. Indeed, by removing the social constitution of space, the naturalism which Dos Passos inherited mystified environment into an autonomous agent. The city is blamed as a scapegoat for environmental, moral, and social deficiencies. In *Manhattan Transfer* the moloch even infects nature: the novel records "zinc water" (MT, p. 251), a "zinc sky" (MT, p. 287), or an "ironcast night" (MT, p. 287); urban dwellers become hollow, "mechanical toy[s]" (MT, p. 375) and nerves are "sharp steel jangled wires" (MT, p. 373). Such environmentalist imagery is pervasive.

Moreover, the very form of the episodes is deterministic. Dos Passos does not record lives, but destinies.[61] As in naturalist one-act plays or short stories, the figures in *Manhattan Transfer* are doomed since they are introduced in moments of crisis and situations from which there is no escape. Bud Korpenning never has any choice; each attempt of his at finding stability, whether he is seen dishwashing, cleaning, or carrying coal, ends in disappointment, rejection, and defeat. When he finally discloses his story of suffering, his sole remaining option is suicide (MT, p. 124). Other characters too are met in crucial situations: Jimmy Herf quits his job, Joe Harland is thrown out of his room, Anna Cohen is fired, several people die or are killed. Here, Dos Passos seems close to the environmentalism of the Chicago School. A multitude of motifs suggest a stifling determination. The first vignette sets the tone for the novel:

> Three gulls wheel above the broken boxes, orangerinds, spoiled cabbage heads that heave between the splintered plank walls, the green waves spume under the round bow as the ferry, skidding on the tide, crashes, gulps the broken water, slides, settles slowly into the slip. Handwinches whirl with jingle of chains. Gates fold upwards, feet step across the crack, men and women press through the manuresmelling wooden tunnel of the ferryhouse, crushed and jostling like apples fed down a chute into a press. (MT, p. 3)

This clearly evokes the mythical "city of destruction" (MT, p. 366) which in its evil and life-forbidding traits reaches back to the beginnings of human history.

The novel contains the cultural pessimism current in the 1920s, a period which was particularly overwhelmed by the effects of capitalist urbanization. Many interpreta-

---

[59] Joseph Warren Beach, *The Twentieth Century Novel: Studies in Technique*, New York, 1932, p. 511.

[60] Robert C. Rosen, *John Dos Passos. Politics and the Writer*, Lincoln, Nebraska, 1981, p. 46.

[61] Jean-Paul Sartre, "A Propos de John Dos Passos et *1919*," *Nouvelle Revue Francaise*, 51 (1938), 292-301; repr. *Dos Passos*, ed. Andrew Hook, Englewood Cliffs, 1974, p. 65.

tions declare this defeatism as the essence of the city and Dos Passos' randomly arranged and yet determined episodes as the meaning of the novel.[62] The form is reduced to a reflection of this explanation. The doomed and dissociated city represents moral chaos.[63]

Yet the episodes by themselves are only segments of the complex image projected by *Manhattan Transfer*. A utopian quality is contained in the vision of new, meaningful connections beyond the surface discontinuity, in the conception of a potential liberation from determinist space, and in the recognition of a solely contingent nexus through montage.[64] The invisible relations underlying the urban jungle are made transparent in the cubist restructuring of space. The seemingly determined city can be changed. A cubist conception of space is basic to the meaning of *Manhattan Transfer*. Art could, Dos Passos asserted, "mold and influence ways of thinking to the point of changing and rebuilding ... the mind of the group."[65]

Critics have noted the links between Dos Passos and cubism. Eric Mottram, for instance, has described *Manhattan Transfer* as "a pattern of noisy and wilful cubist surfaces."[66] Being well acquainted with leading European and American avantgardists, Dos Passos had an especially close connection to cubism. Many of the artists he was in contact with, Fernand Léger, Robert and Sonia Delaunay, Natalie Gontcharova, Michael Larionov, and Pablo Picasso had been influential in the cubist movement.[67] Above all, he admired the work of Blaise Cendrars, the seminal figure in literary cubism together with Guillaume Apollinaire.[68] Dos Passos later asserted that Cendrars and other "poets who went along with cubism in painting" were very influential for his work.[69] Already in 1921, in notes later published in his travel account *Orient Express*, Dos Passos praised

---

[62] Wrenn, pp. 129f; Millgate, p. 141; McCormick, pp. 141ff.

[63] Gelfant, p. 166.

[64] Lowry, p. 1629.

[65] John Dos Passos, "The Writer as Technician," *American Writers Congress*, ed. Henry Hart, New York, 1935, pp. 78-82; cited in Gelfant, p. 138.

[66] Eric Mottram, "The Hostile Environment and the Survival Artist," *The American Novel and the 1920s*, eds. Malcolm Bradbury and David Palmer, London, 1971, p. 242.

[67] Werner Haftmann, *Malerei im 20. Jahrhundert*, 2 vols., 1954, München, 1979, pp. 123-46; 226; Stolzfus, p. 199; Ludington, pp. 213-35; Virginia Spencer Carr, *Dos Passos. A Life*, New York, 1984, pp. 195ff.

[68] In 1931, Dos Passos translated his poem *Panama or the Adventures of My Seven Uncles*. Blaise Cendrars, *Panama or the Adventures of My Seven Uncles*, trans. John Dos Passos, New York, 1931. Astre, p. 174; Landsberg, p. 113.

[69] Dos Passos cited in Wagner, p. 49.

Cendrars' cubist poetry and called him the "Homer of the Transsiberian."[70] Indeed, the first of all cubist poems which described Easter in New York contained, among more conventional passages, strikingly congenial images to those in *Manhattan Transfer*.[71] The influence ranges from parallels in technique--the assemblage of discontinuous bits, multilinear strands, and the collage of diverse materials--to similarities in diction and imagery. Like Jimmy Herf, who feels cramped in a "squirrelcage" (MT, p. 329), Cendrars had written in *Panama or the Adventures of My Seven Uncles*, the poem which Dos Passos later translated, "I go round and round inside the meridians like a squirrel in a squirrel-cage."[72]

Dos Passos was generally interested in those styles and media which were related to the cubist revolution. Thus, he was deeply impressed by the satiric montages in the paintings of George Grosz. He collaborated in creating sets for Serge Dhiagileff's Ballets Russes and for the Ballets Suédois in Paris; later, in the New Playwrights Theater he himself designed and painted cubist and constructivist stage sets.[73] Also, he followed film-making closely and it is likely that he had seen Charles Sheeler and Paul Strand's documentary montage, *Manhatta*, from 1922.[74]

Dos Passos' concern for the visual had a profound impact on *Manhattan Transfer*. Techniques from the visual arts, especially from cubism, are adjusted and transformed for fictional purposes. Dos Passos' metaphors for the writer disclose his deep concern with visual processes and spatial forms. He views the novelist as an "architect" who "builds reality"[75] so that his composition will "stand up off the page." Also, the writer analyzes the "panorama of history"[76] and produces "simultaneous chronicles"[77] from juxtaposed surfaces.

Dos Passos' style reflects this preoccupation with spatial and architectural forms. His prose adds chunks on chunks without punctuation--"behind them beyond barges tug-

---

[70] John Dos Passos, *Orient Express*, New York, 1927.

[71] Cendrars wrote in *Pâques à New York* in 1912: "The elevated grumbles, leaps, sways, and strains./The bridges shake with railway trains" (Blaise Cendrars, *Pâques à New York*, Paris, 1912). He also called his *Prose Du Transsibérian*, a poem from 1913, the "First Simultaneous Book." Chefdor, p. 40.

[72] Dos Passos, *Orient Express*, p. 198.

[73] He had discovered the work of the German dadaist during World War I. Knox, p. 257. Ludington, pp. 225, 237.

[74] Astre, pp. 169f. Dos Passos later wrote that he had seen the film, but that he could not exactly recollect when he had seen it. He also was familiar with the multilinear films of D. W. Griffith.

[75] Dos Passos, "A Statement of Belief," p. 26.

[76] Dos Passos, "What makes a Novelist?" p. 31.

[77] Wagner, p. 49.

boats carferries the tall buildings, streaked white with whisps of steam and mist, tower gray into sagged clouds" (MT, p. 282)--and he presses words together into new compounds, as in "dollarproud" (MT, p. 11), "manywindowed"(MT, p. 296), or "sulphurgreen" (MT, p. 378). Parataxis organizes the cumulation of segments.[78] Elliptical sentences abound; a flowing rhythm is rejected in favor of conspicuous seams and ruptures that reveal the constructed texture of fictional reality.

> Spring rich in gluten. . . . Chockful of golden richness, delight in every bite, THE DADDY OF THEM ALL, spring rich in gluten. Nobody can buy better bread than PRINCE ALBERT. Wrought steel, monel, copper, nickel, wrought iron. All the world loves natural beauty. LOVE'S BARGAIN that suit at Gumpel's best value in town. Keep that schoolgirl complexion. . . . Joe KISS, starting, lightning, ignition and generators. (MT, p. 351)

The heaping of fragments is more important than the creation of organic coherence or of a profoundly personal perspective. The cataloguing of ubiquitous things, as in Walt Whitman's poetry, distinguishes the democratic architect.[79] Dos Passos uses the speech of his generation "straight,"[80] and juxtaposes discordant diction without modification: he asserted that the writer in the process of composition must become "just an eye and an ear."[81] His democratized, accessible modernism excels with the unconventional arrangement of cubist pieces in "simultaneous" blocks:

> When they passed cross-streets a puff of air came in her face off the river. Sudden jetbright glances of eyes under straw hats, attitudes of chins, lips, pouting lips, Cupid's bows, hungry shadow under cheekbones, faces of girls and young men nuzzled fluttering against her like moths as she walked with her stride even to his through the tingling yellow night. (MT, p. 153)

> At Forty-second Street he woke up. Everything was a confusion of bright intersecting planes of color, faces, legs, shop windows, trolleycars, automobiles. (MT, p. 333)

The modern city in *Manhattan Transfer* differs crucially from James Joyce's image in *Ulysses* with its predominance of inner monologue and mythic patterns. Dos Passos assembles a multiplicity of facets which only a 'camera eye' would detect in the metropolis. This preoccupation with physical details and surfaces renders his treatment unique. It translates the modern city's appearances into the form of the novel, and thus may present the city as both free and determinate, random and ordered, cubist and naturalist.

---

[78]"For Dos Passos," Sartre wrote, "narrating means adding." Sartre, p. 63.

[79]Rideout, p. 158.

[80]Dos Passos, "Introduction," p. viii.

[81]Dos Passos, "What makes a novelist?" p. 32.

John Berger provides an illuminating interpretation of the social potential in the cubist conception of space. Congenial in its political thrust, Berger's reading of cubism can be applied to Dos Passos' metropolis. In his well known essay "The Moment of Cubism," Berger writes: "Cubism changed the nature of the relationship between the painted image and reality, and by doing so it expressed a new relationship between man and reality."[82] The observers' relation to the surroundings changed dramatically. With cubism, Berger explains, "a man was part of the world and indivisible from it. In an entirely original sense, which remains at the basis of modern consciousness, a man *was* the world which he inherited."[83] In contrast to Renaissance perspective, which established a viewpoint outside the world depicted, now the field of vision became the picture itself and the viewers' position shifted to within the frame.

Cubism concentrated on the changing relationships among parts and the interaction of objects. The seemingly disjointed and fragmented surfaces of its images revealed an essential continuity: discontinuous space was linked through a continuity of structure. Hence the diagram became the relational model for cubism. The diagram was "a visible, symbolic representation of invisible processes, forces, structures."[84] Being part of this world, its frontal facing became inadequate. "The spectator," Berger writes, "has to find his place *within* this content whilst the complexity of the forms and the 'discontinuity' of the space remind him that his view from that place is bound to be only partial. Such content and its functioning was prophetic because it coincided with the new scientific view of nature which rejected simple causality and the single permanent all-seeing viewpoint."[85]

Immersed in the world and yet urged to orient themselves in surrounding space, viewers become most fully aware that they *are* space. The world, projected as a process, is changeable.[86] Cubists envisioned a transformed world as it became theoretically possible in the first decade of this century. "Cubism," John Berger concludes, "was the art which reflected the possibility of this transformed world and the confidence it inspired. Thus, in a certain sense, it was the most modern art--as it was also the most philo-

---

[82]Berger, "The Moment of Cubism," p. 171.

[83]Berger, p. 164.

[84]Ibid., pp. 176ff.

[85]Ibid., p. 180.

[86]Berger explains that "the Cubists created the possibility of art revealing processes instead of static entities. The content of their art consists of various modes of interaction: the interaction between different aspects of the same event, between empty space and filled space, between structure and movement, between the seer and the thing seen." Ibid., p. 178.

sophically complex--which has yet existed."[87] The central paradox was that cubism imagined a world transformed and not the political process of transformation. This tension too underlies the cubist city in *Manhattan Transfer*.

Although this concept of cubist space was only an artistic practice and never explicitly formulated as theory, its implications are palpable in the novel. The most conspicuous parallel is that Dos Passos also conceived of his novels as diagrams. Townsend Ludington's biography depicts a sketched diagram for his novel *1919*.[88] The arrangement of facets signifies the diagram of society. Moreover, readers of *Manhattan Transfer* are also thrust into the middle of a "multiplicity of cubist perspectives."[89] The orientation in urban space is suggested in the unique juxtaposition and arrangement of facets. The world can no longer be understood as the product of monocausal forces and can no longer be ordered toward a single hierarchical center, while the new continuity and coherence are only contingent. *Manhattan Transfer* projects a decentered city. In the novel, those figures fail who search for a simple "center of things" (MT, p. 4). All myths about a single center are shattered for Bud Korpenning, whether he is rinsing plates or whether he is looking for it on Broadway or on Brooklyn Bridge. Ellen Thatcher is misled as she believes the consumer world to be "the center of things" (MT, p. 368).

The concept of change is important for the novel. Readers become part of a process as they create links and connections among the city's diverse facets. Positioned amidst the fictional city, reader and character alike become involved and have to commit themselves.[90] As Jean-Paul Sartre explained for *1919*, this implies a commitment for collectivity, for everyman: "In order to understand the words, in order to make sense out of the paragraphs, I first have to adopt his [the collective consciousness'] point of view. I have to play the role of the obliging chorus. This consciousness exists only through me; without me there would be nothing but black spots on white paper."[91] This contingency and openness of fictional reality also implies a new sense of freedom. Readers have the relationship to the urban environment at their disposal; they are no longer placed within determining surroundings, but they may actively decide about the shape of and their role toward urban space. In this sense, once dissected, the rigid space of the city can be changed and remolded collectively.

---

[87]Ibid., p. 185.
[88]Ludington, p. 282.
[89]Rosen, p. 42.
[90]Lowry, p. 1638; Gelfant, p. 160.
[91]Sartre, p. 67.

Finally, the new quality of orientation in cubist Manhattan reflects the latest developments in the scientific understanding of reality in which the simple determination and monocausal explanations of the nineteenth century have been corrected to multicausal models.[92] In the twentieth century, there is no single, apodictically true perspective. The cubist arrangement can only be partial and contingent. Its affinity to scientific thought is also evident in the rational and detached attitude toward the object of scrutiny. As George Becker wrote about Dos Passos' novel, "Intelligence rules here. Passion will come later."[93]

The new attitude toward the city is contained in the novel's unique experiments in form. Dos Passos does not transmute the material itself, but he alters the relations among the constitutive segments of the city. Recording the existing variety of registers, dialects, and diction without major alterations, Dos Passos predominantly alters syntactical relations to build his cubist city. His novel assembles the various episodes in a unique way, indicating thematic, formal, and structural correspondences among the separate strands. Human agency is reintroduced to the city. The determining urban container is dissected and reassembled in an open totality of relations.[94] The special fusion in the novel, in which political choice and aesthetic predilection creatively coincide, engenders a distinctly modern perception of the metropolis and, in an abstract sense, expresses the utopian vision of a world transformed. But collectivity, in *Manhattan Transfer*, is suggested only indirectly in the politics of form and perception.

In *Manhattan Transfer*, the world under scrutiny is yet limited to a city. Dos Passos takes great pains to shape the novel in aesthetic analogy to the visual city. Its form represents Manhattan. Unity of place substitutes for unity of action. Dos Passos translates the urban tension between order and disorder, between collective bulk and individual components, between variety and uniformity, between a continuous skyline and the horizontally discontinuous skyscrapers, between circular closure and outside links into the structure of his novel. As in the earliest hieroglyph for city, the Egyptian ideogram, Manhattan is represented by a cross within a circle, by intersecting lines within city walls.[95]

The analogy between form and subject is elaborate in *Manhattan Transfer*: the formal arrangement underlines the thematic focus on the visual city. The attempt at or-

---

[92]Lowry, p. 1637.

[93]George Joseph Becker, *John Dos Passos*, New York, 1974, p. 55; Rosen, p. 42.

[94]Astre, pp. 183ff; Rosen, p. 46.

[95]Robert S. Lopez, "The Crossroads Within the Wall," *The Historian and the City*, eds. Oscar Handlin and John Burchard, Cambridge, Mass., 1963, p. 27.

der, however, is also evident at the level of episodes. The rejection of the traditional plot does not imply utterly unrelated characters and events. Rather, a subtle and extensive diagram of relations connects the characters, indicates links, and shows through indirection who exerts power, who suffers, and who is defeated.[96]

Dutch Robertson, for instance, who disembarks in New York together with his friend Joe O'Keefe, also returns from war with Jimmy Herf, Ellen Thatcher, and James Merivale. Joe O'Keefe's political activities relate him to Gus McNeil, George Baldwin and the businessman Densch. While Dutch remains unemployed and eventually turns criminal, the others are shown to profit from war, legally and illegally. Densch backs Baldwin as a reform candidate telling him that "I consider it my duty as a citizen to help in cleansing up the filthy conditions of bribery, corruption and intrigue that exist in city government" (MT, p. 327), but leaves the city for Marienbad, as his export firm defaults on ten million dollars (MT, p. 385). His departure and Dutch's trial are juxtaposed (MT, p. 390). Baldwin, the opportunist politician and newly appointed District Attorney (MT, p. 384), is linked through his function and Densch's rhetoric to the judge who sentences Dutch and Francie for their robberies:

> The unalienable rights of human life and property the great men who founded this republic laid down in the constitootion have got to be reinstated ... Therefore in spite of what those sentimental newspaper writers who corrupt the public mind and put into the head of weaklings and misfits of your sort the idea that you can buck the law of God and man, and private property, that you can wrench by force from peaceful citizens what they have earned by hard work and brains ... and get away with it; ... I am going to impose on you two highwaymen the maximum severity of the law. (MT, p. 391)

Similarly, Ellen Thatcher, who thinks that a fashion magazine will "make every reader feel Johnny on the spot in the center of things" (MT, p. 368), is witness to Anna Cohen's accident in Madame Soubrine's sweatshop and, this time directly, helps to gloss over the plight of garment workers by appeasing alarmed consumers (MT, p. 398). Joe Harland, the stigmatized relative of Jimmy Herf and James Merivale, has contacts to Joe O'Keefe. Congo Jake, the friend of Jimmy Herf, marries Nevada Jones, the ex-lover of George Baldwin. A web of direct, indirect, and contingent contacts relates characters to one another.

The cubist image of fictional Manhattan, like the real city, contains symmetrical relations and rational, geometrical forms. The city's rectangular layout set down in 1811, its numbering of streets, the equidistance between city blocks and the continuity of built-up space along canyon-like streets is captured in the elaborate symmetries and repeti-

---

[96]Kathleen Komar, *Pattern and Chaos: Multilinear Novels by Dos Passos, Döblin, Faulkner, and Koeppen*, Columbia, S.C., 1983, pp. 105-11.

tions in the novel's form. As Kathleen Komar has recently indicated, repetition is an important structural principle in *Manhattan Transfer*.[97] It pervades all levels of the novel from the iterations inherent in the dominantly paratactical sentences to the size of the novel's sections. *Manhattan Transfer* is tightly structured into three equally long sections and a symmetrical number of chapters.[98] The first and last section contain five subsections, the middle one eight. Also, the a-chronological sections are arranged in chronological symmetry to the central chapter during war time.[99] This trisection reappears on another level: the novel is constructed from the three narrative levels of thematic titles, lyric preambles, and narrative episodes. Finally, three key figures excel among the multitude of characters.[100]

There is a pronounced will to formal correspondences and order beneath the kaleidoscopic surface. The numericist orientation in the maze is directly related to Manhattan and its layout:

> Let's see how many blocks? . . . Less than twenty, eighteen. It must have been to keep from going crazy that people invented numbers . . . Probably that's what old Peter Stuyvesant thought, or whoever laid the city out in numbers. (MT, p. 373)

The frequent use of the figure 'three' further expands the triadic patterns in the novel. This numericism is far too conspicuous not to be detected, but also not too obtrusive as to disturb the seemingly random surface of *Manhattan Transfer*. The numbers function as a further ordering device. The figure 'three' opens the novel, "three gulls wheel above the broken boxes" (MT, p. 3), and completes the framing in the last page, "carefully he spends his last quarter on breakfast. That leaves him three cents for good luck or bad for that matter" (MT, p. 404). "Three gulls" also appear in the middle section (MT, p. 251). Throughout the novel, the number 'three' is employed in instances where any figure could have been taken.[101] Furthermore, the narrative contains several phrases or pas-

---

[97] Komar, p. 32.

[98] Klotz, p. 359; Schmidt-von Bardeleben, p. 43.

[99] Arranged in chronological order, the three main section are a-chronological. For a detailed discussion see Craig Carver, "The Newspaper and Other Sources of *Manhattan Transfer*," *Studies in American Fiction*, 3 (1975), pp. 167-180. Clark, p. 99.

[100] Originally, Dos Passos had planned to render the triadic order even more conspicuous, as Lois Hughson's manuscript collations indicate. As initially outlined, the novel would have concentrated more fully on the three protagonists. Dos Passos, however, later revised his plans and added several minor characters and unconnected episodes to increase the multiperspective effect in *Manhattan Transfer*. Lois Hughson, "Narration in the Making of *Manhattan Transfer*," *Studies in the Novel*, 8 (1976), 185-98.

[101] To quote some of the many instances, Dos Passos uses three "steps" (MT, p. 157), "three cards" (MT, p. 280), and "three jobs" (MT, p. 282).

sages which are repeated three times, such as the description of Bud's monotonous dishwashing (MT, p. 42), or the phrase "WE HAVE MADE A TERRIBLE MISTAKE" in the preamble to "Longlegged Jack of the Isthmus" (MT, p. 144). The seemingly disconnected variety of facets is tightly organized by abstract relations. The spirit is rational and detached, as in a cubist painting.

The novel translates the surface tension in cityscapes between order and randomness into its fictional form. The extensive patterns express a fascination with well-ordered urban space against an environment in which otherwise arbitrary naturalist forces rule:

> 'But the worst thing was,' went on Rose Segal, 'that while they was fightin up in Goldstein's a rivet flew out the winder and fell nine stories an killed a fireman passin on a truck so's he dropped dead in the street. (MT, p. 357)

The analogy between fictional pattern and urban space is further extended. The island on the Hudson is linked to circular enclosure and spatial delimitation:

> "That's New York. . . . You see New York is on Manhattan Island."
> "Is it really on an island?"
> "Well what do you think of a boy who dont know that his home town is on an island?" The tweedy gentleman's gold teeth glittered as he laughs with his mouth wide open. Jimmy walks on round the deck, kicking his heels, all foamy inside; New York's on an island. (MT, p. 68)

The geometrical order is framed and reinforced by circular motifs and patterns in *Manhattan Transfer*. The circle recurs in images of round objects and in cyclical motion.[102] Again, the first line introduces this motif, as three gulls "wheel" in the air--a motif which is repeated later and reappears in variations, in revolving doors, in a phonograph rasping "round and round" (MT, p. 216), or in "nickelglinting wheels" (MT, p. 376). Dos Passos painstakingly creates the effect of circular patterns. Each section concludes with death as the end of a cycle. Francie's impression of "going round and round" (MT, pp. 390f) is repeated three times before she swoons. A circle is also used to express Jimmy Herf's disorientation: "The trouble with me is that I cant decide what I want most, so my motion is circular, helpless and confoundedly discouraging" (MT, p. 176). Finally, the novel is directly associated with circular motion: "The wheels rumbled in her head, saying Manhattan Trans-fer. Man-hattan Trans-fer" (MT, p. 116). The novel functions as a formal analogy of the island city: it is a delimited, separate and self-contained entity. This circular frame is evoked as the ferry, the figure 'three,' a lunchwagon, a man with a straw hat, and the reference to the smell of tenements appear in the beginning and recur in

---

[102]Clark, pp. 103f.

the end. Bud Korpenning first enters and Jimmy Herf eventually leaves Manhattan on a ferry.

Through its circular imagery and structure, *Manhattan Transfer* creates a framework for the relation among its parts. The pattern repeats the conflict basic to *Manhattan Transfer*. Cubism and naturalism are in tension because the evidence can be read in both ways: Manhattan can be a generic determining environment and a loose frame to an open diagram. More important, the duality of form contains the central contradiction of the political diagram in *Manhattan Transfer*. Only radical collective change may alter conditions, yet the novel excludes collective experience and effort. Overall, the cubist city succumbs to impressions of domination and powerlessness. After World War I, the utopia of a realizable world gave way to a skeptical attitude toward Western civilization. Not by chance, the war is a pivotal point structurally in *Manhattan Transfer*.

The cubist diagram nevertheless intends to provide orientation for meaningful change. The montage of events indicates the agents who produced these stultifying conditions, even if it cannot point toward a source for change. The economic analysis in *Manhattan Transfer*, as much as it may be indebted to Marxist thought, is directed by Thorstein Veblen's scrutiny of American society.[103] In his novel *Big Money*, Dos Passos compares Veblen's critique to a diagram of society. The passage explicitly formulates what Dos Passos' had attempted earlier with his cubist diagram in *Manhattan Transfer*:

> he established a new diagram of a society dominated by monopoly capital,
> etched in irony
> the sabotage of production by business,
> the sabotage of life by blind need for money profits,
>   pointed out the alternatives: a warlike society strangled by the bureaucracies of the monopolies forced by the law of diminishing returns to grind down more and more the common man for profits,
>   or a new matter-of-fact commonsense society dominated by the needs of the men and women who did the work and the incredibly vast possibilities for peace and plenty offered by the progress of technology.[104]

5. The City as Diagram and Circle

The frequently formulated opposition between the modernity of Dos Passos' city image, implying individual agency and freedom on the aesthetic level, and its restrictive

---

[103]Rideout, p. 162; John P. Diggins, "Visions of Chaos and Visions of Order: Dos Passos as Historian," *American Literature*, 46 (1974), p. 344.

[104]John Dos Passos, *U.S.A.*, New York, 1938, p. 812.

determinism, projecting a naturalist entrapment for characters on the narrative level, is transcended in *Manhattan Transfer*. Dos Passos has inherited the naturalist tradition, but he crucially reassesses its dated objectivism and generates an image which proposes the openness of a cubist diagram.

The novel connects the multifaceted parts in a new way through montage. Religious, mythical, and materialist explanations may exist side by side. The inclusive both-and possibility of the twentieth century replaces the causal explanation of reality in the restrictive either-or dichotomy of the nineteenth century. Myth can be seen as a social ideology and ideology may turn into myth. The juxtaposition of epistemological models allows the acknowledgement of multiple sources and punctuates the idea of contingency. Implicitly, the novel questions the one-dimensional and clear-cut solutions of religious fundamentalism or the rigidity in fatalistic views. Socialism also is only one, if important, foil among others. Modern urban life is too complex to be reduced to a single system. "God," Jimmy Herf exclaims, "I wish I could blame it all on capitalism the way Martin does" (MT, p. 265). Three principal explanatory modes which are at once interrelated and separate can be distinguished in *Manhattan Transfer*: the environmental-determinist, the mythic-religious, and the socio-economic mode.

The urban environmentalism has already been mentioned. The arrival in Manhattan is equated with squalor and decay, reversing the journey motif from Walt Whitman's *Crossing Brooklyn Ferry*: "orangerinds, spoiled cabbage heads" float in the water and the "newborn baby" is compared to a "knot of earthworms" (MT, p. 3). The trip across the water can no longer invoke community and signify rebirth. New York too is no longer Whitman's "city of orgies walks and joys" (MT, p. 174), but a place where abortions block the water supply, where traffic congests the center, and where the "pursuit of happiness" (MT, p. 365) becomes meaningless leisure. The gates in the ferryhouse, as in Strand and Sheeler's *Manhatta*, suggest Dante's inferno.[105]

The prevailing upper- and middle-class perspective turns nature into the antipode of the city in *Manhattan Transfer*. The adverse impact of the mechanical world produces the transfer of characteristics: nature acquires machine-like qualities in these surroundings: waves show the "glint of steel" (MT, p. 246), and the blue night glows "the way iron starts to glow in a forge" (MT, p. 124). The urban environment is most strikingly characterized by its loss of fertility. Green, the color which signifies natural growth, is repeatedly used for engines, buses, doors, and other inorganic objects but hardly ever for flora. This artificial environment is "dead green" (MT, p. 171). The enclaves of nature

---

[105]Schleier, p. 101.

found in the city imply barrenness. Dos Passos depicts this unnatural environment with disturbing images: "In the hall they came upon the fair young man quietly vomiting into a firebucket under an artificial palm" (MT, p. 35).

In the environmental perspective, innately urban traits seem to shape lives. In his novel, *The Big Money*, Dos Passos explicitly formulates this standpoint in characterizing the architect Frank Lloyd Wright: "The buildings determine civilization as the cells in the honeycomb the function of bees."[106] The city in *Manhattan Transfer* not only shapes, but also entraps people like animals.[107] The novel repeatedly uses cage motifs: Jimmy Herf, for instance, complains that "we live cramped in our squirrelcage" (MT, p. 329). The city seems omnipresent; escape is impossible:

> Her head ached as if it were bound with hot wire. She went to the window and leaned out into the sunlight. Across Park Avenue the flameblue sky was barred with the red girder cage of a new building. Steam riveters rattled incessantly; now and then a donkeyengine whistled and there was a jingle of chains and a fresh girder soared crosswise in the air. (MT, p. 185)

Closely connected to this mode of explanation is another layer of imagery which expresses an even deeper uneasiness about urban culture. From the mythical-religious viewpoint, the city is linked to cyclical decay and innate sinfulness. The Manhattan of the 1920s is connected to the archetypal image of the necropolis. New York is related to ancient paradigms and the fate of these cities:

> There were Babylon and Niniveh; they were built of brick. Athens was gold marble columns. Rome was held up in broad arches of rubble. In Constantinople the minarets flame like great candles round the Golden Horn . . . Steel, glass, tile, concrete will be the materials of the skyscrapers. (MT, p. 12)[108]

Biblical quotations and motifs appear throughout *Manhattan Transfer*. The chapter titles "Rejoicing City That Dwelt Carelessly" (MT, p. 271) and "The Burthen of Niniveh" (MT, p. 371) are directly taken from Old Testament prophets.[109] Also, Babylonian aberrations thrive: New York has a disproportionately large share of arsonists, kidnappers, burglars, murderers.

---

[106]Dos Passos, *U.S.A.*, p. 1080.

[107]Mizener, pp. 24ff.

[108]Typical for Dos Passos' focus, each archetypal city is charaterized by visual qualities.

[109]Philip Arrington, "The Sense of an Ending in *Manhattan Transfer*," *American Literature*, 54 (1982), p. 438. David Vanderwerken, "*Manhattan Transfer*: Dos Passos' Babel Story," *American Literature*, 49 (1977), 253-67.

But the mythical-religious segments are not privileged explanations. Rather, as George-Albert Astre pointed out, the mythical explanation is constantly contrasted with a historical-materialist view.[110] The validity of religious fundamentalism is questioned within the narrative. The modern city is condemned by an unpleasant tramp:

> Do you know how long the Lord God took to destroy Babylon and Nineveh? Seven minutes. There's more wickedness in one block in New York City than there was in a square mile in Nineveh, and how long do you think the Lord God of Sabbaoth will take to destroy New York City an Brooklyn an the Bronx? Seven seconds. (MT, pp. 380f)

In a letter to his friend Germaine Lucas Champonnière, Dos Passos wrote in 1924 that he found the bible most unpleasant if "devilishly well" written. The Old Testament, he asserted, would always stand against civilization and happiness.[111]

Similarly, the often noted link between *Manhattan Transfer* and the "Unreal City" by T. S. Eliot is complex.[112] Admittedly, passages which announce a "death-in-water" or "death-in-fire" (MT, p. 271) seem clearly to refer to *The Waste Land*. But references to mythical cities need not be linked to Eliot's religious antiurbanism. Prior to the publication of *The Waste Land*, in 1921, Dos Passos had actually visited the site of ancient Babylon.[113] In *Manhattan Transfer*, old civilizations also signify social oppression: "The result has been to put more power in the hands of a few men than there has been in the history of the horrible slave civilizations of Egypt and Mesopotamia" (MT, p. 263).[114]

Correspondingly, choosing nature as a yardstick for the city does not exclude for Dos Passos the fascination with traffic and skyscrapers. Young Jimmy Herf likes machines and wants to live in the city to observe them (MT, p. 100), Phil Sandbourne dreams of revolutionary skyscrapers and moving subway platforms (MT, p. 256). Nature can potentially be brought in harmony with the city. The architect Specker envisions a "communal building . . . Seventyfive stories high stepped back in terraces with a sort of hanging garden on every floor" (MT, p. 170). The exuberant celebration of metropolitan pace and atmosphere invalidates any suggestions of regressing toward agrarian forms of life which the middle-class ideology then proposed in stylizing self-reliant farmers and

---

[110] Astre, p. 153.

[111] Ludington, p. 231.

[112] Lowry, "*Manhattan Transfer*: Dos Passos' Wasteland," pp. 47-52.

[113] Ludington, p. 211.

[114] Similarly, fire imagery need not signify urban destruction. Readers in 1925 would undoubtedly still remember the disastrous fire in the Triangle Sweatshop which destroyed 141 lives in 1911. Dos Passos' accounts of fire accidents, especially Anna's in the end (MT, pp. 397ff), would strike overtones of social criticism. Ellis, pp. 490ff.

Arcadian suburbanites to prototypical democrats.[115] Nature, but not the country, offers positive values for Dos Passos in 1925. Through Bud Korpenning's story, his flight to the city, *Manhattan Transfer* dismantles the illusion of an innocent and pious countryside. The "hard godfearin" (MT, p. 123) father had flogged his son on the farm for years before the victim committed patricide.

The social and economic interpretation of the modern city is the most consistent of the three modes. Both the environmental and the religious mode contain contradictory evidence which denies their claims to universal truth. The anticapitalist thrust alone is unequivocal. Veblen's diagram is basic to *Manhattan Transfer*.[116] The overthrow of big business is the paramount objective. Bourgeois ideology is disclosed in the juxtaposition of contradictory evidence, in episodes which show the discrepancy between what the country's dominant class demands and proclaims and what it actually does.

Many destinies hinge upon the war. In an acerbic montage, reminiscent of George Grosz's biting satires, Densch, who has greatly profited from the war,[117] warns against the unruly mob while dining majestically:

> 'The country is going through a dangerous period of reconstruction . . . the bankruptcy of a continent . . . bolshevism and subversive doctrines rife . . . America . . .' he says, cutting with the sharp polished steel knife into the thick steak, rare and well peppered. He chews a mouthful slowly . . . 'The great principles of democracy, of that commercial freedom upon which our whole civilization depends are more than ever at stake.' (MT, pp. 287f)

Densch later flees the country and escapes indictment (MT, pp. 385ff), whereas Dutch Robertson, the war veteran, is sentenced to twenty years (MT, pp. 390ff). Dutch, who "made the world safe for democracy," could not find employment after the war (MT, p. 294). Also Densch's hymn to freedom with its denunciation of immigrants, "I happen to know from a secret and reliable source that there is a subversive plot among undesirable elements in this country" (MT, p. 287), is juxtaposed to the deportation of American communists (MT, p. 288).

Material conditions deny the full development of the individual's capacities. Ellen Thatcher's path toward hollow materialism and stardom are predetermined by Ed Thatcher's exclusive focus on money. "Big money's what I'll have to have, for my little girl," the accountant knows on the day of her birth (MT, p. 8). The unbearable housing situation is linked to speculation and profits: "No sir as a real estate proposition, Twenty-

---

[115] Some interpretations see the Jeffersonian belief in an agrarian America as a positive foil in *Manhattan Transfer*. Michael Millgate, *American Social Fiction: James to Cozzens*, Edinburgh, 1964, p. 140.

[116] Rideout, p. 161.

[117] He criticizes his wife's expenditures by complaining, "She must think the war's still on" (MT, p. 362).

third Street has crashed . . . How's all the big money in New York been made? Astor, Vanderbilt, Fish. . . . In the real estate of course. Now it's up to us to get in on the next great cleanup. . . . Buy Forty" (MT, p. 29). Information and public opinion are also controlled by big business. With reference to Upton Sinclair's *The Brass Check*, Jojo Oglethorpe claims that "every sentence, every word, every picayune punctuation that appears in the public press is perused and revised and deleted in the interests of advertisers and bondholders. The fountain of national life is poisoned at the source" (MT, p. 195).

Manhattan Transfer shows a pervasive powerlessness of individuals against the machinations of big business and their "sabotage of life by blind need for money profits."[118] The outcome of the first decades is bleak. Corruption and opportunism succeed, visionaries and sympathetic people are defeated. Densch escapes, Ellen Thatcher, George Baldwin, and James Merivale rise to preeminent positions in society; Bud Korpenning and Stan Emery commit suicide, Anna Cohen is badly burnt; Dutch, Francie, and Congo Jake are arrested; Jimmy Herf, finally, leaves in bewilderment. Visions of a better life are thwarted by existing conditions.

Criticism dominates *Manhattan Transfer*. Utopian or positive values are often only implied in the critique. Radical political solutions are talked about, but Dos Passos does not particularly stress them.[119] He is adamant, however, in his objection to simplistic solutions. His open analysis of the system's flaws allows an assemblage of contrary strands without questioning the basic opposition to the degradations of capitalism. Collective changes are propagated, but as Warren Beach pointed out, in the novel "the social nexus is just what is lacking."[120] Dos Passos' vision of change is expressed purely in the politics of form. The altered city is primarily a result of aesthetic and intellectual, but not of social agency. Yet the new mode of perceiving reality is an emancipatory practice. It is a liberation from inadequate models whose hierarchical structure hindered any pluralistic and collective perception.

The absence of an explicit social force which might produce change generates the pervasive ambivalence in *Manhattan Transfer*.[121] The novel argues the need for change and incorporates a strong artistic impulse of change, but it cannot identify forces of change. For a novel which concentrated completely on sights, blind spots of vision are

---

[118] Dos Passos, *U.S.A.*, p. 812.

[119] Mizener, p. 41.

[120] Beach, p. 41.

[121] Granville Hicks called the novel a "poem of hate-and-love." Granville Hicks, "The Politics of John Dos Passos," *Antioch*, 10 (1950), p. 89.

particularly revealing. Thus, the cohesion of ethnic or working-class communities is never brought into focus. Collective agency is denied its visual exponent. Moreover, the thrust toward change often is without direction. In a novel of ceaseless motion and pervasive mobility, the misguided impulse is expressed in circular and cyclical images which imply stasis and futility.[122] The hope in progress, the visions of revolutionary change and the necessity for advancement are evident in symbolic vignettes. The will to advance without an impulse to change is perfectly compressed in the image of the legless man who stares at a dirigible floating over the skyline:

> The young man without legs had stopped still in the middle of the south sidewalk of Fourteenth Street. He wears a blue knitted sweater and a blue stocking cap. His eyes staring up widen until they fill the paperwhite face. Drifts across the sky a dirigible, bright tinfoil cigar misted with height, gently prodding the rainwashed sky and the soft clouds. The young man without legs stops still propped on his arms in the middle of the south sidewalk of Fourteenth Street. Among striding legs, lean legs, waddling legs, legs in skirts and pants and knickerbockers, he stops perfectly still, propped on his arms, looking up at the dirigible. (MT, p. 351)

Manhattan Transfer's complex diagram is the fictional response to and acceptance of modern interdependence. It celebrates aesthetic collectivity by rearranging fictional space in a revolutionary way. In the equation between fictional form and social space, the replacement of social and political action by its aesthetic equivalent has reached its most condensed form. Modernism here expresses the social and political impulse: the novelistic form chiefly represents human agency. Lacking a political force for change, all Dos Passos can do is function as a fictional "architect of history" and provide an acute analysis of society in his urban diagram. Two distinct responses among modern artists develop from here. On the one hand, there is the Brechtian model which attempts to change the world through politicizing art even further and, on the other hand, there is the withdrawal to playful subversion in aesthetic autonomy.

Inchoately challenging determinism in *Manhattan Transfer*, John Dos Passos enlarged the restrictive environmental focus in his next novels. The exclusive concentration on processes in the city contradicted the notion of general interdependence in the twentieth century. The interrelation of the cubist diagram proved more adequate to understand reality than the notion of isolated, homogeneous and self-contained entities. True to his insight that "everybody in the city is part of the industrial mechanism,"[123] he widened his perspective to American society at large in his trilogy *U.S.A.*

---

[122]Gelfant, p. 148.
[123]Dos Passos cited in Rosen, p. 48.

In *U.S.A.* Dos Passos reassessed the circular hieroglyph which he had applied to his New York novel. In the Egyptian ideogram for city, the circle stood for the wall, the border of the city, whereas the cross indicated roads and the city's links to its larger setting.[124] In the twentieth century, the channels and lines that lead into and out of the city have gained preeminent importance. The city must be conceived as a part of an extensive diagram. The circle which defined the walled and autonomous city has been so widened as to become unimportant. Society at large has become the circle. *U.S.A.*, indeed, was the more appropriate frame upon which the diagram of economic and social forces could be examined. At the end of *Manhattan Transfer*, Jimmy Herf has left the city with the ferry, but outside urban boundaries he still walks "along a cement road between dumping grounds full of smoking rubbishpiles. The sun shines redly through the mist on rusty donkeyengines, skeleton trucks, wishbones of Fords, shapeless masses of corroding metal" (MT, p. 404). Even in the urban twenties, destruction could no longer be seen as simply urban.

---

[124]Lopez, p. 27.

12
Richard Wright
Native Son

1. Rebellion and the Black Ghetto

Richard Wright's *Native Son* conveys a gruesome picture of the conditions in black Chicago in the late 1930s.[1] The poverty, plight, and desperation in the South Side ghetto present an image of the modern city that had been hardly acknowledged by American society. Another facet which shocked readers was the reaction of the black victim: for the first time in American fiction, a black protagonist revolted and retaliated.[2] The shock generated by the novel is reflected in Irving Howe's famous assertion that "the day *Native Son* appeared, American culture was changed forever."[3] However, the novel's conflict also extends beyond specific racial suppression on the South Side, or what Gunnar Myrdal later called the "American dilemma."[4] The segregated city in *Native Son* represents a larger division. Though based upon racial issues, the novel transcends questions of ethnic difference and evaluation by discussing, more generally, the relationship between oppressor and oppressed.

For Richard Wright, the "general denial of humanity"[5] to blacks has alienated white and black Americans from one another.[6] The fates of oppressors and oppressed are intricately interrelated, as Wright explains in his autobiography *American Hunger*:

---

[1] Richard Wright, *Native Son*, New York, 1940. References to *Native Son* will be abbreviated to NS and incorporated into the text.

[2] Katherine Fishburn, *Richard Wright's Hero: The Faces of a Rebel-Victim*, Metuchen, N.J., 1977, p. 100.

[3] Irving Howe, "Black Boys and Native Sons," *Dissent*, 10 (1963), 353-68, repr. *Twentieth Century Interpretations of Native Son*, ed. Houston A. Baker, Englewood Cliffs, N.J., 1972, p. 63.

[4] Gunnar Myrdal, Richard Sterner, and Arnold Rose, *An American Dilemma: The Negro Problem and Modern Democracy*, New York, 1944.

[5] Richard Wright, "Introduction," *Black Metropolis*, St. Clair Drake and Horace R. Cayton, New York, 1945, p. xxv.

[6] Kurt Otten, "Der Protestroman Richard Wrights," *Black Literature*, ed. Eckhard Breitinger, München, 1979, p. 334.

> I felt that the Negro could not live a full, human life under the conditions imposed on him by America; and I felt, too, that America, for different reasons, could not live a full, human life. It seemed to me, then, that if the Negro solved his problem, he would be solving infinitely more than his problem alone. I felt certain that the Negro could never solve his problem until the deeper problem of American civilization had been faced and solved.[7]

Challenging a fatal *status quo*, the rebellion of Bigger Thomas is central to *Native Son*.[8] His killing of Mary Dalton is a violent answer to oppression, but also a first step in the antithetical movement toward a new wholeness. As in Upton Sinclair's *The Jungle*, the impulse for an uprising against enslavement and dissociation is connected to the enclosed working-class city.

Bigger Thomas' development stands in contrast to the naturalist determinism in the novel.[9] The environmentalism, so conspicuous in the animal imagery and conditioned behavior in *Native Son*, seems to contest the existence of any free will or emancipatory action. Moreover, white Chicago appears to have succeeded in deleting any viable black identity which could nourish a rebellion. James Baldwin, among other critics, protested that Richard Wright failed "to convey any sense of Negro life as a continuing and complex group reality."[10] The suppression seems so complete as to deny meaningful experience to black Chicagoans.

Wright's view of the ghetto was profoundly influenced by the urban theory of Chicago sociology. His portrait of black Chicago clearly indicates an awareness of statistical evidence, urban studies, and established genres of city fiction. In Chicago, the black novelist met the sociologist Louis Wirth who became one of his tutors for understanding the modern city:[11]

> I ran through volumes that bore upon the causes of my conduct and the conduct of my people. I studied tables of figures relating population density to insanity, relating housing to disease, relating school and recreational opportunities to crime, relating various forms of neurotic behavior to environment, relating racial insecurities to the conflicts between whites and blacks.[12]

---

[7]Richard Wright, *American Hunger*, New York, 1977, p. 41.

[8]Keneth Kinnamon, *The Emergence of Richard Wright*, Urbana, Ill., 1973, p. 138.

[9]For a discussion see Michel Fabre, "Beyond Naturalism?" *The World of Richard Wright*, Jackson, Miss., 1985, 56-76.

[10]James Baldwin, "Many Thousands Gone," *Partisan Review*, 18 (1951), 665-80, repr. *Twentieth Century Interpretations of Native Son*, ed. Houston A. Baker, Englewood Cliffs, N.J., 1972, p. 58.

[11]Constance Webb, *Richard Wright: A Biography*, New York, 1968, p. 108.

[12]Wright, *American Hunger*, pp. 19f.

Native Son innovatively blends Wright's own experiences in the black belt with sociological insights and creates a Chicago which at once appears as a place of unalterable repression and of hopeful change. The two seemingly contradictory strands of determinism and emancipation express the tension which becomes crucial to the novel's meaning. As Wright had suggested in his famous essay "Blueprint for Negro Writing" in 1937, the black writer's task was to show the direction of social action and development.[13] Hence, with his own fictional city, Wright set out to create "with words a scheme of images and symbols whose direction could enlist the sympathies, loyalties, and yearnings of the millions of Bigger Thomases in every land and race."[14] The achievements and contradictions in Wright's proto-existentialist novel[15] are thus strongly related to his views about the path humanity would take in the modern city.

2. South Side Chicago in the 1930s

From the end of the Civil War to the second decade of the twentieth century, the racial imbalance between a Jim-Crow South, with nearly nine tenths of the black population, and a white-immigrant North, with the remaining tenth, was relatively stable. While blacks were useful as cheap and dependent labor in southern cotton production, booming industries in the North recruited European immigrants for their manpower needs.[16] Then major changes in the national economy induced the migration of millions of southern blacks to the new Canaan in the North.

In the course of the economic boom in the United States during World War I, manufacturing employment alone increased from 7 million in 1914 to 9 million in 1919. At the same time, the immigrant figure dropped drastically to one tenth of its pre-war figures. The resulting shortage of labor lured approximately half a million blacks to move North to guarantee further industrial expansion.[17] Thus, it was capitalist interests

---

[13]Richard Wright, "Blueprint for Negro Writing," *New Challenge*, 2 (1937), 53-65, repr. *Richard Wright Reader*, eds. Ellen Wright and Michel Fabre, New York, 1978, 37-49.

[14]Richard Wright, "How 'Bigger' Was Born," *Native Son*, New York, 1940, p. xix.

[15]Donald B. Gibson, "Wright's Invisible Native Son," *American Quarterly*, 21 (1969), 728-738, repr. *Richard Wright: A Collection of Critical Essays*, eds. Richard Macksey and Frank E. Moorer, Englewood Cliffs, N.J., 1984, p. 104.

[16]Stephen Steinberg, *The Ethnic Myth: Race, Ethnicity, and Class in America*, New York, 1981, p. 174.

[17]Steinberg, p. 204.

which lowered racial barriers, induced profound regional upheavals, and nourished the growth of ghettos in the North.

The economic constellation just described--the shortage of manual labor in the North and an increased concentration and mechanization in the cotton industry in the South--continued in the 1920s and 1930s. It led to a substantial enlargement of black communities in northern cities. Between 1910 and 1940 about 1,750,000 black Americans thus migrated to midwestern and eastern states.[18] In 1900, only some thirty thousand blacks lived among one and a half million white Chicagoans, but by 1940 almost three hundred thousand blacks were crammed into the tightly segregated South Side. In the 1920s, the decade that Richard Wright moved with his family to Chicago, the black population doubled as an estimated 124,000 Southerners arrived in the black belt.[19]

The black community in Chicago and other northern cities was rigidly segregated. Unlike other immigrant groups, blacks, even though they also recognized the advantages of ethnic solidarity, self-help, and independence, did not choose the ghetto voluntarily, but were forced into separation by white hostility. At first, propaganda and threats, then violence and bombings were used to keep blacks out of white neighborhoods; eventually, by the mid-1920s, racial covenants to property deeds restricted the access to white quarters and the white housing market.[20] When real estate speculators got the chance to extend the demarcated fringes of the ghetto with techniques known as 'block-busting,' they reaped massive profits forcing blacks to pay excessive rent in the new areas.[21]

As the migration of blacks picked up, segregation in Chicago became even more pronounced. By the 1930s, the vast majority of them lived in areas with more than 90% blacks and almost half of them lived in areas which were more than even 98% black. The white prejudice that black occupation meant slum creation was further cemented by

---

[18]Myrdal, p. 183.

[19]Thomas Lee Philpott, *The Slum and the Ghetto: Neighborhood Deterioration and Middle Class Reform, Chicago, 1880-1930*, New York, 1978, p. 116. Arnold R. Hirsch, *Making the Second Ghetto: Race and Housing in Chicago, 1940-1960*, Cambridge, Mass., 1983, p. 17. The migration meant a double adjustment for blacks as they had to switch from agricultural to industrial employment and from rural to urban surroundings. In 1890, four out of five black Americans still lived in villages and cottages in the cotton belt, but by 1920 four out of five black Americans in the North worked in cities. Chudacoff, p. 206.

[20]Allan Spear, *Black Chicago: The Making of a Negro Ghetto, 1890-1920*, Chicago, 1967, pp. 221, 225.

[21]Housing speculation was not necessarily divided along the color line as the cases of black realtors as Oscar De Priest or Philip Payton Jr., indicate, even though whites clearly predominated as in all other economic fields in the ghetto (Ira Katznelson, *Black Men, White Cities: Race, Politics and Migration in the United States, 1900-30, and Britain, 1948-68*, New York, 1973, p. 98). Ultimately, class and not race decided about the quality of urban space. But as the black bourgeoisie which could afford better housing in outlying zones constituted only a tiny section of black urbanites, class exploitation and color discrimination virtually coincided for the majority of black Americans. Chudacoff, p. 206.

municipal housing and real estate policy. The addition of housing units and the extension of the ghetto limits did not keep step with black migration. This led to severe overcrowding and a subsequent deterioration in the housing situation.[22] Moreover, since blacks worked in the lowest paid jobs, the costs necessary to maintain decent housing were beyond their means. By 1935, a black family did not earn even half of the median income of its white counterpart.[23]

Unhygenic conditions prevailed as blacks crowded into unsanitary neighborhoods and delapidated houses. The lack of jobs and hence of money especially marked in Depression years, meant a lower life expectancy for ghetto dwellers. Tuberculosis occurred twice as often among blacks as among whites. The infant and general mortality rates were significantly higher than those of white Chicago. In the 1930s, in black areas a plague of rats whose attacks maimed and even killed children became so prominent that a municipal campaign to exterminate rodents had to be organized. In 1940, the first year of this campaign, an estimated 1,5 million rats were killed in Chicago.[24]

The Chicago ghetto was almost fully exploited by outside capital because most of the real estate agencies and the retail businesses were controlled by white businessmen.[25] Municipal services were noticeably inferior in the black belt. Even volunteer and neighborhood work followed the color line. As Thomas Philpott has shown, progressive settlement workers "were deeply implicated in making and maintaining the black ghetto in Chicago."[26] Richard Wright himself briefly worked in one of the settlements and later declared the utter failure and fatal deception of such liberal policies:

> Here I felt for the first time that the rich folk who were paying my wages did not really give a good goddam about Bigger, that their kindness was prompted at bottom by a selfish motive. They were paying me to distract Bigger with ping-pong, checkers, swimming, marbles, and baseball in order that he might not roam the streets and harm the valuable white property which adjoined the Black Belt. I am not condemning boys' clubs and ping-pong as such; but these little stopgaps were utterly inadequate to fill up the centuries-long chasm of emptiness which American civilization had created in these Biggers.[27]

On the whole, white society was deeply implicated in the ghettoization of black citizens. The economic disadvantages which poor blacks shared with the other working-

---

[22] Within the first three decades of the twentieth century, the black population in Chicago increased eightfold, while the ghetto territory multiplied only five times. Hirsch, pp. 4, 35.

[23] Myrdal, p. 365.

[24] Hirsch, pp. 18, 25.

[25] Spear, pp. 226f.

[26] Philpott, p. 343.

[27] Wright, "How 'Bigger' Was Born," p. xxvii.

class immigrants were aggravated by racial prejudice and discrimination. It was among lower- and working-class whites and blacks that tensions evolved over the little that was to be gained in the labor market. Aggressively recruited by northern businessmen and used as scabs, the booming number of black migrants in urban factories increased anxieties among working-class whites.[28] These fears were exploited by racist and ethnic politics. The largest organization of the fundamentalist Ku Klux Klan did not operate in the bible belt, but in Chicago, with the strongest local section numbering some fifty thousand members. Racial hatred flared up especially at the beginning of the black migration. The worst outbursts of violence occurred in 1919, a year of severe economic insecurity, when war veterans and black migrants clashed in over twenty serious race riots in cities in the United States. In a week of fighting and rampaging in Chicago, which finally was put down by the state militia, 38 people were killed, 520 injured and over one thousand families left homeless by arsonists.[29] The majority of victims were black.

The black and white elite cooperated in business and politics to prevent real challenges to racial segregation. Black leaders discouraged unionization when recruiting blacks for northern factories, and the labor program of the Chicago Urban League, which was to help poor blacks, identified itself mostly with the needs of large employers.[30] A bitter irony in the face of the actual powerlessness and plight of the community, blacks in Chicago were politically more active, better organized, and achieved more than anywhere else in the country. The black vote, for instance, was a major reason why the Republican Boss Bill Thompson stayed mayor in Chicago in the teens and twenties. Yet machine patronage gave little to the majority of blacks, and the least for black working-class families who only received the most unattractive of municipal jobs.[31] Politics primarily functioned as a buffer, and the color solidarity sometimes expressed by the black elite blurred deeper antagonisms. With Oscar De Priest, a black politician who financed his political campaigns with his profits from ghetto housing, Chicago sent the first black Congressman to Washington, D.C., turning a real estate speculator into a figure of racial pride.[32]

Because of segregation, blacks were forced to rely on their own city institutions and thus founded separate churches, clubs, civic associations, and newspapers. Within

---

[28] Blacks were used several times as strike-breakers in the stockyards and, most important, in the steel strike of 1919. Katznelson, p. 97.

[29] Chudacoff, pp. 206, 220; Teaford, p. 57.

[30] Katznelson, pp. 96f; Spear, p. 173.

[31] Katznelson, pp. 89, 95, 100f; Myrdal, p. 501.

[32] Katznelson, pp. 98, 118.

the ghetto a strong, independent black culture developed which was of some help in coping with the hardships of everyday life. A new collective identity evolved in the urban centers of the North and the city within the city began to acquire positive connotations for blacks. Since the jobs open to black Americans were chiefly menial ones and other paths of recognition were barred to them, black intelligence, creativity, and effort went into culture, entertainment, and sports. Unique contributions to modern culture, blues and jazz most ingeniously expressed black plight and yearnings.[33]

3. Experience in the Black Belt

Native Son describes the truncated lives of a disorganized black working-class family in Chicago in the 1930s. Their mental maps of the South Side delimit their world. Keneth Kinnamon praised this depiction of the black city for its vividness and a "verisimilitude that is almost photographic."[34] Yet the novel is also influenced by modes of perception developed in American urban fiction in the first third of the twentieth century. Richard Wright fuses his black experience with modernist perspectives.[35]

With his concentration on isolation and individuality, Wright resumes a pattern established by earlier city novelists. Stephen Crane, Theodore Dreiser, John Dos Passos, and James T. Farrell, authors whom Wright admired, considerably influenced the city image in *Native Son*. Wright highly valued *Maggie: A Girl of the Streets* and adjusted Crane's image of the dual city and his discussion of failed perception to his novel; Wright considered Dreiser as important as Dostoevsky, his favorite writer, and the handling of the trial section or the use of newspaper clippings in *Native Son* are acknowledged influences of *An American Tragedy* and *Sister Carrie*;[36] he esteemed Dos Passos' urban montage which became germinal for his first novel, the posthumously published *Lawd Today*; finally, he discussed his fiction with James T. Farrell, the author of the Chi-

---

[33]LeRoi Jones, *Blues People*, New York, 1963. Black music, as Richard Wright later asserted, "quickened and lifted the sense of humanity" of millions throughout the world. Richard Wright, "The Shame of Chicago," *Ebony*, 7 (1951), p. 31.

[34]Kinnamon, p. 121.

[35]In his essay "How 'Bigger' was Born," Wright explained: "This association with white writers was the life preserver of my hope to depict negro life in fiction, for my race possessed no fictional works dealing with such problems, had no background in such sharp and critical testing of experience. . . ." Wright, "How 'Bigger' Was Born," p. xvi.

[36]Margaret Walker, *Richard Wright, Daemonic Genius: A Portrait of the Man, A Critical Look at His Work*, New York, 1988, pp. 74, 123ff.

cago trilogy *Studs Lonigan*, who had studied urban sociology at the University of Chicago.[37]

Though influenced by these urban novelists, Wright's fiction also relates directly to the theories of urban ecology taught at the University of Chicago.[38] Mary Wirth, the social worker of the Wright family, had introduced Richard Wright to her husband, Louis Wirth, in the early 1930s. Wirth directed Wright's sociology readings and was his supervisor in a WPA project. Wright thus became acquainted with the ideas of Chicago sociology through Robert E. Park, Robert Redfield, E. Franklin Frazier, and Horace C. Cayton.[39] Later, in 1945, the novelist was asked to write an introduction for Horace C. Cayton and St. Clair Drake's prime sociological study of South Side Chicago, *Black Metropolis*.[40] His own collaboration with Chicago sociologists climaxed in 1941, when he published a study of black migration called *Twelve Million Black Voices* which treated the development of the black folk from feudal to urban ways of life. Wright himself stressed the importance of theory for his perception and understanding of the American city:

> I lived half hungry and afraid in a city to which I had fled with the dumb yearning to write, to tell my story. But I did not know what my story was, and it was not until I stumbled upon science that I discovered some of the meanings of the environment that battered and taunted me. I encountered the work of men who were studying the Negro community, amassing facts about urban negro life, and I found that sincere art and honest science were not far apart, that each could enrich the other. The huge mountain of fact piled up by the Department of Sociology at the University of Chicago gave me my first concrete vision of the forces that molded the urban Negro's body and soul.[41]
>
> It was from the scientific findings of men like the late Robert E. Park, Robert Redfield, and Louis Wirth that I drew the meanings for my documentary book, *Twelve Black Voices*; for my novel *Native Son*; it was from their scientific facts that I absorbed some of that quota of inspiration necessary for me to write *Uncle Tom's Children* and *Black Boy*.[42]

---

[37] Ibid., p. 75. Wright employed one of Dos Passos' central city images, the "squirrelcage," as an epigraph for a section of his novel *Lawd Today*. Richard Wright, *Lawd Today*, New York, 1963, p. 99. Arnold Rampersad, "Foreword," *Lawd Today*, 1963, New York, 1986, p. 3.

[38] Chester Eisinger, *Fiction of the 1940s*, Chicago, 1963, pp. 68f.

[39] Walker, p. 69; Webb, pp. 102, 371; Edward Margolies, *The Art of Richard Wright*, Carbondale, Ill., 1969, p. 11.

[40] Prior to this effort in urban sociology and prior to *Native Son*, Wright had completed several essays on black urban culture in the South Side and in Harlem. See Richard Wright, "Ethnological Aspects of Chicago's Black Belt," (1935), *New Letters*, 39 (1972), 61-67. "Portrait of Harlem," *New York Panorama*, ed. New York WPA, New York, 1938, 132-51, (unsigned article). Michel Fabre, *The Unfinished Quest of Richard Wright*, trans. Isabel Barzun, New York, 1973, p. 627.

[41] Wright, "Introduction," p. xvii.

[42] Ibid., p. xviii.

In *Native Son*, the environmentalism of the Chicago School is evident in the emphasis on the physical conditions, the "steel and stone" (NS, p. 19) of the ghetto. Moreover, Herbert Spencer's teleological evolutionism underlies Bigger Thomas' vision of a future life in the city. Bigger's view reflects ecological concepts of the atomized mass urbanite. Not neighbors and friends of a knowable, and delimited surrounding, but an anonymous mass will surround him in his new life:

> He looked out upon the world and the people about him with a double vision: one vision pictured death . . . and the other vision pictured life, *an image of himself standing amid throngs of men*, lost in the welter of their lives with the hope of emerging again, different, unafraid. (NS, p. 337; my italics)

Yet Richard Wright's image of the South Side cannot be limited to existing literary and scientific models. Rather he innovatively transformed the naturalist and ecological patterns by fusing the ecological model with a dialectical view of society and economics. Class relations produce the urban environment and shape its infrastructure, its buildings, and its communities. Wirthian theory, as Wright pointed out, cannot by itself capture black urban experience:

> In general, the book [*Black Metropolis*] can be thought of in a phrase that Louis Wirth has used to describe the lives of people who live in cities: Urbanism As a Way of Life; but with this important exception: The Jim Crow lives that Negroes live in our crowded cities differ qualitatively from those of whites and are not fully known to whites.[43]

Richard Wright depicts the brutality of ghetto life in *Native Son* by carefully recording the conditions imposed on a black working-class family. The urban experience of Bigger Thomas and his family are exemplary: their story reads like a classical study in ghetto poverty, family disorganization, and juvenile delinquency. At the center of the novel is the youthful protagonist. Even though Wright's authorial voice intervenes at times, most events are filtered through the eyes of Bigger Thomas; readers receive mainly his image of Chicago.[44]

The four family members share a tiny kitchenette which is owned by Henry Dalton's South Side Real Estate Company. The slum apartment tyrannizes the family with its narrowness, squalor, and rodents. Living is tense "in this garbage dump" (NS, p. 12) and Bigger experiences his home as "nothing but shouts and bickering" (NS, p. 16). The environment does not simply squelch individuality, but also the basic humanity of ghetto dwellers. Bigger is alienated from his family, his friends, and his lover: "He lived with

---

[43] Ibid., p. xx.

[44] Joyce Ann Joyce, *Richard Wright's Art of Tragedy*, Iowa City, 1986, p. 65.

them, but behind a wall, a curtain" (NS, p. 14). His life as a youth is characterized by stagnation, meaninglessness, and powerlessness.[45] Brooding and self-hatred alternate with bursts of violence: "He knew that the moment he allowed what his life meant to enter fully into his consciousness, he would either kill himself or someone else" (NS, p. 14).

Richard Wright lays bare the grounds on which street-corner violence and gangs of juveniles must thrive. Under ghetto conditions, the barriers to leading a normal life are almost insurmountable. Bigger is unemployed as the novel opens. As a school dropout, he is not qualified for well paying or satisfying jobs. He also hates working for white people: "Yes, he could take the job at Dalton's and be miserable, or he could refuse it and starve. It maddened him to think that he did not have a wider choice of action" (NS, p. 16). The yearnings evoked by motion pictures, magazines, and advertisements can only be realized with money earned in petty criminal acts, in holdups and robberies. The South Side suffocates his aspirations very early. When Bigger slays Bessie Mears and decapitates Mary Dalton, he is still a youth "not old enough to vote" (NS, p. 349).

The pervasive ways in which a cold and hostile environment determine black existence are masterfully depicted. The opening scene prefigures many of the major issues in the novel. The compositional density testifies to Richard Wright's control of language and to his economy in the selection of detail. Its aesthetic web sets the novel apart from any unimaginative case study or protest fiction with which Wright, as a propagandist and Communist, has been identified.[46] Literature, as Wright argued, was not a "carbon copy of reality."[47]

The shrill, metallic noise in the first line of the novel represents what Wright called "that great iron city, that impersonal, mechanical city."[48] Chicago intrudes as a force from the outside into the life of the Thomas family and jolts them into their day:

> Brrrrrrriiiiiiiiiiiiiiiiinng!
> An alarm clock clanged in the dark and silent room. A bed spring creaked. A woman's voice sang out impatiently:
> "Bigger, shut that thing off!"
> A surly grunt sounded above the tinny ring of metal. Naked feet swished dryly across the planks in the wooden floor and the clang ceased abruptly.
> "Turn on the light, Bigger."
> "Awright," came a sleepy mumble.

---

[45]Fishburn, p. 80.

[46]Robert A. Bone, *The Negro Novel in America*, New Haven, 1965, p. 147.

[47]Wright, "Blueprint for Negro Writing," p. 48.

[48]Wright, "Introduction," p. xvii.

> Light flooded the room and revealed a black boy standing in a narrow space between two iron beds, rubbing his eyes with the backs of his hands. (NS, p. 7)

The oppositions of night and day, darkness and light, and of black and white in the first lines foreshadow the chief dichotomy and conflict in the fictional city.[49] Wright's prose, in its intended "complex simplicity,"[50] evokes a profound dissociation in the duality of sounds in the scene. The smooth nasals ("clanged," "spring," "sang," "thing," "ring") evoking warmth, shelter, and the gradual beginning of a new day, clash with orders and plosives of an aggressive environment ("clock," "dark," "creaked," "shut," "grunt"). Even in its basic phonetic constituents, *Native Son* projects a segregated city and records the split consciousness of this ghetto world. For Wright, this dichotomy transcends city limits:

> Lodged in the innermost heart of America is a fatal division of being, a war of impulses. America knows that a split is in her, and that that split might cause her death; but she is powerless to pull the dangling ends together. An uneasiness haunts her conscience, taints her moral preachments, lending an air of unreality to her actions, and rendering ineffectual the good deeds she feels compelled to do in the world. America is a nation of a riven consciousness.[51]

To use the noise of a clock at the beginning of a city novel is significant. A major symbol of urban ecology, the clock represents the artificial and rationalist quality of the modern environment. In his introductory essay to *Black Metropolis*, Wright quotes Robert Redfield's statement that, in the city, "clocks replaced the sun as a symbolic measurement of time."[52] People in the city do not rise with dawn, but still at night. Clocks continue to play an important role in the novel. A clock appears later in the panic in the bedroom and recalls the circumstances of Bigger's conditioned murder of Mary Dalton (NS, p. 88).

The environment of steel and stone, represented by claustrophobic rooms, remains important throughout the novel. Each section corresponds to a major locale: the Thomas kitchenette, the Dalton mansion, and the prison cell. The contrast of class and race is translated into spatial terms. The narrow kitchenette of the Thomas family is brought into direct contrast with the "spacious" (NS, p. 45) surroundings of the Daltons who are both employer and slumlord for Bigger Thomas. When Bigger returns from the Daltons' mansion where he has indulged himself in the "quiet, warm, clean, rich house" (NS, p. 155), he notices the utter barrenness of his family's slum dwelling:

---

[49] Foreshadowing is a major technique in the novel. Fabre, p. 182.
[50] Wright, "Blueprint for Negro Writing," p. 45.
[51] Wright, "Introduction," p. xxi.
[52] Ibid., p. xxii.

> He looked around the room, seeing it for the first time. There was no rug on the floor and the plastering on the walls and ceiling hung loose in many places. There were two worn iron beds, four chairs, an old dresser, and a drop-leaf table on which they ate. (NS, p. 100)

The contrast between the Daltons and the Thomases stands for a city-wide division of exploiter and exploited. While the South Side is flooded with white values, it lacks the options and conveniences which the white metropolis boasts of in advertisements, postcards, and city guides. Bigger's city does not contain the emblems of progress and civic pride so ostentatiously displayed in Chicago's Loop: there are no high-rise buildings, neither civic institutions nor museums, neither imposing department stores, boulevards, playgrounds, nor parks in South Side Chicago. The black part of the city is unrelentingly bleak. There, separation and segregation are impervious.

In the South Side, the lack of opportunity and the imposed restrictions paralyze blacks. For Bigger, the ghetto is a prison:

> "Goddammit!"
> "What's the matter?"
> "They don't let us do *nothing*."
> "Who?"
> "The *white* folks."
> "You talk like you just now finding out," Gus said.
> "Naw. But I just can't get used to it," Bigger said. "I swear to God I can't. I know I oughtn't think about it, but I can't help it. Every time I think about it I feel like somebody's poking a red-hot iron down my throat. Goddammit, look! We live here and they live there. We black and they white. They got things and we ain't. They do things and we can't. It's just like living in jail. Half the time I feel like I'm on the outside of the world peeping in through a knot-hole in the fence...." (NS, p. 23)

While the black world goes unnoticed through its exclusion--Bigger feels completely "outside of this white world" (NS, p. 207)--white values profoundly affect the South Side and direct black aspirations. Hollywood films rouse the yearning for adventure, success, and recognition that are constantly thwarted by conditions in the ghetto (NS, p. 32ff). Airplanes do fly above the South Side, but without black passengers or pilots. Bigger, whose childhood dream is to become an "aviator" (NS, p. 327), is barred from such a career, no matter how hard he would try in the ghetto. All blacks may do in the slum is "play 'white'" (NS, p. 21), their grim substitute for deferred hopes and experiences. Since there is no real chance for participation in American society, the frustration among streetcorner boys breeds aggression:

> "Maybe they right in not wanting us to fly," Bigger said.
> "'Cause if I took a plane up I'd take a couple of bombs along and drop 'em sure as hell...." (NS, p. 20)

The duality of rich and poor and the inequality of separate white and black cities is not only a physical division because blacks have internalized their oppression. For Bigger, whites live "right down here in my stomach" (NS, p. 24). The constant denial of humanity and the predictable futility of effort result in destructive aggression and self-hatred. In true naturalist manner, Bigger is moved by destructive forces beyond his control:

> These were the rhythms of life: indifference and violence; periods of abstract brooding and periods of intense desire; moments of silence and moments of anger--like water ebbing and flowing from the tug of a far-away, invisible force. Being this way was a need of his as deep as eating. (NS, p. 31)

The ghetto dwellers seem utterly enclosed and alienated. The outrage, which should be directed against the oppressors, is deflected in internal strife among the victims.[53] Similarly, though Bigger plans to rob a white delicatessen shop, fear makes him fight his poolroom companions, an episode which contrasts with the eventual rebellion.

The inverted aggression among blacks is a self-destructive behavior forced on them by white violence. Throughout the novel, Wright hints at white retaliation whenever the black minority transgresses its territory. Bigger is aware of the bombs "thrown by whites into houses . . . when Negroes had first moved into the South Side" (NS, p. 172). The campaign posters supporting Buckley, the corrupt District Attorney, are literal reminders to the segregated constituency not to trespass white laws: "IF YOU BREAK THE LAW, YOU CAN'T WIN!" (NS, p. 16) Consequently, Bigger, who is aware of the threat of being physically harrassed when leaving the ghetto, arms against possible white violence:

> He was going among white people, so he would take his knife and his gun; it would make him feel that he was the equal of them, give him a sense of completeness. Then he thought of a good reason why he should take it; in order to get to the Dalton place, he had to go through a white neighborhood. He had not heard of Negroes being molested recently, but he felt that it was always possible. (NS, p. 44)

Later, Bigger will again be reminded of the enforced Jim Crow position when the Ku Klux Klan burns a cross in the vicinity of the Dalton place (NS, p. 312).

In *Native Son*, actual repression and internalized frustration backfires violently on the white oppressors. The blindness, fear, and hatred of white Chicago, the "cold and distant world" (NS, p. 45), directly lead to the suffocation of Mary Dalton in a moment

---

[53]Paul N. Siegel, "The Conclusion of Richard Wright's *Native Son*," *PMLA*, 89 (1974), 517-23, repr. *Richard Wright: A Collection of Critical Essays*, eds. Richard Macksey and Frank E. Moorer, Englewood Cliffs, N.J., 1984, p. 115.

of tension. The segregation of lives results in fatal, reciprocal ignorance. As Bigger Thomas comes to realize:

> White folks and black folks is strangers. We don't know what each other is thinking. Maybe she was trying to be kind; but she didn't act like it. To me she looked and acted like all other white folks. (NS, p. 325)

As in Stephen Crane's dual city, blindness is a central image in the novel:[54]

> Jan was blind. Mary had been blind. Mr. Dalton was blind. And Mrs. Dalton was blind; yes, blind in more ways than one . . . Bigger felt that a lot of people were like Mrs. Dalton, blind. . . . (NS, p. 102)

This motif is used meaningfully throughout the novel. The opaque city of blacks is extended to the actual blindness of Mrs. Dalton and more generally to a liberal philanthropy which is as "tragically blind" as "sightless eyes" (NS, p. 362). Even their name suggests lack of vision, for "daltonism" is a medical term for a form of color blindness.[55]

For white Chicago, this blindness is perpetuated by falsified accounts and exaggerated stereotypes in the mass media. The racist newspaper reports in *Native Son* are no polemic exaggeration; Wright simply paraphrased clippings from the *Chicago Tribune* about a black murderer who was on trial in Chicago when the novel was written.[56]

> Though the Negro killer's body does not seem compactly built, he gives the impression of possessing abnormal physical strength. He is about five feet, nine inches tall and his skin is exceedingly black. His lower jaw protrudes obnoxiously, reminding one of a jungle beast. . . . All in all, he seems a beast utterly untouched by the softening influences of modern civilization. In speech and manner he lacks the charm of the average, harmless, grinning southern darky so beloved by the American people. . . . (NS, p. 260)

Though critics noted the "tremendous revelatory power"[57] of Richard Wright's portrayal of oppression, his assessment of the South Side in *Native Son* was also criticized by blacks. James Baldwin, for instance, argued that Wright, in the figure of a black thug and murderer, perpetuated a reversed image of Uncle Tom and denied full humanity to his black protagonist.[58] Other critics claimed that Wright failed to show opposition to oppression in the black community and that he did not appreciate its indigenous culture. One critic even hyperbolically argued that in Bigger's portrait, race is deempha-

---

[54] James Nagel, "Images of 'Vision' in *Native Son*," *University Review*, 36 (1969), 109-15, repr. *Critical Essays on Richard Wright*, ed. Yoshinobu Hakutani, Boston, 1982, p. 151.

[55] Kinnamon, p. 120.

[56] Ibid., pp. 121ff.

[57] Brivic, p. 231.

[58] Baldwin, "Many Thousands Gone," p. 58.

sized to a degree that the "experiences might well have been those of a white youth in the ghettoes of Chicago."[59] Indeed, black religion and community evoke a "vast black silent void" (NS, p. 263) in Bigger. Houston A. Baker remarks:

> Innumerable passages in Wright's autobiography give a sense of black communality, a sense of fused strength, yet the narrator [of *Native Son*] denies the presence of such meaningful relations in the microcosm that he sets before the reader.[60]

The neglect of black community traditions by Wright is revealing in many ways. For one, it testifies to the influence of ecological theory which deemphasized communal cohesion. Strong neighborhood ties and stable structures contradict the model's predictions, which expects society to develop from primary bonds to complex individual independence. Richard Wright accepted this interpretation of urban history. Paraphrasing Robert Redfield, he claimed that with urbanization, "kinship with the soil altered, men became atoms crowding great industrial cities, bewildered as too their duties and meaning."[61] Moreover, the stage of urbanism occurred too early for blacks. In *Twelve Million Black Voices* Wright concluded:

> Perhaps never in history has a more utterly unprepared folk wanted to go to the city; we were barely born as a folk when we headed for the tall and sprawling centers of steel and stone.[62]

Judging the city through the lens of Chicago sociology then, meant that Wright had to play down ethnic bonds. Ghettos would dissolve as Louis Wirth had shown in his dissertation, *The Ghetto*, and monads would people the city. All in all, Richard Wright, who, as a black novelist, set himself the task to project a future path for his folk and to "create values by which his race is to struggle, live and die,"[63] could not employ the ghetto community as an effective symbol for the future. Even if ties were visible, they need not be stressed. To advance, Bigger Thomas has to revolt against the alienated ghetto community.

Even though Wright may have been correct in assuming that conditions in the black belt corroded bonds among blacks and that traditional politics buffered uprisings,

---

[59] Thomas D. Jarrett, "Toward Unfettered Creativity: A Note on the Novelist's Coming of Age," *Phylon*, 2 (1950), p. 315.

[60] Houston A. Baker, "Racial Wisdom and Richard Wright's *Native Son*," *Critical Essays on Richard Wright*, ed. Yoshinobu Hakutani, p. 78.

[61] Wright, "Introduction," p. xxii.

[62] Richard Wright, *Twelve Million Black Voices: A Folk History of the Negro in the United States*, New York, 1941, repr. *Richard Wright Reader*, eds. Ellen Wright and Michel Fabre, New York, 1978, p. 204.

[63] Wright, "Blueprint for Negro Writing," p. 43.

his critics can point to the crucial absence of community in his ghetto novel as a distortion of historical facts. In the case of Robert Nixon, the black murderer whose racist treatment by Chicago's newspapers was used in the novel, the black community, the National Negro Congress, and black preachers did organize resistance to white hostility and racism.[64] This fact is neglected by Wright. Instead, Reverend Hammond who thanks Henry Dalton for his good works, is identified with the prolongation of white injustice (NS, p. 273).

Another reason why Wright chose to neglect the black urban way of life is provided by his biography. Long before his move to the city, he had become isolated among his kin.[65] Although he was fascinated by black culture and thought that the "black folk represent the most magical and meaningful picture of human experience in the Western world,"[66] and that blacks were "an intensely practical people endowed with an extraordinary capacity for emotional expression,"[67] he was also critical of the black community. This impatience is most evident in the autobiographical *Black Boy*:

> After I had outlived the shocks of childhood, after the habit of reflection had been born in me, I used to mull over the strange absence of real kindness in Negroes, how unstable was our tenderness, how lacking in genuine passion we were, how void of great hope, how timid our joy, how bare our traditions, how hollow our memories, how lacking we were in those intangible sentiments that bind man to man, and how shallow was even our despair. After I had learned other ways of life I used to brood upon the unconscious irony of those who felt that Negroes led so passional an existence! I saw that what had been taken for our emotional strength was our negative confusions, our flights, our fears, our frenzy under pressure.[68]

Wright remained ambivalent about the black community throughout his life. He fully identified with its liberation, its cause and its unique culture, yet at times he expressed a deep dissatisfaction with it, especially toward its tendency of accommodation.[69] Since he disliked the acquiescence to injustice among his kin as much as among whites, he criticized the black community for its perpetuation of submissiveness. In *Black Boy* he reproduces a traumatic experience in church:

---

[64]Kinnamon, p. 124.

[65]*Black Boy* records this deep gap that had opened between the youth and mainstream black culture.

[66]Wright, *Twelve Million Black Voices*, p. 146.

[67]Richard Wright, "Introducing Some American Negro Folksongs," *Présence Africaine*, 6 (1949), p. 70.

[68]Richard Wright, *Black Boy: A record of childhood and youth*, New York, 1945, p. 45.

[69]Wright composed blues lyrics and wrote about such popular figures as the boxing champion Joe Louis. D. Ray and R. M. Farnsworth, eds., *Richard Wright: Impressions and Perspectives*, Kansas, 1971, pp. 85-88.

> My mother grabbed my hands and I felt hot tears scalding my fingers. I tried to stifle my disgust. We young men had been trapped by the community, the tribe in which we lived and of which we were a part. The tribe, for its own safety, was asking us to be at one with it.[70]

In *Native Son* it is significant that community, women, and religion combine to prevent the emancipation of the rebel.

As a newcomer to the South Side and a "permanent outsider"[71] among mainstream blacks, the novelist developed a detached stance similar to that of Crane and Dreiser. Emancipation and community seemed incompatible. Moreover, his position as an outsider was cemented joining the John Reed Club and the Communist Party, themselves organizations of a minority. Even among his political allies, however, the novelist remained isolated:

> In his own Party unit, a segregated cell located in the Black Belt of the South Side, even his black comrades seemed to consider him, as an intellectual, a curio.[72]

The most important reason for the neglect of black community life in the novel is an aesthetic one. Bigger's position as an outsider and the marginalization of community are closely linked to the novel's political theme. For Wright, only outsiders to the community were capable of rebellion, as he explained in his essay "How 'Bigger' Was Born": "I lived the first seventeen years of my life in the South without so much as hearing of or seeing one act of rebellion from *any* Negro, save the Bigger Thomases."[73]

4. The Dialectics of Oppression

Bigger Thomas' suffocation and decapitation of a white woman is an unreflected, horrid act of rebellion. Still, his act seems inevitable as an act opposing oppression and dissociation. In Bigger, the yearning for wholeness is emotional and unconscious:

> What made Bigger's social consciousness most complex was the fact that he was hovering unwanted between two worlds--between powerful America and his own stunted place in life--and I took upon myself the task of trying to make the reader feel this No Man's Land.

---

[70] Wright, *Black Boy*, p. 169.

[71] Robert Felgar, *Richard Wright*, Boston, 1980, p. 25.

[72] Blyden Jackson, "Richard Wright: Black Boy from America's Black Belt and Urban Ghettos," *Critical Essays on Richard Wright*, ed. Yoshinobu Hakutani, Boston, 1982, p. 57.

[73] Richard Wright, "How 'Bigger' Was Born," *Native Son*, New York, 1940, p. xiii.

> The most that I could say of Bigger was that he felt the *need* for a whole life and *acted* out of that need; that was all.[74]

Richard Wright's vision turns meaningless violence into an existential emblem of hope. Bigger's rebellion against white oppression functions as an antithetical step in an attempt to achieve recognition and reconciliation. Each of the three books in *Native Son* contains a step in a dialectical triad: "Fear" records Bigger's paralysis in the ghetto, "Flight" presents the feeling of freedom after the eruption of violence, and "Fate" indicates an acceptance of guilt and humility and through it a renewed sense of dignity. Bigger dialectically develops from repression to rebellion and, finally, to recognition. Although he has killed, and thus has seriously violated human bonds, in the end Bigger Thomas may still signify the belief in a future synthesis for Wright. Bigger's hope is a new mutuality of equals. For him, in a "response of recognition, there would be union, identity; there would be a supporting oneness, a wholeness which had been denied him all his life" (NS, p. 335).

The dialectical movement of the plot and of Bigger's consciousness, however, cannot be equated with a Marxist dialectic[75]--several critics suggested this when they called Boris Max a Communist mouthpiece of the author and the defense arguments "transparently propagandistic"[76]--rather, Richard Wright transcends the limitations of traditional materialism in *Native Son*. Sheldon Brivic has noted this extension in the novel: "Black people need Marx's ideas in order to overcome economic and political oppression. Marxism, however, cannot provide a full solution to the problems of blacks because it is not related to their specific racial problems."[77] Boris Max's courtroom plea is only one view of ghetto reality, the other is provided by Bigger Thomas himself. Eventually, Bigger seems the only person who is able to grasp the depth of his act, whereas even Boris Max leaves the prison cell as "a blind man" (NS, p. 392).

Wright proposes in his fiction an extension of Marxist philosophy similar to that which Jürgen Habermas recognized in Hegel's fragment on the "dialectic of the moral life."[78] The passage from Habermas' *Knowledge and Human Interests* is worth quoting at length for it provides a philosophical gloss on the process of reflection and recognition in

---

[74]Wright, "How 'Bigger' Was Born," p. xxiv.

[75]For Keneth Kinnamon, the novel is written from a thoroughly Communist viewpoint. Kinnamon, p. 125.

[76]Carl Russell Brignano, *Richard Wright: An Introduction to the Man and his Works*, Pittsburgh, 1973, p. 78; Margolies, p. 104.

[77]Sheldon Brivic, "Conflict of Values: Richard Wright's *Native Son*," *Novel*, 7 (1974), p. 244.

[78]Habermas, *Knowledge and Human Interests*, p. 56.

Native Son. Habermas summarizes the dialectics of the moral life and the punishment that befalls those who destroy a moral totality as follows:

> The 'criminal' annuls the complementarity of unconstrained communication and the reciprocal gratification of needs by putting himself as an individual in place of the totality. In doing so he sets off a process of fate that turns upon him. The struggle ignited between the conflicting parties and the hostility against the other who has been injured and oppressed render perceptible the lost complementarity and past friendship. The criminal is confronted with the negating power of his past life. He experiences his guilt. The guilty one must suffer under the violence of the repressed and sundered life, which he has himself provoked, until he experiences in the repression of the other's life the deficiency of his own, and, in his turning away from the other subject, his alienation from himself. This *causality of fate* is ruled by the power of the suppressed life. The latter can only be reconciled if the experience of the negativity of the sundered life gives rise to yearning for what has been lost and compels the guilty one to identify with the existence of the other, against which he is struggling, as that which he is denying in his own. Then both parties recognize their rigidified position in relation to each other as the result of detachment and abstraction from their common life context.[79]

Native Son projects a movement similar to that suggested in the Hegelian model. White civilization has committed a crime against common humanity and receives its deserved punishment in the violence triggered by the state of society. The totality of morals, the wholeness of society can only be restored if both sides acknowledge their guilt and failings. Bigger Thomas eventually transcends his determined state. Jan Erlone, who forgives Bigger Thomas for his murders, is greeted in the end by Bigger. Resuming the triadic pattern, Bigger's sign of forgiveness toward Jan shows him for the first time as an equal to whites, "'Tell . . . Tell Mister . . . Tell Jan hello. . . .'" (NS, p. 392).

The Hegelian dialectic helps to emphasize Wright's standpoint which proposes to transcend racial antagonism: there is no cultural or ethnic superiority on either side, but only the mutually broken tissue of moral and social obligations. Whether Bigger is a comprehensive archetypal image of blacks, whether he is a symbol of savage subhumanity, a "human monster,"[80] or whether white civilization is not superior after all, these questions of race appear to be fatally misguided from the Hegelian perspective. Bigger is, as Wright argued later, both black and white, his acts testify to the profound alienation and fragmentation on both sides.[81]

For Wright, the white enclosure of the South Side has initiated black violence. In *American Hunger* he explains that "an insurgent act is but a man's desperate answer to those who twist his environment so that he cannot fully share the spirit of his native

---

[79]Habermas, p. 56.

[80]Felgar, p. 98.

[81]Wright, "How 'Bigger' was Born," p. xiv.

land."[82] In the novel, the Dalton real estate operation and the slum kitchenette of the Thomas family are intricately interconnected in a dialectical process. For example, Bigger Thomas' accidental stifling of Mary Dalton is presented verbatim as a reaction to white suffocation. For Bigger, the whites "own everything. They choke you off the face of the earth" (NS, p. 327). The Daltons are deeply implicated in the death of their daughter. When, under tension, Bigger pounds the rat's head in his family's kitchenette, he acts "hysterically" (NS, p. 10). Similarly, when he is surprised in Mary's bedroom, "a hysterical terror" seizes him (NS, p. 84). Likewise, when the rat threatens his family, his sister panics: "Frantically, Vera climbed upon the bed and the woman caught hold of her" (NS, p. 10). Bigger literally responds in this way as he stifles Mary in her bedroom: "Frenzy dominated him ... Frantically, he caught a corner of the pillow and brought it to her lips" (NS, p. 84). The Daltons' real estate policy and white oppression have caused Bigger Thomas to behave in such an uncontrolled way.

Beyond the behaviorist pattern of stimulus and response in which cause and effect are given, Wright, in a Dreiserian twist, implies that no such unequivocal and direct relation need exist. The connection may be only contingent. As much as Bigger "killed by accident" (NS, p. 101), the Daltons only incidentally own his family's house and suffocate his humanity. Ironically, despite Bigger's murder, both sides are not personally hostile--they are part of a wider segregation and fragmentation.

Wright's achievement does not consist in writing a story of deserved retaliation, but rather in his insight into the fatality of dissociation and conditioned terror. For Wright, rebellion can only be a first step. At first, Bigger's newly acquired freedom turns into another flight from responsibility. His cruel battering of Bessie Mears is a continuation of old behavior. The killing of his lover--Bessie is identified with black submission and meekness--appears as an act of fear and of self-hatred.[83] Community, embeddedness, religion, and women are equated with one another and fought by Bigger: "He hated his mother for that way of hers which was like Bessie's. What his mother had was Bessie's whiskey, and Bessie's whiskey was his mother's religion" (NS, p. 226). Subsumed by economic and racial issues, females suffer most of all in *Native Son*.[84]

---

[82]Wright, *American Hunger*, p. 45.

[83]Felgar, p. 97.

[84]Maria K. Mootry concludes, "However brutal and unfair to women (and to our idea of love) Wright seems to be, we must accept his treatment of the relations between men and women for what it is: a metaphor for the struggle of an oppressed people to deal with history with dignity and meaning. . . ." Maria K. Mootry, "Bitches, Whores, and Woman Haters: Archetypes and Typologies in the Art of Richard Wright," *Richard Wright: A Collection of Critical Essays*, eds. Richard Macksey and Frank E. Moorer, Englewood Cliffs, N.J., 1984, p. 127.

The moral grandeur achieved by the brutalized youth in the prison scene before his death is his final withdrawal from the irrational dialectic of brutality and the acceptance of responsibility for his action. Joyce Ann Joyce has stressed the tragic dimension of his struggle and concluded: "*Native Son* charts Bigger's growth from darkness into light, from innocence into experience, and from ignorance into knowledge."[85] The institutionalized justice of mainstream society will punish the victim and trigger further retaliation, although Bigger's acts, when he accidentally stifled Mary Dalton or battered Bessie Mears, were clearly beyond his control.[86] Bigger emerges as morally superior to his judges because he recognizes his own responsibility and guilt. Facing the death sentence, he both justifies his act--"What I killed for must've been good!" (NS, p. 392)--and yet reaches out for a new wholeness and understanding by sending words of reconciliation to Jan Erlone whose beloved he had murdered.

In contrast to the Hegelian or the Marxist model, however, this attempt to envisage a moral totality is portrayed as the act of an isolated individual. It is distinct from the faith in proletarian solidarity that Richard Wright had promoted in his early days in the Communist Party. In 1934, the poet had hoped for wholeness through proletarian collectivity. In Whitmanesque manner he envisioned revolt:

> I am black and I have seen black hands
> Raised in fists of revolt, side by side with the white fists of white workers,
> And some day--and it is only this which sustains me--
> Some day there shall be millions and millions of them,
> On some red day in a burst of fists on a new horizon![87]

The force that "sustains" Richard Wright in *Native Son* is different. He remains distanced from liberal blindness and Bigger's irrational acts, but also from the class formulae of proletarian fiction. The novel records only the laudable acts of outsiders: of Bigger Thomas, the rebellious black, of Jan Erlone, the sensitive Communist, and of Boris Max, the Jewish radical. Compensating for the loss of collective solutions, Richard Wright turns the political action of individuals into "meaningful and prophetic symbol[s]."[88] The hoped-for new society cannot be achieved as lived, communal reality, but only projected as a literary vision. The end hints at an unresolved conflict. Despite the

---

[85] Joyce, p. 71.

[86] David Bakish, *Richard Wright*, New York, 1973. When Bigger prepares to club his beloved, "the reality of it all slipped from him" (NS, p. 222).

[87] Richard Wright, "I Have Seen Black Hands," *New Masses*, 11 (June 26, 1934), 16, repr. *Richard Wright Reader*, eds. Ellen Wright and Michel Fabre, New York, 1978, p. 246.

[88] Wright, "How 'Bigger' Was Born," p. xiv.

will for reconciliation, communication fails. Accepting white forgiveness, Bigger still rejects the vision of a liberated city developed by Boris Max. It seems incommunicable as yet:

> Bigger was gazing in the direction of the buildings; but he did not see them. He was trying to react to the picture Max was drawing, trying to compare that picture with what he had felt all his life. (NS, p. 390)

5. The Modern Black City

The final section of the novel and its questioning of understanding and communication relate to the writer and his subject. In his "Blueprint for Negro Writing," Wright explicitly demanded of the black novelist the task of serving as a guide for other blacks:

> It means that Negro writers must have in their consciousness the foreshortened picture of the *whole*, nourishing culture from which they were torn in Africa, and of the long, complex (and for the most part, unconscious) struggle to regain in some form and under alien conditions of life a *whole* culture again.[89]

In a profound sense, orientation in the city and the novel become analogous in *Native Son*. The path the city would take also suggests the path of a liberated existence in the future. As argued above, urban reality as recorded by Wright denies any possibility of social wholeness. The ethnic community is marginalized because sociological theory denies its validity for the future; political collectivity, based in the class struggle, has been thwarted by the party's insensitivity to black experience;[90] and, finally, the novelist's artistic integrity contradicts the kinds of group solidarity projected in proletarian fiction. A yearning for wholeness is thus solely present as a motivation for Bigger's action:

> Why this black gulf between him and the world: warm red blood here and cold blue sky there, and never a wholeness, a oneness, a meeting of the two? (NS, p. 383)

For Wright, there was no group in America "acceptable to the whole of our country upholding certain humane values."[91] Nevertheless, despite his social disillusionment and political sobering, Wright still clung to a dialectical view of history. Years later, he would

---

[89] Wright, "Blueprint for Negro Writing," p. 47.

[90] George E. Kent, "Richard Wright: Blackness and the Adventure of Western Culture," *CLA Journal*, 12 (1969), 322-343, repr. *Richard Wright: A Collection of Critical Essays*, eds. Richard Macksey and Frank E. Moorer, Englewood Cliffs, N.J., 1984, p. 43.

[91] Wright, "How 'Bigger' Was Born," p. xxxiv.

say of himself: "I am as collectivist and proletarian in my outlook as when I belonged to the Communist Party."[92] After all, Wright chose to portray a rebel because he saw the urgency to revolt against the debasing *status quo* to achieve a new collectivity.

In *Native Son*, the need for collective action and wholeness is transferred to a different level. The novel projects an aesthetic substitute for solidarity and comradeship: Bigger Thomas, the existential rebel whose name *Big-ger* suggests collectivity, functions as a "prophetic"[93] symbol of political action. Richard Wright, the intellectual outsider, envisages a modernist fusion pointing toward a new social and political wholeness.

As Wright admitted, the act of writing had turned into a compensatory form of living:

> As I contemplated Bigger and what he meant, I said to myself: "I must write this novel, not only for others to read, but to free *myself* of this sense of shame and fear." In fact, the novel, as time passed, grew upon me to the extent that it became a necessity to write it; the writing of it turned into a way of living for me.[94]

Wright's urban aesthetic contains his answer. He develops a crucial analogy between his conscious act of writing and Bigger's unconscious rebellion: they both point in the direction of liberation. The puzzling statement that Bigger Thomas' extinction of life was an act of "creation" (NS, p. 366) is illuminated by comparing it with Wright's views on literature. In "Blueprint for Negro Writing," the materialist surprisingly equates creation with a radical scrutiny of the world: a Marxist approach, he says, "endows the writer with a sense of dignity which no other vision can give. Ultimately, it restores to the writer his lost heritage, that is, his role as creator of the world in which he lives, and as creator of himself."[95] To write about the South Side, then, established a certain degree of emancipation from the determined environment.

Moreover, the acts of creation and self-determination are not necessarily identified with a synthesis achieved through class struggle, but the radical analysis of contradictions can be as important. This shift from class action to individual reflection also provides a clue for understanding the qualitative leap from the pervasive impotence in the ghetto to Bigger's liberation and his sense of freedom in the end. Again, the perspective holds the liberation. Consequently, Bigger's development is not a break in the philosophical basis of the novel, as has been suggested by critics, but a synthesis on a dis-

---

[92] Richard Wright quoted in Webb, p. 208.

[93] Wright, "How 'Bigger' Was Born," p. xiv.

[94] Ibid., p. xxii.

[95] Wright, "Blueprint for Negro Writing," p. 44.

tinct level. Through the act of thinking and writing, a liberating agency is restored to a predetermined environment.

The writer's craft may unify the crucial division of experience in *Native Son* where feeling and thought must remain separate in the figures of Bigger Thomas and Boris Max.[96] Literature signified both reason and emotion to Wright. In *Black Boy* he emphasizes the emancipatory effect of reading, as literature gave him access to knowledge and independence; in *Native Son* the trial served to enlighten the audience about racial injustice. Yet, beyond its critical scrutiny of reality, fiction was also able to touch those chords that reason was unable to reach. As Wright explained, the novelist possesses the "ability to fuse and make articulate the experiences of men, because his writing possesses the potential cunning to steal into the most inmost recesses of the human heart, because he can create myth and symbols that inspire a faith in life. . . ."[97] Fiction may thus unify the dissociated city. The complex web of imagery in *Native Son* was to convey its emotional truth. For Wright, the rationalist, "a sequence of interlocking images" can shed a "kind of meaning."[98]

The communication between author and readers, however, is qualitatively different from the communication among fictional characters. Thus, the difficulties of communicating the necessary political direction are not fully overcome within the novel. The collective argument of the white defender and the isolated black victim remain apart as yet. Readers must fuse the two standpoints to achieve the proper perspective on the liberated city.

In summary, Richard Wright may project a hopeful image of Chicago, yet the conflict between isolation and collectivity in the city cannot be transcended in the story itself. If Wright intends to point out the direction of liberation for his characters, he has to know the path American society will take in the city. But here, the philosophical dilemma inherent in urban theory unwittingly surfaces. On the one hand, the modern city, which is equated with rationality, progress, and science, confirms Herbert Spencer's view of an evolution toward a state of complex heterogeneity. This aspect is contained in *Native Son* in the scientific concept of the ecological city. On the other hand, for Wright, the dissociated city clearly exists in the conflict of class interests. These two views, however, are ultimately incompatible. What teleological evolutionism praises as the highest form of social life corresponds with the decadence of the ruling class in the Marxist view.

---

[96] Brivic, p. 238; Bakish, p. 39.

[97] Wright, "Blueprint for Negro Writing," pp. 43f.

[98] Richard Wright, "Roots and Branches," unpublished typescript, quoted in Fabre, "Beyond Naturalism," p. 70.

Undoubtedly, in Wright's eyes, "the fittest were the productive workers, not the parasitic upper classes."[99] The pervasive ideology of space which allowed both Karl Marx and Herbert Spencer to define the city as an embodiment of progress blurred the deeper rift between these philosophical systems. Through ecological theory, liberal assumptions are reintroduced to the assessment of the modern city which Richard Wright otherwise rejected in his novel. The atomized urbanite of Chicago sociology confirmed Wright's image as an outsider.

This tension between a dialectical and an evolutionary model of city development recurs in the dual ending. On the one hand, Bigger Thomas' personal development signifies growth and projects a dialectical synthesis in recognition.[100] On the other hand, motifs and images indicate an incomprehensible process within a determined frame. The thematic and formal closure of the novel argues the futility of change: Bigger, like the chased rat in the opening scene which "squeaked and turned and ran in a narrow circle, looking for a place to hide" (NS, p. 9), is "trapped" (NS, p. 71) in the city jungle and eventually caught by a cordon of white men (NS, p. 241). The shrill mechanical force which has determined lives from the first line reappears in the end and closes the novel in despairing circularity, even resuming the dichotomy ("ring," "clang," "shut") of the beginning:

> He still held on to the bars. Then he smiled a faint, wry, bitter smile. He heard the *ring* of steel against steel as a far door *clanged shut*.(NS, p. 392; my italics)

Gaps and inconsistencies that are related to this dual image of the city occur throughout the novel. The neglect of the indigenous black ghetto is a major contradiction in the novel. In Wright's eyes, only outsiders to the inhibiting community can function as urban rebels, and thus he disregards the evidence of communal resistance in the Nixon case. In fact, the political development in the urban riots in the sixties showed that the black community was very important indeed. The more integrated blacks were, the more radical was their outlook and their action.[101] Further contradictions appear in the projected city experience in *Native Son*: Richard Wright oscillates between images of the known and delimited ghetto and those of the sprawling city of anonymous atoms. At one point, Bigger is intimately familiar with the neighborhood in the South Side, yet a few sentences later, on the same streetcorner, he is bewildered by the chaos of Chicago, by

---

[99]Fabre, "Beyond Naturalism," p. 57.

[100]Otten, p. 336; Fishburn, p. 100.

[101]Larry Isaac, Elizabeth Mutran, and Sheldon Stryker, "Political Protest Orientations Among Black and White Adults," *American Sociological Review*, 45 (1980), 191-213.

Wright's "unreal city."[102] First, Bigger hyperbolically indicates that he is fully familiar with his black environment,

> He looked round the lamp-lit, snow covered street. 'There's plenty of places,' he said. 'I know the South Side from A to Z.' (NS, p. 140)

Then, a few lines later, this familiar corner has turned into the unknowable moloch of urban ecology:

> Snow was falling again; the streets were long paths leading through a dense jungle, lit here and there with torches held high in invisible hands. (NS, p. 141)

For Wright, who intends to create political symbols indicative of a future society, the social form of the envisaged city remains uncertain. It cannot be a city based in knowable communities, as urban and evolutionary theory contest such a development. Nor can Wright accept the rosy image of Spencer's city of bourgeois individuals. This uncertainty about the future organization of society informs the city image of *Native Son*. Though Bigger Thomas imagines a better city, the novel may only present it as a vague, incommunicable vision lacking concrete contours:

> He [Bigger] jumped up and looked out. The snow had stopped falling and the city, white, still, was a vast stretch of roof-tops and sky. He had been thinking about it for hours here in the dark and now there it was, all white, still. *But what he had thought about it made it real with a reality it did not have now in the daylight. When lying in the dark thinking of it, it seemed to have something which left it when it was looked at.* Why should not this cold white world rise up as a beautiful dream in which he could walk and be at home, in which it could be easy to tell what to do and what not to do? If only someone had gone before and lived or suffered or died--made it so that it could be understood! It was too stark, not redeemed, not made real with the reality that was the warm blood of life. He felt that there was something missing, some road which, if he had once found would have led him to a sure and quiet knowledge. (NS, p. 226; my italics)[103]

Related to this vagueness and its substitution with aesthetic categories is a compression of the emotional and the rational in existentialist acts within the narrative. Richard Wright found a solution congenial to that of French existentialists: an outsider unconsciously but justly rebels against a profound sense of uncertainty and oppression.[104] By emphasizing the act in itself, Wright may avoid the question of collectivity

---

[102]Wright, *American Hunger*, p. 1.

[103]The evasion of concreteness in this passage links *Native Son* with other modernist city novels where authentic forms of urban life are alluded to but not elaborated. F. Scott Fitzgeralds's city image in *The Great Gatsby* certainly is the most complex case.

[104]Wright's existentialism grew out of his own experience in the United States. His concept, in contrast to that of Kierkegaard or Heidegger, is social rather than metaphysical. Gibson, p. 103; Otten, p. 335.

and orientation. Bigger's murder is significant primarily as revolt; it is "a supreme and meaningful act" (NS, p. 111). Similarly, the fact that Boris Max, the white defender, sides with Bigger in court is paramount: "It was not the meaning of the speech that gave him pride, but the mere act of it" (NS, p. 371). Kingsley Widmer formulates the paradoxical assumption underlying such existential acts: for Wright, "existential awareness . . . provides an extreme exploration into truth but no mythos to live."[105]

Acts are attempts to bridge the gaps in the dissociated world of the novel. But the meaning of rationally indecipherable acts is difficult to communicate. The novel which tries to anchor events in Bigger's single perspective, while it intends to enlighten the audience about its political motivation, must incorporate authorial comment to convey the meaning of his acts to readers. The unity of viewpoint in *Native Son* is strained.[106] Bigger's perspective is not purely his own; Wright intrudes to expound the acts of his protagonist. While Wright has Bigger listen in bewilderment to the Daltons--"The long strange words they used made no sense to him; it was another language" (NS, p. 48)--he has Bigger reason the robbery of Blum's in terms that are alien to him: "It would be a symbolic challenge of the white world's rule over them. . . ." (NS, p. 18). The novel thus unwittingly reveals its own unresolved conflicts.

The modernist discourse may sublimate uncertainty in its concentration on the media, on the form and gesture of events, but the meaning of acts will remain indefinite and incommunicable in purely narrative terms. Bigger Thomas cannot finally break through his existential isolation. He remains an open, existential symbol for readers who have to interpret his acts in the light of his and Boris Max's explanations. The conclusion of the novel thus remains ambivalent and unresolved--reflected in the many interpretations it has received. The outcome of the trial and the final dialogue implicitly question Wright's hope in rationality: rebellion, necessary to bring about the new society, will be irrational and brutal.

The impossibility of communicating an orientation in the city is concisely contained in the final passage in *American Hunger*, in which Wright ponders the purpose and meaning of his fiction. Incidentally, his reflections are about his next city novel, *Native Son*:

> Well, what had I got out of living in the city? . . . I paced the floor, knowing that all I possessed were words and a dim knowledge that my country has shown me no examples of how to live a human life. All my life I had been full of a hunger for a new life. . . .

---

[105]Kingsley Widmer, "Black Existentialism: Richard Wright," *Richard Wright: A Collection of Critical Essays*, eds. Richard Macksey and Frank E. Moorer, p. 180.

[106]Kent, p. 54.

> Yes, the whites were as miserable as their black victims, I thought. If this country can't find its way to a human path, if it can't inform conduct with a deep sense of life, then all of us, black as well as white, are going down the same drain . . .
> I picked up a pencil and held it over a sheet of white paper, but my feelings stood in the way of my words. Well, I would wait, day and night, until I knew what to say. Humbly now, with no vaulting dream of achieving a vast unity, I wanted to try to build a bridge of words between me and that world outside, that world which was so distant and elusive that it seemed unreal.
> I would hurl words into this darkness and wait for an echo, and if an echo sounded, no matter how faintly, I would send other words to tell, to march, to fight, to create a sense of the hunger for life that gnaws in us all, to keep alive in our hearts a sense of the inexpressibly human.[107]

Bigger's "inexpressible" act of rebellion was highly significant in maintaining the belief in a release from oppression, but Richard Wright also reified the city as determining environment and thus perpetuated one of the myths of naturalism. Moreover, his fictional city denied collective resistance as a viable form of orientation. *Native Son* conceives of the city only globally as a place of liberation and emancipation, but denies possible emancipation through local bonds. *Native Son* is no exception to Wright's assessment of black history. In *Twelve Million Black Voices*, his overview of the general development of blacks, Wright proudly displays the path blacks have taken. In *Black Boy*, however, the account of his childhood in the South, he rejects community as it threatened his emancipation and his unrelenting opposition to white injustice.

To disclose the contradictions in Wright's existentialist city is not to diminish his superb achievement. Wright, who had come a long way to write *Native Son*, chose France as a refuge for his next years to continue his topic and write a novel entitled *The Outsider*. His image of the modern black city as a place of anonymous and atomized urbanites which denies the validity of the ghetto community and only presents it in its substituted form as aesthetic wholeness, need not be accepted as the sole path in the American city. Urban protest movements, local organizations, and ethnic communities too may develop viable forms of resistance against oppression. After all, Bigger Thomas' existential act intended wholeness to be social wholeness. In the modern American city, this has yet to be achieved; Wright's analysis was an important step in the right direction.

---

[107] Wright, *American Hunger*, pp. 134f.

13

Hubert Selby
Last Exit to Brooklyn

1. The City of the Powerless

Last Exit to Brooklyn records the "claustrophobic"[1] world of an inner-city slum in Brooklyn in the late 1940s and 1950s.[2] The five stories of the first part and the montage of episodes in the second part, the "Coda," describe deep alienation and despair among working-class Brooklynites. For Hubert Selby, their desolate city is a "microcosm"[3] of American society in the post-war decades. He indicts a "loveless world"[4] whose pursuit of happiness has deteriorated to consumerist hedonism and escapist nightmares. Selby's Brooklyn is populated by isolated transients whose lives have been ruined and who have become dependent: it is a city of alcoholics, junkies, transvestites, prostitutes, thugs, juvenile delinquents, and petty criminals.

Its diction and viewpoint relate *Last Exit to Brooklyn* to the naturalist tradition. As an acknowledged influence, Stephen Crane, with his treatment of the Bowery slums at the turn of the century, helped shape Selby's urban vision.[5] Like Crane, Selby transcends a mere documentary approach toward slum reality and poetically transforms the recorded experience. *Last Exit to Brooklyn* presents a thoroughly modernist image of the city in which the bleak atmosphere and reformist impulse are intricately linked to the

---

[1] John O' Brien, "The Materials of Art in Hubert Selby," *The Review of Contemporary Fiction*, 1 (1981), p. 378.

[2] The complete novel appeared in 1964, yet some of its stories were published separately in magazines, starting with "The Queen is Dead" whose first section appeared in *Black Mountain Review* in 1956 (John O' Brien, "Interview with Hubert Selby, Jr.," *The Review of Contemporary Fiction*, 1 (1981), pp. 332f). References to *Last Exit to Brooklyn* will be abbreviated to LB and incorporated into the text. Hubert Selby, *Last Exit to Brooklyn*, New York, 1964.

[3] O'Brien, p. 322.

[4] Hubert Selby in a letter to Webster Schott; cited in Webster Schott, "The Stillborn America," *The Nation*, (Dec. 7, 1964), p. 441.

[5] Gilbert Sorrentino, "The Art of Hubert Selby," *Kulchur*, 4 (1964), pp. 40, 43.

innovative strategies of Selby's prose. Profoundly influenced by Beat poetics,[6] his novel is a fifties' melange of a Bohemian subculture, the world of drug addicts and of social dropouts. Selby's Brooklyn, above all, is a city of shared speech in which the urban slang serves as the raw material for the modernist writer and his intention of conveying an "emotional reality."[7] This unpurged jargon, previously unheard in American fiction, presents slum conditions and the view from below. Its uncouth force, brutality, and blasphemy mean to shock readers; like William Burroughs' *Naked Lunch*, the novel presents a frank picture of the "horrors"[8] produced by contemporary American society.

In yet another sense, the record of urban experience in Brooklyn is a reaction to Crane's portrayal of the Lower East Side in the 1890s. *Last Exit to Brooklyn* deals with the transition from the old street-corner slum of squalid tenements to the ameliorated surroundings of the low-income housing projects of the 1950s which liberal sociologists and planners had suggested to improve the lot of the urban underprivileged. Though projecting environmental changes, Selby shows that, even in new buildings, the slum dwellers remain trapped.[9] *Last Exit to Brooklyn* depicts a paralyzed slum world in which the rebellions of its abandoned citizens have become utterly self-destructive.

The absence of change and the pervasive stasis point to a central paradox of Hubert Selby's image of the American city. On its surface, his lower working-class slum seems deprived beyond redemption; there is no escape from this world, a metaphysical fatalism appears to squelch all hope. Compassion seems so remote as to be invalid for this world. Selby presents this world in a "chillingly neutral tone,"[10] and with his heretic use of scripture, he attacks "religion in a frontal way."[11] Because of its frank and relentless portrait of demeaning conditions, the novel even faced an obscenity trial in England.[12]

---

[6]Beat will be used here as general term for the related developments in the 1940s and 1950s in New American poetry, in Beat literature, and in the Black Mountain group--the movements which Selby was connected to. For the personal and philosophical links among the diverse groups see Harald Mesch, *Verweigerung endgültiger Prädikation: Ästhetische Formen und Denkstrukturen der amerikanischen "Postmoderne," 1950-1970*, München, 1984.

[7]Selby cited in O'Brien, p. 320.

[8]Selby cited in Schott, p. 441.

[9]Kreutzer, *New York in der zeitgenössischen amerikanischen Erzählliteratur*, pp. 239, 244.

[10]Paul Levine, "The Intemperate Zone: The Climate of Contemporary American Fiction," *The Massachusetts Review*, 8 (1967), p. 512.

[11]Roland Binet, "The Mirror of Man," *The Review of Contemporary Fiction*, 1 (1981), p. 381.

[12]Binet, p. 380.

In spite of this detachment in the novel, it is important to note that Selby gives voice to people usually voiceless and thus confronts the utterly depraved conditions. Critics have seen in Selby a moralist and a Christian writer who intended to shock his readers into awareness and responsibility.[13] Moreover, his concern for his characters' speech and his trust in the emotional potential of art indicate that culture, even as a diminished residue, is still essential and that change is possible. Paradoxically then, his fiction of despair is a document of hope nourished from the very vicious microcosm which seems so incurably corrupt. *Last Exit to Brooklyn* attempts to break the social stasis using art and its aesthetic energy: the poetic control and transformation of speech should overcome the "loss of control"[14] in the American city of the 1950s.

2. The American Post-War City

Last Exit to Brooklyn is a fictional document of poverty in a prosperous society. The social and political climate in the United States in the 1950s, a decade of economic expansion, cold-war nationalism, and moral conservatism, is best evoked by the names of its two dominant figures, by Senator Joseph McCarthy and President Dwight D. Eisenhower. In contrast, Hubert Selby's novel portrays the underside, the "invisible" segment of a consumer society, to which Harris Salisbury in *The Shook-Up Generation*, Gabriel Kolko in *Wealth and Power in America*, and Michael Harrington in *The Other America* had just drawn general attention.[15]

The widespread prosperity associated with the 1950s was distributed unevenly. While augmenting its wealth, the "affluent society" excluded the lower third of its citizens in rural areas and inner-city slums from membership. In fact, the small share which the people in the lower working class received from the national income had virtually stagnated since the thirties.[16] While the upper and middle class continued to prosper, self-help efforts and federal welfare programs failed to improve the conditions of the

---

[13]Charles D. Peavy, "Hubert Selby and the Moral Satire," *Satire Newsletter*, 6 (1969), pp. 35-39. Hubert Metcalf, "Herman and Hubert: The Odd Couple," *The Review of Contemporary Fiction*, 1 (1981), p. 369.

[14]Selby cited in Sorrentino, p. 28.

[15]Harrington, p. 3; Harris Salisbury, *The Shook-Up Generation*, New York, 1958. Gabriel Kolko, *Wealth and Power in America: An Analysis of Social Class and Income Distribution*, New York, 1962. The page references are to the German edition: Gabriel Kolko, *Besitz und Macht: Sozialstruktur und Einkommensverteilung in den USA*, trans. Hans-Werner Saß, Frankfurt, 1967.

[16]The ten percent at the bottom of American society received about one percent of the national income, while the ten percent at the top received about thirty percent. Kolko, pp. 22, 133.

poor. In the 1950s, 40 to 50 million Americans lacked the basic goods necessary for humane existence.[17]

Stigmatized by the "crushing inheritance of the past,"[18] the post-war slum generation experienced its continued deprivation and futility of effort against the increasing affluence and egoism in mainstream America. The distrust of welfare programs and federal assistance meant that the poor were left to themselves. Under such conditions, breaking the cycle of poverty was only possible for very few individuals in the fifties. For lower working-class families, the rise to a level of economic security in an economy which moved from unionized blue-collar in the direction of non-regulated service jobs could only be attained if both parents worked, that is if women tried to cope with the jobs both at home and at work.[19] Often, this necessity to work harder only resulted in further familial and social disruptions. Children were neglected and left unprotected from violence, brutality, and crime in the neighborhood.

In the centers of the old industrial cities, whole sections of the city deteriorated as the economic basis and social control in communities were destroyed. The disadvantages of class translated into segregated, inferior areas of the city. This concentration of plight was the outcome of conscious social and political decisions. Thus poverty aggravated in inner cities because the upper and middle class withdrew their tax share leaving centers with debts and outmoded infrastructures to themselves, while conversely fending off low-rent housing through suburban zoning laws.[20] Large low-cost housing projects, planned by middle-class professionals, further concentrated the poor in a few areas and thus increased their spatial segregation.

For New York in particular, this meant that in addition to worsening conditions in older slum areas such as the Lower East Side or Harlem, large sections in Brooklyn markedly deteriorated in the 1950s and 1960s. The fourth largest metropolis before its incorporation into Greater New York in 1898, Brooklyn had been a stable middle-class borough of which Ralph Foster Weld wrote as late as 1950 (certainly hyperbolically even then): "In Brooklyn the discouraged observer of mankind may find some kind of hope. It is the civilized world in microcosm; within its own limits it is a demonstration of world

---

[17] The richest one percent owned 26 percent of the national wealth. Morison, p. 727; Harrington, p. 201; Kolko, p. 134.

[18] Harrington, p. 161.

[19] Between 1953 and 1959, one and a half million blue-collar jobs, that is eleven percent of the total, were eliminated from the U.S. economy. Harrington, p. 33; Kolko, p. 134.

[20] Markusen, pp. 90-94.

peace."[21] In the post-war years Brooklyn drastically lost jobs, tax revenues, and even population, while its share of New York's poor continually increased.[22] Indicative of the shift, black working-class families, who earned even less than their white counterparts, migrated to Brooklyn in a degree unparalleled in any major city after 1940. In 1930, only 2.7 percent of Brooklyn's population was Afro-American, but by 1970 their share had risen to 25.2 percent.[23]

In the 1950s, adequate housing for the poor generally was a severe problem. By the end of the decade more Americans lived in slums than on farms. Over a quarter of the national dwelling units, that is 15.6 million units, were substandard, many of them built before 1900.[24] When delapidated slums were bulldozed and replaced by new buildings under the Housing Act of 1949, the ex-residents frequently could not return to their area because of the smaller number of units and the exorbitant rents in them.[25] The provision of cheap housing thus remained insufficient. It has been estimated that in the 1950s, as a result of slum clearances, the United States lost 280,000 dwelling units a year. By 1970, public low-income housing only amounted to one percent of all units in the United States.[26]

Low-rent housing projects, a liberal policy implemented in the 1950s, were a long overdue step for the good of the underprivileged, but as isolated measures, they were wrong from the start. The public housing policy was suggested by ideas developed earlier in the century by Chicago ecologists. Herbert J. Gans explains the connection between urban theory and municipal renewal practice:

> The planner can recommmend changes in the spatial and physical arrangements of the city. . . . He has been attracted to ecological explanations because these relate behavior to phenomena which he can affect. For example, most planners tend to agree with Wirth's for-

---

[21] Ralph Foster Weld, *Brooklyn is America*, New York, 1950, p. 7.

[22] The 1950s was a period of pervasive uncertainty in Brooklyn. The Brooklyn Navy Yard which had employed over 70,000 workers received drastic cutbacks and was closed in the mid-sixties. Affluent Brooklynites left the borough for Long Island suburbs. For the first time since the eighteenth century, Brooklyn's population declined from 2,738,175 to 2,627,319. Ron Miller, Rita Seiden Miller, and Stephen Karp, "The Fourth Largest City in America--A Sociological History of Brooklyn," *Brooklyn U.S.A.: The Fourth Largest City in America*, Brooklyn College, 1976 Symposium, Brooklyn, 1976, pp. 27f.

[23] Harrington, p. 76. While the overall figure for Brooklyn remained the same, the black populace increased tenfold within 40 years. In 1930 there were only 68,921 blacks in Brooklyn compared to 656,194 in 1970. Over 260,000 blacks moved to Brooklyn alone in the forties and fifties. Harold Connolly, *A Ghetto Grows in Brooklyn*, New York, 1977, p. 141.

[24] Harrington, pp. 147f; Kolko, p. 127.

[25] The Housing Act of 1949 had promised 810,000 new units by 1953 to alleviate the plight, but by 1960 just half of the projected apartments had been completed. Harrington, p. 147.

[26] Chudacoff, p. 288; Lichtenberger, p. 175.

mulations, because they stress number and density, over which the planner has some control. If the undesirable social conditions of the city could be traced to these two factors, the planner could propose large-scale clearance projects which would reduce the size of the urban population, and lower residential densities. Experience with public housing projects has, however, made it apparent that low densities, new buildings, or modern site plans do not eliminate anti-social or self-destructive behavior. The analysis of characteristics will call attention to the fact that this behavior is lodged in the deprivations of low socio-economic status and racial discrimination, and that it can be changed only through the removal of these deprivations.[27]

The vast Pruitt-Igoe complex in St. Louis, built in 1954, has become the best known example for this type of misconceived planning in the United States. Inadequately designed, the project soon deteriorated into a social disaster area, and became notorious for its high crime rates. In 1975, after only twenty years, the once acclaimed buildings had to be demolished.[28] Slum conditions similarly have spread in New York City, despite the fact that by the 1960s its Housing Authority had become the nation's largest landlord with over a hundred public projects. The Red Hook buildings which Hubert Selby portrayed were labelled as "Hell's Kitchen."[29]

To conservative critics, such isolated public housing projects simply are monuments to the failure of the welfare state. In their opinion, conditions in inner-city slums cannot and should not be improved. Edward Banfield elaborated on this standpoint in his book *Unheavenly City*: disorder and violence are an ineradicable, generic feature of slums and government had best benignly neglect these areas of the underprivileged.[30] The problems of class in the modern American metropolis are turned into inevitable urban deficiencies.

In the new slums, the contradictions of the ecological approach became palpably evident. Environmental solutions alone could not solve the dilemma as long as the wider context of inequities in education, health, and income remained untouched. The cycle of poverty continued uninterrupted, in spite of improved hygienic conditions and functional architecture. Moreover, slum clearance often destroyed important social bonds that had

---

[27]Gans, p. 514.

[28]E. Barbara Phillips and Richard T. LeGates, *City Lights: An Introduction to Urban Studies*, New York, 1981, pp. 384ff; Mohl, p. 67.

[29]Mark Miller and Carl Werthmann, "Public Housing: Tenants and Troubles," *Dissent*, 8 (1961), p. 282; Zlotnick, p. 175.

[30]Edward C. Banfield concludes: "That Government cannot solve the problems of the cities and is likely to make them worse by trying does not necessarily mean that calamity impends. Powerful accidental (by which is meant, nongovernmental and, more generally, nonorganizational) forces are at work that tend to alleviate and even eliminate the problems. Hard as it may be for a nation of inveterate problem-solvers to believe, social problems sometimes disappear in the normal course of events." Banfield, p. 257.

evolved in the area. The democratized materialism in commodities, leisure, and entertainment, which the nation's position as a super power secured for more people than ever in history, also brought with it a distinct physiognomy of poverty. As Michael Harrington has noted, cheap clothes have made the American poor the best dressed poor in the world.[31] Furthermore, the aspirations and yearnings of the working class have become forcibly affected by the commercial mass media which promotes middle-class standpoints and celebrates the status symbols of consumer society. Commodities, or rather the lack of them, became a constant reminder of disadvantage and defeat. In 1950, only one-quarter of the lower working-class families could afford a private car, whereas 70 percent of the middle-class families possessed their own automobile.[32]

Aggravating the dilemma of the dispossessed, commercial credits and loans created another kind of dependence. By 1950, as Gabriel Kolko has pointed out, the poorest in the working class had debts which on the average amounted to 160% of their annual income. Their insecure economic position, which only allowed a few months' reserve, could be severely disrupted by prolonged illness or unemployment. During the grave depression of 1958, for instance, five million Americans were without jobs.[33] Unable to repay loans, their choice was restricted to either repossession, skyrocketing debts, or, in the worst case, to criminal acts. The intensified consumerist stimulation added yet another hurdle to the barriers in the cycle of poverty which Michael Harrington succinctly delineated:

> The poor get sick more than anyone else in the society. That is because they live in slums, jammed together under unhygienic conditions; they have inadequate diets, and cannot get decent medical care. When they become sick, they are sick longer than any other group in the society. Because they are sick more often and longer than anyone else, they lose wages and work, and find it difficult to hold a steady job. And because of this, they cannot pay for good housing, for a nutritious diet, for doctors. At any given point in the circle, particularly when there is a major illness, their prospect is to move to an even lower level and to begin the cycle, round and round, toward even more suffering.[34]

The basic inequity and major leverage to break the cycle have as yet remained untouched: while the demands of consumers have continually risen, the income of the poor, their share of power and their prospects in the community have stagnated. Thus the 1950s began to accumulate a potential of frustration and despair that exploded in the last decades in street crime and urban unrest. Senseless brutality and a rising number of

---

[31] Harrington, p. 5.
[32] Kolko, p. 128.
[33] Ibid., pp. 117, 138.
[34] Harrington, p. 16.

robberies, muggings, and murders have since made conditions virtually unbearable in parts of the inner city. The crime rate more than doubled alone between 1950 and the late 1960s. In some housing projects, crime rates are twice as high as in the metropolis as a whole.[35] But as Manuel Castells rightly argues, the rise in crime cannot simply be equated with increased deprivation. During the great depression, for example, crime rates remained approximately the same because New Deal policies provided perspectives for the masses of the poor.[36] This social concern was nonexistent in the 1950s and only briefly revived in visions of a *new frontier* in the 1960s. It is this absence of collective hopes and the breakdown of social structures which *Last Exit to Brooklyn* forcibly documents.

In the sixties, the ghetto riots all over the United States sprang from this frustration. As Ida Susser has pointed out, the "unemployed cannot strike and the underemployed cannot win strikes" because they are made dispensable and superfluous in the economy.[37] Riots thus become one mode of protest to create attention and vent anger in the struggle for economic survival. *Last Exit to Brooklyn* depicts the basis for the violence connected with the urban crisis. It indicates, despite the sensationalism and helpless outcry in the mass media that violence is not a particular problem of the slums, but of the consumer society at large. With its images of senseless destruction and brutality, the novel foreshadows the civil disorders of the 1960s and the epidemic of crime in American cities in the 1970s and 1980s.

3. Brooklyn Slum Reality

In *Last Exit to Brooklyn*, Hubert Selby projects the deadening boredom and paralysis of a working-class slum. The novel is divided into two major sections: the first five stories, loosely arranged around a bar, the "Greeks," are set in the late 1940s, while "Landsend," the "Coda" of the novel, takes place in a low-income housing project in the Red Hook area near the Gowanus Canal in the late 1950s.[38] The two periods signify a transition in the architectural environment of the poor: the Greeks' part describes the

---

[35]Herbert Jacob, *The Frustration of Policy: Responses to Crime by American Cities*, Boston, 1984, p. 2; Harrington, p. 158.

[36]Castells, *The Urban Question*, pp. 395, 403.

[37]Susser, p. 8.

[38]Eberhard Kreutzer, "The Psychodynamics of Person and Place: Hubert Selby's *Last Exit to Brooklyn*," *Amerikastudien*, 22 (1977), p. 138.

conditions of the older street-corner slum of unsanitary tenements; "Landsend" records the results of liberal urban planning and welfare programs in public housing. The change of environment is reflected in distinct fictional forms. Thus the traditional stories of the beginning concentrate on a single group, the guys at the Greeks, or on a single protagonist, as Harry Black in the "Strike," and employ conventional plots of decline or naturalist vignettes in the manner of Stephen Crane's *City Sketches*. In contrast, "Landsend," a collage of some forty interwoven scenes, episodes, and housing authority announcements, draws upon John Dos Passos' montage technique from *Manhattan Transfer*.[39] The Brooklyn novel is the fragmented sum of disparate and yet connected parts.

In spite of such aesthetic nuances and distinctions, the basic conditions in the working-class environment remain unchanged. The bleak mood dominates throughout the novel. Nothing has improved with the intervention of planners, on the contrary, as Selby seems to indicate, the brutalization of children in the housing project has aggravated. A passage from "Strike" captures the pervasive sense of inertia and futility:

> He sat at his desk for a while, walked around for a while ... sat ... walked ... sat ... walked ... looked ... sat ... walked ... the only important thing was that the men get there. They had to. The day had to start. He walked ... sat ... smoked ... the python still there. Were there no hands on the clock? He smoked ... Drew a cup of coffee ... It was strong, bitter, yet it passed his mouth and throat without leaving a taste. Only a film. Dont clocks tick anymore? Is even the sun motionless. [sic] The water is boiled, poured over the coffee and it drips through and time passes ... even if it only drips it passes ... through. (LB, p. 152f)

Selby's Brooklynites do not participate in the post-war glamor of cosmopolitan New York, which is merely a subway ride away. Their enclosed territory is "appallingly static."[40]

Throughout the novel, people are shown trapped in circular or cyclical patterns. This stagnation underlies and engenders the impotent rage and "senseless violence"[41] in *Last Exit to Brooklyn*. The first story, "Another Day Another Dollar," introduces this as an important motif. As in *Maggie: A Girl of the Streets*, violence and circularity combine:

> Vinnie said whatthefuck, hed start, and they formed a circle around him and he turned slowly jerking his head quickly trying to catch the one punching him so he would replace him in the center and he was hit in the side and when he turned he got hit again and as he spun around 2 fists hit him in the back then another in the kidney and he buckled and they laughed.... (LB, p. 15)

---

[39] Roland Binet links Selby's "Women Chorus" to Dos Passos. Binet, p. 381.

[40] Eric Mottram, "Free Like the Rest of Us: Violation and Despair in Hubert Selby's Novels," *The Review of Contemporary Fiction*, 1 (1981), p. 360.

[41] Binet, p. 381.

A little later, the very cruelty and aggression of the 'play' turns into an uncontrolled fury as the "guys" club a soldier, one of the hated "doggies":

> The guys jumped off the fender and leaped on the doggies [sic] back and yanked him down and he fell on the edge of the hood and then on the ground. They formed a circle and kicked. He tried to roll over on his stomach and cover his face with his arms, but as he got to his side he was kicked in the groin and stomped on the ear and he screamed, cried, started pleading then just cried as a foot cracked his mouth. . . . (LB, p. 18)

This Brooklyn world is rendered as a prison from which there is no escape. Regardless of their effort, all of Selby's figures fail. Nothing happens or changes. Thus the first part of the novel opens with the guys at the Greeks--"They sprawled along the counter and on the chairs. Another night. Another drag of a night in the Greeks, a beatup all night diner near the Brooklyn Armybase" (LB, p. 13)--and ends, after some two hundred and thirty pages, with the same people and the same motif:

> The guys washed up in the Greeks, drying their hands with toilet paper and tossing wet wads at each other, laughing. It was the first real kick since blowing up the trucks. The first good rumble since they dumped that doggy. They sprawled at the counter and at the tables and ordered coffeeand. (LB, p. 231)

Only violence, which erupts every now and then, may break the boredom and stasis.

Resuming the circular pattern of the first part, "Landsend" describes the cycle of a day, from the slow awakening of people in the Red Hook houses on a Saturday morning to their falling asleep early on Sunday morning after an unbroken series of personal hostilities.[42] Again, no change is likely to occur at the dawn of the new day. The motif of the first sentence, "MIKE KELLY TOLD HIS WIFE to go tahell and rolled over, covering his head with a blanket" (LB, p. 235), is repeated in the last scene, "He shoved her away, laughing at her, and told her to get the fuck out and leave him alone" (LB, p. 310).

The total enclosure of Brooklyn is also documented in the constricted fictional topography and the limited radius of the characters. Either the Brooklynites submit to the destructive rules in their area or they are defeated in the outside world. As Harry may no longer divert union funds for expensive restaurants, his homosexual lovers in Manhattan immediately reject him (LB, p. 225f). Whenever a Brooklynite ventures beyond his working-class area, failure follows. Tralala and Harry who risk sexual affairs in Manhattan are physically harrassed and brutally beaten as they return. Both end where they started: they are left as human junk "amongst the broken bottles rusty cans and rubble of the lot" (LB, p. 116). There is no alternative. The novel abounds with cir-

---

[42]Kreutzer, "The Psychodynamics of Person and Place," p. 144.

cular and cyclical images (LB, pp. 19, 85, 284, 287).[43] Its title thus contains bitter irony: Brooklyn is the sole and final exit.

The stories in the first section, loosely connected to the Greeks, depict exemplary experiences and mental maps of working-class urbanites.[44] For *Last Exit to Brooklyn*, Selby selects key moments and existential crises in their lives: birth, christening, sexual initiation, wedding, labor strike, imprisonment, and death. The recorded events have a powerful immediacy as they retain Selby's autobiographical involvement: "I lived their life. I wasn't looking in. I *was* in."[45]

Last Exit to Brooklyn opens with the "guys"--Vinnie, Harry, Freddy, Tony, and others. Representing the underemployment in the area, they are jobless and may barely spend any money (LB, p. 16). Trouble for them has started very early, at ages when they were not responsible for their actions. Vinnie steals his first car as a twelve-year old:

> The judge was just as surprised as the arresting officer and had some difficulty suppressing a laugh while reprimanding Vinnie and making him promise never to do such a bad thing again. Go home and be a good boy.
> Two days later he stole another car. (LB, p. 28)

American mainstream society is incapable of dealing with such behavior. By the time Vinnie has reached the age of sixteen, his list of petty crimes is a long one. At that age, he is sent to prison for "his first real bit" (LB, p. 29). If not in trouble with the law, kids have to cope with slum violence. Their games reflect their harsh reality: stand in the circle and try to hit others.

How strongly these urban experiences differ from adolescent experiences in middle-class America may be illuminated with the help of a comparison with the most popular urban youth in the fiction of the fifties. Holden Caulfield in Jerome D. Salinger's *The Catcher in the Rye* experiences New York, the Big Apple, quite differently. Spending money lavishly, he has free access to the city of cars, clubs, shows, cinemas, hotels, and even prostitutes. Holden's image of New York is dominated by his upper-class experience. His primary concern, apart from his criticism of the phony adult world, is the city's opposition to nature and the countryside.[46] In contrast with Holden, the guys from the Greeks do not feel sorry for ducks in wintertime or care about falling kids (LB,

---

[43] Kreutzer, p. 139.

[44] Eberhard Kreutzer has remarked that "for all the singular horrors of catastrophe, the cases are symptomatic rather than isolated." Kreutzer, p. 141.

[45] Selby quoted in *Contemporary Authors*, eds. James M. Ethridge, et al., 1962, Detroit, 1977, p. 715.

[46] Jerome D. Salinger, *The Catcher in the Rye*, New York, 1951. For a discussion of the urban experience in Salinger's novel see Kreutzer, *New York*, pp. 170-78.

p. 286), because they know that a slum child is always in danger of being mugged (LB, pp. 258f). Unlike Holden, none of them shrink from sexuality and prostitutes. For Tralala in *Last Exit to Brooklyn*, sex simply is one way of killing boredom and, later when she is a prostitute, of earning a livelihood:

> Tralala was 15 the first time she was laid. There was no real passion. Just diversion. She hungout in the Greeks with the other neighborhood kids. Nothin to do. Sit and talk. Listen to the jukebox. Drink coffee. Bum cigarettes. Everything a drag. She said yes. In the park. 3 or 4 couples finding their own tree and grass. Actually she didnt say yes. She said nothing. Tony or Vinnie or whoever it was just continued. (LB, p. 95)

The ethic code in slums indeed differs strongly from that of middle-class society, as the studies by William F. Whyte and Elliot Liebow have indicated. Chaotic and normless only for the outsider, the cohesion within hierarchically organized groups is strong. In *Last Exit to Brooklyn* the gang at the Greeks has its own code of behavior. Georgette, as an outsider, is fully aware of the tight rules among the guys--"the code forbids drinking from the same glass as a fag" (LB, p. 59)--and knows that one has to submit to its laws: "She knew he wouldnt go with her while others were there, fearing the jeers of queerbait, so was forced to wait and hope the others might leave" (LB, p. 32).

A hierarchy also exists among the social and ethnic groups in the area. Racist remarks and attitudes abound in the novel and culminate in the street fight between the rival spicks and spades (LB, p. 304). To make life even more complicated in working-class quarters, conflict groups are located next to one another. The aggressive soldiers, the hated "doggies," have their barracks close to the Greeks. The stratification among the poor appears as a reflection of the larger hierarchy in American society: they fight for predominance on a minor scale.

Although the world of the Brooklyn slum is fully segregated as it were, it is influenced profoundly by Manhattan and mainstream America. The omnipresence of the mass media connects the slum dwellers to the aspirations and material lures of American society in general:

> Yasee the grill on the new Pontiac? Man, thats real sharp. Yeah, but a lousy pickup. Cant beat a Plymouth fora pickup. Shit. Cant hold the road like a Buick. Outrun any cop in the city with a Roadmaster. If ya get started. Straightaways. Turns. Outrun the law. Dynaflows. Hydramatics. Cant get started. Theyd be all overya before ya got a block. Not in the new 88. Ya hit the gas and it throwsya outta the seat. Great car. (LB, p. 14)

Because of their enclosure and impotence, the slum dwellers are hardly able to cope with the cunning strategies in consumer capitalism, with the open and subliminal lures, omnipresent in billboards, ads, and TV commericals. Economically barred from access to commodities of middle-class society, they reject its rules. What is considered criminal by official law, here figures as a retribution of injustice, as a challenge to authority, and as a boast among insiders. As a character says of his favorite car, "Aint stealin nothin else anymore" (LB, p. 14).

The fetishes of consumer society loom large. The birth, wedding, and christening in "And Baby Makes Three" are secondary to the fascination with motor-cycles (LB, p. 88). The possession of machines provides power and status. The sole tenderness in this reified world seems reserved for them:

> Abraham opened the door of his bigass Cadillac and looked smugly around at the people sitting . . . before getting in and closing the door with a flourish. He stretched his legs, pushing back against the seat, and smiled. It was his. Ghuddam right. All his. He looked at the dashboard with all its knobs and patted it. Every ghuddam hunk of chrome belonged to him, Abe. . . . He threw the car into reverse and backed out, made a screeching u-turn (haha, looka those cats diggin me) and drove to Blackies garage. (LB, p. 25f)

In this environment, the pursuit of happiness is defined as habitual and addictive pleasure. Harry only wishes "takrist there was somethin good on tv. Why cant they have fights on Tuesday nights. They think people only wanna look at fights on Fridays?" (LB, p. 120). The American dream has deteriorated to escapist flights in drugs, alcohol, or sex:

> When she heard that Vinnie had been paroled she went to Brooklyn (first buying 10 dozen bezendrine tablets) and sat in the Greeks all night following Vinnie everywhere and trying to get him alone. She bought him coffeeand, sat on his lap and asked him to go for a walk. . . . Please Vinnie, the dream almost carrying over to consciousness, the bezendrine making it even more difficult not to try to animate the dream *now*. (LB, p. 26f)

"Strike" provides the most encompassing image of manipulation and powerlessness in *Last Exit to Brooklyn*. Ruthless employers and corrupt unions exploit Brooklyn workers who in the labor strife are impotent on the local or municipal level against the (inter)national organization of capital. Thus the company can easily bypass the strike:

> Their other plants, and subcontractors, throughout the country had been geared in ample time to handle all existing orders and any that might come in during the immediate future. All their government contracts were being fulfilled and no new ones would be forthcoming before February of the following year. At least none of any quantity. And too, the manner in which the contracts had been distributed to other plants, and the manner in which the transfers had been noted on the books meant a substantial tax saving would be effected. Of course a few of the younger executives had a burdensome amount of work to do because of the strike, but a substantial bonus at Christmas and a pat on the back would not only satisfy them but would encourage them to work even harder in the future. And the cost of the bonuses would only amount to a minute percentage of the money saved in unpaid wages. (LB, p. 189)

But the union too betrays its workers. They fight for a senseless and eventually resultless cause:

> The union officials were indignant about the companys attitude in being so rigid and in sending trucks through the line and left Mondays meeting declaring they would not meet with them for a few weeks, not until the company reconsidered its arbitrary stand and realized that the men were willing to stay on strike for a year if necessary in order to get a decent contract. The recording secretary remained in the city and the other officials went to Canada for a rest. They needed a rest from the pressures of the strike and the oppressive heat. (LB, p. 189)

As is typical for the novel, such a loss of control generates violence. After weeks of mounting tension, the confrontation between policemen and workers reveals that both sides are powerless and bored. The frustration turns into an open conflict:

> Each day the routine was the same except that it grew more intense and the men were continually looking for an excuse to hit someone, anyone; and the police were just waiting for someone to start something so they too could find relief from the boredom by cracking someones skull. And as the boredom increased so did the resentment: the resentment of the men toward the cops for being there and trying to prevent them from winning the strike; and the police for making it necessary for them to stand around like this for hours each day when they werent even allowed to go on strike if they wanted more money. (LB, p. 166)

The moment the elites think it profitable to settle the strike, the labor struggle immediately ceases--without any gains for the workers. A laconic sentence concludes the futility of the workers' perseverance for months: "At the first meeting after the xmas holidays the strike was settled" (LB, p. 221).

The "Coda" resumes the plight in slums some ten years later. Nothing but the architecture of the housing has changed. People still are powerless and desperate, the violence and loneliness even seem worse: the elderly Ada lives completely isolated in one of the apartments. The situation of children who live in the project is hopeless:

> Some of the bigger kids took a basketball away from the kids on the court and when the owner of the ball started crying for his ball they finally hurled it at him smashing his nose and making it bleed and one of his friends yelled at the fleeing kids calling them black bastards and they came back and told him he was blackeran shit and the other kids said they had black bedbugs and the other kid said his mother fucks for spicks and the kid pulled out a nailfile and slashed the other kid across the cheek and then ran, his friends running with him; and in the far corner of the playground a small group of kids huddled quietly, keeping to themselves, ignoring the fighting and screaming, their arms of comradeship around each others shoulders, laughing and smoking marijuana. (LB, p. 270f)

Even willing parents and mothers hardly have any choice. Either the kids have to face the violence and crime in the project (LB, p. 258f), or their energies will be pent-up and frustrated in small apartments:

> The children went back to their room and Lucy sighed. That boy sure can be nerve-racking. Hes under my feet all day long, always arunnin--running around the house yelling. . . . Why dont you just lettim go out an play? Lucy cringed. Caus--Because I do not want him playing with any patched pants kids, thats why. (LB, p. 277)

Women, especially as wives and mothers, suffer most from the changed conditions. Left alone by their chauvinist husbands, they are overworked with their responsibilities at work and at home.[47] Even everyday chores are time-consuming and often difficult to manage for the poor. Elevators necessary to carry shopping goods to upper floors are out of order or are made unusable as someone has defecated in them (LB, p. 276); women have to wait in line for hours and hours in a laundromat with broken machines (LB, pp. 263-66). Ida Susser has called attention to this dimension of poverty:

> Since they [the poor] subsist at an economic level with little to spare, daily life becomes a drama of survival. The daily round is to contend with, surmount, or succumb to perils that might be absorbed with little effect by the middle-class households. The forces which leave their scars on the poor are not isolated occurences; they are funadamental features of our society.[48]

All in all, Hubert Selby does not romanticize women as victims in the project. They too fight one another. For Lucy, the elderly Ada simply is "the filthy jew. Never changes her clothes" (LB, p. 276). The "members" of the "WOMENS CHORUS" (LB, pp. 257, 279, 286, 292) are among the most vicious and cruel characters of *Last Exit to Brooklyn*. Hankering for sensation, they display a cynical indifference even in a moment of crisis:

> The women watched the baby as it crawled around on the ledge and window sill. Maybe he thinks hes a bird. Hey, ya gonna fly? Laughter. Others looked up and someone screamed and someone else yelled get back, O my God, O my God. . . . The women continued to laugh and wonder when it would fall. (LB, p. 286f)

Last Exit to Brooklyn presents a bleak world: for the slum dwellers, conditions have not improved. Selby's harsh criticism of public housing in "Landsend" is part of a

---

[47]Wives in *Last Exit to Brooklyn* are frequently mere objects for their husbands anger, aggression, or lust. Unless prostitutes or willing one-night-stands, female sexual longings are denied. When Abe eventually returns home after a night out, he beats his wife Nancy as she longs for sex: "He backhanded her across the face . . . and she called him a noaccountblackniggabastard and he punched her in the motherfuckin face. . . . She crawled out to the kitchen and pulled herself up, holding onto the edge of the sink, still yelling he was a blackniggabastard, then let cold water run over her head. Her daughter came over to help her and Nancy continued yelling and then the frustration started her crying and her daughter told her not to cry, Jesus loves us Mommy. Nancy told her to get the fuck away from her" (LB, p. 310f).

[48]Susser, p. 14.

general attack on liberal solutions which do not challenge consumer capitalism.[49] In "Strike," for instance, Selby turns against the unions and their policy and points out that a paid "clique" (LB, p. 142) is used to run the meetings and direct the voting behavior of workers. He also makes it clear that the social workers of the Housing Authority remain distanced from the plight of their clients. Their professional aloofness translates into the impersonal and threatening language of the "Project Newsletter":

> Throwing garbage out of the window is referred to as AIRMAIL. We do not want any AIRMAIL from this Project. . . . AIRMAIL is violation of the Health Code and a violation of the Housing Authority Regulations. Any tenant found guilty of throwing garbage from the windows will be immediately evicted. We want this Project to be a safe and clean place to live. It is up to you to keep it this way. (LB, p. 245)

In addition, Selby reveals that welfare money alone will not remove slum conditions. The episode "The Queue" laconically records the fatality of piecemeal measures: "The welfare checks were cashed and there were long lines outside the Liquor Store across the street from the Project" (LB, p. 300).

Last Exit to Brooklyn offers a depressing description of the "subculture of misery"[50] of the other America. For Selby, the degradations in inner-city slums symbolize defects of American society as a whole: upper- and middle-class environments have similar deficiencies, though there the "symptoms will be manifested differently."[51] In "The Queen is Dead," this suburbia is explicitly derided for its hypocrisy: "I love the ones who almost cry when they are finished and start telling you about how much they love their wife and kiddies. And when they take out the pic--O I hate those freaks" (LB, p. 61f).

For Selby, an important source for the conditions in slums is the people's "lack of control."[52] His assessment of American society in the fifties relates the fictional theme, the powerlessness of the poor, to the analysis of consumer capitalism in William Burroughs' *The Naked Lunch*. Junk, Burroughs' ingenious metaphor for impotence and degradation, embodies the dependency of the trapped and manipulated:

> Junk is the ideal product . . . the ultimate merchandise. No sales talk necessary. The client will crawl through a sewer and beg to buy. . . . The junk merchant does not sell his product to the consumer, he sells the consumer to his product. He does not improve and simplify his merchandise. He degrades and simplifies the client.[53]

---

[49]Mottram, p. 360.
[50]Harrington, p. 12.
[51]Schott, p. 442.
[52]O'Brien, p. 315.
[53]William S. Burroughs, *The Naked Lunch*, 1959, London, 1982, p. 3.

Diagnosing the same patient, Selby meant to provide a "pathological study, showing the disease without offering the cure."[54] He unflinchingly records the symptoms of despair and powerlessness, the eruptions of economic, social, and political impotence in horrid scenes of violence and self-mutilation.

4. The Violence of Powerlessness

The total dependency of Selby's figures manifests itself on two connected levels. First, there is the powerlessness against outside forces; people in the Brooklyn slum are imprisoned within an affluent society. Second, there is the loss of control over their inner lives. This "lack of power," an impotence no less profound, is internalized; characters are devoid of controlled responsibility or free will.[55] The body, their prime barter in the exchange for money and power, is degraded by its excessive exploitation through drugs, sex, and violence. For lower-class figures, physical decline means defeat. Thus the title of Georgette's story "The Queen is Dead" alludes to the lethal outcome of her drugged "dream" (LB, p. 27). Similarly, Tralala's attraction as a prostitute wanes dramatically. Brooklyn, the last exit, means death.

Lacking the political means to achieve change, the slum dwellers disregard and reject society's norms. Breaking the moral and sexual taboos of mainstream society is their way of rebelling. With a meticulous attention to detail, Selby records the repulsive brutality and obscenity of his figures, and like Joyce, unearths "the abyssal, far-reaching power of man's imagination."[56]

Since the slum dwellers oppose authoritarian power blindly, their despair has acquired a completely self-destructive character. Whereas the unreal city in *The Waste Land* or the ash heap in *The Great Gatsby* stated the decay of society and the aridity of modern culture metaphorically, the characters of *Last Exit to Brooklyn* inflict pain and destruction directly on themselves. "Tralala" ends in a crescendo of frenzied violence in which the prostitute, in a horrid apotheosis of her life, ends raped and beaten as human junk among the refuse "lying naked covered with blood urine semen" (LB, p. 116). Such an annihilation of the characters' feelings, minds, and bodies relates to the hollowing out of the American city, once seen by many as the core and apex of culture. Selby discloses

---

[54]Selby quoted in Mottram, p. 363.
[55]Selby quoted in O'Brien, p. 315.
[56]Binet, p. 385.

the dire results of exploitation and segregation. Trying to reach readers outside the working-class slums, he hoped to rouse indignation and have the privileged in suburbia face reality in the inner city. As reactions showed, Selby indeed shocked the public--though some of the attention was clearly misdirected, as the obscenity trial in England indicates.[57]

In spite of its authenticity, Selby's account is not a clinical, "objective reportage"[58] of the Brooklyn slums. The selection and arrangement of events, motifs, and images reveal Selby's interested perspective. Despite the environmentalist ontology and his anti-bourgeois thrust, Selby's critique is moralistic and individualistic. The implicit reform impulse is conservative. Liberal programs fail, but not because they are too limited, inconsistent, and superficial, but because people did not change. In 1981, Selby asserted in retrospect: "One of the things I find insane is that we seem to believe in this country that if we change the society, then the individual will be changed. That doesn't happen." Even though Selby too sees these people as victims of circumstance, for him, "the transformed individual makes a transformed world."[59]

The selection of events and symptoms reveals this bias. Most important, Selby marginalizes and excludes the depiction of labor, although in a working-class environment, labor constitutes the chief basis of existence. The stories "Another Day Another Dollar," "The Queen is Dead," and "And Baby Makes Three" are set in the evening and during leisure time, while the account of project life in "Landsend" refers to a day on the weekend. "Strike," the story which functions as a climax to the portayal of lower working-class life, chooses to concentrate on the factory's closure and Harry Black's homosexuality. Certainly, there are references to work--Tralala looking for clients, housewives doing chores in the household, or policemen protecting the factory--and the underemployment in the slums is a reason for many characters to loaf around. Still, the predominant interest in *Last Exit to Brooklyn* is the leisure, repose, and after-work boredom of working-class characters.

"Strike" reveals Selby's peculiar focus most tellingly. Taking issue with labor conditions, the story bypasses the grinding monotony and impotence at work. In stark contrast to Upton Sinclair's depiction of industrial mechanisms in *The Jungle*, the labor processes in the factory and their effect on the community vanish from sight--although the company employs over a thousand men and thus dictates the lives of several thou-

---

[57]The novel was banned in Italy. Jeffrey Halterman and Richard Layman, eds., *Dictionary of Literary Biography. American Novelists since World War II*, vol. 2, Detroit, 1978, p. 444.

[58]Levine, p. 515.

[59]Selby quoted in O'Brien, pp. 317, 328.

sand residents of the area (LB, p. 128). For Harry Black, who only lives a few blocks from his workplace, the factory as a major force and socializing agent plays an unimportant part. His story mostly takes place during its seven-month closure.

Harry's perception of his co-workers is also revealing. Harry, the laziest laborer in the factory, causes the strike in the very beginning by routinely sauntering through the building (LB, p. 129). As the company's "worst lathe operator" (LB, p. 128), he is the shop steward for the unions. Yet despite Harry's union position and his years of employment in the factory, he seems barely familiar with his colleagues. Strangely, Harry Black does not seem to belong to the factory. During the strike, his co-workers are a mass of faceless buddies, whereas visitors from the Greeks readily receive names and become distinguishable as individuals (LB, pp. 140ff., 160).

This distancing of workers is part of a generally detached perspective in the story. Like Theodore Dreiser in his record of the strike in *Sister Carrie*, Selby distances himself from the people involved. *Last Exit to Brooklyn*, which otherwise excels in its closeness to events and in its "eliciting of detail,"[60] in places becomes very remote in perspective and diction:

> The mass continued to wallow along and across 2nd avenue as a galaxy through the heavens with the swooshing of comets and meteors and the voice that screeched now directed itself to the firemen and they walked slowly toward the grinding mass and a white glove clutched at a head and the glove turned red and occasionally a bloody body would be exuded from the mass and roll a foot or two and just lie there or perhaps wriggle slightly and four or five beaten and bloodied cops managed to work their way free from the gravity of the mass and stood side by side and walked back to the mass swinging their clubs and screaming. (LB, p. 170f)

In a text which otherwise avoids long or complex words in order to reproduce the view from below authentically, the aloofness in tone becomes a major disruption in the novel:

> The voice screeched again giving directions and the two powered battering rams were directed with knowledge and precision and soon the mass was a chaos of colliding particles that bounced tumbled and whirled around against and over each other and soon it was quiet enough to hear the ambulance sirens.... (LB, p. 171)

Linked to this detachment, the labor strife is further marginalized as it is primarily used to project Harry Black's homosexual awakening. Factory, union, and strike become a colorful foil for the sexual conflicts of Harry: the story opens with his interest in his son's penis (LB, p. 119), concentrates in the middle on the crucial recognition of his own homosexuality (LB, p. 196), and ends with Harry as a bewildered and cruel

---

[60]Harry Lewis, "Some Things I want to say about Hubert Selby's Work," *The Review of Contemporary Fiction*, 1 (1981), p. 414.

paederast (LB, p. 229). His final words sum up the sexual focus of "Strike": "GOD / YOU SUCK COCK" (LB, p. 230). For Richard Wertime, "the larger social conflicts with which the story deals . . . [are] rehearsals of Harry's psychosexual self-destruction, around which central action all the other actions turn."[61]

The neglect of specific labor conditions in the working-class city is connected to Selby's ahistorical critique of society, that is to his naturalism and Puritanism.[62] The opening epigraph from the scriptures links the two explanations as it fuses the timeless animal imagery of the Old Testament with that of the naturalist ontology:

> For that which befalleth the sons of men befalleth beasts; even one thing befalleth them: as the one dieth, so dieth the other; yea, they have all one breath; so that a man hath no preeminence above the beast: for all is vanity. (LB, p. 11)

Though the setting and atmosphere are decidely secular, Hubert Selby's determinism appears to be metaphysical. Christian religion provides an important foil for *Last Exit to Brooklyn*, despite the ironic use of Old Testament quotes and the blasphemic attacks on religious belief. In 1964, however, Selby was not yet the Christian writer he later confessed to be. The quotes are as yet one source of explanation among others.[63]

Selby's critique of slum condition is profoundly colored by Puritan attitudes. Despite the omnipresence of sex, the book never shows physical love as erotic, stimulating, or liberating, but almost always as desperate, violent, and repulsive. Denying the pleasureful and emancipatory sides of sex, Selby too excludes other positive forms of sensual or playful subversion. In addition, the range of slum characters he presents is clearly limited to the dull and vile types among prostitutes and thugs.[64] Readers do not find a slum figure like Sea Cat, whom Elliot Liebow praised in *Tally's Corner* to be an "excellent storyteller."[65] Rather, the mood reflects Selby's self-characterization as "a frustrated preacher and a frustrated teacher"[66] who does not romanticize slum dwellers and does not discover any vitality and ebullience among them.

---

[61] R. A. Wertime, "Psychic Vengeance in *Last Exit to Brooklyn*," *Literature and Psychology*, 24 (1974), p. 160.

[62] Peavy, p. 37.

[63] In the interview with John O'Brien in 1981, Hubert Selby remarked in retrospect that "Christ didn't come for the righteous. Who did Christ commune with? The sinners. We are all children of God. That's what got me started with those epigraphs in *Last Exit*. . . ." O'Brien, p. 324.

[64] Richard Wertime writes that "we are intended to have no liking for these characters at Alex's: they are stupid swaggering hoods of the classic 50's variety. . . ." Wertime, p. 155.

[65] Liebow, p. 24f.

[66] O'Brien, p. 318.

Last Exit to Brooklyn combines the description of social defects with the moralist condemnation of a godless world. The two modes of explanation are linked throughout the novel. Harry, the lazy shop steward and worshipper of consumer fetishes, eventually finds himself crucified at the foot of a billboard (LB, p. 230). Similarly, Abraham Washington in "Landsend," whose name both connotes the founding father of the nation and the archetype of the Christian believer, is portrayed as a narcissistic sex-maniac who only worships his Cadillac. The final sentence of *Last Exit to Brooklyn* establishes the link between the loveless and godless world concisely: "Abraham slept" (LB, p. 311).

While the references to the wrathful god of the Old Testament are an important foil for the moralist writer, they do not serve as superior explanations for the conditions of the novel. *Last Exit to Brooklyn* attacks all forms of dependency. According to Eric Mottram, "Selby's work contains the suggestion of a *direction* of cure, a context for violence which is so authoritarian in itself as to be, by his own evidences, invalid."[67]

5. The Avantgarde City

Selby's prose is the most striking feature of the city portrait in *Last Exit to Brooklyn*. The city becomes a place of shared language through Selby's stylized speech. Yet, to write that *Last Exit to Brooklyn* develops a community of speech seems paradoxical for a novel which, on its surface, records the complete breakdown of social and cultural ties. The distinction between the minutely recorded city of his figures and the modernist transformation of their speech is important for a full understanding of Selby's novel.

The Brooklyn idiom reflects lower working-class conditions and conveys a deprived world: the additive style captures its inertia and monotony, the violent obscenities indicate the mutilated emotions of its residents, the mass of expletives intends to shock. On the other hand, the urban slang in the novel also expresses an opposition to middle-class suburbia, for the hoods and bohemians develop a common jargon in their rebellion against hypocrisy and privilege. In fact, recording many terms for the first time, *Last Exit to Brooklyn* became a major source for the supplementary volume to the standard dictionary of slang.[68]

Because of Selby's versatile handling of everyday speech in *Last Exit to Brooklyn*, one could say that the modern city seems again to resume its position as a catalyst for

---

[67] Mottram p. 363.
[68] Kreutzer, *New York*, p. 315.

innovation, change, and rejuvenated communication--against the evident stasis on the level of events. As Raymond Williams has pointed out, James Joyce's *Ulysses*, the representative novel of modern urbanity, contains a similar paradox: "Through its pattern of loss and frustration, there is not only search but also discovery: of an ordinary language, heard more clearly than anywhere in the realist novel before it; a positive flow of that wider human speech which had been screened and strained by the prevailing social conventions: conventions of separation and reduction, in the actual history."[69] While Joyce presents the incredible variety of Irish middle-class sociolects in their distinct private, public, and professional forms, emphasizing their archetypal universality, Selby follows in the tradition of Poe and Baudelaire: interested in the underside of human and urban life,[70] he transforms the variations of urban slang to evoke a distinct aesthetic community.

Selby makes the recorded speech serve nondiscursive functions, as he hyperbolically explains in the following passage:

> My ideal as a writer is to get to the point where the reader doesn't even have to read the words. The story should just come right off the page. I don't want you to read a story, I want you to experience it. I don't want to tell you a story, I want to put you through an emotional experience.[71]

In this use of language, not what is said is most important, but how it affects readers through its form, rhythm, and energy:

> *There was* no end of drunks. Everybody had money during the war. The waterfront *was filled* with drunken seamen. *And* of course the base *was filled* with doggies. *And* they were *always* good for *a few bucks* at least. *Sometimes* more. *And* Tralala *always* got her share. No tricks. *All* very simple. The guys had a ball and she got *a few bucks*. *If there was* no room to go to *there was always* the Wolffe Building *cellar*. *Miles* and *miles* of *cellar*. One screwed and the others played chick. *Sometimes* for hours. But she got what she wanted. *All* she had to do was putout. It was *kicks* too. *Sometimes*. *If* not, so what? It made no difference. Lay on your back. Or bend over a garbage can. Better than working. *And* it *kicks*. For a while anyway. But time *always* passes. (LB, p. 96; my emphasis)

The short passage compresses the unsteadiness and boredom of several years of adolescence in the slum. The form of the language is paramount. The repetition, anaphora, syntactic parallelism, assonance, internal rhyme, and alliteration all evoke a sense of

---

[69] Williams, *The Country and the City*, p. 294.

[70] Michael Stephens, "Hubert Selby, Jr.: The Poet of Prose Masters," *The Review of Contemporary Fiction*, 1 (1981), p. 393.

[71] Selby quoted in O'Brien, p. 319.

sameness and inertia beyond the profanity of the events. The passage indeed suggests years, emotionally.

Selby's focus here is not primarily on the events of the narrative, but on the formal capacities of his prose, of its sound, structure, and syntax. This interest in the autonomous aesthetic of the medium and in the nonrepresentational functions of language link Selby to the major innovations in poetry, painting, and jazz in the fifties. The belief in a nonrepresentational communication and emotional understanding was closely linked to the modern city as the actual setting and catalyst for avantgarde culture and its aficionados. This primacy of the emotional discourse allowed artists to envision new collective forms of communication beyond class and education. The penchant for music in the avantgarde made many envisage democratic modes of resistance and liberation through jazz, rock'n'roll, and other forms of popular music.

Selby was in close contact to the leading artists of his time. One of the prime mentors of the new American poets, William Carlos Williams, first read his prose and encouraged him to continue. Robert Creeley, another influential poet, published his first story in the *Black Mountain Review*. In New York, Selby was part of a circle of likeminded poets and Beats: he knew Gilbert Sorrentino, Le Roi Jones, Joel Oppenheimer, Allen Ginsberg, and Fee Dawson. He also frequented the Cedar Tavern, the venue of the abstract expressionist painters.[72] Their innovations in the use of color and their concern for the energy, rhythm, and gesture of the aesthetic medium have been compared to Selby's prose.[73] Above all, there was a common enthusiasm among poets and painters for jazz, especially for Bebop and cool jazz, whose musicians became cult figures for the avantgarde. Like Jack Kerouac who used jazz rhythms for the prosody of his spontaneous writing, Selby stressed the importance of music for his art.[74] For Selby and Kerouac, to convey the "purity of speech"[75] was a paramount goal.

The primacy of the medium and of nondiscursive modes of communication united the diversity of artistic efforts in the fifties. As inheritors of surrealist traditions such as the *écriture automatique*, the Beats saw nonrepresentational art, drugs, Zen, and sex as means to liberate the individual and enhance subjectivity. *Last Exit to Brooklyn* is a

---

[72]Stephens, p. 389; Joel Oppenheimer, "Memories," *The Review of Contemporary Fiction*, 1 (1981), p. 398.

[73]The trance of Jackson Pollock's drip labyrinths, the drive and tension in Franz Kline's canvases, or the controlled gesture in Willem de Kooning's portraits are congenial to the emotional precision in Selby's prose. Lewis, p. 414; Stephens, p. 390.

[74]There are several references to jazz in the novel (LB, pp. 68, 74). Schott, p. 441.

[75]Jack Kerouac, "Essentials of Spontaneous Prose," repr. *Boundary*, 2 (1975), p. 743; quoted in Mesch, p. 154.

contribution to this cult of authenticity. The communication of true subjectivity through spontaneous, processual, or abstracted uses of the aesthetic medium was perceived as a major alternative to the alienated culture of mainstream society.[76] This interest in the emotional capacity of art is reflected in Hubert Selby's assertion to "*feel* for people." Above all, he aspired to convey the "emotional reality" of the modern city.[77]

Last Exit to Brooklyn even contains passages in which this emancipatory potential of art is directly alluded to--in which the new understanding briefly emerges. Significantly, the rhythms of Charlie 'Bird' Parker and the reading of Poe's "The Raven" are shown to lift boundaries between hoods and Bohemians for a moment:

> ... and the Bird was blowing a final chorus, high, and the set wouldnt end, but the Bird would slowly fade and you never know when he really stopped and the sounds would hang and roll in your ear and would all be love--Quoth the Bird evermore--and the flames bowed and licked the edge of the candles and even Harry didnt fight his lethargy and try to break the spell and Georgette lowered the book to her lap with full dramatic presence and the final words still whirled with the light and stayed in the ear as the sea in a shell and Georgette sat on a wondrous throne in a wondrous land where people loved and kissed and sat silent together, holding hands and walking through magic nights and Goldie got up and kissed the Queen and told her it was beautiful ... Vinnie struggled with the softness he felt, trying honestly to understand it, then let it slide and slapped Georgette on her thigh, gently, as one does a friend, and smiled, at her ... and groped for words, battling with the boundaries then saying, Hey, that was alright Georgie boy.... (LB, p. 69)

The love, longing, and softness are fully conveyed through sound, while repetition and variation produce the musical flow of the prose. Vinnie significantly feels the power of art, although as a hood, he cannot understand why his hard shell has softened.

On the other hand, it is obvious from the previous analysis that Selby's innovations are far from pure, autonomous, and democratic, rather, the aesthetic transformation of urban slang in *Last Exit to Brooklyn* reflects the very contradictions that pervade Selby's image of working-class Brooklyn. In the egalitarian, Whitmanesque tradition, Selby indeed shows a democratic concern for ubiquitous details and applies William Carlos Williams' maxim from *Paterson*, "no ideas but in things,"[78] to his slum world. On the other hand, his abstracted use of speech reflects the elitist and esoteric sides of the Beat counterculture. In their words: you either 'dig' it, or you don't.[79] Thus Selby's aesthetic stylization of speech removes it from the Red Hook world and clashes with his

---

[76] Mesch, pp. 17-22.

[77] O'Brien, pp. 319f.

[78] William Carlos Williams, *Paterson*, 1946, New York, 1963, p. 6. Selby explicitly refers to Williams' program in his interview with John O'Brien. O'Brien, p. 327.

[79] On the theory behind the hipster and Beat jargon, see Mesch, p. 152.

concern for the "local and particular."[80] The poetic slumming in *Last Exit to Brooklyn* is as distant from the poor as the bureaucratic jargon of the Project Newsletter. Ironically, it also is "a slow flight *above* a segment of a city, offering to the mute spectator bits and pieces of raw life as the guided tour progresses."[81] A Bohemian elitism nonetheless is elitist.[82]

This distance to working-class culture also has a basis in Selby's social background. If there is a strong autobiographical element in his account of the Brooklyn slum, his upbringing also provided distance: "Even as I was hanging out with those guys down at the army base--those guys I wrote about in *Last Exit*--, every now and then I would find myself wandering off to the museum alone."[83] For Selby, the "art of literature" becomes the opposite to degradation--he mystifies art and the artist as "absolute," "supreme," and "pure."[84] At the time of composition, when Selby felt a "terrible, intense hatred for God,"[85] art seems to have replaced the metaphysical frame. Selby's latent Puritanism then translated into the formal rigidity and cohesion in the novel and the length with which he presented degrading details and scenes.[86] Selby later admitted himself, that after rereading his novel he noticed his "obsession with control."[87] Indeed, his work in its moral absoluteness and formal rigor, may be said to stand in the tradition of Puritan epics like John Milton's *Paradise Lost*.[88]

Of course, the modernity and achievement of *Last Exit to Brooklyn* are not its latent religious rigidity, but its inherent challenge to the paralysis and hopelessness of the fifties' slum world. The drive, speed, rhythm, musicality, and energy which in places

---

[80] Robert Buckeye, "Some Preliminary Notes Towards A Study of Selby," *The Review of Contemporary Fiction*, 1 (1981), p. 374.

[81] Binet, p. 381.

[82] Selby recalls that putting out the "little magazines" in the 1950s, he and his Beat friends were "feeling superior to everybody." O'Brien, p. 335.

[83] O'Brien, pp. 334f.

[84] Selby cited in O'Brien, pp. 315, 327f.

[85] Ibid., p. 333.

[86] His Puritan background--"I used to get my mouth washed out with soap for saying things like 'lousy.'" (Ibid., p. 319)--, seems to surface in the excessive preoccupation with perversion and filth, the urinating in other people's windows (LB, p. 242) or the defecating in elevators (LB, p. 248). Webster Schott poignantly noted that in *Last Exit to Brooklyn* "obscenities [are] as common as prepositions." Schott, p. 441.

[87] O'Brien, p. 328.

[88] Kenneth Tindall compared Selby's prose to "Racine's tragedies with their stripped-down vocabulary." Kenneth Tindall, "The Fishing at Coney Island: Hubert Selby Jr. and the Cult of Authenticity," *The Review of Contemporary Fiction*, 1 (1981), p. 370. For his novel *The Demon*, Selby applied the structure of the morality play. O'Brien, p. 330.

characterize Selby's prose challenge the overall atmosphere of stasis.[89] In terms of Charles Olson's "Projective Verse," the novel is an "energy field."[90] The aesthetic and emotional effects rank paramount. Thus Selby will change the perspective within a sentence to create the sharp divisions and disruptions in this world: "The cop stepped over to the soldier and told him if he didnt shut up right now hed lock him up, *and your friend along with you*" (LB, p. 21; my emphasis). Moreover, since Selby presents atrocity without any explicit comment for his readers, he renders his world with a situational immediacy unachieved before. Violence and despair explode with full force and yet their emotional and moral impact on readers is controlled by the artist. With the help of the guys, Tralala, who soon will be beaten unconscious herself, brutally clubs a customer of hers from the base:

> Ya lousy fuckin hero. Go peddle a couple of medals if yaneed money so fuckin bad. She spit him in the face again, no longer afraid he might say something, but mad. Goddamn mad. A lousy 50 bucks and he was cryin. And anyway, he shouldve had more. Ya lousy fuckin creep. She kicked him in the balls. He grabbed her again. He was crying and bent over strugglin to breathe from the pain of the kick. If I don't have the pass I cant get in the Base. I have to get back. Theyre going to fly me home tomorrow. I havent been home for almost 3 years. Ive been all shot up. Please, PLEASE. Just the wallet. Thats all I want. Just the ID Card. PLEASE PLEASE!!! The tears streaked the caked blood and he hung on Tonys and Als grip and Tralala swung at his face, spitting, cursing and kicking. Alex yelled to stop and get out. I dont want trouble in here. (LB, p. 99)

Selby controls the brutality in the scene so that it verges on the brink of being unbearable. In the explosion of despair and hatred, the soldier's "PLEASE PLEASE," his repeated plea is not heard. The passage conveys a physiognomy of cruelty that traditional forms of narrative could not capture: Tralala appears as inhumanly disfigured as the women in de Kooning portraits. Selby accomplishes an enhanced emotional precision to express the despair in Tralala's atrocities. Above the chaos of violence in the scene, the language has the controlled density of poetry. The prose, mercilessly flat, produces the oppressive mood through assonance, internal rhymes, ("peddle," "couple," "medal"; "bad, "mad"), and varied repetitions ("lousy," "mad," "he was cryin"). The scene is rhythmically structured to lead up to the crescendo of "spitting, cursing, and kicking." The desperation and inhumanity are aggravated by the vicious anticlimax in which a laconic, "I dont want trouble in here," reduces the atrocity to an everyday annoyance.

While the seeming artlessness and detachment of Selby's prose seem to gainsay an involvement in this world, urban conditions in *Last Exit to Brooklyn* are confronted

---

[89]Sorrentino, p. 41.

[90]Stephens, p. 392.

through the innovative treatment of conditions. Selby attempts to sublimate the surface violence into the aesthetic energy of the medium: as such it is to disrupt and challenge the pervasive paralysis of the slum world. The compassion for the plight of the Red Hook dwellers is transformed into a quasi-political potential of the fictional speech: Selby wants to overcome the urban isolation and deprivation by a new emotional communication in the metropolis. The meticulous attention to speech thus not only attempts a catharsis in readers, but, above all, carries the hope for change: "Selby reconstructs [the] world in such a way to make it strange and new."[91] As Herbert Marcuse would later argue generally in *The Aesthetic Dimension: Toward a Critique of Marxist Aesthetics*, Selby's aesthetic form contains the progressive moment and radical impulse.[92] Indeed, as Hubert Selby remarked, art for him implied the possibility of change. This belief in culture, in its urban forms, allows him to continue the modernist search.[93] The dual aesthetic in recording the plight of slum dwellers, after all, affords glimpses of change. While Selby's critique of the housing projects is conservative, his montage is innovative and suggests the dynamics of change.

With this poetic transformation of conditions in the Brooklyn slum, the city potentially remains a place of creativity, progress, and change. Reflecting prevalent thoughts in the artistic avantgarde of the 1950s, the mode of emancipation is decidedly emotional, subjective, and esoteric. The conditions in the city are not chiefly challenged through explicit political programs as in Upton Sinclair's or Richard Wright's novels, rather the aesthetic transformation and fictional form achieve importance as in Stephen Crane's or John Dos Passos' city novels.

Last Exit to Brooklyn, despite its criticism of urban planning, thus indicates that the modern city need not inevitably be destructive, chaotic, and brutal. For Selby, the impulse to change and to experiment beyond old patterns, if only in a limited, aesthetic sense, was instrumental of writing the novel. With his precision of speech he denies and fights the social loss of control in the American city. The energy of his prose is directed at improving modern conditions. But as the gaps in his image of the slum world indicate, the aestheticizing of urban debris is not enough to overcome the profound despair in the modern city. To translate this aesthetic impulse back into valid social and political programs seems more important than ever in the crime- and drug-ridden American metropolis of the 1980s.

---

[91] O' Brien, "The Materials of Art in Hubert Selby," p. 379.

[92] Mottram, p. 354.

[93] Selby cited in O' Brien, "Interview," p. 327.

14

Thomas Pynchon
The Crying of Lot 49

1. The Grid Metropolis

The grid is a crucial metaphor in Thomas Pynchon's novel *The Crying of Lot 49*.[1] It signifies order and control and represents the sprawling metropolis of late consumer capitalism. Connecting the grid to the post-industrial Californian city, Thomas Pynchon follows Lewis Mumford who had written in *The City in History* in 1961: "The electric grid, not the Stone Age container, provides the new image for the invisible city and the many processes it serves and furthers. It is not merely the pattern of the city itself, but every institution, organization, and association composing the city that will be transformed by this development."[2] The grid had indeed become an appropriate metaphor to mark the end of the dichotomy between the city and the country in the United States. By 1970, nine out of ten Californians lived in the sprawling urban areas. For Thomas Pynchon, the grid encompasses the entire nation: San Narciso stands for America (CL, p. 123).

The grid, as connectedness and closure, appears in innumerable forms and contexts in *The Crying of Lot 49*. Above all, there is the visible grid of transportation systems: the pattern of rectangular streets, the web of freeways, and the transcontinental network of tracks (CL, p. 124). An embodiment of the corporate economy, the grid of routes "can be traced back to the Inverarity estate" (CL, p. 117). The grid thus crystallizes the new quality of control and homogeneity as envisioned in Herbert Marcuse's *One-Dimensional Man*.[3] It is further linked to technology, to the flow of energy in a

---

[1] References to *The Crying of Lot 49* will be incorporated in the text abbreviated to CL. Thomas Pynchon, *The Crying of Lot 49*, 1966, London, 1979.

[2] Mumford, p. 645. Thomas Pynchon has denied any reading of books by Lewis Mumford, but recommended Mumford's writings on the city form in a letter in 1969. David Seed, *The Fictional Labyrinths of Thomas Pynchon*, London, 1988, pp. 241, 263.

[3] Frank D. McConnell, *Four Postwar American Novelists: Bellow, Mailer, Barth, and Pynchon*, Chicago, 1977, p. 172.

"printed circuit" (CL, p. 14) and to the "web of telephone wires" (CL, p. 124). It generally represents communication channels: the postal monopoly of Thurn and Taxis, the oligopoly of television and radio stations, and the underground links among the Tristero. Finally, the grid stands for the labyrinth of meaning and the proliferation of semantic patterns in the novel itself.[4] The novel is a tapestry of meaning which is "the world" (CL, p. 13).

Despite the overall presence of grids, Oedipa Maas, the middle-class housewife who has become the executor of the will of Pierce Inverarity, a California land speculator and entrepreneur, still divides settlements along traditional lines. She distinguishes between the city and nature, between articifial developments and biological growth, between a corrupted West and a cleansing Pacific. As in F. Scott Fitzgerald's *The Great Gatsby*, the suburban imagery discloses her biased perspective as that of a slumming private eye. The novel, however, does not sanction any of Oedipa's views as she searches for the legacy of America. Hooking readers onto Oedipa's quest, *The Crying of Lot 49* denies a final denouement and remains characterized by a pervasive ambiguity.[5]

The entropy metaphor, however, which organizes the search in the novel, resumes Oedipa's bias on a more abstract level. Pynchon's metaphor, a concept from thermodynamics and information theory, connects cultural decay to laws of nature and to the supposedly irreversible heat-death. In an earlier short story "Entropy," the writer had suggested that thermodynamical processes and "American consumerism" had "a similar tendency from the least to the most probable, from differentiation to sameness, from ordered individuality to a kind of chaos."[6] A major contradiction in the novel, entropy underlies Oedipa's sorting of clues seemingly unchallenged and thus enhances her subjective effort to an apparently impartial thrust at truth. Yet the transference of insights from natural science to history and society is highly questionable--particularly in *The Crying of Lot 49*, where the diagnosis of the city reflects the interested mental map of a "Young Republican" suburbanite (CL, p. 51).

Extending the search of modernist fiction, *The Crying of Lot 49* partly supersedes this dilemma as it raises the question of the validity of cultural and aesthetic order in general. Pynchon's fiction challenges outdated projections of order.[7] Through the "ever-

---

[4]Dietmar Claas, *Entgrenztes Spiel: Leserhandlungen in der postmodernen amerikanischen Erzählkunst*, Stuttgart, 1984, p. 78.

[5]Thomas H. Schaub, *Pynchon: The Voice of Ambiguity*, Chicago, 1981, p. 21.

[6]Thomas Pynchon, "Entropy," *Kenyon Review*, 22 (1960), repr. Thomas Pynchon, *Slow Learner*, Boston, 1984, p. 88.

[7]Molly Hite, *Ideas of Order in the Novels of Thomas Pynchon*, Columbus, Ohio, 1983, p. 10.

subversive medium of fiction,"[8] he undermines all closed systems--even the predictable uncertainty in entropic ones. Yet the pervasive ambiguity in *The Crying of Lot 49* also subverts the notion of an unambiguous ambiguity in the end: the last words repeat the title and refer readers back to the closed openness of the quest. Readers, who like Oedipa had passively "settled back" (CL, p. 127) to await a solution are forced to conduct their own search in the contemporary city.

2. California in the 1960s

With the emergence of the United States as a super power after World War II, the economy expanded rapidly. From 1945 to 1967, the gross national product nearly quadrupled. Constituting but six percent of the globe's population, Americans produced half of the world's goods.[9] Corporate concentration further advanced. By the 1950s, the top four percent of manufacturing enterprises already controlled six out of ten jobs in the field, that is a total labor force of over 14 million people. In the course of the 1950s, an additional two thousand companies worth over ten million dollars disappeared in mergers. By 1963, there were no privately owned firms among the 200 largest non-financial corporations.[10]

With the general economic expansion, many people rose to or within the middle classes. The enlarged corporate and state bureaucracies further accelerated the growth of white-collar employment. In 1957, for the first time in American history, there were more white-collar than blue-collar workers in the United States.[11] Betweeen 1950 and 1970, middle-class suburbs gained three fourths of the jobs created. While the inner cities grew by just 10 million in this period, the suburbs added 85 million people. Within thirty years, from 1940 to 1970, the suburban population doubled. By 1970, more people lived in the suburbs than in central cities.[12]

---

[8]Thomas Pynchon, "The Heart's Eternal Vow," rev. of Gabriel Garcia Marquez, *Love in the Time Cholera*, *New York Times Review of Books*, (Apr. 10, 1988), p. 47.

[9]It rose from $ 213 billion to $ 775 billion. Morison, p. 703.

[10]Rodriguez, p. 204; Morison, p. 706; Charles H. Hession and Hyman Sardy, *Assent to Affluence. A History of American Economic Development*, Boston, 1969, p. 831.

[11]Hession, p. 831. San Francisco had the nation's highest percentage of white collar employees. Blume, p. 360.

[12]Robert Fishman, *Bourgeois Utopias*, New York, 1987, p. 182; Chudacoff, pp. 264f.

Federal spending for research in advanced military and aerospace technologies boosted companies in the South and the West. Government employment and spin-off innovations meant subsidized growth making California the largest state by the last third of the century. The southern part of California tripled its population from 3.7 million in 1940 to 11.8 million in 1970.[13] The Los Angeles-Long Beach Metropolitan Area mushroomed from a population of three hundred thousand in 1910, to almost three million in 1940, and to seven million in 1970. During the 1960s, 1.2 million people moved to Los Angeles.[14]

Choosing California as the setting for his novel, Thomas Pynchon presents the cityscape that was on the frontier of social change. The mere fact that by 1970 91 percent of Californians lived in urban areas indicates the degree to which this society had changed.[15] The West of the United States most conspicuously displayed the distinct form of spatially decentralized control which developed in the post-war years: here, the rise in military-aeronautic expenditures had generated the booming megalopolitan sprawl of countless single-family houses, private cars, and freeways; here, the one-dimensional "manipulation of needs by vested interests"[16] through the mass media and their proliferation of a homogenized consumer culture had its center in Hollywood.

The sprawling Californian cities were on the forefront of the national trend toward the decentralized "suburban metropolis."[17] The automobile, often mentioned as a cause, was but a tool in this development. Los Angeles, for instance, had spread long before.[18] Yet individualized traffic accelerated the development and aggravated conditions. Within two decades, the number of cars in the United States tripled from 25 million in 1945 to 75 million in 1965.[19] Government assisted this private consumption and the oligopoly of car manufacturers by paying ninety percent of the cost for highway construction. By 1973, it had spent sixty times more on freeways than on public transporta-

---

[13] Helmut Blume, *USA*, vol. 2, Darmstadt, 1979, p. 351. In 1940, California with 6.9 million inhabitants was only half the size of New York, then the most populous state with 13.5 million people. By 1970, however, California with almost twenty million residents had become the largest state in the Union. Blume, p. 134.

[14] Chudacoff, p. 274; Warner, p. 134; Blume, p. 351; Castells, p. 420.

[15] Estall, p. 50.

[16] Marcuse, *One-Dimensional Man*, p. 3.

[17] Fishman, p. 156.

[18] The original intention behind the low density in Los Angeles was conservative as the single-family home was perceived to be the perfect domestic environment. The real estate lobby which was very strong in the city turned this into municipal policy. By 1967, two thirds of the houses in the area were single-family dwelling units. Warner, p. 136; Fishman, pp. 156, 162ff.

[19] Burkhard Hofmeister, *Nordamerika*, Frankfurt, 1970, p. 222.

tion in cities.[20] Endlessly sprawling cities ensued. By 1960, the terrain of Los Angeles spanned seventy miles from east to west; two thirds of its area was yielded to the voracious needs of freeways, streets, parking lots, and garages.[21]

With the mass production of cars and the facilitated access to credit, the residential fringes of cities boomed. In 1950 alone, one million single-family houses were begun in the suburbs. The Depression era had paved the way for the massive exodus in the post-war decades when the Federal Housing Act of 1934 chiefly provided mortgages for middle-class housing. This bias in funding speeded up the split between the pauperized center and the prosperous suburbs. The building programs testified to powerful lobbies. Due to the concentration in the construction sector, large companies came to dominate the industry after the war and prefabricated Levittowns mushroomed.[22] Two thirds of the 15 million dwelling units erected in the 1950s were constructed by large builders.[23]

Political and legal measures, such as harsh zoning laws, assisted the withdrawal to the suburbs. Through zoning, real estate speculators and developers fended off lower-income groups because their intrusion would have deflated land values; homeowners similarly feared the loss of property value and of social homogeneity. High acreage requirements, strict construction codes, the exclusion of apartment buildings, and the minimizing of public services helped the suburbanites to keep their dream middle-class and white.[24] In addition, the fringe communities refused annexation by central municipalities and thus drained the city core of a substantial share of expenditures.[25] The impoverished city was thus left to finance the outdated infrastructure and cultural attractions in the metropolitan area--the concert halls, libraries, museums, zoos, and parks--paying more than users from the wealthy fringe.[26]

The suburbanization after World War II may be evaluated as a massive rejection of social responsibility by privileged groups. Within the suburbs themselves, middle-class women paid the toll for this withdrawal. Trapped by the patriarchal division of work and

---

[20] Castells, p. 387.

[21] Morison, p. 706. The first freeway from Pasadena to central Los Angeles was constructed in 1940; after 1950 twenty-three highways were added producing a close network of some 650 miles of road. Blume, p. 354.

[22] Chudacoff, pp. 265, 288; Barry Checkoway, "Large Builders, Federal Housing Programs, and Postwar Suburbanization," *Marxism and the Metropolis*, eds. W. Tabb and L. Sawers, New York, 1984, pp. 160f.

[23] Checkoway, pp. 154f.

[24] Chudacoff, pp. 226, 246f.

[25] Industrial areas were zoned so that the companies need not pay for public facilities of adjacent working-class communities. Markusen, p. 96.

[26] Johnston, p. 148; Markusen, pp. 90-9.

home, females were left to themselves and their domestic constriction of house-keeping and child-rearing, feeling isolated and removed from viable cultural and social activities.[27]

The proliferation of the electronic mass media accompanied the trend toward individualized commodity consumption. By the end of the 1950s, 85 percent of American households had a television set.[28] An oligopoly of three national networks controlled television programs. These commercial media hardly functioned in the prime sense of communication, "the passing of ideas, information, and attitudes from person to person,"[29] but primarily served as tools for consumer stimulation and entertainment. Concentration also occurred in other fields of communication: from 700 competing daily papers in 1910, only 64 had survived in cities by 1967. In many urban areas the commercial TV network, radio station, and newspaper today lie in the hand of a single corporation.[30] Above all, Hollywood with its massive output of films and TV programs molded the American imagination. For Thomas Pynchon, indeed, the circuit imagery in *The Crying of Lot 49* is a significant metaphor. In his essay, "A Journey Into the Mind of Watts," which was published in the same year as the novel, he wrote that "Los Angeles, more than any other city, belongs to the mass media."[31]

The spread of commodities and the extensive suburbanization which even reached the upper level of the working class by the 1960s could not blur the fact that economic power was distributed unevenly: in 1956, one percent owned 26 percent of all the nation's riches while 30 percent lived in poverty.[32] For some groups, the plight continued unchanged. Thus in 1970, only five percent of the black population lived in suburbs.[33] The increasing division into flourishing and decaying sections in the sprawling metropolis accelerated the differences in urban ways of life with the neglected areas and

---

[27] See Sylvia F. Fava, "Women's Place in the New Suburbia," *New Space for Women*, eds. Gerda R. Wekerle, Rebecca Peterson, and David Morley, Boulder, Col., 1980, 129-49.

[28] By the mid-sixties, there were over eight thousand shopping centers in the United States. Johnston, p. 219; Kreutzer, p. 28.

[29] Raymond Williams, *Communications*, Harmondsworth, 1962, p. 9.

[30] Morison, p. 706.

[31] Thomas Pynchon, "A Journey Into the Mind of Watts," *New York Times Magazine*, (June 12, 1966), 34f., 78, 80ff., 84, repr. London, 1983, p. 5.

[32] Morison, p. 727.

[33] Howard Chudacoff stresses the ethnic discrepancy: "Since World War II the division between cities and suburbs has assumed a racial dimension--whites on the outside, blacks on the inside. Between 1950 and 1966, 70 percent of the increase in the nation's white population occurred in suburbs, while 86 percent of the increase in the black population took place in central cities." Chudacoff, p. 273.

disadvantaged groups further vanishing from sight. In the 1970s, Peter Orleans examined composite images of Los Angeles by different social groups. The Los Angeles of Spanish or black working-class citizens expressed the extreme enclosure and constricted radius as their mental maps only extended a few blocks in their environs. In contrast, upper-class citizens who had an overview of the whole area, refused to acknowledge the existence of plight and disadvantage and omitted the lower-class areas from their maps.[34]

In the 1960s, the latent conflict in cities exploded and the riots of the disadvantaged forced mainstream America to take note of the crisis at last. The Watts unrest in Los Angeles was the first of its kind and became paradigmatic.[35] Tensions in black Los Angeles erupted in August 1965 after the arrest of a black youth for drunken driving and his demeaning treatment by white policemen. In almost a week of rioting, 34 people were killed and over a thousand injured. The large participation of the community--from 30,000 to 80,000 blacks were involved at different stages--indicates the high degree of disillusionment with American consumer society. During the riots, which were stopped by sending 14,000 national guards into the area, almost four thousand blacks were arrested.[36]

The issues in the conflict were not restrictively urban ones. Rather, one should consider that the general prosperity had not helped people in Watts. From 1960 to 1965, the percentage of blacks living in poverty remained the same, while the absolute figures of poverty even increased in Watts, from 247,000 to 260,000 people.[37] What became important from a sociological and planning standpoint was the fact that the outbreak of hostilities in bungalow areas contradicted the urbanist myth about density and its dangers. High urban density did not produce the riots. To put it pointedly, Los Angeles was approximately fifteen times less crowded than Manhattan.[38]

Rioting, then, was one response to the disillusionment with American society in the 1960s. The spread of urban protest and of counterculture movements was another. Civil rights demonstrations, anti-war rallies, student protests, grass-root organizations and radical back-to-nature experiments openly testified to the large disagreement with the American establishment and its moral majority in the suburbs. Such movements are the real counterparts of the Tristero, the organization of the disinherited in the novel.

---

[34]Orleans, pp. 121ff.

[35]Joachim Klewes, "'I feel buried here in Watts . . .' Eine Fallstudie des Aufstandes in Los Angeles 1965," *Soziologie der Masse*, eds. Helge Pross and Eugen Buß, Heidelberg, 1984, p. 118.

[36]Some six hundred buildings were destroyed or damaged during the ghetto riots. Klewes, pp. 119f.

[37]Nathan Cohen, ed., *The Los Angeles Riots: A Socio-psychological Study*, New York, 1970, p. 8.

[38]Jackson, "The Capital of Capitalism: The New York Metropolitan Region, 1890-1940," p. 325f.

After the publication of *The Crying of Lot 49*, the muted post horns of Pynchon's Tristero organization appeared all over the United States.[39]

3. The Slumming Suburbanite as Detective

The Californian cityscape in *The Crying of Lot 49* is presented from a thoroughly middle-class standpoint. Oedipa Maas, a housewife from Kinneret-Among-The-Pines, projects her suburban perspective on the encompassing grid that "was less an identifiable city than a group of concepts--census tracts, special purpose bond-issue districts, shopping nuclei, all overlaid with access roads to its own freeway" (CL, p. 14). Written as a third-person narrative, the novel conveys her mental map. For the investigation into suburban conformity, urban entropy, and the sixties' underground, the unreliable narrator is a perfect fictional tool. Sporadically, an omniscient narrator intrudes to indicate what has escaped his heroine.[40]

The first chapter introduces the world of middle-class suburbia. Plastic, parties, psychoanalysts, shopping centers, and muzak dominate. With a remarkable narrative economy, the opening sentence establishes the atmosphere and the crucial link between the organization families and the organizations themselves. Suburbia has inherited the legacy of big business:

> One summer afternoon Mrs Oedipa Maas came home from a Tupperware party whose hostess had put perhaps too much kirsch in the fondue to find that she, Oedipa, had been named executor, or she supposed executrix, of the estate of one Pierce Inverarity, a California real estate mogul who had once lost two million dollars in his spare time but still had assets numerous and tangled enough to make the job of sorting it all out more than honorary. (CL, p. 5)

Mass commodities and the mass media dominate the consumer society. With telling names from satire, the "Maas" suburbanites stand for this *mass* culture. Reified, they even merge with commodities: Oedipa and her car, "she and the Chevy" (CL, p. 15), become a synthetic object. The professions of Wendell 'Mucho' Maas--he first works as a salesman for used cars and then as a radio disc jockey--signify the complete penetration

---

[39] Heinz Ickstadt, "Thomas Pynchon. *Die Versteigerung von Nr. 49*," *Zum Romanwerk von Thomas Pynchon*, ed. Heinz Ickstadt, Hamburg, 1981, pp. 123f; Annette Kolodny and Daniel James Peters, "Pynchon's *The Crying of Lot 49*: The Novel as Subversive Experience," *Modern Fiction Studies*, 19 (1973), p. 79.

[40] Georgiana M. M. Colvile, *Beyond and Beneath the Mantle: On Thomas Pynchon's The Crying of Lot 49*, Amsterdam, 1988, pp. 11, 22, 82.

of postindustrial space by means of communications. Hence, San Narciso may remind Oedipa of a "printed circuit" of the "transistor radio" (CL, p. 14):

> The ordered swirl of houses and streets, from this high angle, sprang at her now with the same unexpected, astonishing clarity as the circuit card had. Though she knew even less about radios than about Southern Californians, there were to both outward patterns a hieroglyphic sense of concealed meaning, of an intent to communicate. There'd seemed no limit to what the printed circuit could have told her (if she only tried to find out); so in her first minute of San Narciso, a revelation also trembled just past the threshold of her understanding. (CL, p. 15)

Oedipa Maas ventures to break away from this grid.[41] She is a "prisoner among the pines and salt fogs of Kinneret" (CL, p. 12) and experiences a strong "sense of buffeting, insulation" (CL, p. 12). As the novel starts, Oedipa Maas seems completely isolated, a consumerist monad in the suburban grid engulfed by an insulation both physical and emotional.[42] Through extensive references, Thomas Pynchon makes her experience express the general victimization of housewives in patriarchal suburbs. Whereas in Betty Friedan's *The Feminine Mystique* the environment of female suburbanites is associated with concentration camps, *The Crying of Lot 49* has Dr Hilarius, an ex-Nazi doctor who experimented on Jews, run drug tests on a sample of middle-class housewives (CL, p. 10).[43]

Oedipa Maas' impulse to break the suburban enclosure is initiated by the death of Pierce Inverarity. In the beginning of the novel, she recalls her first, futile attempt at escape, fleeing to Mexico with Inverarity. Oedipa then resigned as a surrealist tapestry seemed to signify the impossibility of escape. She had believed that the grid of control was everywhere:

> In Mexico City they somehow wandered into an exhibition of paintings by the beautiful Spanish exile Remedios Varo: in the central paintings of the triptych, titled 'Bordando el Manto Terrestre', were a number of frail girls . . . prisoners in the top room of a circular tower, embroidering a kind of tapestry which spilled out the slit windows and into a void, seeking hopelessly to fill the void: for all the other buildings and creatures, all the waves, ships and forests of the earth were contained in this tapestry, and the tapestry was the world. Oedipa, perverse, had stood in front of the painting and cried. (CL, p. 13)

---

[41] Throughout the novel, the adjusted and aquiescent husband serves as a contrast to Oedipa Maas. He is a suburbanite who tries to exist within the bounds of a manipulated culture. Eventually, his identity will dissolve, when in a parody on Timothy Leary's liberation through drugs, Mucho Maas experiences incoherent LSD-hallucinations (CL, p. 99).

[42] The insulation may provide protection at times, though. As Roseman tries to play "footsie" (CL, p. 12) with her under the table, her thick boots protect her from his approaches; later, Metzger cannot feel her breasts under all the clothes she wears (CL, p. 25).

[43] Betty Friedan, *The Feminine Mystique*, New York, 1963, p. 305ff.

This time, the search for Inverarity's legacy, for "America" (CL, p. 123), develops into a sustained attempt to disclose and destroy her own webs of dependency. Oedipa's concern for the urban underworld, for the city below the grid of artificial cityscapes of real estate speculators such as Inverarity, turns her into an involved citizen which, in real life suburbia, has been notoriously lacking. According to Michael Harrington's *The Other America*, the ordinary tourist rarely leaves the main highway and "the middle-class women coming from Suburbia on a rare trip may catch the merest glimpse of the other America on the way to an evening at the theater."[44] Thomas Pynchon himself asked the white middle class to descend from the highway in his essay "A Journey into the Mind of Watts":

> The two cultures do not understand each other, though white values are displayed without let-up on black people's TV screens, and though the panoramic sense of black impoverishment is hard to miss from atop the Harbor Freeway, which so many whites must drive at least twice every working day. Somehow it occurs to very few of them to leave at the Imperial Highway exit for a change, to go east instead of west only a few blocks, and take a look at Watts. A quick look. The simplest kind of beginning. But Watts is country which lies, psychologically, uncounted miles further than most whites seem at present willing to travel.[45]

At the beginning of her search, Oedipa Maas is fully embedded in her suburban perspective. Like Harrington's suburbanites, she looks "down a slope, needing to squint for the sunlight, on to a vast sprawl of houses" (CL, p.14). In connection with Los Angeles, such a view from above is decidedly social. In L. A., the paradigmatic grid city and model for Pynchon's San Narciso, height implies class:

> The principal class distinction was no longer distance from the center--the poor living closer in, the richer further out--but elevation. The wealthy seized upon the hill as a sign of wealth and status, while more modest developments limited themselves to spreading along the endless flatlands. . . . For the wealthy, the high ground offered not only splendid views and purer air but also the exclusivity that distance provided in the railroad suburb. . . . The archetypal hill suburb was, of course, Beverly Hills.[46]

Throughout the novel, even when Oedipa descends "from atop" the freeway to have a look at life below, her search remains tied to middle-class perspectives and assumptions. Her class perception is reflected in her mental map and in the fact that she has access to all areas. This distinguishes her urban experience from the constricted city of the out-

---

[44]Harrington, pp. 3, 4. See also Seed, pp. 150f.

[45]Pynchon, p. 4.

[46]Fishman, p. 167.

cast. To find out more about the Tristero, "The Disinherited" (CL, p. 110), she has to walk and ride the bus just like any outcast (CL, p. 85).

Oedipa Maas' concern for the underprivileged in the city stands in the old tradition of middle-class interest in slums and the humanitarian help for the "other half." Like the reformer Jacob A. Riis, who campaigned for the noble Bowery poor at the turn of the century, Oedipa Maas turns into a would-be reformer who searches for an authentic counterculture in the urban underworld. Indeed, it is among the dispossessed, in one of the few nonsatiric moments of the novel, that the slumming suburbanite is depicted as truly compassionate when assisting a drunken sailor:

> She was overcome all at once by a need to touch him, as if she could not believe in him, or would not remember him, without it. Exhausted, hardly knowing what she was doing, she came the last three steps and sat, took the man in her arms, actually held him, gazing out of her smudged eyes down the stairs, back into the morning. She felt wetness against her breasts and saw that he was crying again. (CL, p. 87)

But a few moments later, her split allegiance and inconsistent attitudes are revealed as she imagines herself as a "lady bountiful,"[47] a glamorous social worker from suburbia:

> She ran through then a scene she might play. She might find the landlord of this place, and bring him to court, and buy the sailor a new suit at Roos/Atkins, and a shirt, and shoes, and give him the bus fare to Fresno after all. But with a sigh he had released her hand, while she was so lost in the fantasy that she hadn't felt it go away, as if he'd known the best moment to let go. (CL, p. 88)

Trying to escape from her prison, she still is influenced by old attitudes and media fantasies.

Oedipa's wish to assist others is one side of her quest, but she also becomes the detective, the person to solve a riddle, as her archetypal name suggests.[48] Finding out more about Pierce Inverarity's legacy, she intends to put her deranged world in order. Oedipa's quest is in the tradition of private eye narratives. The ideological dimension and urban implication of such stories has been described by Raymond Williams. The detective may "penetrate the intricacies of the streets":

> The opaque complexity of modern city life is represented by crime; the explorer of a society is reduced to the discoverer of single causes, the isolable agent and above all his means, his technique.[49]

---

[47]Seed, p. 150.
[48]McConnell, p. 170.
[49]Williams, *The Country and the City*, p. 273.

Oedipa Maas' search yields two main results. The first is her record of the debased Californian cityscape. The second result are the links and connections which she creates and which express her hopes for an alternative. With Robert Merrill, it can be said however:

> In a very real sense it doesn't matter which of Oedipa's "alternatives" is true. Either Tristero or the legacy America--in either case we have the contemporary landscape Pynchon reveals both to Oedipa and to the reader.[50]

Pynchon does not verify her hopes. He undermines and parodies the detective genre which he draws upon by not offering a solution to Oedipa's investigations.[51]

The contemporary landscape which *The Crying of Lot 49* presents is the cityscape of postindustrial capitalism. Pierce Inverarity is heir to Jay Gould (CL, p. 3), the notorious monopolist and exploiter in the early days of industrial capitalism, but his multiple identities (CL, p. 6) signify the trend toward deindividualized corporate power. The images of grids, webs, and tapestries time and again evoke this new quality of control. Even the counterorganizations of the Tristero are linked to its web as all access routes to them also lead to Inverarity's holdings (CL, p. 117). For Thomas Pynchon, spatial forms directly express cultural and political conditions. In a letter in 1969, he explained: "The physical shape of a city is an infallible due [sic] to where people who built it are at. It has to do with our deepest responses to change, death, being human."[52]

The power grid of big business thus dominates San Narciso and dictates the fate of consumer society. In its title, *The Crying of Lot 49* hints at the sale of California (and implicitly of the West, the mythic territory of freedom and prosperity) to the highest bidder among real estate speculators.[53] By the 1960s, the grid of capitalism extends beyond a single city or region:

> There was the true continuity, San Narciso had no boundaries. No one knew yet how to draw them. She had dedicated herself, weeks ago, to making sense of what Inverarity had left behind, never suspecting that the legacy was America. (CL, p. 123)

The corporate economy also controls the media and new technologies. Inverarity's commercials for a residential project pay for the programs that Oedipa Maas and her co-executor Metzger watch in 'Echo Courts' (CL, pp. 19f., 27). The "Yoyodyne" company drains individuals of their creativity as it robs inventors and engineers of their patents (CL, p. 61). It is even in control of the nation's future: outer space, which in the

---

[50] Robert Merrill, "The Form and Meaning of Pynchon's *The Crying of Lot 49*," *Ariel*, 8 (1977), p. 69.

[51] Tony Tanner, *Thomas Pynchon*, London, 1982, p. 58.

[52] Pynchon quoted in Seed, p. 241.

[53] The figure 49 stands for the year of the goldrush and is a nickname for the state. Ickstadt, p. 111.

early sixties was envisioned as the *new frontier*, is part of the corporate empire. The government-contracted Yoyodyne Galactronics is a giant in the aerospace industry (CL, p. 15).

Completely manipulated, as it is, the San Narciso society has fallen in love with itself and reproduces its narcissistic images in the mass media. "Mucho" Maas represents, as his telling name implies, the wasteland of mass culture in concentrated form. Selling and buying used cars, the "motorized, metal extensions" (CL, p. 8) of the people, he participates in strengthening the grid of dependence. He shares their degeneration:

> Clipped coupons promising savings of 5 or 10c, trading stamps, pink flyers advertising specials at the markets, butts, tooth-shy combs, help-wanted ads, Yellow Pages torn from the phone book, rags of old underwear or dresses that already were period costumes, for wiping your own breath off the inside of a windshield . . . all the bits and pieces coated uniformly, like a salad of despair, in a grey dressing of ash, condensed exhaust, dust, body wastes--it made him look sick, but he had to look. (CL, p. 8)

The owners do not notice this wasteland any longer, accepting it as if "it were the most natural thing" (CL, p. 8). Though Mucho Maas is disturbed by the sign of the National Automobile Dealer's Association NADA (CL, p. 100), he becomes disillusioned as he is edited and censored when working for the mass media (CL, p. 9).

Beneath the surface of this one-dimensional society, Oedipa Maas detects the traces of a countermovement to the establishment. The disinherited in W.A.S.T.E., an acronym for WE AWAIT SILENT TRISTERO'S EMPIRE (CL, p. 116), stand for a different America. They are the human detritus of this reified world.[54] Their withdrawal from mainstream society is represented by a muted postal horn, an emblem for their independent mail and communication systems. In the terminology of Marshall McLuhan, the medium is their message: WASTE uses garbage cans as mailboxes (CL, p. 89).[55]

> Last night she might have wondered what undergrounds apart from the couple she knew of communicated by WASTE system. By sunrise she could legitimately ask what undergrounds didn't. . . . For here were God knew how many citizens, deliberately choosing not to communicate by US Mail. It was not an act of treason, nor possibly even of defiance. But it was a calculated withdrawal, from the life of the Republic, from its machinery. Whatever else was being denied them out of hate, indifference to the power of their vote, loopholes, simple ignorance, this withdrawal was their own, unpublicized, private. Since they could not have withdrawn into a vacuum (could they?), there had to exist the separate, silent, unsuspected world. (CL, p. 86)

Yet readers of *The Crying of Lot 49* cannot be certain whether the Tristero system actually exists, or how vast and connected its underground organizations are. Even Jesus

---

[54]Ibid., p. 107.

[55]On the links between McLuhan and Pynchon see Schaub, pp. 25ff; Seed, pp. 140-46.

Arrabal's political hope, the Conjuración de los Insurgentes Anarquistas, may be a self-deception because the name of the organization may after all stand as acronym for the C.I.A. (CL, p. 82).[56]

Though the novel leaves open whether the Tristero organization is real or imaginary, there are extratextual clues about the significance of the counterculture and the importance of a search for alternatives to escape control. In his essay on the black rebellion in the Watts section of Los Angeles, Pynchon projects the massive riots as authentic attempts to break the oppression of the dominant white world.[57] He identifies white Los Angeles as an "unreal" media world which the "real" culture of the suppressed blacks opposes:

> It is, after all, in white L.A.'s interest to cool Watts any way it can - to put the area under a siege of persuasion; to coax the Negro poor into taking on certain white values. Give them a little property, and they will be less tolerant of arson; get them to go in hock for a car or color TV, and they'll be more likely to hold down a steady job. Some see it for what it is-- this come-on, this false welcome, this attempt to transmogrify the reality of Watts into the unreality of Los Angeles. Some don't. Watts is tough; has been able to resist the unreal.[58]

The division into the "real" and the "unreal" is then extended to express the contrast between the black slum dwellers below and the white suburbanites on the freeways:

> Overhead, big jets now and then come vacuum-cleanering in to land; the wind is westerly, and Watts lies under the approaches to L.A. International. The jets hang what seems only a couple of hundred feet up in the air; through the smog they show up more white than silver, highlighted by the sun, hardly solid; only the ghosts, or possibilities, of airplanes.
> From here, much of the white culture that surrounds Watts--and, in a curious way, besieges it--looks like those jets: a little unreal, a little less than substantial. For Los Angeles, more than any other city, belongs to the mass media. What is known around the nation as the L.A. Scene exists chiefly as images on a screen or TV tube, as four colored magazine photos. . . . It is basically a white Scene, and illusion is everywhere in it, from the giant aerospace firms that flourish or retrench at the whims of Robert McNamara, to the "action" that everybody mills along the Strip on weekends looking for, unaware that they, and their search which will end, usually, unfulfilled, are the only action in town.[59]

The oppositions developed in the essay recur in *The Crying of Lot 49*. According to the novel, "High above the LA freeways, / And the traffic's whine, / Stands the well-known Galactronics / Branch of Yoyodyne" (CL, p. 57). Another occasion, Oedipa Maas is

---

[56]Colvile, p. 56.

[57]See also Heinz Ickstadt, "Kommunikationsmüll und Sprachcollage: Die Stadt in der Fiktion der amerikanischen Fiktion der Postmoderne," *Die Unwirklichkeit der Städte*, ed. Klaus R. Scherpe, 197-224.

[58]Pynchon, p. 10.

[59]Ibid., p. 5.

asked by the drunken sailor to drop a Tristero message in a garbage can "under the freeway" (CL, p. 86):

> For an hour she prowled among the sunless, concrete underpinnings of the freeway, finding drunks, bums, pedestrians, pederasts, hookers, walking psychotics, no secret mailbox. But at last in the shadows she did come on a can with a swinging trapezoidal top, the kind you throw trash in: old and green, nearly four feet high. On the swinging part were handpainted the initials W.A.S.T.E. (CL, p. 89)

Oedipa Maas, despite her stamina to descend and have a look at the disinherited, also resembles the white social workers in Watts who adhere to their stereotyped images of blacks:

> Sadly, they [the social workers] seem to be smiling themselves out of any meaningful communication with their poor. Besides a 19th-century faith that tried and true approaches--sound counselling, good intentions, perhaps even compassion--will set Watts straight, they are also burdened with the personal attitudes they bring to work with them. Their reflexes--especially about conformity, about failure, about violence--are predictable.[60]

Black youths when applying for jobs, should, their white counselors tell them, "look as much as possible as a white applicant."[61] Like the inadequate and outdated "Great Depression techniques applied to a scene that has long outgrown them,"[62] but which whites still propose in Watts, Oedipa eventually ponders on "spreading some kind of a legacy among them all, all those nameless, maybe as a first instalment" (CL, p.125). Welfare money alone, Pynchon seems to imply, cannot solve the conflict.

In contrast to *The Crying of Lot 49*, the essay is firm about the need to destroy the manipulated communication channels of the white world. Art may create "honest rebirths" from the debris:

> Along with theatrical and symphonic events, the festival also featured a roomful of sculptures fashioned entirely from found objects--found, symbolically enough, and in the Simon Rodia tradition, among the wreckage the rioting had left. Exploiting textures of charred wood, twisted metal, fused glass, many of the works were fine, honest rebirths.
> In one corner was this old, busted hollow TV set with a rabbit-ears antenna on top; inside where its picture-tube should have been, gazing out with scorched crevices and sockets, was a human skull. The name of the piece was "The Late, Late, Late Show."[63]

The final image presents the neglected reality behind the media world and recalls the victims of unreality. As Pynchon has remarked recently, he believes that it is important

---

[60]Ibid., p. 9.

[61]Ibid., p. 9.

[62]Ibid., p. 4.

[63]Ibid., p. 11.

to talk and write about those people and problems that are neglected by the media and by history. Writing for him is revolutionary, if it redeems these silences.[64]

In *The Crying of Lot 49*, the dispossessed of the Tristero remain invisible and without a proper representative. Oedipa's brief observations are not confirmed by other characters and are increasingly questioned by the protagonist herself, who fears that they are hallucinations or a gigantic hoax imposed on her by Inverarity. There is, however, one more significant link between the "real" subculture of blacks in the essay and the "real alternative" (CL, p. 118) of the Tristero: the opponent in *The Crying of Lot 49* may stand for the unreal because the name Inver(ar)ity can be read as lack of veracity.[65]

In the novel, the criticism of and the envisioned alternatives to contemporary California are strongly affected by Oedipa's middle-class perspective. While the novel questions virtually all of the options she detects, it never casts doubt upon the ideological basis of her binary choices. Oedipa still interprets the "essentially man-made landscape"[66] along the lines of the traditional middle-class dichotomy between the natural and artificial. Though the myth of a rejuvenating way of life in suburbia was severely challenged by the all-encompassing influence of the grid in real life, the middle-class detective of the novel holds on to the old suburban ideology of space. Her assessment of the Californian megalopolis thus stands in the tradition of suburban fiction to which F. Scott Fitzgerald's *The Great Gatsby* or Walker Percy's *The Moviegoer* belong.

Oedipa Maas opposes the recent developments that threaten to obliterate options for a separate suburban life-style. The grid metropolis signifies the unreal mass media, the printed circuit of a radio; its size implies inflated, unsound growth: "Address numbers were in the 70 and then 80,000s. She had never known numbers to run so high. It seemed unnatural" (CL, p. 15). The "infected city" (CL, p. 80) is sick. It has become addicted to its own traffic:

> What the road really was, she fancied, was this hypodermic needle, inserted somewhere ahead into the vein of a freeway, a vein nourishing the mainliner LA, keeping it happy, coherent, protected from pain, or whatever passes, with a city, for pain. But were Oedipa some single melted crystal of urban horse, LA, really, would be no less turned on for her absence. (CL, p. 16)

---

[64]In his review of *Love in the Time of Cholera*, Pynchon asserts the necessity to write about "a history which has brought so appallingly many down, without ever having spoken, or having spoken gone unheard, or having been heard, left unrecorded. As revolutionary as writing well is the duty to redeem these silences. . . ." Pynchon, "The Heart's Eternal Vow," p. 49.

[65]True to the pervasive ambiguity of the novel, Inverarity may signify both untruth and in truth. Frank Kermode, "Decoding the Trystero," *Pynchon. A Collection of Critical Essays*, ed. Edward Mendelson, Englewood Cliffs, 1978, p. 162.

[66]Seed, p. 148.

Metropolitan decay needs nature's counterforces. The Tristero communicate via "green" mailboxes (CL, p. 89), while unreal suburbia is introduced through Tupperware and the "greenish dead eye of the TV tube" (CL, p. 5). The references to *The Great Gatsby* and *The Waste Land* are but logical extensions of this pattern. Pierce Inverarity's housing development, Fangoso Lagoons, is "artificial" (CL, p. 19) and directly relates to T. S. Eliot's city poem: "Some immediacy was there again, some promise of hierophany: printed circuit, gently curving streets, private access to the water, Book of the Dead" (CL, p. 20). Oedipa clings to the myth of the West, the initial model for the middle-class crabgrass frontier. The Pacific should perform the cleansing now that the land is corrupted:

> Oedipa had believed, long before leaving Kinneret, in some principle of the sea as redemption for Southern California (not, of course, for her own section of the state, which seemed to need none), some unvoiced idea that no matter what you did to its edges the true Pacific stayed inviolate and integrated or assumed the ugliness at any edge into some more general truth. (CL, p. 37)

In true continuation of the metaphysical responses toward the secular London waste land or the Long Island valley of ashes, the decay of the bourgeois world acquires a transcendental dimension in *The Crying of Lot 49*. Looking down on the city from middle-class heights, Oedipa "and the Chevy seemed parked at an odd religious instant" (CL, p. 15). The grid, in its "hieratic geometry" (Cl, p. 37), promises an "hierophany" (CL, p. 20). Indicative of Pynchon's ingenuity to multiply and relate meanings, Oedipa's last name compresses the connections, as Maas connotes to mass as in mass culture, natural matter, and religious mass.[67] Oedipa's longing for absolute certainty is linked to religious images.[68] Her projection of binary options, Tristero or no Tristero, hoax or paranoia, is specifically related to the manichaeism of the Scurvhamites: it was this Puritan sect which managed to suppress Wharfinger's play, the Jacobean backdrop to the decadence of contemporary California (CL, p.107).

On the whole, Pynchon's novel, however, dissolves the restrictive duality inherent in manichean visions or other simplistic dichotomies.[69] Its pervasive ambiguity challenges the rigidity of the proposed binary options in Calvinist theology, computer science, or Bakunin's anarchism. It also questions its own literary autonomy, by linking

---

[67] Colvile, p. 26. Her name also signifies the grid imagery as the Dutch *Maaswerk* stands for the woof of a tapestry. Pierre-Yves Pétillon, *La grande-route*, Paris, 1979, p. 179; quoted from Colvile, p. 12.

[68] For an affirmative reading, see Edward Mendelson, "The Sacred, the Profane, and *The Crying of Lot 49*," *Pynchon. A Collection of Critical Essays*, ed. Edward Mendelson, Englewood Cliffs, 1978, pp. 112-46.

[69] Hite, p. 71.

Calvinism to literary theory: "Puritans were utterly devoted, like the literary critics, to the Word" (CL, p. 107). Similarly, Driblette, the director of Wharfinger's play, advises Oedipa not to take a Puritan attitude toward "words, words" (CL, p. 53), and to fill them with life instead: "You can put together clues, develop a thesis, or several, about why characters reacted to the Trystero possibility the way they did.... You could waste your life that way and never touch the truth" (CL, p. 54).

Though Pynchon undermines the binary pattern of the Puritans and the computers, he is obsessed by their power and attracted by the implication of unambiguous solutions. As a spray can goes wild and whirls at random through the room in Echo Courts, it is significantly "God or a digital machine," which "might have computed in advance the complex web of its travel...." (CL, p. 24).

4. Ambiguity in the Entropic City

Oedipa Maas' intention to "*project a world*" (CL, p. 56), is not an isolated case in *The Crying of Lot 49*. Thomas Pynchon himself is a prolific creator of fiction. His novel presents a huge array of grids, tapestries, and scientific metaphors and is preoccupied with the possibility or impossibility of order.[70] As Pynchon explained in 1984, the combination of themes and metaphors in his early short fiction and in *The Crying of Lot 49* resulted from the political and artistic situation in the late 1950s and early 1960s.[71] Pynchon regards his entropy metaphor and his "thermodynamical gloom"[72] as an image of the paralysis of American society:

> One of the most pernicious effects of the '50's was to convince the people growing up during them that it would last forever.... While Eisenhower was in, there seemed no reason why it should all not just go on as it was.[73]

---

[70]Manfred Pütz, "Thomas Pynchon's *The Crying of Lot 49*: The World is a Tristero System," *Mosaic*, 7 (1974), pp. 125ff.

[71]Pynchon considers his Californian novel as part of these early efforts. Thomas Pynchon, "Introduction," *Slow Learner*, Boston, 1984, p. 22.

[72]Pynchon, p. 14.

[73]Ibid., p. 14.

An "unpolitical '50's student," Pynchon believed that scientific models and encyclopaedic totality were alternatives to a "too autobiographical" literature. [74] Such statements may explain the impersonal, technical style of Pynchon's fiction and also reveal that the natural sciences were attractive because they seemed to provide models for analyzing the world in objectively predictable, universal terms.

In *The Crying of Lot 49*, the concept of entropy, with its evocation of conformity, sameness, probability, and chaos, was a congenial metaphor to express the conditions in the contemporary cityscape.[75] Entropy generally is, "throughout his fiction . . . the most pervasive of metaphors."[76] Pynchon first applied it in his short story with the same title:

> I happened to read Norbert Wiener's *The Human Use of Human Beings* (a rewrite for the interested layman of his more technical *Cybernetics*) at about the same time as *The Education of Henry Adams*, and the "theme" of the story ["Entropy"] is mostly derivative of what these two men had to say. A pose I found congenial in those days . . . was that of somber glee at any idea of mass destruction or decline. . . . Given my undergraduate mood, Adams' sense of power out of control, coupled with Wiener's spectacle of universal heat-death and mathematical stillnes, seemed just the ticket.[77]

The complex, but basically dual use of entropy in *The Crying of Lot 49* has been described by other critics in detail. As a concept in thermodynamics, entropy serves as a measure of the irreversible decline, disorder, and eventual equilibrium of low-quality energy of a closed system. As a concept in information theory, entropy, in a diametrical sense, serves as a measure for the amount of information; the higher the entropy, the more information is available.[78] Maxwell's Demon (CL, pp. 59, 72f.), a scientific model of entropy developed by the physicist James Clerk Maxwell in 1871, anticipated the two uses of entropy in thermodynamics and information theory. Maxwell's Demon tries to counter the irreversible decline of energy by collecting information about the distribution and location of molecules to sort them out, that is, he decreases the entropy by creating order among low and high energy particles. The Demon serves as the overarching metaphor for Oedipa Maas' role as a private eye in contemporary California; its suggests

---

[74]Ibid., p. 6. Pynchon writes: "Somewhere I had come up with the notion that one's personal life has nothing to do with fiction, when the truth, as everyone knows, is nearly the opposite. . . . I preferred fancy footwork instead." Ibid., p. 21.

[75]Robert Sklar, "The Anarchist Miracle: The Novels of Thomas Pynchon," *Pynchon. A Collection of Critical Essays*, ed. Edward Mendelson, Englewood Cliffs, 1978, p.94.

[76]Joseph W. Slade, "'Entropy' and Other Calamities," *Pynchon. A Collection of Critical Essays*, ed. Edward Mendelson, Englewood Cliffs, 1978, p. 77.

[77]Pynchon, p. 13.

[78]Anne Mangel, "Maxwell's Demon, Entropy, Information: *The Crying of Lot 49*," *Mindful Pleasures*, eds. George Levine and David Leverenz, Boston, 1976, pp. 87-100.

parallels which at times may seem "too neat."[79] But Oedipa Maas cannot overcome entropic loss and consequently loses herself in a labyrinth of disorderly meaning. Maxwell's concept has been criticized. As several scientists have pointed out in the twentieth century, sorting out information also uses up energy.[80]

Pynchon uses a complicated and contradictory scientific concept whose "qualities and quantities will not come together to form a unified notion,"[81] even for himself, and whose theoretical underpinnings are unclear and unsteady to date.[82] He may be criticized for not considering whether it is legitimate to apply laws of nature to history and society. For Pynchon, entropy, and science in general, apparently are not so problematic as other constituents of reality. In a sense, the insistence on the unambiguous and inescapable heat-death of nature reinforces Oedipa Maas' suburban imagery and lifts her assessment to a level which, if more sophisticated, is related to the ontological tendency in bourgeois myths that Roland Barthes has examined and criticized in his *Mythologies*.[83]

The entropy metaphor and its application to the contemporary Californian cityscape are problematic for other reasons too. Key concepts of entropy such as irreversibility and probability are vulnerable intellectually in their theoretical foundation.[84] Moreover, as Pynchon himself later acknowledged, the gloom he associated with entropy is not universally accepted among its theorists.[85] Indeed, the validity of the concept as a whole can be doubted and denied. The astronomer David Layzer has argued that, contrary to what generations of thinkers assumed, the continual creation of macroscopic systems prevents the universe from running down.[86]

Apart from the status of theory, its claim to impartiality and universality is problematic. Jeremy Campbell summarizes the fallacy of objective disarray basic to the concept of entropy:

---

[79] Mangel, p. 90.

[80] Ibid., p. 92f; Schaub, pp. 27ff. Jeremy Campbell writes: "Maxwell's demon can obtain perfect information about all the molecules in the whirling microcosm of his vessel of gas, but only because he is an ideal, mythical being. His chamber is immaculately sealed against all kinds of chance impacts and influences from the outside world. The demon inhabits a perfectly closed system, but no such system exists in the real world." Jeremy Campbell, *Grammatical Man: Information, Entropy, Language, and Life*, New York, 1982, p. 87. In the discussion of scientific thought, I heavily draw on Campbell's summary of developments in the field.

[81] Pynchon, p. 14.

[82] Campbell, p. 32.

[83] Barthes, pp. 144f.

[84] Campbell, pp. 32, 55.

[85] Pynchon, p. 14.

[86] Campbell, pp. 84-89.

> Part of the trouble arises because, while entropy refers to the physical state of a physical system, it is a measure of the disorderliness of that system, and disorder is not a wholly objective property. The human observer cannot be excluded completely, because the idea of order is inextricably linked to the mind's awareness. Muddle, to some extent, is in the brain of the beholder. One person's disorder may be another's order, depending on how much knowledge that person possesses about the details of the apparent confusion.[87]

Such qualms about scientific cognition relate to the general discussion of the epistemological basis of the natural sciences in Jürgen Habermas' *Knowledge and Human Interests*. Entropy, as used in thermodynamics and information theory and as applied in the novel, relies on the 'ideal decoder,' a descendant of the ahistorical and autonomous subject of Immanuel Kant, on which the natural sciences have by and large depended.[88] As Thomas H. Schaub has indicated, Norbert Wiener seems to assume that for sense organs, "there is little difference between man and machine, both receive and transmit messages, and both survive in their environment through this feedback process. . . ."[89] In Thomas Pynchon's "Entropy," the narrowed perspective, that is the concentration on the object of investigation or the message of the information channel rather than on the interests of participants in the process, is evident:

> Tell a girl: "I love you." No trouble with two-thirds of that, it's a closed circuit. Just you and she. But that nasty four-letter word in the middle, that's the one you have to look out for. Ambiguity. Redundance. Irrelevance, even. Leakage. All this is noise. Noise screws up your signal, makes for disorganization in the circuit.[90]

Though Pynchon at times satirizes such a grotesquely serious application of science, the scientific models he has chosen presuppose an autonomous encoder and decoder and fail to consider the materialist, psychoanalytical, or post-structuralist misgivings about such assumptions. Significantly, the sickness that may befall Oedipa Maas in *The Crying of Lot 49* is paranoia, a mental derangement which solipsistically centers in the individual.

Partiality, which inheres in any act of cognition, logically increases if the object of investigation is not taken from microscopic or macroscopic nature, but from the realm of culture and, in particular, if the observer investigates into the social organization of modern cities. Oedipa's view of a chaotic underground and her metaphysical imagery for dependency in contemporary society are decidedly interested projections. Oedipa too

---

[87]Ibid., pp. 32f.

[88]See especially the chapters on Kant, Hegel, and Marx. Habermas, pp. 5-63.

[89]Schaub, p. 28.

[90]Pynchon, "Entropy," pp. 90f.

faces the dilemma which slumming middle-class members generally have in the modern city: outsiders may discern chaos due to their ignorance of subcultural behavior; or they may posit metaphysical depravity where there are difference, contradiction, and change. It is a major weakness that the novel which focuses so much on perception, vision, and discovery (Georgiana Colvile counted 36 "eyes" in the novel[91]), marginalizes the issue of social constrictions in 'scientific' models. Because of Pynchon's "technical bent of mind,"[92] it is, however, no surprise that the question of alternatives to the manipulated Californian grid should be conveyed in images from information theory and computer science.

As Scott Sanders remarks, Pynchon opposes the degradations inherent in technology, but he also tends to mystify it in his fiction.[93] Indeed, the connection which the writer establishes between science, puritanism, and paranoia, renders his fiction apocalyptic.[94] Puritanism with its metaphysical conspiracy plot and the binary options of either being elect or preterite, has an affinity to modern, digital dichotomies and to the conspiracy syndrome of paranoids. For Sanders, paranoia is the last retreat for the Puritan imagination.[95] Mental illness serves as a psychological correlative to the mystification of technological irreversibility in a one-dimensional society:[96]

> If one accepts Herbert Marcuse's argument that we live in a society which is organized along increasingly rational lines to serve increasingly irrational ends, then one can see how the individual may suspect himself to be the victim of a vast and sinister plot. The citizen of advanced industrial society encounters a world which is intricately and obscurely organized, that operates from remote centers of power, that is governed by a technocratic elite of specialists who command esoteric knowledge, and who control him by devious means....[97]

By linking conditions in society to "God or a digital machine" (CL, p. 24), to superhuman technology or metaphysical evil, Pynchon removes the control in consumer capitalism from human involvement and renders conditions unalterable.

---

[91]Colvile, p. 22.

[92]Roger B. Henkle, "Pynchon's Tapestries on the Western Wall," *Pynchon. A Collection of Critical Essays*, ed. Edward Mendelson, Englewood Cliffs, 1978, p. 110.

[93]Scott Sanders, "Pynchon's Paranoid History," *Mindful Pleasures*, eds. George Levine and David Leverenz, Boston, 1976, p. 158.

[94]Claas, p. 78.

[95]Sanders, p. 140.

[96]For a discussion of Marcuse's "totalitarianism" in his study of the advance of the technological rationality and the romantic elements in his thought, see Jay, pp. 220-40.

[97]Sanders, p. 156.

The satiric mode in *The Crying of Lot 49* partly seems a response to his bleak analysis of the world and an expression of his "thermodynamical gloom." Its cynicism and grim humor are, in terms of Freud's analysis of jokes, the last resort of the overwhelmed victim to oppose the inevitable. Satire provides a mode for talking about frustration and impotence in the face of seemingly inescapable catastrophes.[98] In fact, Pynchon has related the apocalyptic atmosphere in his early fiction to the feeling of powerlessness in the face of advanced technology, especially of "The Bomb":

> Except for that succession of the criminally insane who have enjoyed power since 1945, including the power to do something about it, most of the rest of us poor sheep have always been stuck with simple, standard fear. I think we all have tried to deal with this slow escalation of our helplessness and terror in the few ways open to us, from not thinking about it to going crazy from it. Somewhere on this spectrum is writing fiction about it....[99]

Far from being solely a defensive mechanism, Dionysian laughter also destabilizes the grids of power and order. Thus the rigidity of technological-scientific metaphors is to some extent overcome by Pynchon through the innovative use of the "ever-subversive medium of fiction."[100] On the narrative level, Pynchon consciously undermines all systems of order be they social, scientific, or religious. The multiplicity of meaning in his tightly woven prose gainsays any uniform mode of interpretation. This disruption of closed systems also accounts for the literary strategy behind his choice of the model of detective fiction: hooking readers onto plots, he surprises their expectations by dissolving their control over the fictional world. In his own words, he opposes holistic systems with "moments of productive silence."[101] F. Scott Fitzgerald's definition of a first-rate mind seems to apply: Pynchon holds two opposed ideas without breaking apart.[102] Obsessed with grids of control and aspiring to totality through an encyclopaedic inclusiveness, *The Crying of Lot 49* refrains from closure and undermines the paralysis in deterministic systems. But like F. Scott Fitzgerald, who hid his contradictions and absences with "blankets of excellent prose,"[103] Thomas Pynchon cloaks his unsteady uni-

---

[98] Such Dionysian laughter is a widespread attitude among post-structuralists as Martin Jay remarks: "Manic explosions of laughter rather than the tortured anguish of an Adorno or Sartre are their response to the frustrations of utopian hopes." Jay, p. 512.

[99] Pynchon, pp. 18f.

[100] Pynchon, "The Heart's Eternal Vow," p. 47.

[101] Pynchon, "Introduction," pp. 22f.

[102] Fitzgerald, *The Crack-Up*, p. 69.

[103] Fitzgerald, *Letters*, p. 341.

verse of things with the "comfortable and pious metaphor"[104] of science and in this resembles the poet Fausto Majistral in *V.*

The Crying of Lot 49 resumes the search of early modernists by extending their predominantly static views of aesthetic order. The capacities of language and form replace and embody social responses. Pynchon's fiction achieves special autonomy as he denies the public a biographical, social, and religious context for his work.[105] All readers have is *The Crying of Lot 49* and the instability of its patterns. In it, Pynchon challenges and extends traditional concepts of order:

> His own fictional worlds ... are pluralistic--governed not by a rigid, absolute, and universal idea of Order but by multiple partial, overlapping, and often conflicting *ideas* of order. And these worlds are familiar, even when they are most bizarre and surreal, because they evoke a multilayered reality in which multiple means of putting things together manage to coexist without resolving into a single, definitive system of organization.[106]

The will to break the suburban closure in *The Crying of Lot 49* and its quasi-metaphysical degeneration, also rests on options, however faint, to be able to develop a new basis for society: "To say that no distinction exists would be to sacrifice the very rationale of this comic reportage. . . ."[107] In the Watts essay, the real subculture of blacks provided the contrast for judging the unreal American society. In the novel, in less obvious ways, Pynchon also refers beyond the instability of "words, words" (CL, p. 53). The search remains circular as the final words of the text repeat the title[108] and must be resumed beyond its class-based, suburban frame to subvert the closed system. If writing was a subversive act for Thomas Pynchon, and if reading the novel similarly is a subversive act as Annette Kolodny and Daniel Peters have asserted, the ambiguous ending also asks readers not to settle back passively to "await the Crying of Lot 49" (CL, p. 127), but to remember that Oedipa's quest may be meaningful in real life.[109] Though this conclusion may be speculative, it should be kept in mind that Pynchon himself was stimulated by reality, by alternatives that only political involvement provides.

---

[104]Thomas Pynchon, *V.*, 1963, London, 1975, p. 326.

[105]Schaub, p. 125.

[106]Hite, p. 10.

[107]Richard Poirier, "Embattled Underground," *New York Times Review of Books*, (May 1, 1966), p. 43; quoted in Seed, p. 149.

[108]Oedipa moves from one typical suburban event, the Tupperware party, to another one, the diversion in an auction room, in the end. Colvile, p. 91.

[109]Kolodny, p. 86.

As critics have pointed out, active love and empathy are among the unambiguous, positive values that can be culled from Pynchon's fiction.[110] Love appears in several of the nonsatiric passages in his novels and also surfaces as a powerful force in a recent essay.[111] His hope in political alternatives is evident in the distinct diction in the final Tristero passages:[112]

> If San Narciso and the estate were really no different from any other town, any other estate, then by that continuity she might have found the Tristero anywhere in her Republic, through any one of a hundred lightly concealed entranceways, a hundred alienations, if only she'd looked. She stopped a minute between the steel rails, raising her head as if to sniff the air. Becoming conscious of the hard, strung presence she stood on--knowing as if maps had been flashed for her on the sky how these tracks ran on into others, others, knowing they laced, deepened, authenticated the great night around her. If only she'd looked. . . . She thought of other, immobilized freight cars, where the kids sat on the floor planking and sang back, happy as fat, whatever came over the mother's pocket radio; of other squatters who stretched canvas for lean-tos behind smiling billboards along the highways, or slept in junkyards in the stripped shells of wrecked Plymouths, or even, daring, spent the night up some pole in a linesman's tent like caterpillars, swung among a web of telephone wires, living in the very copper rigging and secular miracle of communication, untroubled by the dumb voltages flickering their miles, the night long, in the thousands of unheard messages. (CL, p. 124)

Oedipa's search is an inchoate attempt to break the closed grid, but, like the commitment of the social workers in Watts, it also is marred by a failure to perceive and accept the distinct subcultures.[113] Molly Hite sees her metaphysical impulse as a major deficit: "Because she aims at complete transcendence, she keeps construing events as clues that will carry her forward, away from humanity, toward a supernatural level of being that subsumes humanity to its own inscrutable purposes."[114] Oedipa's recurrent wish to lapse into paranoia (CL, p. 126) clearly is counterproductive and, as Scott Sanders remarked, a "totalitarian's dream."[115] The successful breeding of fear and mistrust among citizens is the best way to foster acquiescence and to preclude political change.

The Crying of Lot 49 will not sanction any straight reading. The novel remains open, the search multiplies rather than settles questions. Yet readers also are reassured

---

[110]Slade, p. 80; Henkle, p. 105; Merrill, p. 69.

[111]Pynchon, "The Heart's Eternal Vow," p. 47.

[112]In a revision, Thomas Pynchon even toned down some of the excessive rhetoric. Seed, p. 149.

[113]Pynchon similarly declared for the sixties' movements that "The success of the 'new left' later in the '60's was to be limited by the failure of college kids and blue-collar workers to get together politically. One reason was the presence of real, invisible class force fields in the way of communication between the two groups." Pynchon, "Introduction," p. 7.

[114]Hite, p. 86f.

[115]Sanders, p. 158.

that there can be no unambiguous ambiguity or a nonfragmented fragmentation. Oedipa's options, the seemingly objective "matrices of a great digital computer" (CL, p. 125) must be extended by the silences in the text.[116] Moreover, the ontological instability of the world which postmodernism perceives, may after all only be the instability of those who perceive it. *The Crying of Lot 49* challenges all views about closure and ambiguity without excluding the possibility of change within the contemporary grid.

All in all, Thomas Pynchon undoubtedly reifies the relations in the sprawling cities as natural and mystifies the degree of technological control. But he also suggests the possibility of change. His hope, which is primarily an aesthetic one in *The Crying of Lot 49*, is for the materialization of that long-standing dream of an uninhibited plurality and nonrepressive freedom which is yet denied to the global villagers in the grid of the Western world.

---

[116]Molly Hite explains: "*The Crying of Lot 49* is thus not only the story of Oedipa's quest but the story of what Oedipa misses or discounts because she is on quest. The novel comprehends what she passes over as well as what she construes as evidence; it includes her exclusions." Hite, p. 80.

15

Conclusion

> Jesus! What a nut *he* was! I wondeh what eveh happened to 'im, anyway! I wondeh if someone knocked him on duh head, or if he's still wanderin' aroun' in duh subway in duh middle of duh night wit his little map! Duh poor guy! Say, I've got to laugh, at dat, when I t'ink about him! Maybe he's found out by now dat he'll neveh live long enough to know duh whole of Brooklyn. It'd take a guy a lifetime to know Brooklyn t'roo an' t'roo. An' even den, you wouldn't know it all.[1]

> The New Deal Carry-out shop is on a corner in downtown Washington, D.C. It would be within walking distance of the White House, the Smithsonian Institution, and other major public buildings of the nation's capital, if anyone cared to walk there, but no one ever does.[2]

> I remember in the early fifties when I moved into a Jewish slum on the Lower East Side of New York. The first day in my apartment, I went into a store on my block. After I had paid for my purchase, the man behind the counter said, 'You live in 740, don't you?' The community was self-enclosed; it knew everyone, and could figure out the street number of a stranger within twenty-four hours.[3]

The relationship between urban fiction, the segregated city, and modern society--as examined in this study--is a complex and complicated one. Clearly, the metropolitan setting in its vastness, fragmentation, and flux has been a crucial catalyst for a wide variety of experiences and for the diverse modes of modernist expression and fictional form. As clearly, the social and literary modes emerging in the modern city cannot be reduced to single causes and deterministic relationships. Consequently, the search for meaning in American city novels has not resulted in definitive *modern* or *urban* answers. This study has emphasized both the selectivity and partiality of each of the projected city images and uncovered the implicit denial of universality in the gaps, ruptures, and incongruities of each novel.

---

[1]Thomas Wolfe, "Only the Dead Know Brooklyn," *From Death to Morning*, 1935, New York, 1963, p. 97.

[2]Liebow, *Tally's Corner*, p. 17.

[3]Harrington, *The Other America*, p. 150.

Nevertheless, the discussions of American urban experience have also revealed stable patterns, recurring tensions and contradictions which have shaped the pluralism of forms and the partiality of responses in the twentieth-century city. As the study has indicated, economic priorities and related class interests have dictated the content, form, and pace of changes in the modern American metropolis. The city's expanse, verticality, dissociation, or heterogeneity have been related to specific historical processes and conditions. Throughout the modern period, a fundamental conflict has underlain the particulars of fragmentation and directed the unfulfilled yearnings for wholeness and community: whereas daily life in the city has become more and more dominated by capitalist processes which have outpaced the control by individual communities and municipalities, traditional cultural responses have proved increasingly inadequate to cope with the scope and weight of these changes. In an economic system which has precluded all-encompassing democratic decisions and the collective control of changes, the rights of individuals and groups in the American city have frequently been suspended, undermined, or annulled. Capitalist considerations and upper- and middle-class interests have generally decided the direction of changes. Subsequently, as political, cultural, and communal initiatives have become less and less relevant to the problems of work and life in the modern city, they have lost their social validity. Each city novel provides its unique assessment of this basic conflict between capitalist priorities and cultural deficits.

As Jürgen Habermas has argued, the most important step for the project of modernity is to reintegrate the separated spheres of life: the economic and cultural, the aesthetic and social, the rational and emotional, the mental and manual have to be recombined in a comprehensive democratic process.[4] Insisting on the necessity of such a reintegration, this study has indicated that such a synthesis cannot be anachronistically conceived of in terms of premodern concepts of totality, nor can it fall behind the poststructuralist challenge to holistic modern forms. Both socially and physically, the modern city signifies pluralism. The interpretation of the city novels has disclosed a great diversity of experience and an unprecedented need for differentiation which traditional concepts of urbanism, modernism, or orthodox materialism were not able to provide.

The investigation into conditions in the American city has also questioned the accuracy of certain urbanist explanations. The quotations at the beginning of this chapter emphasize the diversity of the modern American city. Thomas Wolfe evokes the overwhelming vastness and variety of the metropolis, Elliot Liebow the closure, difference, and proximity of its cultures, and Michael Harrington, finally, the supervision and cohe-

---

[4]Habermas, "Die Moderne: ein unvollendetes Projekt," pp. 457ff.

sion in some of its neighborhoods. Such a pluralism of forms and diversity of needs has frequently been levelled by traditional perspectives. Their city was anonymous, amoral, and destructive. Its wasteland was unreal. Yet, Nick Carraway's view of a New York valley of ashes from which workers have disappeared and which no longer provides nourishment like the original "fresh, green breast" (GG, p. 187) and the view of Ona Lukoszaite and Jurgis Rudkus from a similarly devastated cityscape, intending to transform the Chicago "dumping ground" (TJ, p. 33) through their labor, only resemble one another superficially:

> About half-way between West Egg and New York the motor road hastily joins the railroad and runs beside it for a quarter of a mile, so as to shrink away from a certain desolate area of land. This is a valley of ashes--a fantastic farm where ashes grow like wheat into ridges and hills and grotesque gardens; where ashes take the form of houses and chimneys and rising smoke and, finally, with a transcendent effort, of ash-grey men, who move dimly and already crumbling through the powdery air. Occasionally a line of grey cars crawls along an invisible track, gives out a ghastly creak, and comes to rest and immediately the ash-grey men swarm up with leaden spades and stir up an impenetrable cloud, which screens their obscure operations from your sight. (GG, p. 29)

> A little way further on, and Jurgis and Ona, staring open-eyed and wondering, came to the place where this "made" ground was in the process of making. Here was a great hole, perhaps two city blocks square, and with long files of garbage wagons creeping into it.... They stood there while the sun went down upon this scene, and the sky in the west turned blood red, and the tops of the houses shone like fire. Jurgis and Ona were not thinking of the sunset, however--their backs were turned to it, and all their thoughts were of Packingtown, which they could see so plainly in the distance. The line of the buildings stood clear-cut and black against the sky; here and there out of the mass rose the great chimneys, with the river of smoke streaming away to the end of the world.... To the two who stood watching while the darkness swallowed it up, it seemed a dream of wonder, with its tale of human energy, of things being done, of employment for thousands upon thousands of men, of opportunity and freedom, of life and love and joy. When they came away, arm in arm, Jurgis was saying, "Tomorrow I shall go there and get a job!" (TJ, p. 34)

The crucial distinctions in perspective and assessment become blurred if such images are homogenized as embodiments of the modern metropolitan wasteland. It is the differences in images that are important in the search for meaning in modernity.

Historical differentiations in reactions to metropolitan disruption also deserve careful attention. In the early stages of the modern city, the emerging urbanism and modernism, while certainly class-based in their formulations, were understandable responses to the massive upheavals under industrial capitalism. They were valid answers as the development of the modern city and of capitalist society converged. The fatal sedimentation occurred later when these specific reactions became reified to unchanging and unsurpassable verities about the state of modern cities.[5] As was pointed out on dif-

---

[5]Howe, "The City in Literature," pp. 55ff.

ferent occasions in this study, traditional sociological and literary theories cemented such notions of the urbanist and modernist city.

Since city and society seemed to converge in the beginning of the century, the fictional city was often used to embody general directions in modernity and to express visions of a future state of affairs. For Theodore Dreiser, the consumer city in *Sister Carrie* stands for a natural evolution toward progress, heterogeneity, and individualism. For Upton Sinclair, the city in *The Jungle* represents the certainty of a Socialist revolution and the collective liberation of the working class. To F. Scott Fitzgerald, the New York of *The Great Gatsby* captures the modern contrariness that he envisions in his dialectical aesthetic program. For John Dos Passos, finally, the metropolis in *Manhattan Transfer* is the congenial subject to capture the contingency of a modern cubist totality.

The city images of the novels are, however, not restricted to represent future trends of modernity. Many city novels start from the awareness of fundamental divisions in the metropolis. In them, the city signifies varied and contradictory tendencies. Not uniformity or exemplariness, but fragmentation and multiplicity appear as the most characteristic facts of modernity. Stephen Crane was the first to highlight the segregation of the modern American metropolis in the duality of Bowery and Uptown and express his misgivings about unequivocal visions in modernity. Richard Wright, too, saw the split between a black and white Chicago as the most characteristic feature. Hubert Selby recorded fragmentation and degeneracy in an enclosed working-class slum indicating the distinct forms of powerlessness among social outcasts. Thomas Pynchon, finally, projected the underground organizations of the Tristero as counterforces to the Californian grid and hoped to disrupt its entropic homogeneity.

If a tendency toward fragmentation and multiplicity can be gleaned from the diversity of portraits in the twentieth century, the distinction developed above does not hold an explanatory model for modern city fiction. Most novels can be classified both ways. The use of city images as metaphoric anticipations of future trends cannot be restricted to the early stages of the modern city.[6] There also is no one-directional development from modernist to postmodernist forms that might be causally linked to an increasing fragmentation and heterogeneity in the modern American city.[7] The history of the modern city contains different answers for different groups.

---

[6]While *The Crying of Lot 49* stresses the fragmentation in the real and unreal cultures of the city, it also projects the urban grid as historically representative for American consumer society.

[7]Such a tendency toward dispersal and dissolution has been suggested by Burton Pike and Ihab Hassan. Pike, *The Image of the City in Modern Literature*, pp. 129-136; Hassan, "Cities of Mind, Urban Words: The Dematerialization of Metropolis in Contemporary American Fiction," pp. 93-112. See also Ihab Hassan, *Paracriticism: Seven Speculations of the Times*, Urbana, Ill., 1975.

In all novels, the city images are the products of partial assessments and interests. Thus, Theodore Dreiser marginalizes those diverse collective responses that do not go along with middle-class individualism. Upton Sinclair denies ethnic variety and cohesion among his Americanized stockyard workers. John Dos Passos cannot discern communal bonds in his montage of multiple Manhattan fragments. Similarly, novels which stress disparity in cities also tend to marginalize incompatible strands in their analysis. Stephen Crane does not detect order and familiarity in his working-class neighborhood as they disprove his findings of a generic chaos. Likewise, Richard Wright denies the validity of ethnic bonds and black solidarity since he experienced an acquiescent Southern community as inhibiting. Hubert Selby, finally, who concentrates on the loss of control of working-class slum dwellers, marginalizes conditions at work. Each city novel presents important facets of modern experience, but each excludes complementary and contradictory elements at one and the same time. While authentic, each city image cannot claim to be universally representative of *the* modern city.

Both the diversity in experience and the social bias in the assessment of conditions reappear in the aesthetic transformation of the city novels. Ideological perspective and fictional form are strongly interrelated in American city images. The fundamental division in modern experience has taken a special form here: as communal and political responses became invalidated in the metropolis by the power of material change, the basis for assessing developments and problems has become increasingly disconnected from actual groups in the city. Judgment, agency, and value are frequently expressed by the formal elements of the novels. Linguistic and aesthetic categories achieve an unprecedented importance.[8] Raymond Williams has stressed the social and psychological implications of this specialization and separation. He explains the initial link between the early modern city and the inchoate forms of modernism:

> The most important general element of the innovations in form is the fact of immigration to the metropolis, and it cannot too often be emphasised how many of the major innovators were, in this precise sense, immigrants. At the level of theme, this underlies, in an obvious way, the elements of strangeness and distance, indeed of alienation, which so regularly form part of the repertory. But the decisive aesthetic effect is at a deeper level. Liberated or breaking from their national or provincial cultures, placed in quite new relations to those other native languages or native visual traditions, encountering meanwhile a novel and dynamic common environment from which many of the older forms were obviously distant, the artists and writers and thinkers of this phase found their only community available to them: a community of the medium; of their own practices.[9]

---

[8] Bradbury, "The Cities of Modernism," pp. 100f.
[9] Williams, "The Metropolis and the Emergence of Modernism," p. 21.

Indeed, in the modern city novels, the concern for craft and form achieves paramount significance. A specialized aesthetic questioning partly replaces the more direct moral, social, and political forms of involvement of previous periods. In each novel, what matters is the degree of separation in economic and political concerns of author and group. Thus the proletarian and upper-class ideals of Upton Sinclair and F. Scott Fitzgerald allow their works to remain conventional in form since they still relate their judgment to the social worlds depicted: the overwhelming change in the modern city is to be mastered by literary as well as by social values.[10] In other city novels, however, there are no explicit social groups or political ideals to guide the judgment of conditions in the modern metropolis. Consequently, the modernist assessments by Hubert Selby and Thomas Pynchon refer primarily to values in the avantgarde community. The validity of Selby's picture is related to William Carlos Williams' poetry, Beat poetics, and abstract expressionist painting. Similarly, Thomas Pynchon, a student of writing courses by Vladimir Nabokov, primarily relates to the tradition of modernist fiction.

As this study has indicated, an assessment only on the grounds of the literary achievements tends to hide the social and cultural forces which triggered and directed the modernist impulses in the first place. While autonomous to some degree, each modernist city image depends on, and reacts to, wider economic and political developments. The relation between aesthetic program and social values is often not a smooth one: literary innovation and philosophical context clash and leave incongruities and gaps in the city image.

Upton Sinclair, for instance, hopes for the rejuvenation of the industrial city through a revolutionary change in ownership and hence considers the criticism of aesthetic and literary modes of expression as secondary. His radical analysis of conditions is conveyed in most conventional terms. Similarly, the experience Theodore Dreiser records in *Sister Carrie* clearly has become incompatible with the attitudes he superimposes in his philosophical explanations. Hubert Selby, finally, reverts to outmoded forms of Christian submissiveness and Puritan inner-direction as solutions to the loss of control in consumer society. These novels reveal the insufficient fusion of literary strategy and political ideologies in the ruptures in the style, atmosphere, and form of the fictional city image.

Aesthetic mode and fictional form often substitute and displace the explicit social impulse in the modern city novel. Modernist aesthetics attempt to withstand, control, or

---

[10] Nevertheless, in both cases the political program is revealed as desideratum rather than as a potential option or lived reality. Intending to incite emancipation and action, Sinclair ends by preaching socialism, while Fitzgerald finds that he has to blanket the absence of gentlemanly behavior in his lyrical prose.

challenge the deficiencies of the modern metropolis. Not particular movements, forces, or ideals, but the literary form provides the political and social agency that the urban experience of the fictional characters is lacking. In Dos Passos' montage of fragmented spaces, both the dissolving and decentering of the metropolitan environment restores the impulse toward change and emancipation that is absent in the Manhattan episodes themselves. Likewise, F. Scott Fitzgerald who does not point out a political force among the social classes to change the degenerate city, develops a negation of conditions through the dialectical aesthetics of *The Great Gatsby*. For Richard Wright, in his political novel, the act of writing paradoxically becomes the most appropriate mode to fuse black resistance and white radicalism. In *The Crying of Lot 49*, the disruption of linguistic stability and fictional patterns is primarily meant to destabilize a completely manipulated society in which Pynchon does not verify the existence of any opposition movement.

In some novels, literary or aesthetic values constitute the sole frame for orientation. Modern art alone, not any social or political option, is to withstand deprivation in the modern city. For Stephen Crane, the duality of the Bowery and Uptown indicates a fundamental urban disparity and chaos from which the writer distances himself with the help of irony. For Hubert Selby, the brutality of the city is primarily mastered by transforming it into a musical, emotional reality. This position has conservative implications: it denies that existing conditions could be changed.

Regardless of the artistic intention in each of the novels, this study has shown modernist expressions as reactions to social processes and specific historical experiences in the American city. When examined carefully, the emptiness, negativity, or contradiction of the modernisms could be related to particular social and political issues and conflicts. Each novel reveals a specific incongruity. Thus Stephen Crane attempts to master the chaos of the modern city in ironic detachment, while the naturalist record exactly reveals his distanced perception as deficient and as a possible source of the urban chaos itself. Contrary to Theodore Dreiser's positivist program of rendering a scientific totality in *Sister Carrie*, Carrie Meeber's yearning, at the climax of the novel, cannot be spelled out in rational terms.[11] The lyrical prose in *The Great Gatsby*, intended as an expression of superior values, only blankets and romanticizes nonexistent social behavior. Richard Wright's complex simplicity of style, in the service of political enlightenment, turns out as a hurling of words into darkness. Mystifying the process of communication

---

[11]Blanche Gelfant recently concluded: "Theodore Dreiser's *Sister Carrie* is a mystery still. She hungers, as we know, but not for man's love, and not for anything we can clearly define. She dreams and desires, epitomizing finally an indeterminate and ineffable desire which can never be fulfilled." Blanche Gelfant, "The City's 'Hungry' Woman as Heroine," p. 269.

and understanding, Hubert Selby imagines that readers experience his musical prose directly without reading the words. Only when placed in the context of specific historical and social conditions in the American city do the modernist elements acquire a more precise meaning.

In the twentieth century, the modernist discourse has tended to reify purely aesthetic categories. To varying degrees, the academic methods of formalism, structuralism, and deconstructionism have contended the supersession and replacement of explicitly social and political concerns by aesthetic, linguistic, and formal ones.[12] Such approaches often link the modern city and the modern novel in a quasi-causal interdependence: using a circular explanation, the modernist history of city fiction is verified by an urbanist history of the metropolis. The categories of fragmentation and montage, of segregation and dissociation, of heterogeneity and collage reciprocally testify to a universal validity, without acknowledging their basis in very partial assessments of modern society. Fragmented and aporetic modernisms are often set in analogy to a heterogeneous and opaque metropolis. In many respects, postmodern art and deconstruction theory perpetuate this bias of modernism. Postmodernism in its playful, subversive use of preceding modernist trends and the dissolution of the human subject become related to the alleged dissolution and disappearance of the city in the post-industrial megalopolis.[13]

Urbanism and modernism have subsumed or excluded a variety of valid forms of social and artistic expression by universalizing and reifying specific conditions of the early modern city. Contrary to this tradition, the interpretations in the present study stress the wide pluralism of experience. Each mode of living and urban perspective creates its cultural and artistic answer: any modernist form may only claim to be one among many. There is no reason why a community based on aesthetic traditions and modernist innovations should be superior to a community based on ethnic folklore or on social and political values. Indeed, Upton Sinclair's conventional tale of the industrial cityscape is as modern, radical, and biased as John Dos Passos' cubist metropolis.

The great achievement of modernist fiction has been to generate a wide variety of literary expressions to capture and convey the fundamental contingency and insecurity in modernity. The end of literature or art, however, which has often been predicted on account of the narrowed territory for purely aesthetic innovation, only signifies the dead

---

[12]Williams, pp. 13f., 21f; see also chapter 5.

[13]William Sharpe and Leonard Wallock link the lacking center of the postindustrial city, that is the dissolving urbanist city, to the lacking center in Derrida's post-structuralist theory. Sharpe and Wallock, "From 'Great Town' to 'Nonplace Urban Realm': Reading the Modern City," p. 22.

end of the specialized aesthetic response to problems in modernity.[14] Clearly, modernism is not a history of simplification or decadence as has often been implied by orthodox Marxist or conservative critics. Samuel Beckett's dramatic silences or Mark Rothko's color meditations cannot be surpassed in their reduction, purity, and concentrated power of expression. They are the apex of a particular process that began in the early modern cities of Western civilization.

The modernist specialization, however, has generated another division which has been thoroughly counterproductive. On the one hand, there are the purely academic modernisms, restricted to small literary circles, avantgarde venues, and museums which have become dissociated from the vast majority of people and their experience. On the other hand, there are popular modernist forms in film, television, music, design, and fashion which are denigrated as mass entertainment.[15] However, this dichotomy of elitist modernism and depraved mass culture only duplicates and cements yet another division of modernity. These different spheres also need to be reintegrated. Most of the popularized modernisms today are used affirmatively to serve consumer stimulation and commodity fetishism in advertisements, music videos, and promotional films.

The reintegration of specialized spheres to truly modern and democratic forms of difference and equality still is the paramount goal for the uncompleted project of modernity. The critical analysis of modern city novels may help to see this more clearly. As Marshall Berman has pointed out, "the modernisms of the past can give us back a sense of our modern roots, roots that go back two hundred years."[16] The need to reassess divisions and to reintegrate separated spheres is also evident for the country and city, another dichotomy that has accompanied much of modern history. The American city novels examined in this study cannot be said to espouse antiurban sentiments, although they certainly criticize conditions in cities. The ambivalent attitude toward the urban environment is related to wider issues and ideological interests: each account transcends the narrow limits of a purely environmental division.

In sum, the examination of modern American city fiction has yielded two main results. First, it has found a pluralism in urban experience and modernist expression questioning older views which suggested a more uniform development in the modern city and the modern novel. Second, it has also indicated how thoroughly cultural expressions were affected by material pressures exerted by a capitalist economy. Hence, there

---

[14]Pike, pp. 130ff.

[15]Williams, pp. 14, 22f.

[16]Berman, p. 35.

can be no purely literary conclusion to this investigation of modern city fiction. The path to truly pluralistic forms of life in modernity can only mean that the undemocratic concentration of economic power in the hands of a few individuals and corporations must be challenged. If a minority decides over the technological direction of society and determines the conditions of production, the shape and quality of urban housing, and the forms of culture, a democratic pluralism cannot be said to have been achieved. On a similar note, Sam Bass Warner concluded his history of the American city: "As things now stand neither the consumer nor the employee has any real control over the work of the city and hence no control over the essence of his culture and his daily environment."[17] Yet the examination of novelistic responses also suggests that there is no one single way of achieving equality and variety: hierarchical, homogeneous models for the reintegration of separated spheres must be challenged--regardless of whether these are based in nineteenth-century positivism, idealism, or materialism.

The demands of openness and pluralism also apply to this study. It cannot and, in fact, does not pretend to be exhaustive or conclusive as to the trends it has described. Though stressing the paramount importance of democratic control over conditions in cities, this study does not claim to provide an apodictically correct path to accomplish this goal. Furthermore, the relation between social experience in the city and the aesthetic mode of transformation is certainly fundamental, but this focus has led to the neglect of other important facets of the city and modernity. The psychological, sensual, and sexual dimensions to urban space and experience deserve closer scrutiny.[18] Similarly, due to the scarcity of detailed information and the limitations of a single study, the urban perspectives of women, American Indians, Jews, Hispanics, and other ethnic groups were neglected or not treated adequately. Especially the female experience in the city has only recently acquired the detailed attention it deserves. Nevertheless, it is a hoped-for consequence of the present study that future examinations in this field will not simply assume the existence of a monolithic, homogeneous, and generic city.

The search for meaning in modernity will continue to take place in urban environments. Voices that proclaim the disappearance of the city only disclose their narrow conception of the topic.[19] Clearly, on the surface, urban modes of life in the Ameri-

---

[17] Warner, p. 274.

[18] Sydney Janet Kaplan, for instance, shows Katherine Mansfield's awareness of the modern city's "potential as a catalyst for sexual release." Kaplan, p. 170.

[19] Urban sprawl in the late twentieth century creates difficulties in terminology for those theorists and critics who see the city primarily as a determining entity. The diffusion in space has complicated their environmentalist explanation. The post-industrial city thus is approached with contradictory coinages and concepts. Melvin M. Webber, for instance, sees the city as a "nonplace urban realm," John D. Kasarda as a "polycen-

can city have dramatically changed in the post-war decades. On a deeper, pictorial level, however, the relationship between city and society displays an essential continuity. Both the first Egyptian ideogram for the city and the latest grid imagery of the American megalopolis are congenially connected. The cross in the circle and the cross in the square signify the essential interdependence between city and society. They indicate the existence of a locally circumscribed entity, and they stress the link to wider structures beyond the immediate environs. At the close of the twentieth century, this encompassing framework for cities and modernity must be understood as the interrelated structures on the globe and its entirety of resources, cultures, and people.

---

tric ecological field," Burton Pike as a "nowhere city," or Robert Fishman as a "technoburb." For a discussion of this dilemma in traditional urban theory see Sharpe and Wallock, pp. 7-46. Webber and Kasarda cited in Sharpe and Wallock, p. 33; Pike, p. 117; Fishman, *Bourgeois Utopia*, p. 182.

Selected Bibliography

Urban Literature and Urban Studies

Urban Literature

Baldwin, James. *Go Tell It on the Mountain*. New York, 1953.
Barthelme, Donald. *City Life*. New York, 1970.
Bellow, Saul. *The Victim*. New York, 1947.
Cahan, Abraham. *Yekl: A Tale of the New York Ghetto*. New York, 1886.
Calvino, Italo. *Invisible Cities*. Trans. William Weaver, New York, 1972.
Cather, Willa. *The Song of the Lark*. Boston, 1915.
Cendrars, Blaise. *Pâques à New York*. Paris, 1912.
Crane, Stephen. *Maggie: A Girl of the Streets*. New York, 1893.
Crane, Stephen. *The New York City Sketches of Stephen Crane*. Eds. Robert W. Stallmann and E. R. Hagemann, New York, 1966.
Dos Passos, John. *Manhattan Transfer*. Boston, 1925.
Dos Passos, John. *U.S.A.* New York, 1938.
Dreiser, Theodore. *Sister Carrie*. New York, 1900.
Dreiser, Theodore. *Sister Carrie*. Eds. John C. Berkey, James L. West III, Neda M. Westlake, and Alice M. Winters. Philadelphia, 1981.
Dreiser, Theodore. *An American Tragedy*. New York, 1925.
Eliot, Thomas Stearns. *The Waste Land*. London, 1922.
Farrell, James T. *Studs Lonigan*. New York, 1935.
Fitzgerald, F. Scott. *The Great Gatsby*. New York, 1925.
Ginsberg, Allen. *Howl and Other Poems*. San Francisco, 1956.
Howells, William Dean. *A Hazard of New Fortunes*. New York, 1890.
Joyce, James. *Ulysses*. 1922, New York, 1934.
Percy, Walker. *The Moviegoer*. New York, 1960.
Pynchon, Thomas. *V.* New York, 1963.
Pynchon, Thomas. *The Crying of Lot 49*. New York, 1966.
Roth, Henry. *Call it Sleep*. New York, 1934.
Salinger, Jerome D. *The Catcher in the Rye*. New York, 1945.
Selby, Hubert. *Last Exit to Brooklyn*. New York, 1964.
Sinclair, Upton. *The Jungle*. New York, 1906.
Sinclair, Upton. *The Jungle*. Ed. Gene DeGruson, Memphis, Tenn., 1988.
West, Nathanael. *The Day of the Locust*. New York, 1939.

Whitman, Walt. *Leaves of Grass*. New York, 1891.
Wolfe, Thomas. *You Can't Go Home Again*. New York, 1934.
Wolfe, Thomas. *From Death to Morning*. New York, 1935.
Wright, Richard. *Native Son*. New York, 1940.
Wright, Richard. *Lawd Today*. New York, 1963.
Yezierska, Anzia. *Bread Givers*. New York, 1925.

Criticism of Urban Literature

Aaron, Daniel. "The Unholy City: A Sketch." *American Letters and Historical Consciousness*. Eds. J. Gerald Kennedy and Daniel M. Fogel, Baton Rouge, 1987, 177-190.

Arden, Eugene. "The Evil City in American Fiction." *New York History*. 35 (1954), 259-79.

Arden, Eugene. "The New York Novel: A Study in Urban Fiction." Diss. The Ohio State University, 1953.

Bolt, Christine. "The American City: Nightmare, Dream, or Irreducible Paradox?" *The American City: Literary and Cultural Perspectives*. Ed. Graham Clarke, New York, 1988, 13-35.

Bradbury, Malcolm. "The Cities of Modernism." *Modernism, 1890-1930*. Eds. Malcolm Bradbury and James Mc Farlane. Harmondsworth, 1976, 96-104.

Bradbury, Malcolm, and James Mc Farlane, eds. *Modernism, 1890-1930*. Harmondsworth, 1976.

Bremer, Sidney H. "American Dreams and American Cities in Three Post-World War I Novels." *South Atlantic Quarterly*. 79 (1978), 274-85.

Bremer, Sidney H. "Lost Continuities: Alternative Urban Visions in Chicago Novels, 1890-1915." *Soundings*. 64 (1981), 29-51.

Bremer, Sidney H. "Willa Cather's Lost Sisters," *Women Writers and the City: Essays in Feminist Literary Criticism*. Ed. Susan Merrill Squier. Knoxville, 1984, 210-29.

Clarke, Graham, ed. *The American City: Literary and Cultural Perspectives*. New York, 1988.

Clarke, Graham. "A 'Sublime and Atrocious' Spectacle: New York and the Iconography of Manhattan Island." *The American City: Literary and Cultural Perspectives*. New York, 1988, 36-61.

Conrad, Peter. *The Art of the City: Views and Versions of New York*. New York, 1984.

Cowan, Michael. *City of the West: Emerson, America, and Urban Metaphor*. New Haven, 1967.

Cowan, Michael. "Walkers in the Street: American Writers and the Modern City." *Prospects*. 6 (1981), 281-311.

Crider, Gregory L. "William Dean Howells and the Antiurban Tradition: A Reconsideration." *American Studies*. 19 (1978), 55-64.

Dickstein, Felice Witzum. "The Role of the City in the Works of Theodore Dreiser, Thomas Wolfe, James T. Farrell, and Saul Bellow." Diss. The City University of New York, 1973.

Dunlap, George A. *The City in the American Novel 1789-1900: A Study of American Novels Portraying Contemporary Conditions in New York, Philadelphia, and Boston.* 1934, New York, 1965.

Festa-McCormick, Diana. *The City as Catalyst: A Study in Ten Novels.* Rutherford, 1979.

Fiedler, Leslie. "Mythicizing the City." *Literature and the Urban Experience.* Eds. Michael C. Jaye and Ann Chalmers Watts. New Brunswick, N.J., 1981, 113-21.

Fine, David M., ed. *Los Angeles in Fiction: A Collection of Original Essays.* Albuquerque, 1984.

Fine, David M. *The City, the Immigrant, and American Fiction, 1880-1920.* Metuchen, N.J., 1977.

Fisher, Philip. "City Matters: City Minds." *The Worlds of Victorian Fiction.* Ed. Jerome H. Buckley, Cambridge, Mass., 1975, 371-389.

Gelfant, Blanche Housman. *The American City Novel.* Norman, Oklahoma, 1954.

Gelfant, Blanche Housman. "Residence Underground: Recent Fictions of the Subterranean City." *Sewanee Review.* 83 (1975), 406-38.

Gelfant, Blanche Housman. "Sister to Faust: The City's 'Hungry' Woman as Heroine." *Women Writers and the City: Essays in Feminist Literary Criticism.* Ed. Susan Merrill Squier. Knoxville, 1984, 265-87.

Göbel, Walter. "Schreckbild Stadt: Chicago im naturalistischen Roman." *Zeitschrift für Literaturwissenschaft und Linguistik.* 12 (1982), 88-102.

Gullason, Thomas A. "The Prophetic City in Stephen Crane's 1893 Maggie." *Modern Fiction Studies.* 24 (1978), 129-37.

Haas, Rudolf. "Großstadtmotive im Spiegel moderner amerikanischer Prosa." *Die neueren Sprachen.* 6 (1957), 497-510.

Hanley, Richard Eugene. "Place to Place: A Study of the Movement Between the City and Country in Selected Twentieth-Century American Fiction." Diss. State University of New York at Binghampton, 1981.

Hapke, Laura. "Down There on a Visit: Late Nineteenth-Century Guidebooks on the City." *Journal of Popular Culture.* 20 (1986), 41-56.

Hassan, Ihab. "Cities of Mind, Urban Words: The Dematerialization of Metropolis in Contemporary American Fiction." *Literature and the Urban Experience.* Eds. Michael C. Jaye and Ann Chalmers Watts. New Brunswick, N.J., 1981, 93-112.

Högel, Rolf. "Chicago, 1880-1900: Seine Darstellung in Theodore Dreisers Roman *Sister Carrie*." *Der Fremdsprachliche Unterricht.* 15 (1981), 17-25.

Hoffmann, Gerhard. *Raum, Situation, erzählte Wirklichkeit: Poetologische und historische Studien zum englischen und amerikanischen Roman.* Stuttgart, 1978.

Homberger, Eric. "Chicago and New York: Two Versions of American Modernism." *Modernism, 1890-1930.* Eds. Malcolm Bradbury and James Mc Farlane. Harmondsworth, 1976, 151-161.

Howe, Irving. "The City in Literature." *The Critical Point.* New York, 1973, 39-58.

Hussey, Barbara Lee. "The Disappearance of the City in the Modern Novel: From Spatiality to Textuality." Diss. Purdue University, 1980.

Ickstadt, Heinz. "Gesichter Babylons: Zum Bild der Großstadt im modernen amerikanischen Roman." *Jahrbuch für Amerikastudien.* 16 (1971), 60-76.

Ickstadt, Heinz. "Öffentliche Fiktion und bürgerliches Leben--der amerikanische Roman der Jahrhundertwende als kommunikatives System." *Amerikastudien--Theorie, Geschichte, interpretatorische Praxis*. Eds. Martin Christadler and Günter Lenz. Stuttgart, 1977, 223-47.

Ickstadt, Heinz. "Exploring the Abyss: Die Entdeckung des Sozialen Untergrunds in der Amerikanischen Fiktion des Späten Neunzehnten Jahrhunderts." *Amerikanische Ghettoliteratur: Zur Literatur ethnischer, marginaler und unterdrückter Gruppen in Amerika*. Ed. Berndt Ostendorf, Darmstadt, 1983, 27-49.

Ickstadt, Heinz. "Black vs. White City: Kultur und ihre soziale Funktion im Chicago der Progressive Period." *Amerikastudien*. 29 (1984), 199-214.

Ickstadt, Heinz. "New York und der Stadtroman der Amerikanischen Moderne." *Medium Metropole: Berlin, Paris, New York*. Eds. Friedrich Knilli und Michael Nerlich. Heidelberg, 1986, 111-124.

Ickstadt, Heinz. "Kommunikationsmüll und Sprachcollage: Die Stadt in der Fiktion der amerikanischen Fiktion der Postmoderne." *Die Unwirklichkeit der Städte*. Ed. Klaus R. Scherpe, 197-224.

Isernhagen, Hartwig. "Die Bewußtseinskrise der Moderne und die Erfahrung der Stadt als Labyrinth." *Die Stadt in der Literatur*. Eds. Cord Meckseper and Elisabeth Schraut, Göttingen, 1983, 81-104.

Jähner, Harald. "Tour in die Moderne: Die Rolle der Kultur für städtische Imagewerbung und Städtetourismus." *Die Unwirklichkeit der Städte*. Ed. Klaus R. Scherpe, Hamburg, 1988, 225-242.

Jaye, Michael C., and Ann Chalmers Watts, eds. *Literature and the Urban Experience*. New Brunswick, N.J., 1981.

Kaplan, Amy Beth. "Realism Against Itself: The Urban Fiction of Twain, Howells, Dreiser, and Dos Passos." Diss. Johns Hopkins University, 1982.

Klotz, Volker. *Die erzählte Stadt: eine Herausforderung des Romans von Lesage bis Döblin*. München, 1969.

Knilli, Friedrich, and Michael Nerlich, eds. *Medium Metropole: Berlin, Paris, New York*. Heidelberg, 1986.

Kreutzer, Eberhard. *New York in der zeitgenössischen amerikanischen Erzählliteratur*. Heidelberg, 1985.

Lees, Andrew. *Cities Perceived: Urban Society in European and American Thought, 1820-1940*. London, 1985.

Levy, Diane Wolfe. "City Signs: Towards a definition of Urban literature." *Modern Fiction Studies*. 24 (1978), 65-74.

Lloyd, W. J. "Landscape Imagery in the Urban Novel: A Source of Geographic Evidence." *Environmental Knowing*. Eds. Gary T. Moore and Reginald G. Golledge. Stroudsburg, Pennsylvania, 1976, 279-85.

Machor, James L. *Pastoral Cities: Urban Ideals and the Symbolic Landscape of America*. Madison, 1987.

Marx, Leo. *The Machine in the Garden: Technology and the Pastoral Ideal*. New York, 1964.

Marx, Leo. "Pastoral Ideals and City Troubles." *Journal of General Education*. 20 (1969), 251-71.

Marx, Leo. "The Puzzle of Anti-Urbanism in Classic American Literature." *Literature and the Urban Experience*. Eds. Michael C. Jaye and Ann Chalmers Watts. New Brunswick, N.J., 1981, 63-80.

McDermott, John J. "Nature, Nostalgia, and the City: An American Dilemma." *Soundings*. 55 (1972), 1-20.

Modern Fiction Studies. "The Modern Novel and the City." 24 (1978).

Morrison, Toni. "City Limits, Village Values: Concepts of the Neighborhood in Black Fiction." *Literature and the Urban Experience*. Eds. Michael C. Jaye and Ann Chalmers Watts. New Brunswick, N.J., 1981, 35-43.

Oates, Joyce Carol. "Imaginary Cities: America." *Literature and the Urban Experience*. Eds. Michael C. Jaye and Ann Chalmers Watts. New Brunswick, N.J., 1981, 11-33.

Ostendorf, Berndt, ed. *Amerikanische Ghettoliteratur: zur Literatur ethnischer, marginaler und unterdrückter Gruppen in Amerika*. Darmstadt, 1983.

Pike, Burton. *The Image of the City in Modern Literature*. Princeton, 1981.

Plett, Heinrich F., and Renate Plett. "New York. Variationen über das Thema Metropolis im amerikanischen Drama der zwanziger Jahre." *Zeitschrift für Literaturwissenschaft und Linguistik*. 12 (1982), 103-33.

Raleigh, John Henry. "The Novel and the City: England and America in the Nineteenth Century." *Victorian Studies*. 11 (1968), 291-328.

Rankin, David L. "Urban and Rural Syntax: An Analysis based on American Fiction from 1920-62." Diss. Renselaer Polytechnic Institute, 1973.

Rose, Alan H. "Sin and the City: The Uses of Disorder in the Urban Novel." *Centennial Review*. 16 (1972), 203-20.

Scherpe, Klaus R., ed. *Die Unwirklichkeit der Städte. Großstadtdarstellungen zwischen Moderne und Postmoderne*. Hamburg, 1988.

Scherpe, Kaus R. "Nonstop nach Nowhere City? Wandlungen der Symbolisierung, Wahrnehmung und Semiotik der Stadt in der Literatur der Moderne." *Die Unwirklichkeit der Städte. Großstadtdarstellungen zwischen Moderne und Postmoderne*. Hamburg, 1988, 129-152.

Schmidt-von Bardeleben, Renate. *Das Bild New Yorks im Erzählwerk von Dreiser und Dos Passos*. München, 1967.

Sharpe, William, and Leonard Wallock. "From 'Great Town' to 'Nonplace Urban Realm': Reading the Modern City." *Visions of the Modern City: Essays in History, Art, and Literature*. Eds. William Sharpe and Leonard Wallock. 1984, Baltimore, 1987, 7-46.

Sharpe, William, and Leonard Wallock, eds. *Visions of the Modern City: Essays in History, Art, and Literature*. 1984, Baltimore, 1987.

Siegel, Adrienne. "When Cities were Fun: The Image of the American City in Popular Books, 1840-1870." *Journal of Popular Culture*. 9 (1975), 573-82.

Sizemore, Christine W. "Reading the City as palimpsest: The Experiential Perception of the City in Doris Lessing's *The Four-Gated City*." *Women Writers and the City: Essays in Feminist Literary Criticism*. Ed. Susan Merrill Squier. Knoxville, 1984, 176-190.

Smith, Carl S. *Chicago and the Literary Imagination, 1880-1920*. London, 1984.

Spears, Monroe K. *Dionysus and the City: Modernism in Twentieth-Century Poetry*. New York, 1970.

Squier, Susan Merrill, ed. *Women Writers and the City: Essays in Feminist Literary Criticism*. Knoxville, 1984.

Stout, Janis P. *Sodoms in Eden: The City in American Fiction before 1860*. Westport, Conn., 1976.

Timms, Edward, and David Kelley, eds. *Unreal City: Urban Experience in Modern European Literature and Art*. Manchester, 1985.

Titche, Leon L., Jr. "Döblin and Dos Passos: Aspects of the City Novel." *Modern Fiction Studies*. 17 (1971), 125-35.

Trachtenberg, Alan. "The American Scene: Versions of the City." *Massachusetts Review*. 8 (1967), 281-95.

Trachtenberg, Alan, Peter Neill and Peter C. Bunnell, eds. *The City: American Experience*. New York, 1971.

Walker, Robert H. "The Poet and the Rise of the City." *American Urban History*. Ed. Alexander Callow, New York, 1969, 363-73.

Weimer, David R. *The City as Metaphor*. New York, 1966.

White, Morton, and Lucia White. *The Intellectual Versus the City: From Thomas Jefferson to Frank Lloyd Wright*. Cambridge, Mass., 1962.

Williams, Raymond. *The Country and the City*. New York, 1973.

Williams, Raymond. "The Metropolis and the Emergence of Modernism." *Unreal City: Urban Experience in Modern European Literature and Art*. Eds. Edward Timms and David Kelley. Manchester, 1985, 13-24.

Wirth-Nesher, Hana. "The modern Jewish Novel and the City: Franz Kafka, Henry Roth, and Amos Oz." *Modern Fiction Studies*. 25 (1978), 91-101.

Zeitschrift für Literaturwissenschaft und Linguistik. "Stadt und Literatur." Ed. Wolfgang Haubrichs. 12 (1982).

Zipris, Lester Roy. "Lure of the City: Urban Landscape and Metaphor in American Literature, 1870-1920." Diss. State University of New York, 1981.

Zlotnick, Joan. *Portrait of an American City: the Novelists' New York*. Port Washington, N.Y., 1982.

Urban Studies

Abrams, Philip. "Towns and Economic Growth: Some Theories and Problems." *Towns in Societies*. Eds. Philip Abrams and E. Wrigley. Cambridge, 1978, 9-33.

Aronson, Sidney H. "The City: Illusion, Nostalgia, and Reality." *Readings in Introductory Sociology*. Eds. Dennis H. Wrong and Harry L. Gracey. New York, 1972, 288-300.

Ashton, Patrick J. "Urbanization and the Dynamics of Suburban Development under Capitalism." *Marxism and the Metropolis*. Eds. William Tabb and Larry Sawers. New York, 1984, 54-81.

Badcock, Blair. *Unfairly Structured Cities*. Oxford, 1984.

Badger, R. Reid. *The Great American Fair: The World's Columbian Exposition and American Culture*. Chicago, 1979.

Berg, Barbara J. *The Remembered Gate: Origins of American Feminism, The Woman and the City, 1800-1860*. New York, 1978.

Berger, Bennett. *Working-Class Suburb: A Study of Auto Workers in Suburbia*. 1960, Berkeley, Cal., 1968.

Bergmann, Hans. "Panoramas of New York, 1845-1860." *Prospects*. 10 (1985), 119-37.

Blume, Helmut. *USA*. 2 vols. Darmstadt, 1979.

Bodnar, John. "The European Origins of American Immigrants." *Essays from the Lowell Conference on Industrial History 1982 & 1983*. Ed. Robert Weible. North Andover, Mass., 1984, 259-275.

Bowden, Charles, and Lew Kreinberg. *Street Signs Chicago: Neighborhood and Other Illusions of Big-City Life*. Chicago, 1981.

Boyle, Miriam J., and M. E. Robinson. "Cognitive Mapping and Understanding." *Geography and the Urban Environment*. 1 (1979), 59-82.

Bridenbaugh, Carl. *Cities in the Wilderness: Urban Life in America, 1625-1742*. New York, 1938.

Bridenbaugh, Carl. *Cities in Revolt: Urban Life in America, 1742-1776*. New York, 1955.

Briggs, Asa. "The Environment of the City." *Encounter*. 59 (1982), 23-35.

Brownell, Blaine. "The Agrarian and Urban Ideals: Environmental Images in Modern America." *Journal of Popular Culture*. 5 (1971), 576-87.

Bulmer, Martin. *The Chicago School of Sociology*. Chicago, 1984.

Callow, Alexander B., Jr., ed. *American Urban History*. New York, 1969.

Carey, James T. *Sociology and Public Affairs: The Chicago School*. Beverly Hills, 1975.

Carter, Harold. *The Study of Urban Geography*. 1972, London, 1981.

Castells, Manuel. *The Urban Question*. Trans. Alan Sheridan. London, 1977.

Castells, Manuel. *City, Class, and Power*. London, 1978.

Checkoway, Barry. "Large Builders, Federal Housing Programs, and Postwar Suburbanization." *Marxism and the Metropolis*. Ed. William Tabb and Larry Sawers. New York, 1984, 152-73.

Chudacoff, Howard P. *The Evolution of American Urban Society*. Englewood Cliffs, N.J., 1981.

Connolly, Harold. *A Ghetto Grows in Brooklyn*. New York, 1977.

Conzen, Michael P. "The American Urban System in the Nineteenth Century." *Geography and the Urban Environment*. 4 (1984), 295-347.

Downs, Roger M., and David Stea, eds. *Image and Environment*. Chicago, 1973.

Downs, Roger M., and David Stea. *Maps in Minds*. New York, 1982.

Drake, St. Clair, and Horace C. Cayton. *Black Metropolis: A Study of Negro Life in a Northern City*. 1945, 2 vols. New York, 1970.

Duncan, Susanna. "Mental Maps of New York." *New York*. (Dec. 19, 1977), 51-62.

Estall, Robert. *A Modern Geography of the United States*. Harmondsworth, 1976.

Falke, Andreas. "Die amerikanischen Städte zwischen Niedergang und Revitalisierung: Stadtentwicklung, Politik und soziale Probleme in den 80er Jahren." *Amerikastudien*. 33 (1988), 21-51.

Fischer, Claude S. *The Urban Experience*. New York, 1978.

Fishman, Robert. *Bourgeois Utopias*. New York, 1987.

Forrest, Ray, J. Henderson, and Peter Williams, eds. *Urban Political Economy and Social Theory*. Aldershot, 1982.

Fraser, Derek, and Anthony Sutcliffe, eds. *The Pursuit of Urban History*. London, 1983.

Fried, Marc, Ellen Fitzgerald, Peggy Gleicher, and Chester Hartman, et al. *The World of the Urban Working Class*. Cambridge, Mass., 1973.

Frisby, David. *Georg Simmel*. Chichester, 1984.

Frisby, David. *Fragments of Modernity: Theories of Modernity in the Work of Simmel, Kracauer, and Benjamin*. Cambridge, 1985.

Gans, Herbert J. "Urbanism and Suburbanism As Ways of Life: A Re-evaluation of Definitions." *Human Behavior and Social Processes*. Ed. Arnold Rose. Boston, 1962, 625-48.

Gans, Herbert J. *The Urban Villagers: Group and Class in the Life of Italian-Americans*. New York, 1962.

Gans, Herbert J. *The Levittowners: Ways of Life and Politics in a New York Suburban Community*. New York, 1967.

Gebhardt, Eike. "Die Stadt als moralische Anstalt: Zum Mythos der kranken Stadt." *Die Unwirklichkeit der Städte*. Ed. Klaus R. Scherpe, Hamburg, 1988, 279-303.

Geller, Daniel M. "Responses to Urban Stimuli: A Balanced Approach." *Journal of Social Issues*. 36 (1980), 86-98.

Glaab, Charles N., and A. Theodore Brown. *A History of Urban America*. New York, 1967.

Gottdiener, Mark. *The Production of Urban Space*. Austin, Texas, 1985.

Gottdiener, Mark, and Alexandros Ph. Lagopoulos, eds. *The City and the Sign: An Introduction to Urban Semiotics*. New York, 1986.

Gottdiener, Mark. "Urban Semiotics." *Remaking the City: Social Science Perspectives on Urban Design*. Eds. John S. Pipkin, Mark La Gory, and Judith R. Blau. Albany, N.Y., 1983, 101-14.

Gottmann, Jean. *Megalopolis: The Urbanized Northeastern Seaboard of the United States*. Cambridge, Mass., 1961.

Hammack, David C. *Power and Society: Greater New York at the Turn of the Century*. New York, 1982.

Handlin, Oscar, and John Burchard eds. *The Historian and the City*. Cambridge, Mass., 1963.

Harloe, Michael, and Elizabeth Lebas, eds. *City, Class, and Capital*. London, 1981.

Harring, Sidney L. *Policing A Class Society: The Experience of American Cities, 1865-1915*. New Brunswick, N.J., 1985.

Harvey, David. *Social Justice and the City*. London, 1973.

Hirsch, Arnold R. *Making the Second Ghetto: Race and Housing in Chicago, 1940-1960*. Cambridge, Mass., 1983.

Holton, R. J. *Cities, Capitalism, and Civilization*. London, 1986.

Holzner, Lutz. "Stadtland USA - Zur Auflösung und Neuordnung der US-amerikanischen Stadt." *Geographische Zeitschrift*. 73 (1985), 191-205.

Hummon, David M. "Urban Views: Popular Perspectives on City Life." *Urban Life*. 15 (1986), 3-36.

Jackson, Kenneth T. "The Capital of Capitalism: The New York Metropolitan Region, 1890-1940." *Metropolis 1890-1940*. Ed. Anthony Sutcliffe. London, 1984, 319-53.

Jackson, Kenneth T. *Crabgrass Frontier: The Suburbanization of the United States*. New York, 1985.

Jacob, Herbert. *Crime and Justice in Urban America*. Englewood Cliffs, N.J., 1980.

Jacob, Herbert. *The Frustration of Policy: Repsonses to Crime by American Cities*. Boston, 1984.

Jacobs, Jane. *The Death and Life of Great American Cities*. New York, 1961.

Jaret, Charles. "Recent Neo-Marxist Urban Analysis." *Annual Review of Sociology*. 9 (1983), 499-524.

Johnston, R. J. *The American Urban System. A Geographical Perspective*. New York, 1982.

Katz, Michael B. *In the Shadow of the Poorhouse: A Social History of Welfare in America*. New York, 1986.

Katznelson, Ira. *Black Men, White Cities: Race, Politics and Migration in the United States, 1900-30, and Britain, 1948-68*. New York, 1973.

Katznelson, Ira. *City Trenches: Urban Politics and the Patterning of Class in the United States*. New York, 1981.

Katznelson, Ira, and Aristide Zolberg, eds. *Working-Class Formation: Nineteenth-Century Patterns in Western Europe and the United States*. Princeton, 1986.

Knox, Paul. *Urban Social Geography: An Introduction*. London, 1982.

Leeds, Anthony. "Cities and Countryside in Anthropology." *Cities of the Mind: Images and Themes of the City in the Social Sciences*. Eds. Lloyd Rodwin and Robert M. Hollister. New York, 1984, 291-312.

Lefebvre, Henri. *La Révolution Urbaine*. Paris, 1970.

Ley, David. *A Social Geography of the City*. New York, 1983.

Lichtenberger, Elisabeth. *Stadtgeographie*. 2 vols. Wien, 1985.

Liebow, Elliot. *Tally's Corner*. Boston, 1967.

Logan, John R., and Mark Schneider. "Racial Segregation and Racial Change in American Suburbs, 1970-1980." *American Journal of Sociology*. 89 (1983), 874-88.

Lopez, Robert S. "The Crossroads Within the Wall." *The Historian and the City*. Eds. Oscar Handlin and John Burchard. Cambridge, Mass., 1963, 27-43.

Lubove, Roy. *The Progressives and the Slums. Tenement House Reform in New York City, 1890-1919*. Greenwood, 1962.

Lynch, Kevin. *The Image of the City*. Cambridge, Mass., 1960.

Lynch, Kevin. "Reconsidering *The Image of the City*." *Cities of the Mind: Images and Themes of the City in the Social Sciences*. Eds. Lloyd Rodwin and Robert M. Hollister. New York, 1984, 151-62.

Markusen, Ann R. "Class and Urban Social Expenditure: A Marxist Theory of Metropolitan Government." *Marxism and the Metropolis*. Eds. William Tabb and Larry Sawers. New York, 1984, 82-100.

Martins, Mario Rui. "The Theory of Social Space in the Work of Henri Lefebvre." *Urban Political Economy and Social Theory*. Eds. Ray Forrest, J. Henderson, and Peter Williams. Aldershot, 1982, 160-85.

Mayerson, Charlotte Leon, ed. *Two Blocks Apart: Juan Gonzales and Peter Quinn*. New York, 1965.

McKelvey, Blake. *The Urbanization of America, 1860-1915*. New York, 1963.

Milgram, Stanley. "The Experience of Living in Cities." *Science*. 167 (1970), 1461-68.

Milgram, Stanley, et al. "A Psychological Map of New York City." *American Scientist*. 60 (1972), 194-200.

Miller, Mark and Carl Werthmann. "Public Housing: Tenants and Troubles." *Dissent*. 8 (1961), 282-88.

Mohl, Raymond. "The Transformation of Urban America Since the Second World War." *Amerikastudien*. 33 (1988), 53-71.

Moore, Gary T. "Knowing about Environmental Knowing: The Current State of Theory and Research on Environmental Cognition." *Remaking the City: Social Science Perspectives on Urban Design*. Eds. John S. Pipkin, Mark La Gory, and Judith R. Blau. Albany, N. Y., 1983, 21-49

Mowry, George. *The Urban Nation, 1920-1960*. New York, 1960.

Müller, Lothar. "Die Großstadt als Ort der Moderne: Über Georg Simmel." *Die Unwirklichkeit der Städte*. Ed. Klaus R. Scherpe, Hamburg, 1988, 14-36.

Muller, P. O. *The Outer City*. Washington, D.C., 1976.

Muller, Peter O. *Contemporary Suburban America*. Englewood Cliffs, N.J., 1981.

Mumford, Lewis. *The Culture of Cities*. New York, 1938.

Mumford, Lewis. *The City in History: Its Origins, its Transformation and its Prospects*. 1961, Harmondsworth, 1966.

Newman, Peter. "Urban Political Economy and Planning Theory." *Urban Political Economy and Social Theory*. Eds. Ray Forrest, J. Henderson, and Peter Williams, Aldershot, 1982, 186-202.

Orleans, Peter. "Differential Cognition of Urban Residents: Effects of Social Scale on Mapping." *Image and Environment*. Eds. Roger M. Downs and David Stea. Chicago, 1973, 115-30.

Pahl, Raymond E. "The rural-urban continuum." *Readings in Urban Sociology*. Ed. Raymond E. Pahl. London, 1968.

Park, Robert E. "The City: Suggestions for the Investigation of the Human Behavior in the City Environment." *The American Journal of Sociology*. 20 (1915), 577-612.

Park, Robert E., Ernest W. Burgess and Roderick McKenzie, eds. *The City*. Chicago, 1925.

Park, Robert E. "Human Ecology." *The American Journal of Sociology*. 32 (1936), 1-15.

Perry, David C., and Alfred J. Watkins. *The Rise of Sunbelt Cities*. Beverly Hills, 1977.

Persons, Stow. *Ethnic Studies at Chicago, 1905-1945*. Urbana, Ill., 1987.

Pfeil, Elisabeth. *Großstadtforschung*. Hannover, 1972.

Phillips Barbara E., and Richard T. LeGates. *City Lights: An Introduction to Urban Studies*. New York, 1981.

Philpott, Thomas Lee. *The Slum and the Ghetto: Neighborhood Deterioration and Middle Class Reform, Chicago, 1880-1930*. New York, 1978.

Pipkin, John S., and Mark La Gory, Judith R. Blau, eds. *Remaking the City: Social Science Perspectives on Urban Design*. Albany, N. Y., 1983.

Radford, John P. "The Social Geography of the Nineteenth Century U.S. City." *Geography and the Urban Environment*, 4 (1984), 257-93.

Riis, Jacob A. *How the Other Half Lives*. 1890, New York, 1957.

Rodriguez, Nestor R., and Joe R. Feagin. "Urban Specialization in the World-System: An Investigation of Historical Cases." *Urban Affairs Quarterly*. 22 (1986), 187-220.

Rodwin, Lloyd, and Robert Hollister, eds. *Cities of the Mind*. New York, 1984.

Rosenwaike, Ira. *Population History of New York City*. Syracuse, 1972.

Rutman, Darrett B. *Winthrop's Boston: Portrait of A Puritan Town, 1630-1649*. Chapel Hill, 1965.

Saarinen, Thomas F., David Seamon, and James L. Sell, eds. *Environmental Perception and Behavior: An Inventory and Prospect*. Chicago, 1984.

Saunders, Peter. *Social Theory and the Urban Question*. London, 1981.

Schlesinger, Arthur. *The Rise of the City 1878-1898*. New York, 1933.

Schmitt, Peter J. *Back to Nature: The Arcadian Myth in Urban America*. New York, 1969.

Sennett, Richard. *Families Against the City: Middle Class Homes of Industrial Chicago, 1872-1890*. New York, 1974.

Sennett, Richard. "Middle-Class Families and Urban Violence: The Experience of a Chicago Community in the Nineteenth Century." *Nineteenth-Century Cities: Essays in the New Urban History*. Eds. Stephan Thernstrom and Richard Sennett. New Haven, 1969, 386-420.

Shergold, Peter R. *Working-Class Life: The American Standard in Comparative Perspective, 1899-1919*. Pittsburgh, 1982.

Sies, Mary Corbin. "The City Transformed: Nature, Technology, and the Suburban Ideal, 1877-1917." *Journal of Urban History*. 14 (1987), 81-111.

Simmel, Georg. "The Metropolis and Mental Life." *The Sociology of Georg Simmel*. Trans., and ed. Kurt H. Wolff, repr. *Cities and Society*. Eds. Paul K. Hatt and Albert J. Reiss. 1951, New York, 1963, pp. 635-46.

Slayton, Robert Allen. *Back of the Yards: the Making of a Local Democracy*. Chicago, 1986.

Smith, Michael Peter. *The City and Social Theory*. New York, 1979.

Smith, Neil. *Uneven Development*. New York, 1984.

Spear, Allan. *Black Chicago: The Making of a Negro Ghetto, 1890-1920*. Chicago, 1967.
Steffens, Lincoln. *The Shame of the Cities*. 1904, New York, 1957.
Stimpson, Catherine R., Elsa Dixler, Martha J. Nelson, and Kathryn B. Yatrakis, eds. *Women and the City*. Chicago, 1980.
Strauss, Anselm L. *Images of the American City*. New York, 1961.
Strauss, Anselm L., ed. *The American City*. London, 1968.
Susser, Ida. *Norman Street: Poverty and Politics in an Urban Neighborhood*. New York, 1982.
Sutcliffe, Anthony, ed. *Metropolis 1890-1940*. London, 1984.
Suttles, Gerald D. *The Social Order of the Slum*. Chicago, 1968.
Taylor, William R. "Psyching Out the City." *Uprooted Americans*. Eds. Richard L. Bushman, et al., Boston, 1979, 247-86.
Trachtenberg, Alan. "Image and Ideology: New York in the Photographer's Eye." *Journal of Urban History*. 10 (1984), 453-64.
Wade, Richard C. *The Urban Frontier. 1790-1830*. Cambridge, Mass., 1959.
Ward, David. *Cities and Immigrants: A Geography of Change in Nineteenth-Century America*. New York, 1971.
Warner, Sam Bass. *The Urban Wilderness: A History of the American City*. New York, 1972.
Warner, Sam Bass. "The Management of Multiple Urban Images." Eds. Derek Fraser and Anthony Sutcliffe. *The Pursuit of Urban History*. London, 1983, 383-94.
Wekerle, Gerda R., Rebecca Peterson, and David Morley, eds. *New Space for Women*. Boulder, Col., 1980.
Whyte, William F. *Street Corner Society: The Social Structure of an Italian Slum*. 1943, Chicago, 1955.
Whyte, William F. "On Street Corner Society." *Urban Sociology*. Eds. Ernest W. Burgess and Donald J. Bogue. Chicago, 1964, 156-68.
Wilson, Robert A., and David A. Schulz. *Urban Sociology*. Englewood Cliffs, N.J., 1978.
Wirth, Louis. *The Ghetto*. Chicago, 1928.
Wirth, Louis. "Urbanism as a Way of Life." *The American Journal of Sociology*. 44 (1938), 1-24.
Louis Wirth. *On Cities and Social Life*. Ed. Albert J. Reiss. Chicago, 1964.
Wortman, Marlene Stein. "Domesticizing the Nineteenth-Century American City." *Prospects*. 3 (1977), 531-72.
Wright, Gwendolyn. *Building the Dream: A Social History of Housing in America*. New York, 1981.
Zukin, Sharon. "A Decade of the New Urban Sociology." *Theory and Society*. 9 (1980), 575-601.

Literary Criticism

Stephen Crane

Crane, Stephen. *Stephen Crane: Letters*. Eds. Robert W. Stallmann and Lillian Gielkes. New York, 1960.

Bergon, Frank. *Stephen Crane's Artistry*. New York, 1975.

Bradbury, Malcolm. "Sociology and Literary Studies. II. Romance and Reality in *Maggie*." *Journal of American Studies*. 3 (1969), 111-21.

Brennan, Joseph X. "Ironic and Symbolic Structure in Crane's *Maggie*." *Nineteenth Century Fiction*. 16 (1962), 303-15.

Cady, Edwin H. *Stephen Crane*. Boston, 1980.

Colvert, James B. "Structure and Theme in Stephen Crane's Fiction." *Modern Fiction Studies*. 5 (1959), 199-208.

Colvert, James B. *Stephen Crane*. New York, 1984.

Fine, David M. "Abraham Cahan, Stephen Crane, and the Romantic Tenement Tale of the Nineties." *American Studies*. 14 (1973), 95-107.

Fitelson, David. "Stephen Crane's *Maggie* and Darwinism." *American Quarterly*. 16 (1964), 182-94.

Graff, Aida Farrag. "Metaphor and Metonymy: The Two Worlds of Crane's *Maggie*." *English Studies in Canada*. 8 (1982), 422-36.

Haack, Dietmar. "Stephen Crane und die 'kühne Metapher'." *Jahrbuch für Amerikastudien*. 14 (1969), 116-23.

Holton, Milne. *Cylinder of Vision: The Fiction and Journalistic Writing of Stephen Crane*. Baton Rouge, 1972.

Katz, Joseph, ed. *Stephen Crane in Transition: Centenary Essays*. De Kalb, Ill., 1972.

Pizer, Donald. "Stephen Crane's *Maggie* and American Naturalism." *Criticism*. 7 (1965), 168-75.

Slotkin, Alan. "Dialect Manipulation in 'An Experiment in Misery'." *American Literary Realism*. 14 (1981), 273-76.

Stallmann, Robert Wooster. "Crane's *Maggie*: A Reassessment." *Modern Fiction Studies*. 5 (1959), 251-59.

Trachtenberg, Alan. "Experiments in Another Country: Stephen Crane's *City Sketches*." *Southern Review*. 10 (1974), 265-85.

Westbrook, Max. "Stephen Crane's Social Ethic." *American Quarterly*. 14 (1962), 587-96.

Theodore Dreiser

Dreiser, Theodore. *A History of Myself*. New York, 1922.

Dreiser, Theodore. *The Color of a Great City*. New York, 1923.

Dreiser, Theodore. *My City*. New York, 1929.

Dreiser, Theodore. *Dawn*. New York, 1931.

Bowlby, Rachel. *Just Looking: Consumer Culture in Dreiser, Gissing and Zola.* New York, 1985.

Davidson, Kathy N., and Arnold E. "Carrie's Sisters: The Popular Prototypes for Dreiser's Heroine." *Modern Fiction Studies.* 23 (1977), 395-407.

Elias, Robert H. *Theodore Dreiser: Apostle of Nature.* 1948, New York, 1970.

Fisher, Philip. *Hard Facts: Setting and Form in the American Novel.* New York, 1985.

Flanagan, John T. "Theodore Dreiser's Chicago." *Revue des Langues Vivantes.* 32 (1966), 131-44.

Katope, Christopher G. "*Sister Carrie* and Spencer's *First Principles*." *American Literature.* 41 (1969), 64-75.

Kwiat, Joseph J. "The Education of Theodore Dreiser in the World of the City: 'Exercises' for the Early Novels."*Americana-Austriaca.* 5 (1980), 91-109.

Lehan, Richard. *Theodore Dreiser: His World and His Novels.* Carbondale, Ill., 1969.

Lingemann, Richard. *Theodore Dreiser: At the Gates of the City, 1971-1907.* New York, 1986.

McWilliams, Dean. "The Profound Superficiality of Dreiser's 'Sister Carrie'." *The DLSU Graduate Journal.* 13 (1988), 44-66.

Markels, Julian. "Dreiser and the Plotting of Inarticulate Experience." *Massachusetts Review.* 2 (1961), 431-48.

Matthiesen, F. O. *Theodore Dreiser.* New York, 1951.

Michaels, Walter Benn. "*Sister Carrie*'s Popular Economy." *Critical Inquiry.* 7 (1980), 373-90.

Moers, Ellen. "The Finesse of Dreiser." *American Scholar.* 33 (1963), 109-14.

Moers, Ellen. *Two Dreisers.* New York, 1969.

Müller, Kurt. "Identität und Rolle in Theodore Dreisers *Sister Carrie.* Teil 1: Rollenverhalten, Identität und soziale Struktur." *Literaturwissenschaftliches Jahrbuch im Auftrage der Görres-Gesellschaft.* 21 (1980), 253-82.

Müller, Kurt. "Identität und Rolle in Theodore Dreisers *Sister Carrie.* Teil 2: Überanpassung und Anomie." *Literaturwissenschaftliches Jahrbuch im Auftrage der Görres-Gesellschaft.* 22 (1981), 209-39.

Petrey, Sandy. "The Language of Realism, the Language of False Consciousness." *Novel: A Forum on Fiction.* 10 (1977), 101-13.

Pizer, Donald. *The Novels of Theodore Dreiser: A Critical Study.* Minneapolis, 1976.

Schröder-Drescher, Christa. *Das Bild Chicagos in der Cowperwood Trilogie Theodore Dreisers mit besonderer Berücksichtigung von The Titan.* Frankfurt, 1980.

See, Fred G. "The Text as Mirror: *Sister Carrie* and the Lost Language of the Heart." *Criticism.* 20 (1978), 144-66.

Swanberg, W. A. *Dreiser.* New York, 1965.

Szuberla, Guy Alan. "Dreiser at the World's Fair: The City Without Limits." *Modern Fiction Studies.* 23 (1977), 369-79.

Upton Sinclair

Sinclair, Upton. "What Life Means to Me." *Cosmopolitan*. 41 (1906), 591-95.

Sinclair, Upton. "Is 'The Jungle' True?" *Independent*. 40 (1906), 1129-33.

Sinclair, Upton. *Mammonart*. Pasadena, Cal., 1925.

Sinclair, Upton. *American Outpost*. New York, 1932.

Sinclair, Upton. "Foreword to *The Jungle*." New York, 1965.

Barrett, James R. *Work and Community in 'The Jungle': Chicago's Packinghouse Workers, 1894-1922*. Urbana, Ill., 1988.

Folsom, Michael Brewster. "Upton Sinclair's Escape from *The Jungle*: The Narrative Strategy and Suppressed Conclusion of America's First Proletarian Novel." *Prospects*. 4 (1979), 237-66.

Folsom, Michael Brewster. "The Unredeemed Landscape: Industrial America in the Imagination of Whittier, Bellamy, and Sinclair." *Essays from the Lowell Conference on Industrial History 1982 & 1983*. Ed. Robert Weible. North Andover, Mass., 1984, 68-80.

Harris, Leon. *Upton Sinclair: Amercian Rebel*. New York, 1975.

Herms, Dieter. *Upton Sinclair, ein amerikanischer Radikaler. Eine Einführung in Leben und Werk*. Frankfurt, 1978.

Homberger, Eric. *American Writers and Radical Politics, 1900-1939*. New York, 1987.

Mookerjee, R. N. *Art for Social Justice: The Major Novels of Upton Sinclair*. Metuchen, N.J., 1988.

Scriabine, Christine. "Upton Sinclair and the Writing of *The Jungle*." *Chicago History*. 10 (1981), 26-37.

Spaunhorst, Franz-Peter. *Literarische Kulturkritik als Dekodierung von Macht und Werten am Beispiel ausgewählter Romane von Upton Sinclair, Frank Norris, John Dos Passos und Sinclair Lewis*. Frankfurt, 1986.

Szuberla, Guy A. "Dom, Namai, Heim: Images of the New Immigrant's Home." *Prospects*. 10 (1985), 139-68.

Yoder, Jon A. *Upton Sinclair*. New York, 1975.

F. Scott Fitzgerald

Fitzgerald, F. Scott. "Introduction." *The Great Gatsby*. New York, 1934, vii-xi.

Fitzgerald, F. Scott. *The Crack-Up*. Ed. Edmund Wilson. New York, 1945.

Bewley, Marius. "Scott Fitzgerald's Criticism of America." *The Sewanee Review*. 62 (1954), 223-46.

Bruccoli, Matthew J. *Some Sort of Epic Grandeur*. London, 1981.

Dahl, Curtis. "Fitzgerald's Use of American Architectural Styles in *The Great Gatsby*." *American Studies*. 25 (1984), 91-102.

Donaldson, Scott. "The Political Development of F. Scott Fitzgerald." *Prospects*. 6 (1981), 313-55.

Fraser, Keath. "Another Reading of *The Great Gatsby*." *English Studies in Canada*. 5 (1979), 330-43.

Garrett, George. "Fire and Freshness: A Matter of Style in *The Great Gatsby*." *New Essays on The Great Gastby*. Ed. Matthew J. Bruccoli. Cambridge, 1985, 101-16.

Gervais, Ronald J. "The Socialist and the Silk Stockings: Fitzgerald's Double Allegiance." *Mosaic*. 15 (1982), 79-92.

Godden, Richard. "*The Great Gatsby*: Glamor on the Turn." *Journal of American Studies*. 16 (1982), 343-71.

Huonder, Eugen. *The Functional Significance of Setting in the Novels of Francis Scott Fitzgerald*. Bern, 1974.

Korenman, Joan S. "A View From the (Queensboro) Bridge." *Fitzgerald/Hemingway Newsletter*, 7 (1975), 93-96.

Light, James F. "Political Conscience in the Novels of F. Scott Fitzgerald." *Ball State University Forum*. 4 (1963), 13-25.

Lisca, Peter. "Nick Carraway and the Imagery of Disorder." *Twentieth Century Literature*. 13 (1967), 18-28.

Miller, James E. "Fitzgerald's Gatsby: The World as Ash Heap." *Critical Essays on The Great Gatsby*. Ed. Scott Donaldson. Boston, 1984, 242-58.

Mizener, Arthur. *The Far Side of Paradise: A Biography of F. Scott Fitzgerald*. New York, 1950.

Ornstein, Robert. "Scott Fitzgerald's Fable of East and West." *College English*. 18 (1956), 139-43.

Parr, Susan Resneck. "The Idea of Order at West Egg," *New Essays on The Great Gastby*. Ed. Matthew J. Bruccoli. Cambridge, 1985, 59-78.

Posnock, Ross. "'A New World, Material Without Being Real': Fitzgerald's Critique of Capitalism in *The Great Gatsby*." *Critical Essays on The Great Gatsby*. Ed. Scott Donaldson. Boston, 1984, 201-13.

Slater, Peter Gregg. "Ethnicity in *The Great Gatsby*." *Twentieth Century Literature*. 19 (1973), 53-62.

Stern, Milton R. *The Golden Moment. The Novels of F. Scott Fitzgerald*. Urbana, Ill., 1970.

Turnbull, Andrew. *Scott Fitzgerald*. New York, 1962.

Way, Brian. *F. Scott Fitzgerald and the Art of Social Fiction*. London, 1980.

John Dos Passos

Dos Passos, John. "Statement of Belief." *Bookman*. 68 (Sept. 24, 1928), 26.

Dos Passos, John. *The Best Times: An Informal Memoir*. New York, 1966.

Dos Passos, John. "What makes a Novelist?" *National Review*. 20 (1968), 29-32.

Arden, Eugene. "*Manhattan Transfer*: An Experiment in Technique." *University of Kansas Review*. 22 (1955), 1953-58.

Astre, George-Albert. *Thèmes et structures dans l'oeuvre de John Dos Passos*. Paris, 1956.

Beach, Joseph Warren. *American Fiction, 1920-40*. New York, 1941.

Becker, George Joseph. *John Dos Passos*. New York, 1974.

Carver, Craig. "The Newspaper and Other Sources of *Manhattan Transfer*." *Studies in American Fiction*. 3 (1975), 167-80.

Clark, Michael. *Dos Passos's Early Fiction, 1912-1938*. Selingsgrove, 1987.

Colley, Iain. *Dos Passos and the Fiction of Despair*. Totawa, N.J., 1978.

Diggins, John P. "Visions of Chaos and Visions of Order: Dos Passos as Historian." *American Literature*. 46 (1974), 329-46.

Hughson, Lois. "Narration in the Making of *Manhattan Transfer*." *Studies in the Novel*. 8 (1976), 185-98.

Isernhagen, Hartwig. *Ästhetische Innovation und Kulturkritik. Das Frühwerk von John Dos Passos, 1916-1938*. München, 1983.

Komar, Kathleen. *Pattern and Chaos: Multilinear Novels by Dos Passos, Döblin, Faulkner, and Koeppen*. Columbia, S.C., 1983.

Knox, George. "Dos Passos and Painting." *Texas Studies in Literature and Language*. 6 (1964), 22-38.

Landsberg, Melvin. *John Dos Passos' Path to U.S.A.* Boulder, 1972.

Lowry, E. D. "The Lively Art of *Manhattan Transfer*." *PMLA*. 84 (1969), 1628-38.

Ludington, Townsend. *John Dos Passos. A Twentieth Century Odyssey*. New York, 1980.

Mizener, Sharon Fusselman. *Manhattan Transients*. Hicksville, N.Y., 1977.

Rosen, Robert C. *John Dos Passos. Politics and the Writer*. Lincoln, Nebraska, 1981.

Sartre, Jean-Paul. "A Propos de John Dos Passos et *1919*." *Nouvelle Revue Francaise*. 51 (1938), 292-301.

Spindler, Michael. "John Dos Passos and the Visual Arts." *Journal of American Studies*. 15 (1981), 391-406.

Stolzfus, Ben. "John Dos Passos and the French." *Comparative Literature*. 15 (1963), 146-63.

Wagner, Linda W. *Dos Passos: Artist as American*. Austin, 1979.

Richard Wright

Wright, Richard. "Ethnological Aspects of Chicago's Black Belt." *New Letters*. 39 (1972), 61-67.

Wright, Richard. "Portrait of Harlem." *New York Panorama*. Ed. New York WPA. New York, 1938, 132-51.

Wright, Richard. "How 'Bigger' Was Born." *Native Son*. New York, 1940.

Wright, Richard. *Twelve Million Black Voices: A Folk History of the Negro in the United States*. New York, 1941.

Wright, Richard. "Introduction." *Black Metropolis*. Eds. St. Clair Drake and Horace R. Cayton. New York, 1945, xvii-xxxiv.

Wright, Richard. "The Shame of Chicago." *Ebony*. 7 (1951), 24-32.

Wright, Richard. *American Hunger*. New York, 1977.

Baker, Houston A. "Racial Wisdom and Richard Wright's *Native Son*." *Critical Essays on Richard Wright*. ed. Yoshinobu Hakutani, Boston, 1982, 66-81.

Bakish, David. *Richard Wright*. New York, 1973.

Baldwin, James. "Everybody's Protest Novel." *Zero*. 1 (1949), 54-8.

Baldwin, James. "Many Thousands Gone." *Partisan Review*. 18 (1951), 665-80.

Bone, Robert A. *The Negro Novel in America*. New Haven, 1965.

Brignano, Carl Russell. *Richard Wright: An Introduction to the Man and his Works*. Pittsburgh, 1973.

Brivic, Sheldon. "Conflict of Values: Richard Wright's *Native Son*." *Novel*. 7 (1974), 231-45.

Fabre, Michel. *The Unfinished Quest of Richard Wright*. Trans. Isabel Barzun. New York, 1973.

Felgar, Robert. *Richard Wright*. Boston, 1980.

Gibson, Donald B. "Wright's Invisible Native Son." *American Quarterly*. 21 (1969), 728-38.

Howe, Irving. "Black Boys and Native Sons." *Dissent*. 10 (1963), 353-68.

Jackson, Blyden. "Richard Wright: Black Boy from America's Black Belt and Urban Ghettos." *Critical Essays on Richard Wright*. Ed. Yoshinobu Hakutani. Boston, 1982, 48-65.

Kinnamon, Keneth. *The Emergence of Richard Wright*. Urbana, Ill., 1973.

Margolies, Edward. *The Art of Richard Wright*. Carbondale, Ill., 1969.

Mootry, Maria K. "Bitches, Whores, and Woman Haters: Archetypes and Typologies in the Art of Richard Wright." *Richard Wright: A Collection of Critical Essays*. Eds. Richard Macksey and Frank E. Moorer. Englewood Cliffs, N.J., 1984, 117-27.

Nagel, James. "Images of 'Vision' in *Native Son*." *University Review*, 36 (1969), 109-15.

Siegel, Paul N. "The Conclusion of Richard Wright's *Native Son*." *PMLA*. 89 (1974), 517-23.

Walker, Margaret. *Richard Wright, Daemonic Genius: A Portrait of the Man, A Critical Look at His Work*. New York, 1988.

Webb, Constance. *Richard Wright: A Biography*. New York, 1968.

Widmer, Kingsley. "Black Existentialism: Richard Wright." *Richard Wright: A Collection of Critical Essays*. Eds. Richard Macksey and Frank E. Moorer. Englewood Cliffs, N.J., 1984, 173-81.

Hubert Selby

Binet, Roland. "The Mirror of Man." *The Review of Contemporary Fiction*. 1 (1981), 380-88.

Buckeye, Robert. "Some Preliminary Notes Towards A Study of Selby." *The Review of Contemporary Fiction*. 1 (1981), 374-75.

Kreutzer, Eberhard. "The Psychodynamics of Person and Place: Hubert Selby's *Last Exit to Brooklyn*." *Amerikastudien*. 22 (1977), 137-45.

Lewis, Harry. "Some Things I want to say about Hubert Selby's Work." *The Review of Contemporary Fiction*. 1 (1981), 413-15.

Mottram, Eric. "Free Like the Rest of Us: Violation and Despair in Hubert Selby's Novels." *The Review of Contemporary Fiction*. 1 (1981), 353-63.

O' Brien, John. "Interview with Hubert Selby, Jr.," *The Review of Contemporary Fiction*. 1 (1981), 315-35.

O' Brien, John. "The Materials of Art in Hubert Selby." *The Review of Contemporary Fiction*. 1 (1981), 376-79.

Sorrentino, Gilbert. "The Art of Hubert Selby." *Kulchur*. 4 (1964), 27-43.

Stephens, Michael. "Hubert Selby, Jr.: The Poet of Prose Masters." *The Review of Contemporary Fiction*. 1 (1981), 389-97.

Wertime, Richard A. "Psychic Vengeance in *Last Exit to Brooklyn*." *Literature and Psychology*. 24 (1974), 153-66.

Thomas Pynchon

Pynchon, Thomas. "A Journey Into the Mind of Watts." *New York Times Magazine*. (June 12, 1966), 34f., 78, 80ff., 84.

Colvile, Georgiana M. M. *Beyond and Beneath the Mantle: On Thomas Pynchon's The Crying of Lot 49*. Amsterdam, 1988.

Cowart, David. *Thomas Pynchon. The Art of Allusion*. Carbondale, Ill. 1980.

Hite, Molly. *Ideas of Order in the Novels of Thomas Pynchon*. Columbus, 1983.

Ickstadt, Heinz, ed. *Ordnung und Entropie. Zum Romanwerk von Thomas Pynchon*. Hamburg, 1981.

Ickstadt, Heinz. "Thomas Pynchon. *Die Versteigerung von Nr. 49*." *Zum Romanwerk von Thomas Pynchon*. Hamburg, 1981, 104-27.

Kermode, Frank. "Decoding the Trystero." *Pynchon. A Collection of Critical Essays*. Ed. Edward Mendelson. Englewood Cliffs, N.J., 1978, 162-66.

Kolodny, Annette, and Daniel James Peters. "Pynchon's *The Crying of Lot 49*: The Novel as Subversive Experience." *Modern Fiction Studies*. 19 (1973), 79-87.

Mendelson, Edward. "The Sacred, the Profane, and *The Crying of Lot 49*." *Pynchon. A Collection of Critical Essays*. Englewood Cliffs, N.J., 1978, 112-46.

Merrill, Robert. "The Form and Meaning of Pynchon's *The Crying of Lot 49*." *Ariel. A Review of International English Literature*. 8 (1977), 53-70.

Pütz, Manfred. Thomas Pynchon's *The Crying of Lot 49*: The World is a Tristero System." *Mosaic*. 7 (1974), 125-37.

Sanders, Scott. "Pynchon's Paranoid History." *Mindful Pleasures*. Ed. George Levine and David Leverenz. Boston, 1976, 139-59.

Schaub, Thomas H. *Pynchon: The Voice of Ambiguity*. Chicago, 1981.

Seed, David. *The Fictional Labyrinths of Thomas Pynchon*. London, 1988.

Tanner, Tony. *Thomas Pynchon*. London, 1982.

Literary Theory and General Studies

Barthes, Roland. *Mythologies*. Trans. Annette Lavers. London, 1972.

Bercovitch, Sacvan, and Myra Jehlen, ed. *Ideology and Classic American Literature*. Cambridge, 1986.

Berger, John. *Ways of Seeing*. Harmondsworth, 1972.

Berger, John. *The Sense of Sight*. New York, 1985.

Berman, Marshall. *All That is Solid Melts Into Air*. 1982, Harmondsworth, 1988.

Campbell, Jeremy. *Grammatical Man: Information, Entropy, Language, and Life*. New York, 1982.

Dowd, Douglas F. *The Twisted Dream: Capitalist Development in the United States since 1776*. Cambridge, Mass., 1977.

Eagleton, Terry. *Literary Theory*. Oxford, 1983.

Ewen, Stuart. *Captains of Consciousness: Advertising and the Social Roots of Consumer Culture*. New York, 1976.

Ewen, Stuart. *Channels of Desire: Mass Images and the Shaping of American Consciousness*. New York, 1982.

Friedan, Betty. *The Feminine Mystique*. New York, 1963.

Goldmann, Lucien. *Towards a Sociology of the Novel*. Trans. Alan Sheridan. London, 1975.

Habermas, Jürgen. *Knowledge and Human Interests*. Trans. Jeremy J. Shapiro. Boston, 1971.

Habermas, Jürgen. "Die Moderne: ein unvollendetes Projekt." *Kleine politische Schriften, I-IV*. Frankfurt, 1981, 444-64.

Harrington, Michael. *The Other America: Poverty in the United States*. Baltimore, 1963.

Hofstadter, Richard. *Social Darwinism in American Thought*. 1944, Boston, 1955.

Howard, June. *Form and History in American Naturalism*. Chapel Hill, 1985.

Jameson, Frederic. *The Political Unconscious*. London, 1981.

Jay, Martin. *Marxism and Totality*. Oxford, 1984.

Kolko, Gabriel. *Wealth and Power in America: An Analysis of Social Class and Income Distribution*. New York, 1962.

Lears, T. J. Jackson. *No Place of Grace: Antimodernism and the Transformation of American Culture, 1880-1920*. New York, 1981.

Lévi-Strauss, Claude. *Tristes Tropiques*. New York, 1961.

Lukács, Georg. *Theory of the Novel*. Trans. Anna Bostock. Cambridge, Mass., 1971.

Marcuse, Herbert. *One-Dimensional Man*. Boston, 1964.

Macherey, Pierre. *A Theory of Literary Production*. Trans. Geoffrey Wall, London, 1978.

Marcuse, Herbert. *The Aesthetic Dimension: Toward a Critique of Marxist Aesthetics*. Boston, 1978.

Mesch, Harald. *Verweigerung endgültiger Prädikation: Ästhetische Formen und Denkstrukturen der amerikanischen "Postmoderne," 1950-1970.* München, 1984.

Morison, Samuel Eliot, Henry Steele Commager, and William E. Leuchtenberg. *A Concise History of the American Republic.* 1977, New York, 1983.

Myrdal, Gunnar, Richard Sterner, and Arnold Rose. *An American Dilemma: The Negro Problem and Modern Democracy.* New York, 1944.

Schleier, Merrill. *The Skyscraper in American Art, 1890-1931.* Ann Arbor, Mich., 1986.

Spindler, Michael. *American Literature and Social Change.* Bloomington, 1983.

Walcutt, Charles Child. *American Literary Naturalism.* Minneapolis, 1956.

Index

Abrams, Philip 3, 14, 50
Afro-Americans 7, 33, 41-43, 66, 68, 170, 245-72, 277, 305-6, 312-5, 323
Althusser, Louis 7, 106
Architecture 1, 15, 39, 70-72, 137-40, 193-96, 204, 213, 216-17, 226, 229, 276-78, 280
Astre, George-Albert 240

Badcock, Blair, 20, 22
Badger, R. Reid 139
Baker, Houston A. 259
Baldwin, James 246, 258
Banfield, Edward C. 278
Barrett, James R. 172
Barthelme, Donald 3, 13
Barthes, Roland 82-82, 319
Baudelaire, Charles 47, 294
Beach, Joseph Warren 224, 226-27, 242
Beat Movement 274, 295-99, 331
Becker, George Joseph 233
Beckett, Samuel 334
Bellow, Saul 3
Benjamin, Walter 47, 167, 182
Berg, Barbara J. 83, 102
Berger, Bennett 60-61
Berger, John 45-46, 145, 215, 231-32
Bergon, Frank 127, 130
Berman, Marshall 210, 334
Bewley, Marius 209
Blake, Fay M. 145
Bloodworth, William 183-84, 190
Boston 18-22, 33, 64, 80
Bradbury, Malcolm 2, 99, 122, 124, 130
Brecht, Bertolt 105, 167, 182, 243
Bremer, Sidney H. 101-2, 197
Brennan, Joseph X. 115, 123
Bridenbaugh, Carl 21-22
Brignano, Carl Russell 262
Brivic, Sheldon 262
Brooklyn 10-11, 98, 195, 273-99
Broughton, Philip 43
Brownell, Blaine 80, 82
Bryce, James A. 40
Burnham, Daniel 138, 140-41
Burroughs, William S. 274, 288

Cahan, Abraham 102
Calvino, Italo 13
Campbell, Jeremy 319-20
Carey, James T. 59
Castells, Manuel 3, 9, 45, 51-52, 55, 67, 280

Cather, Willa 3
Cayton, Horace C. 252
Cendrars, Blaise 228-29
Chicago 1, 10, 31, 39-40, 49, 70, 80, 98, 133-91, 245-72, 328-29
Chicago School of Socoiology 5, 46-60, 62, 74, 78, 91, 137, 142, 150-51, 221, 227, 246, 252-53, 269, 277,
Chudacoff, Howard P. 20, 26, 41, 62, 137, 140, 305
Clarke, Graham 95
Class 4-7, 27, 31, 33-36, 40, 43-44, 57-59, 61, 63, 66-69, 82, 85, 88, 91, 104, 114, 119, 124-25, 136-47, 157-58, 168-77, 183, 190-91, 194-204, 216-26, 247-61, 275-89, 307-17, 327-28, 331
Colvert, James B. 121
Colvile, Georgiana 321
Conrad, Peter 93-94
Corbin, Alfred 71, 159
Cowan, Michael 95
Cowley, Malcolm 202
Crane, Hart 93
Crane, Stephen 2, 10, 14, 16, 57, 77-78, 88, 91, 102, 108, 110-32, 223, 251, 258, 273-74, 281, 299, 329-332
Crying of Lot 49, The 3, 10, 101, 108, 300-25, 332
Cubism 214-15, 226-38, 243-45, 329, 333

Darwin, Charles 54
Darwinism, Social 53-54, 58, 129-30, 133, 158
Davidson, Arnold E., and Kathy N. 149-50
Derrida, Jacques 105-6, 333
Dickstein, Felice Witzum 96
Dickens, Charles 182, 205
Dos Passos, John 2, 9-10, 15, 57, 88, 96, 103, 108, 132, 213-44, 251, 281, 299, 329-33
Dostoyevsky, Fyodor 184, 251
Drake, St. Clair 252
Dreiser, Theodore 2, 10, 57-58, 88, 96-97, 103, 108, 132-165, 173, 178, 214, 251, 264, 291, 329-332
Dunham, H. Warren 55
Dunlap, George A. 86, 96
Durkheim, Emile 48, 62

Eagleton, Terry 11
Eble, Kenneth 109
Eisenstein, Sergej 222
Elias, Robert H. 158
Eliot, Thomas Stearns 1, 8, 91, 203, 214, 240, 316
Ellul, Jacques 79
Emerson, Ralph Waldo 76-77, 161
Engels, Friedrich 68-70
Ewen, Stuart 139, 146

Index 359

Existentialism 222, 247, 270-272
Expressionism 108, 132

Faris, Robert E. L. 55
Farrell, James T. 59, 88, 91, 223, 251
Fehl, Gerhard 70
Festa-McCormick, Diana 94
Fiedler, Leslie 91-92
Film 222, 229-30, 238, 305
Fine, David M. 101-02
Fischer, Claude S. 78
Fisher, Philip 99, 141, 151, 154
Fishman, Robert 303, 309, 336
Fitelson, David 121
Fitzgerald, F. Scott 2, 10, 88, 97, 99, 108-9, 190, 192-212, 223, 301, 315, 322, 331-32
Fleming, Robert E. 96
Folsom, Michael Brewster 182
Ford, Henry 178-79
Fragmentation 2-4, 6, 9, 11, 13-32, 40, 45, 50, 59-60, 63, 66-67, 72-73, 85, 87-90, 104-5, 107-8, 110, 130-31, 195, 264, 281, 325-33
Fraser, Keath 211
Frazier, Franklin E. 252, 264
Freud, Sigmund 90, 322
Fried, Marc 64-65
Friedan, Betty 308
Frisby, David 57

Gans, Herbert J. 5, 45, 51, 55, 58-59, 142, 221-22, 277-78
Garland, Hamlin 127
Garrett, George 199
Gelfant, Blanche 2, 78, 87-89, 94-95, 100-1, 121, 141, 151, 156-57, 197, 213, 220
Gender 3, 5, 12, 33-34, 36, 38, 68, 81, 83, 94, 101-2, 116-17, 125-26, 141, 143-44, 162, 175, 196, 207, 264, 305, 335
Ginsberg, Allen 15, 295
Glaab, Charles N. 20, 75
Godden, Richard 209-10
Göbel, Walter 98, 141
Goldmann, Lucien 105, 160
Gottdiener, Mark 20, 69
Gottmann, Jean 28
Graff, Aida Farrag 111
Great Gatsby, The 2, 10, 88, 93, 108, 192-212, 214, 223, 289, 301, 315-16, 332
Grosz, George 229, 241
Gullason, Thomas A. 121, 130

Haas, Rudolf 96, 126
Haack, Dietmar 131

Habermas, Jürgen 6-7, 11, 106-7, 191, 262-63, 320, 327
Hanley, Richard Eugene 95-96
Hapke, Laura 80
Harring, Sidney L. 171
Harrington, Michael 275, 279, 309, 326-27
Harris, Leon 187
Harvey, David 3
Hassan, Ihab 93
Hassam, Childe 204
Hatt, Paul K. 55
Hawthorne, Nathaniel 76, 97
Hegel, G. W. F. 208, 262-63, 265
Hicks, Granville 242
Hite, Molly 324-25
Hoffmann, Gerhard 94-95
Holton, Milne 117, 121
Holton, R. J. 4, 45
Howard, June 134, 163
Howe, Irving 1, 100, 245
Howells, William Dean 3, 76, 99, 103, 121, 140
Hughson, Lois 235
Hummon, David M. 85
Huonder, Eugen 209
Hussey, Barbara Lee 98

Ickstadt, Heinz 39, 58-60, 66, 70, 93, 99, 208
Ideology 5-8, 11-13, 52, 54, 72, 79, 82, 106-7, 136-41, 157, 162-63, 238, 315, 330
Immigrants 25, 36-37, 40, 112-14, 166-91, 217-18, 223, 247, 335
Isernhagen, Hartwig 99, 222

Jacob, Herbert 53
Jacobs, Jane 161
James, Henry 76, 183, 194
Jay, Martin 2, 7, 10-11, 107, 321-22
Jefferson, Thomas 143, 207-8, 241
Johnston, R. J. 20
Joyce, Joyce Ann 265
Joyce, James 6, 183, 230, 289, 294
Jungle, The 2, 10, 88, 102, 145, 166-91, 246, 290, 329

Kaplan, Amy Beth 103, 157
Kaplan, Sydney Janet 335
Katz, Michael B. 36
Katznelson, Ira 6-7, 33, 37, 60, 248
Kerouac, Jack 295
Kinnamon, Keneth 251
Klotz, Volker 1, 98-99
Knox, Paul 64
Kolko, Gabriel 275, 279
Kolodny, Annette 323

Kooning, Willem de 298
Komar, Kathleen 235
Kreutzer, Eberhard 15, 86-88, 97-98, 101, 283

Larsen, Lawrence 15, 206
Last Exit to Brooklyn 3, 10, 14, 98, 108, 273-299
Lawrence, D. H. 216
Lears, Jackson T. 136, 158
Lees, Andrew 75, 128
Lefebvre, Henri 6
Lehan, Richard 200, 204
Lessing, Doris 101
Levine, Paul 274
Lévi-Strauss, Claude 15
Levy, Diane Wolfe 98
Lewis, Sinclair 214
Ley, David 67
Liebow, Elliot 65, 284, 292, 326-27
Lisca, Peter 204
Los Angeles 1, 29, 67-68, 300-25
Lowry, E. D. 222
Lubove, Roy 33, 112-13
Ludington, Townsend 232
Lukács, Georg 2, 7, 210
Lynn, Kenneth S. 128, 152
Lynch, Kevin 4, 67, 101

Macherey, Pierre 7, 13, 106-7
Machor, James L. 8, 74, 82, 84
Maggie: A Girl of the Streets 2, 10, 14, 16, 77, 88, 110-32, 223, 251
Mangel, Anne 319
Manhattan Transfer 2, 10, 88, 93-94, 132, 213-44, 281, 329
Marcuse, Herbert 11, 105, 299, 321
Martin, Jay 141
Marx, Karl 8, 48, 181, 210, 268-69
Marx, Leo 7, 76, 97
Marxism 6-7, 54, 164, 213, 237, 262, 265, 267, 334
Matthiesen, F. O. 161
Mayerson, Charlotte Leon 63
McLuhan, Marshall 312
Mencken, H. L. 211
Mental map 4, 17, 67-69, 142, 197, 205, 214, 251, 301, 307, 309
Merrill, Robert 311
Mesch, Harald 274
Michaels, Walter Benn 156
Milgram, Stanley 68, 205, 224-25
Modernism 2, 13, 15-17, 99-100, 132, 214-15, 220, 226-38, 243, 251, 266-74, 293-99, 328-35
Mookerjee, R. N. 190
Mootry, Maria K. 264
Morrison, Toni 102

Mottram, Eric 228, 281, 293
Müller, Kurt 153
Muller, Peter O. 61
Mumford, Lewis 6, 28, 61, 70, 77-78, 90, 216, 300
Myrdal, Gunnar 245

Nabokov, Vladimir 331
Native Son 3, 10, 245-72
Naturalism 1, 98, 108, 115, 121, 129, 132, 134, 149, 152-53, 159, 161, 163, 173, 176, 182, 186, 214-15, 226-38, 272-74, 292-93, 332
New York 1, 10, 15-16, 21-22, 25, 28, 30-35, 62-63, 68-69, 89, 110-65, 192-244, 276-78, 306, 328-29, 332
Nietzsche, Friedrich 210

Oates, Joyce Carol 91
O'Brien, John 292
Olson, Charles 298
Orleans, Peter 67- 68, 306

Pahl, Raymond E. 3, 51-52
Park, Robert E. 3, 46-49, 51-54, 57-58, 62, 138, 146, 150, 252
Peel, J. D. Y. 53
Percy, Walker 315
Peters, Daniel 323
Philpott, Thomas Lee 249
Pike, Burton 2, 90, 336
Pizer, Donald 121, 149, 153
Plett, Heinrich F., and Renate 95
Poe, Edgar Allan 294, 296
Poenicke, Klaus 132
Poirier, Richard 146
Posnock, Ross 211
Postmodernism 13, 93, 325, 329, 333
Priest, Oscar de 250
Pynchon, Thomas 3, 300-25, 329, 331-32

Radford, John P. 113
Realism 7, 103, 131, 156, 164
Redfield, Robert 252, 255, 259
Riesman, David 153
Riis, Jacob A. 57, 62, 69, 112, 114-15, 119, 310
Rose, Alan H. 92
Roth, Henry 69, 94, 223
Rothko, Mark 334
Rutman, Darrett B. 18-19

Salinger, Jerome D. 283-84
Salisbury, Harris 275
Sartre, Jean-Paul 230, 232
Sanders, Scott 321, 324
Saunders, Peter 45, 48-49, 52

Index   361

Schaub, Thomas H. 320
Scherpe, Klaus R. 100
Schmidt-von Bardeleben, Renate 96
Schmitt, Peter J. 76, 194
Schott, Webster 297
Selby, Hubert 3, 10, 14, 98, 108, 132, 273-99, 329-33
Semiotics 17, 60, 69-72
Sennett, Richard 38, 136, 140
Sharpe, William 105-6
Shergold, Peter R. 38
Sies, Mary Corbin 83-84, 194
Simmel, Georg 46-49, 51-55, 57-58
Sinclair, Upton 1-2, 10, 77-78, 88, 102, 166-91, 242, 246, 290, 299, 329, 331, 333
Sister Carrie 2, 10, 88, 93, 101, 108, 132-65, 173, 178, 291, 329, 331-32
Sizemore, Christine W. 101
Slade, Joseph W. 318
Slayton, Robert Allen 170, 172, 177
Slums 1, 27, 34-36, 41, 56-57, 62-66, 71, 84, 112-14, 123, 132, 169-70, 173, 217, 247-61, 273-90, 296, 310, 312-15
Smith, Carl S. 96, 101
Smith, Michael Peter 45, 56
Smith, Neil 83
Sombart, Werner 38
Spears, Monroe K. 92
Spencer, Herbert 53-54, 58, 133, 143, 146, 148, 151, 157-58, 253, 268-69
Spengler, Oswald 8, 92-93, 203, 214
Squier, Susan Merrill 101
Steffens, Lincoln 206
Stern, Milton R. 208
Stieglitz, Alfred 71, 159
Stimpson, Catherine R. 3
Stout, Janis P. 80
Strauss, Anselm L. 69, 73
Studs Lonigan 88, 223, 252
Suburbs 7, 29, 31, 40-42, 60-62, 83-84, 141-143, 176, 194-97, 200, 205-6, 208, 301-5, 307-10, 313, 319
Susser, Ida 280, 287

Thoreau, Henry David 76-77
Tocqueville, Alexis de 33
Trachtenberg, Alan 71, 78, 97, 116, 137, 159
Tuan, Yi-Fu 86
Turner, Frederick Jackson 21, 81, 193, 196, 208

Ulysses 6, 230, 291
Urbanization 4-5, 18-46, 80-85, 111, 136, 169, 195, 216, 227, 247-48, 302-3

Urbanism 4-5, 46-60, 62, 72, 91-92, 97, 130, 151, 141-47, 149-52, 196-97, 221-22, 306, 333

Veblen, Thorstein 148, 237, 241

Wade, Louise Carroll 172
Wade, Richard C. 21
Walcutt, Charles Child 121
Walker, Robert H. 78
Warner, Sam Bass 9, 20, 30-32, 38, 70-72, 335
Waste Land, The 1, 203, 240, 289, 316
Weber, Max 48, 54
Weimer, David R. 10, 86, 97, 121
Weld, Ralph Foster 276
Wertheim, Stanley 122
Wertime, Richard A. 292
Westbrook, Max 121
Wharton, Edith 3
White, Lucia and Morton 71, 74, 76-78, 135, 151
Whitman, Walt 15, 32, 76, 94-95, 180, 214, 230, 238, 265, 296
Whyte, William F. 56-57, 65, 128, 284
Widmer, Kingsley 271
Wiener, Norbert 320
Williams, Carlos William 295-96, 331
Williams, Raymond 2, 6-8, 15, 53, 74, 89, 99, 103-4, 294, 310, 330
Wilson, Edmund 208, 211
Winthrop, John 18
Wirth, Louis 46-47, 50-53, 55-56, 58, 62, 65, 78, 87, 94-95, 150, 222, 246, 252-53, 259
Wirth-Nesher, Hana 94
Wolfe, Thomas 3, 326-27
Wordsworth, William 204
Wortman, Marlene Stein 34
Wright, Frank Lloyd 239
Wright, Richard 3, 10, 59, 92, 132, 245-72, 299, 329-32

Yezierska, Anzia 3

Ziff, Larzer 127
Zipris, Lester Roy 97
Zlotnick, Joan 96
Zola, Emile 184
Zorbaugh, Harvey W. 62

NEUE STUDIEN ZUR ANGLISTIK UND AMERIKANISTIK

Band 1 Ingeborg Weber-Brandies: Virginia Woolf "The Waves": Emanzipation als Möglichkeit des Bewußtseinsromans. 1974.

Band 2 Meinhard Winkgens: Das Zeitproblem in Samuel Becketts Dramen. 1975.

Band 3 Klaus Simonsen: Erzähltechnik und Weltanschauung in Samuel Butlers literarischen Werken "Erewhon Revisited" und "The Way of All Flesh". 1974.

Band 4 Renate Mann: Jane Austen: Die Rhetorik der Moral. 1975.

Band 5 Bernhard Reitz: Das Problem des historischen Romans bei George Eliot. 1975.

Band 6 Wolfgang Sänger: John Millington Synge: The Aran Islands. Material und Mythos. 1976.

Band 7 Norbert Schmuhl: Erfahrungen des Aufbruchs. Zur Perspektivität und Aperspektivität in James Joyces Ulysses. 1976.

Band 8 Reinhard Mischke: Launcelots allegorische Reise. Sir Thomas Malorys Le Morte Darthur und die englische Literatur des fünfzehnten Jahrhunderts. 1976.

Band 9 Kurt Müller: Konventionen und Tendenzen der Gesellschaftskritik im expressionistischen amerikanischen Drama der zwanziger Jahre. 1977.

Band 10 Ursula Schaefer: Höfisch-ritterliche Dichtung und sozialhistorische Realität. Literatursoziologische Studien zum Verhältnis von Adelsstruktur, Ritterideal und Dichtung bei Geoffrey Chaucer. 1977.

Band 11 Ewald Mengel: Harold Pinters Dramen im Spiegel der soziologischen Rollentheorie. 1978.

Band 12 Norbert Bolz: Eine statistische, computerunterstützte Echtheitsprüfung von "The Repentance of Robert Greene". Ein methodischer und systematischer Ansatz. 1978.

Band 13 Klaus Peter Jochum: Discrepant Awareness: Studies in English Renaissance Drama. 1979.

Band 14 Rudi Camerer: Die Schuldproblematik im Spätwerk von Charles Dickens. 1978.

Band 15 Peter Stapelberg: Sean O'Casey und das deutschsprachige Theater (1948-1974). Empirische Untersuchungen zu den Mechanismen der Rezeption eines angloirischen Dramatikers. 1979.

Band 16 Hans Ulrich Seeber: Moderne Pastoraldichtung in England. Studien zur Theorie und Praxis der pastoralen Versdichtung in England nach 1800 mit besonderer Berücksichtigung von Edward Thomas (1878-1917). 1979.

Band 17 Klaus Martens: Negation, Negativität und Utopie im Werk von Wallace Stevens. 1980.

Band 18 Angela Lorent: Funktionen der Massenszene im viktorianischen Roman. 1980.

Band 19 Rotraut Spiegel: Doris Lessing: The Problem of Alienation and the Form of the Novel. 1981.

Band 20 Edda Kerschgens: Das gespaltene Ich: 100 Jahre afroamerikanischer Autobiographie. Strukturuntersuchungen zu den Autobiographien von Frederick Douglas, Booker T. Washington und W.E.B. Du Bois. 1980.

Band 21 Josef Oswald: The Discordant, Broken, Faithless Rhythm of Our Time. Eine Analyse der späten Dramen Eugene O'Neills. 1981.

Band 22 Dietrich Strauß: Die erotische Dichtung von Robert Burns. Bedingungen, Textüberlieferung, Interpretation, Wertungen. 1981.

Band 23 Jill Bonheim: Paul Scott: Humanismus und Individualismus in seinem Werk. 1982.

Band 24 Claudia Stehle: Individualität und Romanform. Theoretische Überlegungen mit Beispielen aus dem 19. Jahrhundert. 1982.

Band 25 Helga Stelzer: Narzißmus-Problematik und Spiegel-Technik in Joseph Conrads Romanen. 1983.

Band 26 Katherine Bastian: Joyce Carol Oates´s Short Stories Between Tradition and Innovation. 1983.

Band 27 Regine Rosenthal: Die Erben des Lazarillo. Identitätsfrage und Schlußlösung im pikarischen Roman. 1983.

Band 28 Beate Lahrmann-Hartung: Sean O´Casey und das epische Theater Bertolt Brechts. 1983.

Band 29 Hans-Wolfgang Schaller: William Dean Howells und seine Schule. Strukturzüge im amerikanischen Realismus und Naturalismus. 1983.

Band 30 Elmar Schenkel: Natur und Subjekt im Werk von John Cowper Powys. 1983.

Band 31 Sabine Volk: Grenzpfähle der Wirklichkeit. Approaches to the Poetry of R.S. Thomas. 1985.

Band 32 Erika Hulpke: Die Vielzahl der Übersetzungen und die Einheit des Werks: Bildmuster und Wortwiederholungen in T.S. Eliot, *Collected Poems/Gesammelte Gedichte*. 1985.

Band 33 Eike Schönfeld: Der deformierte Dandy: Oscar Wilde im Zerrspiegel der Parodie. 1986.

Band 34 Kurt Greinacher: Die frühen satirischen Romane Aldous Huxleys. 1986.

Band 35 Susanne Mayer: Die Sehnsucht nach den anderen. Eine Studie zum Verhältnis von Subjekt und Gesellschaft in den Autobiographien von Lillian Hellman, Maya Angelou und Maxine Hong Kingston. 1986.

Band 36 Klaus Martens: Die antinomische Imagination. Studien zu einer amerikanischen literarischen Tradition (Charles Brockden Brown, Edgar Allan Poe, Herman Melville). 1986.

Band 37 Richard Matthews/Joachim Schmole-Rostosky (eds.): Papers on Language and Mediaeval Studies Presented to Alfred Schopf. 1988.

Band 38 Christian von Raumer: Khaki-clad Civilians. Soziale Erfahrung in der britischen Prosaliteratur des Ersten Weltkriegs. 1987.

Band 39 Claudia Ebel: Der entwurzelte Hindu. Eine Untersuchung zum postkolonialen Kulturkonflikt in V.S. Naipauls Trinidadromanen. 1989.

Band 40 Sabine Krome: Das Vaterbild in ausgewählten Romanen William Styrons. 1989.

Band 41 Rita Stoll: Die nicht-pronominale Anrede bei Shakespeare. 1989.

Band 42 Helmut Schönhöffer: Krankheit im anglo-amerikanischen Drama der Moderne. Gesellschaftskritik im Spiegel der Machtanalyse Michel Foucaults. 1989.

Band 43 Irene Neher: The Female Hero's Quest for Identity in Novels by Modern American Women Writers. The Function of Nature Imagery, Moments of Vision, and Dreams in the Hero's Development. 1989.

Band 44 Thomas Kühn: Sir Thomas Brownes *Religio Medici* und *Pseudodoxia Epidemica*. Eine ideengeschichtliche Untersuchung mit besonderer Berücksichtigung des Begriffs "reason". 1989.

Band 45 Martina Wächter: Darstellung und Deutung der Vergangenheit in den Dramen Arthur Millers. 1989.

Band 46 Jan Vester: Wirklichkeit und Text / Wirklichkeit als Text. Exemplarische Studien zum amerikanischen Naturalismus. 1989.

Band 47 Daniel Göske: Herman Melville in deutscher Sprache. Studien zur übersetzerischen Rezeption seiner bedeutendsten Erzählungen. 1990.

Band 48 Ulrich Adolphs: Die Tyrannei der Bilder - Sam Shepards Dramen. 1990.

Band 49 Vera Nünning: Die Ästhetik Virginia Woolfs. Eine Rekonstruktion ihrer philosophischen und ästhetischen Grundanschauungen auf der Basis ihrer nichtfiktionalen Schriften. 1990.

Band 50 Michael Meyer: Struktur, Funktion und Vermittlung der Wahrnehmung in Charles Tomlinsons Lyrik. 1990.

Band 51 Heinz Eikmeyer: Angst und Furcht in den Dramen Harold Pinters. 1990.

Band 52 Gerd Hurm: Fragmented Urban Images. The American City in Modern Fiction from Stephen Crane to Thomas Pynchon. 1991.